IRISH COMPANY LAW
FOR BUSINESS

Henry Ellis LLM, PhD, PGC Ed, FCII

Professor of Corporate, Commercial and Economic Law
University of Limerick

JORDANS

1998

Published by
Jordan Publishing Limited
21 St Thomas Street
Bristol BS1 6JS

Whilst the publishers and the author have taken every care in preparing the material included in this work, any statements made as to the legal or other implications of particular transactions are made in good faith purely for general guidance and cannot be regarded as a substitute for professional advice. Consequently, no liability can be accepted for loss or expense incurred as a result of relying in particular circumstances on statements made in this work.

British Library Cataloguing-in-Publication Data
A catalogue record for this book is available from the British Library.

ISBN 0 85308 467 X

Typeset by Mendip Communications Ltd, Frome, Somerset
Printed by MPG Books Ltd, Bodmin, Cornwall

PREFACE

This book attempts to present company law in a visible private enterprise context and a reader-friendly manner by adopting a new 'business relationship' approach to the subject.

Irish (and UK) companies are essentially contract-based. Accordingly, the text focuses on the individual contractual relationships which arise from the formation, management and use of companies. This novel approach should facilitate a greater understanding of the complexities of company law, particularly amongst those involved in carrying out day-to-day transactions on behalf of or with companies.

The basic business relationships arising in company law can involve the company itself, its investors, directors and creditors. These relationships, and the roles of officials such as receivers, liquidators and examiners, are introduced in Part I.

Legislative aims

Company law has developed within the broad statutory aims of:

(1) permitting the use of companies as business associations in order to stimulate the growth of trade and enterprise; and
(2) protecting investors in, and creditors of, companies.

These legislative aims are explained in Part I.

Company law is both lengthy and complex. For example, the Companies Act 1963 consists of 399 sections (and 13 Schedules). The Companies Act 1990 contains a further 262 sections. Much of this law is very detailed. Accordingly, one can easily lose sight of its underlying principles.

To assist readers to keep the fundamental aims of company law in mind as they become immersed in its detailed provisions, I have used transparent chapter titles such as:

> Protection for Investors in Public Companies (Chapter 10);
> Protection of Company's Capital Base for Creditors (and Investors) (Chapter 13);
> The Investors' Statutory Contract (Chapter 29);
> Creditors' Remedies against the Company (Chapter 34);
> Unsatisfied Creditors' Remedies against the Company's Members and Officers (Chapter 36); and
> Examinership and its Effects on Creditors' Rights (Chapter 37).

Core ideas in company law

Before delving into the detailed laws affecting the various parties to corporate contracts, it is necessary to understand core concepts underlying company law. Part II, therefore, is devoted to explaining the meaning and relevance of:

(1) a company's separate legal personality;
(2) the 'veil' of incorporation; and
(3) the concept of limitation of liability.

Separate legal personality

A House of Lords ruling in 1897 is probably the most significant court decision in company law.

In *Salomon v Salomon & Co*, the court made it clear that a company would be recognised judicially as an entirely separate person from its principal share-holders. Thus, the House of Lords gave precedence to *form* over *substance*; in effect accepting that once the form of a company was within the letter of the law, the court would not look behind the company form to identify the beneficial owners of its shares. Chapters 3 and 4 deal with separate corporate personality.

The veil of incorporation

Generally, the courts consider themselves bound by the principle in *Salomon*'s case that the company is a separate person distinct from its members. As a result, there is said to be a 'veil' drawn between the company and its members. The courts will not normally 'lift' this veil to look at the economic reality of who owns the company.

There are exceptional circumstances where the courts will look behind the corporate form to see who actually owns and controls a company. This action is known as 'lifting the veil of incorporation'.

The veil may be lifted by statutory provision to require group accounts from holding companies and to identify specific inter-group transactions. Again, under taxation law, the shareholders of a 'close' company may incur personal taxation liabilities for its profits. However, legislation generally does not render investors liable for the debts of the company.[1]

So long as a shareholder acts in good faith, because of the privilege of limitation of liability, he is unlikely to incur liability for company debts. Where, however, a shareholder moves outside his expected passive role and becomes involved in

---

1 Under s 36 of the 1963 Act, a reduction in the number of members below the legal minimum may lead to the remaining member(s) being held liable for the debts of the company. This statutory exception is not of great practical value to company creditors – particularly since the introduction of the single member company.

fraudulent trading by the company, he may be held personally liable by statute[1] for company debts.

The process of lifting the veil always overrules the separate legal personality of the company. Usually, this is necessary to give effect to statutory provisions designed to bring greater transparency into transactions involving connected companies.

The judiciary may also lift the veil at common law, eg to prevent the use of corporate form for an unequitable purpose.[2] Generally, though, the courts will only lift the veil to make the members liable for company debts, where the company has been used as a 'cloak' for fraud or other criminal activities. Accordingly, notwithstanding any lifting of the veil, investors will normally retain the privilege of limited liability, providing they do not become involved in corporate transactions nor attempt to influence the directors and officers in the management of the company. This could happen by investors acting as 'shadow' directors or by corporate members interfering in their capacity as a 'related' company.

This book attempts to rationalise the 'jungle of judgments' relating to lifting the veil in Chapter 6. The extent to which a liquidator can utilise the related company relationship to increase an insolvent company's assets is dealt with in Chapter 42.

Limitation of liability

In company law, limitation of liability essentially means that a shareholder can only lose the amount of his investment in a company if it fails. He is not liable to the creditors of an insolvent company for company debts.

The limited liability company or corporation was invented as a means of attracting the large aggregations of capital required for construction and other major business projects during the Industrial Revolution of the 19th century. Such projects required capital contributions from a wide range of passive investors not actually involved in running the businesses.

The original intention of the legislature seemed to envisage granting limited liability to investors in substantial companies. The real significance of the House of Lords decision in the *Salomon* case is that it confirmed that the privilege of forming a limited liability company was also available to the owners of small businesses which had been operating as sole traders. A result of the *Salomon* decision was to generate an explosion in the growth of private companies which today form the vast majority of companies registered in Ireland.

---

1 Under s 297A of the 1963 Act.
2 For example by a person attempting to escape his liability to pay royalties under a licence agreement by transferring the licence to a company formed for that purpose. This happened in *Cummins v Stewart* [1911] 1 IR 236.

The stimulus to the incorporation of small businesses, originally generated by the *Salomon* case, received statutory reinforcement recently. Following implementation of the EU Single Member Company Directive on 1 October 1994, nearly 2,000 such companies were registered in Ireland by December 1995.

The relative advantages and disadvantages of trading in corporate and non-corporate forms are set out in Chapter 5.

Business relationships in company law

Having introduced the various corporate business relationships in Part I and explained the fundamental legal principles underlying company law in Part II, the remaining text focuses on the detailed rules and procedures primarily affecting:

(1) the company itself;
(2) its directors and officers;
(3) its members; and
(4) its creditors.

The company itself

Part III deals with company registration procedures and early corporate transactions, including choice of name, the tort of passing off and the position of promoters.

Part IV sets out the legal provisions relating to companies' capital, governance and contractual capability. The effects of ultra vires transactions are dealt with in Chapters 17 and 18.

The protection available to a company against its creditors is detailed in Part IX, whilst the contents of Part X includes corporate financial restructuring, changes in ownership, and winding up of companies.

Directors and officers

The directors are the company's human managing agents.

Because of the concept of limitation of liability, investors in a failed company are not generally liable for the debts of their company. As a result, creditors of an insolvent company cannot realistically consider suing the shareholders for its debts. Creditors may, however, have another potential source of funds to supplement the company's assets. This source is the company's directors and officers.

The Increasing Liabilities of Directors. The enactment of the Companies Act 1990 greatly increases the potential legal liability of directors to contribute to the assets of an insolvent company. Two leading court decisions reinforce this trend towards increasing the liability of company directors.

In *Re Hefferon Kearns (No 2): Dublin Heating Co Ltd v Hefferon and Ors,*[1] Lynch J interpreted the new reckless trading provisions in the 1990 Act, whilst the High Court in *Mantruck Services Ltd (in liquidation): Mehigan v Duignan*[2] held a director liable to pay in excess of £90,000 for failing to keep proper books of account under the 1990 Act. These cases are analysed in Chapter 21.

Because of the increasing risk of directors incurring personal liability for the company's debts, a chapter has been included on Directors' and Officers' Professional Indemnity Insurance (Chapter 22). In my view, the prudent company director of the 1990s should always effect this type of insurance, thereby transferring part of his financial risk to an insurance company. The advantage of this course of action is that the insurance cover will protect the director's personal assets and provide a managed fund for meeting any claims of unpaid company creditors.

Directors' duties and liabilities generally, including the recent statutory provisions permitting the restriction and disqualification of directors, are explained in Part V.

Directors can also incur other serious criminal sanctions (see below).

The role of company law in providing for the monitoring of the directors' stewardship of their shareholders' company is outlined in Part VI. This Part includes chapters on the auditor's role and responsibilities (Chapter 26) and investigations into a company's affairs and ownership (Chapter 27). The requirements of the Electoral Act 1997 on the disclosure of donations are noted in Chapters 24 and 25.

Company members

The members (or shareholders) are the owners of a company in which they have invested capital.

Investors' individual rights and responsibilities are dealt with in Part VII. The implications of the European Communities (Public Limited Companies Subsidiaries) Regulations 1997[3] on share purchases are noted in Chapter 28, whilst disclosure and transfer of shareholders' interests is dealt with in Chapter 31.

The impact of changes in company ownership or the liquidation of the company on shareholders' rights is included in Part X.

Corporate Governance and Audit Committees. The roles of, and interaction between, directors and members in operating the company are dealt with in Chapters 14 to 16.

---

1 [1993] IR 3 191 (HC).
2 (Unreported) 8 October 1996 (HC).
3 SI 1997/67.

The establishment of an audit committee can be an important way of improving corporate governance by ensuring greater accountability of a company's directors and officers to its members.

An audit committee should consist of a majority of non-executive directors and be chaired by one of them. It can provide a forum for the regular questioning of executive directors on behalf of the wider company membership. The setting up of audit committees was recommended by the Cadbury Committee in the United Kingdom for all listed companies.

The requirements for establishing audit committees are not generally included in texts on company law, so I have followed this precedent.

Company creditors

Part VIII explains the various types of company creditor and the security (if any) held by creditors over the company's property. It includes chapters on the consequences of receivership.

The protection against creditors available to a company by the examinership process is dealt with in Part IX, whilst the rights of creditors on the financial restructuring and winding up of companies are included in Part X.

Companies and agency law (and trusts)

A company, being simply an artificial legal person, has neither mind nor body, so cannot operate except by using agents. The agency law principles underlying the authority of a company's directors, officers, managers and employees who act on its behalf are outlined in Chapter 18.

The role of directors as 'quasi-trustees' is explained in Chapter 14. Chapter 31 deals with the equitable interests of share purchasers.

Companies and criminal law

Companies cannot initiate criminal proceedings, but they may themselves be prosecuted.

Problems can arise in the imposition of criminal responsibility on a company. In particular, difficulty may be encountered in ascribing 'mens rea' or 'guilty intention' to an artificial legal person. Generally, such mental intention is ascribed to a company if the board of directors or managing director initiated the wrongful act in question.

Whilst the criminal liability of companies is outlined in Chapter 4, the problems associated with 'mens rea' and corporate bodies is a developing area of jurisprudence, one which, I consider, is more appropriately dealt with in a textbook on criminal law.

Criminal responsibility of directors

The reality of the power of directors to make decisions on behalf of a company is recognised in company law by the imposition of criminal responsibility on directors for a wide range of their actions. For example, under s 297 of the Companies Act 1963, where a director carries on the business of the company with intent to defraud, he may, on conviction on indictment, be liable to imprisonment for up to 7 years and/or a fine not exceeding £50,000.

Again, where an officer knowingly or recklessly makes a statement to the auditors of the company which is misleading, false, or deceptive, he may be criminally prosecuted under s 197 of the Companies Act 1990. The term 'officer' in s 197 includes any employee of the company.

Speaking to the Institute of Directors in December 1997, the Tánaiste and Minister for Enterprise, Trade and Employment, Ms Mary Harney, said:

> 'There are probably more than 200,000 people who have voluntarily accepted responsibilities as directors for the care and management of companies. Directors are responsible for the day-to-day operation of the companies under their control.

> The law does not differentiate between executive and non-executive directors for that purpose. I am conscious that the vast bulk of directors strive to act in an honourable and responsible fashion to meet their obligations to their share-holders, creditors, employees and to the public at large.

> However, there are still quite a large number of companies that fail to provide basic information on their membership and financial standing. In recent months, the Companies Registration Office has had its staff increased by nearly 50 per cent. With a new IT system coming onstream in early 1998, the registrar of companies intends to take a much more pro-active stance in relation to companies failing to file statutory returns with his Office.

> He has given defaulting companies a period of grace to bring their affairs up to date. If this expires without result, he will proceed, not only against the companies concerned, but against selected directors where this is warranted. The conse-quence of convictions recorded against directors may be to disqualify them from holding any directorships in the State.'

The Tánaiste also commented that she would:

> '... be examining in the near future what extra resources should be allocated within my own Department to initiate prosecutions for offences for which I have responsibility under the Companies Acts.'

I do not consider it appropriate to include a chapter dealing specifically with all the criminal responsibilities of company directors. Instead, I have simply indicated in Chapter 21 and Appendix B the nature and sources of the most serious offences which can be committed by them.

Recent Stock Exchange developments

One of the advantages of holding shares in a public company is the availability of a stock market in which to find a buyer for them. During 1997, a new Developing Companies Market was started up within the Stock Exchange, following the closure of the Smaller Companies Market in 1996. A new computerised CREST system to streamline the paperwork involved in buying and selling shares was also introduced.

The Stock Exchange Act 1995 had separated the UK and Irish Stock Exchanges, resulting in the creation of the Irish Stock Exchange Ltd. This separation process was further cemented by the Irish Takeover Panel Act 1997. Under this Act, an independent Irish Takeover Panel was started on 1 July 1997. This development is noted in Chapter 40.

Implications of competition law

Due to the increasing number of company takeovers and mergers, the lines of demarcation between company and competition law are becoming somewhat blurred. Accordingly, Chapter 40 includes an outline of the overlapping powers of the Minister for Enterprise, Trade and Employment and the Competition Authority in controlling the economic consequences of takeovers and mergers.

Future reforms

Company law is a vital element in generating and sustaining economic development. As the Minister for Science, Technology and Commerce stated:[1] 'The Company Law Code is a crucially important aspect of the structure of the modern state, and it is important that it be continually updated'. To this end, a Companies (Amendment) Bill is being prepared which will reform aspects of the law of examinership and remove the statutory audit requirement for small companies whose turnover does not exceed £100,000. These reforms will implement some of the recommendations of the Company Law Review Group.[2]

Again, the Tánaiste, Ms Mary Harney, informed the Institute of Directors that:

> 'Through its work over many years, the Oireachtas has given us a valuable and detailed code of companies legislation. Its duty and that of Government is to ensure that this framework remains relevant and effective for the times we live in.
>
> I was disappointed to learn that s 240 of the Companies Act 1990 only allows either the DPP or myself to take summary proceedings in relation to an offence under the Companies Acts, where those proceedings are instituted within three years of the date of the offence. Recent experience suggests that this deadline has often passed before the possible offence is discovered.

---

1 (Then) Mr Michael Smith, TD, in *Companies Report '96*, prepared by the Department of Enterprise, Trade and Employment, Stationery Office, Dublin, August 1997.
2 Contained in its First Report (Stationery Office, Dublin, 1995).

It is my intention that the forthcoming Companies (Amendment) Bill ... will lengthen the period allowed for the initiation of summary proceedings.'

The Government is also reviewing the Registration of Business Names Act 1963 and considering whether an Executive Unit be established to tackle the issue of restrictions on directors.

At an EU level, the Government has signed the draft Convention on the Mutual Recognition of Insolvency Proceedings. Revised proposals have been issued for a Takeover Directive and attempts are being made to break the deadlock on the establishment of a 'European Company'.

These current developments illustrate further the dynamic nature of company law and the range of economic activities affected by it.

Acknowledgements

I would like to express my thanks to a number of people.

The calculation of the inflation factor in updating the amount received by Mr Salomon for the sale of his business (in Chapter 3) was carried out for me by my colleague Dr Tony Leddin, Senior Lecturer in Economics.

Mr Tom Healy, Chief Executive of the Irish Stock Exchange, appraised me of current and recent developments at the Exchange, and gave me permission to reproduce its list of member firms in Appendix A.

Mr John Bissett of Coyle Hamilton Corporate Broking and Ms Jacqueline McNamee of AIG (Europe) Ltd assisted me with my enquiries into Directors and Officers Professional Indemnity insurance.

My departmental colleague, Ms Siun O'Keefe, clarified some of the intricacies of competition law.

Mrs Mary O'Brien 'unscrambled' my handwriting and typed the manuscript with her usual high levels of accuracy, speed and good humour.

Mr Jack Anderson and Ms Sinead Kennedy checked the proofs, each making contributions which improved both the accuracy and the content of the text.

Finally, Mr Richard Hudson and the staff at Jordans were most helpful in dealing with the many different aspects of publishing this book. In it, I have attempted to state the law as at 1 July 1997.

Henry Ellis
Law Department
University of Limerick
February 1998

CONTENTS

Preface v
Table of Cases xxxix
Table of Statutes li
Table of Statutory Instruments lxiii
Table of EU Legislation lxv
Table of Abbreviations lxix

INTRODUCTION lxxi

Key concepts in company law lxxi
Types of company permitted lxxi
Formation of a company lxxii
How a company carries on business lxxii
Financial difficulties lxxiii
Terminating the 'life' of a company lxxiii
Business relationships in company law lxxiii

PART I   THE BUSINESS RELATIONSHIPS IN COMPANY LAW 1

Chapter 1   Origins and Scope of Company Law 3
The statutory framework 3
Separate legal personality of a company 4
· The veil of incorporation 4
Limited liability of investors 4
The artificial nature of a company 4
The company's human agents 5
Company capital and initial finance 5
Company organisation by means of its human agents 5
Investors' rights and responsibilities 5
Disclosure of interests 7
Transfer of interests 7
Compulsory purchase 7
Directors and officers – the company's managing agents 7
Directors' duties 8
Directors' liability for company debts 8
Disqualification of directors 8
The company secretary 8
Monitoring the directors' management of the company 8
Company employees 9
Contractual capacity of the company and its agents 9
Company control and ownership 9
External or third party relationships 10
Creditors' rights against the company 10
Rights against insolvent company's assets 11
Creditors' rights against directors and others 11
Creditors' rights to terminate the life of a company 12

Protecting the company against its creditors   12
Compromising company debts and corporate restructuring   13
Changes in company ownership by takeover or merger   14
Winding up a company   14
  Dissolving the company   14

Chapter 2   Company Law Objectives – Protection of Investors and Creditors   15
Internal and external interests   15
  Internal interests   15
  External (or third party) interests   15
Investor protection   16
  Limitation of liability   16
    Price paid for limitation of liability   17
  Other protections for investors   17
Creditor protection   18
  Public nature of constitutional documents   18
  Maintenance of company's capital   19
  Creditors' powers to intervene   19
  Creditors' rights of recovery against the company   20
    Secured creditors   20
    Unsecured creditors   20
    Ranking of creditors' claims   20
  Priorities in a distribution   20
  Creditors' other rights of recovery   21
    Significance of the two 1990 Acts   21

PART II   FUNDAMENTAL PRINCIPLES OF COMPANY LAW   23

Chapter 3   The Concept of Corporate Personality   25
The effect of incorporation   25
  Separate legal personality of the company and *Salomon*'s case   25
    Liquidator's contention   25
    The case on appeal   26
    Essence of judgment   26
    One-man companies   26
    Subsequent case-law   27
    Importance of the *Salomon* decision   27
The veil of incorporation   28
  Company ownership and management   28

Chapter 4   Limited Liability and Other Consequences of Incorporation   31
Introduction   31
  Memorandum of association and limitation of liability   31
    Effect of registration of a company   31
Other consequences of separate legal personality   32
  A company can sue and be sued in its own name   32
  A company can own property   33
    Company assets   34
  A company has perpetual succession   34
  Formation of a company may increase potential borrowing opportunities 35
  Incorporation facilitates the transfer of investors' interests   35
  Taxation implications   35

Chapter 5   Companies, Sole Traders and Partnerships Compared 37
Advantages and disadvantages 37
Sole traders 37
Advantages 37
Disadvantages 37
Partnerships 38
Advantages 38
Disadvantages 39
Conclusion 39
Registered companies 39
Advantages 40
Disadvantages 40
Conclusion 41

Chapter 6   Lifting the Veil of Incorporation which Protects Investors 43
The nature of the 'veil' metaphor 43
Peeping behind the veil 44
Related companies 44
Veil lifted by the court 45
Directors and officers 46
The purpose of peeping 46
Penetrating the veil 47
Extending the veil 48
Ignoring the veil 48
Some conclusions on lifting the veil 49
Groups of companies at common law 50
Statutory lifting of the veil and directors 51
Directors' rather than investors' liabilities 51

**PART III   COMPANY REGISTRATION AND EARLY CORPORATE
TRANSACTIONS** 53

Chapter 7   Restrictions on Choice of Company Name 55
Significance of company name 55
Registration of Business Names Act 1963 56
Refusal to register a name 56
Penalties 56
Publication of registered business name 56
Directors' particulars on letterheadings 57
Mistaken registration 57
The tort of passing off 57

Chapter 8   Choice of Company Type and Registration Procedures 59
Introduction 59
Companies limited by shares 59
Companies limited by guarantee 60
Unlimited companies 60
Public and private companies 61
Public companies 61
Private companies 62
Factors affecting choice of corporate form 62
Procedures for the formation of a company 63

Memorandum of association   63
Articles of association   63
Approval of proposed company name   64
Lodgement of documents   64
Off the shelf companies   64
Publication in *Iris Oifigiúil*   65
Single-member private companies, limited by shares or by guarantee 65
Minimum share capital for new public limited company   65
Unlimited companies   65
Make up of register of companies   66
Change of status   66
Change to single-member company   66
Change from single-member company   66
Change from public company into private company   66
Minority protection   67
Re-registration of private company as public company   67
Third party rights   67
Conversion of unlimited company into limited company and vice versa 68

Chapter 9   Promoters and Pre-Incorporation Contracts   69
Promoters   69
Definitions of promoter   69
Promoter's fiduciary relationship   70
Duties of disclosure   70
Common law remedies of the company   71
Rescission   71
Recovery of profits   71
Damages for misfeasance   72
Statutory rights of the company   72
Effects of breaching the 1983 Act   72
Remuneration of promoters   73
Provision in articles of association   73
Information to be included in a prospectus   73
Promoters and pre-incorporation contracts   73
Pre-incorporation and pre-trading contracts   74

**PART IV   COMPANIES' CAPITAL, GOVERNANCE AND CONTRACTUAL
CAPABILITY**   75

Chapter 10   Protection for Investors in Public Companies   77
The need for protection   77
Public company formation procedures   78
The European Communities (Stock Exchange) Regulations 1984   78
The Admissions Directive   78
The Listing Particulars Directive   79
The Interim Reports Directive   79
Methods of raising capital   79
An offer for sale   79
A placing   79
A public offer   80
A rights issue   80

National investment markets 80
  The Listed Market 81
    The Listing Rules 81
  The Unlisted Securities Market (USM) 82
  The Developing Companies Market (DCM) 82
Prospectuses 83
  Public offers 83
  Contents of prospectus 84
    The minimum subscription 84
    Reports to be attached 84
    Registration 84
  Pre-emption rights 85
Contractual aspects of public subscriptions 85
  Protecting public investors at allotment stage 86
    Directors' authority 86
    Allotment procedures 86
    Minimum subscription 86
  Payment for allotted shares 87
    Non-cash consideration 87
    Directors' liabilities 87
  Void and voidable allotments 88
  Returns of allotments 88
  Shareholders' liability 88
  Other remedies and protections 88
Investors' remedies for misrepresentations 89
  Investors' remedies 89
  Common law remedies 89
    Rescission 89
    Limits on rescission 89
    Damages for fraud 90
    Damages for negligence 90
    Other common law remedies against the directors and promoters 90
    Concealment 90
  Statutory remedies under s 49 91
    Position of expert 91
    Persons named in prospectus without authority 92
    Meaning of untrue statement 92
Criminal liability for misrepresentations 92
  Defence 92
Statement in lieu of prospectus 92

Chapter 11 Commencement of Business by Public and Non-Irish Companies 95
Introduction 95
  The Trading Certificate 95
  Liability of directors for pre-trading contracts 95
Non-Irish companies 96
  Accounts and publicity 96
  Cessation of business in Ireland 97
  Irish branches 97
  Details of external companies 97
Other business associations 97

European Economic Interest Groupings (EEIGs)   97

Chapter 12   Composition of a Company's Capital Base   99
Definition of capital   99
  Investment capital   99
    Balance sheet position   99
  Loan capital   99
    Capital employed   99
  Gearing   100
  Fixed and circulating capital   100
  Working capital   100
  Share capital   100
Types of share capital   100
  Nominal (or authorised) capital   100
  Issued capital   101
  Paid-up and uncalled capital   101
  Reserve capital   101
Classes of shares   102
  Class rights   102
  Preference shares   102
  Ordinary shares   102
    Non-voting ordinary shares   103
  Deferred shares   103
  Distinctions between preference and ordinary shares   103
Variation of class rights   104
  Objections   104
  The issuing of additional shares of a similar class   104
  The s 38 procedure   105
Shareholders' rights generally   105

Chapter 13   Protection of A Company's Capital Base for Creditors (and
  Investors)   107
Statutory rules   107
Restrictions on the direct reduction of share capital   108
  Share premium fund to be treated as capital   108
  Permitted use of share premium fund   108
Permitted reduction in share capital under s 72   108
  Application to the court   109
  Fairness between competing class rights   109
  Variation of class rights   110
  Objections by creditors   110
  Court order for reduction   111
  Liability of shareholders for reduced shares   111
Other permitted reductions in share capital   111
  Re-registration under s 15   111
  Forfeiture, etc, under s 43   112
Statutory capital maintenance rules   112
  Redemption of redeemable shares   112
    Conditions for redemption   112
    Cancellation of shares on redemption   113
    Capital redemption reserve fund   113

Payment of a premium on redemption 113
Treasury shares 113
Re-issuing of treasury shares 114
Restrictions on a company purchasing its own shares 114
Section 41 of the 1983 Amendment Act 114
Purchasing shares under the 1990 Act 115
Market purchase 115
Off-market purchases 115
Contingent purchase contracts 116
Transfer or release of company's right to buy its own shares 116
Payments by a company for its own shares 116
Effect of company's failure to redeem or purchase its own shares 116
Purchase by subsidiary of shares in its holding company 116
Disclosure of share purchases 117
Extraordinary meeting following serious loss of capital 117
Section 40 requirements to call a meeting 117
Other capital maintenance rules 118
Giving loans by a company for the purchase of its own shares 118
Conditions for valid loans or guarantees 118
Objections 119
Effect of breach of s 60 procedures 119
Third party notice of breach 119
Permitted loans under s 60 120
Restriction on public companies 120
Dividends and debts 120
Prohibition against issuing shares at a discount 120
Payment by instalments 121
Issuing shares at a premium 121
Payment of dividends only out of profits 121
Distribution 121
Profits of public companies 122
Specialist companies 122
The relevant accounts 122
Alteration of capital 122
Increase in and diminution of share capital 123

Chapter 14   Roles of Directors and Investors in Operating the Company 125
The underlying relationships 125
The company 125
Company management 125
The director's role 125
Definition of directors 126
Directors as quasi-trustees 126
Duties as quasi-trustees 127
Directors as agents 127
The member's role 128
Legal relationship with the company 128
Appointment of directors by members 129
First directors 129
Subsequent directors 130
Rotation of directors 130
Increase or reduction in numbers of directors 130

Removal of directors   130
Defects in appointment   131
Disqualification of directors   131
Remuneration of directors   131
Loans to directors   132
Disclosure of directors' salaries and emoluments   132
General duty of disclosure on directors (and secretary)   132
Particulars of directors to be shown on company letter headings   132
Assignment of office by directors   132
Removal of directors   133
Natural justice   133
Directors' service contracts   133
The managing director's contract   134
1990 Act limitations on directors' service contracts   134
Inspection of directors' service contracts   135
Authority of directors   135
The company secretary's role   135
Functions as chief administrative officer   135
Authority of the secretary   136
Qualifications required   136
Appointment of secretary   137

Chapter 15   Company Meetings and Resolutions   139
Types of meetings   139
Company meetings   139
Annual General Meetings (AGMs)   139
Notice   139
Waiver of notice   140
Adjourned AGMs   140
Single-member companies   140
Business at AGMs   140
Location of AGM   140
Extraordinary General Meetings (EGMs)   141
Notice   141
Business at EGM   141
Power to order the holding of a meeting   141
Proceedings at general meetings   142
Quorum of members   142
Chairman   142
Adjournment   143
Voting   143
Proxies   143
Resolutions   144
Ordinary resolution   144
Special resolution   144
Unanimous agreement   144
Adjourned meetings   145
Amendments   145
Extended notice   145
Minutes of meetings   145
Inspection of minute books   145
Registration and copies of certain resolutions   146

When special resolutions are required 146
Democratic control of the company 147

Chapter 16   Majority Control and the Protection of Minority Investors 149
The taking of decisions 149
  Alteration of the articles of association 149
  Corporate rights versus individual rights 149
Judicial protection for minority investors 150
  Bona fide for the benefit of the company as a whole 150
  Cases of hardship 151
  Other minority remedies 151
Section 205 remedy for oppression by the majority 151
  Only available to investors 152
  Offending conduct 152
  The second limb 152
  Remedies available to the court 153
    Proceedings may be held in camera 154
  Examinership 154
Investigations into the affairs of the company 154
Petitioning for the winding up of the company 154
Other examples of statutory protection for minorities 154
The rule in *Foss v Harbottle* and minority interests 155
  Application of the rule 156
  Apparent judicial exceptions to the rule 156
  The derivative action 157
Interests, other than investors' interests, to be considered 158

Chapter 17   A Company's Contractual Powers, Name and Registered Office 159
Constitutional documents 159
  Constructive notice 159
Effect of ultra vires transactions 160
  Effect of doctrine on drafting of objects clauses 160
Evolution of the modern objects clause 160
  Bell Houses (or catch-all) clauses 161
Company powers 161
  Power to make gratuitous payments 162
  Power to lend money 164
  Other express powers 164
Investors and the ultra vires doctrine 164
  Alteration of objects clause 165
Creditors and the ultra vires doctrine 165
  Section 8 protection 165
    Acts lawfully and effectively done 166
    Person relying on s 8 must not be actually aware 166
    Regulation 6 protection 167
    Regulation 6 and s 8 compared 167
    Regulation 10 168
    Position of company under ultra vires contracts 168
Company name 168
  Power to dispense with the word 'limited' 169
  Change of name 169

Publication of name   169
Officers' liability for use of name incorrectly   169
Registered office   170
Registers and documents to be kept at registered office   170
Service of proceedings on a company   170

Chapter 18   Company Contracts and the Powers of its Human Agents   171
Form of company contracts   171
The seal   171
The company's human agents   172
Agency law principles   172
Definition of agent   172
Authority of agent   172
Actual and ostensible authority   173
Usual authority of company's agents   173
Board of directors   174
Internal limits on borrowing powers and lender protection   174
Exceptions to the rule in *Turquand*'s case   175
Protection of lenders under art 79   175
Managing director   176
Chairman   176
Individual directors   176
Company secretary   176
Shareholders   176
Third party protection and the doctrine of ostensible authority   176
Conditions necessary   177
Managing directors and chairman   177
Directors and managers   178
The company secretary   178
The ultra vires doctrine and company agents   178

PART V   DIRECTORS' PROCEEDINGS, DUTIES AND LIABILITIES   181

Chapter 19   Directors' Proceedings and Common Law Duties   183
Directors   183
Proceedings of directors   183
Committees   184
Chairman's and managing directors' roles   184
Duties of directors   184
The company's best interests   185
Employees' interests   185
The interests of creditors   185
Directors' duties generally   186
Common law duties   186
Fiduciary duties   186
Responsibility for company property and monies   186
Not making a secret profit   187
Avoiding conflicts of interest   188
Maintaining voting impartiality   188
The proper exercise of directors' fiduciary powers   188
Duties of care and skill   190

Degree of skill	190
Diligence	191
Delegation of responsibilities	191
Concluding summary	191
Chapter 20 Statutory Strengthening of Directors' Duties	193
The Companies Act 1990	193
Strengthening of directors' honesty requirements	193
Transactions involving directors (and others)	193
Connected persons	193
Shadow directors	194
Disclosure of interest in proposed contracts	194
Specific transactions regulated	194
Directors' service contracts	195
Substantial property transactions with directors	195
Effect of breach of s 29	195
Penalising the dealing in options to trade in certain shares and debentures	195
Prohibition of loans and credit to directors and connected persons	196
General prohibition on granting of credit to directors	196
'Permitted' credit transactions	196
Transactions below a certain value	197
Intra-group loans and transactions	197
Business transactions and advances on directors' expenses	197
Civil remedies for the making of prohibited loans, etc	197
Personal liability for company debts	197
Disclosure of transactions involving directors, and others, in the accounts	198
When disclosure is not required	198
Particulars to be disclosed in companies' accounts	199
Disclosure of directors' and others' interests in shares and debentures	199
Share dealings by directors, secretaries and their families	199
Sanction for non-compliance	199
Register of directors' and other interests	200
Disclosure of interests in directors' reports or accounts	200
Insider dealing by connected persons	200
Unlawful dealing in securities by insiders	201
Lawful dealings	201
Connected persons	201
Other companies and tippees	201
Liability for insider dealing	202
Time-limits	202
Criminal sanctions	202
Exempt transactions	202
Stock Exchange supervision of insider dealing regulations	202
Annual report	203
EU dimension	203
Fraudulent trading	203
Raising of directors' competency levels	203
Keeping proper books of account	203
Purpose of books of account	203
Contents of books of account	204
Criteria for proper books of account	204
Personal liability of directors and officers	204

Reckless trading 204

Chapter 21   Legal Liabilities of Directors and Others 207
The two perspectives 207
Directors' liability to the company 207
Remedies against directors by the company 207
Relief of directors from liability for breach of duty 208
Section 391 relief 208
Relief in the articles of association 208
Insurance 208
Directors' liability to outsiders as agents of the company 209
Common law liabilities to outsiders 209
Ultra vires and unauthorised transactions 209
Personal contractual liability 209
Tortious liability of a director 210
Corporate crimes 210
Criminal sanctions in the Companies Acts against directors and others 210
Statutory liabilities of directors to outsiders 211
Directors' personal liability for the debts of an insolvent company 212
Liability for failure to keep proper books of account 212
Defence 212
Types of company losses 212
Judicial interpretation 213
Liability for reckless trading 214
Who can initiate proceedings? 214
What is reckless trading? 214
Defence 214
Judicial interpretation of reckless trading provisions 215
Scope of s 297A 216
Meaning of 'recklessness' 216
Under s 297A(2)(a) – the objective test 216
Under s 297A(2)(b) – the subjective test 216
Liability for fraudulent trading 217
Criminal sanctions for fraudulent trading 219

Chapter 22   Directors' and Officers' Professional Indemnity Insurance 221
Claims for compensation 221
Who is able to sue? 221
Legal proceedings against directors and officers by minority investors 222
Legal proceedings by non-members 223
Events giving rise to legal proceedings against directors 225
Cover provided by D&O policies 225
Policy exclusions 226
Basis of cover 227
Section 200 and D&O policies 227
The future of D&O insurance 227
Modern attitude towards directors' responsibilities 228

Chapter 23   Restriction and Disqualification of Directors 229
The Companies Act 1990 229
Part VII of the 1990 Act 229
Restrictions on directors 230
Effect of s 150 restriction declaration 230

Exemption and relief	230
Duties of liquidators and receivers	231
Effect of restriction declarations on companies	231
Restrictions on the company	231
Relief for the company	232
Disqualification of directors	232
Disqualification order	232
Mandatory disqualification	232
Discretionary disqualification	232
Who may apply for the making of a disqualification order?	233
Relief from disqualification order	233
Enforcement and sanctions	233
Civil consequences	234
Other directors	234
Acting under direction of disqualified person	234
Register of orders	235
Undischarged bankrupts	235

PART VI MONITORING THE DIRECTORS' STEWARDSHIP OF THE COMPANY — 237

Chapter 24 Financial Records, Accounts and Reports	239
Basic financial records	239
Books of account	239
Sanctions for breach of s 202	240
Criminal sanctions	240
Defences	240
Officers	240
Other criminal sanctions	241
Civil liability of officers for debts of the company	241
The annual accounts	241
Group accounts	241
Failure to prepare annual accounts	242
Preparation of annual accounts	242
Shareholders' accounts and filed accounts	242
Form and content of accounts	243
Formats	243
Balance sheet layout	243
Profit and loss account layout	245
Vertical and horizontal layouts	246
Accounting principles	246
Valuation rules	247
Fixed and current assets	248
Revaluation reserve	248
Information required by way of notes to the accounts	248
Balance sheet	248
Profit and loss account	249
Details of subsidiaries	249
Other information required in accounts	249
Directors' salaries, etc	249
Disclosures of transactions involving directors, and others	249
Medium-sized and small private companies	249
Tests to be satisfied	250

Directors' report 250
  Expanded directors' report 251
  Extra statement for directors of small or medium-sized companies 251
Auditors' report 252
  Contents of auditors' report 252
  Expanded auditors' report 252
  Special auditors' report 252
  Recommendation in Partnership 2000 253
Profits available for distribution 253
Dividends 253
Approval of annual accounts 254

Chapter 25 Statutory Registers, Books and the Annual Return 255
Maintaining registers 255
Statutory registers 255
  The register of members 255
  Extra registers for plcs 256
  Register of directors and secretaries 256
  Register of directors' interests in shares and debentures of the company 257
  Register of debenture-holders 257
Statutory books and minutes 257
  Minute books 258
Annual returns 258
  Information to be included in annual return 258
  Companies not having a share capital 259
  Documents to be attached to the annual return 259
    Medium-sized and small private companies 260
    Concessions for medium-sized private companies 260
    Concessions for small private companies 260
    Section 12 exemptions in relation to notes to the accounts 261
  Summary of 1986 Act concessions for medium-sized and small companies 261
  Large companies 261
  Certificates to be attached by private companies 262
  Time-limit for filing of annual return 262

Chapter 26 The Auditor's Role and Responsibility 263
The auditor 263
Appointment of auditors 263
  First auditors 263
  Subsequent auditors 263
    Retiring auditors 263
    Appointment by Minister 264
  Qualifications for appointment 264
    Recognition of accountancy bodies 264
    Registration of auditors 265
    Individually recognised auditors 265
    Prosecution 265
  Persons disqualified from acting as auditors 265
Remuneration of auditors 266
Termination of auditor's appointment 266
  Resignation of an auditor 266
  Removal and replacement of an auditor 266

Extended notice 267
General position of auditors 267
Auditors' rights 267
Auditors' duties 268
If proper books of account are not being kept 269
Directors' emoluments 269
Auditors and the 1983 Act 269
Penalties for false statements to auditors 270
Civil liability of auditors 270
Auditors' standard of care 270
Auditors' liability under contract 270
Contracting out of liability 271
Auditors' liability in tort 271
Contracting out of liability for negligent acts 272
Auditors' concern over size of potential liability 272

Chapter 27   Investigations into a Company's Affairs and Ownership 275
Appointment of inspectors 275
Investigation of a company's affairs 275
Who can apply for appointment of inspectors? 275
Applications by the Minister 276
Duties of company officers and agents 276
Secret transactions 277
Examination on oath 277
Related companies 277
Inspector's sanctions 277
Inspector's reports 278
Copies 278
Acting upon the inspector's report 278
Expenses of investigation into company's affairs 278
Investigation by an inspector into the ownership of a company 279
Inspector's powers 280
Minister's powers to investigate company ownership 280
Powers to enter and search premises 281
Security of information obtained 281
Power to impose restrictions on shares 281
Criminal offence 282
Lifting of restrictions on shares 282
Limits on investigating foreign companies 282

PART VII   INVESTORS' INDIVIDUAL RIGHTS AND RESPONSIBILITIES 283

Chapter 28   Acquiring and Relinquishing Company Membership 285
Membership 285
Who can become members? 285
Infants and minors 285
Companies 285
Buying its own shares 286
Purchasing the shares of its holding company 286
Deceased members 287
Bankrupt members 287
How persons may become members 287

By subscribing to the memorandum   287
By agreeing to become members   287
Transfer of shares   288
   Directors' powers   288
Transmission of shares   288
Estoppel   289
Condition precedent to membership   289
Register of members   289
Rectification of the register   289
Trusts not be entered in the register   290
How persons relinquish membership   290

Chapter 29   The Investors' Statutory Contract   293
Significance of membership   293
   Corporate majority decisions and individual members' rights 293
Shares   294
   What is a share?   294
      Essential nature   294
      Essentially a contract   295
   The s 25 contract   295
   Shareholders' rights   297
   Shareholders' duties   298
   Public subscriptions for shares   298
   Calls   298
   Types of shares   298
   Variation of class rights   298
   Amount and numbering of shares   299
   Share certificates   299
      Object of certificate   299
      Effect of certificate   299
   Comment on case-law   300
   Share warrants   301
Conversion of shares into stock   301

Chapter 30   Dividends and Calls on Shares   303
Shareholders' rights and liabilities   303
Shareholders' principal rights   303
   Dividends   303
      Right to a dividend   303
      Amount of dividend payable   304
      Mode of payment   305
      Shares in lieu of dividends   305
      Effect of declaration of dividend   305
Financial liabilities of shareholders   305
   Making a call for payment   306
      Limits   306
      Early payment of calls   306
      Late payment   307
   Non-payment of calls   307
   Forfeiture of shares   307
      Notice of forfeiture   307
      Effect of forfeiture   307

Surrender of shares 308
Lien on members' shares 308
Notice of other interests 308

Chapter 31 Disclosure and Transfers of Shareholders' Interests 309
The register 309
Disclosure of interests in shares 309
  Share dealings by directors, secretaries and their families 309
  Disclosure of significant interests in shares of a plc 309
  Register of significant interests 310
    Investigations of interests in shares 310
  Notification of thresholds to Stock Exchange 311
  Notification of interests of concert parties 311
  Disclosure orders for interests in private companies 311
  Exempted companies 312
  Who can apply for a disclosure order? 312
  Scope of disclosure order 312
  Contravention of disclosure order 313
Transfer of shares 313
  Assignment of interest 313
    The Stock Transfer Form 313
    Contents 314
    Procedure 315
  Consequences 315
  Registration of the transferee 315
  Directors' powers to refuse registration in private companies 315
  Summary – private company share transfers 316
  Directors' powers to refuse registration in plcs 317
  Notice of refusal to register 318
    Delays 318
  Consequences of non-registration 318
  Non-registration and subsequent transfers 318
    Competing claims 318
  Forged transfers 319
  Certification of transfer 319
  Rights issues and voluntary share transfers 320
  Computerised transfers of shares 320
    A new vocabulary 320
  The 1996 Regulations outlined 321
  Involuntary share transfers 321
  Compulsory purchase of shares 322
Share warrants 322

PART VIII CREDITORS' RIGHTS AGAINST THE COMPANY AND ITS OFFICERS 323

Chapter 32 Company Creditors and their Securities (Charges) 325
Creditors 325
  Creditors' rights generally 325
  Company information for creditors 326
  Unsecured creditors 326
  Preferential creditors 327

Secured creditors   327
A company's borrowing powers   327
Debentures   328
  Debentures and shares   328
  Security for company borrowing   329
Charges   329
Mortgages and fixed charges   330
  Charges by way of mortgage   330
    Legal and equitable interests   330
  Fixed charges   330
Floating charges   331
  Crystallisation of a floating charge   331
  Effect of crystallisation   332
    De-crystallisation   332
  Advantages to companies of floating charges   332
  Disadvantages to lenders   332
    Avoidance under ss 288 and 289   333
    Solvency   333
    Loss of priority under s 98   333
    Commercial risks   333
    Reservation of title clauses   334
    Subsequent fixed charges   334
    Negative pledge clauses   334
Fixed or floating charge?   335

Chapter 33   Debentures, Registration and Priority of Charges   337
The debenture   337
Types of debenture   337
  Registered and bearer debentures   337
  Redeemable and perpetual debentures   337
Forms of debenture   338
  The charge   338
  The conditions   338
  Interpretation of wording   339
  Trustees for the debenture-holders   339
Registration of charges securing debentures   340
  Register of charges   340
  Extension of registration time and correction of errors in the register   341
  Register of debenture-holders   341
Transfer of debentures   341
  Transfer generally 'subject to equities'   342
  Priority of charges   342
    Effect of registration on priorities   342
Re-issue of debentures   343
Debenture stock   343
Debenture-holders' remedies   343
Debts due from debenture-holders   343

**Chapter 34   Creditors' Remedies Against the Company – Consequences of
  Receivership**   345
Rights of action   345
Unsecured creditors' remedies   345

Debenture-holders' remedies 345
Appointment of receiver 346
Appointment under a fixed charge 346
Appointment under a floating charge 346
Jeopardy 346
Appointment by the court 347
Qualifications of receiver 347
Notice of appointment 347
Invoices and letterheads 347
Notifications and information 348
Powers of receivers and managers 348
Application to court for directions or objections 349
Application of monies realised 349
Effect of appointment of a receiver 349
The status of a receiver 350
Receivers appointed by the debenture-holders 350
Receivers appointed by the court 350
The receiver and company contracts 351
Existing contracts 351
New contracts 351
Substituting new for existing contracts 351
Contracts of employment 352

Chapter 35 The Receiver's Rights and Duties – Premature Ending of his Powers 353
Rights of receiver 353
Remuneration 353
Indemnification 353
Defective appointment 353
Receiver's duties 353
Duty when selling property 354
Sale of non-cash assets 354
Duties in applying the proceeds of sale of assets 354
Duty to report misconduct 355
Receiver's specific statutory tasks 355
Notification 355
Statement of particulars 355
Verification of particulars 355
Copies to registrar and debenture-holders 356
Delivering of half-yearly returns to the registrar 356
Enforcement of receiver's duty to make returns 357
Liabilities of receivers 357
Application to the court for directions 357
Premature termination of receiver's powers 357
Resignation 357
Removal 358
Receivers, examiners and liquidators 358
Effect on receiver of appointment of examiner 358
Effect on receiver of appointment of liquidator 359

Chapter 36   Unsatisfied Creditors' Remedies Against the Company's
    Members and Officers   361
Creditors' remedies   361
Unsatisfied creditors' remedies against the members   361
    Immunity of members   362
Unsatisfied creditors' claims against directors and officers   362
    Directors' and officers' liabilities towards creditors   363
        Failure to keep proper books of account   363
        Reckless and fraudulent trading   363
        Restriction and disqualification   364
    The post-1990 legal environment   364

PART IX   PROTECTION AVAILABLE TO A COMPANY AGAINST ITS
    CREDITORS   365

Chapter 37   Examinership and its Effects on Creditors' Rights   367
The effect of examinership   367
Power of the court   367
    Related companies   369
    Interim examiner   369
    Security for costs   369
    Examiner's liability for company contracts   370
        Right to indemnity   370
    Qualifications of an examiner   370
Who can petition the court?   370
    Notification of examiner's appointment   371
        By the examiner   371
        In letterheadings etc   371
    Consequences of examinership   371
    Company immunities   372
    Receivers   372
    Provisional liquidators   372
Powers of examiner   373
    Further powers of the court over company management   373
    Seeking the production of documents and evidence   374
    Examination on oath   374
    Directors' statement of affairs   374
    Meetings   375
    Discovery of detrimental conduct   375
        Remedies   375
    Certification of expenses   375
    Applications to the court for direction   376
    Power to deal with charged property   376
    The right to seek a transfer of the directors' powers   376
Effect of examinership on creditors' rights   377
    Costs of examinership paramount   377
    Secured creditors   377
    Unsecured creditors   378

Chapter 38   The Examiner's Opinion and the Future of the Company   379
Duty of examiner   379
Information in examiner's report   379

Examiner's opinions 379
Examiner's recommendation 380
When examiner's recommendation is positive 380
Examiner's report under s 18 381
Avoidance of certain company contracts 381
The proposed rescue package 381
Impairment 382
Committee of creditors 382
Plenary meetings 383
Confirmation by the court 383
Objections 383
Court's decision 384
Revocation on grounds of fraud 384
Cessation of protection order 384
When examiner's report is negative 384
Power of the court 385

**PART X   FINANCIAL ARRANGEMENTS AND RESTRUCTURING;
CHANGE(S) IN OWNERSHIP AND WINDING UP OF COMPANIES** 387

**Chapter 39   Financial Arrangements Between the Company, its Creditors
and Members** 389
Payment of outstanding company debts 389
Section 201 schemes of arrangement and compromises 389
Who may apply to the court? 390
The statutory meetings 390
Class meetings 390
Information for members and creditors 390
Approval of members and creditors 391
Court sanction of scheme 391
Objections by minorities 391
Amalgamations 392
Registration of the court order 392
Uses for schemes of arrangement 392
Reconstructions 393
Amalgamations 393
Reconstructions under section 260 393
Procedure 393
Effect of winding-up order 394
Dissenting members' rights 394
Section 260 and a creditors' voluntary winding up 394
Amalgamations generally 395

Chapter 40   Company Takeovers and Mergers 397
Introduction 397
Takeover procedure 397
Power to compulsorily acquire shares of minority 397
Rights of dissentient members 398
Onus of proof 398
Proving unfairness 398
Dissentient's opportunity to sell 399
Legal controls over profiteering 399

Compensation for loss of office on mergers etc   400
The City Code on Takeovers and Mergers   400
     The City Code and s 204   401
The Irish Takeover Panel   401
  Rulings and directions   402
  Appeals   402
The European Communities (Mergers and Divisions of Companies)
  Regulations 1987   402
  Procedure   403
  Liability of directors and independent persons   403
  Confirmation by the court   403
     Copy to registrar   403
  The European Communities (Safeguarding of Employees' Rights on
     Transfer of Undertakings) Regulations 1980   404
  Controlling the economic impact of mergers and takeovers   404
  The Mergers, Takeovers and Monopolies (Control) Act 1978   404
     Procedure   405
  The Competition Act 1991   405
  Powers of the Competition Authority   406
  Sanctions available to aggrieved persons   406
     Defences   406
  The 1978 and 1991 Acts   406
  The Competition (Amendment) Act 1996   407
  Abuse of a dominant position   408
Intra-EU and international trading   408

**Chapter 41   Initiation of Winding-Up Procedure by Creditors, Members and
  Others**   411
Limited liability companies   411
Methods of dissolution   411
Methods of winding up   411
  Winding up by the court   412
     Grounds for compulsory winding up   412
     Inability to pay its debts   412
     Just and equitable grounds   414
     Oppression of a member   415
  Who may petition the court to wind up the company?   415
     Petitions by contributories, by the Minister and by members   416
     Effect of winding-up order   416
     Effects of application to wind up   416
  Commencement of winding up by the court   416
  Members' voluntary winding up   417
     Circumstances in which company may be wound up voluntarily   417
     Publication of resolution   417
     Commencement of winding up   417
     Consequences of voluntary winding up   417
     Statutory declaration of solvency   417
     Independent verification   418
     Objections by creditors   418
     Liability of directors for declaration of solvency   418
     Appointment of liquidator   418
  Creditors' voluntary winding up   419

Initiation of a creditors' voluntary winding up	419
Appointment of liquidator	419

Chapter 42 The Official Liquidator's Role 421

Winding-up orders	421
Conducting the winding-up proceedings	421
Actions stayed	421
The statement of affairs	421
Appointment of official liquidator	422
Impartiality	422
Publicity	423
Title	423
Terms of appointment	423
Position	423
Resignation and removal of liquidator	423
Procedures to be followed by liquidators	424
Procedure for calling meetings	424
Committees of inspection	424
Powers of the liquidator	425
Without prior approval	425
With prior approval	425
Duties of the liquidator	426
Duty to take company's property into his custody	426
Duty to settle list of contributories	426
Meaning of contributory	427
Present members' liability	427
Past members' liability	427
Lists of contributories	427
Rectification	427
Liability of contributories	427
Directors as contributories	428
Duty to admit or reject proof of debts	428
Bankruptcy rules and set off	428
Time-limits	428
Procedure for ascertaining creditors	429
Duty to realise the company assets	429
Maximising company assets	429
Related companies	430
Pooling of assets of related companies	430
Minimising the company's liabilities	431
Avoidance of floating charges	431
Floating charges and connected persons	432
Floating charges and officers	432
Fraudulent preferences	432
Disclaimer of onerous property and contracts	433
Getting in the company's assets	433
Duty to pay the company's debts	433
Where the company is solvent	433
Where the company is insolvent	433
Secured creditors with fixed charges	433
Costs of the liquidation	434
Section 285 ranking of debts	434

Preferential creditors   434
Floating chargees   435
Unsecured creditors   435
Members and contributories of the company   435
Duty to co-operate with the court and the relevant authorities   436
Termination of liquidation and dissolution of the company   436

Chapter 43   Members' Voluntary Liquidation Procedures   437
Members' voluntary winding up   437
Effect of liquidator's appointment   437
Duties and powers of liquidator   437
Duty to call meetings   438
Annual meetings   438
Final meetings   438
Dissolution of the company   439
Powers of the liquidator in a reconstruction   439
If company is insolvent   439
Consequence for the winding-up procedure   440
Appointment of new liquidator by creditors   440
Annual and final meetings   440

Chapter 44   Creditors' Voluntary Winding-Up Procedures   441
Introduction   441
Meeting of creditors   441
Appointment of liquidator   441
Effect of appointment of liquidator   442
Committee of inspection   442
Composition   442
Procedures   442
Duties of the liquidator   443
Annual meetings   443
Final meetings   443
Dissolution of the company   443

APPENDICES

Appendix A   The Irish Stock Exchange and its Member Firms   447

Appendix B   Potential Criminal Liabilities of Company Directors 449

Appendix C   Additional Reading   451

INDEX   453

TABLE OF CASES

References are to paragraph numbers, except for roman numerals, which are references to pages of the Preface.

ADT v BDO Binder Hamlyn [1996] BCC 808 — 26.30
AT & T Istel Ltd v Tully [1993] AC 45, [1992] 3 All ER 523, [1992] 3 WLR 344 (HL) — 27.11
Aaron's Reefs Ltd v Twiss [1896] AC 273, 65 LJPC 54, 74 LT 794 (HL); *affirming* [1895] CA 2 IR 207 — 10.45
Adams v Cape Industries plc [1990] Ch 433, [1991] 1 All ER 929, [1990] 2 WLR 657 — 6.16
Alexander v Automatic Telephone Co [1900] 2 Ch 56, 69 LJ Ch 428, 82 LT 400 (CA) — 30.10
Allen v Gold Reefs of West Africa [1900] 1 Ch 656, 69 LJ Ch 266, 82 LT 210 (CA) — 16.4, 19.19
Allied Irish Banks Ltd v Ardmore Studios International (1972) Ltd (unreported) 30 May 1973 (HC) — 18.12
Allied Irish Coal Suppliers Ltd v Powell Duffryn International Fuels Ltd [1997] 1 ILRM 306 (HC) — 6.16
Aluminium Fabricators Ltd, Re [1984] ILRM 399 (HC) — 2.7, 21.32
Aluminium Industrie Vaassen BV v Romalpa Aluminium [1976] 2 All ER 552, [1976] 1 WLR 676, [1976] 1 Lloyd's Rep 443, 120 SJ 95 (CA) — 32.28
Angelis v Algemene Bank Nederland (Ireland) Ltd and Others (unreported) 4 July 1974 (HC) — 15.13, 34.7
Anglo Overseas Agencies Ltd v Green [1961] 1 QB 1, [1960] 3 All ER 244, [1960] 3 WLR 561, 104 SJ 765 — 17.13
Arclex Optical Corporation v McMurray [1958] Ir Jur Rep 65 (HC) — 19.15
Armstrong v Jackson [1917] 2 KB 822 — 9.7
Ashbury Railway Carriage and Iron Co Ltd v Riche (1875) LR 7 HL 653, 44 LJ Exch 185, 33 LT 450 — 17.3, 17.5
Ashmark Ltd (No 2), Re (unreported) 8 December 1989 (HC) — 41.12
Atlantic Magnetics Ltd, Re [1993] 2 IR 561 (SC) — 37.2, 37.33
Attorney-General v Great Eastern Rly Co (1880) 5 App Cas 473, [1874–80] All ER Rep Ext 1459 — 17.2
Attorney-General for Ireland v Jameson [1904] 2 IR 644 (ChD) — 29.5, 29.7

Bahia and San Francisco Railway Co, Re (1868) LR 3 QB 584, 37 LJQB 176 — 29.20
Balgooley Distillery Co, Re (1886–87) 17 LR Ir 239 — 13.24
Bank of Ireland Finance v Rockfield Ltd [1979] IR 21 (SC) — 13.41, 13.42
Bannantyne v Direct Spanish Telegraph Co (1886) 34 ChD 287, 56 LJ Ch 107, 55 LT 716 (CA) — 13.5, 13.7
Barnett Hoares & Co v South London Tramways Co (1887) 18 QBD 815 (CA) — 14.34
Battle v Irish Art Promotion Centre Ltd [1968] IR 252 — 3.8
Beauforte (Jon) (London), Re; Applications of Grainger Smith & Co (Builders), John Wright & Son (Veneers) and Lowell Baldwin [1953] Ch 131, [1953] 1 All ER 634, [1953] 2 WLR 465 — 17.3, 17.15
Belfast Empire Theatre of Varieties Ltd, Re [1963] IR 41 (HC) — 30.8, 42.10

Bell Houses v City Wall Properties [1966] 2 QB 656, [1966] 2 All ER 674,
    [1966] 2 WLR 1323, 110 SJ 268, [1965] CLY 482 (CA)   17.5, 17.6
Bishopsgate Investment Management Ltd v Maxwell [1993] BCC 120 (CA)   19.19
Bloomenthal v Ford [1897] AC 156 (HL)   29.20
Bluth (Don) Entertainment Ltd and Related Companies, Re (1994) *Irish Times
    Law Reports*, 4 July (SC)   37.28, 37.33
Bolton (HL) Engineering Co Ltd v Graham (TJ) & Sons Ltd [1957] 1 QB 159,
    [1956] 3 All ER 624, [1956] 3 WLR 804 (CA)   18.1
Bond Worth Ltd, Re [1980] Ch 228, [1979] 3 All ER 919, [1979] 3 WLR 629 32.28
Borland's Trustee v Steel Bros & Co Ltd [1901] 1 Ch 279, 70 LJ Ch 51, 49 WR
    120   29.6
Bradford Banking Co v Henry Briggs & Co (1886) 12 App Cas 29, 56 LJ Ch
    364, 56 LT 62 (HL)   30.20
Bray Travel Ltd and Bray Travel (Holdings) Ltd, Re (unreported) 13 July 1981 6.7
Brightlife, Re [1987] Ch 200, [1986] 3 All ER 673, [1987] 2 WLR 197   32.19
Brinsmead (TE) & Sons, Re [1897] 1 Ch 45   41.7
Broderip v Salomon [1895] 2 Ch 323   3.3
Bugle Press, Re, Application of H C Treby, Re, Houses and Estates [1961] Ch
    270, [1960] 3 All ER 791, [1960] 3 WLR 956 (CA)   6.13, 6.14, 40.6
Bula Ltd, Re (unreported) 18 July 1986 (HC)   41.6
Burkinshaw v Nicholls (1878) 3 App Cas 1004, 48 LJ Ch 179 (HL)   29.20
Burt, Boulton & Hayward v Bull [1895] 1 QB 276   34.19
Butler Engineering Ltd, Re (unreported) 1 March 1996 (HC)   37.2

C & A Modes v C & A (Waterford) Ltd [1976] IR 198   7.10
Campbell v Paddington Corporation [1911] 1 KB 869   21.12
Canadian Aero Service v O'Malley (1973) 40 DLR (3d) 371, [1974] SCR 592
    (SC Can)   19.14
Candler v Crane, Christmas & Co [1951] 2 KB 164, [1951] 1 All ER 426, 95 SJ
    171 (CA)   26.29
Caparo Industries v Dickman [1990] 2 AC 605, [1990] 1 All ER 568, [1990] 2
    WLR 358 (HL)   26.30, 26.31
Caratal (New) Mines Ltd, Re [1902] 2 Ch 498, [1902] WN 120   15.22
Carlton Holdings, Re [1971] 2 All ER 1082, [1971] 1 WLR 918, 115 SJ 301   40.3
Carrigan (PJ) Ltd and PJ Carrigan v Norwich Union Fire Insurance Society Ltd
    and Scottish Union and National Insurance Company Ltd (No 2)
    (unreported) 11 December 1987 (HC)   4.8
Carroll Industries plc v O'Cualacháin [1988] IR 705   24.22
Carvill (Michael Meade) v Irish Industrial Bank Ltd [1968] IR 325 (SC) 14.29
Casey v Bentley [1902] 1 IR 376 (CA)   29.6, 31.27
Cavan Crystal Group Ltd, Re (unreported) 26 April 1996 (HC)   23.5
Chic, Ltd [1905] 2 Ch 345   41.7
China Steamship Co, Re, ex parte Mackenzie (1869) LR 7 Eq 240, 38 LJ Ch
    199   33.17
City Equitable Fire Insurance Co Ltd, Re [1925] Ch 407   19.20, 19.25
Clarets Ltd, Re; Spain v McCann and Stonehurst Bank (Ireland) Ltd [1978]
    ILRM 215   33.19
Clark v Workman [1920] 1 IR 107 (ChD)   19.17, 19.19, 29.8, 29.10
Clemens v Clemens Bros [1976] 2 All ER 268   16.5
Clubman Shirts Ltd, Re [1983] ILRM 323   16.11

Cockburn v Newbridge Sanitary Steam Laundry Co [1915] 1 IR 237   16.22
Comhlucht Páipéar Riomhaireachta Teo v Udarás Na Gaeltachta [1990] 1 IR
    320   42.47
Contract Packaging Ltd, Re (1992) *The Irish Times,* January 16, 17, 18   21.32
Cook v Deeks [1916] AC 554, 85 LJPC 161 (PC)   16.22
Cooley Distillery/Irish Distillers Case, Competition Authority Decision No 285,
    25 February 1994   40.29
Corporate Affairs Commission v David James Finance Ltd [1975] 2 NSWLR
    710   10.19
Corran Construction Co Ltd v Bank of Ireland Finance Ltd (unreported) 8
    September 1976 (HC)   42.40
Cotman v Brougham [1918] AC 514, 87 LJ Ch 379 (HL)   17.5
Coveney v Persse [1910] 1 IR 194   32.30
Cox v Dublin City Distillery (No 2) [1915] 1 IR 345   18.12
Creation Printing Co Ltd, Re, Crowley v Northern Bank Finance Corporation
    Ltd and Another [1981] IR 353 (SC)   32.25, 42.37
Credit Finance Bank plc, Re (unreported) 9 June 1982 (HC)   15.18
Credit Finance Bank plc, Re (unreported) 19 June 1989 (HC)   13.7
Crowe (W & L) Ltd & Another v ESB (unreported) 9 May 1984 (HC)   34.23
Cummins v Stewart [1911] 1 IR 236   vii

DHN Food Distributors v Tower Hamlets London Borough Council; Bronze
    Investments v Same; DHN Food Transport v Same [1976] 1 WLR 852,
    [1976] JPL 363, *sub nom* DHN Food Distributors v London Borough of
    Tower Hamlets [1976] 3 All ER 462 (CA)   6.7, 6.10
DPP v Kent & Sussex Contractors Co Ltd [1944] KB 146, [1944] 1 All ER 119   21.13
Daimler Co v Continental Tyre and Rubber Co (Great Britain) [1916] 2 AC
    307 (HL)   6.9
Daly (John) & Co Ltd, Re (1887–88) 19 LR Ir 83   41.12
Daniels v Daniels [1978] Ch 406, [1978] 2 All ER 89, [1978] 2 WLR 73   16.22, 22.3
Dairy Lee Ltd; Stakelum v Canning [1976] IR 314 (HC)   14.5, 42.49
Derry v Peek (1889) 14 App Cas 337, [1886–90] All ER Rep 1, 58 LJ Ch 864
    (HL)   10.42
Desmond v Glackin (No 2) [1993] 3 IR 67 (HC)   27.15
Dockrell & Co v Dockrell & Co (1941) 75 ILTR 226 (HC)   7.10
Doherty (GS) Ltd v Doherty and Another (unreported) 19 December 1969
    (SC)   16.5
Dorchester Finance Co Ltd v Stebbings [1989] BCLC 498 (ChD)   19.21
Dovey v Cory [1901] AC 477 (HL)   19.25
Dublin County Council v Elton Homes Ltd [1984] ILRM 297 (HC)   6.14
Dublin North City Milling Co Ltd, Re [1909] 1 Ir R 179   31.24
Dubned Exports Ltd, Re (unreported) 9 May 1986 (HC)   41.6
Dun Laoghaire Corporation v Parkhill Development [1989] IR 477   6.14

Ebrahimi v Westbourne Galleries [1973] AC 360, [1972] 2 All ER 492, [1972] 2
    WLR 1289 (HL)   41.7
Edenpark Construction Ltd, Re (unreported) 17 December 1993 (HC)   37.19, 37.28
Eley v Positive Government Security Life Assurance Co Ltd (1876) 1 ExD 88
    (CA)   14.12, 29.9

Erlanger v New Sombrero Phosphate Co (1878) 3 App Cas 1218, 48 LJ Ch 73,
  39 LT 269 (HL)   9.3, 9.7
Europemballage Corpn and Continental Can Co Inc v Commission of the
  European Communities [1973] ECR 215, [1973] CMLR 587, ECJ   40.32
Ewing v Buttercup Margarine Co [1917] 2 Ch 1, 86 LJ Ch 441 (CA)   7.9
Exchange Banking Co, Flitcroft's Case, Re (1882) 21 ChD 519 (CA)   13.1

Farm Fresh Frozen Foods Ltd, Re [1980] ILRM 131   33.12
Fitzpatrick v Fitzpatricks Footwear Ltd (unreported) 18 November 1970 (HC) 14.26
Floating Dock Co of St Thomas Ltd, Re [1895] 1 Ch 691, 64 LJ Ch 361, 39 Sol
  Jo 284   13.7
Forest of Dean Coal Mining Co, Re (1878) 10 ChD 450, 27 WR 594, 40 LT 287 14.5
Foss v Harbottle (1843) 2 Hare 461, 67 ER 189   16.5, 16.19, 16.21, 16.22, 16.23, 19.5,
                                                 21.3, 22.3, 22.4, 22.14, 29.2
Frederick Inns Ltd, Re [1994] 1 ILRM 387 (SC); [1991] ILRM 582 (HC)   16.24,
                                               17.9–17.11, 17.17, 17.20, 19.8
Freeman & Lockyer (a Firm) v Buckhurst Park Properties (Mangal) Ltd [1964]
  2 QB 480, [1964] 1 All ER 630, [1964] 2 WLR 618 (CA)   18.20, 18.21, 18.22

Galloway v Halle Concerts Society [1915] 2 Ch 233, 84 LJ Ch 723, [1914–15]
  All ER Rep 543   30.10
Galway and Salthill Tramway Co, Re [1918] 1 IR 62, 52 ILT 41 (HC)   41.5
Garvey v Ireland [1981] IR 25 (SC)   14.28
General Auction Estate & Monetary Co v Smith [1891] 3 Ch 432   32.12
German Date Coffee Co Ltd, Re (1882) 20 ChD 169 (CA)   17.5, 41.7
Gerrard (Thomas) & Son Ltd, Re [1968] Ch 455, [1967] 2 All ER 525, [1967]
  3 WLR 84   26.26
Glover v BLN Ltd, Lincoln and Nolan, Lincoln and Nolan (Sales) and Lincoln
  and Nolan (Parts) [1973] IR 388 (SC)   14.28
Gluckstein v Barnes [1900] AC 240, 69 LJ Ch 385, 82 LT 393 (HL)   9.5, 9.8
Great Eastern Railway v Turner (1873) 8 Ch App 149   14.6
Great Wheel Polgooth Co Ltd, Re (1883) 53 LJ Ch 42   9.2
Greenhalgh v Arderne Cinemas [1945] 2 All ER 719; *affirmed* [1946] 1 All ER
  512   12.24
Greenhalgh v Arderne Cinemas [1951] Ch 286, [1950] 2 All ER 1120, 94 SJ
  855 (CA)   16.5
Greenore Trading Co Ltd, Re [1980] ILRM 94 (HC)   16.10
Grierson, Oldham & Adams Ltd, Re [1968] Ch 17, [1967] 1 All ER 192, [1967]
  1 WLR 385   40.5
Griffiths v Secretary of State for Social Services [1974] QB 468, [1973] 3 All ER
  1184, [1973] 3 WLR 831   34.16, 34.24
Guinness v Saunders [1988] 2 All ER 940, [1988] 1 WLR 863, (1988) 4 BCC
  377 (CA)   20.6

Hafner, Re, Olhausen v Powderly [1943] IR 426 (SC)   31.22
Halpin v Cremin [1954] IR 19 (HC)   32.19
Hammond Properties Ltd v Gajdis [1968] 3 All ER 267   18.6
Healy v Healy Homes Ltd [1973] IR 309 (HC)   24.3

Heaney v Ireland [1994] ILRM 420   27.11

Hedley Byrne & Co v Heller & Partners [1964] AC 465, [1963] 2 All ER 575, [1963] 3 WLR 101 (HL)   26.30

Hefferon Kearns Ltd (No 1), Re [1992] 1 ILRM 51, [1993] IR 3 177   21.27, 22.5

Hefferon Kearns Ltd (No 2), Re: Dublin Heating Co Ltd v Hefferon and Ors [1993] IR 3 191 (HC)   ix, 20.48, 21.26, 22.5

Hellenic & General Trust Ltd, Re [1975] 3 All ER 382, [1976] 1 WLR 123, 119 SJ 845   39.4, 39.14

Hely-Hutchinson v Brayhead Ltd [1968] 1 QB 549, [1967] 2 All ER 14, [1967] 2 WLR 1312   18.13, 18.22

Henderson v Bank of Australasia (1890) 45 ChD 330 (CA)   15.25

Hickey (WJ) Ltd (in Receivership), Re; Uniacke v Cassidy Electrical Supply Co Ltd [1988] IR 126 (HC)   32.28

Hickman v Kent or Romney Marsh Sheep Breeders' Association [1915] 1 Ch 881 (ChD)   29.9

Hilger Analytical Ltd v Rank Precision Industries [1984] BCLC 301, (1983) *The Times*, December 13   33.17

Hoare & Co Ltd, Re (1933) 150 LT 374   40.5

Hoare & Co Ltd (No 1), Re [1904] 2 Ch 208, [1904] WN 123 (CA)   13.5

Hodgson v Nalgo [1972] 1 All ER 15, [1972] 1 WLR 130, (1971) 116 SJ 56   16.22

Hogg v Cramphorn Ltd; Same v Same [1967] Ch 254, [1966] 3 All ER 420, [1966] 3 WLR 995   19.18

Holidair Ltd, Re [1994] 1 ILRM 481 (SC)   32.21, 32.30, 33.9, 37.34

Hopkins v Shannon Transport Systems Ltd (unreported) 10 July 1972 (HC)   9.5, 9.7, 20.6

Horsley & Weight, Re [1982] Ch 442, [1982] 3 All ER 1045, [1982] 3 WLR 431, (1982) 79 LS Gaz 919 (CA)   13.1, 13.35

Houghton & Co v Nothard, Lowe and Wills Ltd [1927] 1 KB 246   18.13

Houldsworth v City of Glasgow Bank (1880) 5 App Cas 317   10.42

Howard v Patent Ivory Manufacturing Co (1888) 38 ChD 156   18.13

Hull (Alexander) & Co Ltd v O'Carroll, Kent & Co (1955) 89 ILTR 70   34.8

Hunting Lodges Ltd, Re [1985] ILRM 75   21.31

Hutton v West Cork Railway Co (1883) 23 ChD 654 (CA)   17.9, 19.6

IRC v Crossman [1937] AC 26 (HL)   29.6

Industrial Development Consultants v Cooley [1972] 2 All ER 162, [1972] 1 WLR 443, (1971) 116 SJ 255   19.14, 19.15

International Retail Ltd, Re (unreported) 19 September 1979 (HC)   33.14

Irish Permanent Building Society v Registrar of Building Societies and Irish Life Building Society [1981] ILRM 242   3.9

Irish Tourist Promotions Ltd, Re (unreported) 22 April 1974 (HC)   41.6, 41.7

Irish Visiting Motorists' Bureau Ltd, Re (unreported) 27 January 1972 (HC)   16.11

Jackson v Munster Bank Ltd, ex parte Dease (1885) 15 LR Ir 356   19.13, 19.22

Jacobus Marler Estates Ltd v Marler, Re (1913) 85 LJPC 167n, (1913) 114 LT 640n   9.15

Jetmara Teo, Re (unreported) 10 May 1991 (HC)   38.9

Jones v Lipman [1962] 1 All ER 442, [1962] 1 WLR 832, 106 SJ 531   6.12, 6.14

Keenan Bros Ltd, Re [1985] IR 401 (SC)   32.18
Keenan Bros Ltd (in Liquidation), Re [1985] IR 641 (SC)   33.8, 33.9
Kelleher v Continental Irish Meat Ltd (unreported) 9 May 1978 (HC)   42.40
Kelly v Haughey Boland & Co [1989] ILRM 373   26.30
Kelly's Carpetdrome Ltd, Re (unreported) 1 July 1983 (HC)   2.7, 6.10, 21.32
Kilgobbin Mink and Stud Farms Ltd v National Credit Co Ltd (unreported) 16
    February 1978 (HC)   18.23
Kinsella and Others v Alliance and Dublin Consumers Gas Co & Others
    (unreported) 5 October 1982 (HC)   15.18, 28.16, 29.1
Kitson & Co Ltd, Re [1946] 1 All ER 435 (CA)   17.5, 41.7
Kleinwort Benson v Malaysia Mining Corp Berhad [1989] 1 All ER 785, [1989]
    1 WLR 379, [1989] 1 Lloyd's Rep 556 (CA)   6.16
Kreditbank Cassel GmbH v Schenkers [1927] 1 KB 826   18.13

Lagunas Nitrate Co v Lagunas Syndicate [1899] 2 Ch 392, 68 LJ Ch 699, 81 LT
    334 (CA)   9.7
Lakeglen Construction Ltd, Re [1980] IR 347 (HC)   33.8
Lee v Lee's Air Farming [1961] AC 12, [1960] 3 All ER 420, [1960] 3 WLR 758
    (PC)   3.7
Lee v Neuchatel Asphalte Co (1889) 41 ChD 1, 58 LJ Ch 408 (CA)   13.49
Lee, Behrens & Co Ltd, Re [1932] 2 Ch 46, [1932] All ER Rep 889, 101 LJ Ch
    183   17.8, 19.6
Leech v Stokes [1937] IR 787   26.26
Leeds & Hanley Theatres of Varieties Ltd (No 1), Re [1902] 2 Ch 809, 72 LJ
    Ch 1, 87 LT 488 (CA)   9.7, 9.9
Levy v Abercorris Slate and Slab Co (1887) 37 ChD 260, [1886–90] All ER Rep
    509, 57 LJ Ch 202   32.10
Lloyd v Grace, Smith & Co [1912] AC 176, [1911–13] All ER Rep 51 (HL)   21.12,
                                                                        29.21
Lloyd Cheynham & Co v Littlejohn & Co [1987] BCLC 303, 1986 PCC 389
    (QBD)   24.20
Lombard & Ulster Banking Ltd v Bank of Ireland (unreported) 2 June 1987
    (HC)   13.42
Lombard & Ulster Banking (Ireland) Ltd v Amarec Ltd (in Liquidation)
    (1978) 112 ILTR 1 (HC)   33.13
Lundy Granite Co, Lewis's Case, Re (1872) 26 LT 673   14.21
Lyons, Keleghan and Murphy v Curran [1993] ILRM 375   27.8

Macaura v Northern Assurance Co [1925] AC 619, 94 LJPC 154, 59 ILTR 45,
    [1925] All ER Rep 51 (HL)   4.7, 4.8
MacDougall v Gardiner (No 2) (1875) 1 ChD 13, 45 LJ Ch 27, 33 LT 521 (CA) 16.20
Mantruck Services Ltd (in Liquidation): Mehigan v Duignan (unreported) 8
    October 1996 (HC)   ix, 21.20, 24.9, 36.6
Masser (AH) Ltd, Re (unreported) 6 October 1986 (HC)   33.8
Maunsell Bros Ltd v London & North Western Rly Co [1917] 2 KB 836   4.5
McCormick v Cameo Investments Ltd [1978] ILRM 191 (HC)   16.18, 40.4
McGowan v Gannon [1983] ILRM 516   35.5
Medical Battery Co, Re [1894] 1 Ch 444, 63 LJ Ch 189, 42 WR 191   41.7

Menier v Hooper's Telegraph Works (1874) LR 9 Ch App 350, 43 LJ Ch 330,
    30 LT 209   16.5
Meux's Brewery Co Ltd, Re [1919] 1 Ch 28   13.10
Minister for Justice v Siúicre Éireann, Greencore plc [1992] 2 IR 215   27.13
Movitex Ltd v Bulfield (1986) 2 BCC 99, 403, [1988] BCLC 104   21.6
Moylan v Irish Whiting Manufacturers Ltd (unreported) 14 April 1980 (HC)   16.22
Multinational Gas and Petrochemical Co v Multinational Gas and
    Petrochemical Services Ltd [1983] Ch 258, [1983] 2 All ER 563, [1983] 3
    WLR 492 (CA)   21.4
Murph's Restaurant Ltd, Re [1979] ILRM 141   16.9, 41.7
Murphy (Daniel) Ltd, Re [1964] IR 1 (HC)   42.37

NFU Development Trust, Re [1973] 1 All ER 135, *sub nom* National Farmers'
    Union Development Trust, Re [1972] 1 WLR 1548, 116 SJ 679   39.2, 39.3
National Farmers' Union Development Trust, Re. *See* NFU Development Trust,
    Re
National Motor Mail-Coach Co Ltd, Re, Clinton's Claim [1908] 2 Ch 515 (CA)   9.12
Nelson Guarantee Corporation Ltd v Hodgson [1958] NZLR 609 (SC NZ)   26.20
New Brunswick and Canada Railway and Land Co v Muggeridge (1860) 1 Dr &
    Sm 383 (ChD)   10.45
Newborne v Sensolid (Great Britain) [1954] 1 QB 45, [1953] 1 All ER 708,
    [1953] 2 WLR 596, 97 SJ 209 (CA)   9.15
Newbridge Sanitary Laundry Ltd, Re [1917] 1 IR 237   41.7
Newdigate Clothing Co Ltd, Re [1912] 1 Ch 468 (CA)   34.21
Nolan (EP) Contractors (Longford) Ltd, Re (1996) *The Irish Times*, June 22   23.4
Northern Bank Finance Co Ltd v Quinn and Achates Investment Co [1979]
    ILRM 221   17.18, 17.19
Northern Bank Finance Corporation Ltd v Charlton [1979] IR 149 (SC)   9.7
Northside Motor Co Ltd, Re; Eddison v Allied Irish Banks (unreported) 24 July
    1985 (HC)   13.41
North-West Transportation Co v Beatty (1887) 12 App Cas 589, 56 LJPC 102,
    57 LT 426 (PC)   19.5

Oakbank Oil Co v Crum (1882) 8 App Cas 65, 48 LT 537 (HL)   29.18
Old Bushmills Distillery Co Ltd, Re, ex parte Brett [1897] IR 488 (CA)   32.22
Old Silkstone Collieries, Re [1954] Ch 169, [1954] 1 All ER 68, [1954] 2 WLR
    77, 98 SJ 27 (CA)   13.8
Omnium Electric Palaces Ltd v Baines [1914] 1 Ch 332 (CA)   9.5
O'Keefe v Ferris, Ireland and the Attorney-General [1993] 3 IR 165; [1997] *Bar
    Review*, 178n (SC)   21.34
O'Neill v Ryan, Ryanair and Others (unreported) 24 November 1989
    (HC)   16.21, 19.5
Ooregum Gold Mining Co of India Ltd v Roper [1892] AC 125, 61 LJ Ch 337,
    66 LT 427 (HL)   13.46
Overend, Gurney & Co, Re, Oakes v Turquand (1867) LR 2 HL 325, [1861–73]
    All ER Rep 738, 36 LJ Ch 949 (HL)   10.41

Pacific Colocotronis, The. *See* UBAF Ltd v European American Banking Corp; Pacific Colocotronis, The

Pageboy Couriers Ltd, Re [1983] ILRM 510   41.6

Panorama Developments (Guildford) Ltd v Fidelis Furnishing Fabrics Ltd [1971] 2 QB 711, [1971] 3 All ER 16, [1971] 3 WLR 440 (CA)   14.34, 18.18, 18.25

Parke v Daily News [1962] Ch 927, [1962] 2 All ER 929, [1962] 3 WLR 566   17.8, 19.6

Pavlides v Jensen [1956] Ch 565, [1956] 2 All ER 518, [1956] 3 WLR 224   16.22

Pender v Lushington (1877) 6 ChD 70, 46 LJ Ch 317   16.21

Percival v Wright [1902] 2 Ch 421, 71 LJ Ch 846, [1902] WN 134   14.8, 19.5, 20.28

Polly Peck International plc (in administration) (No 3), Re [1996] 2 All ER 433   6.16

Poole v National Bank of China [1907] AC 229, 76 LJ Ch 458, 96 LT 889   13.6

Power (John) & Son Ltd, Re [1934] IR 412 (SC)   13.8, 39.8

Power Supermarkets Ltd v Crumlin Investments Ltd (unreported) 22 June 1981 (HC)   6.6, 6.7, 6.9, 6.10, 6.11, 6.16

Primor plc v Stokes Kennedy Crowley; Primor plc v Oliver Freaney & Co (1995) *The Irish Times*, 20 December (SC)   26.32

Private Motorists Provident Society & Moore v Attorney-General [1984] ILRM 988 (SC)   29.6

Prudential Assurance Co v Chatterley-Whitfield Collieries [1949] AC 512, [1949] 1 All ER 1094 (HL)   13.7

Prudential Assurance Co v Newman Industries (No 2) [1982] Ch 204, [1982] 1 All ER 354, [1982] 2 WLR 31 (CA)   22.4

Pye (Ireland) Ltd, Re (unreported) 11 March 1985 (HC)   39.5

R Ltd, Re [1989] ILRM 757 (SC)   16.14

R v Board of Trade, ex parte St Martin's Preserving Co Ltd [1965] 1 QB 603, [1964] 2 All ER 561, [1964] 3 WLR 262 (DC)   27.2

R v Great North of England Railway Co [1924] QB 315   4.5

R v ICR Haulage [1944] KB 551, 113 LJKB 492, [1944] 1 All ER 691   21.13

R v Registrar of Joint Stock Companies ex parte More [1931] 2 KB 197, 100 LJKB 638, 145 LT 522 (CA)   41.7

R v Shacter [1960] 2 QB 252, [1960] 1 All ER 61, [1960] 2 WLR 258 (CCA)   26.18, 26.27

Rayfield v Hands [1960] Ch 1, [1958] 2 All ER 194, [1958] 2 WLR 851   14.12

Rearden v Provincial Bank of Ireland [1896] 1 IR 532 (ChD)   30.20

Reed v Explosives Co Ltd (1887) 19 QBD 264   34.24

Regal (Hastings) v Gulliver [1967] 2 AC 134n, [1942] 1 All ER 378 (HL)   19.14

Rex Pet Foods Ltd v Lamb Bros (Ireland) Ltd (unreported) 5 December 1995 (HC)   6.4, 6.5

Rock v Ireland (unreported) 10 November 1995 (HC)   27.11

Roundabout, The, Ltd v Beirne [1959] IR 423   3.11, 6.14

Royal British Bank v Turquand (1856) 6 E & B 327, Exch Ch   18.12, 18.13, 18.14, 18.26, 21.10, 32.9

Ruben v Great Fingall Consolidated [1906] AC 439 (HL)   18.13, 29.20, 29.21

Russell Murphy, Re [1976] IR 15   33.23

Salomon v Salomon & Co [1897] AC 22, 66 LJ Ch 35, [1895–9] All ER Rep 33 (HL)   vi, vii, viii, 3.2, 3.6, 3.7, 3.10, 6.1, 6.16, 9.5

Saunders v UK (1994) *The Independent*, September 30, ECHR   27.11

Savoy Hotel, Re [1981] Ch 351, [1981] 3 All ER 646, [1981] 3 WLR 441   39.2

Scott v Scott [1943] 1 All ER 582   30.4

Scottish & Newcastle Breweries Ltd v Blair 1967 SLT 72   17.27

Securities Trust Ltd v Associated Properties Ltd and Estate Development Ltd
    (unreported) 19 November 1980 (HC)   13.41, 40.4

Securities Trust Ltd v Hugh Moore and Alexander Ltd [1964] IR 417 (HC)   10.43,
    26.30, 29.10

Shannon Transport Systems Ltd, Re (unreported) 3 February 1975 (HC)   41.6

Sheffield Corporation v Barclay [1905] AC 392, 64 LJKB 747, 93 LT 83 (HL)   31.30

Shindler v Northern Raincoat Co Ltd [1960] 2 All ER 239, [1960] 1 WLR 1038,
    104 SJ 806   14.30

Sidebotham v Kershaw, Leese & Co [1920] 1 Ch 154, 89 LJ Ch 113, 122 LT 325
    (CA)   16.6

Simpson v Molson's Bank [1895] AC 270, 64 LJPC 51 (PC)   28.19

Sisk (John) & Son v Flinn (unreported) 18 July 1984 (HC)   26.30, 26.31

Smith v Anderson (1880) 15 ChD 247, 50 LJ Ch 39 (CA)   14.7

Smith v Croft (No 2) [1988] Ch 114, [1987] 3 All ER 909, [1987] 3 WLR 405   16.23

Smith (Howard) v Ampol Petroleum [1974] AC 821, [1974] 1 All ER 1126,
    [1974] 2 WLR 689 (PC)   19.18

Smith & Fawcett Ltd, Re [1942] Ch 304, [1942] 1 All ER 542 (CA)   19.6, 19.18, 31.21

Smith, Stone & Knight Ltd v Birmingham Corpn [1939] 4 All ER 116, 37 LGR
    665   6.7

South of England Natural Gas and Petroleum Co, Re [1911] Ch 575   10.19

Southard & Co, Re [1979] 3 All ER 556, [1979] 1 WLR 1198, (1979) 123 SJ 718
    (CA)   41.6

Southern Foundries (1926) Ltd v Shirlaw [1940] AC 701, [1940] 2 All ER 445
    (HL)   14.30

Spackman v Evans (1868) LR 3 HL 171, 37 LJ Ch 752   26.18

Springline Ltd, Re (1997) *Irish Times* Law Reports, 22 December   37.33

Standard Chartered Bank v Walker [1982] 3 All ER 938, [1982] 1 WLR 1410,
    [1982] Com LR 233 (CA)   35.6

State, The (Thomas McInerney & Co Ltd) v Dublin County Council [1985]
    ILRM 513   6.3

Station Motors Ltd, Re (unreported) 22 November 1984 (HC)   42.40

Sussex Brick Co, Re [1904] 1 Ch 598, 73 LJ Ch 308, 90 LT 426 (CA)   31.26

Sussex Brick Co, Re [1961] Ch 289n, [1960] 1 All ER 772n, [1960] 2 WLR
    665n   40.5

Swabey v Port Darwin Gold Mining Co (1889) 1 Meg 385 (CA)   14.21

Tangney v Clarence Hotel Co Ltd [1933] IR 51 (HC)   31.24

Tea Corporation Ltd, Re; Sorsbie v Tea Corporation Ltd [1904] 1 Ch 12 (CA)   39.8

Tempany v Hynes [1976] IR 101 (SC)   32.20

Tesco Stores Ltd v Brent London Borough Council [1993] 2 All ER 718,
    [1993] 1 WLR 1037, [1993] COD 280 (DC)   4.5

Tesco Supermarkets Ltd v Nattrass [1972] AC 153, [1971] 2 All ER 127, [1971]
    2 WLR 1166 (HL)   4.5, 21.13

Thairlwell v Great Northern Rly Co [1910] 2 KB 509, 79 LJKB 924   30.4

Transplanters (Holding Co) Ltd, Re [1958] 2 All ER 711, [1958] 1 WLR 822,
    102 SJ 547   26.18

Trevor v Whitworth (1887) 12 App Cas 409, 57 LJ Ch 28, 57 LT 457 (HL)   13.24
Truck and Machinery Sales Ltd v Marubeni Kumatsu Ltd (unreported) 23
    February 1996 (HC)   41.6
Twycross v Grant (1877) 2 CPD 469, 46 LJCP 636, 36 LT 812   9.2

UBAF Ltd v European American Banking Corp; Pacific Colocotronis, The
    [1984] QB 713, [1984] 2 All ER 226, [1984] 2 WLR 508 (CA)   18.25
Ulster Investment Bank Ltd v Euro Estates Ltd [1982] ILRM 57 (HC)   18.12
Underwood (AL) Ltd v Bank of Liverpool and Martin [1924] 1 KB 775, 93
    LJKB 690, 131 LT 271 (CA)   18.13
United Meat Packers, Re (unreported) 2 March 1992 (HC), 13 March 1992
    (SC)   37.34

Verit Hotel and Leisure (Ireland) Ltd; Carway v Attorney-General [1997] 1
    ILRM 110   23.3

Wall v London and Northern Assets Corpn [1898] 2 Ch 469, 67 LJ Ch 596, 79
    LT 249 (CA)   15.16
Wallersteiner v Moir (No 2); Moir v Wallersteiner (No 2) [1975] QB 373,
    [1975] 1 All ER 849, [1975] 2 WLR 389 (CA)   22.5
Wallis & Simmonds (Builders) Ltd, Re [1974] 1 All ER 561, [1974] 1 WLR 391,
    [1974] 1 Lloyd's Rep 272   33.12
Watteau v Fenwick [1893] 1 QB 346   18.6, 18.8, 18.24
Welding Plant Ltd, Re (unreported) 27 June, 25 July 1984   42.40
Welton v Saffery [1897] AC 299, [1895–9] All ER Rep 567, 66 LJ Ch 362 (HL)   14.12
Western Counties Steam Bakeries & Milling Co, Re, Parson's and Robjent's
    Case [1897] 1 Ch 617, 66 LJ Ch 354, 76 LT 239   26.27
Westport Property Construction Co Ltd, Re (unreported) 13 September 1996
    (HC)   37.2
Westwinds Holding Co Ltd, Re (unreported) 21 May 1974 (HC)   16.11
Whaley Bridge Calico Printing Co v Green and Smith (1880) 5 QBD 109, 49
    LJQB 326, 41 LT 674   9.2
White v Bristol Aeroplane Co [1953] Ch 65, [1953] 1 All ER 40, [1953] 2 WLR
    144, 97 SJ 64 (CA)   12.24
Whitechurch (George) Ltd v Cavanagh [1902] AC 117, 71 LJKB 400, 50 WR
    218 (HL)   14.34
Williams (H.) (Tallaght) Ltd (in Receivership and Liquidation), In the Matter
    of [1997] *Irish Times* Law Reports, 27 January   42.50
Williams Group (Tullamore) Ltd, Re (unreported) 8 November 1985 (HC)   16.12
Wilson v Kelland [1910] 2 Ch 306, 79 LJ Ch 580, 26 TLR 485   33.19
Wilson (Inspector of Taxes) v Dunnes Stores (Cork) Ltd (unreported) 22
    January 1976 (HC)   30.8
Wogans (Drogheda) Ltd (No 2), Re (unreported) 7 May 1992 (HC)   37.11
Woodchester Case, Competition Authority Decision No 6, 4 August 1992   40.29
Woolf v East Nigel Gold Mining Co (1905) 21 TLR 660   14.21
Woolfson v Strathclyde Regional Council (1978) 248 EG 777, [1979] JPL 169,
    (1978) 38 P & CR 521 (HL)   6.7, 6.10
Wymes v Crowley (unreported) 27 February 1987 (HC)   34.16

Yenidje Tobacco Co Ltd, Re [1916] 2 Ch 426, [1916–17] All ER Rep 1050   41.7
Yorkshire Woolcombers' Association, Re [1903] 2 Ch 284 (CA)   32.18

2

TABLE OF STATUTES

References are to paragraph numbers, except for roman numerals which are references to pages of the Preface or Introduction.

Age of Majority Act 1985	28.1	s 18(2)	4.3
Anti-Discrimination Pay Act		s 20	8.27
1974	22.7	s 21	7.3
		(2)	28.10
		s 22	7.2
		(2)	7.2
Bankruptcy (Ireland)		s 23	7.2, 17.25
(Amendment) Act 1872		(1)	15.30
ss 97, 98	28.8	(2)–(4)	7.7
		s 24	17.24
		s 25	1.12, 14.12, 16.2, 16.3, 29.7–
Companies Act 1862	1.2		29.10, 29.18, 30.1, 30.8
Companies Act 1959	15.20	s 29	17.1
Companies Act 1963	v, 1.2, 2.7, 8.1,	s 31	10.25, 28.9
	10.1, 10.6, 10.16, 13.20,	(1)	28.10
	15.26, 20.12, 24.1, 24.29,	(2)	14.11
	25.13, 42.14, 42.28	s 32	6.16, 13.33, 21.15
Pts VIII, IX	11.9	s 33	8.7, 8.23, 8.25, 25.20
Pt XI	11.4	s 36	vi, 6.17, 36.2
s 2	10.18, 14.5	s 37(1), (2)	9.15
(1)	32.12	ss 38, 39	18.1
s 5	8.6, 8.7, 8.9	ss 43–48	10.2
s 6	8.10	s 43	10.6, 10.23
(1)	17.23	(3)	15.29
(c)	17.1	s 44	App B
(2)	4.2	(1)	10.6
(4)(a)	29.17	(3)	10.19
s 7	8.10	(4)(a),(b)	10.19
s 8	2.12, 17.5, 17.15, 17.17, 17.18,	s 45	10.6, 10.19
	17.20, 17.22, 18.26, 21.10,	s 46	10.6, 10.23, App B
	32.9	(3)	10.40
(1)	17.16, 17.18, 17.22	s 47	10.6
(2)	17.14, 32.2	(1)(b)	10.23
s 10	13.14, 13.25	s 48	10.6
(1)	17.14	s 49	9.2, 10.38, 10.46, 10.47
(2)	15.30	(6)	10.48
(3)	2.9, 16.18, 32.2	(8)(a)	9.2
(4)–(6)	16.18	s 50	10.50, 10.51, App B
(7)	16.18, 32.2	s 52(1)	10.49
(8)–(11)	16.18	ss 53–59	10.28
s 13	8.11	s 53	10.28, 10.29
s 14	8.11	(4)	10.32
s 15	13.25, 15.8, 16.2	(6)	10.32
(1)	15.30	s 55	10.33, 10.36

Companies Act 1963 – *cont.*

s 56	10.32
s 57	10.32
(1)	10.33
(2)	10.32
(4)	10.34
s 58	10.34
s 60	13.33, 13.38, 13.41, 13.42, 13.43, 13.45, 16.18, 23.8
(1)	13.38, 13.39, 13.41, 13.42
(2)	13.39, 13.41
(3)	13.41
(5)	6.18, 13.39, 21.15
(12)	13.45
(13)	13.43, 13.44
(14)	13.41, 13.42
(15)	13.41
(15A)	13.39
(15B)	13.44
(15C)	13.44
s 61(1), (2)	10.19
s 62	13.48
(1)	13.3
(2)	13.4
s 64	13.18
s 67	12.14
s 68	13.55, 29.23
(1)(d)	13.55
s 69	13.55, 29.23
s 72	13.1, 13.5, 13.25, 32.2
s 72(2)	13.5, 15.30
(a)	13.7
s 73(2)	13.9, 13.10
(a)–(c)	13.9
(3)	13.10
ss 74, 75	13.11
s 76	13.12
(2)	13.12
s 78	12.22, 12.25, 16.18
(1)–(5)	12.23
ss 79–90	33.16
s 79	31.16, 31.33
s 80	29.17
s 81	31.14, 31.15, 31.33, 31.36, 33.16
s 82	31.14, 31.15, 31.36
s 83	31.14, 31.20, 33.16
s 84	31.14, 31.25
s 85	31.18, 31.31
s 87	29.19
s 88	29.22, 31.38
(3)	31.38

ss 91–93	14.35
s 91	14.35, 25.7, 33.15
s 92	25.7, 33.15
s 93	33.10
s 94	33.4
s 95	33.20
s 96	33.20
s 98	32.23, 32.26, 32.27, 35.8
ss 99–102	32.13
s 99	25.7, 32.28, 32.30, 33.19
(1), (2)	33.11, 33.12
(9)	32.11
ss 103–105	14.35, 33.13
s 103	14.35, 25.7
ss 104, 105	33.13
ss 106–110	14.35
s 106	32.13, 33.14, 33.19
s 107(1)	34.10
s 113	17.28
s 114(1)	7.5, 17.26
(4)	17.27
(5)	17.23
s 115	6.2
(2)	10.52
s 116(1)	25.3
ss 117–124	14.35
s 117	25.3
s 119	25.3
s 121	25.3
s 122	28.18
(5)	28.18
s 123	28.19, 31.27
s 124	28.17
s 125	25.10, 25.21
s 126	25.12
s 127	25.21
s 128	25.18
s 131	15.3
(3)	15.13, 15.15, 16.18
s 132	15.10, 15.13
(1)	16.18
s 133	15.4
(2)(b)	15.11
(3)	15.5
s 134(b)	15.13
(c)	15.15
(d)	15.16
s 135	15.13
s 137(1)(b)	16.18
s 140	15.9
s 141	15.4, 15.22

Companies Act 1963 – *cont.*

s 141(2)	15.22
(3)	15.22
(6)	15.20
(8)	15.23
s 142	14.18, 14.27, 26.17
s 143	15.29
s 144	15.24
s 145	15.27, 19.2, 25.9
s 146	15.28, 25.9
s 147	24.2
(1)	24.1
s 148	24.10, App B
(3)	24.12
s 149	24.13, App B
(5), (7)	24.13
ss 150–158	6.16
s 152	6.11
s 155(5), (6)	12.18
s 156	24.10
s 158	24.34, App B
(7)	24.12
s 159	32.3
ss 160–163	26.2
s 160	26.27
(1)	26.4
(2), (3)	26.5
(5)	26.16
(6)	26.3
ss 165–173	16.16, 27.1
s 174	14.13, 14.34
s 175	14.34, 14.38
s 179	14.14
s 180	14.14, 14.20
s 181	14.19, 16.22
s 182	14.27, 14.28, 14.29, 14.30, 14.31
(2)–(6)	14.27
(7)	14.27, 14.29
s 183	23.21
s 184	14.20, 23.1
s 185	14.21
s 187	40.8, 40.9
s 188	40.8, 40.9
s 190	14.24, 14.35
s 191	14.23, 14.24, 26.22
(1), (2)	24.30
(8)	26.22
s 192	14.22, 14.24, 20.12
(3)	20.12, 20.22
s 194	19.16, 20.6, 25.8
(1)–(7)	20.6

s 195	14.35, 25.5
s 196	7.6, 14.25
s 197	21.15, 42.27
s 198	21.15, 42.27
(1)	15.30
s 199	14.26
s 200	21.6, 22.12, 22.13, 22.14, 26.28
(b)	26.28
ss 201–203	1.36, 16.18, 39.20
s 201	1.35, 39.1, 39.2, 39.3, 39.10, 39.12, 39.13, 39.14
(1)	39.4
(7)	39.2
s 202(1)(b)(3)	39.6
(2)	39.6
s 203	39.10, 39.13, 39.14
(1)(a)	41.2
(b)	39.10
(e)	39.9
s 204	6.13, 16.18, 39.14, 40.3, 40.4, 40.6, 40.11
(1)	40.3, 40.4, 40.7
(2)	40.3
(4)	40.7
s 205	2.9, 13.14, 13.25, 16.7, 16.10, 16.11, 16.12, 16.15, 16.17, 16.22, 22.5, 29.2, 29.11, 37.16, 41.7, 41.8, 41.9
(1)	16.8, 16.9, 16.12
(3)	16.13
(7)	16.14
s 207(2)	42.27
ss 208–211	42.21
s 213	22.5, 29.2, 34.2, 41.5, 41.7
(a)	15.30
(e)	41.5
(f)	41.5, 41.7
(g)	16.17, 41.5, 41.8
s 214	1.31, 17.9, 41.6
(a), (b)	37.3
s 215	41.9
(a)	41.10
(d)	41.10
(e)	41.10
ss 217, 218	41.12
s 220	41.13
s 221	42.1
s 222	42.3
s 223	41.11
s 224(1)	42.4
(3)	42.4

Companies Act 1963 – *cont.*

s 226(2)	42.2
s 227	42.7
s 228(c)	42.11
s 229	42.19
s 230	42.19
s 231	42.15
(2)(a)	42.16
s 233	42.14, 44.8
ss 237–249	42.32
s 241	42.31
s 242	42.53
s 244	42.47
s 249(1)	42.55
s 251	29.11, 41.14
(1)(a)	15.29
(b)	15.30
(c)	15.29
s 252	41.16
s 253	41.17
ss 254, 255	41.18
s 256	6.18, 41.20
(3), (4)	41.20
(6)	21.15
(8), (9)	41.22
ss 257–264	41.21
ss 258, 259	43.1
s 260	1.36, 39.13, 39.15, 39.16, 39.19, 39.20, 43.9, 44.9
(1)	39.15, 39.16
(2)	39.16
(3), (4)	39.18
(5)	39.17
(6)	39.18
s 261	41.24, 43.11
(2)	43.10
s 262	43.5
s 263	41.2, 43.5
(4)	43.8
s 264	43.13
ss 266–273	44.1
s 266	41.25, 44.2, 44.7
s 267	44.3
(2)	41.26
s 268	39.19
(1), (2)	44.7
s 269	44.4
s 270	44.4
s 271	39.19, 44.9
s 272	44.10

s 273	41.2, 44.11
(4), (5)	44.12
ss 275–282	43.4
s 275	42.53, 43.4
s 276	43.4
s 276A	44.3
s 277	44.4
s 279	43.4
s 280	42.47, 43.4
s 281	42.47, 44.4
s 283(1)	42.28
(2)	42.30
s 284	42.18, 42.29
s 285	2.20, 32.5, 32.6, 42.18, 42.45, 42.47, 42.48
(2)–(5)	42.49
(7)(a)	42.50
(b)	32.26, 42.51
(14)	42.50
ss 286–292	42.36
s 286	42.40
s 288	32.23, 32.24, 32.27, 42.37
(1), (2)	32.24
(4)	32.24, 42.38
s 289	32.23, 32.24, 32.25, 32.27, 42.39
s 290	42.41
s 293	21.14, App B
(1)	24.8
s 295	21.14, App B
s 297	x, 2.22, 21.33, App B
(1)	21.33, 21.34, 21.35
(2)	21.35
s 297A	vii, 1.30, 20.47, 21.22, 21.27
(1), (2)	20.47
(1)	21.23, 21.33
(b)	21.34, 22.6
(2)(a)	21.21, 21.24, 21.25, 21.28, 21.29
(b)	21.24, 21.25, 21.26, 21.30
(3)	21.24
(6)	21.25, 21.26, 21.30
(9)	21.32
s 298	2.10, 21.15, 22.7, 26.27, 42.10, 42.33
s 299	42.54
(2)	35.9
(3)–(5)	42.54
s 300	42.5
s 300A	42.6

Companies Act 1963 – *cont.*

s 301	42.6
s 301A	42.6
s 303	42.7
s 311	41.2
s 312	42.12
ss 314, 315	34.9
s 316	34.22, 35.3, 35.18
(1)	34.14
(2)	34.22
(3)	35.4
s 316A(1), (2)	35.6
(3)	35.7
s 317(1)	34.11
s 318	35.2
s 319	34.12, 35.10, 35.15
s 320	35.10, 35.15
s 321	35.15
s 322	35.16
s 322A(1), (2)	35.21
s 322B	35.24
(1)	35.24
s 322C	35.20
s 323	34.13
ss 324–327	11.9
ss 328–343	11.9
ss 329, 330	11.9
ss 351–360	11.4
ss 354, 355	11.5
s 356	11.4
s 357	11.6
s 361	10.6
(1)(b)	10.6
(2)	10.6
s 364	10.6
s 377	11.9
s 378	14.35
s 379(1)	17.30
s 389	8.13
s 391	21.5, 21.6, 22.12
s 397	8.13
Sch 1, Table A	lxxii, 8.11, 8.13, 18.9, 29.9
Pt I	
arts 2–46	29.9
art 2	12.15
art 3	12.22, 12.25, 31.24
art 4	12.24
art 7	28.19
art 8	29.19
arts 11–14	30.19

arts 15–21	12.13, 30.10
art 18	30.13
art 21	30.12
art 22	31.16, 31.19
arts 22–28	28.13
art 23	31.16
art 24	28.13, 31.18, 31.24
art 25	31.29
arts 29–31	28.14
arts 29–32	31.36
arts 30, 31	28.14
arts 33–39	30.15
art 35	30.16
art 37	30.17
art 42	29.23
arts 44, 45	13.55
art 46	13.2
arts 47–74	29.9
art 51	15.11
art 53	15.8, 15.12
arts 53–74	15.14
arts 54, 55	15.15
arts 56, 57	15.16
art 58	15.17
arts 59–62	15.18
art 61	15.16
arts 63–67	15.18
art 67	15.16
arts 69–71	15.19
art 74	15.19
arts 75–112	29.9
art 76	14.21
art 79	18.10, 18.11, 18.14, 18.26, 21.10
art 80	9.13, 18.10
art 81	18.10
arts 83–87	19.16
art 85	14.5
art 91	14.20
arts 92–94	14.16
art 97	14.17
art 98	14.17, 14.18
arts 99, 100	14.18
art 101	19.2
art 102	19.2
art 104	19.2
arts 105–107	19.3
art 109	19.2
art 110	14.30, 18.15
art 111	18.15
arts 113, 114	14.38, 29.9

Companies Act 1963 – *cont.*	
Sch 1, Table A, Pt I – *cont.*	
art 115	18.1, 18.17
arts 116–129	29.9
art 116	30.4
art 117	30.4
art 118	30.4
art 119	30.4
art 120	30.5
art 123	30.6
art 130	26.2, 29.9
art 131	29.9
art 132	29.9
arts 133–137	29.9
art 138	21.6
Sch 1, Table A, Pt II	
art 3	28.13, 31.21
Sch 1, Table B	12.11, 17.4
Table C	8.3
Table D	8.3
Table E, Pt I	8.18
Pt III	8.18
Sch 2	10.52
Sch 3, Part I	10.20
paras 1–18	10.21
para 9	9.14
para 13	9.14
Part II	10.22
Sch 5, Pts I, II	25.11
Sch 6	24.15
Sch 9	11.9
Companies Act 1990	v, viii, ix, 1.2, 1.30, 2.23, 6.5, 6.16, 6.18, 8.1, 13.24, 13.26, 19.5, 19.16, 19.25, 20.1, 20.12, 20.30, 20.41, 21.33, 21.34, 21.35, 22.1, 22.7, 22.15, 24.29, 31.3, 31.7, 36.9, 37.1
Pt II	16.16, 27.1
Pt III	19.16, 20.3, 20.7
Pt IV	19.16, 28.19, 31.2
Pt V	19.16
Pt VII	2.23, 14.20, 23.1, 23.2
Pt X	26.8
Pt XI	13.17, 13.34, 28.6
s 7	22.5, 27.1, 27.2
(1)	27.3
(a), (b)	16.16
s 8	27.2, 27.4, 27.17
s 9	27.8
s 10	App B
(3)	27.6
s 10(4), (7)	27.7
s 11(3)	27.11
s 12(1)	27.12
s 13(1)	27.13
s 14	27.1, 27.8, 27.14
(2)	27.14
(5)	27.16
s 15	27.17
(2)	27.17
s 16(3)–(5)	27.20
(6)	27.20, 27.22
(7)–(13)	27.20
(14)–(17)	27.20, 27.21
(18)	27.20
s 17	27.23
s 18	27.11
s 19	27.17, 27.19
s 20	27.18, 27.19
s 21	27.19
s 23	27.19
ss 25–27	20.3
s 25(2)(a)–(c)	20.12
s 26	20.4
s 27	14.5, 20.5, 20.6, 25.8
(3)	20.6
s 28	14.31, 20.8
ss 28–47	20.2
s 29	20.10
(2)	20.9, 20.15, 42.16
(5)	20.10
s 30(2)	20.11
ss 31–38	20.12
s 31	20.11, 20.18, 20.20, 21.15
(1)	20.13
ss 32–37	20.13, 20.14
s 32	20.15, 21.15
s 33(1), (2)	20.15
ss 34, 35	20.16
ss 36, 37	20.17
s 38	6.18, 21.15
(1)	20.18
s 39	6.18, 21.15
(1)	20.19
s 40	20.18, 21.15
ss 41–47	20.20, 24.31
s 41	20.22
(6)	20.21
(7)(a), (b)	20.21
(8)	20.20
ss 42–44	20.22
s 45	20.21, 20.22

Companies Act 1990 – *cont.*	
s 46	20.22
s 47	20.6
s 50	14.32, 20.8
s 51	14.35, 25.5, App B
s 52	16.24
(1), (2)	19.7
s 53	App B
ss 53–56	14.35, 20.2
ss 53–58	20.26
ss 53–66	20.23
s 53	25.6
(1)	20.24, 20.25
(2)	20.25
(7)	20.25
s 58	App B
s 59	20.26, 25.6
ss 60–62	20.26
s 60(8)	20.26
s 63	20.27, 25.6
s 64	25.6, App B
s 65	20.27
ss 67–71	25.4
s 72	31.4
s 73	31.4, 31.8
s 74	31.8
(4), (5)	31.8
s 75	31.8
s 80	25.4, 31.5, 31.6
s 81	25.4, 31.6
ss 82–85	31.6
s 88	31.6
ss 91–96	31.7
s 97	31.10
s 98	31.9
s 100	31.12
s 102	31.11
s 103(4)	31.12
s 104	31.13
ss 107–121	20.2, 20.28
s 107	20.29, 20.31
s 108	20.29, 20.36, 20.37
(2), (3)	20.32
(10)	20.30
(11)	20.31
s 109	20.33
(4)	20.34
s 110	20.36
ss 111–114	20.35
s 114	App B
s 115(3)	20.37
s 115(5), (6)	20.37
s 116	20.39
s 119	2.39
s 120	20.38
s 123	1.31, 41.6
s 124	42.15, 42.16
s 128	41.20
s 135	42.40
s 136	32.23, 42.37
s 137	21.14, 21.15
s 138	1.30, 6.8, 6.18, 20.40, 20.47, 21.2, 21.15, 21.22, 26.18, 36.7
s 140	6.10, 42.34
(2)	42.34
(5)	6.5
(a)–(f)	42.34
s 141	6.5, 6.10, 42.35
(3)	42.11, 42.35
(4)–(6)	42.35
s 142	42.33
s 146	42.6
s 148	42.33
ss 149–158	23.2
s 149	23.3
(1)	23.3
(b)	23.3
s 150	23.3, 23.4, 23.13
(1)	23.3
(2)	23.5
(3)	23.18
s 151	23.6
s 152	23.5
ss 153, 154	23.6
s 155	23.8
(5)	23.7
s 156	23.8
s 157	23.9
ss 159–160	23.2
s 159	23.11
s 160	23.14, 42.5
(1)(b)	23.12
(2), (3), (9)	23.13
s 161	App B
ss 161–169	23.2
ss 161, 162	23.16
s 163	6.18, 23.17
(4)	23.18
s 164	App B
ss 164, 165	23.19
ss 167, 168	23.20

Companies Act 1990 – *cont.*

s 169	23.21
s 170	34.9
s 171	34.14
s 172	35.6
s 175	35.21
s 176	35.24
s 177	35.20
s 179	35.9
s 180	37.1, 37.11, 38.2
s 181	37.1, 37.2
s 185(2)–(4)	26.15
s 186	26.15
s 187(1)	26.7
(a)(iii)–(vi)	26.7
(2)	26.12
s 188	App B
s 191	26.8
s 193(1)	24.37, 26.20
(3)	26.19
(4)	24.38
(e), (f)	24.38
(6)	26.19, 26.20
s 194	26.21, App B
(1)	26.21
s 195	26.12
s 196	26.19
s 197	xi, 26.24, App B
s 198	26.9
s 199	26.7, 26.10
s 200	26.7
ss 202–204	6.18, 21.15
s 202	20.42, 20.45, 21.2, 21.18, 21.20, 24.2, 24.4, 24.7, 26.21, App B
(1)–(4)	24.2, 24.6
(5)–(9)	24.2
(10)	24.2, 24.5, 24.6, 24.7
s 203	21.15, 24.7, App B
s 204	2.22, 21.19, 21.20, 21.21, 24.9, 36.6
(1)	21.17, 36.6
(b)	21.19
s 206	12.21
(2)	13.21
(e)	13.21
s 207	13.17, 13.19
(1)	12.21
(2)	13.26
s 208	13.19, 13.20, 13.22, 13.26
s 209	13.22, 13.26
(5), (6)	13.23

s 210	13.18, 13.32
ss 211–230	13.25
s 211(2)	13.26
s 212(2)(a)	13.28
(b)	13.27
s 213	13.28, 13.30, 13.31, 13.32
(3)–(7)	13.28
s 214	13.30, 13.31, 13.32
(1)	13.29
s 215	13.27, 13.30, 13.31, 13.32
s 217	13.30
s 219(2)	13.32
s 222	13.34
s 224	13.33, 28.6
(2)	28.6
s 225	13.33
s 226	13.34
s 228	28.6
s 236	14.37
(c)	14.37
s 238	10.19
s 240	xii
s 243	App B
(1)	24.8
ss 244, 245	25.21
s 250	11.9

Companies (Amendment) Act 1977

s 4	14.35, 33.15

Companies (Amendment) Act 1982

s 3	8.13, 14.38
s 8	14.35, 25.5
s 10	32.6
s 12	25.21, 41.2
s 13	5.7
s 20	25.3
Sch 1	24.12

Companies (Amendment) Act 1983   2.14, 10.1, 13.24, 13.52, 23.8

Pt IV	13.49, 30.4
s 3	14.14
s 4	8.6
s 6(6)	11.2
(7), (8)	11.2
s 7	8.6
s 9	8.25
(3)	8.25, 26.23
(10)	8.26
s 10	8.25
s 12(3)(a)	15.29

Companies (Amendment) Act
  1983 – *cont.*
  s 14   8.23
  s 15   8.24, 13.13, 13.14, 15.30
    (2)   13.14
    (3)   16.18
    (6), (7)   8.24
  s 19   8.6, 8.17
  s 20   10.26, 10.27
  s 21   8.7
  s 22   10.29
  s 23   10.24
    (11)   22.5
  s 24   10.24
  ss 26–37   9.10, 10.30
  s 27   13.46, 29.21
    (1), (2)   29.21
  ss 30–33   10.31
  s 30   9.10, 9.11
    (5)–(8)   26.23
    (10)   9.11
    (12)   26.23
  s 32   9.10, 9.11, 26.23
    (3)   9.10
    (8)   9.11
  s 38   12.25
  s 40   2.14, 13.35, 13.36, 15.10, 24.38,
                                           26.23
  s 41   13.25
    (1)   13.25
  s 43   13.13
    (1)   13.15, 30.17
    (3)(a)   13.15
  s 44   13.25, 30.19
  ss 45–51   13.49
  s 45   24.42, 30.4
  s 45A   30.4
  s 46   13.51
    (1)   13.51
    (2)   8.25, 13.51, 26.23
  ss 47, 48   13.52
  s 49   13.53, 24.42
    (3)   24.40, 24.42, 26.23
    (6)   26.23
  s 51(2)   13.50
  s 52   8.27, 16.18
  s 53   8.27
  Sch 1   10.28
    para 16   26.28
Companies (Amendment) Act
  1986   24.13, 24.14, 24.15, 24.23,
                                           25.18

  s 2   24.13
    (1)–(3)   25.19
  s 3(4)   24.14
  s 4   24.15
    (3), (4)   24.19
  ss 5, 6   24.21
  s 7   25.13
  ss 8, 9   24.32
  s 10   24.33
    (1), (2)   25.16, 25.18
  s 11   24.33
    (1)   25.15
    (2)   25.15, 25.18
  s 12   24.33
    (1)   25.17, 25.18
    (2)   25.15
  s 13   24.35
  s 14   24.35, 28.6
    (d)   24.35
  s 15   24.39, 25.19
  s 16   6.5, 24.28
  s 18   25.19
    (2)   24.36
    (3), (4)   24.40
  s 22   App B
  Sch, Pt I   24.16, 24.17, 24.18, 25.15
  Sch, Pt II   24.22, 24.23
  Sch, Pt III   24.22, 24.23
    para 21(3), (4)   24.22
    para 22   24.24
  Sch, Pt IV   24.23
    paras 23–25   25.17
    paras 26–37   24.26, 25.17
    paras 39–43   24.27, 25.17
    para 44   25.17
Companies (Amendment) Act
  1990   1.30, 1.31, 1.32, 2.22, 2.23,
                                      36.7, 37.1
  s 2   37.2
  s 3   37.11
  s 4(4)   16.15
    (5)   37.4
  s 5(1)   37.15
    (2)   37.35
    (d)   37.34
    (3)   37.35
  s 6(1)   35.23, 37.17
  s 7   37.19
    (5)   37.26
    (6), (7)   37.29
  s 8   37.19, 37.21

Companies (Amendment) Act
    1990 – *cont.*
  s 8(3)   37.25
  s 9   37.20, 37.31
  s 10   37.28, 37.31, 37.33, 37.34
      (1)   37.27
  s 11(1)   37.30
      (2)   37.30, 37.33
      (3)   37.30
      (4)   37.30, 37.33
  s 12(1)   37.12
      (2)   37.13
  s 13(6)   37.8, 37.9
      (7)   37.29
  s 14(1)   37.23
  s 15(3)–(5)   38.1
  s 16   38.2
  s 17   38.4, 38.17, 38.18
      (1)   38.18
  s 18   38.4, 38.5, 38.6
      (3), (4)   37.15
  s 20   38.7
      (1)   38.7
  s 21   38.10
  s 22   38.8
  s 23   38.11
  s 24   38.4, 38.12
      (2)   38.9
          (c)   38.9
  s 25   38.13
  s 26   38.16
  s 27   38.15
  s 29   37.27, 37.28, 37.33
      (2)   37.27
      (3)   37.33
  s 33   21.22
Companies Clauses
    Consolidation Act 1845   39.18
Competition Act 1991   22.7, 40.29, 40.30
  s 4   40.25, 40.29
      (1)   40.25, 40.26, 40.27, 40.29
      (2)   40.25
  s 5   40.24, 40.31
  s 6   40.27
  s 14   40.24
Competition (Amendment) Act
    1996   40.29, 40.30
Conveyancing Act 1881
  ss 17–23   34.5
  s 24(8)   34.15
Corporation Tax Act 1976   22.7

Data Protection Act 1988   22.7

Electoral Act 1997   ix, 25.11
  s 26   24.34
Employment Equality Act 1977   22.7

Finance Act 1980
  s 38   4.13
Finance Act 1986
  s 115   32.31
Finance Act 1995
  s 174   32.31
Finance Act 1997   22.7, 22.8

Income Tax Act 1967   22.7
Industrial and Provident
    Societies Acts 1893 to 1978   23.11
Irish Takeover Panel Act 1997   xii, 40.12,
                                            40.13

Joint Stock Companies Act 1844   1.2, 1.3,
                                              36.3
Joint Stock Companies Act 1856   1.2, 1.3

Landlord and Tenant
    (Amendment) Act 1980   6.10
Limited Liability Act 1855   1.2, 36.3
Limited Partnerships Act 1907   5.7

Mergers, Takeovers and
    Monopolies (Control) Act
    1978   39.14, 40.19, 40.22, 40.23,
                                    40.29, 40.30
  s 1(3)(a)   40.23
  s 14   39.14
Minimum Notice and Terms of
    Employment Act 1973   42.49

Partnership Act 1890   5.5, 5.6, 41.7

Redundancy Payments Acts
    1967–1979   42.49

Registration of Business Names	
Act 1963 xii, 5.6, 7.1, 7.2, 7.8, 17.23	
s 3(d)	7.2
s 4	7.2
s 7	7.2
ss 10, 11	7.4
s 14(1)	7.3
(3)	7.1
Restrictive Practices	
(Amendment) Act 1987	40.22
Safety, Health and Welfare at	
Work Act 1989	22.7, 24.34

Solicitors Act 1954	
s 58	8.13
Statute of Limitations Act 1957	42.30
Stock Transfer Act 1963	31.16
s 2(1)	31.33
Trades Disputes Act 1906	6.14
Unfair Dismissals Act 1977	42.49

Table of Foreign Statutes

New Zealand

Workman's Compensation Act	
1922	3.7

United Kingdom

Companies Act 1948	
s 209	40.6
Companies Act 1985	
s 310	22.13
(3)(a)	22.13
Trade Descriptions Act 1968	
s 24	4.5

TABLE OF STATUTORY INSTRUMENTS

References are to paragraph numbers, except for roman numerals which are references to pages of the Preface.

Companies Act 1990 (Auditors) Regulations 1992, SI 1992/259   26.8
Companies Act 1990 (Uncertified Securities) Regulations 1996, SI 1996/68   31.33, 31.34
    Chs II–VI   31.35
    reg 4(1)   31.33
    Sch   31.35

District Court Rules 1997, SI 1997/93
    s 9(3)   7.2

European Communities (Accounts) Regulations 1993, SI 1993/396
    reg 4   24.32
    reg 7   24.13
European Communities (Branch Disclosure) Regulations 1993, SI 1993/395   11.7
European Communities (Companies) Regulations 1973, SI 1973/163   17.20
    reg 4   8.15
    reg 6   2.12, 17.19, 17.20, 17.22, 18.26, 21.10, 32.9
       (1), (2)   17.19, 17.20
       (3)   17.19
    reg 10   8.15, 17.21
European Communities (Companies) (Group Accounts) Regulations 1992, SI 1992/201   24.11
    reg 4   24.11
European Communities (European Economic Interest Groupings) Regulations 1989, SI 1989/191   11.10
European Communities (Mergers and Divisions of Companies) Regulations 1987, SI 1987/137   40.15, 40.16, 40.17
European Communities (Non-Life Insurance) Framework Regulations 1994, SI 1994/359
    reg 7(1)   8.8
European Communities (Public Limited Companies) Regulations 1997   ix
European Communities (Public Limited Companies Subsidiaries) Regulations 1997, SI 1997/67   13.33, 28.6
    regs 4–6   28.6
European Communities (Safeguarding of Employees' Rights on Transfer of Undertakings) Regulations 1980, SI 1980/306   3.11, 34.16, 40.21
European Communities (Single-Member Private Limited Companies) Regulations 1994, SI 1994/275   5.10, 8.7
    reg 3(1)   8.7
    reg 4   8.16
    reg 5   8.21
    reg 6   8.22

European Communities (Single-Member Private Limited Companies)
    Regulations 1994, SI 1994/275 – *cont.*
   reg 8   15.7, 24.10
     (3)   26.19
   reg 9   15.7
European Communities (Stock Exchange) Regulations 1984, SI 1984/282   10.2,
               10.3, 10.6, 10.15, 10.16, 10.18, 10.52, 31.7
   reg 10   10.15
   reg 12   10.6
     (3)   10.6
   reg 13   10.6
   Sch 1   10.6
   Sch A   10.15
European Communities (Stock Exchange) (Amendment) Regulations 1991,
    SI 1991/93   10.2
European Communities (Transferable Securities and Stock Exchange)
    Regulations 1992, SI 1992/202   10.21

Mergers, Takeovers and Monopolies (Control) Act (Newspapers) Order
    1979, SI 1979/17   40.23

Rules of the Supreme Court 1986, SI 1986/115   42.12, 42.31

TABLE OF EU LEGISLATION

References are to paragraph numbers, except for roman numerals which are references to pages of the Preface.

1968   First Company Law Directive
Directive 68/151/EEC; First Council Directive of 9 March 1968 on
   coordination of safeguards which, for the protection of the interests of
   members and others, are required by Member States of companies
   within the meaning of the second paragraph of Article 58 of the Treaty,
   with a view to making such safeguards equivalent thoughout the
   Community (1968 OJ L65/8)   8.15
   Art 9   17.19

1977   Acquired Rights Directive
Directive 77/187/EEC; Council Directive of 14 February 1977 on the
   approximation of the laws of the Member States relating to the
   safeguarding of employees' rights in the event of transfers of
   undertakings, businesses or parts of businesses (1977 OJ L61/26) 40.21

1977   Second Company Law Directive
Directive 77/91/EEC; Second Council Directive of 13 December 1976 on
   coordination of safeguards which, for the protection of the interests of
   members and others, are required by Member States of companies
   within the meaning of the second paragraph of Article 58 of the Treaty,
   in respect of the formation of public limited liability companies and the
   maintenance and alteration of their capital, with a view to making such
   safeguards equivalent (1977 OJ L26/1)   28.6
   Art 17   13.35

1978   Third Company Law Directive
Directive 78/855/EEC; Third Council Directive of 9 October 1978 based on
   Article 54(3)(g) of the Treaty concerning mergers of public limited
   liability companies (1978 OJ L295/36)   40.16

1978   Fourth Company Law Directive
Directive 78/660/EEC; Fourth Council Directive of 25 July 1978 based on
   Article 54(3)(g) of the Treaty on the annual accounts of certain types of
   companies (1978 OJ L222/11)   24.13

1979   Admission Directive
Directive 79/279/EEC; Council Directive of 5 March 1979 coordinating the
   conditions for the admission of securities to official stock exchange
   listing (1979 OJ L66/21)   10.4

1980   Listing Particulars Directive
Directive 80/390/EEC; Council Directive of 17 March 1980 coordinating the
requirements for the drawing-up, scrutiny and distribution of the listing
particulars to be published for the admission of securities to official stock
exchange listing (1980 OJ L100/1)   10.5, 10.15

1982   Interim Reports Directive
Directive 82/121/EEC; Council Directive of 15 February 1982 on information
to be published on a regular basis by companies the shares of which have
been admitted to official stock exchange listing (1982 OJ L48/26)   10.6

1982   Sixth Company Law Directive
Directive 82/891/EEC; Sixth Council Directive of 17 December 1982 based
on Article 54(3)(g) of the Treaty, concerning the division of public
limited liability companies (1982 OJ L378/47)   40.16

1983   Seventh Company Law Directive
Directive 83/349/EEC; Seventh Council Directive of 13 June 1983 based on
the Article 54(3)(g) of the Treaty on consolidated accounts (1983 OJ
L193/1)   24.11

1988   Directive on Disclosure of Significant Shareholdings
Directive 88/627/EEC; Council Directive of 12 December 1988 on the
information to be published when a major holding in a listed company is
acquired or disposed of (1988 OJ L348/62)   31.7

1989   Prospectus Directive/Public Offers Directive
Directive 89/298/EEC; Council Directive of 17 April 1989 coordinating the
requirements for the drawing-up, scrutiny and distribution of the
prospectus to be published when transferable securities are offered to
the public (1989 OJ L124/8)   10.21

1989   Twelfth EC Company Law Directive
Directive 89/667/EEC; Twelfth Council Company Law Directive of 21
December 1989 on single-member private limited-liability companies
(1989 OJ L395/40)   viii, 8.7

1989   Mergers Control Regulation
Council Regulation (EEC) 4064/89 of 20 December 1989 on the control of
concentrations between undertakings (1989 OJ L395/1)   40.32

1990   Prospectus Directive
Directive 90/211/EEC of 23 April 1990   10.21

Directive 92/101/EEC   13.33, 28.6

Regulation 1310/97 amending Regulation 406/89 on control of
concentrations between undertakings (1997 OJNL 180 of 9.7.97, p1)   40.32

1957   Treaty of Rome
   Art 85   40.25, 40.32
   Art 86   40.31, 40.32
   Art 87   40.32
   Art 235   40.32

Irish Constitution
   Art 38   27.11

TABLE OF ABBREVIATIONS

To avoid unnecessary repetition, the following abbreviations are frequently used in the text when indicating principal statutory sources:

Statute	Abbreviations
Companies Act 1963	The 1963 Act *or* CA 1963
Companies Act 1963, Sch 1, Table A, Part I	Table A
Companies (Amendment) Act 1977	The 1977 Amendment Act
Companies (Amendment) Act 1982	The 1982 Amendment Act
Companies (Amendment) Act 1983	The 1983 Amendment Act
Companies (Amendment) Act 1986	The 1986 Amendment Act
Companies (Amendment) Act 1990	The 1990 Amendment Act
Companies Act 1990	The 1990 Act

INTRODUCTION

The origin of company law was nineteenth-century legislation enacted to stimulate the growth of trade and enterprise. This legislation sought to achieve its aims by introducing a facility whereby investors and entrepreneurs were permitted to create corporate bodies (companies) through which they could carry on business. Investors could also, if they wished, have their liability for the losses of their companies limited.

Key concepts in company law

Understanding the legal 'architecture' which permits investors and entrepreneurs to carry on business by means of companies, necessitates an explanation of the fundamental ideas underpinning company law. Accordingly, before focusing on detailed company law rules, requirements and procedures, Part II of this book contains explanations of:

(1) what is meant by the separate legal or corporate personality of the company;
(2) what limited liability means for investors and the company; and
(3) what is meant by 'the veil of incorporation', and when, in exceptional circumstances, this veil might be 'lifted' to remove investors' immunity from liability for the debts of the company, or to restrain them from using the company as a means of evading their personal legal obligations.

To illustrate the practical effects of corporate personality and limited liability, the relative advantages and disadvantages of carrying on business as a sole trader, in partnership or by means of a company are compared (in Chapter 5).

Types of company permitted

The companies legislation permitted the formation of several types of company.

Persons seeking to promote companies under the Companies Acts were permitted to form companies which were either limited by shares or by guarantee. Promoters could also, if they so desired, choose to forgo the benefits of limited liability and form unlimited companies. Chapter 8 mentions the factors to be considered by company promoters before deciding on the type of corporate form most appropriate to their needs.

All companies can be classified as either private or public (plc), generally according to the numbers of their shareholders or members. Private companies need a minimum of one member and are subject to a maximum limit of

50 members. Public companies must have at least seven members but are subject to no upper limit on membership numbers.

In Ireland, over 90 per cent of all companies are private.

Formation of a company

Promoters can form a company by following a statutory procedure known as registration. The documentation to be submitted to the registrar of companies when forming a new company includes its 'constitutional' documents: its memorandum and articles of association.

The *memorandum of association* is the more fundamental document. It sets out the company's name, objects and nominal capital. It also records (if applicable) the fact that the liability of the members is to be limited.

The *articles of association* consist of the rules governing the internal management of the company. These deal with such matters as the appointment and powers of directors, shareholders' rights and liabilities, and proceedings at company meetings. Table A is a model set of articles for the management of public and private companies limited by shares, set out in the First Schedule to the Companies Act 1963. Many companies adopt all, or part, of Table A for their articles.

When the registrar of companies is satisfied that the registration application is in order, he issues a certificate of incorporation. This certificate is essentially the company's 'birth' certificate.

From the date of incorporation mentioned in the certificate of incorporation, the subscribers to the memorandum, together with such other persons who may from time to time become members of the company, become a body corporate with the name contained in the memorandum of association. From this moment, the company has a separate legal existence from its members.

How a company carries on business

Although a company is recognised as a separate legal person by the law, it has no 'mind or body' like a human being. As a result, it can only carry on its business by using human agents.

Members of the company cannot act as agents for it; this restriction is part of the 'price' paid by members for the privilege of incorporating companies. The members do, however, elect a board of directors who will act as the company's managing agents.

Directors must act in a fiduciary or trustworthy manner in relation to the property and assets of the company. Such property and assets are owned by the company, however, and not by the directors.

The directors also act as agents for the company when negotiating contracts for it with 'outsiders', eg when borrowing money for the company from banks, or buying goods and services for it generally. 'Outsiders' owed money by the company are usually styled 'creditors'.

Financial difficulties

If the company encounters financial difficulties, secured creditors may appoint a receiver and manager over the company's property. Ultimately, unpaid creditors may petition the court to terminate the 'life' of the company.

Terminating the 'life' of a company

A company is brought into existence by utilising a legal procedure known as registration. A company's existence may be terminated by following another procedure. The usual procedure for ending the 'life' of a company is known as 'winding up' or 'liquidation'.

Even unsecured creditors, if they are owed at least £1,000, can petition the court to appoint a liquidator to wind up a company.

Business relationships in company law

The core business relationships affecting registered companies involve:

(1) the company itself;
(2) its promoters;
(3) its directors and officers;
(4) its members (or investors);
(5) its creditors; and
(6) if the company encounters financial or other difficulties, office-holders such as:
    (a) inspectors;
    (b) receivers (and managers);
    (c) examiners; and/or
    (d) liquidators.

Company law provides a framework of rules and procedures which govern these business relationships. The interaction between the relationships will be developed in Part I, before concentrating on the law affecting individual business relationships in Parts II to X.

PART I

THE BUSINESS RELATIONSHIPS IN COMPANY LAW

Chapter 1

ORIGINS AND SCOPE OF COMPANY LAW

THE STATUTORY FRAMEWORK

1.1 Incorporated business associations, which in Ireland are styled as 'companies', are active in any Western European (and, indeed, world) market economy involving the selling and buying of goods, products and services.

In Ireland, company law provides the legal framework within which investors, entrepreneurs and labour organise themselves into corporations which become recognised as separate and independent persons in the eyes of the law.

1.2 The political pressure to permit associations of individuals to trade as companies culminated in the 1840s. Government felt that economic activity would be stimulated if entrepreneurs were permitted to register companies – a much faster and more efficient process than that of obtaining a royal charter. As a result of this political/economic pressure, the Joint Stock Companies Act was passed in 1844. The Act provided for the registration of companies without the need to obtain a royal charter. It did not, however, include provisions limiting the liability of shareholders.

Shortly after the 1844 Act, political lobbying on behalf of investors commenced to add the protection of limited liability to the benefits of company registration.

The principle of limited liability was introduced by the Limited Liability Act 1855. This Act was quickly repealed by the Joint Stock Companies Act 1856 which retained the principle of limited liability but also introduced the constitutional documents of the modern registered company, requiring a memorandum of association and a set of articles of association.

The first 'modern' Companies Act was enacted in 1862. It contained over 200 sections and consolidated all the previous statutes. The current legislation regulating companies is contained largely in the Companies Acts 1963 to 1990, which contain over 800 sections and 19 Schedules.

1.3 It is worth noting, at this stage, that the current framework of Irish company law reflects many ideas introduced over 150 years ago which may not be entirely appropriate for business enterprises entering the third millennium. In particular, the emphasis given to public companies in the legislation does not reflect the present structure of Irish business associations, where private companies make up an overwhelming majority. Notwithstanding this, a major revision of company law seems unlikely in the foreseeable future. Accordingly, corporate business transactions in Ireland will continue to take place within the legal framework of a large and complex body of company law, originating in England in 1844, and consisting of thousands of individual rules.

The significance of the 1844 and 1856 legislation was that these Acts introduced the methods of registering a company with separate legal personality and limited liability for its investors.

SEPARATE LEGAL PERSONALITY OF COMPANY

1.4 A registered company is treated, in law, as a separate and distinct person from its shareholders. In Chapter 3, we examine this concept of statutory corporate personality and show how the judiciary have interpreted it.

The veil of incorporation

1.5 The corporate personality of a registered company is also often likened to a veil, protecting the shareholders of a company against legal actions against them for the debts of the company. There are, however, exceptional occasions when the courts will 'lift this protective veil' and allow a company's creditors to pursue actions against its shareholders. In Chapter 6, an attempt is made to unravel the confusing miscellany of case-law on this subject. The legislature has also made provision, in some circumstances, for the veil of incorporation to be lifted. Examples are also included in Chapter 6 of the *exceptional statutory* cases where the veil of incorporation offers *no protection* to shareholders.

LIMITED LIABILITY OF INVESTORS

1.6 The liability of a registered company which fails financially is limited to the assets of the company remaining at the time of the liquidation. Because the company's liability is limited, so too is that of its investors. This is because, generally, a company's creditors cannot make its shareholders liable for the debts of the company, which is a separate person and quite distinct from them at law. It is only in the exceptional cases where the court or statute penetrates the veil of incorporation (or separate personality of the company), that the shareholders may be rendered liable for the debts (or other activities) of the company. As indicated in the Preface, this is usually only likely to happen when a shareholder acts improperly or becomes involved with the management or affairs of the company. For example, if it is proved that the company was formed for some fraudulent or illegal purpose, or to evade the members' legal obligations, a court may 'lift the veil' and make the shareholders liable for the company's debts.

THE ARTIFICIAL NATURE OF A COMPANY

1.7 A company is, obviously, very different to a human legal person. A company has 'neither body, mind nor soul'. If the law recognises a person with neither body, mind nor soul as a full legal person, the question arises as to how such a company can exercise its legal rights: in particular, how does a company operate and trade? The short answer is by a series of agency contracts with humans. Companies can therefore only operate by using human agents.

The company's human agents

1.8 Before any company is registered, some person (or persons) must have the idea and energy to start the incorporation procedure. Such a person is styled a *promoter*.

A promoter enters into contracts both with the company and on its behalf, even before it is registered. There were some problems at common law relating to the validity of pre-incorporation contracts made by promoters, but this situation was remedied in 1963. In Part III of this book, the rights and liabilities of promoters are explained. This part also outlines the formal procedure to be taken to register and incorporate a private company and explains the importance of the memorandum and articles of association.

1.9 Once the registrar of companies issues a certificate of incorporation, the company is legally 'born'. What this means is that the law now recognises the *company* as an artificial but legal person which is entitled to trade in its own right. A company, therefore, has the legal power to enter into contracts with investors, or trading contracts, to borrow money and to give security for its borrowings.

Company capital and initial finance

1.10 A private company is entitled to commence trading once it receives its certificate of incorporation from the registrar of companies. Public companies, on the other hand, have to raise their capital from the public before the registrar licenses them to commence business by means of a Trading Certificate. Chapters 10 and 11 illustrate how investors in public companies are protected before such a company is allowed to trade. The composition of a company's capital base, and the statutory restrictions on any reduction of it, are dealt with in Chapters 12 and 13.

COMPANY ORGANISATION BY MEANS OF ITS HUMAN AGENTS

1.11 When a company is being formed, the human agents most directly connected with it will be its investors or shareholders. However, shareholders cannot negotiate contracts and act as agents for the company. Their input is limited to electing the board of directors. It is this body of human agents which has the authority to manage the company. They constitute the 'mind'[1] of the company. All company decisions emanate from the board of directors. The board may, however, delegate powers to a *Managing Director* or indeed, to senior employees (executives). Provided directors' decisions are lawful and within their powers ('intra vires'), they cannot be overruled by the members.

Chapter 14 deals with the respective roles of investors and directors in operating the company.

Investors' rights and responsibilities

1.12   The 'corporate rights' of investors to elect the board of directors is the extent of their entitlement to corporate governance.

Investors' individual contractual rights against the company are the subject of Part VII. Depending on the class of share, these include the right to vote, to attend meetings, and to payment of a dividend. Investors, in their contract terms, accept the fact that resolutions passed at company meetings are controlled by the majority. The procedures involved in these meetings between company owners (investors) and human managing agents (directors) are detailed in Chapter 15.

Again, whilst, generally, minority shareholders have to accept majority decisions at company meetings, there are exceptional cases where a minority of members have a right to appeal a majority decision to the courts. These exceptional circumstances are explained in Chapter 16.

A person invests in a company by purchasing its shares. However, their full contractual benefits will not accrue to shareholders until they become members of the company. This entails having their names included in the register of members.

In Chapter 28, we look at who can become company members and the different ways of acquiring (and relinquishing) membership.

Essentially, a member has a contract with the company. This is known as a s 25 contract.

The terms of a s 25 contract are contained in the company's articles of association. The 'bundle' of members' rights under their contracts are specified in Chapter 29, and Chapter 30 focuses on members' rights to be paid a dividend, and their liabilities to meet instalments due (calls) on partly paid shares.

---

1 But not its body and soul! A company's business premises and staff employed also give it a physical presence.

Disclosure of interests

1.13 The statutory duties on members to disclose their interests in shares are outlined in Chapter 31, which also deals with the process of transferring the ownership of shares when they are being sold.

Transfer of interests

1.14 The transfer process involves two stages. The first is an assignment by the seller of his interest in the shares to the purchaser. The second stage involves the registration of the purchaser as a member in place of the seller.

Company directors have rights to refuse the registration of a purchaser of shares. If the directors exercise these rights, then the purchaser concerned will hold only an equitable, rather than a legal, interest in the shares purchased.

The consequences of non-registration of a share transfer are also dealt with in Chapter 31.

Compulsory purchase

1.15 Following a successful *takeover bid*, the purchasing company may be entitled compulsorily to acquire the shares of the dissenting minority – see below.

Directors and officers – the company's managing agents

1.16 While the investors may own the company, they are not entitled to manage it or to negotiate contracts on its behalf. This function is given to the directors. It is they who control the day-to-day trading activities of the investors' company.

The directors are elected by the investors. Accordingly, Chapter 14 deals with the appointment and removal of directors. A director elected by the investors is an office holder rather than an employee of the company, ie he is typically a non-executive director.

Directors may also enter into service contracts (of employment) with the company. For example, the managing director or, indeed, any other executive director, has a dual role. He is an office holder; he is also an employee of the company of which he is a director. These distinctions are explained in Chapter 14.

In view of the critical role of directors under company law, Part V is devoted to looking at their legal responsibilities in discharging their duties to the company.

Directors' duties

1.17 Directors' common law fiduciary duties and duties of care and skill are introduced in Chapter 19. Chapter 20 then shows how these duties were strengthened by statutory intervention in 1990.

Directors' liability for company debts

1.18 As a result of their increasingly more onerous duties, directors now run a real risk of being made personally liable for the debts of a 'failed' company: a liability incurred by them as managing agents, not as investors.

Directors may also be sued for breach of duty by the company, although the shareholders have the power to waive such rights.

The extent of directors' potential legal liabilities, and the advantage of transferring at least some of them to an insurance company, are outlined in Chapters 21 and 22.

Disqualification of directors

1.19 The sanctions of restriction and disqualification of directors, which were introduced in 1990, are outlined in Chapter 23.

The company secretary

1.20 Every company must appoint an officer known as the company secretary. His role is essentially to ensure that the company complies with the provisions of the Companies Acts and is outlined in Chapter 14.

The authority of the company secretary to bind the company in contracts with 'outsiders' is mentioned in Chapter 18.

Monitoring the directors' management of the company

1.21 The law prescribes the keeping of statutory registers, books, records and accounts in which the business transactions of the company must be recorded. Certain of these documents must be open to inspection by the investors.

The directors must prepare annual accounts and lay them before the members in general meetings. The company's independent auditors will report to the members on the accounts. Approval of the annual accounts by the members is, essentially, a vote approving the directors' management of their company.

The directors must also submit an annual return to the registrar of companies.

Chapters 24 to 26 detail the statutory requirements for monitoring the directors' stewardship of the company. These include the role and responsibilities of the independent auditor.

If directors are unhelpful and refuse to provide information to members or creditors, the latter may apply to the court seeking the appointment of an Inspector to investigate the conduct of the company's affairs. The Minister can also have an Inspector appointed to investigate company ownership – see Chapter 27.

Company employees

1.22 In practice, when managing the company, the directors will employ staff on the company's behalf, and delegate its day-to-day operational tasks to them. Nevertheless, company law does not encompass the rights and duties of company employees. This is the province of labour/employment law. As far as company law is concerned, the relevant fact is that a company can act as an employer in much the same way as a human person.

Notwithstanding, some ambiguities have arisen in connection with the duties of directors who are also employees, eg managing and other executive directors. Therefore, discussion of the blurring of the distinction between the role (or roles) of directors as office holders and employees is included in Chapter 19.

CONTRACTUAL CAPACITY OF THE COMPANY AND ITS AGENTS

1.23 A company, as a recognised legal person, can enter into contracts (by using its directors and employees as human agents). Generally, however, a company can only enter into contracts within the powers contained in the objects clause of its memorandum of association. If it enters into a contract outside its objects, that contract is 'ultra vires' and void at common law. In Chapter 17, we show how the legislature has intervened to protect creditors against ultra vires contracts. The provision of the Companies Acts relating to the company's name and registered office (address) are also noted in this chapter. Restrictions on the initial choice of a company name are dealt with in Chapter 7.

The agency law principles underlying the authority of directors, officers and employees to act on the company's behalf are explained in Chapter 18. This chapter also deals with the form of company contracts.

COMPANY CONTROL AND OWNERSHIP

1.24 A feature of company law is that it separates control of a company from its ownership. As mentioned above, a company is controlled by its board of directors. It is, however, owned by its *shareholders or members*. The members of a company are simply *investors* who contribute to the company's *capital.*

In practice, the same person may be both a shareholder and a director. In fact, in many small private companies, including the recently introduced *single-member company*, the majority shareholder may also be the managing director. Nevertheless, in company law, these roles are seen as distinct: the person involved 'wearing two hats' – one when acting as member, the other when acting as director.

In company law, legal relationships between the company, its directors and members (shareholders) can be classified as matters *internal to the company*. However, the company also enters into legal relationships with persons external to it. Such relationships usually arise out of trading or borrowing transactions.

EXTERNAL OR THIRD PARTY RELATIONSHIPS

1.25 When a company enters into a trading transaction and that trader remains unpaid for the goods or services supplied to the company, the 'third party' or external trader becomes a creditor of the company.

Similarly, if the company borrows money,[1] the lender will be a creditor for the monies remaining unpaid on the loan. If, as would usually be the case, the lender insists on the company furnishing security before granting it the loan, the lender will be classified as a 'secured creditor'.

Creditors' rights against the company

1.26 The different types of company creditors and the nature of their security on the company's assets are noted in Chapter 33.

Secured creditors are generally known as debenture-holders; their contract with the company being evidenced by a debenture deed.

The usual terms of a debenture are outlined in the deed. Charges on the company's assets as security for the debenture must be registered with the registrar of companies. The company must also maintain a register of debenture holders.

Debentures can be transferred (sold and bought) in much the same way as shares.

The remedies of unpaid creditors, both unsecured and secured, are detailed in Chapter 34.

1.27 Secured creditors can appoint a receiver over the company's property for its failure to repay monies borrowed. The consequences of receivership for

---

1 Sometimes classified as 'loan' capital as distinct from capital supplied by shareholders (investment capital).

the company, and the rights, powers and duties of the receiver are explained in Chapter 35.

Because of the privilege of limited liability which investors enjoy, if a company is insolvent on winding up, the creditors have little chance of recovering company debts from them. Recent statutory developments have made the company's managing agents, ie its directors and officers, a much better target – see **1.30** below. Chapter 36 focuses on unsatisfied creditors' remedies against the company's investors and officers.

Rights against insolvent company's assets

1.28   The most frequent reason for liquidating a company is because it has become insolvent, ie unable to pay its debts to creditors.

As the liability of investors is limited to the fully paid up value of their shares, if there is a lack of company funds to meet all the claims of creditors, what does the law prescribe?

Suppose, for example, that Alpha Ltd, a private company, is to be wound up with assets totalling £800,000 and liabilities of £2.4 million. Which creditors (if any) will be paid, and, assuming some are, how much of their debts will they receive? To answer this question, one has to classify the various company creditors.

1.29   The general rule regarding ranking of payments is that secured creditors are entitled to be paid in preference to unsecured creditors. As most companies being wound up will have insufficient assets to pay all their creditors, the likely losers in this scenario will be the unsecured creditors.

Again, if there are insufficient assets to pay the unsecured creditors, the shareholders, who rank below them, will also lose their total investments in the company.

The full ranking of creditors' debts and creditors' rights generally is outlined in Chapter 2 and in Parts VIII and X. These parts also explain the distinctions between a company liquidation and receivership, and the differing roles of a liquidator and a receiver.

Creditors' rights against directors and others

1.30   At this stage, it is clear that the principle of limited liability protects investors if the company in which they are members is wound up. The creditors only have rights against company assets, and these rights depend on their legal ranking as creditors. In practice, such rights may only be useful to secured creditors.

This situation is unsatisfactory, from a creditor's point of view. As a result, unsatisfied creditors have looked for sources of redress, other than the company assets.

The obvious target for creditors were the company's directors, who, in certain circumstances, can be held *personally* liable (without limitation) for the unpaid debts of the company. For example, under s 297A of the Companies Act 1963,[1] an officer of the company, such as a director or manager, can be held by a court to be personally responsible for all the debts of the company, where it appears that he was knowingly a party to the carrying on of the business in a reckless manner.

During 1990, two important Companies Acts were passed. The first[2] introduced the office of Examiner into Ireland – see **1.32** below. The second[3] greatly increased the responsibilities and liabilities of company directors.

Creditors' rights to terminate the life of a company

1.31   Under s 214 of the Companies Act 1963,[4] a creditor (secured or unsecured) who is owed a sum exceeding £1,000 may, if the company, after due written notice, fails to pay the amount, petition or apply to the court to wind up that company. In fact, the majority of petitions to the court to wind up companies are presented by creditors.

From a company's perspective, therefore, creditors are given real powers under company law. They possess the ultimate sanction of bringing the life of the company to an end, without seeking the consent, or even against the express wishes, of that company's directors and shareholders.

It was the possibility of the use by creditors of that ultimate sanction against Mr Larry Goodman's companies, in 1990, which led to a special sitting of the Dail in August, and the passing of the Companies (Amendment) Act 1990. This Act introduced the office of Examiner in Ireland.

Protecting the company against its creditors

1.32   The policy underlying the appointment of an Examiner is that companies in financial difficulties might be given time to place their finances on a firmer footing, thereby avoiding a winding up with all its negative consequences for company, directors, shareholders, employees and creditors alike. Accordingly, under the 1990 Amendment Act, an application for the appointment of an Examiner by the court may be presented by any or all of the following persons:

(1)   the company;
(2)   the directors;
(3)   a creditor (including an employee); and
(4)   a member holding at least 10 per cent of the voting shares.

---

1   Inserted by s 138 of the Companies Act 1990.
2   Companies (Amendment) Act 1990.
3   Companies Act 1990 – see Chapter 2 and Part V.
4   Amended by s 123 of the Companies Act 1990.

1.33 If, on hearing the petition, the court appoints an Examiner, the company is deemed to be *under the protection* of the court for a period of three months. During this three-month period, no receiver may be appointed over any part of the company's property; no proceedings for the winding up of the company may be commenced, nor resolution for its winding up passed.

This three-month 'breathing space' from its creditors, for a debtor company, may enable the Examiner to work out a financial arrangement to save the company – hence the term 'debtor protection', in company law.

The protection of a company against its creditors and the role of the Examiner are explained further in Part IX.

1.34 Chapter 37 looks at examinership in detail, and shows its effects on creditors' rights. How the Examiner's Opinion and Recommendation will affect the future of the company is explained in Chapter 38. Generally, if the Examiner's Report expresses the view that the company is viable, he will propose a 'rescue' package to meetings of creditors and investors. Once the court confirms these financial proposals, they become binding on all creditors, investors and the company itself.

If the court refuses to confirm the proposed rescue package, or, if the Examiner's Report expresses the view that the company is not capable of survival as a going concern, the court may, inter alia, order the winding up of the company.

Compromising company debts and corporate restructuring

1.35 In a successful examinership, the company may be 'saved' by the Examiner coming to an arrangement or compromise with the company's creditors. It is not, however, necessary for the company to be placed in examinership in order simply to compromise its debts. This can be done by entering into a scheme of arrangement or compromise under s 201 of the Companies Act 1963.

Chapter 39 outlines the procedures for a s 201 compromise between a company and its investors or creditors. Such an arrangement needs the approval of a majority of the investors and creditors.

1.36 Where a scheme provides for the transfer of company assets to a new company, this is often referred to as a *reconstruction*.

An *amalgamation* is a joining together of two or more companies to form a single new company.

Both reconstructions and amalgamations may be carried out under ss 201 to 203 of the 1963 Act in connection with schemes of arrangements with creditors, or under s 260 of the 1963 Act in the course of a voluntary winding up.

Changes in company ownership by takeover and merger

1.37 The term *takeover* is often used to describe a bid by a company to purchase the majority or all of the shares in a 'target' company. If the bid is not contested, the transaction will be described as a *merger*. It is the prior agreement (or the lack of it) to an amalgamation of companies that distinguishes the process of merger from that of takeover. Mergers are usually the result of an agreed takeover bid.

Chapter 40 outlines the statutory takeover procedures, including the power of the bidding company to compulsorily acquire the shares of a minority of investors in the target company and the rights of the dissident investors. As takeovers and mergers afford an opportunity for directors and shareholders to make sizeable profits, the legal and other controls designed to prevent excessive profit-taking are discussed: as is the government interest in ensuring that the takeover or merger does not result in a monopoly situation which could reduce competition and lead to product (or services) price increases for consumers.

Winding up a company

1.38 The procedure for terminating the 'life' of a company is known as winding up.

Part X shows how the winding-up procedure can be initiated by creditors, members and others. Irrespective of who initiates the liquidation, the task of realising the company's assets and paying its creditors falls upon the liquidator. The role and responsibility of an official liquidator appointed by the court is examined in Chapter 42, whilst the duties of liquidators appointed by investors and creditors in 'voluntary' liquidations are compared in Chapters 43 and 44.

Dissolving the company

1.39 When the liquidator has completely wound up the affairs of the company, the final procedure is for the company to be dissolved. For example, in a creditors' voluntary winding up, three months after the registrar of companies has received the liquidator's final account, the company will be deemed to be dissolved.

A company ceases to exist as a separate legal entity only when it has been dissolved.

Chapter 2

COMPANY LAW OBJECTIVES – PROTECTION OF INVESTORS AND CREDITORS

INTERNAL AND EXTERNAL INTERESTS

2.1 The many and various business interests affected by corporate transactions were outlined in Chapter 1. Some of these interests are internal to the company; others are external.

Internal interests

2.2 Shareholders (or members), as investors, supply a company's capital. However, they take no part in the day-to-day management of the company. Nevertheless, investors have contracts with the company and enjoy both corporate and individual rights[1] against the company on the basis of these contracts.

Companies are managed by the directors, who may be non-executive or executive. The board of directors will employ persons to carry out the work of the company.

In the normal course of business, therefore, one might encounter a range of contractual relationships which concern largely the internal affairs of the company.

2.3 Examples of such *internal* relationships include the following contracts between:

(1) a company and its *members*, involving both (a) corporate and (b) individual aspects of membership rights;
(2) a company and its *directors* as office holders and, perhaps, also as employees;
(3) a company and its *promoter* (or *promoters*);
(4) a company and its *employees*;
(5) an investor and another investor (or investors);
(6) an investor may also have dealings with *directors* and *employees*, acting on behalf of the company.

External (or third party) interests

2.4 When a company engages in business and borrows money, it enters into contracts with traders and banks. Neither of these interests are involved with the internal affairs of running the company. Such interests are classified, therefore, as *external*, or *third party interests*.

---

1 See Chapters 1 and 16.

External (or third party) corporate transactions include the following between:

(1) a *company* and a third party, eg the company buys a lorry from a garage. The garage is a third party creditor of the company until paid;
(2) a *promoter* (on behalf of the company) and a third party;
(3) a *director* (or *directors*) (on behalf of the company) and a third party;
(4) an *employee* (on behalf of the company) and a third party;
(5) a *promoter* and a third party;
(6) an *investor* and a third party (buying his shares).

2.5   When a company finds itself in financial difficulties, it may have to enter into special arrangements with its creditors, have a receiver appointed over its property by secured creditors, or be wound up by a liquidator appointed by either the court, its investors or creditors. The resulting legal relationships arising from these events are detailed in Parts VIII and X. The effect of the appointment of an Examiner on creditors' rights and the future viability of the company is dealt with in Part IX.

The body of company law contains a framework underpinning each of these internal and external legal relationships. The core policy objectives underlying company law seek, essentially, to protect two broad categories of interests, ie those of investors (internal) and creditors (external). One can, therefore, state succinctly the twin core aims of company law as being Investor Protection and Creditor Protection.

INVESTOR PROTECTION

2.6   In the 1850s, entrepreneurs were not satisfied solely with the introduction of a simpler procedure to register a company. They also sought, successfully, to have losses arising out of their investments (shares) in companies capped.

Limitation of liability

2.7   The most fundamental form of investor protection is the privilege of trading with limited liability. Investors (or shareholders) in companies registered under the Companies Acts were protected by having their liability for losses sustained in the event of the company collapsing limited to the amount (if any) unpaid on their shares. Thus, the most the shareholder would lose was the amount which he had invested in a company which failed. The advantage of this privilege has been underlined recently by the huge losses incurred by investors in Lloyd's Syndicates. These investors, called 'Names', invested without the privilege of limited liability. When the syndicates made very heavy trading losses, they were able to pass them on to their 'Names'.

The limitation of liability available to investors in registered companies, since 1855, has been most successful in protecting them against the type of Lloyd's Names scenario. As a general immunity for shareholders against claims made by company creditors, this fundamental form of investor protection has withstood the test of time. The only erosion of it has been where the 'veil of incorporation' has been lifted. In these quite exceptional cases,[1] a court may be able to effectively ignore the investors' fundamental immunity and render them liable to the company creditors for contract debts or other personal obligations. For example, in *Re Aluminium Fabricators Ltd*,[2] O'Hanlon J stated:

> 'The privilege of limitation of liability which is afforded ... in relation to companies incorporated under the [1963] Act with limited liability, cannot be afforded to those who use a limited company as a cloak or shield beneath which they seek to operate a fraudulent system of carrying on business for their own personal enrichment and advantage.'

Price paid for limitation of liability

2.8　The price paid by investors for having their liability limited includes that of being debarred from taking any part in the day-to-day management of the company.

Whilst investors own the company, they are nonetheless, prohibited from managing it (as members) or negotiating contracts with third parties on the company's behalf. Thus, in company law, ownership and management diverge. These principles of company law are reflected in public companies where ownership is separate from management. However, for the over 95 per cent of all Irish companies which are private, the larger shareholders will also be directors. These member directors embrace two different relationships within the one person. For company law purposes, one has to distinguish and classify the actions of a member director into those exercised by him as a shareholder and those exercised as a director. Again, the formation of a registered company involves a formal registration procedure before the registrar issues the Certificate of Incorporation. Once registered, the company (acting through its directors) must comply with the provisions of the Companies Acts relating to publicity, maintenance of registers, submissions of returns and accounts, etc.

Many of the 'downside' aspects of limitation of liability are obvious in the comparison of companies, partnerships and sole traders, outlined in Chapter 5.

Other protections for investors

2.9　The whole idea of limited liability is clearly a fundamental protection for investors. However, the detailed provisions of the Companies Acts 1963 to 1990 give investors many more protections. These include protection against certain actions taken by fellow (majority) shareholders and by company directors.

In relation to resolutions at meetings, the basic rule in company law is majority control. A simple majority (51 per cent) of ordinary shareholders is normally

---

1　See Chapter 6.
2　[1984] ILRM 399 (HC). See also Chapter 6 and the case of *Re Kelly's Carpetdrome Ltd.*

sufficient to control most decisions taken at company general meetings. Nevertheless, even in such situations there are statutory protections for minority investors. These minority protections range from s 205[1] remedies in cases of oppression to s 10(3) rights of objecting to a change in the memorandum of association.

2.10 Indeed, the majority of shareholders may need protection more from the actions of the directors than from the other shareholders. Accordingly, there are many rules of company law which attempt to protect investors from the actions of directors in abusing their positions of power and of trust. For example, under s 298,[2] the court may compel any director who has misapplied or retained any property[3] of the company, or who has been guilty of any misfeasance or breach of trust, to repay or restore the property.

Again, directors may be liable to compensate investors who were induced to purchase shares in a public company by incorrect information in a prospectus.[4]

CREDITOR PROTECTION

2.11 Persons entering into trading contracts with, or lending[5] money to, the company are generally referred to as creditors.

In reality, a company is akin to a legally recognised 'front' permitting investors to become involved in the financing of trade. As a result, the policy underlying company law also builds into the legislation elements of protection for the creditors of registered companies.

There are, broadly, three aspects to creditor protection in company law. The first relates to the public nature of the memorandum and articles of association of registered companies. The second aspect is the protection company law gives to maintaining the integrity of a company's share capital fund, and the third is the power given to creditors to interfere in the management of a company which places their interests in jeopardy.

Let us now look briefly at the type of actual protection within these broad categories of creditor protection.

Public nature of constitutional documents

2.12 The constitutional documents of a company are its memorandum and articles of association. These are available for inspection by any persons trading with or lending money to the company. Reference to them would enable

---

1 Of the 1963 Act. See Chapter 16.
2 Of the 1963 Act.
3 Or money.
4 See Chapter 10.
5 With or without security – see Part VIII.

potential creditors to check basic information such as authorised capital and the company's objects before granting it credit.

Often, trade creditors do not avail themselves of the opportunity of checking a company's memorandum of association. Notwithstanding, s 8[1] and reg 6 of the European Communities (Companies) Regulations 1973[2] may protect them.

Maintenance of company's capital

2.13   The registrar will not issue a trading certificate to a public company until satisfied that its minimum capital requirements have been raised from the public.[3]

Company law aims to protect and maintain[4] the capital fund of the company so that it is available to meet the company's contractual obligations. The law does this by stipulating that capital may only be reduced if proper safeguards are in place.

Again, a company is only permitted to buy its own shares in a few exceptional cases. It is also restricted in the circumstances in which it can lend money to a third party to buy the (lending) company's shares.

2.14   The Companies (Amendment) Act 1983 introduced a minimum share capital for a public limited company. The amount of the minimum paid-up capital, effectively £7,500, is quite modest.

Under s 40 of the 1983 Amendment Act, where the net assets of the company are half, or less, of the amount of the company's called-up share capital, the directors must convene an extraordinary general meeting for the purpose of considering what measures, if any, should be taken to deal with the situation.

Laudable capital maintenance rules such as those outlined above lose much of their effectiveness when one realises that their impact, if any, on private companies, is minimal.

Creditors' powers to intervene

2.15   The rights of creditors to liquidate the company were outlined in Chapter 1. Secured creditors have the power to appoint a receiver over the company's property.

Whilst creditors are not members of the company, and take no active part in the management of it, if the company is placed in receivership or is being wound up, *creditors are given more authority in controlling the company's affairs.* Examples

---

1 Of the Companies Act 1963.
2 SI 1973/163 – see Chapter 17.
3 See Chapters 10 and 11.
4 See Chapters 12 and 13.

include the power of the creditors to decide who becomes liquidator in a creditors' voluntary winding up.[1]

Creditors' rights of recovery[2] against the company

2.16 If the company fails to pay any monies owing to a third party creditor, the latter's rights depend on whether his debt is secured or unsecured. The contract document under which a company acknowledges its indebtedness under a loan is called a *debenture*.[3]

Secured creditors

2.17 Debentures usually give a fixed and/or floating charge over the company's assets as security.

When a loan is made to a company, the debenture trust deed involved normally gives the lender the power to appoint a receiver (and, perhaps, manager) in the event of the company defaulting on its repayments. The power bestowed on a receiver and manager would include the right to sell the company's assets. Thus, a creditor secured by a fixed charge can realise his security and effectively remain outside of the company liquidation procedure.

Unsecured creditors

2.18 When an unsecured creditor is owed money by the company, he can petition for its winding up and seek to recover his debt from the company's liquidated assets. The problem such a creditor faces, however, is that there may not be monies realisable to pay his debts. This unsatisfactory situation arises because of the ranking of creditors' claims in a winding-up situation.

Ranking of creditors' claims

2.19 A *fixed* charge is a mortgage of land or fixed plant and machinery. The property must be identified and any necessary formalities for the creation of the charge must be observed. The company cannot sell the assets covered by a fixed charge without the consent of the debenture holder. However, the company can sell assets which are the subject of a *floating charge*. The latter charge is an equitable mortgage of a type of the company's assets, without specifying any particular items, eg stock in trade.

Priorities in a distribution

2.20 Holders of fixed charges are entitled to realise their security. If the realised security is insufficient to repay them, then they can prove for the shortfall as unsecured creditors in the liquidation.

---

1 See Parts VIII and X.
2 See Part VIII for a more detailed treatment.
3 The term 'debenture' may also be used to describe the loan itself.

After the holders of fixed charges have realised their security, the liquidator will pay the remaining company creditors in the following order:

(1) *preferential* creditors, eg arrears of rates, income tax, wages and salaries of employees, redundancy payments, etc;[1]
(2) creditors secured by *floating* charges;
(3) *unsecured* creditors.

If a surplus remains after paying the preferential creditors, those secured by floating charges would be paid. The unsecured creditors are only paid if monies remain after paying category (2) above. In many liquidations, it would be unlikely that assets existed to pay the unsecured creditors, who constitute the most vulnerable group of external interests.

Creditors' other rights of recovery

2.21 If one can use the phrase 'typical' liquidation, it might be said that, in such a case, not only would the unsecured creditors not be paid, but some or all of those holding floating charges, and even preferential creditors,[2] might also lose out. Because of these creditor losses, it would not be unusual to find creditors seeking avenues of redress other than the company's own assets.

The company investors are protected by the separate personality of the company and the veil of incorporation. Much of the case-law dealing with *lifting the veil* relates to company creditors seeking to overturn the investors' immunity for company debts. However, this is a rather limited 'window of opportunity'.

A more fertile source of legal redress, particularly since 1990, is an action against the company's managing agents, ie its directors and officers.

Significance of the two 1990 Acts

2.22 The Companies Act 1990 increased the scope of remedies available to creditors by extending significantly the legal liability of company officers. For example, the s 297[3] remedy of rendering directors liable for fraudulent trading, which had not proved very satisfactory in practice, was extended to make officers (and others) liable also for reckless trading.

Again, s 204[4] renders any company officer liable for the debts of the company if proper books of account have not been kept. The headline 'Mantruck director ordered to pay liquidator £91,000'[5] illustrates the effectiveness of this provision. In that case, a director, John Duignan, was ordered to pay by Shanley J in the High Court, because the company, Mantruck Services, failed to keep

---

1 See s 285 of the 1963 Act.
2 For example, the Revenue Commissioners are often cited as unpaid creditors when a company is liquidated.
3 Of the 1963 Act.
4 Of the 1990 Act.
5 In the *Sunday Business Post* of 13 October 1996. This was the first award under s 204.

proper books and records. In view of these new onerous liabilities of company officers towards creditors, a chapter on directors' and officers' professional indemnity insurance has been included in Part V.

2.23   Part VII of the 1990 Act introduces new preventative measures to protect potential company creditors, by providing for the making of Disqualification and Restriction Orders against directors – see Part V.

Creditors' rights are dealt with in detail in Part VIII.

The Companies (Amendment) Act 1990, which preceded the 1990 Act, actually takes some rights away from creditors. It does this by allowing the appointment of an Examiner to delay the creditors (particularly secured creditors) from exercising their remedies against the company for a period of three months.[1]

---

1 See Chapter 1 and Part IX.

PART II

FUNDAMENTAL PRINCIPLES OF COMPANY LAW

Chapter 3

THE CONCEPT OF CORPORATE PERSONALITY

THE EFFECT OF INCORPORATION

3.1   When a company is formed, the effect of its incorporation is to create a distinct legal entity with rights and obligations quite separate from those possessed by its members (shareholders). One therefore has to consider the company as a separate person in its own right.

Separate legal personality of the company and *Salomon*'s case

3.2   Whilst introduced in the early nineteenth century, the concept of corporate legal personality was not fully appreciated until the landmark case of *Salomon v Salomon & Co*,[1] in 1897.

Salomon developed a thriving business as a sole trader. He then converted it into a limited liability company, the shareholders being himself, his wife and their five children.[2] Salomon placed a value of £39,000 (approximately £1.3 million at 1990s values) on his business and received from the company as consideration for the sale of his business to it, cash, a debenture or secured loan of £10,000 and 20,001 £1 shares out of the issued capital of £20,007. Salomon's wife and children each held one of the remaining six £1 shares.[3]

An economic depression occurred in the boot and shoe trade in which Salomon & Co traded. To assist the company, Salomon borrowed money on the security of the debentures and lent it to the company. Despite this financial assistance, the company failed and was forced into liquidation.

Liquidator's contention

3.3   The liquidator of Salomon & Co claimed that the company was entitled to be indemnified by Salomon against all its unsecured liabilities because, he contended, the company was '*a mere nominee* and agent' of Salomon.

The liquidator was successful as far as the Court of Appeal. In *Broderip v Salomon*,[4] it was held that the company was the agent of Salomon, and therefore Salomon, as principal, was liable for the debts of his agent, the company.

---

1   [1897] AC 22.
2   At that time, a minimum of seven members was required.
3   Probably as Salomon's nominees.
4   [1895] 2 Ch 323.

The case on appeal

3.4   On appeal, the Court of Appeal upheld the decision against Salomon, suggesting that the company was a trustee holding the business in trust for Salomon. However, when Salomon appealed to the House of Lords, he won the case: their Lordships reversing unanimously the Court of Appeal decision.

In the House of Lords judgment, Lord Macnaghten stated:

> 'The *Company is at law a different person altogether* from the [members] ... and, though it may be that after incorporation the business is precisely the same as it was before, and the same persons are managers, and the same hands receive the profits, the company is not in law the agent of the [members] or for them. *Nor are the [members] liable*, in any shape or form, except to the extent and in the manner provided by the Act.' (author's emphasis)

Essence of judgment

3.5   The House of Lords held, essentially, that Salomon & Co had been properly formed and was a separate legal person in its own right, despite the dominant position of Salomon within it.

As Salomon had paid for his shares in full by selling his business to the company, his liability to company creditors was discharged because the full nominal value of the company shares had been paid.

One-man companies

3.6   The company was not an 'alias' (or alter ego – other self) for Aaron Salomon, nor his agent or trustee. It was, in fact, a 'one-man' company. To quote from Lord Macnaghton's judgment again:

> 'It has become the fashion to call companies of this class "one man companies". This is taking a nickname, but it does not help one much in the way of argument. If it is intended to convey the meaning that a company which is under the absolute control of one person is not a company legally incorporated, although the requirements of the Act ... may have been complied with, it is inaccurate and misleading: if it merely means that there is a predominant partner possessing an overwhelming influence and entitled practically to the whole of the profits, there is nothing in that that I can see contrary to the true intention of the Act ... or against public policy, or detrimental to the interests of creditors. If the shares are fully paid up, it cannot matter whether they are in the hands of one or many. If the shares are not fully paid, it is as easy to gauge the solvency of an individual as to estimate the financial ability of a crowd ...'

Salomon's case established that corporate legal personality would be recognised even when one shareholder effectively controlled the company and had himself decided on the value of assets used to pay for his shares.

Subsequent case-law

3.7   The principle *that a company is a legal person separate and distinct from its members*, emanating from *Salomon*'s case, was applied by the Privy Council, in 1960.

In *Lee v Lee's Air Farming Ltd*,[1] Lee held 2,999 shares in the company: his wife held the remaining share. Lee was killed in an air crash whilst working for the company. Mrs Lee claimed statutory[2] workman's compensation for injuries to her husband whilst an employee of the company. It was disputed on the grounds that Lee and Lee's Air Farming Ltd were the same person.

The Privy Council applied *Salomon*'s case and held that Lee was a separate person from the company he formed. Accordingly, Mrs Lee was entitled to compensation.

3.8   In *Battle v Irish Art Promotion Centre Ltd*,[3] the managing director, a major shareholder in the company, sought to represent the company in legal proceedings. The Supreme Court held that he had no authority to represent the company in legal proceedings, O'Dalaigh CJ stating:

> 'One sympathises with the purpose which the [managing director] has in mind, . . . to safeguard his business reputation; but, as the law stands, he cannot as major shareholder and Managing Director now substitute his persona for that of the company.'

3.9   More recently, in the case of *Irish Permanent Building Society v Registrar of Building Societies and Irish Life Building Society*,[4] the fundamental principle of separate corporate personality was again applied by Barrington J. The principle has clearly received judicial recognition in the Irish jurisdiction.[5]

Importance of the **Salomon** decision

3.10   *Salomon*'s case was very significant in that it finally established the legality of the 'one-man' company and showed that incorporation was available to small businesses as well as to large enterprises. Nevertheless, the decision causes some concern because it demonstrated how it was possible to limit, not merely money invested in the company, but also how to reduce the speculative risk by loaning money to the company (by debenture) rather than investing in more shares.

The main consequence of incorporation for a registered company is that it becomes a legal person distinct from its members. A registered company is therefore a legalised 'front' through which the company owners (its investors) can trade. Because the separate legal personality of the company acts as a bar to

---

1   [1960] 3 All ER 420.
2   Under the New Zealand Workman's Compensation Act 1922.
3   [1968] IR 252.
4   [1981] ILRM 242.
5   See article by G. McCormack 'Judicial Application of Salomon's Case in Ireland', *Law Society Gazette*, May 1984, pp 97–100.

outsiders (eg company creditors) taking action against its investors, commentators have likened this personality to a 'veil'.

THE VEIL OF INCORPORATION

3.11　The corporate personality is often likened to a veil; the idea being that investors are shielded from legal actions behind this 'veil of incorporation'. The case of *The Roundabout Ltd v Beirne*[1] illustrates the protection given to members by the veil of incorporation.

Marian Park Inn Ltd was a public house trading in Dublin using non-union staff. During May 1958, all the staff joined a union. As a result of this action, the company's three directors closed the premises and dismissed the staff. The union then picketed the premises.

One month later, a new company re-opened the bar premises. This new company was The Roundabout Ltd. Its directors included the three former directors of the Marian Park Inn Ltd. The new company sought an injunction against the union to prevent them picketing the premises whilst used by The Roundabout Ltd. It was argued in favour of the injunction that the business was being conducted by a new legal person and the union had no trade dispute with The Roundabout Ltd. Dixon J agreed and granted the injunction against the union picketing, commenting:

> 'Each company is what is known as a legal person. I have to regard the two companies as distinct in the same way as I would regard two distinct [human] individuals.

McCormack[2] criticises this decision as being a case where legal technicalities were allowed to prevail over industrial relations and common sense, pointing out that Lord Denning had viewed with suspicion the notion that statutory provisions governing industrial disputes could be eroded in this fashion.

Lord Denning was prepared to consider lifting the veil of incorporation in such circumstances – see Chapter 6.[3]

Company ownership and management

3.12　An important implication of separate corporate personality and the veil of incorporation is that company law draws a clear distinction between ownership and management. The shareholders or investors own the company. In doing so, they are protected against the company's creditors by the veil of

---

1 [1959] IR 423 at p 426.
2 G. McCormack 'Judicial Application of Salomon's Case in Ireland' *Law Society Gazette*, May 1984, at p 98.
3 Since the European Communities (Safeguarding of Employees' Rights on Transfer of Undertakings) Regulations 1980, SI 1980/306; incorporation may not now be used to evade responsibility under collective agreements in a takeover situation – see **40.21**.

incorporation. However, because of this protection, shareholders are not entitled (as investors) to take part in the management of their company, nor to enter into contracts on its behalf.

Investors elect directors to manage their company. In practice, a large shareholder may also be a director and take part in the management of the company. In such instances, however, the management tasks are undertaken by virtue of that person's role as director, not because he is (also) an investor.

This divergence of ownership and management reinforces the principle of limited liability for company investors by restricting their roles essentially to the contributing of capital and the election of company officers to manage the enterprise.[1]

---

1 See Chapters 14 to 16.

Chapter 4

LIMITED LIABILITY AND OTHER
CONSEQUENCES OF INCORPORATION

INTRODUCTION

4.1 The previous chapter illustrates how the investors in a company are immune from liability for the debts of a company which they own. However, complete immunity from liability is not permitted. Each investor is liable to be called upon to contribute the full nominal value of his shares if they are not already fully paid up. If a shareholder has agreed to pay more than the nominal value, then his liability is limited to the amount he has agreed to pay.

For example, suppose Alpha Ltd issues 100p shares and X invests in them. If X pays 100p for each share, then that is the limit of his liability. Again, suppose Alpha issued the shares below par value, say at 50p paid per share. If Y bought 5,000 of these shares – an investment of £2,500 – then in the event of Alpha Ltd's liquidation, Y could be called upon to contribute a further £2,500 to the liquidated company's assets – but no more.

The liability of an investor may be limited either by share or by guarantee.

Memorandum of association and limitation of liability

4.2 Section 6(2) of the Companies Act 1963 provides that the memorandum of association of a company limited by shares or by guarantee must also state that the liability of its members is limited.

In addition, the memorandum of a company limited by guarantee must state that each member undertakes to contribute to the assets of the company, in the event of its being wound up while he is a member, for payment of the debts and liabilities of the company contracted before he ceases to be a member[1] ... such amount as may be required, not exceeding a specified amount.

In the case of a company having a share capital, the memorandum of association is also required, unless the company is an unlimited company, to state the amount of share capital with which the company proposes to be registered, and its division into shares of a fixed amount.

Effect of registration of a company

4.3 On the registration of the memorandum of a company, the registrar will certify that the company is incorporated and, in the case of a limited company, that the company is limited.

---

1 Or within one year after he ceases to be a member.

Section 18(2)[1] stipulates that from the date of incorporation, the subscribers of the memorandum, together with such other persons who may become members of the company, shall be a body corporate with the name contained in the memorandum, capable of exercising all the functions of an incorporated company, and having perpetual succession and a common seal, but with such liability on the part of the members to contribute to the assets of the company in the event of its being wound up as is mentioned in the 1963 Act.

Since this liability is limited to the amount unpaid on any shares, and as most shares are issued fully paid, shareholders generally incur no liability for the debts of the company.

OTHER CONSEQUENCES OF SEPARATE LEGAL PERSONALITY

4.4   The other effects of separate corporate personality are set out below.

A company can sue and be sued in its own name

4.5   A company can enter into trading and other *contracts* and be liable under them. (See Chapters 17 and 18.)

A company can also sue for any *torts* committed against it. It is also responsible for torts committed by it. Because of the non-human or artificial nature of a company, responsibility in tort will usually devolve through vicarious liability. Vicarious liability arises when one person is held liable in law for the actions of another. Vicarious liability in tort usually arises where an employer is held responsible for negligent acts committed by his employees in the course of their employment. A principal may also be liable for torts committed by his agents.

There are limits to the degree to which companies can incur vicarious liability under criminal law. As Viscount Reading CJ stated in *Maunsell Bros Ltd v London & North Western Railway Co*,[2] 'it may be the intention of Parliament . . . to impose [such] a liability upon a principal [company]. Many statutes are passed with this object'.

At common law, the (tortious) doctrine of vicarious liability does not generally[3] apply to criminal actions by company employees.

Staughton LJ summarised this confusing aspect of criminal law in *Tesco Stores Ltd v Brent London Borough Council*[4] thus:

---

1 Of the 1963 Act.
2 [1917] 2 KB 836.
3 But a company may be vicariously liable for the crime of public nuisance at common law – see *R v Great North of England Railway Co* [1924] 9 QB 315.
4 [1993] 2 All ER 718.

'*Tesco Supermarkets Ltd v Nattrass* [see **21.13**] was, as it seems to me, concerned with three topics. The first was the general rule as to criminal liability of a corporate body. In the ordinary way a company is not guilty of a crime unless the criminal conduct and the guilty mind exist not merely in a servant or agent of the company of junior rank but in those who truly manage its affairs. Statutes may and sometimes do provide otherwise. There are offences for which, in derogation of the general rule, a company may incur liability through the behaviour of its servants.

Secondly, it was evident in *Tesco Supermarkets Ltd v Nattrass* that the offence in question there was one which could be committed by a company through one of its junior employees acting on its behalf. Otherwise there would have been no need to consider whether the company could rely on a defence which the statute provided ... [Section 24 of the Trade Descriptions Act 1968] provided for the vicarious liability of the company for an employee ...

The third point considered in *Tesco Supermarkets Ltd v Nattrass*, which was critical to the decision, was that s 24 of the 1968 Act was concerned with the conduct of the company itself by those who managed its business. The "person" charged in the section clearly meant the company. The words "he", "himself" and "his" meant the company by its directing mind and will.'

Whilst Staughton LJ's comments are helpful, it is clear that the legislature has not yet developed a coherent policy on the promulgation of laws dealing with corporate criminality.[1]

Again, companies cannot be jailed. However, they may be fined and their directors and officers imprisoned – see **21.14**.

A company can own property

4.6   One major advantage of incorporation is that the property of the company can be distinguished from that of its members. Company property is owned by the company. Members have no proprietary interests in it.

4.7   In *Macaura v Northern Assurance*,[2] a majority shareholder was owed money by the Irish Canadian Sawmill Co Ltd, Skibbereen, County Cork. As a precaution, he insured a company stock of timber against loss. A fire occurred and the member claimed from the insurance company involved. They refused to pay him, on the grounds that he had no insurable interest.[3]

The House of Lords held that the insurers were entitled to repudiate the claim, Lord Sumner commenting:

'It is clear that the applicant had no insurable interest in the timber provided. It was not his. It belonged to the [company] ... [The appellant] owned almost all the shares in the company, and the company owed him a good deal of money, but, neither as creditor or shareholder, could he insure the company's assets ... His

---

1 See J. Gobert 'Corporate Criminality: New Crimes for the Times' (1994) *Criminal Law Review* 722–734, and also Chapter 21.
2 [1925] AC 619, [1925] All ER Rep 51, 59 ILTR 45.
3 A financial involvement necessary to acquire legal rights under an insurance contract.

relation was to the company, not to its goods, and after the fire he was directly prejudiced by the paucity of the company's assets, not by the fire.'

4.8 A more recent case where the insurance of company property by a shareholder was raised as a defence by an insurance company is *P.J. Carrigan Ltd and P.J. Carrigan v Norwich Union Fire Insurance Society Ltd and Scottish Union and National Insurance Company Ltd (No 2).*[1] These insurers contended that the premises insured by them were owned by the first plaintiff, P.J. Carrigan Ltd (the company), whilst the insured person was the second plaintiff, P.J. Carrigan, who had no insurable interest in the property.

The facts in this case were complex and detailed. However, the result was a finding against the insurers, Lynch J stating:

> '... my findings that the second plaintiff is the insured and has an insurable interest ... involves a rejection of the plaintiff's case and of the second plaintiff's evidence that the Company is the insured and was also the sole owner of the Glebe [the insured property].'

Even though the decision went against the insurance company, it did so on evidential grounds. Accordingly, because of Lynch J's comments it would seem that the principle of separate company ownership of property, reinforced by the *Macaura* decision, is still good law in Ireland.

Company assets

4.9 It is indisputable that all assets of the company are the property of the company and a shareholder, even a controlling one, cannot insure the company's real property or simply help himself to the company's cash. As a result, a managing director, even though he may own 99 per cent of the company's shares, cannot lawfully:

(1) lodge cheques payable to the company into his own bank account; nor
(2) draw cheques to meet his own personal expenditure on the company's bank account.

A company has perpetual succession

4.10 A company, being an artificial person, does not die when its human members expire. What happens, in these circumstances, is that the deceased member's shares pass, as part of his estate, to the beneficiaries named in his will. If the member leaves no will, the shares pass as part of his property according to the rules of intestate succession.

Because a company exists until it is wound up, property, once transferred to the company, remains the property of the company.

Again, because the company never dies, no question of death duties on real property will arise. Furthermore, any change in company investors will have no

---

1 (Unreported) 11 December 1987 (HC).

effect on company property as it is owned by the company, and not its shareholders.

Formation of a company may increase potential borrowing opportunities

4.11 A company, by owning property, also has the power to borrow money by mortgaging that property. In particular, a company can give, as security, a floating charge[1] over its stock-in-trade. This is a facility not available to sole traders and partnerships.

A floating charge is one that is linked to any or all of the company's assets of a certain type, but not to any specific item.

Incorporation facilitates the transfer of investors' interests

4.12 Shares are items of property. Where a company has transferable shares, ownership of the company can be changed or divided without affecting the company itself. Similarly, the death of an investor will not affect the company (see **4.10** above).

Taxation implications

4.13 Whilst the company is viewed in law like a human legal person, it is treated differently to sole traders, and partnerships, for taxation purposes.

Companies are taxed on the whole of their trading profits (and capital gains) under a single rate of corporation tax.[2] Income tax is payable on the fees and salaries of directors, who can claim refunds of certain Pay Related Social Insurance (PRSI) contributions.[3] Income tax is also payable on profits distributed to shareholders in the form of dividends.

Companies controlled by five or fewer shareholders or participators who are directors, are known as 'close' companies. The provisions in taxation law for the apportionment of certain income of close[4] companies have the effect of lifting the veil of incorporation and rendering their shareholders subject to extra personal taxation.

The detailed provisions of corporate taxation law are outside the scope of this work.[5] Promoters should, therefore, avail themselves of professional taxation

---

1 See Chapters 32 and 33.
2 Certain manufacturing companies may be entitled to a reduced rate of corporation tax under s 38 of the Finance Act 1980, as amended.
3 As a result, they are entitled to reduced social security benefits.
4 See Chapter 6.
5 See G. Saunders *Tolley's Taxation in the Republic of Ireland 1996/97* (Tolley Publishing Co Ltd, 1996); A. Moore (ed) *Tax Acts, 1996–97* (Butterworth (Ireland) Ltd) and B. Giblin and S. Keegan (eds) *Irish Tax Reports (1922–1996)* (Butterworth (Ireland) Ltd, 1997).

advice before proceeding to form a company. However, as a general rule, the larger the scale of the business enterprise to be started, the greater the probability that taxation advantages will favour trading by means of a company. Once a certain scale of operational size has been reached, use of the corporate form becomes almost a practical necessity. In fact, in the case of a large group of companies, the trading losses of group members may be offset against the profits of others – thereby reducing the overall taxation liability of the group as a whole. This taxation treatment of companies within a group is yet another example of the veil of incorporation being lifted – this time clearly for the benefit of the shareholders of the holding company.

Chapter 5

COMPANIES, SOLE TRADERS AND PARTNERSHIPS COMPARED

ADVANTAGES AND DISADVANTAGES

5.1 Perhaps the best way of visualising the distinctive features of a company is to compare the advantages and disadvantages of trading in partnership and carrying on business as a sole trader.

Sole traders

5.2 This type of business structure is inexpensive to start up and the legal requirements are minimal. When a person starts up in business[1] he must use a trading name. If this is a name, other than his own, it must be registered with the Registry of Business Names. He must also notify the local Inspector of Taxes.

Advantages

5.3 The main advantages of operating in business as a sole trader are that:

(1) business may be commenced with the minimum of formality and legal expense;
(2) the trader has full control over all aspects of decision making within his enterprise;
(3) the sole trader is entitled to all profits made; and
(4) he is free to sell his business, if he wishes, or make arrangements for the business to be carried on after his death by another family member.

Disadvantages

5.4 The main disadvantages for sole traders are:

(1) *unlimited liability for the debts of the business.* What this means is that if the enterprise fails, the sole trader's house and other personal possessions are liable to be sold to pay off his business creditors;
(2) *restricted scope for raising capital.* The three main sources of capital available to a sole trader are his own savings, bank borrowings by him, possibly secured by the mortgaging of his private house, and accumulated profits from prior years' trading (if available).

---

1 Assuming he is not setting up in a profession where mandatory educational qualifications are required, eg medicine, law or accountancy, or engaging in an activity which requires special licensing, such as money lending, bookmaking or running a public house.

It might be thought that sole traders (or, as we shall see later, partnerships) may find it easier to borrow money because of their unlimited personal liability. This is not so, because companies have a device known as a 'floating' charge available to them.

A floating charge[1] is essentially a mortgage over the non-fixed assets of a company, such as its stock-in-trade. It does not prevent the company dealing with these assets in the ordinary course of business.

A floating charge may be very useful in raising capital when a company has no (unsecured) fixed assets such as land or premises which can be included in a mortgage, but instead has an extensive and valuable stock-in-trade;

(3) there are circumstances also where *taxation* may be more severe on a sole trader than one operating through a private company.

Partnerships

5.5 Partnership is an unincorporated business association. It is a contract between two or more people 'to carry on a business in common with a view to profit.' Business may be defined as a series of acts which, if successful, will produce a gain. Generally, therefore, a business cannot consist of one isolated act, such as two persons deciding to purchase a house with the objective of selling it at a profit. The legal principles underlying partnerships are set out in the Partnership Act 1890.

Advantages

5.6 The main advantages for partnerships are:

(1) the starting up of a partnership is basically free from statutory regulation, apart from the 1890 Act and the Registration of Business Names Act 1963.[2] Neither of these Acts could be regarded as intrusive. Essentially, therefore, the creation of a partnership is purely a matter of agreement between its members. This agreement may be express or even implied;

(2) each partner is entitled to take part in the management of the firm;[3]

(3) the legal relationships between the different partners are regulated by the partnership articles. These articles are freely alterable in any way agreed between all the partners;

(4) *partnership articles are private documents;* they are not open to inspection by the public. *No person dealing with the partnership is presumed to have a knowledge of their contents;*

(5) *partners can enter into contracts on behalf of the firm.* Thus, individual partners are agents of the firm in negotiating contracts which are apparently connected with the ordinary business of the partnership.

---

1 See also Part VIII.
2 See Chapter 7.
3 The collective noun 'firm' is the proper term to denote a partnership. It is not correct to apply it to a company, although this is often done mistakenly.

Disadvantages

5.7   The main disadvantages for partnerships are:

(1) a partnership is *not a distinct or separate legal person* and therefore cannot exist apart from the members who compose it. As a result, the death or bankruptcy of a partner will normally bring the partnership to an end automatically;

(2) partnerships may be formed[1] in which the liability of some of the members is limited. However, in such circumstances, at least one member must always remain fully liable for the firm's debts;

(3) in the event of financial failure by a firm, its creditors have personal rights against the individual partners, whose liability is unlimited.[2] Thus, persons trading as partners do not enjoy limited liability;

(4) a partner may not transfer his interest or share in the firm without the consent of all his other partners;

(5) a partnership may not consist of more than 20 members, or 10 members if formed to carry on banking business. The maximum limit of 20 members was removed for firms of solicitors and accountants by the Companies Amendment Act 1982.[3]

Conclusion

5.8   Partnerships are unincorporated associations of business persons, easy to form, with little statutory supervision or regulation of their trading activities. Essentially, firms are not separate legal persons from their constituent partners and, as a result, partners can be fully liable for the trading debts of an insolvent firm. Partnerships share this major economic disadvantage with sole traders. The way to trade, knowing that, in the event of a down turn in business and financial failure, one's legal liability to creditors is limited, is to operate by means of a registered company.

Registered companies

5.9   Unlike the starting up in business as a sole trader or in partnership, the creation of a company involves elaborate legal formalities to comply with the provisions of the Companies Acts. In return for registering a company in this manner, its owners create a separate legal person and their liability for its debts may be limited. The advantages and disadvantages of registered companies are summarised below.

---

1 Under the Limited Partnerships Act 1907.

2 Unless a limited partner.

3 Section 13.

Advantages

5.10 The main advantages for registered companies are:

(1) every company is a legal person or entity separate and distinct from its members. As it is non-human, it never 'dies'. A company therefore enjoys what is known as perpetual succession;

(2) the creditors of an insolvent company generally only have rights of action against the company and its assets. They do not have rights of action against the individual investors (shareholders) personally for company debts;

(3) when forming registered companies, the liability of investors for company debts may be limited to a definite amount, either by share nominal value or by guarantee;

(4) an investor's shares in a public company are generally transferable without the consent of the other investors;

(5) public companies may be formed with no upper limit on the maximum number of investors. The minimum number of investors for a public company is seven. For private companies, the minimum number of investors used to be two until 1994. Then the European Communities (Single-Member Private Limited Companies) Regulations[1] permitted the formation of single member private companies.

Disadvantages

5.11 The main disadvantages for registered companies are:

(1) the elaborate registration procedure required to form a new company could be considered a disadvantage. However, this may be of little practical disadvantage to a start up situation because of the market facility of being able to buy off the shelf companies (there is a further body of specialist company law relating to the formation and management of banks and insurance companies);

(2) the powers of a company are strictly limited by its memorandum of association. Alterations of corporate objectives in the objects[2] clause are restricted, require a special procedure and may involve a court action if minority members are dissatisfied with them;

(3) the memorandum and articles of a company – its constitutional documents – are open to inspection by the public. As a result, every person dealing with the company is presumed to be aware of their contents;[3]

(4) unlike partnerships, the management of companies is subject to strict statutory regulation affecting such matters as issuing of shares, proceedings at meetings, maintenance of registers, rights and responsibilities of directors and auditors, keeping and submission of accounts and the rendering of returns;

---

1 SI 1994/275 – see Chapter 8.
2 See Chapters 15 and 16.
3 But see Chapter 17 and creditor protection against 'ultra vires' contracts.

(5) again, unlike partnerships, members are unable to enter into contracts on behalf of their company. Members are not the agents of the company. They take no direct part in company management. Management of companies is delegated to their human agents, ie the directors and officers.

Conclusion

5.12 From this brief comparison of the legal elements of sole traders, partnerships and companies, it is clear that the two most fundamental advantages enjoyed by companies are:

(1) the fact that a company exists as a separate legal person quite distinct from the members who own it; and
(2) following on from and combined with separate personality, the advantage to investors of having their liability limited. This is possible because, generally,[1] in the event of a company failure, the only rights of redress creditors have are against company assets. Members, because of the principle of limited liability, enjoy immunity against such creditors' claims unless a creditor can convince a court to lift the veil of incorporation. The exceptional (and rare) instances where the veil of incorporation is lifted, to remove an investor's immunity against the creditors of a company, are examined in the next chapter.

Using corporate form to trade may also have taxation advantages.[2]

---

1 There are also exceptional instances where, eg, directors may be liable for the debts of a failed company – see Chapters 1 and 2 and Part V.
2 See Chapter 4.

Chapter 6

LIFTING THE VEIL OF INCORPORATION WHICH PROTECTS INVESTORS

THE NATURE OF THE 'VEIL' METAPHOR

6.1 We have seen how the separate corporate personality of a company has been likened to a veil. Corporate personality is viewed as a veil which prevents outsiders taking legal action against company members, even though the outsiders can ascertain the identities of members and the number of shares which they hold. However, this blocking of action against members by the veil of incorporation is a general rule. As explained in the Preface, there have been instances where judges have allowed outsiders to take action against the members of companies. In these exceptional cases, it has been said that the veil of incorporation has been lifted.

There are many examples of lifting the veil. The problem is how to rationalise the circumstances in which a judge is likely to deviate from the strict rule of the separate legal entity of the company (the rule in *Salomon's* case), and lift the veil of incorporation. As McCormack[1] comments:

> 'The doctrine of separate corporate personality is relaxed in certain exceptional instances where it tends towards an inequitable conclusion. It is not easy to discern any unifying set of guidelines among this wilderness of single distances. Cases are decided on a fairly ad hoc basis with little regard for satisfactory concepts that admit of more generalised application. This approach breeds uncertainty. Judges need to intellectualise their decisions to a greater extent. Until this task is achieved, the subjective judgment is likely to hold sway.'

The need to rationalise the 'jungle of judgements' relating to the veil metaphor was the subject of an interesting article by Ottolenghi.[2] Ottolenghi suggests that before asking *when* the veil is lifted, one should ascertain what is actually done by the courts and the legislature. The practice of lifting the veil is not always detrimental to a company or its shareholders. Sometimes this action may benefit them as well as the (outsider) company creditors. Accordingly, he suggests that in lifting the veil, four different attitudes towards the company can be detected.[3] These attitudes may be classified as:

(1) peeping behind the veil;
(2) penetrating the veil;
(3) extending the veil; and
(4) ignoring the veil.

---

1 G. McCormack 'Judicial application of Salomon's case in Ireland' *Law Society Gazette*, May 1984, p 100.
2 S. Ottolenghi 'From Peeping Behind the Corporate Veil to Ignoring it Completely' *Modern Law Review*, May 1990, pp 338–353.
3 Each of these attitudes may be used in different circumstances and for different reasons.

Peeping behind the veil

6.2 'Peeping' may consist of the court lifting the veil to identify ownership of the company, and then 'dropping' the veil again. The statutory definition of holding company,[1] is an example of a statutory peeping behind the veil. Once the court has obtained the relevant information, the veil is then 'pulled down' once more and the company may be treated as a separate legal entity.

The courts may also peep behind the veil as a preliminary information seeking exercise before making a decision on whether or not to lift it.

6.3 In *The State (Thomas McInerney & Co Ltd) v Dublin County Council,*[2] the company argued that because it and the landowner, another company, were subsidiaries of the holding company, the veil should be lifted and the plaintiff company deemed to be the owner of the land in question.

Carroll J refused to lift the veil, stating:

> 'This is not a case where justice demands that the corporate veil be lifted ... It is not for a corporate group to claim that the veil should be lifted to illuminate one aspect of its business while it (the veil) should be left *in situ* to isolate the individual actions of its subsidiaries in other respects ...'

In short, Carroll J was saying that the veil of incorporation could not be lifted, or left in place, at the plaintiff company's whim.

6.4 In *Rex Pet Foods Ltd v Lamb Bros (Ireland) Ltd,*[3] 'peeping' by the court elicited that a change of management, occurring in March 1982, was a perfectly normal commercial transaction and did not affect the separate corporate entity of the plaintiff company, which had become a subsidiary of the defendant company.

A declaration was sought when Rex Pet Foods Ltd went into receivership, seeking to treat both companies as one legal entity, thereby aggregating their joint assets. The High Court refused to lift the veil in the absence of evidence to suggest that any funds of the plaintiff company were wrongfully siphoned off into the defendant company.

Related companies

6.5 Since the *Rex Pet Foods Ltd* decision, there has been legislative action aimed at giving creditors access to funds of related companies.

A related company is defined in s 140(5) of the Companies Act 1990. On the application of the liquidator or any creditor of a company which is being wound up, the court, if it is satisfied that it is just and equitable to do so, may order that any company that is or has been related to the company being wound up shall

---

1 Section 115 of the Companies Act 1963. A holding company must normally prepare group accounts – see Chapter 24.
2 [1985] ILRM 513.
3 (Unreported) 5 December 1985 (HC).

pay an amount equivalent to the whole or part of the debts provable in that winding up.

Where two or more related companies are being wound up, the court may order the aggregation of assets and that the companies be wound up together as one company. In deciding whether or not to make such an order, the court will consider the following factors:[1]

(1) the extent to which any of the companies took part in the management of any of the other companies;

(2) the conduct of any of the companies towards the creditors of any of the other companies;

(3) the extent to which the circumstances that gave rise to the winding up of any of the companies are attributable to the actions or omissions of any of the other companies;

(4) the extent to which the businesses of the companies have been intermingled.

Clearly, the related company concept introduced by the Companies Act 1990 is another example of the legislature lifting the veil of incorporation. It is designed to give a liquidator the opportunity of maximising company assets – see Chapter 41.

Veil lifted by the court

6.6   There are examples where the court, after 'peeping' behind the veil, then proceeds to lift it.

In *Power Supermarkets Ltd v Crumlin Investments Ltd*,[2] the plaintiff company held part of a shopping centre under a lease. *This lease had a clause which prohibited the granting of further leases to traders in the grocery business.* This clause was designed to protect Power Supermarkets from competition.

Dunnes Stores Group, which operates a chain of supermarkets in competition with Power Supermarkets, purchased[3] Crumlin Investments Ltd, the defendant company. Following the purchase, Crumlin Investments Ltd were prepared to let a unit in the shopping centre to Dunnes Stores (Crumlin) Ltd, another subsidiary company in the Dunnes Stores Group, which intended to engage in the grocery business there. Power Supermarkets sought an injunction to restrain Crumlin Investments Ltd from infringing the terms of their lease. Costello J granted the injunction, stating:

'It seems to me to be well established . . . that a court may, if the justice of the case so requires, treat two or more related companies as a single entity so that the business

---

1 See s 141 of Companies Act 1990. See also s 16 of the Companies (Amendment) Act 1986 for definition of new term 'associated' company introduced by that Act.

2 (Unreported) 22 June 1981 (HC).

3 The purchasing company was, in fact, Cornelscourt Shopping Centre Ltd, a wholly owned subsidiary of Dunnes Stores Ltd, which, in turn, was a wholly owned subsidiary of Dunnes Holding Co.

notionally carried on by one will be regarded as the business of the group, or another member of that group, if it conforms to the economic and commercial realities of the situation. It would ... be very hard to find a clearer case than the present one for the application of this principle.'

Costello J concluded that if he did not treat the two defendant companies as a single economic entity, it could involve a considerable injustice to the plaintiff company, whose legal rights under their lease might be defeated:

'by the mere technical devise of the creation of a company with a £2 issued capital which had no real independent life of its own.'

6.7   When giving his judgment in the *Power Supermarkets Ltd* case, Costello J approved the decisions in *Smith, Stone and Knight Ltd v Birmingham Corporation* and *D.H.N. Food Distributors Ltd v Tower Hamlets London Borough Council.*[1] In the *D.H.N.* case, three group companies were regarded as a single legal entity because they constituted, in reality, a single economic entity.

Doubts have been expressed by the House of Lords as to the correctness of the decision to lift the veil in the *D.H.N.* case. These doubts were expressed in *Woolfson v Strathclyde Regional Council.*[2] Notwithstanding, in *Re Bray Travel Ltd and Bray Travel (Holdings) Ltd*,[3] the principles enunciated by Costello J in the *Power Supermarkets Ltd* case were approved and followed by the Supreme Court.

Directors and officers

6.8   From these illustrations, it is clear that 'peeping' behind the veil takes place only when the courts or the legislature desire to identify those who really govern companies or give controlling instructions to their directors.

A court does not have to 'peep behind the veil' when recourse is made to a company's directors. The directors are a company's human managing agents. They stand in front of the veil so there is no need to look behind the company's separate corporate personality to identify them. Thus, the fact that s 138 of the Companies Act 1990 imposes personal liability on officers or others in respect of fraudulent and reckless trading[4] does not entail a lifting of the veil. These liabilities:[5]

'are better regarded as "punitive" measures, a sort of statutory *caveat* directed at those who purport to act in the name of the company, knowing that the company would not honour their acts.'

The purpose of peeping

6.9   Peeping behind the veil is not, in itself, a step necessarily leading to personal responsibility of shareholders for company debts or actions. Rather, it

---

1   [1939] 4 All ER 116 and [1976] 1 WLR 852, respectively.
2   1978 SLT 159, 38 P & CR 521 (HL).
3   (Unreported) 13 July 1981.
4   See Part V.
5   To quote from Ottolenghi's article.

is the preliminary investigative act of examining certain features relating to the company which can only be achieved by 'peeping' behind the veil. These features would include the company's type (holding, subsidiary, related, etc), character (alien[1]), residence (for tax purposes), control, etc. Having carried out its preliminary examination of the issues which necessitated peeping behind the veil of incorporation, the court must then decide what to do with the information it has elicited. This will entail a positive decision by the court either:

(1) that the veil should not be lifted and the separate corporate personality remains intact; or

(2) that the circumstances are such that the court must penetrate the veil. The instances when the court might take this action, already illustrated by the *Power Supermarkets* case in **6.6** above, are outlined below.

Penetrating the veil

6.10   As mentioned above, in the case of *Woolfson v Strathclyde Regional Council,* the House of Lords expressed doubts on whether the lower court decision in the *D.H.N.* case properly applied the *principle that it is appropriate to pierce the corporate veil only where special circumstances exist indicating that it is a mere facade* concealing the true facts. This seems to imply that the veil, generally, should only be lifted to permit legal actions be taken *against* shareholders, and *not by* them. This is reflected also in the exceptional instances where the legislature pierces the veil.

The purpose of penetrating the veil of incorporation is sometimes to make (controlling) shareholders personally responsible for the debts of the company.[2] For example, in *Re Kelly's Carpetdrome,*[3] Costello J imposed personal liability for company debts, not only on the directors but also on the persons who beneficially owned the company.

The pooling of the assets of a related company under ss 140 and 141 of the Companies Act 1990 (see **6.5** above) is another example of statutory penetration of the veil; as is the classification of 'close company' for the purposes of taxation.

Close companies are those controlled by five or fewer shareholders. Taxation law provisions for the apportionment of certain income of a close company amongst its investors have the effect of treating the investors as if they each own portions of the company property; thereby rendering them liable to extra personal taxation.

---

1 In determining the ownership of agricultural land, the Land Commission will look at the nationality of an owner company's shareholders rather than the place of registration of the company. See also *Daimler v Continental Tyre and Rubber Co* [1916] 2 AC 307 (HL).

2 Effectively depriving them of the privilege of limited liability.

3 (Unreported) 1 July 1983 (HC).

The Landlord and Tenant (Amendment) Act 1980[1] is another example of statutory penetration of the veil – this time, exceptionally, for the benefit of the company's controlling shareholder.

In practice, the veil is usually penetrated to impose responsibility upon shareholders for the improper use of corporate form (as happened in the *Power Supermarkets* case) or to establish their economic interest in the company assets.

Extending the veil

6.11   When a court peeps behind the veil to find that the company in question is one of a group of companies, it may, instead of treating each company as a separate corporate entity, treat the whole group as one single corporate entity. This technique has the effect of extending, rather than piercing, the veil by treating all group companies as a single business entity, perhaps reflecting the economic or commercial reality of the situation.

The legislative requirement[2] for a group of companies to provide group accounts also illustrates this extension of the veil.

The decision in *Power Supermarkets Ltd v Crumlin Investments Ltd* (see **6.6**) would be classified (by this writer) as piercing the veil on grounds of an improper use of corporate form.

Ignoring the veil

6.12   There are circumstances when it is said that the courts will *ignore* the separate personality of a company. This situation can arise where the company was formed for some fraudulent, illegal or improper purpose or for the evasion of legal obligations. Names used by the courts to describe such companies are 'puppet', 'sham', 'scheme', 'cloak' (for fraud) and 'bubble company', to mention a few. In the case of *Jones v Lipman*,[3] X contracted to sell his house to Jones. He then decided to avoid the sale. In order to frustrate a court order of specific performance[4] being made against him, X formed a company and then sold his house to it.

The court held that Jones was entitled to a decree of specific performance against the defendant and his company, Russell J stating that the company was:

> 'the creation of the defendant, a devise and a sham, a mask which he holds before his face in an attempt to avoid recognition (by the law).'

---

1 By virtue of the Landlord and Tenant (Amendment) Act 1980, a tenant's statutory right to renewal of his tenancy is not lost because he has converted his business to a private company.
2 Section 152 of the Companies Act 1963.
3 [1962] 1 All ER 442.
4 Compelling X to complete the transaction.

6.13 Again, in *Re Bugle Press Ltd*,[1] members holding 90 per cent of the shares in a company, Y Ltd, formed a new company, X Ltd. X Ltd then made an offer to buy the shares of Y Ltd. The investors holding 90 per cent of Y Ltd's shares accepted X Ltd's offer. X Ltd then served notice on the 10 per cent minority shareholder of Y Ltd, stating that they wished to compulsorily acquire his shares under the equivalent of s 204 of the 1963 Act – see Chapter 40. He opposed the scheme on the basis that it amounted, in effect, to an expropriation of his shares by the majority shareholders of Y Ltd.

The minority shareholder's claim succeeded. The court lifted the veil and identified the actual identity of the majority shareholders involved.

6.14 Where the controllers of a company have committed nothing worse than mismanagement, the court will not lift the veil – see *Dublin County Council v Elton Homes Ltd*.[2]

It is difficult to reconcile the *Jones v Lipman* and *Re Bugle Press* decisions with the principle followed in *Roundabout Ltd v Beirne*.[3] It has been suggested that this decision might be distinguished on the grounds that the new company was formed, not to circumvent a legal duty, but to by-pass the immunity of the pickets under the Trades Disputes Act 1906.

Some conclusions on lifting the veil

6.15 It seems clear from the cases mentioned above that in each instance where the issue of corporate personality is raised, the court must carry out a preliminary investigation into the particular facts. This involves an activity which we have labelled 'peeping' behind the veil.

If, after carrying out this preliminary corporate examination, action is taken by the court to remove the immunity of shareholders, then it is obvious that the veil of corporation has been lifted. The author has difficulty with the concept of a court ignoring the veil, and, in all cases where a court removes the immunity of shareholders, would classify this action as simply lifting or piercing the veil of incorporation. There seems little doubt that a *court will pierce the veil* where a company was formed for a fraudulent, illegal or improper purpose or an obvious evasion of legal obligations. These are the instances which were[4] classified as ignoring the veil.

A *court, on the other hand, may extend the veil* to ignore the separate legal entities of various companies within a group and treat the whole group as one economic entity. However, when taking such an action, the court does not isolate or identify the shareholders of the holding company. It does not, therefore, *pierce the veil of incorporation* to attack the immunities of the holding company's

---

1 [1960] 3 All ER 791 (CA).
2 [1984] ILRM 297 (HC). See also *Dun Laoghaire Corporation v Parkhill Development* [1989] IR 477.
3 See Chapter 3.
4 Incorrectly, in the author's view.

members: it merely extends it to identify the holding company in order to implement the policy underlying the relevant statutory provision.

Groups of companies at common law

6.16   It should be noted, however, that whilst company law may make special provision for holding companies and subsidiaries,[1] their position at common law is one of separate legal entities. The subsidiary is not necessarily to be treated as the implied agent of the holding company. This situation was considered as recently as July 1996, by Laffoy J in *Allied Irish Coal Suppliers Ltd v Powell Duffryn International Fuels Ltd.*[2]

In this case, the plaintiff alleged that the defendant and its parent company constituted a single economic entity, and asked the court to exercise its discretion to regard them as such on the basis of the decision in *Power Supermarkets Ltd v Crumlin Investments Ltd.*

Laffoy J commented:

> '... the situation here ... is that the plaintiff traded with the defendant during 1983 and 1984 in the knowledge that the latter was a subsidiary of the [parent] plc.
>
> The plaintiff does not allege that there was privity of contract between it and the plc, nor does it assert that the statements which it alleges were fraudulent or negligent or were made by or on behalf of the plc. In essence, what the plaintiff seeks by joinder of the plc *is to render the assets of the plc available to meet the liabilities of its subsidiary.*
>
> The issue I have to address is whether the principle enunciated in the *Power Supermarkets* case, can be applied to achieve this end.' (author's emphasis)

The judge then decided that the principle whereby a court, when the justice of the case so requires, treats two or more related companies as a single business entity (so that the business notionally carried on by one will be regarded as the business of the group, if this conforms to the economic and commercial realities of the situation) could not be utilised to render the assets of a parent company available to meet the liabilities of its trading subsidiary to a party with which it had traded. For her to have done so appeared to Laffoy J:

> '... to be fundamentally at variance with the principle of separate corporate legal personality laid down in *Salomon v Salomon* and the concept of limited liability.'

This common law position that a holding company is generally not liable for the trading debts of its subsidiary, may be subject to the provisions of the Companies Act 1990 on the pooling of assets of related companies, which are outlined above. These statutory provisions, however, only come into operation where a company is being wound up.

---

1   See Companies Act 1963, s 32 (as amended) dealing with membership and ss 150 to 158 prescribing group accounts.

2   [1997] 1 ILRM 306. See also *Adams v Cape Industries plc* [1990] Ch 433, *Kleinwort Benson Ltd v Malaysian Mining Corporation* [1989] 1 All ER 785 – a case dealing with a 'letter of comfort' issued by the holding company – and *Re Polly Peck International plc (in administration) (No 3)* [1996] 2 All ER 433.

Generally, a court *may* pierce the veil of incorporation if the justice of the case demands it. In addition, it may identify individual shareholders in order to determine the company's character, status and where it resides, particularly to prevent the avoidance of *tax* liabilities.

Statutory lifting of the veil and directors

6.17 The minimum membership requirement of s 36 of the 1963 Act is a clear example of direct statutory lifting and piercing the veil, thus making the members liable for the debts of their company. Most other instances of statutory liability for company debts are directed at directors and officers, rather than members, so the veil of incorporation becomes irrelevant. It does not have to be lifted to identify and/or sue company directors and officers.

Directors' rather than investors' liabilities

6.18 The legal liability of directors and others for fraudulent and reckless trading have already been mentioned in **2.22**.

If it can be shown that a *director or officer* was *knowingly* a party to the carrying on of business in a *reckless* manner, or if *any person* is a party to the carrying on of any business of the company with intent to defraud creditors of the company, then by virtue of s 138 of the Companies Act 1990, a court may hold them personally liable for the debts of the company, without any limitation of liability.

Again, if a company is being wound up and a court finds that proper books of account have not been kept, the court may declare that one or more *officers* (and former officers) of the company who were at fault shall be personally liable for the debts of the company.[1]

There are several other examples of[2] directors and managers, rather than investors, being rendered liable for company debts. The question now to be considered in more detail, however, is whether these instances of potential unlimited liability for company directors (and others) involve a lifting of the veil. Ottolenghi, as mentioned in **6.8** above, considers it does not. If one limits the protection of the veil of incorporation simply to company shareholders, then clearly Ottolenghi is correct. These onerous statutory liabilities on directors and officers, essentially, render them liable as a company's human managing agents for company debts. In practice, such potential liabilities of companies' managing agents[3] will probably offer a much more fertile source of funding to potential company creditors than the older methods of attempting to recover from investors by seeking to pierce the veil. Put very simply, whilst investors still substantially enjoy the privileges of limited liability,[4] creditors now

---

1 See ss 202 to 204 of the Companies Act 1990.
2 Eg Companies Act 1963, ss 60(5) and 256 (as amended), and Companies Act 1990, ss 38, 39 and 163.
3 Who should consider purchasing relevant insurance cover to indemnify them against these liabilities.
4 Only losing it in the exceptional cases where the veil of incorporation is actually 'pierced'.

enjoy significant new avenues and sources of recovery for company debts from directors and officers; the Companies Act 1990, having raised the legal duties of directors and managers considerably.[1] Since 1990, therefore, the likely reaction of unpaid company creditors will be to pursue the company's officers, rather than its members, for recovery of their monies.

1 See Part V.

PART III

COMPANY REGISTRATION AND EARLY CORPORATE TRANSACTIONS

Chapter 7

RESTRICTIONS ON CHOICE OF COMPANY NAME

SIGNIFICANCE OF COMPANY NAME

7.1 Having looked at the fundamental principles of company law, we now address the preliminary matters of company registration and certain transactions arising during the initial company registration phase. In this connection, choice of a company name can be of significance for promoters.

Suppose J. Mannion and R. Whyte decide to form a company for the purpose of canning peas and selling these products through usual wholesale and retail outlets.

If the company is named, as one might expect, Mannion and Whyte Ltd, it is clear that the company will have had no trade record in the vegetable canning business. If, however, the company name was to be, for example, Crosse and Blackwell Ltd, it is likely that this name would make it easier for Mannion and Whyte's company to succeed in business, because customers would confuse it with the well-established Crosse & Blackwell Ltd.

There are statutory controls in place to prevent promoters such as Mannion and Whyte using names for their companies which could take unfair advantage of the reputation of other established businesses. These controls largely take the form of compulsory regulation of business names for new companies under the Registration of Business Names Act 1963 ('RBNA 1963').

Before registering a name under the RBNA 1963, the registrar will take care to see that the name is not likely to mislead the public or affect the reputation of an existing business. However, s 14(3) of the RBNA 1963 does point out that even if a business name is registered under the Act, registration 'shall not be construed as authorising the use of that name, if apart from such registration, the use thereof could be prohibited'. Section 14(3), therefore, makes it clear that even if a business name is registered, if the name is likely to mislead the public into believing that the company is linked to another established company so as to take advantage of its reputation, the latter company may take action to protect its business reputation in tort: in particular by relying on the tort of passing off.

Let us now focus on these two broad categories of protection against misleading business names, ie statutory protection under the RBNA 1963 and the tort of passing off.[1]

---

1 Company officials may also incur a legal liability if they use an incorrect name for the company. This aspect is dealt with in Chapter 17 in the context of the name clause in the memorandum of association.

Registration of Business Names Act 1963

7.2   There are few legal restrictions on either sole traders or partners using their own names for the purposes of their trading enterprises. However, if either type of 'trader' uses a business name, other than their own true surname, this business name must be registered under the RBNA 1963. So, too, must 'every body corporate having a place of business in the State and carrying on business under a business name which does not consist of its corporate name without any addition.'[1]

The information to be registered under the Act includes:[2]

(1) the business[3] name;
(2) the general nature of the business and principal place where it is carried on;
(3) the company's corporate name and particulars of its principal office;
(4) the date of the adoption of the business name by that company.

The Register is maintained by the Companies Registration Office. The registrar keeps an index of business names registered under the RBNA 1963. The certificate of registration must be displayed prominently at the principal place of business. Any changes of name must also be registered.[4]

Section 9(3) of the District Court Rules 1997[5] provides for a person using a trade name to be sued under that name.

Refusal to register a name

7.3   Under s 14(1) of the RBNA 1963, the Minister may refuse to permit the registration of a name which, in his opinion, is undesirable. Section 21 of the Companies Act 1963 contains a similar provision. Registrations refused under ss 14(1) or 21 are subject to appeal to the courts.

Penalties

7.4   The penalties for non-observance of the RBNA 1963 are set out in ss 10 and 11. These include a maximum fine of £100 and/or, on summary conviction, imprisonment for up to six months.

Publication of registered business name

7.5   Every company must affix or print its name legibly on the outside of every office in which its business is carried on. Each company must also engrave its

---

1 Section 3(d) of the RBNA 1963, reinforced by s 22 of the Companies Act 1963.
2 See s 4 of the RBNA.
3 The use of the abbreviations 'Ltd', 'Teo', 'plc' or 'cpt' alone need not give rise to registration under the RBNA – see s 22(2) of the Companies Act 1963.
4 See s 7 of the RBNA 1963 and s 23 of the Companies Act 1963.
5 SI 1997/93.

name on the company seal and print or write it in all business letters and cheques – see s 114(1) of the Companies Act 1963.

Directors' particulars on letterheadings

7.6 Generally, under s 196 of the Companies Act 1963, in all business letters which are sent by a company to any person, the following particulars relating to a director must be included:

(1) his present Christian name, or initials, and present surname;
(2) any former Christian names and surnames; and
(3) his nationality, if not Irish.

Mistaken registration

7.7 If, through inadvertence or otherwise, a company is registered with a name which, in the opinion of the Minister, is too similar to the name of a company in existence which is already registered, the newer company may change its name voluntarily with the approval of the Minister, or if the Minister so directs within six months of registration, must change its name within six weeks of being ordered to do so.[1]

During 1995, 1,684 name changes were approved by the Minister. He also directed 13 companies to change their names because of some or all of the following factors: the degree of similarity between the two names either phonetically or in spelling; similarities in the objects of the two companies; or the proximity to each other of the registered offices of the companies.

THE TORT OF PASSING OFF

7.8 As mentioned above, registration of a company name under the RBNA 1963 will be no bar to proceedings taken against the company if the registered name too closely resembles that of an existing company or business. The company with the offending name may be liable for the tort of 'passing off'.

A tort is a civil wrong. The tort of passing off, essentially, encompasses the civil wrong of representing a business which is being carried on by another as being carried on by oneself.

7.9 The purpose of this tort is to protect a plaintiff company's proprietary interest in the goodwill of its business. In *Ewing v Buttercup Margarine Co Ltd*,[2] the plaintiff, who carried on business under the trade name of Buttercup Dairy Co, was successful in restraining a company from being registered under the business name of the Buttercup Margarine Co Ltd.

---

1 See s 23(2), (3) and (4) of the Companies Act 1963.
2 [1917] 2 Ch 1 (CA).

7.10   The protection available to companies in a passing off action is not limited by State boundaries, as the case of *C & A Modes v C & A (Waterford) Ltd*[1] illustrates.

C & A Modes was registered in England and, in 1972, had no branches in the Republic of Ireland. It did, however, advertise there. The defendant company, C & A (Waterford) Ltd, was registered in 1972. It was also, like C & A Modes, involved in the retail clothing business. In the Supreme Court judgment, Henchy J stated:

> 'Goodwill does not necessarily stop at a frontier ... What has to be established for the success of the plaintiff's claim ... is that by his business activities ... he has generated within the State a property right in a goodwill which will be violated by the passing off.'

The Court held that C & A (Waterford) Ltd's name involved a passing off which violated the English company's property right to goodwill. Accordingly, the Court granted an injunction to prevent the continued use of the offending business name. Clearly, therefore, promoters will have to take care when deciding on an appropriate business name for their company.

---

1 [1976] IR 198. See also *Dockrell & Co v Dockrell & Co* (1941) 75 ILTR 226 (HC).

The memorandum of association of an unlimited company simply contains name and objects clauses. It does not include clauses limiting the liability of members in the event of the winding up of the company.

Unlimited companies are not common or, indeed, suitable for trading purposes. However, they may be formed for tax management purposes, with the intention that the company will not actively transact business.

PUBLIC AND PRIVATE COMPANIES

8.5 All companies, whether limited by shares or guarantee, or unlimited, will be formed as either a public or a private company.

Public companies

8.6 These companies must have a minimum number of seven members.[1] Public companies must be formed with a *minimum share capital*[2] of £30,000, of which at least 25 per cent must be paid up. Their names must end with plc or cpt.[3]

The main advantage of forming a public company is that there are no maximum limits on the number of members, and the shares of members are freely transferable by sale on the Stock Exchange or elsewhere. Accordingly, members are facilitated in realising their investment if they desire to sell their shares.[4]

The largest industrial, financial and trading companies are public companies whose shares are quoted on Stock Exchange lists. Daily newspapers, such as the *Irish Times*, normally publish the previous day's market information for shares of public companies under the heading 'Dublin Closing Prices'. The information published is each company name, market guide price, and date of previous bargain, business done and closing quotation. These prices are based on those prevailing at 4.30 pm the previous day. Footnotes to this information will disclose whether the business done was by a connected party, a bargain in a small amount, or whether the price was ex-dividend.

The list of Dublin Closing Prices published in daily newspapers, by courtesy of the Irish Stock Exchange, contains share prices for listed public companies. These include AIB, Arnotts, Bank of Ireland, CRH, DCC, Flogas, Fyffes, Golden Vale, Guinness, Irish Life, Irish Permanent, Lyons, New Ireland, Smurfit, United Drug, Waterford Foods and Woodchester.

---

1 Section 5 of the CA 1963.
2 The formation of public companies limited by guarantee, and having a share capital, is prohibited by s 7 of the Companies (Amendment) Act 1983. The authorised minimum share capital is prescribed in s 19 of that Act.
3 Section 4 of the Companies (Amendment) Act 1983.
4 For a profit or at a loss – see also Chapter 10.

Private companies

8.7 Private companies cannot have more than 50 members[1] and are not allowed to sell their shares to the public.[2] Because of this limitation, the company, in turn, restricts the rights of investors to transfer (sell) their shares.

Section 5 of the CA 1963 provided that a private company had to be formed with at least *two* members. This provision is now reformed by the European Communities (Single-Member Private Limited Companies) Regulations 1994 (the 1994 Regulations).[3]

Article 3(1) of the 1994 Regulations stipulates that:

> 'notwithstanding any enactment or rule of law to the contrary, a private company limited by shares or by guarantee *may be formed by one person*, and *may have one member*, to the extent permitted by the Companies Acts and these Regulations.'

FACTORS AFFECTING CHOICE OF CORPORATE FORM

8.8 Any investors and/or entrepreneurs wishing to trade as a business association must initially decide on the type of company to form. The relevant factors to consider might include:

(1) the objectives of the business, ie is the enterprise commercial, as distinct from professional services; are its aims educational, charitable or non-profit-making?

(2) does the proposed enterprise need large amounts of capital? If so, will public investment be necessary?

(3) is the company required by external regulations, eg a professional body or statutory requirement,[4] to adopt a particular form?

(4) whether the promoters wish to maintain a level of confidentiality concerning the company's financial position once it has commenced trading.

Taking these, and other factors into account, the promoters will decide on whether the company is to be limited by shares or by guarantee, or (very rarely) unlimited. They then have to follow the appropriate procedure for registering the company. Registration will be complete upon the issue by the registrar of a certificate of incorporation.[5]

---

1 Excluding employees and former employees – see s 33 of the CA 1963.

2 Section 33 of the 1963 Act, and s 21 of the Companies (Amendment) Act 1983.

3 SI 1994/275, implementing the 12th EU Company Law Directive No 89/667/EEC – published in [1989] OJ L395/40.

4 Eg Art 7(1) of the European Communities (Non-Life Insurance) Framework Regulations 1994, SI 1994/359, stipulates that only business associations adopting the form of a company limited by shares, or by guarantee or unlimited will be licensed to transact non-life insurance business in Ireland. These regulations also provide substantial minimum capital requirements for insurance companies.

5 The company's 'birth certificate'.

Procedures for the formation of a company

8.9   As a consideration for the privileges of incorporation and, indeed, limitation of liability,[1] registration of a company requires compliance with a formal statutory procedure.

Section 5 of the CA 1963 provides that any two (now one – see **8.7** above) or more persons, by subscribing to a memorandum of association, can form an incorporated company.

Memorandum of association

8.10   This document is central to the constitution of the company. Section 6[2] specifies that the memorandum of every company must state:

(1)   the company name;
(2)   the objects of the company;
(3)   that the liability of its members is limited either by share or by guarantee;
(4)   in the case of a company having a share capital, the amount of this capital, and its division into shares of a fixed amount.

The memorandum[3] must be printed, stamped as a deed, and be signed by each subscriber, in the presence of at least one witness.[4]

Articles of association

8.11   These are regulations governing the internal management of the company. Together with the memorandum of association, they form the constitution of a company. The two documents are broadly distinguishable by the fact that the memorandum, generally, governs the *external* actions of a company in relation to its structure and objects, whilst the articles govern the *internal* workings and relationships within a company. This internal perspective of the articles focuses on such matters as appointment and powers of directors, shareholders' rights and liabilities, and procedures at meetings.[5]

The articles must be printed, paragraphed and numbered, stamped as a deed, signed by the subscribers and witnessed.[6] The legislature has provided a model set of articles in Table A of the Companies Act 1963.

Section 13 of the CA 1963 permits companies to adopt all or any of the regulations in Table A. Most new companies would adopt this model with such

---

1 Unlike the formation of an unincorporated association, such as a partnership, which can be created informally.
2 Of the CA 1963.
3 The contents of the memorandum of association will be examined more closely in Chapters 17 and 21.
4 Section 7 of the CA 1963.
5 The articles of association are dealt with more fully in Chapters 14, 15 and 16 and Parts V, VI and VII.
6 Section 14 of the CA 1963.

exclusions, additions and amendments as deemed necessary to meet that particular company's needs.

Approval of proposed company name

8.12   It is advisable to write to the registrar of companies submitting a list of proposed names, asking if he would approve all or any of them. The Minister, as we saw in Chapter 7,[1] may object to a name. Effectively, it is the registrar who carries out this supervisory function.

Lodgement of documents

8.13   The following documents must be prepared and lodged with the registrar:

(1) the memorandum of association;
(2) the articles (if Table A not adopted);
(3) a statutory declaration of compliance with the requirements of the Companies Acts in respect of registration signed either by the solicitor[2] involved in the company formation, or by a person named in the articles as a director or secretary of the company;
(4) a statement in prescribed form containing particulars of the directors, the company secretary and the registered office. This statement must be signed by, or on behalf of the subscribers and persons named in it as directors and secretary;[3]
(5) a cheque for the stamp duty.

If the registrar is satisfied that the requirements of the Companies Acts have been complied with, he will issue a certificate of incorporation. The company comes into existence from that moment, as under s 389 of the CA 1963, a certificate of incorporation is deemed to be 'prima facie' evidence of incorporation.

Off the shelf companies

8.14   What we have illustrated in the above procedure is a 'made to measure' company. But in many instances, people simply wish to change their business from being operated on a sole trader basis into a company. To facilitate this conversion, it is possible to buy a 'shelf company'.

Off the shelf companies are generally formed with standard articles, and the objects clause drafted in such a way as to make it suitable for most commercial purposes. The company name, however, can be made specific.

---

1 See **7.3**.
2 See s 397 of the CA 1963 for competitive restriction in s 58 of the Solicitors Act 1954.
3 See s 3 of the Companies (Amendment) Act 1982.

Off the shelf companies may be purchased from company formation agents, some of whom advertise their services in the daily newspapers. A company formation agent will usually send a client the certificate of incorporation, together with the memorandum and articles of association.

Publication in *Iris Oifigiúil*

8.15 Article 4 of the European Communities (Companies) Regulations 1973[1] (the 1973 Regulations) provides that, within six weeks of the issue of the certificate of incorporation, the company is required to publish in *Iris Oifigiúil* that the certificate has been issued by the registrar, and the memorandum and articles of association, together with notice of the address of the registered office, delivered to him.

The company is not required to publish the contents of these documents: merely the fact that they have been issued or delivered.

Single-member private companies, limited by shares or by guarantee

8.16 Regulation 4 of the 1994 Regulations stipulates that only one person need subscribe his name to the memorandum of association of a single-member company.

Minimum share capital for new public limited company

8.17 If the new company to be formed is a public one, then the minimum share capital requirement applies. This was introduced by s 19 of the Companies (Amendment) Act 1983 and is £30,000,[2] of which at least 25 per cent must be paid up.

Unlike a private company, a public company cannot commence business immediately after the issuing of the certificate of incorporation – see **9.16** and **11.1**.

Unlimited companies

8.18 If persons wished to form an unlimited company, then the memorandum would omit the capital and limitation of liability clauses. Table E, Part I of the CA 1963 contains the model memorandum of association for this type of company, whilst Table E, Part III sets out the appropriate articles of association for a private unlimited company.

---

1 SI 1973/163, implementing the First EU Company Law Directive No 68/151/EEC. These regulations also specify how a failure to publish the prescribed information may affect third parties dealing with the company (see Art 10).
2 The Minister has the power to increase this amount.

Make up of register of companies

8.19   On 31 December, 1995, 91.6 per cent of all companies registered were private, 0.3 per cent public, 2.8 per cent unlimited and 3.3 per cent guarantee.

CHANGE OF STATUS

8.20   It is possible for companies, once formed, to subsequently change their status. As a result, a 'two-member' company may convert to a single-member company, and vice versa. Similarly, a private company may change to become a public company.

Change to single-member company

8.21   If the number of investors in a private company is reduced to one and all the shares in that company are registered in that same investor's name, then that company will become a single-member company.

Regulation 5 of the 1994 Regulations also provides that when the company becomes a single-member company due to the reduction in members, that fact and the identity of the sole investor must be notified[1] in prescribed form to the registrar of companies, within 28 days of the reduction in membership.

Change from single-member company

8.22   Regulation 6 sets out a similar procedure to that outlined above, where the number of investors in a single-member company increases. In this event, when membership increases to at least two, but not more than 50, the single-member company becomes a private company. Here again, the company must notify the registrar of the change.

Change from public company into private company

8.23   Section 14 of the Companies (Amendment) Act 1983 sets out the circumstances in which a public company may re-register as a private company, together with the procedures involved.

Essentially, a special[2] resolution has to be passed. This resolution must:

(1)   alter the memorandum so that it no longer states that the company is to be a public limited company; and

---

1 If the company fails to notify the registrar, it and its officers who are to blame will be guilty of a criminal offence, and subject, on summary conviction, to a fine not exceeding £1,000.
2 Ie one requiring a 75 per cent majority – see Chapter 15.

(2) alter the articles to include the provisions necessary under s 33,[1] eg maximum of 50 members and restrictions on members' rights to sell shares.

Minority protection

8.24 Section 15 of the 1983 Act gives a minority of five per cent, or at least 50 members, or those holding five per cent of the value of the company's issued share capital, the right to apply to the court to cancel the special resolution authorising the change in status of the company.

The powers of the court to deal with the minority's complaint are elaborated in s 15(6) and (7).

Re-registration of private company as public company

8.25 Formation of a new plc is quite rare. Most public limited companies start life as successful private companies which subsequently convert to plcs.

Prior to 1983, a special resolution deleting the restrictive articles of association necessary under s 33 might have sufficed to make the change. Now, however, detailed additional requirements and procedures are prescribed by ss 9 and 10 of the Companies (Amendment) Act 1983. These extra requirements are, essentially, aimed at ensuring that a plc possesses the statutory minimum nominal and paid up share capital, and that its net assets at least equal the total of its called up share capital and undistributable reserves (defined in s 46(2)). Proof of the minimum asset requirement will require a written statement by the company auditors that, in their opinion, its balance sheet[2] net assets were sufficient to cover the prescribed aggregated liabilities.

The directors must also forward a copy of the relevant balance sheet, accompanied by an unqualified report by the company's auditors in relation to that balance sheet and make a statutory declaration.[3]

If, and when, the registrar is satisfied with the application, he will:

(1) retain the application and supporting documentation; and
(2) issue the company with a (new) certificate of incorporation stating that the company is a plc.

Third party rights

8.26 Section 9(10) makes it clear that re-registration will not affect any rights or obligations of the company, or render defective any legal proceedings by or against the company.

---

1 Of the CA 1963.
2 Which must have been prepared not more than seven months before the application for re-registration.
3 See s 9(3).

Conversion of unlimited company into limited company and vice versa

8.27 Under s 20 of the CA 1963, as amended by s 53 of the 1983 Act, an unlimited company may be converted into a company limited by shares or by guarantee. The procedure is again based on the passing of a special resolution.

Since s 52 of the Companies (Amendment) Act 1983 came into force, a limited company may convert into an unlimited company. However, because of the serious nature of this change, in effect foregoing the investor's fundamental protection of limitation of liability, all investors must assent to the re-registration of the company as unlimited.

Chapter 9

PROMOTERS AND PRE-INCORPORATION CONTRACTS

PROMOTERS

9.1　The persons who generate the idea of starting up a company and then taking steps to register it, are known as *promoters*.

Definitions of promoter

9.2　In the case of *Whaley Bridge Calico Printing Co v Green*,[1] Bowen J defined the term promoter as:

> 'a term not of law, but of business, usefully summing up in a single word a number of business operations familiar to the commercial world, by which a company is brought into existence.'

Again, in *Twycross v Grant*,[2] a promoter is described as:

> 'one who undertakes to form a company with reference to a given object, and to set it going, and who takes the necessary steps to accomplish that purpose.'

There exists a narrower statutory definition of promoter. For the purposes of civil liability, in respect of mis-statements in a prospectus under s 49 of the CA 1963,[3] a promoter is defined as meaning:

> 'a promoter who *was a party* to the *preparation of the prospectus* ... but does not include any person by reason of his acting in a professional capacity for persons engaged in procuring the formation of the company.'[4] (author's emphasis)

This statutory definition should be viewed as restricted to actions under s 49. For the remainder of this chapter, the term 'promoter' is used in the wider legal context embraced within the judicial definitions illustrated above. It should be remembered, though, that even within the wider definition of promoter, a solicitor or accountant who provides professional services in connection with forming the company will not, simply by providing these services, be deemed a promoter.[5] If, however, the professional is more closely involved with the creation of the company, actively desiring that it be registered, he may well be deemed to be one of its promoters.

1　(1880) 5 QBD 109.
2　(1877) 2 CPD 469.
3　See **10.46**.
4　Section 49(8)(a).
5　In *Re Great Wheel Polgooth Ltd* (1883) 53 LJ Ch 42, it was held that a person who merely acts as the agent or employee of a promoter is not himself a promoter.

9.3 Whilst, at times, the tests for identifying a promoter may not be precise, nevertheless, once a person is classified as a promoter his legal position is quite unambiguous. A promoter is not a trustee or agent of the company. He stands in a fiduciary relationship towards the company which he promotes. As a result, he must not make, either directly or indirectly, a profit at the expense of the company, without its knowledge and consent. As Lord Cairns said in *Erlanger v The New Sombrero Phosphate Co*:[1]

> 'It is now necessary that I should state … in what position I understand the promoters to be placed with reference to the company which they proposed to form. They stand, in my opinion, undoubtedly in a fiduciary position. They have in their hands the creation and moulding of the company; they have the power of defining how, and when, and in what shape, and under what supervision, it shall start into existence and begin to act as a trading corporation. If they are doing all this in order that the company may … become, through its managing directors, the purchaser of the property of themselves, (the promoters), it is, in my opinion, incumbent upon the promoters to take care that in forming the company they provide it with … a board of directors, who shall both be aware that the property which they are asked to buy is the property of the promoters, and who shall be competent and impartial judges as to whether the purchase ought or ought not to be made.'

Promoter's fiduciary relationship

9.4 The promoter's fiduciary relationship means that he is under a legal duty towards the company to *disclose* any potential profit and to *account* for it.

If, therefore, the promoter wishes to sell his own property to the company, he will have to disclose his personal interest and account to the company for profits which he might otherwise have retained. It is not the profit which the law forbids; it is the non-disclosure of it.

Duties of disclosure

9.5 If a promoter wishes to sell his own property to the company, he should disclose his interest to either:

(1) a board of independent directors,[2] or the company in general meeting;[3] or
(2) to the intended investors;[4] or
(3) to the public by means of listing particulars or a prospectus.[5]

A promoter cannot contract out of his fiduciary duties by inserting provisions to that effect in the company's articles of association.[6]

---

1 (1878) 3 AC 1218 (HL).
2 *Hopkins v Shannon Transport Systems Ltd* (unreported) 10 July 1972 (HC).
3 *Gluckstein v Barnes* [1900] AC 240.
4 *Salomon v Salomon & Co* [1890] AC 22. Aaron Salomon had disclosed his interest and potential profit to all other members of the company (his family).
5 See **10.14** and **10.18** below.
6 *Omnium Electric Palaces Ltd v Baines* [1941] 1 Ch 332.

Common law remedies of the company

9.6 The remedies of the company against promoters were originally developed at common law. However, since 1983, there have been statutory rules introduced to protect the company.

Rescission

9.7 At common law, if any profit is not disclosed, the company's remedy can vary according to when the property in question was acquired by the promoter, ie whether the property was acquired before or after the person became a promoter.

When the promoter was not in a fiduciary relationship to the company when he acquired the property, then the company's remedy for non-disclosure of profits by the promoter is rescission. This means that the company can withdraw from the contract with the promoter, return the property to him and recover the contract price paid for it.[1]

Rescission is an option available to the company whose contract for the sale of the property to the promoter is a voidable one. Consequently, the company have the option of continuing with the contract, if they so desire. As Pringle J stated:[2]

> 'So far as these contracts being reprobated by the company, they were, in fact approbated to a substantial extent. It appears to be clear that failure by a promoter or a director to make full disclosure of his contracts with the company renders the contract voidable by the company, but *not* void.' (author's emphasis)

The right of rescission will generally be lost:

(1) if the parties cannot be restored to their original positions, as in *Lagunas Nitrate Co v Lagunas Syndicate*,[3] or

(2) if innocent third parties have acquired rights for value under the contracts, as in *Re Leeds and Hanley Theatres of Varieties Ltd*[4] and in *Northern Bank Finance Corporation Ltd v Charlton*.[5]

Recovery of profits

9.8 Where the promoter is in a fiduciary position to the company both:

(1) when he acquired the property; and

(2) when he sold it to the company,

the company may not only rescind the contract as above, it may also either:

---

1 *Erlanger v The New Sombrero Phosphate Co* (1878) 3 AC 1218 (HL).

2 In *Hopkins v Shannon Transport Systems Ltd* (unreported) 10 July 1972 (HC).

3 [1899] 2 Ch 392 (CA). See also *Armstrong v Jackson* [1917] 2 KB 822 where rescission was granted even though that meant the person guilty of fraud lost money as a result of the loss in value of the shares in question.

4 [1902] 2 Ch 809 – here property had already been sold.

5 [1979] IR 149 (SC).

(1) retain the property, paying no more for it than the promoter. This will have the effect of depriving the promoter of his profit; or

(2) recover the secret profit from the promoter. It was held in *Gluckstein v Barnes* that a secret profit of £20,000 had to be repaid by the promoters to the company.

Damages for misfeasance

9.9 If the remedies in **9.7** and **9.8** above are either not available or are inappropriate, the company may sue the promoters for damages for breach of their fiduciary duty. The measure of the damage will be the amount of the secret profit made by the promoter.[1]

Statutory rights of the company

9.10 The common law remedies of a company against a promoter are available to both private and public companies. In the case of the latter, however, they have become less significant because of ss 26 to 37[2] of the Companies (Amendment) Act 1983, which have regulated aspects of company dealings involving non-cash assets. For example, s 30 would make it necessary for any property being offered by a promoter to the company, as consideration for its shares, to be valued by an *independent expert*. Similarly, s 32 also provides for an independent expert's valuation of assets where a public company, within two years of commencing business, acquires an asset from a subscriber[3] to its memorandum, and the consideration for that asset amounts to one tenth or more of the nominal value of the company's issued capital. In addition, under s 32, the terms of the sale must have been approved[4] by an ordinary resolution of the company, and a copy of the agreement delivered to the registrar of companies.

Effects of breaching the 1983 Act

9.11 Where there is a breach of s 30, the promoter/allottee will be liable to pay the company an amount equal to the true value of the shares, and will also be liable to pay interest.[5]

In the event of a breach of s 32, the company will be entitled to recover its consideration, or an amount equivalent to it, from the relevant person/promoter and the agreement, so far as not carried out, shall be void.[6]

---

1 *Re Leeds and Hanley Theatres of Varieties Ltd* [1902] 2 Ch 809.
2 See **10.30**.
3 Who need not necessarily be a promoter.
4 See s 32(3).
5 Section 30(10).
6 Section 32(8).

Remuneration of promoters

9.12 A promoter has no legal right to recover his expenses. As Cozens-Hardy, MR said:[1]

> 'There is no foundation for any general proposition (that a promoter is entitled to recover his expenses). Indeed, the contrary is well settled. If A voluntarily pays B's debt, B is under no obligation to repay A ...'

Provision in articles of association

9.13 To overcome the unsatisfactory situation over recovery of promoters' expenses, art 80 of Table A stipulates that:

> 'The directors ... may pay all expenses incurred in *promoting* and *registering* the company ...' (author's emphasis)

An article, such as art 80, gives the directors the discretion to pay the promoters' expenses. As, in many instances, the promoters will also be the company's first directors, they will, in practice, be re-imbursed their expenses.

Information to be included in a prospectus

9.14 Any prospectus issued by the company must include 'any amount or benefit paid or given within the preceding five years to any promoter'[2] and short details of any property transaction in which the vendor is a promoter or director of the company.[3]

Promoters and pre-incorporation contracts

9.15 There are similarities between the positions in law of a promoter and an agent.[4] A promoter can be viewed as an agent of the company in its dealings with third parties.

In agency law, for a principal to adopt contracts entered into on his behalf by his agent, that principal must be in existence at the time the contract was made. Otherwise, the agent, and not the principal, is the person who can enforce that contract. For example, in the case of a contract entered into by a promoter on behalf of the company before the certificate of incorporation is issued (a pre-incorporation contract), the company, as principal, is not yet in existence. As a result, the company could not sue on a pre-incorporation contract.[5] To overcome the agency difficulties over pre-incorporation contracts, the CA 1963 provides as follows:[6]

---

1 In *Re National Motor Mail-Coach Co Ltd, Clinton's Claim* [1908] 2 Ch 515 (CA).
2 See CA 1963, Sch 3, para 13.
3 Ibid, para 9.
4 *Jacobus Marler Estates Ltd v Marler* (1913) 85 LJPC 167n.
5 *Newborne v Sensolid (Great Britain) Ltd* [1954] 1 QB 45 (CA). The promoter could not enforce such a contract either.
6 Section 37(1) and (2).

(1) any pre-incorporation contract may be *ratified*[1] by the company after its formation; and

(2) prior to ratification, a promoter shall be personally bound by the contract and entitled to the benefit thereof, unless he has expressly agreed to the contrary.

Pre-incorporation and pre-trading contracts

9.16 The distinctions between pre-incorporation and pre-trading contracts, and directors' liabilities in respect of the latter, are explained in Chapter 11.

---

1 Ie approved or validated retrospectively.

PART IV

COMPANIES' CAPITAL, GOVERNANCE AND CONTRACTUAL CAPABILITY

Chapter 10

PROTECTION FOR INVESTORS IN PUBLIC COMPANIES

THE NEED FOR PROTECTION

10.1 We have seen[1] that once the registrar issues a certificate of incorporation to a private company, it can immediately commence trading. In 1995, there were 134,769 private companies registered (91.6 per cent of the total).

The shareholders of a private company buy their shares in the company secure in the knowledge that the basic investors' protection of limitation of liability applies to their investment. Each purchase of such shares is a relatively straightforward transaction: both purchaser and vendor of the shares being aware that the general public are prohibited from subscribing for the shares and debentures of a private company.

Investors buying shares in private companies will almost certainly also possess some personal knowledge of the company and its affairs. By contrast, those buying shares in public companies would not normally have access to relevant information about them. Accordingly, as we shall illustrate in this chapter, the companies legislation includes a large amount of 'investor protection' measures for persons buying shares in public companies. The main reasons underlying these protective measures are:

(1) to facilitate the reasonable assessment by prospective investors of the value and price of the shares offered for public sale; and

(2) to contribute to the effective use by shareholders of voting or other rights which they may possess as company members (or, indeed, debenture holders).

The statutory protection to investors in public companies is based upon compelling the companies to provide minimum information to potential investors by the issuing of prospectuses or listing particulars. Investors are given legal remedies for misrepresentations in these documents. They may also be entitled to on-going notification by the company of any 'price sensitive' information.

On 31 December 1995, out of a total 147,058 companies registered in Ireland, only 557 (0.3 per cent) were public. Because of the low number of public companies, the importance given to them in the Companies Act 1963 has sometimes been questioned. However, it should not be forgotten that whilst the number of public companies is small, each public company may have literally thousands of shareholders. Therefore, the provisions relating to public companies in the companies legislation will affect a disproportionately large

---

1 In Chapter 9.

number of individual investors. Nevertheless, the dominance of private companies as the most favoured business association for trading, seems implicitly to have been recognised by the Companies (Amendment) Act 1983 which defines a public company simply as one 'which is not a private company'.

PUBLIC COMPANY FORMATION PROCEDURES

10.2   The normal pattern in company development would be to register a private company – often a family business. As this business grows and its need for extra capital exceeded the owners' capacity, the owners/directors[1] would decide that they needed to re-register as a public company to gain access[2] to the wider capital base. Such a decision to 'go public' is known as 'floating' a company. This would be the usual method of forming a public company.

The flotation of a company will generally take place when a private company decides to 'go public' and 'converts' to plc status, rather than forming an entirely new plc.

When a public company wishes to raise money from the public by offering to sell them its shares,[3] the company[4] is expected to comply with the requirements of ss 43 to 48 of the 1963 Act relating to prospectuses, or the listing rules of the Stock Exchange.

The Stock Exchange requirements reflect EU reforms which were implemented in Ireland by the European Communities (Stock Exchange) Regulations 1984[5] (the 1984 Regulations).

The European Communities (Stock Exchange) Regulations 1984

10.3   The 1984 Regulations implemented the following three directives:

The Admissions Directive[6]

10.4   This Directive prescribes the conditions which must be fulfilled before securities may be admitted to official Stock Exchange listing. The term 'securities' includes shares, debentures, options, futures, differences and long-term insurance contracts.

---

1 Usually the same persons.
2 And, perhaps, also to liquidate some of their 'paper' assets (shares) in the company.
3 Or debentures.
4 Or its agents.
5 SI 1984/282, as amended by SI 1991/18.
6 Directive 79/279/EEC of 5 March 1979.

The Listing Particulars Directive[1]

10.5 This Directive seeks to ensure that the admission of securities to official listing is dependent upon the publication of an information sheet styled the Listing Particulars.

The Interim Reports Directive[2]

10.6 This Directive prescribes the regular publication of information by companies whose shares have been admitted to official Stock Exchange listing.

The three EU Directives are reproduced in full as the first Schedule to the 1984 Regulations.

The Irish Stock Exchange is established as the competent authority under the Regulations, for deciding on the admission of securities to listing. When application is made to the Irish Stock Exchange for admission to official listing, and the relevant particulars are approved by them, reg 12 of the 1984 Regulations applies. Regulation 12(3) makes it clear that these listing particulars shall be deemed to be a prospectus within the Companies Act 1963.[3]

A copy of the listing particulars must be delivered to the registrar of companies, on or before their publication – reg 13.

Methods of raising capital

10.7 There are several methods by which a new or converted public company can raise capital from the public. These include:

An offer for sale

10.8 An offer for sale involves the company selling all the new shares to an issuing house, who, in turn, sells them to the public.

An issuing house, such as a merchant bank, would expect to sell the shares to the public at a higher price than they paid for them. In return for this, though, the issuing company is guaranteed against the failure of the issue, which has effectively been underwritten by the bank.

A placing

10.9 This transaction is similar to an offer for sale but the issuing house 'places' the shares with their clients – often large institutional investors. The

---

1 Directive 80/390/EEC of 17 March 1980.
2 Directive 82/121/EEC of 15 February 1982.
3 In such case, ss 43, 44(1), 45, 47, 361(1)(b), 361(2) and 364 of the 1963 Act will not apply. Section 48 of the 1963 Act was repealed in 1983 but s 46 still remains in existence and applicable. Section 46 deals with the furnishing of written evidence by an expert of his consent to the issue of a prospectus containing statements by him. Sections 361 and 364 refer to prospectuses related to companies incorporated outside of Ireland.

issuing house may or may not have purchased the shares before placing them with their clients.

A public offer

10.10   Whilst a company uses an intermediary in selling its shares in 10.8 and 10.9 above, where it makes a public offer it deals directly with the public.

A rights issue[1]

10.11   This is a method of raising finance from the present members of the company. Members are offered a new issue of shares in proportion to their existing shareholdings. Such issues are usually made by renounceable letters of allotment (see **31.32**).

When contemplating raising capital from the public, directors will have to consider which is the appropriate national securities market, taking into account the size of their company and its particular business.

NATIONAL INVESTMENT MARKETS

10.12   As we saw, a flotation involves selling[2] shares to the public either directly by a Public Offer or indirectly to the clients of an issuing house. This process only applies to companies formed as plcs or converting to public companies.

A flotation will be much more attractive if those shares, when purchased, can be traded on the Stock Exchange. For all practical purposes, therefore, the directors of a public company will have to seek a listing, or at least a public market, for the company's shares.

There were two major potential public markets for shares within the Irish Stock Exchange. These were the *Listed Market* and *Unlisted Securities Market* (USM). A restricted *Smaller Companies Market* (SCM) had also developed for indigenous companies with a minimum market capitalisation of £200,000.

10.13   During 1997, the budget introduced in January included taxation incentives for investors in the planned *Developing Companies Market* (DCM). The DCM is the Irish equivalent of the Alternative Investment Market in London. It is intended to cater for small and medium-sized developing companies who do not seek a full stock market listing. It will have less onerous listing requirements than a full listing, and thus be less costly to enter.

---

1 This must be distinguished from a 'bonus' issue which is a capitalisation of profits, giving investors additional shares in lieu of dividend payments.

2 The company may also fix a minimum price for its shares and invite bids for them. This method is known as offering shares by tender, but is rarely used in Ireland.

A company choosing to enter the DCM in Dublin could also seek a listing on the Alternative Investment Market in London. However, this dual listing can have significant taxation implications in Ireland.

Prior to introducing the DCM, the Stock Exchange had shut down the DCM's immediate predecessors. These were the SCM and the USM – see **10.12**. The discontinuance of the SCM was attributed to the stock market crash of 1987 and the fact that many of the companies which had availed of it were start-up operations which subsequently failed.

The reduction of the required trading record for Official Listing to three years had minimised the distinction between the Listed and Unlisted Markets. Accordingly, in 1996, the Exchange decided to effectively merge the successful USM with the Listed Market.

The Listed Market

10.14   Mature companies of substantial market value would generally seek Official Listing. To be admitted, a company must produce *listing particulars* giving as complete a picture of itself as possible to the Exchange and potential investors, ie its trading history, financial record, management, business prospects, etc. The Stock Exchange's detailed listing requirements are set out in the Listing Rules.

The Listing Rules

10.15   The Official Listing requirements are set out in the *Yellow Book* and are a substitute for the statutory requirements relating to prospectuses.[1] The detailed listing particulars[2] *include*:

(1) the names of the issuer, persons responsible for listing particulars, the auditors and other advisors;
(2) the securities concerned and any underwriting arrangements;
(3) general information about the issuer and its capital;
(4) details of the group's activities;
(5) financial information;
(6) management information;
(7) recent development and prospects; and
(8) additional information on debt securities.

In addition, an applicant is expected to disclose all such information as investors and advisers may reasonably require to make an informed assessment of:

(1) the issuer's assets and liabilities, its financial position, profit and loss, and prospects; and
(2) the rights attaching to the securities.

---

1 See **10.18** below.
2 See the Listing Particulars Directive in Sch A to the 1984 Regulations.

The basic requirement for a company seeking to have its shares listed is that it has a three-year trading record, and 25 per cent of its issued shares are owned by the public[1] (achieving a reasonable spread of shareholders).

Refusal by the Stock Exchange to grant a listing (or to withdraw one) is subject to review by the court.[2]

During 1996, listing particulars were registered for just one applicant company, pursuant to the 1984 Regulations.

Once listed, companies are under a continuing duty to provide all information necessary to ensure an orderly market and to protect investors' interests. This would include any information that could materially affect its share price.

The Unlisted Securities Market (USM)

10.16　　The USM was formed in 1980. It had been developed to encourage smaller companies, with a three-year business record, to seek additional capital from the public.

Because the 1984 Regulations only apply to listed securities, applicants to the USM were subject to the provisions of the 1963 Act relating to prospectuses. They were also subject to the regulations of the Stock Exchange for operating the USM. As mentioned above, this market was discontinued in 1996.

The Developing Companies Market (DCM)

10.17　　The entry requirements for access to the DCM include a minimum trading record of one year, compared with three years for full or official listing.

At least 10 per cent of the company's shares must be issued to the public. In practice, one would expect most companies to exceed this figure and to offer 20 to 30 per cent of their shares to the public . This would allow the founding shareholders to broaden the investor base without reducing their own voting power below 51 per cent levels.

Whilst there is a minimum company valuation requirement of £700,000 stg for full listing, none exists for listing on the DCM.

Both Official List and DCM companies will be under the continuing obligation to disclose 'price sensitive' information. This could include potential or planned takeovers. For example, in the case of listed companies contemplating a takeover in which the target company represented more than 25 per cent of its own size under a number of headings (eg net assets, property, etc), the listed company must issue a detailed circular to shareholders and obtain their approval at an extraordinary general meeting.

---

1 Ie by persons other than the company's owners, directors and close associates.
2 Regulation 10 of the 1984 Regulations.

For DCM companies, the comparable takeover transaction size threshold is 100 per cent. This increased threshold size will tend to dispense with the requirement of issuing a circular to shareholders by a DCM company seeking to expand its business by acquiring another company.

Further information on share listing matters may be obtained from either the Stock Exchange or its member firms. Appropriate details are included in Appendix A.

PROSPECTUSES

10.18   Where shares are being offered to the public, and the European Communities (Stock Exchange) Regulations 1984 do not apply, the Companies Acts provide that potential investors must be furnished with detailed information by the issuer to inform and protect them. The prescribed information must be communicated to the public by the issuing of a prospectus. For example, DCM companies, not being listed within the meaning of the 1984 Regulations, would be required to issue a prospectus under the 1963 Act.

A prospectus is defined in s 2 of the 1963 Act as 'any notice, circular, advertisement or other invitation, offering to the *public* for subscription or purchase, any shares or debentures of a company' (author's emphasis).

Public offers

10.19   Section 61(1) further construes an offer to the public as including an offer:

> 'to any section of the public, whether selected as members or debenture holders[1] of the company, or as clients of the person issuing the prospectus or in any other manner ...'

A public offer may not, however, extend to include an invitation restricted to the company's employees. For example, in *Corporate Affairs Commission v David James Finance Ltd,*[2] an invitation restricted to 12,500 company employees was held not to be made to the public.[3] However, by contrast, in *Re South of England Natural Gas and Petroleum Co,*[4] a promoter issued 3,000 copies of a prospectus marked 'For private circulation only' to shareholders of certain companies in which he had an interest. It was held, in this case, that an invitation was made to the public.

---

1   Amended by s 238 of the Companies Act 1990 dealing with debentures to be repaid within five years.
2   [1975] 2 NSWLR 710.
3   See also the limitation in s 61(2) of the 1963 Act.
4   [1911] Ch 575.

Any document which falls within the definitions of a prospectus must meet the statutory information disclosure requirements stipulating that no form of application for shares in a company which are being offered to the public shall be issued without being accompanied by a prospectus[1] complying with the Act.[2]

Contents of prospectus

10.20   The specific information which must be contained in a prospectus is set out in Part I of Sch 3 to the 1963 Act. This includes details of the company's capital, its directors, promoters, auditors and property acquired or to be purchased. The prospectus will also seek to elicit whether or not the promoters and directors have any personal interests in the company and/or its assets.

The minimum subscription

10.21   Fundamental matters dealt with in the prospectus include specifying the *minimum subscription*.[3] This is the minimum amount which, in the opinion of the directors, must be raised to pay the purchase price of any property to be acquired, to pay any preliminary expenses and commissions, to repay borrowings and to provide working capital.

The full details required to be included in a prospectus are set out in paras 1 to 18 of Sch 3, Part I of the 1963 Act, as amended by the European Communities (Transferable Securities and Stock Exchange) Regulations 1992[4].

Reports to be attached

10.22   Part II of Sch 3 prescribes the reports which must accompany the prospectus. For example, there must be a report by the auditors on the profits and losses of the company and its subsidiaries in each of the previous three years and a statement of their assets and liabilities at the latest date to which accounts were made up. If any business is to be acquired from the proceeds of the new issue, similar reports are required on that business.

Registration

10.23   A copy of the prospectus must be delivered to the registrar before it can be issued.[5] This copy must be signed by every person named in it as director or proposed director.[6]

---

1 Section 44(3) of the 1963 Act.
2 For limited exceptional cases where no prospectus need be issued, see s 44(4)(a) and (b) and s 45 of the 1963 Act.
3 See Sch 3, para 4.
4 SI 1992/202, which implemented EC 'Prospectus' Directives 89/298/EEC of 17 April 1989 and 90/211/EEC of 23 April 1990.
5 Section 47(1)(b).
6 Or by his agent, if authorised in writing.

A prospectus will be dated, unless the contrary is proved, as being issued on the date of its publication.[1]

The following documents must be attached to the copy delivered to the registrar:

(1) the consent of every expert required by s 46;
(2) a copy of every material contract; and
(3) if the auditors or accountants have made any adjustments to the accounts, a signed statement specifying these adjustments and giving the reasons for them.

Documents (1) and (3) are required only in the cases of prospectuses issued generally to the public.

There were 97 prospectuses registered during 1996.

Pre-emption rights

10.24 Section 23 of the Companies Act 1983 introduced the concept of pre-emption rights to Ireland. Pre-emption rights are, essentially, rights of first refusal. As a consequence, the effect of s 23 is to preclude a company allotting 'equity'[2] or ordinary shares unless it has firstly made an offer to its existing shareholders, to buy on equivalent terms, a number of the new shares in proportion to their existing shareholdings.

Where, however, the directors are authorised by the articles of association or by special resolution of the company in general meeting, they may allot equity securities as if pre-emption rights did not apply to the allotment.[3]

When considering the raising of finance for a public company which has been converted from a private one, the directors must, therefore, also bear in mind any pre-emption rights of the existing members.

CONTRACTUAL ASPECTS OF PUBLIC SUBSCRIPTIONS

10.25 In terms of contract law, when a prospectus is issued to the public, it is deemed an 'invitation to treat', ie the public are invited to make offers to purchase the shares which are for sale. To initiate such a deal, the purchaser completes the application form usually attached to the prospectus and forwards it, with his cheque, to the issuing company, or its agents.

---

1 Section 43.
2 It does not apply to preference shares nor to shares held under an employees' share scheme.
3 See s 24 of the 1983 Act.

When the directors of the issuing company allot shares and advise the applicant that he has been allotted the shares he applied for, then this constitutes acceptance[1] and a valid[2] contract comes into force.

Protecting public investors at allotment stage

10.26   Prior to 1983, there had been little statutory restriction on the power of directors to allot shares. Section 20 of the 1983 Act has changed this situation by stipulating that, to do so now, directors will need the authority of either the articles of association or an ordinary resolution at a general meeting.

Directors' authority

10.27   This authority to allot shares may be given to the company directors for a specific issue. Alternatively, it may be a general authority covering all issues for no longer than five years. Both types of authority must state the maximum amount of shares that may be allotted, and the date on which it is to expire.

Such instances of authority to allot can be varied, revoked or renewed by the company in general meeting. In addition, directors authorised by s 20 may also be given the power to restrict or withdraw the statutory pre-emption rights for periods up to five years.

Allotments made by directors without s 20 authority will not be invalid. However, the directors will be liable to a fine.

Allotment procedures

10.28   Sections 53 to 59 of the 1963 Act[3] further protect potential public investors by restricting the directors' powers to allot shares. For example, s 53 provides that no allotment can be made of any share capital of a company offered to the public for subscription unless the sum raised in cash exceeds the amount of the *minimum subscription.*[4]

Minimum subscription

10.29   Section 53 has been extended by s 22 of the 1983 Act so that any offer for shares *must be fully subscribed* before allotment can take place, unless the listing particulars or prospectus expressly states that a part subscription is acceptable.

---

1 Although the applicant does not become a member until his name has been included in the register of members – see Chapter 28. However, this requirement does not apply to the original subscribers to the memorandum – see s 31 of the 1963 Act.
2 The manner of acceptance, whether oral, written, posted or even implied by the applicant's conduct, will be subject to the rules of contract law – accordingly, see R. Friel *The Law of Contract* (Round Hall Press, 1995), pp 52–59.
3 As amended by the Companies (Amendment) Act 1983 – see Sch 1.
4 See above.

The requirements of ss 53 and 22 need not cause problems, in practice, when the public money is raised by either an Offer for Sale or a Placing. If a company were to offer its shares for sale directly to the public, the risk of failure could be avoided by an underwriting agreement.

An *underwriting agreement* is a contract whereby, before a company offers shares to the public, the underwriters (eg a merchant bank) agree, in return for a commission, to take all or part of the offered shares which were not subscribed for by the public.

Payment for allotted shares

10.30 Sections 26 to 37 of the Companies (Amendment) Act 1983 introduced further restrictions on payment for shares. Generally, shares must be paid up in money or money's worth, including goodwill and expertise (shares taken by a subscriber to the memorandum of a plc must be paid up in cash).

Shares cannot be issued at a discount. They may only be allotted if 25 per cent of their nominal value and all of any premium, has been paid up.

Non-cash consideration

10.31 A public company may only allot shares in return for non-cash assets if the transfer of the assets is to take effect within five years of the allotment. If acceptable non-cash assets are to be used as consideration for shares, ss 30 to 33 make provision for their independent expert valuation.

The non-cash consideration valuation process may also apply in the case of a purchase by a plc of non-cash assets from its subscribers or members. Generally, the asset must be acquired within two years of the company's receipt of its Certificate of Trading,[1] and the consideration for the asset must be valued by an independent person in accordance with s 32.

Directors' liabilities

10.32 If, after 40 days, insufficient share applications have been received to cover the amount of the minimum subscription, applicants' monies must be refunded to them. Failure to refund these monies within 48 days can render the directors jointly and severally liable to repay that money – see s 53(4) and (6) of the 1963 Act. Directors may also be subject to a fine if they begin to allot shares *before* the fourth day[2] after the date the prospectus is issued, or if permission to trade in the shares has not been applied for or granted.[3]

---

1 See Chapter 12.
2 Section 56 of the 1963 Act.
3 Section 57. The directors may also be legally liable to repay the investors – see s 57(2).

Void and voidable allotments

10.33 Where a prospectus states that application has been or will be made for permission for the shares offered to be dealt with on the Stock Exchange, then, if application has not been made within three days after the first issue of the prospectus, or granted within six weeks from the date of the closing of the subscription lists, any allotment shall be void.[1]

Section 55 also deals with irregular allotments. It provides that any allotment made in contravention of the minimum subscription requirement will be voidable within one month after the date of the allotment.

Returns of allotments

10.34 Section 58 provides that whenever a company makes any allotment of its shares, it must, within one month thereafter, deliver prescribed details to the registrar, including the nominal amount of the total shares in the allotment, the individual allottees' names and addresses, and the amount, if any, paid or due and payable on each share.

Where a company fails to comply with s 58, any officer who is in default may be fined up to £500. Some relief is available: s 57(4) empowers the court, if satisfied that the delay was accidental or inadvertant, to make an order extending the time for the delivery of the returns 'for such period as the court may think proper'.

Shareholders' liability

10.35 The immediate liability of the shareholder is to pay for his shares in cash, or, with the consent of the company, in money's worth such as a non-cash asset, in accordance with the terms of the issue.

The full extent of a shareholder's contractual liabilities and rights is dealt with in Chapters 29 to 31.

Other remedies and protections

10.36 An applicant is not limited solely to his statutory rights under s 55. He also has other legal remedies for incorrect pre-contractual information.

When a member of the public is induced to enter into a contract for the purchase of shares by an untrue or misleading statement in the listing particulars or prospectus, it may give rise to either civil or criminal liability.

---

1 Section 57(1) of the 1963 Act.

INVESTORS' REMEDIES FOR MISREPRESENTATIONS

10.37   The remedies available to a misled investor may entail legal action against all or some of the following persons:

(1) the company;
(2) the issuing house;
(3) individuals responsible for producing the statutory documentation, including the directors; and
(4) the experts (if any).

Investors' remedies

10.38   Subscribers for shares have both common law and statutory remedies. Common law remedies are based on actionable misrepresentations and rights in contract (rescission) and the torts of deceit and negligence. Investors' statutory remedies arise under s 49 of the 1963 Act.

Common law remedies

10.39   Where a prospectus contains an incorrect statement which has induced a person to subscribe for shares on the faith of it, the misled subscriber may rescind (withdraw) from the contract, and, depending on the circumstances, sue for damages.

Rescission

10.40   A subscriber for shares may apply to the court for the contract to be set aside if he was induced to enter into it by incorrect statements of fact in the prospectus, even though these statements were made innocently, eg a false statement made innocently by an 'expert', ie an engineer, accountant or other professional man whose profession gives authority to any statement made by him.[1]

Limits on rescission

10.41   Rescission may not be available in certain circumstances, eg undue delay by the subscriber in attempting to avoid the contract; where he does anything after he becomes aware of the misrepresentation which is inconsistent with the right to repudiate, such as attempting to sell the shares; or where proceedings have been commenced to wind up the company.[2]

---

1 Section 46(3) of the 1963 Act.
2 *Re Overend, Gurney & Co* (1867) LR 2 HL 325.

Damages for fraud

10.42   Any person induced by fraud to take shares has the right at common law to claim damages in the tort of *deceit*. Such a contract would usually be induced by a fraudulent misrepresentation.

An action for deceit will not be successful unless, as enunciated in the case of *Derry v Peek*:[1]

> 'a man makes a statement to be acted upon by others, which is false, and *which is known by him to be false*, or is made by him *recklessly or without care whether it is true or false*.' (author's emphasis)

It was held in *Derry v Peek* that a mis-statement, made in an honest but mistaken belief, was not deceit, even though the belief was not founded on reasonable grounds.

A subscriber may not retain the shares and obtain damages against the company.[2] This does not, however, affect his rights of action against those responsible for the fraudulent misrepresentation, eg the directors or promoters.

Damages for negligence

10.43   In principle, subscribers would appear to enjoy the right to claim damages for a negligent[3] misrepresentation against both the company and the persons responsible for issuing the prospectus.

Other common law remedies against the directors and promoters

10.44   Apart from his remedies against the company, a subscriber may also be able to pursue legal action against any person responsible for the incorrect statement in the prospectus. These persons include directors, promoters and experts.

The subscriber can sue the directors, promoters and experts for damages, based on the tort of deceit, in cases where he has been misled by a fraudulent misrepresentation or, indeed, by the concealment of material facts.

Concealment

10.45   In *Aaron's Reefs Ltd v Twiss*,[4] it was held that the concealing of material facts from the prospectus was fraudulent, and the subscriber was entitled to a remedy, Fitzgibbon LJ stating:

---

1 (1889) 14 App Cas 337.
2 *Houldsworth v City of Glasgow Bank* (1880) 5 App Cas 317.
3 *Securities Trust Ltd v Hugh Moore and Alexander Ltd* [1964] IR 417 (HC).
4 [1895] CA 2 IR 207, a decision subsequently affirmed in the House of Lords – see [1896] AC 273. In *New Brunswick and Canada Railway & Land Co v Muggeridge* (1860) 1 Dr & Sm 383 (ChD), Kindersley V-C stated that those issuing prospectuses 'are bound to state everything with strict and scrupulous accuracy, and not only to abstain from stating as fact that which is not so, but to omit no

'if a prospectus contains any material representation of fact which is false and fraudulent, it cannot be the law that a reference in the statutory form to a document which would reveal the falsehood can place the framers of the prospectus in the same position as if they had not made the misrepresentation. It is no answer to a plea of false and fraudulent representation to say that the person who made it had supplied the person whom he defrauded with means by which he might have discovered the fraud before he acted upon it.'

This judgment seems to suggest that misrepresentation may occur, even though the statutory disclosure requirements have been met.

Statutory remedies under s 49

10.46 Section 49 of the 1963 Act imposes civil liability on those responsible for the issuing of the prospectus. However, a director or promoter may avoid liability by proving that:

(1) consent to become a director was withdrawn before the prospectus was issued and it was issued without his knowledge or consent; or
(2) the prospectus was issued without his knowledge or consent and on finding this he forthwith gave reasonable public notice of that fact; or
(3) after issue and before allotment he became aware of the mis-statement, withdrew his consent and gave reasonable public notice and reasons for the withdrawal; or
(4) he had reasonable grounds for believing and did believe the statement to be true;
(5) as regards an untrue statement in an expert's report, that it was an accurate copy or extract of the statement or report and he had reasonable grounds to believe that the 'expert' was competent to make the statement and had given the consent required by the Act before the issue of the prospectus.

Position of expert

10.47 An expert can escape liability for a mis-statement made by him if he proves that:

(1) he withdrew his consent to the issue in writing before the registration of the prospectus; or
(2) after registration and before allotment he withdrew his consent, giving reasonable public notice of it and the reason therefor; or
(3) he was competent to make the statement and had reasonable grounds to believe and did believe that the statement was true up to the time of allotment.

---

one fact within their knowledge, the existence of which might in any degree affect the nature, or extent, or quality of the privileges and advantages which the prospectus holds out as inducements to take shares.'

A person who has suffered loss or damage because of an untrue statement in a prospectus has an easier evidential task in obtaining compensation under s 49, than in tort, because of the reversal of the burden of proof by s 49.

Persons named in prospectus without authority

10.48   A person named as a director and who does not consent to become one, is entitled to be indemnified by the other directors against all damages and costs for which he is made liable – see s 49(6).

Meaning of untrue statement

10.49   Section 52(1) defines a statement as untrue if it is misleading in the form and content in which it is included.

CRIMINAL LIABILITY FOR MISREPRESENTATIONS

10.50   By virtue of s 50 of the 1963 Act, a person who authorises the issue of a prospectus containing an untrue statement is liable:

(1) on indictment, for up to two years' imprisonment and/or a fine not exceeding £2,500; or
(2) on summary conviction, for up to six months' imprisonment and/or a fine not exceeding £500.

Defence

10.51   A person will not be liable under s 50 if he can prove that either:

(1) the statement was immaterial; or
(2) he had reasonable grounds to believe, and did, up to the time of the issue of the prospectus, believe that the statement was true.

STATEMENT IN LIEU OF PROSPECTUS

10.52   When a company has not issued a prospectus inviting the public to subscribe for its shares, it is not permitted to commence business or exercise any borrowing powers unless a Statement in Lieu of Prospectus[1] has been delivered to the registrar.

The Second Schedule to the 1963 Act sets out a form of Statement and the particulars which have to be contained in it when delivered to the registrar by a private company in converting to an unlimited public company.

---

1 Section 115(2) of the 1963 Act.

A Statement may also be required from an unlimited public company which does not issue a prospectus.

Apart from these exceptional cases, the requirements of the Companies Acts on prospectuses, and of the 1984 Regulations on listing particulars, are so widespread that the Statement in Lieu has little relevance today.

Chapter 11

COMMENCEMENT OF BUSINESS BY PUBLIC AND NON-IRISH COMPANIES

INTRODUCTION

11.1 A company registered as a public company will be unable to commence trading or borrow money until it has been issued with a Trading Certificate by the registrar of companies. The registrar will not issue this certificate until he is satisfied that the company has met the statutory requirements regulating the raising of capital from the public.[1]

The Trading Certificate

11.2 The registrar will issue a Trading Certificate only if he is satisfied that the nominal value of the company's allotted share capital exceeds the statutory minimum, and he has received a statutory declaration signed by a director[2] confirming this fact. The declaration must also contain details of:

(1) the amount of the preliminary expenses of the company and the persons by whom any of those expenses have been paid or are payable; and
(2) any amount or benefit paid ... or given to any promoter of the company, and the consideration for it.

Once issued, the Trading Certificate is conclusive evidence that the company is entitled to commence business and to exercise its borrowing powers.[3]

Liability of directors for pre-trading contracts

11.3 When considering early contracts made by a private company, we saw[4] that there are only two categories which may arise. These are contracts:

(1) made on behalf of the company by promoters before the company was incorporated ie 'pre-incorporation' contracts made before the Certificate of Incorporation was issued; and
(2) made after incorporation.

Resulting from s 6(7) of the 1983 Act, however, there are three categories of contract to be considered in the corresponding circumstance for public companies. These contracts are:

(1) pre-incorporation contracts made by promoters, as above; and

---

1 See Chapter 10.
2 Or secretary.
3 Section 6(6) of the Companies (Amendment) Act 1983.
4 In Chapter 9.

(2) contracts made after incorporation but before the issuing of the Trading Certificate. These are known as pre-trading contracts; and

(3) contracts made after the Trading Certificate has been issued.

The law relating to responsibility of promoters is the same for both private and public companies. Section 6(8) of the Companies (Amendment) Act 1983, however, imposes civil[1] liability on directors for pre-trading contracts. This liability can arise where the company fails to honour its contractual obligations within 21 days from being called upon to do so. In these circumstances, the directors are jointly and severally liable to indemnify the other party to the pre-trading contract. The indemnity is for any loss or damage suffered by that party as a result of the company's failure to discharge its obligations.

NON-IRISH COMPANIES

11.4 Companies incorporated outside of Ireland who wish to trade into the State by starting up an establishment there, must comply with Part XI[2] of the 1963 Act. This involves, inter alia, delivering to the registrar within one month of starting up the Irish place of business, the following documents:

(1) certified copies of its *memorandum* and *articles* of association;

(2) a list of *directors* containing specified details of each director;

(3) details of the *company secretary*;

(4) the names and addresses of one or more persons resident in Ireland and authorised to accept service of legal proceedings on behalf of the company, ie the company's authorised *legal representatives*;[3] and

(5) the *address* of the company's principal place of business in Ireland.

Any alterations in (1) to (5) above must be notified to the registrar.

Accounts and publicity

11.5 A non-Irish company trading in Ireland may[4] have to submit accounts to the registrar, and show its country of origin in:

(1) every *prospectus* issued in Ireland;

(2) every place where it carries on business in Ireland; and

(3) on its billheads, letter headings and company publications and notices.[5]

---

1 And criminal – see s 6(7).
2 Comprising ss 351 to 360.
3 See s 356.
4 See s 354.
5 Section 355.

Cessation of business in Ireland

11.6   If a non-Irish company ceases to have a place of business in the State, it must also notify the registrar.[1]

Irish branches

11.7   The particulars required of companies with a branch, as distinct from an established place of business, in Ireland, are set out in the European Communities (Branch Disclosures) Regulations 1993.[2]

Details of external companies

11.8   The statistics for numbers of non-Irish or external companies show a significant growth in branch operations and a reduction in established places of business during 1994 and 1995. The official numbers were:[3]

	1995	*1994*
Branches (EU)	424	106
Branches (non-EU)	75	27
Places of Business	2,124	2,431
Total of External Register	2,623	2,564

OTHER BUSINESS ASSOCIATIONS

11.9   Parts VIII[4] and IX[5] of the 1963 Act apply to companies formed and registered under older Companies Acts or other statutes. These companies are now subject to the relevant provisions of the current legislation, which has superseded the older Acts.

European Economic Interest Groupings (EEIGs)

11.10   A legal framework exists[6] which permits groupings of persons, companies and other legal entities to co-operate effectively in economic activities across national frontiers within the EU, whilst at the same time preserving their legal and economic independence.

---

1 Section 357.
2 SI 1993/395.
3 Source – *Companies Report Year Ending 1995*, Department of Enterprise and Employment.
4 Sections 324 to 327.
5 Sections 328 to 343. This Part includes companies registered under the Joint Stock Companies Act – see ss 329 and 330. The provisions of the Act which apply to chartered companies are outlined in the 1963 Act, Sch 9, as amended by s 250 of the 1990 Act. Section 377 of the 1963 Act makes provision for unregistered companies.
6 Under the European Communities (European Economic Interest Groupings) Regulations 1989, SI 1989/191.

There are similarities between the structures of an EEIG and a registered company. Instead of a memorandum and articles of association, the contract forming the grouping must be registered with the registrar. Relevant information must also be published in *Iris Oifigiúil* and an annual return furnished to the registrar.

The trading profits and losses of an EEIG belong, not to the grouping, but are returned to the individual members.[1]

There were five EEIGs registered in Ireland on 31 December 1995.

---

1 An EEIG has some characteristics of a partnership. However, it is recognised by the law as a separate corporate entity.

Chapter 12

COMPOSITION OF A COMPANY'S CAPITAL BASE

DEFINITION OF CAPITAL

12.1   Capital may be loosely defined as the money, property and assets used in operating a business. Depending on its source, it may be classified either as investment or loan capital.

Investment capital

12.2   In the context of company law, most persons would tend to view capital as the money which a company possesses as a result of issuing shares to its members. The company, of course, will make use of its investors' monies to buy premises, plant and raw materials and to pursue its business objectives generally. The aggregate fund of the monies contributed by investors, essentially, becomes the major source of a company's capital requirements. This source of corporate funding is styled investment capital.

Balance sheet position

12.3   Because of the separate legal personality of a company, its investment capital is ultimately owed to members. Investment capital is, therefore, shown on the Liabilities, rather than the Assets, side of the company's Balance Sheet.

Loan capital

12.4   A company may not wish to raise all its capital from investors. Instead, it may obtain a loan from a bank. Such finance would have to be repaid. The contract under which the monies are borrowed is known as a debenture. A debenture is, therefore, an acknowledgement of debt issued by a company. Generally, under debentures, the company pays a fixed interest and uses its assets as security. Finance raised by the issue of debentures is known as loan capital.[1]

Capital employed

12.5   The expression 'capital employed' is used to denote the total amount of a company's shareholders' funds plus its long-term borrowings, ie investment capital plus loan capital.

---

1   The respective rights of creditors and company under debentures are dealt with in Part VIII.

Gearing

12.6   The ratio of loan capital to a company's total capital employed is known as 'gearing'. When a company is described as 'highly geared', it indicates that the level of its borrowings is high, compared to its investment[1] capital. A 'lowly geared' company, by contrast, has relatively low borrowings or loan capital.

Fixed and circulating capital

12.7   'Fixed capital' is that held by the company in the form of fixed assets. Fixed assets denote property or machinery which a company owns and uses, but does not buy or sell as part of its regular business, eg machinery used by the company as part of its manufacturing process.

'Circulating capital' refers to capital in the form of cash or debtors, raw materials, finished products and work in progress required for the company to carry on its business.

Working capital

12.8   'Working capital' has a narrow technical meaning. It refers to capital in the form of cash, stocks and debtors (less creditors) used by a company in its day-to-day operations.

Share capital

12.9   The term 'share capital' is widely used to denote the total value of a company's shares. It also includes the types and nature of shares making up the company's capital (see **12.15** below).

TYPES OF SHARE CAPITAL

12.10   Money received by the company in return for the issue of its shares, is generally styled 'share capital'. The word 'capital', when used in the context of the share capital of a company, needs to be refined into different categories. These categories are designated as nominal, issued, paid-up, uncalled and reserve (share) capital.

Nominal (or authorised) capital

12.11   By virtue of the capital clause in its memorandum of association, every company 'limited by shares' must set out the amount of capital with which it

---

1 Or *equity* capital, ie that contributed by 'ordinary' shareholders, as distinct from preference shareholders.

proposes to be registered. Once the amount of the nominal (or authorised) capital has been declared in the memorandum, it cannot be increased or reduced unless the appropriate formalities have been observed.

The capital clause in the memorandum also provides for the division of the nominal capital into a stated number of shares, each of a fixed amount.

The model capital clause in Table B[1] reads 'The share capital of the company is £200,000 divided into 200,000 shares of £1 each'.

The amount of a company's authorised capital will depend upon its business requirements, both short and long term.

Issued capital

12.12 A company is not required to issue all of its authorised capital immediately. In the example given above from Table B, if that company decides to issue 100,000 shares at £1 each, then £100,000 will be the amount of the issued share capital.

Paid-up and uncalled capital

12.13 The paid-up capital is that part of the issued capital which has been paid up by the investors. For example, if a company wishes, it could issue, say, 100,000 shares of £1 each, and decide that the shareholders would not be called upon to pay the full £1 at once. The company may issue the shares on condition that 60p is paid initially, leaving the balance of 40p to be called up later. In this example, the paid-up capital would amount to £60,000, and the uncalled capital £40,000.

The articles of association[2] will normally give the directors the power to make calls on investors in respect of any monies unpaid on their shares.

Reserve capital

12.14 Reserve capital is explained in s 67 of the 1963 Act, which provides that a limited company may, by special resolution, determine that any portion of its share capital which has not already been called up, shall not be capable of being called up except in the event of the company being wound up.

Reserve capital is, accordingly, not available to the directors; it is available only for the creditors on the winding up of the company.

---

1 Of the 1963 Act, Sch 1.
2 See Table A, 1963 Act, arts 15 to 21 (and Chapter 30).

CLASSES OF SHARES

12.15   There can be more than one class of share. For example, the articles of association[1] may provide that:

> 'Without prejudice to any special rights previously conferred on the holders of any existing shares or class of shares, any share in the company may be issued with such preferred, deferred or other special rights or such restrictions, whether in regard to dividend, voting, return of capital or otherwise, as the company may from time to time by ordinary resolution determine.'

Class rights

12.16   Each class of share will possess special rights confined to its own class and styled 'class rights'. Class rights often relate to the *voting rights* and/or *dividend payment entitlements* of the holders of a particular class of share.

The two most usual classes of shares are preference and ordinary shares.

Preference shares

12.17   A preference share is a share which entitles its holder to *preference* (over other shares) *when profits have been made available for dividends*. A preference share may indicate a fixed dividend, eg a six per cent preference share. In many cases, there may be preference as to repayment of capital by the company to the shareholder in case of a winding up.

The fixed dividend must be paid to the preference shareholders before the holders of the ordinary shares receive any dividend.

Preference shares may be:

(1)   cumulative; this means that if the dividend is not paid in any year or years, the arrears accumulate and must be paid off before the ordinary shares receive dividends; or
(2)   non-cumulative; meaning that if no dividend is paid in any year it is lost forever.

There is a presumption that preference shares are cumulative. To be otherwise, they must be expressly stated in the articles as being non-cumulative.

Ordinary shares

12.18   Section 155(5)[2] defines equity share capital as a company's 'issued share capital excluding any part thereof which, neither as respects dividend nor as respects capital, carries any right to participate beyond a specified amount in

---

1 See Table A, 1963 Act, art 2.
2 Of the 1963 Act.

a distribution'. The class of shares to which s 155(5) refers is known as 'ordinary shares'.

Ordinary shareholders only become entitled to dividends if and when:

(1) the company has made a profit; and
(2) the preference shareholders have been paid their fixed dividend.

Ordinary shareholders do, however, have voting rights, and, effectively, have the power to control the company.

Finance raised by ordinary shares is sometimes called 'risk capital', since the holders of these shares are not entitled to dividends nor to return of capital until prior claims have been satisfied. For example, if the company is in financial difficulties, the profits available for dividends may only be enough to pay a dividend on the preference shares; in such circumstances, the ordinary shareholders receive no payment. On the other hand, if the company is prospering, the preference shareholders[1] will be limited to their fixed dividend, while the directors may recommend a dividend of, say, 10 per cent for the ordinary shareholders.

Non-voting ordinary shares

12.19 A company may also issue ordinary shares without voting rights attached. In this way, the directors of the company can raise more capital from investors without diluting control of the company by the existing 'equity' shareholders.

Deferred shares

12.20 Deferred shares are also known as Founders' or Management shares. The rights of these shareholders will depend on the articles. Generally, deferred shareholders would be entitled to participate in dividends after the ordinary shares had been paid a fixed dividend.

Deferred shares are rarely issued now.

Distinctions between preference and ordinary shares

12.21 Ordinary shareholders possess full voting rights. Preference share-holders are not entitled to vote at general meetings, except, perhaps in cases where their dividend is in arrears and/or their special class rights are being altered. In fact, the fixed dividend payable to preference shareholders is a manner of payment similar to the fixed interest payment made to debenture holders in respect of loan capital.

---

1 Unless the company has issued a class of share known as *Participating Preference Shares*. Such shareholders may also be entitled to part of the profits in excess of that used to pay the fixed dividend of the preference shareholders, always providing this right has been expressly conferred by the articles of association.

The possibility of the purchasing back by the company of redeemable[1] preference shares, further strengthens the similarities between this category of investment capital and loan capital.

In the event of a company's liquidation, if its articles of association expressly provide, preference shareholders may be entitled to a return of their capital in priority to the ordinary shareholders.

VARIATION OF CLASS RIGHTS

12.22   Section 78[2] deals with variation of the rights of special classes of shares. The term 'variation' also includes abrogation or cancellation of class rights. If provision is made in the memorandum or articles for variation of class rights, subject to the consent of any specified proportion of those shareholders, then the class rights can be altered. For example, art 3[3] contains the following 'modification of class rights' clause:

> 'If at any time the share capital is divided into different classes of shares, the rights attached to any class may, whether or not the company is being wound up, be varied or abrogated with the consent in writing of the holders of three-fourths of the issued shares of that class, or with the sanction of a special resolution passed at a separate general meeting of the holders of the shares of the class.'

Objections

12.23   If the holders of 10 per cent or more of the shares in question object to the alteration of their rights, s 78(1) gives them the right to apply to the court to have the variation cancelled. The procedures to be followed when making this appeal to the court are set out in s 78(2) to (5).

The issuing of additional shares of a similar class

12.24   In *White v Bristol Aeroplane Co*,[4] the court held that the rights of existing shareholders are not varied by the issue of new shares ranking pari passu[5] with them. Article 4[6] reflects this judicial decision by providing:

> 'The rights conferred upon the holders of the shares of any class issued with preferred or other right shall not, unless otherwise expressly provided by the terms of issue of the shares of that class, be deemed to be varied by the creation or issue of further shares ranking *pari passu* therewith.'

---

1 Defined by s 206 of the Companies Act 1990 as shares which are liable, at the option of the company or the shareholder, to be redeemed. However, even ordinary shares may now be issued as redeemable under the 1990 Act – s 207(1) and Chapter 13.
2 Of the 1963 Act.
3 Of Table A in the 1963 Act, Sch 1.
4 [1953] Ch 65 (CA).
5 Equally.
6 Of Table A in the 1963 Act, Sch 1.

Similarly, when the voting power of one class of ordinary (10p) shareholders was diluted by the action of another group of ordinary (50p) shareholders who by resolution subdivided their shares into five 10p shares each, the court in *Greenhalgh v Arderne Cinemas Ltd*[1] held that the rights of the original 10p shareholders, although possibly 'affected as a matter of business', were not varied as a matter of law.

The s 38 procedure

12.25   If a company has not made provision in its memorandum or articles to cater for the variation of class rights, s 38[2] effectively makes it mandatory for the procedures in s 78 and art 3 to apply; including the provision for a 10 per cent minority right of objection to the court – see Chapter 16.

SHAREHOLDERS' RIGHTS GENERALLY

12.26   Members' 'individual rights' and liabilities arising out of their contracts with the company are dealt with in Part VII.[3]

---

1   [1946] 1 All ER 512 (CA)
2   Of the 1983 Act.
3   Chapters 28 to 31.

Chapter 13

PROTECTION OF A COMPANY'S CAPITAL BASE FOR CREDITORS (AND INVESTORS)

STATUTORY RULES

13.1 One of the main planks of creditor, and indeed, investor[1] protection contained in the Companies Acts, is the legislature's desire to protect a company's share capital, which makes up its capital base. The underlying reason for this was explained by Jessel MR in *Re Exchange Banking Co, Flitcroft's Case*,[2] who stated:

> 'The creditor has no debtor but that impalpable thing, the corporation, which has no property except the assets of the business ...
>
> The creditor, therefore, ... has a right to say that the corporation shall keep its capital and not return it to the shareholders ... If directors ... improperly pay away the [company] assets to the shareholders, they are liable to replace them.'

A company, and its directors acting on its behalf, can quite properly expend contributed capital for any purpose which is intra vires the company.[3] Buckley LJ confirmed this in *Re Horsley and Weight Ltd*.[4] He further stated, however, that:

> 'The company's creditors are entitled to assume that the company *will not* in any way *repay* any paid up share capital to the shareholders except by means of a duly authorised reduction of capital. They are entitled to assume that the company's directors will conduct its affairs in such a manner that no unauthorised repayment will take place.' (author's emphasis)

The statutory rules protecting the share capital[5] base of the company can be divided into two broad categories. The first category consists of the restricted circumstances in which s 72[6] may permit a *direct repayment* to shareholders, or a reduction in their liabilities to the company in respect of their shares, ie restrictions on the direct reduction of share capital.

The second category of statutory rules protecting the capital base is intended to prevent any *indirect repayment* of the share capital to members. These rules are generally referred to as the 'capital maintenance rules'.

---

1 Particularly in public companies where most of the members would not be directors. Effectively, therefore, investors entrust their invested funds in the company to the care of directors over whom, in practice, they may have little control.
2 (1882) 21 ChD 519.
3 See Chapter 14.
4 [1982] 3 All ER 1045 (CA).
5 This protection is based upon the supposition that each company will possess a substantial amount of share capital. This is, very often, not the case. Many small private companies will have been formed with only insignificant (£2) amounts of share capital.
6 Of the 1963 Act.

RESTRICTIONS ON THE DIRECT REDUCTION OF SHARE CAPITAL

13.2 A company's articles of association may, like Table A, art 46,[1] provide that the company can, by *special resolution*, reduce its share capital, but only as permitted, and with the consents required, by law.

A company's share capital is viewed in law as a fund, a form of financial buffer out of which creditors may be paid in the event of the company failing. As a result, creditors are protected by the legislature specifying:

(1) the limited circumstances in which share capital may be reduced; and
(2) the procedures to be followed by the company, acting through its directors, to effect a permitted direct reduction of capital.

Share premium fund to be treated as capital

13.3 If a company issues shares of £1 nominal value for, say, £1.25, the extra 25p is deemed to be a premium. Section 62(1)[2] provides that, in these circumstances, a sum equal to the total amount of the premiums in that issue of shares must be kept in a separate account called *the share premium account.*

Permitted use of share premium fund

13.4 Section 62(2) permits the share premium funds to be used:

(1) in *paying up unissued shares* (other than redeemable shares) to be allotted to shareholders as fully paid bonus shares, in writing off:
    (a) the preliminary expenses of the company; or
    (b) the expenses of, or the commission paid or discount allowed, on any issue of shares or debentures; or
(2) in *providing for the premium payable* on redemption of any redeemable preference shares, or of any debentures.

Except in the cases of the limited uses permitted by s 62(2), the share premium fund is to be treated as if it were share capital, and is subject to the statutory restrictions on reduction of capital.

PERMITTED REDUCTION IN SHARE CAPITAL UNDER SECTION 72[3]

13.5 Subject to confirmation by the court, a company may, if so authorised by its articles, reduce its share capital by *special resolution.*

---

1 Of the 1963 Act.
2 Ibid.
3 Ibid.

The power given in s 72 is general. If the company adopts the proper procedure, it can reduce its capital 'in any way'. However, s 72(2) specifies three particular instances in which capital may be reduced. These are for:

(1) the extinction or reduction of the liability on shares in respect of *capital not paid up*;[1] or
(2) the cancellation of paid-up share capital which is 'lost or unrepresented'[2] by available assets; or
(3) the paying-off of any paid-up share capital which is in excess of the needs of the company.

Application to the court

13.6   When the company has passed a resolution for reducing its share capital, it may apply to the court. When the interests to be borne in mind are simply those of shareholders, the court may apply the following criteria:

(1) will the reduction be fair to the interest of members of the public who may be induced to take shares in the company? and
(2) will the reduction be fair and equitable as between the different classes of shareholders?[3]

Fairness between competing class rights

13.7   A useful method for the court to decide what is fair between the different classes of members is to view the consequences of the reduction request in the light of a theoretical winding up of the company. If, therefore, preference shareholders enjoy no special rights as to repayment of capital, a reduction of capital should be borne rateably by the preference and ordinary shareholders.[4] However, if the articles confer preferential rights as to repayment of capital on the preference shareholders, the ordinary shares would be expected to bear the loss first.[5] The opposite is also the case. If, for example, capital is being returned as surplus to the company's requirements in accordance with s 72(2), it should be returned, firstly, to the preference shareholders.[6] As Costello J stated in *Re Credit Finance Bank plc*:[7]

> 'The reality is, the (restructuring) scheme is fair between the classes of shareholders involved – the preference shareholders and the ordinary shareholders. It is true that the preference shareholders are to be repaid, but this is perfectly permissible.'

---

1 Eg uncalled capital.
2 Eg writing off trading losses, as in *Bannantyne v Direct Spanish Telegraph Co* (1886) 34 ChD 287. Evidence of the loss must be given to the court – see *Re Hoare & Co Ltd* [1904] 2 Ch 208 (CA).
3 *Poole v National Bank of China* [1907] AC 229.
4 *Bannantyne v Direct Spanish Telegraph Co* (1886) 34 ChD 287.
5 *Re Floating Dock Co of St Thomas* [1985] 1 Ch 691.
6 *Prudential Assurance Co v Chatterly-Whitfield Collieries* [1949] AC 512.
7 (Unreported) 19 June 1989 (HC).

Variation of class rights

13.8   If a proposed reduction of share capital is, in effect, a variation of class rights, the court may refuse to confirm the reduction unless the necessary consent of the class had been obtained in the proper manner.[1] In *Re John Power & Son Ltd*,[2] the court approved the principle that a reduction in capital which is not in accordance with class rights must either:

(1)   be approved at a separate meeting of that class; or
(2)   be proved to be fair and equitable. When considering whether the majority acted fairly and equitably, the court must look at the scheme, confirm that the majority are acting bona fide, and:

> 'see that the minority is not being overridden by a majority having interests of their own clashing with those of the minority which they seek to coerce ... and then see the scheme is a reasonable one ... [to which no] reasonable man might say that he could not approve of it.'

Objections by creditors

13.9   Section 73(2) stipulates that where a proposed reduction of share capital involves either:

(1)   diminution of liability in respect of unpaid share capital; or
(2)   payment to any shareholder of any paid-up share capital; and
(3)   in any other case where the court so directs,

the court shall *settle a list of creditors* in accordance with s 73(2)(a), (b) and (c). Creditors who do not consent to the reduction must be paid off, or their claims secured by payment into court.

13.10   Section 73(3) provides the court with the power to direct that, in the circumstances indicated in (1) and (2) above, s 73(2) shall not apply to any class or classes of creditors. This power is necessary because in instances where no asset out of which their claims could be satisfied is being given up by the company, the creditors should have no right to object to the proposed return of capital. For example, in *Re Meux's Brewery Co Ltd*,[3] the company's capital was made up as follows:

Paid-up Share Capital £1,000,000 (Investment)
Secured Debentures £1,000,000 (Loan)

In 1904, losses amounting to £800,000 were incurred. By 1917, this deficiency had been reduced to £640,000 and the company proposed to reduce its capital to £360,000.[4] The debenture-holders, as creditors, objected.

---

1   *Re Old Silkstone Collieries Ltd* [1954] Ch 169 – also see Chapter 12.
2   [1934] IR 412 (SC).
3   [1919] 1 Ch 28.
4   £1,000,000 paid-up capital less incurred losses of £640,000.

The court held that, as the reduction involved no diminution of unpaid capital, or repayment to shareholders of paid-up capital, creditors were not, prima facie, entitled to object unless they had good grounds for so doing. In this case, the court held that the debenture-holders had no good grounds to object to the proposed reduction.

Court order for reduction

13.11   The court may make an order confirming the reduction on such terms as it thinks fit. Where the court makes such an order, it may also specify in it that the words 'and reduced' be added to the company name.[1]

A copy of the court order and the appropriate minute, showing the reduced share holdings within the company, must be delivered to the registrar of companies.[2] This minute, when registered, shall be deemed to be substituted for the capital clause in the company's memorandum of association.

Liability of shareholders for reduced shares

13.12   Section 76 sets out the liability of members in respect of the reduced shares. Section 76(2) contains some protection for a creditor who had been unaware of the proceedings for reducing the company's capital.

OTHER PERMITTED REDUCTIONS IN SHARE CAPITAL

13.13   Other exceptional examples of reductions in a company's share capital are permitted under ss 15 and 43 of the 1983 Amendment Act.

Re-registration under s 15

13.14   Section 15 applies to a special resolution by a public company to be re-registered as a private one. Section 15(2) gives a minority of shareholders opposed to the re-registration the right to appeal to the court for its cancellation.

When making an order under s 15, the court may, if it thinks fit, provide for the purchase of the shares of dissenting members, and 'for the reduction, accordingly, of the company's capital'.

The court has a similar discretion when responding to a petition by a minority of members in cases of oppression under s 205,[3] or to objections to a change of objects clause in the memorandum under s 10 of the 1963 Act.

---

1   Section 74 of the 1963 Act.
2   Ibid, s 75.
3   See Chapter 16.

Forfeiture, etc, under s 43

13.15 Section 43(1)[1] provides for the forfeiture, etc, of shares held by or on behalf of a public company. Where such shares are forfeited, surrendered or acquired, the company[2] must cancel them and reduce the amount of the share capital by the nominal value of the shares.[3]

STATUTORY CAPITAL MAINTENANCE RULES

13.16 To prevent an *indirect reduction* of share capital, a number of statutory rules exist which deal with the following matters:

(1) redemption of redeemable shares;
(2) restrictions on the acquisition by a company of its own shares or shares in a parent company;
(3) a requirement on the board of directors to call an extraordinary general meeting of the company to consider any serious loss of capital;
(4) the giving of financial assistance (loans) by a company for the purchasing of its own shares;
(5) a prohibition on issuing shares at a discount; and
(6) a requirement that dividends may only be payable out of profits.

We shall now consider each of these statutory requirements separately.

Redemption of redeemable shares

13.17 'Redeemable' shares include any shares which, at the option of the company or the shareholder, are liable to be redeemed.

Under s 207,[4] a company may, if so authorised by its articles, issue redeemable shares. It may also redeem these shares provided it follows the procedures for so doing contained in Part XI.[5]

Conditions for redemption

13.18 The conditions applying to the issue and redemption[6] of shares include:

(1) the nominal value of the non-redeemable issued capital must exceed 10 per cent of the value of the company's total issued share capital before redeemable shares can be issued or redeemed;

---

1 Of the 1983 Amendment Act – see Chapter 31.
2 Unless the shares or any interest in them is previously disposed of.
3 Section 43(3)(a).
4 Of the 1990 Act.
5 Ibid.
6 A company also has the power to convert shares into redeemable shares, and dissenting shareholders have a right to object – see s 210. See also s 64 of the 1963 Act for a company's restricted power to issue redeemable preference shares.

(2) the redeemable shares must be fully paid up;

(3) the terms of the redemption must provide for payment on redemption; and

(4) generally, these shares must be redeemed out of profits available for distribution.

Cancellation of shares on redemption

13.19 Shares redeemed pursuant to s 207 may be cancelled on redemption. Section 208 provides that where this happens and the shares are:

(1) redeemed wholly out of profits; or

(2) redeemed wholly or partly out of the proceeds of a fresh issue; and

(3) the amount of those proceeds is less than the nominal value of the shares redeemed (the *aggregable* difference); then

(4) a sum equal to the shares redeemed wholly out of profits[1] and, in the case of a redemption out of the proceeds of a fresh issue, the aggregable difference, must be transferred to a reserve fund.

Capital redemption reserve fund

13.20 The reserve fund created as in (4) above is known as a capital reserve fund, and the provisions of the 1963 Act relating to the reduction of capital[2] apply as if this fund was paid-up share capital of the company. In short, the fund is treated in the same way as paid-up share capital for the purposes of statutory restrictions on its reduction.

Payment of a premium on redemption

13.21 Section 206(2)(e) provides that the premium, if any, payable on redemption, must be paid out of profits except in the circumstances detailed in s 206(2). This exceptional case allows a company to pay a premium on redemption out of the proceeds of a fresh issue of shares made specifically for the purposes of the redemption.

Treasury shares

13.22 Instead of cancelling redeemed shares and creating a capital redemption reserve fund, a company may instead hold them as treasury shares under s 209. The company may not exercise voting rights, nor pay itself a dividend, in respect of treasury shares which it holds.

Treasury shares may be either cancelled[3] or re-issued.

---

1 As in (1) above.

2 Except as provided in s 208 of the 1990 Act.

3 If cancelled, the provisions of s 208 apply – see **13.19** above.

Re-issuing of treasury shares

13.23 Section 209(5) and (6) set out the detailed procedures to be followed by a company re-issuing treasury shares. Generally, the share capital of the company will not be regarded as having been increased by the re-issue of such shares. In addition, the company, in general meeting, must fix the price range for these shares in advance of their being re-issued for '*off-market*' purchases, ie sales otherwise than on a recognised Stock Exchange.

Restrictions on a company purchasing its own shares

13.24 In *Re Balgooley Distillery Co*,[1] the company had produced a large stock of whiskey which it had difficulty in selling. It then sold whiskey to a director in exchange for a number of his paid-up shares. The court held that the contract was valid and intra vires the company.

In *Trevor v Whitworth*,[2] a company, whose articles of association empowered it to do so, purchased its own shares. Here, the House of Lords overruled the *Balgooley Distillery* decision and held that for the company to purchase its own shares was, in effect, a reduction in capital. Accordingly, such a transaction was ultra vires and void, Lord Macnaghten saying:

> 'If the purchase of shares in (the company) was not one of the objects (stated in the memorandum) of that company, how could its capital be properly employed in that purchase?'

This common law 'ban' on a company purchasing its own shares has now been eased by the emergence of statutory exceptions in the 1983 Amendment Act and the 1990 Act.

Section 41 of the 1983 Amendment Act

13.25 Whilst s 41(1) restates the common law prohibition against a company purchasing[3] its own shares, it does allow for the following exceptional cases:

(1) the *redemption* of redeemable shares;[4]
(2) the *forfeiture* of shares for failure to pay any sums due to the company under them;[5]
(3) the acquisition of any shares in a reduction of capital made under s 72;[6]
(4) the purchase of shares as a result of a court order in response to minority objections;[7] and

---

1 (1886–87) 17 LR Ir 239.
2 (1887) 12 AC 409.
3 Section 44 of the 1983 Amendment Act also regulates the exercising of a lien or the taking of a charge on its own shares by a public company.
4 See **13.17** above.
5 See **13.15** above.
6 See **13.5** above.
7 Under s 10, s 15 or s 205 of the 1963 Act.

(5) reflecting a further desire by the legislature to extend these exceptional cases, the purchase of shares pursuant to ss 211 to 230 of the 1990 Act.

Let us now focus on this significant widening of companies' powers in 1990.

Purchasing shares under the 1990 Act

13.26   Under the 1990 Act, the purchase of its own shares by a company involves two types of transaction, ie market purchase and non-market purchase. However, s 211(2) makes it clear that the provisions of ss 207(2), 208 and 209 are to apply to purchases of its own shares in the same way as they apply to the redemption of shares. This ensures the replacement of the share capital purchased by the company with either:

(1) a fresh issue of shares; or
(2) a capital redemption reserve fund.

Market purchase

13.27   When a company buys its shares on a *recognised Stock Exchange* and is subject to a *marketing arrangement*, the transaction is styled a market purchase.

A company's shares are subject to a marketing arrangement on a recognised Stock Exchange if they are either:

(1) listed[1] on that Stock Exchange; or
(2) the company has been afforded facilities for dealings in those shares to take place in that Stock Exchange without prior permission[2] for individual transactions.

Generally, a company can buy its own shares (including redeemable shares) providing it is authorised to do so by a general meeting. This authority may be a general one or limited to a particular contract for the purchase of its shares by the company.

In the case of a *public company*, the authority must:

(1) specify the maximum number of shares which may be acquired; and
(2) state both the maximum and minimum prices which may be paid for the shares.

The company's authority may be varied, revoked or renewed by the company, again in general meeting.[3]

Off-market purchases

13.28   An off-market purchase[4] is basically any purchase which is not a market purchase.

---

1 Eg see Chapter 10.
2 Obtained from the authority governing that Stock Exchange – see s 212(2)(b).
3 Section 215.
4 See s 212(1)(a).

Section 213 provides that a company must not make an off-market purchase of its own shares unless it is authorised to make that contract by special resolution before the contract is entered into.

If the votes of the seller of the shares are responsible for the carrying of the special resolution to buy his shares, then the resolution may be ineffective.[1]

The other formalities involved with an off-market purchase are contained in s 213(4)–(7).

Contingent purchase contracts

13.29   A contingent purchase contract is one which does not amount to a contract by the company to purchase its own shares but under which, at some future time, it may become entitled to or obliged to purchase those shares.[2] A company may only purchase its shares on a contingent basis, if the contract is approved in advance and all the off-market purchase rules are observed.

Transfer or release of company's right to buy its own shares

13.30   Section 217 provides that any attempted assignment of the rights of a company under any contract authorised under s 213, s 214 or s 215 will be void. The company may, however, relinquish its right under such a contract provided that, in the case of an off-market or contingent purchase, the company's release is authorised by special resolution.

Payments by a company for its own shares

13.31   Generally, payments made by a company in respect of a share purchase or release under ss 213, 214 and 215 must be made out of its distributable profits.

Effect of company's failure to redeem or purchase its own shares

13.32   Section 219(2) makes it clear that a company will not be liable to pay damages for any failure on its part to redeem or purchase shares issued (or converted) under ss 210, 213, 214 and 215.

Purchase by subsidiary of shares in its holding company

13.33   Notwithstanding ss 32 and 60 of the 1963 Act, a subsidiary is now allowed to purchase shares in its holding company. The conditions regulating such transactions are contained in ss 224 and 225.[3]

---

1 See s 213(3).
2 Section 214(1).
3 Of the 1990 Act – see **28.6**.

The European Communities (Public Limited Companies Subsidiaries) Regulations 1997[1] implement EC Directive 92/101 to apply harmonised EU conditions on the purchase of shares in a public company by its subsidiary.

Disclosure of share purchases

13.34 Every company which has purchased shares pursuant to Part XI of the 1990 Act must, within 28 days after the shares were delivered to the company, send prescribed[2] details to the registrar of companies. It must also keep a copy of the contract at its registered office for the 10 years following the performance of the contract.[3]

EXTRAORDINARY MEETING FOLLOWING SERIOUS LOSS OF CAPITAL

13.35 The statutory rules preventing reductions in capital considered above are essentially aimed at preventing the re-payment of share capital to the members. Notwithstanding, it must be remembered that if the company's objects include trading, the statutory controls on loss of capital will not prevent a company incurring trading losses. As Buckley LJ commented in *Re Horsley & Weight Ltd*:[4]

> 'a company, and its directors acting on its behalf, can quite properly expend contributed capital for any purpose which is intra vires the company ... it is a misapprehension to suppose that the directors of a company owe a duty to the company's creditors to keep the contributed capital of the company intact.'

In short, company law does not insulate a company's capital base against erosion by losses suffered in the ordinary course of business trading. As a result, s 40[5] of the 1983 Amendment Act seeks to alert shareholders in the event of their company incurring a serious loss of capital.

Section 40 requirements to call a meeting

13.36 Where the net assets of a company fall to half or less of the amount of the company's called-up share capital, the directors must call an extraordinary general meeting of the company.

This meeting must be called within 28 days of a director becoming aware of the short fall in capital. The meeting must be held within a further 28[6] days. The

---

1 SI 1997/67 – see **28.6**.
2 See s 226.
3 See s 222.
4 [1982] 3 All ER 1045 (CA).
5 Implementing art 17 of the Second EC Company Law Directive (Directive 77/91/EEC).
6 Ie within 56 days of the director becoming aware of the drop in capital.

purpose of the meeting will be to consider what measures, if any, should be taken to deal with the serious financial situation.

Directors who fail to convene this meeting shall be guilty of a criminal offence. Section 40 applies to both public and private companies.

OTHER CAPITAL MAINTENANCE RULES

13.37 Other capital maintenance rules concern the giving of financial assistance by a company for the purchasing of its own shares; a prohibition against issuing shares at a discount and a requirement that dividends must only be paid out of profits.

Giving loans by a company for the purchase of its own shares

13.38 Where a company attempts to give financial assistance to another person to enable him to buy the lending company's own shares, this transaction would be viewed as an indirect reduction in capital. Accordingly, such transactions are regulated by s 60 of the 1963 Act.

Section 60(1) contains a general ban on a company giving loans or guarantees for the purchase, by any person, of its shares, or those of its holding company.

Conditions for valid loans or guarantees

13.39 Section 60(2)[1] refines the general prohibition against loans and guarantees by providing that s 60(1) will not apply if:

(1) the loan or guarantee was *sanctioned by a special resolution* passed within the previous 12 months; and
(2) the company has furnished with each notice of the meeting a copy of a *statutory declaration* stating:
    (a) the form which the assistance is to take;
    (b) the persons to whom the assistance is to be given;
    (c) the purpose for which the company intends those persons to use the assistance;
    (d) that the declarants have made a full inquiry into the affairs of the company and that, having done so, they have formed the opinion that the company, having carried out the transaction whereby such assistance is to be given, will be able to pay its debts in full as they become due.

Any director making this statutory declaration without reasonable grounds for his opinion, can incur criminal[2] sanctions.

---

1 See also s 60(15A).
2 Section 60(5).

Objections

13.40   Holders of 10 per cent or more of the nominal value of the issued capital may appeal to the court to cancel the special resolution.

Effect of breach of s 60 procedures

13.41   Any transaction in breach of s 60 requirements and procedures will be *voidable* at the company's option against *any person who had notice* of the breach.[1] Where the company is in breach, *every officer* in default will be *criminally liable.*[2]

In *Securities Trust Ltd v Associated Properties Ltd and Estates Development Ltd,*[3] the court held that for a special resolution under s 60 to be valid, *the giving of financial assistance had to be intra vires* the company. In the case, lending money was not one of the objects in the memorandum and an article of association expressly provided that none of the funds of the company could be used for the purchase of its shares. Not surprisingly, therefore, the company's resolution under s 60 was deemed null and void.

The case of *Re Northside Motor Co Ltd; Eddison v Allied Irish Banks*[4] dealt with the directors' statutory declaration. In his judgment, Costello J said:

> 'In my view, if a *resolution and/or statutory declaration are materially inaccurate and misleading,* they fail to comply with . . . s 60(2) and (3). As this happened in this case, the guarantee ... was illegal under s 60(1) and the money paid on foot of it recoverable by the liquidator.' (author's emphasis)

Third party notice of breach

13.42   Section 60(14) seems implicitly to render a transaction in breach of s 60 procedures voidable by the company only against a person who had notice of the breach. This assumption was confirmed by the High Court in *Lombard & Ulster Banking Ltd v Bank of Ireland.*[5] In this case, Costello J stated:

> 'even though the transaction was ... one which was rendered illegal by s 60(1), the company is not at liberty to avoid it as the plaintiffs had *no notice* of what had happened.' (author's emphasis)

Again, in *Bank of Ireland Finance v Rockfield Ltd,*[6] the Supreme Court interpreted notice in this context to mean *actual,* as distinct from *constructive,* notice.

---

1 Section 60(14), reinforced by the Supreme Court decision in *Bank of Ireland Finance Ltd v Rockfield Ltd* [1979] IR 21.
2 Section 60(15).
3 (Unreported) 19 November 1980 (HC).
4 (Unreported) 24 July 1985 (HC).
5 (Unreported) 2 June 1987 (HC).
6 [1979] IR 21. Constructive notice in this case was an omission by the plaintiffs to check a matter which they ought to have done. Nevertheless, because it was not actual notice, the plaintiff's action was successful.

Permitted loans under s 60

13.43   Section 60(13) exempts the following three categories of transactions from the s 60 restrictions:

(1) where lending is part of the ordinary business of the company, and the loan is made in the ordinary course of its business;
(2) certain loans for the purchase of fully paid shares by (or for the benefit of) employees, former employees, directors or subsidiary companies;
(3) loans to persons, other than directors, bona fide in the employment of the company or any subsidiary of the company, with a view to enabling those persons to purchase or subscribe for fully paid shares in the company or its holding company.

Restriction on public companies

13.44   Where a public company seeks to avail of the s 60(13) exemptions, it may only do so if its net assets are not reduced[1] as a result of the loan made.

Dividends and debts

13.45   Section 60 does not prohibit the payment of a dividend by the company, or the discharging of any liability lawfully incurred by it.[2]

Prohibition against issuing shares at a discount

13.46   Generally, shares may not be issued at a discount, ie sold at a price less than their nominal value. For example, in *The Ooregum Gold Mining Co of India Ltd v Roper*,[3] the market value of the £1 ordinary shares was 12½p. Because of the low market value of their ordinary shares, the company issued £1 preference shares, crediting 75p, as paid, and seeking only 25p per share to render them fully paid up. The court held that the issue was ultra vires the company, and the allottees were liable to pay £1 per share, Lord Macnaghten commenting:

> 'The dominant and cardinal principle of the [Companies] Acts is that the investor shall purchase immunity from liability beyond a certain limit on the terms that these shall be and remain a liability up to the limit [ie the nominal value of the share].'

The common law prohibition against issuing shares at a discount is preserved by s 27 of the 1983 Amendment Act which provides that 'the shares of a company shall not be allotted at a discount'.

---

1   See s 60(15B) and (15C).
2   Section 60(12).
3   [1892] AC 125.

Payment by instalments

13.47   Issuing shares at a discount should be distinguished from issuing them for full value, but not necessarily on allotment. If the company does not require payment in full on allotment, the shares are classified as partly paid shares.

Issuing shares at a premium

13.48   There is no prohibition against a company issuing shares at a premium, ie receiving a price greater than the par value. For example, if a company issues £1 ordinary shares at £1.50, then they are issued at a premium of 50p.

When a company issues shares at a premium,[1] a sum equal to the value of the premiums received on those shares must be transferred to a special account known as the *Share Premium Account*. Generally, the fund in the Share Premium Account is to be treated as share capital except that it may be used to allot members of the company bonus shares.[2]

Payment of dividends only out of profits

13.49   At common law, it was possible for a company to pay dividends out of its profits without first making good a previous loss. As Lindley LJ stated:[3]

> 'There is nothing at all in the Acts about how dividends are to be paid, nor how profits are to be reckoned; all that is left ... to the commercial world. It is not a subject for an Act of Parliament to say how accounts are to be kept; what is to be put into a capital account ... and an income account, is left to men of business.'

A change in public policy almost a century later manifested itself in Part IV of the 1983 Amendment Act. Part IV, consisting of ss 45 to 51, enacts rules governing the distribution of profits and assets. The *fundamental rule* in s 45 is that a company must not make a distribution except out of profits available for the purpose. The profits available for this purpose are the company's accumulated realised profits, less its accumulated realised losses.

Accumulated profits less accumulated losses means that losses of previous years must be deducted from any current distributable surplus before arriving at a distributable profits figure.

Any increase in the value of a retained asset cannot be taken into account when reckoning a company's profit because it is not *realised*.

Distribution

13.50   The term 'distribution' is defined in s 51(2) of the 1983 Amendment Act. It includes every distribution of a company's assets to members of the company, whether in cash or otherwise. This includes the payment of

---

1 Whether for cash or otherwise.
2 See s 62 of the 1963 Act and **13.4** above.
3 In *Lee v Neuchatel Asphalte Co* (1889) 41 ChD 1 (CA).

dividends,[1] it does not, however, because of s 51(2), include distributions made by way of:

(1) an issue of bonus shares;
(2) the redemption of preference shares;
(3) the redemption or purchase of shares out of the proceeds of a fresh issue made for that purpose;
(4) the reduction of share capital by extinguishing or reducing the liability of members on any of its shares which are not paid up; and
(5) a distribution of assets to members of the company on its winding up.

The rules on distributable profits apply to both private and public companies. The latter, however, are subject to an additional restriction.

Profits of public companies

13.51 Under s 46(1), a plc may only make a distribution of profits:

(1) if the amount of its net assets is not less than the aggregate of the company's called-up share capital and its undistributable reserves; and
(2) if, and to the extent that, the distribution does not reduce the amount of those assets to less than that aggregate.

Undistributable reserves are defined in s 46(2). They include any surplus of revalued accumulated unrealised profits over accumulated unrealised losses.

The effect of s 46 is to regulate the valuation of a plc's net worth by ensuring that all assets are considered and their values aggregated.

Specialist companies

13.52 There are special rules in the 1983 Amendment Act for determining the distributable profits of investment[2] and life assurance[3] companies.

The relevant accounts

13.53 Whether or not a company has distributable profits will have to be determined by reference to the latest properly audited accounts[4] – see Chapter 24.

ALTERATION OF CAPITAL

13.54 A reduction in capital must be distinguished from a diminution of and an increase in capital.

---

1 See Part VII of this book.
2 Section 47.
3 Section 48.
4 Section 49.

Increase in and diminution of share capital

13.55 By virtue of ss 68 and 69,[1] a company may *increase* its share capital, or, indeed, make other alterations which do not reduce its capital, providing they are authorised by the articles. For example, arts 44 and 45 of Table A provide as follows:

> '**44.** The company may from time to time by *ordinary resolution* increase the share capital by such sum, to be divided into shares of such amount, as the resolution shall prescribe.
>
> **45.** The company may by *ordinary resolution*:
> (a) consolidate and divide all or any of its share capital into shares of larger amount than its existing shares;
> (b) subdivide its existing shares, or any of them, into shares of smaller amount than is fixed by the memorandum of association subject, nevertheless, to section 68(1)(d) of the Act;
> (c) cancel any shares which, at the date of the passing of the resolution, have not been taken or agreed to be taken by any person.'

The art 45 alterations would be classified as a diminution, rather than a reduction in share capital.

---

1 Of the 1963 Act.

Chapter 14

ROLES OF DIRECTORS AND INVESTORS IN OPERATING THE COMPANY

THE UNDERLYING RELATIONSHIPS

14.1   When considering the management of the company, difficulties sometimes arise in understanding the underlying relationships between:

(1) the company; and
(2) the directors and investors (or shareholders).

The company

14.2   The company is a separate legal personality on its own account. It is quite distinct from the members (or investors) who own it. The company can own property and enter into contracts in its own right. However, being an artificial creation of the law, a company can only make decisions and act through human agents. The management of a company must therefore be carried out by such agents.

Company management

14.3   It is useful at this stage to refine the term 'management' in the context of company law. The day-to-day management of the company's affairs is the responsibility of its directors and officers. Investors, as owners, have no right to act on behalf of the company in the day-to-day management of its affairs.

A second tier of company management is the taking of decisions to amend the company's memorandum and/or articles of association. Such corporate decisions affecting fundamental constitutional aspects of the company, may impinge directly on investors' contractual rights. Accordingly, investors have a part to play in the voting for and against such changes.

THE DIRECTOR'S ROLE

14.4   Directors are the human agents who have the powers and responsibilities for the day-to-day management of the company. Because of the separation of ownership and management,[1] members, as members, are *not* entitled to take part in the day-to-day management of the company which, in fact, as investors, they own.

---

1 See Chapter 4.

Definition of directors

14.5   In *Re Forest of Dean Coal Mining Co*,[1] Jessel MR said:

> 'It does not matter what you call [directors], so long as you understand what their true position is, which is that they are merely commercial men, managing a trading concern for the benefit of themselves and all other shareholders in it.'

Section 2 of the 1963 Act defines directors as including any person occupying the position of director, by whatever name called.

Section 27 of the 1990 Act introduced the new concept of a *shadow director* into Irish law. A shadow director is a person in accordance with whose directions or instructions, the directors of a company are accustomed to act.

A director is an office holder, not an employee of the company. He may, however, be both a director and an employee. As Kenny J said in *Dairy Lee Ltd; Stakelum v Canning*:[2]

> 'A director holds his office under articles of association of the company and so, as a director, is not an employee or a clerk or servant of the company. Article 85 of the articles in Table A which applied to this company, permits him to hold any other office or place of profit under the company in conjunction with his office of director for such period and on such terms as to remuneration and otherwise as the directors may determine. The result is that a director may be employed by the company not as a director but as a salaried employee.'

The term *executive director* is used to denote a director who is also a full-time employee/manager of the company. A *non-executive director* is simply an office holder. He does not also have a contract of employment with the company.

14.6   The function of directors is not to act as employees of the company. Their role is essentially to manage it. When carrying out their managerial role they act at times like trustees, at other times like ordinary agents. For example, in *Great Eastern Railway v Turner*,[3] Lord Selborne stated:

> 'The directors are mere trustees or agents of the company – trustees of the company's money and property – agents in the transactions which they enter into on behalf of the company.'

Directors as quasi-trustees

14.7   In *Smith v Anderson*,[4] James LJ said:

> 'A trustee is . . . the owner of property and deals with it as a principal . . . A director never enters into a contract for himself, but . . . for his principal, ie for the company . . . for whom he is acting (as agent).'

Directors are not trustees because:

---

1   (1878) 10 ChD 450.
2   [1976] IR 314 (HC).
3   (1872) LR 8 ChApp 149.
4   (1880) 15 ChD 247.

(1) the company's property and monies are owned by the company – not by the directors; and

(2) their duties of care and skill[1] are lower than those required of trustees. As a result, their position may more correctly be described as that of 'quasi-trustees'.

Duties as quasi-trustees

14.8 As quasi-trustees, directors stand in a fiduciary position in relation to the company and owe the following fundamental duties to it:

(1) they must *account for their control* over the company's money; any money improperly paid out must be refunded;

(2) they must *exercise their powers honestly* in the interests of the company and not for themselves;

(3) they must *not make any secret profit* for themselves when acting for the company; and

(4) they must *not be interested in a contract* with the company unless the articles permit it.

The directors owe these duties to the company, and not to the individual shareholders who own it.[2]

Directors as agents

14.9 Directors are also human agents who enable the non-human company to carry on its business.

When directors, as agents in transactions, make contracts on behalf of the company, they generally incur no personal liability under these contracts.[3] It is the company, as principal, who will be liable under them.

At common law, directors will only become liable under such contracts if, when negotiating them, they exceeded the powers given to them by the memorandum and articles of association.[4] They may also be liable for breach of warranty of authority (in agency law) or breach of a statutory duty.

14.10 The duties of a director may be classified, broadly, as:

(1) *Fiduciary duties*: in *Conflicts of Interest; Efficiency, Fairness and Corporate Structure*, A.G. Anderson[5] comments:

---

1 See Part V.

2 See *Percival v Wright* [1902] 2 Ch 421.

3 Always assuming the directors have acted intra vires the company's objects and within their own authority.

4 See Chapter 15.

5 In *UCLA Law Review*. Extracts reproduced in H.R. Hahlo and J.H. Farrar *Hahlo's Cases and Materials on Company Law* (Sweet & Maxwell, third edition, 1987), p 365.

'Fiduciary duties economise on transaction costs by simply obliging the fiduciary to act in the best interests of his beneficiary and to refrain from self interested behaviour not specifically allowed. ...

Fiduciary duties and conflict of interest reflect a compromise between efficiency and fairness. The rules are efficient because they are a substitute for more costly contracts or regulation; they are fair because they restrict cheating to some extent ...'

(2) *Duties of care and skill,* ie levels of competency expected from directors; and
(3) *Statutory duties*: these supplement both common law fiduciary duties and duties of care and skill.

These directors' duties, and their liabilities in respect of breaches of them, are dealt with in Chapters 19 to 23.

THE MEMBER'S ROLE

14.11 Any person who has purchased shares and 'who agrees to become a member of the company and whose name is entered in its register of members, shall become a member of the company'.[1]

The rights of investors, as members, stem from their legal relationship with the company, which can vary depending on the particular kind of shares they hold.

Generally, the members have no right to take part in the day-to-day running of the company: that is the function of the directors. The members exercise their rights over the company's strategic policies by voting on various resolutions which may be put to them from time to time, at the company's annual general meeting.

Members who hold ordinary shares have the voting right to appoint, and if necessary, change the board of directors.

Legal relationship with the company

14.12 There is a legal relationship between the company and its members, and between members and other investors. The fulcrum for these relationships is s 25 of the 1963 Act. Section 25 states that the articles of association bind both the company and the members, to the same extent as if the articles had been signed and sealed by each member individually, and that each member had given a covenant to observe the articles. It will be seen therefore, that the focal point of the relationship between the company and its investors is the articles of association. Each shareholder, on becoming a member, is deemed to have made a contract with the company to observe the articles.[2]

---

1 Section 31(2) of the 1963 Act.
2 This contract extends to agreeing to any alterations of the memorandum and articles, if and when validly made.

Each investor, as a member, is thus contractually bound to the company, through the articles, and the company is bound to each member. But the contract only binds the company and the investors, as members. Members cannot exercise rights against the company in any other capacity. For example, in *Eley v Positive Government Security Life Assurance Co*,[1] a member who had acted as the company's solicitor, was not allowed to treat the articles of association as a contract for the provision of legal services by himself to the company.

Each investor is also contractually bound to all the other members. The articles regulate the rights of company members between themselves. As Lord Hershell said, in *Welton v Saffery*:[2]

> 'It is quite true that the articles constitute a contract between each member and the company, and that there is no contract in terms between the individual members of the company; but the articles do not any the less, in my opinion, regulate their rights inter se. Such rights can only be enforced by or against a member through the company, or through the liquidator representing the company; but I think that no member has, as between himself and another member, any right beyond that which the contract with the company gives.'

If the articles give a member an individual right, it may be directly enforced by him without joining the company as a party.[3]

APPOINTMENT OF DIRECTORS BY MEMBERS

14.13   Private and public companies must have a minimum of two directors[4] (every company must also have a secretary, who may be one of the directors).

First directors

14.14   The names of the *first directors* must be delivered to the registrar of companies with the memorandum of association.[5]

It is not necessary for directors to have shareholding in a company. In practice, though, many directors will also be members.[6]

If the articles provide for the directors to hold *qualification* shares, ie to purchase a minimum number of shares, they must obtain these share qualifications within two months of their appointment.[7] The first appointees must consent, in writing, to becoming directors of the company.[8]

---

1   (1876) 1 Ex D 88.
2   [1897] AC 299.
3   *Rayfield v Hands* [1960] Ch 1.
4   Section 174 of the 1963 Act.
5   Section 3 of the 1983 Amendment Act.
6   Particularly of private companies.
7   Or such shorter time as the articles may specify – s 180 of the 1963 Act.
8   See s 179 of the 1963 Act, for details.

Subsequent directors

14.15   Appointments subsequent to the first directors must be made in the manner provided by the articles. If no provision is made in the articles, they must be elected by the members in general meeting.

Rotation of directors

14.16   Table A[1] provides as follows:

'**92.** At the first annual general meeting of the company all the directors shall retire from office, and at the annual general meeting in every subsequent year, one-third of the directors for the time being, or, if their number is not three or a multiple of three, then the number nearest one-third shall retire from office.

93. The directors to retire in every year shall be those who have been longest in office since their last election but as between persons who became directors on the same day, those to retire shall (unless they otherwise agree among themselves) be determined by lot.

94. A retiring director shall be eligible for re-election.'

Increase or reduction in numbers of directors

14.17   Table A, arts 97 and 98 deal with changes in numbers of directors as follows:

'**97.** The company may from time to time by ordinary resolution increase or reduce the number of directors and may also determine in what rotation the increased or reduced number is to go out of office.

98. The directors shall have power at any time and from time to time to appoint any person to be a director, either to fill a casual vacancy or as an addition to the existing directors, but so that the total number of directors shall not any time exceed the number fixed in accordance with these regulations. Any director so appointed shall hold office only until the next following annual general meeting, and shall then be eligible for re-election but shall not be taken into account in determining the directors who are to retire by rotation at such meeting.'

Removal of directors

14.18   Again, provision is made in Table A for the members to remove any director and to replace him, the relevant articles providing:

'**99.** The company may, by ordinary resolution, of which extended notice has been given in accordance with section 142 of the Act, remove any director before the expiration of his period of office notwithstanding anything in these regulations or in any agreement between the company and such director. Such removal shall be without prejudice to any claim such director may have for damages for breach of any contract of service between him and the company.

---

1 In the 1963 Act, Sch 1.

100. The company may, by ordinary resolution, appoint another person in place of a director removed from office under regulation 99 and without prejudice to the powers of the directors under regulation 98 the company in general meeting may appoint any person to be a director either to fill a casual vacancy or as an additional director. A person appointed in place of a director so removed or to fill such a vacancy shall be subject to retirement at the same time as if he had become a director on the day on which the director in whose place he is appointed was last elected a director.'

The rights of a removed director are dealt with at **14.27** below.

Defects in appointment

14.19 The acts of a director on behalf of the company will be valid, notwithstanding any defects which may afterwards be discovered in his appointment or qualifications.[1]

Disqualification of directors

14.20 Table A, art 91, provides that the office of director must be vacated if the director:

(1) ceases to be a director by virtue of s 180 of the 1963 Act, ie fails to obtain his qualification shares; or
(2) is adjudged bankrupt in the State or in Northern Ireland or Great Britain or makes an arrangement or composition with his creditors generally; or
(3) becomes prohibited from being a director by reason of any order made under s 184 of the Act; or
(4) becomes of unsound mind; or
(5) resigns his office by notice in writing to the company; or
(6) is convicted of an indictable offence unless the directors otherwise determine; or
(7) is for more than six months absent without permission of the directors from meetings of the directors held during that period.

In Chapter 23, we shall consider disqualification and restriction of directors under the 1990 Act, Part VII of which replaces s 184 in (3) above.

Remuneration of directors

14.21 Directors are not employees of the company. They are elected office holders who control and manage the company's affairs. Accordingly, they are not entitled to remuneration for their services unless, as is usual, there is provision for such payments in the articles.[2] For example, art 76 of Table A provides that:

---

1 See s 181 of the 1963 Act for an example of a procedural defect in appointing a director.
2 *Woolf v East Nigel Co* (1905) 21 TLR 660.

'The remuneration of the directors shall from time to time be determined by the company in general meeting. . . . The directors may also be paid all travelling, hotel and other expenses properly incurred by them in attending meetings . . . or in connection with the business of the company.'

Section 185 of the 1963 Act prohibits tax-free payments to directors.

If remuneration is voted to the directors under the articles, it then constitutes a debt due from the company and may, if necessary, be paid out of capital.[1] Furthermore, the company cannot retrospectively amend its articles to remove the directors' entitlement to accrued remuneration.[2]

Loans to directors

14.22   Section 192[3] specifies the information which must be included in the company's annual accounts in relation to loans made to any director.

Disclosure of directors' salaries and emoluments

14.23   Section 191 contains the particulars of directors' salaries and payments which must be given in the company's annual accounts.

General duty of disclosure on directors (and secretary)

14.24   Every director (and secretary) must give notice to the company, in writing, of relevant loans or emoluments for the purpose of compliance[4] with ss 192 and 191.

Particulars of directors to be shown in company letter headings

14.25   Particulars relating to its directors must be shown in all the company's business letters. These particulars are the director's name, initials and nationality, if not Irish.[5]

Assignment of office by directors

14.26   Any transfer by a director, of his office, to another person, even with the agreement of the company,[6] will be of no effect unless and until it is approved

---

1   *Re Lundy Granite Co* (1872) 26 LT 673.
2   They may, however, be able to do so prospectively – see *Swabey v Port Darwin Gold Mining Co* (1889) 1 Meg 385 (CA).
3   Of the 1963 Act.
4   Also with s 190 relating to the register of directors' shareholdings.
5   See s 196.
6   Ie through the board of directors.

by a special resolution of the company. These provisions in s 199[1] are applicable to assignments inter vivos.[2] They are inappropriate where the assignment is made by will or codicil.[3]

REMOVAL OF DIRECTORS

14.27   Section 182 of the 1963 Act gives the members of a company the power to remove any director from office by ordinary resolution, except a director in a private company who was appointed for life.

Extended notice[4] of 28 days must be given of any resolution to remove a director. The detailed procedures are contained in s 182(2)–(7). Under them, the director in question is entitled to make written representations to the meeting in his defence. Section 182(7) also makes it clear that the section does not invalidate the dismissal of a director by the board alone, if such a dismissals procedure is expressly authorised by the articles.

Natural justice

14.28   When dismissing a director, even under s 182, the company must also comply with the requirements of natural justice. As Walsh J stated in *Glover v BLN Ltd*:[5]

> 'In my view, it was necessarily an implied term of the contract that this inquiry and determination should be fairly conducted ...
>   The plaintiff was neither told of the charges against him nor was he given any opportunity of dealing with them before the board of directors arrival at its decision to dismiss him.'

The court, accordingly, held that there had been a breach of natural justice and the plaintiff was entitled to damages for wrongful dismissal.

In the *Glover* case, the plaintiff was an executive director, ie he was an employee of the company as well as an office holder. However, where a non-executive director is dismissed, the rules of natural justice still apply. This was confirmed by *Garvey v Ireland*,[6] which seems to imply a constitutional right to fairness of procedures generally in the making of such decisions.

DIRECTORS' SERVICE CONTRACTS

14.29   There has been a tendency during the last few decades to appoint company executives to the board. Such appointees may be styled 'technical',

---

1 Of the 1963 Act.
2 Ie between living persons.
3 *Fitzpatrick v Fitzpatricks Footwear Ltd* (unreported) 18 November 1970 (HC).
4 See s 142.
5 [1973] IR 388 (SC).
6 [1981] IR 25 (SC).

'financial', 'personnel' or even managing director. All these executive directors effectively hold two posts. One post is the office of director; the second post is the 'service' or employment contract with the company – a fact acknowledged by s 182(7) which provides, inter alia:

> 'nothing in this section shall be taken as depriving a person removed thereunder of compensation or damages, – payable to him in respect of the determination of any (other) appointment terminating with that as director.'

The Supreme Court in *Carvill v Irish Industrial Bank Ltd*[1] confirmed that the dismissal of a director under s 182 was without prejudice to any rights he may have to damages for breach of a contract of employment.

The managing director's contract

14.30   Article 110 of Table A provides that:

> 'The directors may from time to time appoint one or more of themselves to the office of managing director for such period and on such terms as to remuneration and otherwise as they think fit, and, subject to the terms of any agreement entered into any particular case, may revoke such appointment.'

The directors may confer or delegate any of their powers to the managing director.

A company may be liable in damages if the appointment of a managing director is prematurely terminated, either as a consequence of an alteration of the articles,[2] or his removal from office under s 182, if this action is inconsistent with his contract of service.[3]

1990 Act limitations on directors' service contracts

14.31   Section 28 of the 1990 Act seeks to prevent the possible abuse of s 182 whereby directors could, as a board, agree long-term service contracts for themselves with the company without having to obtain the approval of the shareholders. The significance of these long-term contracts were that if the members did dismiss any directors, the compensation payable to them would usually be based on the unexpired portion of their service contracts.

If the effect of a clause in a director's service contract is to extend the contract for a period exceeding five years,[4] then under s 28, that clause is void unless it is first approved by the company in general meeting.[5]

---

1 [1968] IR 325.
2 *Southern Foundries (1926) Ltd v Shirlaw* [1940] AC 701.
3 Cf *Shindler v Northern Raincoat Ltd* [1960] 1 WLR 1038.
4 During which time his employment cannot be terminated by the company giving reasonable notice, or can only be terminated in specified circumstances.
5 See s 28 for the appropriate procedures.

Inspection of directors' service contracts

14.32 A copy of each director's service contract, or, if not in writing, a written memorandum setting out its terms, must be kept by the company for inspection by its members.[1]

Authority of directors

14.33 The authority of the directors to act as agents of the company is examined later in Chapter 18 and Part V.

THE COMPANY SECRETARY'S ROLE

14.34 Clearly, the directors are officers of the company. The term 'company officer' extends to include the company secretary (see ss 174 and 175 of the 1963 Act).

The traditional judicial attitude[2] to the company secretary was that:

> 'he is a mere servant, his position is that he is to do what he is told, and no person can assume that he has any authority to represent anything at all ...'

In 1902, Lord MacNaghten[3] described his duties as 'of a limited and of a somewhat humble character'. This judicial attitude changed in 1971 following the Court of Appeal's decision in *Panorama Developments Ltd v Fidelis Furnishing Fabrics Ltd*.[4] As a result of this decision, the secretary is no longer regarded as a mere clerk but as *the chief administrative officer* of the company with ostensible authority to enter into many contracts on the company's behalf.

Functions as chief administrative officer

14.35 Whilst the functions of the secretary are not defined in the Companies Acts, it is clear that he is the official with special responsibility for ensuring compliance with the companies legislation. In particular, the secretary will:

(1) keep the registered books of the company, including the registers of:
    (a) members;[5]
    (b) directors and secretaries;[6]
    (c) directors' and secretaries' shareholdings[7] (including those of spouses and children);
    (d) debenture-holders.[8]

---

1 Section 50 of the 1990 Act.
2 Per Lord Esher in *Barnett Hoares & Co v South London Tramways Co* (1887) 18 QBD 815 (CA).
3 In *George Whitechurch Ltd v Cavanagh* [1902] AC 117.
4 [1971] 3 All ER 16.
5 Sections 117 to 124 of the 1963 Act.
6 Section 195, as amended by s 8 of the 1982 Amendment Act and s 51 of the 1990 Act.
7 Section 190, as amended by ss 53 to 66 of the 1990 Act.
8 Sections 91 to 93 of the 1963 Act.

A register of charges[1] must be kept centrally by the registrar of companies for each company.

Section 378[2] allows the registered books to be kept in book form or in any other manner, whilst s 4 of the 1977 Amendment Act permits the use of computers, etc, for the maintenance of certain company records;

(2) making the proper returns to the registrar, eg the Annual Return;[3]

(3) notifying the registrar of any changes to the memorandum or the articles of association;

(4) giving the required period of notice for meetings to members;

(5) preparing and recording the minutes of general meetings[4] and meetings of the board of directors;

(6) issuing share certificates and dealing with the transfer of shares;

(7) witnessing the use of the seal of the company; and

(8) delivering particulars of charges entered into by the company, to the registrar.

In large public companies, an external company may be employed to carry out some of these functions, and the secretary's duties may be expanded into managerial functions.

Authority of the secretary

14.36   The extent of the authority of a company secretary to act as agent for the company is dealt with in Chapter 18, at **18.18** and **18.25**.

Qualifications required

14.37   The increasing recognition given to the role of the company secretary is emphasised further by the introduction of qualifications for the secretaries of public companies by the 1990 Act. Section 236 provides that it shall be the duty of the directors to take all reasonable steps to secure that the secretary of the company is a person who appears to them to have the requisite knowledge and experience to discharge the functions of secretary of the company and who:

(a) on the commencement of this section held the office of secretary of the company; or

(b) for at least three years of the five years immediately preceding his appointment as secretary held the office of secretary of a company; or

(c) is a member of a body for the time being recognised for the purposes of this section by the Minister; or

(d) is a person who, by virtue of his holding or having held any other position or his being a member of any other body, appears to the directors to be capable of discharging those functions.

---

1 Sections 103 to 110 of the 1963 Act – see **33.11**.

2 Of the 1963 Act.

3 See Part VI.

4 See Chapter 15.

On 31 December 1995, the following two bodies were recognised by the Minister under s 236(c):

(1) The Institute of Chartered Secretaries and Administrators;
(2) The Irish Institute of Secretaries and Administrators.

It should be noted, though, that it is not obligatory for a secretary of a plc to be a member of a recognised body.

Appointment of secretary

14.38 Every company must have a secretary, who may be one of the directors.[1] The first secretary is the person[2] named as such in the statement delivered to the registrar.[3] Subsequent appointments will be made by the directors, and any secretary[4] so appointed, may be removed by them.[5]

---

1 Section 175 of the 1963 Act.
2 Or body corporate.
3 Under s 3 of the 1982 Amendment Act.
4 Or joint secretaries.
5 See arts 113 and 114 of Table A.

Chapter 15

COMPANY MEETINGS AND RESOLUTIONS

TYPES OF MEETINGS

15.1   Meetings play a key part in the operation of any company by its human agents, ie its officers and members. There are three different types of meeting. These are:

(1) *company meetings* attended by members and directors;
(2) *board meetings* attended by the directors and secretary. These meetings are dealt with in Chapter 19; and
(3) *third party meetings*, ie meetings necessary[1] between company creditors and management. Consideration of third party meetings will be deferred until Part X.

COMPANY MEETINGS

15.2   Company meetings fall into the two categories of Annual and Extra-ordinary General Meetings. In addition, if the interests of a particular class of shareholders are to be affected, the company may have to convene separate 'class meetings' – see **12.22** and **13.8**.

Annual General Meetings (AGMs)

15.3   The Annual General Meeting (AGM) is the most important meeting of the company investors. It must be held every 12 months, and not more than 15 months must elapse between each meeting.[2]

Notice

15.4   Section 133 sets out the statutory periods of notice for calling company meetings.[3] In respect of AGMs, the minimum period of written notice is 21 days. Any provision in a company's articles specifying a shorter notice period will be void.

---

1 In the event of a company liquidation.
2 Except that the company has 18 months to hold the first AGM after the company is formed – see s 131 of the 1963 Act which also makes provision for failure by the directors to call an AGM.
3 Except those at which a special resolution is to be passed which fall to be considered under s 141.

Waiver of notice

15.5   If all the members, together with the auditors, agree, a meeting called with less than 21 days' notice shall be deemed to have been duly called.[1]

Adjourned AGMs

15.6   Generally, adjourned meetings do not need any particular notice unless:

(1) the articles require it;
(2) new business is to be placed on the agenda; or
(3) the adjournment took place without a date being fixed for the next meeting.

Single-member companies

15.7   The sole member of a single-member company may decide to dispense with the holding of AGMs. If he so decides, all the powers exercisable by the company in general meeting shall be exercisable by the sole member, without the need to hold a general meeting for the purpose.

The conditions under which sole members are given these privileges are set out in regs 8 and 9 of the European Communities (Single-Member Private Limited Companies) Regulations, 1994 – see **8.7**.

Business at AGMs

15.8   Generally, the following items are deemed ordinary business at an AGM:

(1) declaring a dividend;
(2) considering the accounts;
(3) considering the balance sheets;
(4) considering the reports of directors and auditors;
(5) electing replacement directors;
(6) re-appointing retiring auditors;
(7) fixing the remuneration of the auditors.

Consideration of these items give the investors an opportunity of judging the effectiveness of the directors' stewardship of their company – see Part VI.

All other items are special business.[2] So, too, is all business transacted at an Extraordinary General Meeting.

Location of AGM

15.9   Generally, the AGM must be held in Ireland.[3]

---

1 Section 133(3).
2 See art 53 of Table A. Examples would include a proposal to alter the articles under s 15 of the 1963 Act.
3 Section 140 of the 1963 Act.

Extraordinary General Meetings (EGMs)

15.10 EGMs may be requisitioned by the members under s 132.[1] The directors must call such a meeting if the requisitionists hold at least one-tenth of the paid-up voting capital or, if there is no share capital, hold a minimum of one-tenth of the total voting rights in the company.

The requisition must state the objects of the meeting and be signed by the requisitionists and deposited at the registered office of the company. If the directors do not convene the meeting within 21 days, the requisitionists themselves may do so.

The directors must also call an EGM in the event of a serious loss of capital.[2]

Notice

15.11 Section 133(2)(b) prescribes the following periods of written notice for meetings which are *not* AGMs or a meeting for the passing of a special resolution:

(1) 14 days for public companies (generally); and
(2) 7 days for private or unlimited companies.

If the passing of a special resolution is proposed at the EGM, the minimum notice will be 21 days. The notice should also contain the exact wording of the resolution to be proposed and must be served in accordance with art 51.

Business at EGM

15.12 All items of business at an EGM are classified as special business.[3]

Power to order the holding of a meeting

15.13 If default is made in holding an AGM, the *Minister* may, on the application of any member of the company, call, or direct the calling of, an AGM.[4]

Again, if for any reason it is impracticable to call a meeting, the *court* may, either on its own motion, or on the application of any director or member, order a meeting to be held.[5] In *Angelis v Algemene Bank Netherland (Ireland) Ltd and Others*,[6] it was held that the court will only convene such a meeting where it is otherwise impracticable to convene it. In that case, the requisition served on the directors to convene a meeting was invalid so they were not bound to act on

---

1 Of the 1963 Act.
2 Under s 40 of the 1983 Amendment Act – see **13.35**.
3 Per art 53 of Table A.
4 Section 131(3).
5 Section 135.
6 (Unreported) 4 July 1974 (HC).

it. Accordingly, the court did not order the meeting because the directors could have convened it if the requisition had been valid. As to the invalidity, Kenny J said:

> 'It seems to me to be probable that the plaintiff agreed to resign as a director of the company and therefore he cannot convene a meeting of directors. By letter dated 14 June 1974 he purported to convene a directors' meeting for the 17 June 1974. If this be read as a requisition to call a meeting of the company, then it was clearly invalid because under s 132 of the Companies Act 1963 the directors have a period of 21 days within which to convene a meeting.'

Any *two or more members* holding at least 10 per cent of the issued capital may also call a meeting, unless the articles provide otherwise – see s 134(b).

Proceedings at general meetings

15.14   The proceedings at general meetings will be regulated by the company's articles of association. As many companies adopt Table A, the contents of arts 53 to 74 are outlined hereunder.

Quorum of members

15.15   Section 134(c) and arts 54 and 55 deal with the quorum required. No business can be transacted at a general meeting unless a quorum of members is *present at the time when the meeting proceeds to business.*

Section 134(c) provides that for a private company, two members constitute a quorum, and for all other companies, three members. These members must be personally present at the meeting – *proxies* cannot be counted for this purpose.

In the case of a single-member company, one member present in person or by proxy will constitute a quorum. This may also apply when an AGM is called by the Minister under s 131(3).

Article 55 sets out the procedure to be followed if, within half an hour, there is no quorum present.

Chairman

15.16   Any member present at the meeting may be elected chairman,[1] unless the articles provide otherwise. However, the articles normally make such provision. For example, under art 56, the chairman of the board of directors is to preside as chairman of every AGM. If he is unavailable, the chairman will be elected from one of the directors present: the decision being made by the directors. If no director is present or willing to act as chairman, the members may choose one of their members to chair the meeting – see art 57.

---

1 Section 134(d).

During the meeting, the chairman must allow the minority of shareholders a reasonable amount of time in which to put forward their case.[1]

Article 61 confers a casting or second vote on the chairman. It is he who will decide on the validity of any disputes as to qualifications of members to vote – art 67.

Adjournment

15.17 The chairman may, with the consent of the meeting, or must, if directed by it, adjourn the meeting – art 58.

Voting

15.18 Any resolution put to the vote of the meeting will be decided on a show of hands, *unless* a poll is demanded in accordance with art 59.[2]

Article 63 provides that, subject to the right to vote being attached to the share class, on a show of hands every member present and every proxy shall have one vote.

When the voting is by poll,[3] every member will have one vote for each share which he holds.

In *Kinsella and Others v Alliance and Dublin Consumers Gas Co & Others*,[4] it was held that it was only those persons whose names were entered in the register of members who were entitled to vote at a general meeting.[5]

Voting may be either personally or by proxy.

Proxies

15.19 Any member who is unable to attend a general meeting, is entitled to appoint another person to attend and vote as his proxy. Articles 69 to 71 set out the procedures for the appointment of a proxy. A draft proxy appointment form is contained in art 71.

A body corporate which is a member, may, by resolution of its directors or general meeting, appoint a person to act as its representative at a general meeting.[6]

---

1 *Wall v London and Northern Assets Corp* [1898] 2 Ch 469.
2 See also arts 60 to 62.
3 In *Re Credit Finance Bank plc* (unreported) 9 June 1982 (HC), it was decided that it is permissible to vote by poll without having a show of hands first.
4 (Unreported) 5 October 1982 (HC).
5 See also arts 64 to 67 which deal with, inter alia, joint shareholders, incapacity of members and arrears in paying up calls made on shares.
6 Article 74.

RESOLUTIONS

15.20 There are two[1] kinds of resolution: ordinary and special.

Ordinary resolution

15.21 An ordinary resolution is one which is passed by a simple majority of the members present and voting, or by a majority of votes cast where voting is in a poll.

Special resolution

15.22 A special resolution is defined in s 141 as any resolution which:

(1) is passed by not less than three-quarters of the votes actually cast;
(2) at a general meeting;
(3) after at least 21 days' notice of the meeting;
(4) which notice specifies the intention to propose the resolution as a special resolution.

Thus, at the option of the proposer, any resolution could become a special resolution but there are very few proposals which require to be passed as special resolutions. However, under s 141(2), less notice can be given if a majority of the number of members having the right to attend and vote, and holding between them at least 90 per cent of the nominal value of the shares giving such right, agree to the shortened notice.

Unless a poll is demanded, a declaration by the chairman that the resolution is carried shall be conclusive evidence of the fact, without proof of the actual numbers of votes cast in favour of or against the resolution.[2] If, though, the chairman acted fraudulently or made a mistake, the declaration is not conclusive. For example, in *Re Caratal (New) Mines Ltd*,[3] a special resolution was proposed. The chairman then stated 'Those in favour 6; those against 23; but there are 200 voting by proxy, and I declare the resolution carried'. The court held that the declaration was not conclusive and the resolution not passed because those 'voting' by proxy were not permitted to vote on a show of hands.

Unanimous agreement

15.23 A resolution in writing, signed by *all* the members entitled to attend and vote, may be deemed to be the equivalent of a special resolution – see s 141(8).

---

1 Prior to the Companies Act 1959, there were also extraordinary resolutions – s 141(6) of the 1963 Act.
2 Section 141(3).
3 [1902] 2 Ch 498.

Adjourned meetings

15.24 Where a resolution is passed at an adjourned meeting, it will be deemed to have been passed on the date of the adjourned meeting.[1]

Amendments

15.25 If an amendment is proposed to the resolution before the meeting, it must be voted upon first. If the chairman refuses to allow a prior vote on the amendment, the resolution, if passed, may not be binding.[2]

Extended notice

15.26 Where the 1963 Act requires extended notice for a resolution, it means notice of at least 28 days prior to the meeting must be given.

MINUTES OF MEETINGS

15.27 Every company must have minutes prepared recording all the proceedings of general meetings.[3] These minutes must be recorded in book or computer recorded form.

Any minute, if purported to be signed by the chairman of the meeting at which the proceedings were had, or by the chairman of the next succeeding meeting, shall be evidence of the proceedings.

Where minutes have been made of the proceedings at any general meeting of the company then, until the contrary is proved, the meeting shall be deemed to have been duly held and convened, and all proceedings had thereat to have been duly had, and all appointments of directors or liquidators shall be deemed to be valid.

Inspection of minute books

15.28 The books containing the minutes of proceedings of any general meeting must be held at the registered office of the company and open for inspection during business hours.[4]

---

1 Section 144.
2 *Henderson v Bank of Australasia* (1890) 45 ChD 330 (CA).
3 And also meetings of directors and/or committees of directors – see s 145.
4 Section 146.

REGISTRATION AND COPIES OF CERTAIN RESOLUTIONS

15.29   Section 143 of the 1963 Act applies to:

(1) special resolutions;
(2) resolutions which have been agreed to by all the members of a company, but which, if not so agreed to, would not have been passed as special resolutions;
(3) resolutions or agreements which have been agreed to by all the members of some class of shareholders but which, if not so agreed to, would not have been effective for their purpose unless they had been passed by some particular majority[1] and all resolutions[2] which effectively bind all the members of any class of shareholders though not agreed to by all those members;
(4) resolutions increasing the share capital of a company;
(5) resolutions that a company be wound up voluntarily passed under s 251(1)(a) or (c);
(6) resolutions attaching rights or restrictions to any share;
(7) resolutions varying any such rights or restrictions;
(8) resolutions classifying any unclassified share;
(9) resolutions converting shares of one class into shares of another class;
(10) resolutions of the directors of a company that an old public limited company be re-registered as a plc.[3]

A printed copy of every resolution or agreement falling within s 143 must, within 15 days after its passing or making, be forwarded to the registrar of companies and be recorded by him.

When special resolutions are required

15.30   Special resolutions are required to make fundamental changes to the company. These fundamental alterations would include:

(1) change of name – s 23(1). This change also requires the written approval of the Minister;
(2) altering its objects – s 10(2);
(3) alteration of, or addition to, its articles – s 15(1) (see Chapter 16);
(4) reduction of share capital – s 72(2). This change is also subject to confirmation by the court;
(5) power to make the liability of its directors unlimited – s 198(1);
(6) resolving that the company be wound up:
    (a) by the court – s 213(a); or

---

1 Or otherwise in some particular manner.
2 Or agreements.
3 See s 12(3)(a) of the 1983 Amendment Act. A resolution of the directors under s 143(3) must also be sent to the registrar.

    (b) voluntarily – s 251(1)(b); and

(7) the re-registration of a public company as a private one under s 15 of the 1983 Amendment Act.

DEMOCRATIC CONTROL OF THE COMPANY

15.31 From our examination of the law governing company meetings, it is obvious that, in most instances, a simple majority of members is sufficient to control decision making. In certain, more fundamental, company matters, which require the passing of a special resolution, a 75 per cent majority is required. Once this majority is mustered, the special resolution concerned may be passed. It would appear, therefore, that company control operates under a form of democratic system. This should mean that the wishes of the majority generally prevail. In the next chapter, we shall consider the implications of majority control for minority investors.

Chapter 16

MAJORITY CONTROL AND THE PROTECTION OF MINORITY INVESTORS

THE TAKING OF DECISIONS

16.1　As we saw in the previous chapter, major decisions are taken within the company by the passing of majority resolutions at meetings. Such decisions illustrate the exercise of 'collective' as distinct from 'individual' shareholders' rights.

For example, a simple majority of votes will ensure the passing of an ordinary resolution at a general meeting: a special resolution requires a 75 per cent majority. Thus, a form of democratic system exists which allows majority investors to control many corporate decisions, such as altering the constitutional document which forms the basis of the contract between investors and the company, ie the articles of association.

Alteration of the articles of association

16.2　The articles of association contain the terms of the contract between shareholders and the company. This agreement is known as a 's 25 contract' – see Chapter 29.

Notwithstanding their fundamental nature, the articles can be altered by special resolution. This is permitted by s 15 of the 1963 Act. Any alteration (or addition) approved by a 75 per cent majority will be as valid as if it had been contained originally in the articles.

Because of the democratic nature of the company control, a minority of members who voted against the change of articles, may have to accept the decision of the majority.

A member could take action if he was deprived of his individual right to vote. If granted this right, and, after validly exercising it, he is outvoted by the majority of other members, the ordinary shareholder must generally accept his fate. Thus, the majority 'will' prevails where corporate decisions are concerned.

Corporate rights versus individual rights

16.3　When decisions are taken within the company, for example, to appoint directors, etc. these are corporate decisions affecting the company as a whole, ie affecting corporate rights. They are not decisions affecting the *individual* rights of shareholders.

Investors have s 25 contracts with the company. They possess *individual* rights under these contracts. If, for example, the directors wrongfully withhold a member's dividend or deprive him of his right to vote, that member can proceed directly against the directors. It is only corporate rights which are subject to majority control. Even in these circumstances, however, both the courts and the legislature have intervened to protect minority members in exceptional cases.

JUDICIAL PROTECTION FOR MINORITY INVESTORS

16.4 Whilst accepting the principle of majority rule, the courts have intervened to protect minority members when the motivation of the majority shareholders is suspect.

In *Allen v Gold Reefs of West Africa*,[1] Lindley MR stated:

> '[The power conferred on companies to alter their articles] must, like all other powers, be exercised subject to those general principles of law and equity which are applicable to all powers conferred on majorities and enabling them to bind minorities. It must be exercised, not only in the manner required by law, but also bona fide for the benefit of the company as a whole, and it must not be exceeded.'

Bona fide for the benefit of the company as a whole

16.5 An alteration of the articles by special resolution must not discriminate between the majority shareholders and the minority, so as to give the former an advantage over the latter. In *Greenhalgh v Arderne Cinemas*,[2] Evershed MR declared:

> 'It is now plain that "bona fide for the benefit of the company as a whole" means . . . that the shareholder must proceed upon what, in his honest opinion, is for the benefit of the company as a whole . . . The phrase, "the company as a whole", does not (at any rate in such a case as the present) mean the company as a commercial entity, distinct from the corporators: it means the corporators as a general body . . . A special resolution of this kind would be liable to be impeached if the effect of it were to discriminate between the majority shareholders and the minority shareholders, so as to give the former an advantage of which the latter were deprived . . . It is therefore not necessary to require that persons voting for a special resolution should, so to speak, dissociate themselves altogether from their own prospects and consider whether the proposal is for the benefit of the company as a going concern.'

It appears, therefore, that whether an alteration is for the benefit of the company is for the investors to decide. The court will only interfere if no reasonable man would think the alteration was for the benefit of the company. This situation could arise because the alteration discriminated in the majority's favour by giving them some advantage denied to the minority and so amounting to fraud on the minority.

---

1 [1900] 1 Ch 656 (CA).
2 [1951] Ch 286 (CA). See also *Clemens v Clemens Brothers Ltd* [1976] 2 All ER 268, which suggests that the majority must act inequitably in relation to the minority.

Fraud in this context means action less than circumscribed within the tort of deceit. It could include, for example, an abuse of power corresponding to a breach of fiduciary duty or other inequitable action. In addition, the minority members themselves need not have suffered individual loss – it may have been the company itself that was injured. For example, in *Menier v Hooper's Telegraph Works*,[1] the majority (a rival company) used their voting power to put the company into voluntary liquidation. This left the majority in possession of the company assets. It was held that the action of the majority amounted to an expropriation of the company's property; and accordingly could be restrained by the minority.

Cases of hardship

16.6   An alteration made bona fide and for the benefit of the company as a whole will not be impeached by the court merely because it inflicts hardship on a particular investor. For example, a resolution passed at a general meeting enabling the directors to acquire, at a fair value, the shares of a minority investor who had an interest in a competing business, was permitted as bona fide in the interests of the company.[2]

Other minority remedies

16.7   The minority shareholders may have statutory avenues open to them to overturn an alteration of the articles rather than simply relying on impugning the motivation of the majority. So, for example, they might be able to utilise s 205 of the 1963 Act on the ground that the affairs of the company were being conducted in disregard of their interests.

SECTION 205 REMEDY FOR OPPRESSION BY THE MAJORITY

16.8   Under s 205(1), any member of a company who complains that the affairs of the company are being conducted or that the powers of the directors of the company are being exercised in a manner oppressive to him or any of the members (including himself), or in disregard of his or their interests as members, may apply to the court for an order.

---

1 (1874) LR 9 Ch App 350. See also other examples of fraud on the minority in the exceptions to the rule in *Foss v Harbottle*, and *G.S. Doherty Ltd v Doherty and Anr* (unreported) 19 December 1969 (SC).

2 *Sidebottom v Kershaw, Leese & Co* [1920] 1 Ch 154.

Only available to investors

16.9 Although the wording in s 205(1) confines this remedy to investors, the oppression suffered by a petitioning investor may be incurred in some other capacity such as director. This happened in *Re Murph's Restaurant Ltd.*[1]

Offending conduct

16.10 Oppressive conduct means actions causing financial loss to the members *qua* members. The course of actions must be 'burdensome, harsh and wrongful' or depart from standards of fair dealing or suggest a lack of probity. For example, in *Re Greenore Trading Co Ltd*,[2] a large shareholder agreed to purchase shares from another member. However, he used company funds to pay for the bulk of this share purchase by him. The petitioner, who originally owned 33⅓ per cent of the company's issued share capital, sought relief under s 205. The High Court granted it, Keane J saying:

> 'The patent misapplication[3] of the company's monies for the purpose of giving (the oppressing member) a dominant position in its affairs seems to me to be ... "burdensome, harsh and wrongful" *quoad* the petitioner.'

16.11 Again, fraudulent conduct by one member of a company holding 50 per cent of its shares, was deemed oppressive to the other member[4] in that company in *Re Westwinds Holding Co Ltd.*[5] An investor may also claim relief under s 205 even if another remedy, such as a derivative action, is available to him.

When a 20 per cent shareholder in a company was not informed that the directors had transferred the business of the company under an arrangement whereby the members had received no prior information concerning the transfer, the High Court held that the failure to provide adequate information to the petitioner amounted to oppression – see *Re Clubman Shirts Ltd.*[6]

Acts may be oppressive even if carried out honestly and in good faith, according to Kenny J in *Re Irish Visiting Motorists' Bureau Ltd.*[7]

The second limb

16.12 Section 205(1) empowers the court to grant a remedy in two distinct sets of circumstances. The first is where the affairs of the company or the powers of the directors have been exercised in an oppressive manner. In *Re Williams Group (Tullamore) Ltd*,[8] Barrington J commented:

1 [1979] ILRM 141.
2 [1980] ILRM 94 (HC).
3 Which included forging the petitioner's signature to sell property belonging to the company.
4 Also holding a 50 per cent shareholding.
5 (Unreported) 21 May 1974 (HC).
6 [1983] ILRM 323.
7 (Unreported) 27 January 1972 (HC).
8 (Unreported) 8 November 1985 (HC).

'If one regards "oppression" as a course of conduct which is "burdensome, harsh and wrongful" or as conduct which involves lack of probity or fair dealing towards some members of the company, there is no history of such a course of conduct in the present company prior to the events giving rise to the present case. On the contrary, the ordinary shareholders appear to have been treated extremely well.

Moreover, in the present case, we are not dealing with a course of conduct but with an individual transaction. It appears however than an isolated transaction can give rise to relief under the Irish section: . . .'

The judge noted that s 205 'offers relief not only when the affairs of the company are being conducted in an oppressive manner, but also (and alternatively) where they are being conducted *in disregard of the interests of some member or members*' (author's emphasis).

In this case, the articles of association had provided that, so long as there were preference shareholders, the ordinary shareholders were not entitled to attend and vote at general meetings.

The preference shareholders resolved to issue a new class of shares to both classes of members.

Whilst accepting that the majority of preference shareholders had acted in good faith, Barrington J concluded that the affairs of the company were being conducted in disregard of the interests of the ordinary shareholders. Accordingly, he granted them relief under s 205.

The second limb of relief is, therefore, where the 'affairs of the company' or the powers of the directors are being exercised in disregard of a member's interests as a member. The term 'affairs of the company' essentially means the conduct of the members when acting collectively. The word 'interests' embraces a wider notion of investor protection than 'rights'. Thus, reference to the 'interests' of members may enable the court to grant relief by considering matters outside a petitioner's purely legal rights as a company member.

Remedies available to the court

16.13 The court may make any order it thinks fit to bring to an end the conduct in question. For example, the court may make an order:[1]

'directing or prohibiting any act or cancelling or varying any transaction or for regulating the conduct of the company's affairs in future, or for the purchase of the shares of any members of the company by other members of the company or by the company and in the case of a purchase by the company, for the reduction accordingly of the company's capital or otherwise.'

---

1 Section 205(3).

Proceedings may be held in camera

16.14   If, in the opinion of the court, the hearing of the proceedings would involve the disclosure of confidential information, the proceedings may be held in camera.[1]

Examinership

16.15   Section 4(4) of the Companies (Amendment) Act 1990 excludes from relief under s 205 claims concerning the conduct of the company's affairs while it is under the protection of the court – see Part IX of this book.

INVESTIGATIONS INTO THE AFFAIRS OF THE COMPANY

16.16   The powers under ss 165 to 173 of the 1963 Act are now replaced and strengthened by Part II of the 1990 Act.

On the application of a minority of the members,[2] the court may appoint one or more inspectors to investigate the affairs of a company.

PETITIONING FOR THE WINDING UP OF THE COMPANY

16.17   Any member entitled to petition the court under s 205, may also petition for the winding up of the company on the grounds mentioned in s 213(g) of the 1963 Act.

OTHER EXAMPLES OF STATUTORY PROTECTION FOR MINORITIES

16.18   Other examples of statutory protection of minority investors include:

(1) where the company resolves by special resolution to *amend the objects clause of its memorandum of association,* an application can be made to the court to cancel the majority decisions:
  (a) by minority shareholders; and
  (b) by certain holders of not less than 15 per cent of the company's debentures – see s 10(3)–(11);[3]
(2) if the majority shareholders decide to pass a resolution *varying the rights of special classes of shares,* then the holders of 10 per cent of the class in question who did not consent to or vote in favour of the resolution may apply to the court to have the variation of their rights cancelled;[4]

---

1 See s 205(7) and *Re R Ltd* [1989] ILRM 757 (SC).
2 See s 7(1)(a) and (b) of the 1990 Act, and Chapter 27.
3 Of the 1963 Act.
4 Section 78 of the 1963 Act and **12.22**.

(3) where the company passes a special resolution to approve the giving of *financial assistance for the purchase of its shares*,[1] minority investors can apply to the court to block the resolution;

(4) where minority shareholders dissent from the decision of the majority investors to sell their shares in a *company reconstruction or amalgamation*, they have rights to object to the court under ss 201 to 204.[2] In *McCormick v Cameo Investments Ltd*,[3] 90 per cent of the members approved a take-over scheme under which it was proposed that the defendant company would purchase all the plaintiff's shares in the company. He claimed that the scheme was unfair and sought relief under s 204. The High Court held that the scheme was reasonable because the price offered for the shares was a fair one;

(5) minority investors can requisition the directors to call an extraordinary general meeting under s 132(1)[4] and, in the case of default in holding an AGM, apply to the Minister, who may direct that the meeting is called;[5]

(6) where a public company converts to private status, minority members can object to the court under s 15(3).[6] In addition, *all* members must agree to the re-registration of a limited company as unlimited;[7] and

(7) minority investors have the right to demand a poll by virtue of s 137(1)(b) of the 1963 Act.

THE RULE IN *FOSS v HARBOTTLE* AND MINORITY INTERESTS

16.19   What is known as the rule in *Foss v Harbottle* also involves consideration of minority interests being adversely affected by fraud in the management of the company.

An investor initiated legal proceedings against the directors of a company in order to compel them to make good losses sustained by the company as a result of their fraud. The legal action by the investor failed, because there was nothing to prevent the company itself from taking the proceedings against the directors.

The policy reasons underlying the rule in *Foss v Harbottle*[8] are that:

(1) litigation at the suit of a minority of the members is futile if the majority do not wish it; and

(2) without the rule, there would be a multiplicity of legal actions.

---

1 Section 60 of the 1963 Act and **13.37**.
2 Of the 1963 Act.
3 [1978] ILRM 191.
4 Of the 1963 Act.
5 See s 131(3).
6 Of the 1983 Amendment Act.
7 Section 52 of the 1983 Amendment Act.
8 (1843) 2 Ha 461.

16.20   As Mellish LJ said in *MacDougall v Gardiner*:[1]

> 'If the thing complained of is a thing which in substance the majority of the company are entitled to do, or if something has been done irregularly which the majority of the company are entitled to do regularly, or if something has been done illegally which the majority of the company are entitled to do legally, there can be no use in having litigation about it, the ultimate end, of which is only that a meeting has to be called, and then ultimately the majority gets its wishes.'

In this case, the court would not intervene where the chairman's actions in conducting a meeting were culpable. If the chairman was wrong, the company, not a member, was the proper person to sue.

Application of the rule

16.21   The rule in *Foss v Harbottle* is restricted to actions in respect of corporate decisions and rights (see **16.3** above). In such instances, where a wrong is done to the company which could validly be approved by a majority of the investors in general meeting, the proper plaintiff is the company itself.

The rule in *Foss v Harbottle* has no application where an investor's individual or personal rights are infringed. For example, in *Pender v Lushington*,[2] a member was able to sue and compel the company to record his vote. But there are limits to the classification of investors' individual rights. In *O'Neill v Ryan, Ryanair and Others*,[3] the High Court held, effectively, that the reduction in the value of a member's shareholding arising from a wrong done to the company was not an actionable individual right. In fact, Lynch J stated:

> 'I am of the opinion that the plaintiff's present action ... is a classic case to which the rule in *Foss v Harbottle* applies and I accordingly dismiss the plaintiff's action.'

Apparent judicial exceptions to the rule

16.22   The following judicial decisions are often cited as exceptions to the rule in *Foss v Harbottle*.

(1)   where the act done is ultra vires the company or *is illegal*;[4]
(2)   where the majority of members have committed a *fraud*[5] on the minority. For example, in *Cook v Deeks*,[6] three directors wrongfully obtained a contract in their own names, when acting on behalf of the company. They then used their voting power (possessing 75 per cent of the ordinary shares) to pass a special resolution wherein the company declared it had

---

1   (1875) 1 ChD 13.
2   (1877) 6 ChD 70.
3   (Unreported) 24 November 1989 (HC).
4   *Cockburn v Newbridge Sanitary Steam Laundry Co* [1915] 1 IR 237.
5   Negligent acts may also be actionable, but only if they confer a benefit on the majority at the expense of the company – see *Daniels v Daniels* [1978] Ch 406; *Pavlides v Jensen* [1965] Ch 565 and Chapter 22.
6   [1916] 1 AC 554.

no interest in the contract. On being sued by the minority shareholder, the directors were ordered to account to the company for the profits which they had made;

(3) where the act requires a special resolution but has been done by ordinary resolution – a procedural irregularity.[1] Similarly, if the company meeting has not been convened in time.[2]

If one considers the exceptions outlined above, it will be seen that they are not wrongs done *to* the company, but are wrongs done *by* it.

If the majority act illegally, oppressively, or in breach of proper procedures, it is the company who will be deemed to be so acting. Because of this, the only persons who are in a position to instigate legal action to prevent the wrongdoing by the company, are the minority shareholders. Accordingly, the common law permits them to sue[3] to prevent the company's wrongful acts. Thus, the rule in *Foss v Harbottle* is restricted to wrongs done *against* the company, *not by it.* That is why the author has classified them as apparent, rather than real. The real exceptions to the rule in *Foss v Harbottle* have been created by statute. In fact, the alternative remedies in s 205 of the 1963 Act now generally provide more relevant and comprehensive grounds for an action by minority investors, than reliance by them on the apparent judicial exceptions to *Foss v Harbottle.*

The derivative action

16.23   In the apparent exceptions to the rule in *Foss v Harbottle*, the minority shareholders would be compelled into taking legal action on behalf of the company, because the controlling owners and/or managing agents, the majority shareholders and/or directors, had committed the wrongful act against the company. Because the rights of the minority are derived from the company, the proceedings are known as a *derivative action.*

Where a derivative action succeeds, judgment is made in favour of the company, and not the minority shareholders who sued on its behalf. If the majority of the members are opposed to the litigation, the plaintiff minority shareholder may be debarred from proceeding with their derivative action.[4]

---

1 Such as a breach of s 181 of the 1963 Act – see *Moylan v Irish Whiting Manufacturers Ltd* (unreported) 14 April 1980 (HC).
2 *Hodgson v National and Local Government Officers Association* [1972] 1 WLR 130.
3 They may also be entitled to be indemnified by the company for all necessarily incurred legal expenses – see **22.3**.
4 See *Smith v Croft (No 2)* [1988] Ch 114.

INTERESTS, OTHER THAN INVESTORS' INTERESTS, TO BE CONSIDERED

16.24 Company control also involves the consideration of interests, other than those of company members. In managing the company, directors are expected to consider primarily the interests of the company,[1] rather than the interests of its shareholders. Of course, the majority shareholders have the power to appoint the directors.

A report produced by 'The Centre for Tomorrow's Company'[2] supported calls for a more open and sophisticated dialogue between companies[3] and investors, covering corporate objectives, as well as financial matters.

The Centre advocated transparency and consistency by large businesses in their dealings with employees, customers, suppliers and shareholders commenting:

> 'They have to choose how they propose to hold dialogue with shareholder groups. They cannot expect to treat shareholders as a watertight compartment.
>
> It is in the interests of shareholders that annual reports and a.g.m.s are designed to communicate the value added by business to customers, suppliers, employees and the community. . . .
>
> Annual Reports[4] which show the extent to which all of these relationships are being developed will give a forward indicator of the company's success in continuing to create long-term shareholder value.'

These comments certainly are desirable practices. Recent Irish case-law[5] indicates that directors are under a legal duty to consider the interests of creditors if their company is in a position of imminent insolvency. Section 52 of the 1990 Act also seems to suggest that directors must consider the interests of its employees.[6]

---

1 See Chapter 19.
2 An independent organisation in the UK representing the views of leading businesses. This report was summarised in the *Irish Times*, 30 December 1996.
3 Initiated by the directors.
4 See Chapter 24.
5 *Re Frederick Inns Ltd* [1994] 1 ILRM 387 (SC).
6 But see Chapter 19.

Chapter 17

A COMPANY'S CONTRACTUAL POWERS, NAME AND REGISTERED OFFICE

CONSTITUTIONAL DOCUMENTS

17.1 We saw in Chapter 3 that a company is recognised as a distinct but artificial person in law. Being an artificial legal person, a company's 'powers of contracting' have to be contained within its constitutional documents. Of particular relevance is the objects clause in a company's memorandum of association.

The memorandum of every company *must* state its objects.[1] The stating of the company's objects in its memorandum achieves the dual aim of protecting:

(1) the *investors*[2] (shareholders), who can elicit the purposes to which the capital they have contributed is being applied; and
(2) external persons such as *creditors*, dealing with the company, who can discover from the memorandum, a public document, the extent of the company's (including borrowing) powers.

If a company acts outside the scope of its powers it is deemed to be acting 'ultra vires'.

Constructive notice

17.2 The thinking underlying the common law doctrine of ultra vires was that the memorandum of association, once approved and registered with the registrar of companies, became a public document.

Since the public had access to public documents, no company creditor could later plead that he did not know of the limitations of the company's trading powers; he should have checked them out first before doing business with that company. Creditors were deemed to have constructive notice of the contents of public documents.

The corollary to the creditors' position is that the company must restrict its trading activities to the objects stated in its memorandum. If it goes outside of those objects, or begins to trade in areas not foreseen by the drafters of the objects clause, then the company is acting 'ultra vires', or 'outside of its powers'.

In *Attorney-General v G.E. Ry Co*,[3] it was held that the doctrine of ultra vires:

---

1 Section 6(1)(c) of the 1963 Act.
2 Under s 29 of the 1963 Act, a company must forward a member a copy of the memorandum (and articles), if requested by him, subject to the payment of a small charge.
3 (1880) 5 App Cas 473.

'ought to be reasonably . . . understood and applied, and . . . whatever may fairly be regarded as incidental to, or consequential upon, those things which the legislature has authorised, ought not (unless expressly prohibited) to be held, by judicial construction, to be "ultra vires".'[1]

EFFECT OF ULTRA VIRES TRANSACTIONS

17.3   In *Ashbury Railway Carriage Co Ltd v Riche*,[2] it was judicially decided that an ultra vires contract was void, and not even the subsequent assent of the whole body of shareholders could ratify it. Persons dealing with the company were deemed to have constructive notice of its powers, even if they have not inspected its memorandum of association. As a result, at common law, third parties would have no rights against the company[3] under an ultra vires contract. For example, in *Re Jon Beauforte (London) Ltd*,[4] a company's objects clause empowered it to transact business as costumiers and gown makers. It subsequently diverted into the business of making veneered panels, which were ultra vires.

The company decided to build a factory to manufacture veneer panels. Builders (and other suppliers) were contracted to build the factory. Neither the builders nor any of the suppliers of goods and materials for the factory knew that the building of the factory was ultra vires. Nevertheless, the court held that none of them could prove for their debts in the company's liquidation, as they had acquired no contractual rights under their ultra vires contracts.

Effect of doctrine on drafting of objects clauses

17.4   The severe consequences at common law for company contracts deemed ultra vires by the courts, led to objects clauses becoming lengthy – quite different to the succinct model in Table B.[5]

EVOLUTION OF THE MODERN OBJECTS CLAUSES

17.5   In the earlier cases, it was sometimes held by the courts that the company had a *main object*[6] and, possibly, several subsidiary objects. The main object was generally to be found in the first paragraph of the objects clause.

In *Re German Date Coffee Co Ltd*,[7] it was held that as the main object was no longer capable of achievement, the *substratum* of the company was gone; the company

1 Per Lord Selborne, LC.
2 (1875) LR 7 HL 653.
3 They might, however, enjoy rights of recovery against the directors – see Part V.
4 [1953] Ch 131.
5 See 1963 Act at p 701.
6 Eg in *Ashbury Railway Carriage Co Ltd v Riche* (1875) LR 7 HL 653.
7 (1882) 20 ChD 169 (CA).

was not empowered to carry out its subsidiary objects and had to be wound up. However, a company will not be wound up if the substratum or main object has not become impossible to achieve.[1] The 'main objects' rule will not be applied by the courts if the memorandum states that each of the objects is to be regarded as a main (or independent) object. The validity of this approach originated in the case of *Cotman v Brougham.*[2]

The effects of these cases on object clauses had been to make them give the company power to undertake a number of trading purposes, and to declare that each individual head of trading was an independent main object.

There were other UK cases which shaped the drafting of present day objects clauses.[3] However, because of the reform initiated in Ireland by s 8 of the 1963 Act, these cases are not being dealt with in the text, except for one: the *Bell Houses*[4] case.

Bell Houses (or catch-all) clauses

17.6   The *Bell Houses* case upheld the validity of the following objects clause:

> 'to carry on any other trade or business whatsoever, which can, in the opinion of the directors, be advantageously carried on by the company in connection with, or ancillary to, any of the above businesses or the general business of the company.'

The Court of Appeal's ruling effectively allows a company to undertake any business which the directors, acting in good faith, thought might be advantageously carried on. This type of 'catch-all' clause virtually overturns the effectiveness of the ultra vires rule.

COMPANY POWERS

17.7   In addition to the various separate objects contained in the 'objects' clause, the modern memorandum would also generally contain a number of powers which are considered reasonably conducive to the furtherance of the company's objects.[5] These might include the powers:

(1)   to sell the undertaking of the company for shares in another company or other consideration;

(2)   to take shares in another company;

(3)   to borrow money and to issue bills of exchange. This is implied in the case of a trading company, but an express power removes any difficulty if there is a doubt as to whether the company answers that description;

---

1   As in *Re Kitson & Co Ltd* [1946] 1 All ER 435 (CA).
2   [1918] AC 514 (HC).
3   But see L. MacCann 'The Capacity of the Company' *Irish Law Times*, April 1992, pp 79–86.
4   *Bell Houses Ltd v City Wall Properties Ltd* [1966] 2 All ER 674 (CA).
5   Many of these express powers would probably be implied.

(4) to amalgamate or enter into profit-sharing agreements with other companies, and to borrow money jointly with other companies;
(5) to acquire similar businesses;
(6) to sell or otherwise dispose of any part of the property of the company.

Power to make gratuitous payments

17.8 In *Re Lee, Behrens & Co Ltd*,[1] the directors decided that the company should covenant to pay a pension to the widow of the former managing director. The court held this transaction ultra vires and void because it was not:

(1) for the benefit of the company; or
(2) reasonably incidental to its business.

Again, in *Parke v Daily News Ltd*,[2] the company had sold the major part of its business and proposed to distribute the purchase price amongst former employees. The court held that such a gratuitous payment was ultra vires, void, and incapable of ratification by the majority of shareholders. Once again, the proposed payment was not reasonably incidental to, or consequential upon, the company's business.

17.9 It might be argued that gratuitous payments generally are in the interests of a company by generating a certain amount of good will. This argument, however, will not succeed where the donor company is being wound up, as in *Hutton v West Cork Railway Co*[3] and in *Re Frederick Inns*.[4]

The *Frederick Inns* case involved the Belton group of companies which owned and managed nine public houses in Dublin. The corporate structure used for this enterprise was a holding company, Motels Ltd, and nine subsidiary companies. The case was concerned with the holding company, Motels Ltd, and three specific subsidiaries, namely:

(1) Frederick Inns Ltd;
(2) The Rendezvous Ltd; and
(3) The Graduate Ltd.

Since the late 1970s, the group was in a position of constantly owing money to the Revenue Commissioners in respect of VAT, PAYE/PRSI and Corporation Profits Tax.

By June 1984, the group's liabilities to the Revenue Commissioners had risen to £2.8 million.

On 12 June 1984, the Collector General sent each of the ten companies ten separate letters demanding the amount due from it and giving notice that, in

1 [1932] 2 Ch 46.
2 [1962] Ch 927.
3 (1883) 23 ChD 654 (CA).
4 [1991] ILRM 582 (HC) and [1994] 1 ILRM 387 (SC).

the event of failure to pay, the letter would be used as evidence[1] that the company was unable to pay its debts, and a petition for winding up would be issued.

Subsequent to these letters, negotiations took place between representatives of the Revenue Commissioners and some of the group's directors. These negotiations resulted in an arrangement whereby the three subsidiaries identified above would be sold, and £1.4 million paid to the Revenue out of the proceeds.

This arrangement was duly carried out, with one variation: £1.2 million was paid to the Revenue Commissioners instead of the £1.4 million.

The £1.2 million was made up of the following contributions:

Frederick Inns Ltd	£200,000
The Rendezvous Ltd	£100,000
The Graduate Ltd	£123,000 approx
Motels Ltd	£777,000 approx
Total	£1,200,000

All four companies were insolvent when each of the instalments was paid. The Revenue Commissioners were aware of these facts.

The Revenue Commissioners applied the £1.2 million received to reducing the amounts owing by *all ten* companies in the group.

17.10   In the High Court, Lardner J held that each of the companies in the group was a separate legal entity, and that the Revenue Commissioners were not entitled to treat the group as one single entity. He stated:

> 'Insofar as payments to the Revenue . . . were intended to be applied in reduction of the tax liabilities of other companies in the group, they can only be regarded as voluntary payments made without consideration for the benefit of third parties and . . . in the absence of any evidence that such excess payments were for the benefit of the paying companies, they are clearly ultra vires.'

Specifically, Lardner J gave the following reasons for his finding the excess payments of tax ultra vires. He said:

> 'payment . . . of any sum in excess of its (own) tax liability was ultra vires the paying company insofar as:
>
> (a)   it effected a gratuitous reduction or alienation of its assets and
> (b)   it was done when the company was insolvent.'

On appeal, the Supreme Court upheld Lardner J's decision.

---

1 For the purpose of s 214 of the 1963 Act.

Power to lend money

17.11   In the appeal to the Supreme Court, it was submitted that an express power to lend money in the memorandum of association of Frederick Inns Ltd could be relied upon.

The express power read as follows:

> 'To advance and lend money from time to time either with or without mortgage or other security at such rates of interest and generally upon such terms and conditions and in such manner as may be thought expedient.'

Blaney J's response was:

> 'I reject this submission also. The four companies did not lend any monies to the other six. What they did was to pay part of their debts which was something very different.'

Other express powers

17.12   It would not be unusual to include an express power 'to pay pensions to employees of the company and to their wives and other dependants.'

An objects clause often concludes with a general 'catch-all' power to do 'all such business and things as may be incidental or conducive to the attainment of the above objects, or any of them'. However, such a power should be interpreted as authorising the company only to do that which is incidental or conducive to the main object(s)[1] of the company. This is because objects are the activities which a company was formed to carry out; powers merely assist in the attainment of these objects.

INVESTORS AND THE ULTRA VIRES DOCTRINE

17.13   In *Anglo Overseas Agencies Ltd v Green*,[2] Salmon J said that:

> 'The principal purpose of (the main objects) rule is that (investors) may know how the money they invest is to be used.'

The original idea was that the ultra vires rule would protect investors, as enunciated by Salmon J. However, the development of lengthy object clauses, including express powers and catch-all objects and powers as illustrated above, has eroded the effectiveness of the ultra vires doctrine in protecting investors. It is arguable, however, whether such protection is really necessary for investors.

In Ireland, most companies are private. In many of these, the investors will also be the directors and actually making decisions on behalf of the company.

---

1 Unless there is a 'Bell Houses' type catch-all clause in the memorandum – see **17.6**.
2 [1961] 1 QB 1.

In public companies, the objects clause is an internal matter affecting investors and directors. Each investor is entitled to a copy of the memorandum, and, if sufficient interest is mustered, investors can alter the objects clause.

Alteration of objects clause

17.14   Section 10(1)[1] allows the company, by special resolution, to amend the provisions of its memorandum by:

(1)   abandoning;
(2)   restricting; or
(3)   amending any existing object; or
(4)   by adopting a new object.

Thus, the majority of shareholders have it within their power to restrict or amend their company's objects clause if they consider it gives too much discretion to the directors. They can also apply to the court, under s 8(2) of the 1963 Act, to restrain a company from carrying out an ultra vires act. Ultimately, of course, the majority of investors can remove the directors if they are dissatisfied with the manner of their transacting the business of the company.

CREDITORS AND THE ULTRA VIRES DOCTRINE

17.15   Where the company entered into an ultra vires contract with a third party, at common law this transaction was void. This meant that neither the company nor the third party could acquire rights or incur liabilities under it. The *Re Jon Beauforte (London) Ltd* case (see **17.3**) illustrated this fact, and, particularly the unjust nature of a third party or creditor's legal position. The legislature has attempted to protect the creditors' legal position by enacting s 8 in the 1963 Act.

Section 8 protection

17.16   To mitigate the harshness of the common law position, s 8(1) of the 1963 Act modifies the ultra vires rule thus:

> 'Any act or thing done by a company which if the company had been empowered to do the same would have been lawfully and effectively done, shall, notwithstanding that the company had no power to do such act or thing, *be effective in favour of any person relying on such act or thing who is not shown to have been actually aware*, at the time when he so relied thereon, that such act or thing was not within the powers of the company, but any director or officer of the company who was responsible for the doing by the company of such act or thing shall be liable to the company for any loss or damage suffered by the company in consequence thereof.' (author's emphasis)

---

1 Of the 1963 Act.

Essentially, s 8(1) gives protection against ultra vires contracts provided that:

(1) such contracts are 'lawfully and effectively done'; and
(2) the person[1] relying on the contract 'is not shown to be actually aware, . . . that the act was ultra vires'.

Acts lawfully and effectively done

17.17 The usual interpretation of this requirement would be that the ultra vires act must otherwise be in accordance with company and general law. However, the complicated *Frederick Inns* case (see **17.9**) seems to have distinguished between 'lawful' and 'effectively done'.

In that case, Blaney J raised two separate questions, namely:

(1) is the transaction within the power or capacity of the company? (lawful); and
(2) if so, has that power been validly exercised so as to bind the company? (effectively done).

He then decided that the transaction was within the power of the company, but that this power had not been validly exercised by[2] the directors, saying:

> 'It is clear that it could not be held that the payments by the four companies were "lawfully and effectively done". At the time the payments were made, the four companies were under the management of their directors pending imminent liquidation. Because of the insolvency of the companies the shareholders no longer had any interest. The only parties with an interest were the creditors. The payments made could not have been lawful [and effective] because they were made in total disregard of their interests. And since the payments were not lawfully [and effectively] made, the Revenue Commissioners cannot rely on s 8 of the Companies Act 1963 to remedy the fact that the payments were ultra vires.'[3]

Person relying on s 8 must not be actually aware

17.18 The intention of s 8 is to overturn the constructive notice which the third party was deemed to have of a company's objects in its public constitution, or memorandum of association.

Because of s 8, it will no longer be necessary for those dealing with companies to read their objects clauses. If a contract is ultra vires, such persons would be protected by s 8 as they were not actually aware of this fact.

---

1 The wording of s 8(1) is wide enough to include both external and internal interests, eg directors.
2 The directors can only validly exercise powers on behalf of the general body of shareholders. When a company is insolvent, the interests of the creditors intrude. Creditors then become prospectively entitled to displace the normal power of the shareholders (and consequently directors) to deal with the company's assets. This seems to be the line of reasoning underlying Blaney J's decision.
3 Bracketed words inserted by author.

However, where a person enters into an ultra vires contract with a company, having firstly read that company's memorandum and failing to realise that the transaction in question was ultra vires, s 8(1) will not protect him. As Keane J stated in *Northern Bank Finance Co Ltd v Quinn and Achates Investment Co*:[1]

> 'I see no reason in logic or justice why the legislature should have intended to afford the same protection to persons who had actually read the memorandum and simply failed to appreciate the lack of vires.'

Regulation 6 protection

17.19   Regulation 6 of the European Communities (Companies) Regulations 1973[2] implemented art 9 of the First EU Directive on Company Law.[3]

Regulation 6(1) reads as follows:

> 'In favour of a person dealing with a company in *good faith*, any transaction entered into by an *organ of the company*, being its board of directors or any *person registered* under these regulations as a person authorised to bind the company, shall be deemed to be within the capacity of the company and any limitation of the powers of that board or person, whether imposed by the memorandum or articles of association or otherwise, may not be relied upon as against any person so dealing with the company.
>
> Regulation 6(2) provides that "any such person shall be presumed to have acted in good faith unless the contrary is proved".' (author's emphasis)

Regulation 6(3) clarifies the registration procedure mentioned in reg 6(1). The registration of a person authorised to bind the company shall be effected by delivering to the registrar of companies a notice giving the name and description of the person concerned.

Clearly, under reg 6, an outsider may enforce an ultra vires transaction against the company, provided it was negotiated with the board of directors or a registered person, and, at the time of entering into the contract, the outsider was unaware that it was beyond the powers or capacity of the company.

Regulation 6 and s 8 compared[4]

17.20   In reg 6(1), the person seeking to enforce the ultra vires contract must have dealt with the company in *good faith*. In s 8, he need only be 'actually unaware'. The criterion of good faith may imply a duty to investigate, even though reg 6(2) imports a presumption of good faith on the part of the third party. Under s 8, the ultra vires contract must simply be negotiated by the

---

1   [1979] ILRM 221.

2   SI 1973/163.

3   Directive 68/151/EEC.

4   For a more detailed comparison, see L. MacCann 'The Capacity of the Company (Part II)', *Irish Law Times*, July 1992, pp 151–159. MacCann considered that Keane J did not distinguish between 'actual notice' and 'actual knowledge' in the *Northern Bank Finance Co* case – see **17.18** above. See also P. Ussher 'Company Law – Validation of Ultra Vires Transactions' [1981] DULJ 76.

company. The protection under reg 6 is limited to contracts negotiated by 'its board of directors or any person registered under the 1973 regulations'.

In the *Frederick Inns* case, Blaney J stated:

> 'I think it is clear that none of the companies had any person registered under the regulations as a person authorised to bind the company. The payment appears to have been agreed to be made as a result of informal meetings between accountants acting on behalf of the companies and Mr Burke on behalf of the Revenue Commissioners. In these circumstances, ... the Revenue Commissioners cannot rely on Regulation 6 as validating the payment.'

Finally, reg 6 only applies to limited companies.

Regulation 10

17.21   Regulation 10 of the 1973 Regulations also protects persons, where documents should have been published in *Iris Oifigiúil,* but were not. These documents cannot be relied upon by the company against a third party.

Position of company under ultra vires contracts

17.22   Section 8 and reg 6 only benefit the other parties to the ultra vires contract. The company itself cannot enforce an ultra vires contract against the other party. However, it may have an *action for damages against any director or officer* of the company who was responsible for the ultra vires transaction under s 8(1).

COMPANY NAME

17.23   As the company is an artificial person created under the law, it must be given a name. The problems associated with the choice of undesirable business names have already been dealt with[1] so we can now concentrate on the requirements of the memorandum of association and the Companies Acts generally.

The memorandum of every company must state:[2]

(1) in the case of a public limited company, the name of the company, with 'public limited company' or 'cuideachta phoibli theoranta' as the last words of the name;
(2) in the case of a company (other than a public limited company) which is limited by shares or by guarantee, the name of the company, with 'limited' or 'teoranta' as the last word of the name.

---

1 In Chapter 7 dealing with the Registration of Business Names Act 1963 and the tort of passing off.
2 Section 6(1) of the 1963 Act. Section 114(5) permits the use of the abbreviations 'Ltd', or 'Teo', and 'plc' or 'cpt'.

Power to dispense with the word 'limited'

17.24 Section 24[1] gives the Minister the power to dispense with 'limited' or 'teoranta' in the name of a company formed for promoting commerce, art, science, religion or any other useful object, which will not apply its profits (if any) to pay dividends to its members.

During 1996, the Minister authorised 30 companies to omit 'Limited' from their names. Authorised companies included 'Ashbourne Care', 'Cork University Foundation' and 'Victim Support'.

Change of name

17.25 A company may, by special resolution, change its name.[2] A change of name will not affect company contracts in existence prior to the name change.

Publication of name

17.26 Section 114(1) of the 1963 Act provides that every company must:

(1) paint or affix, and keep painted or affixed, its name on the outside of every office or place in which its business is carried on, in a conspicuous position, in letters easily legible;
(2) have its name engraved in legible characters on its seal;
(3) have its name mentioned in legible characters in all *business letters* of the company and in all notices and other official publications of the company, and in all bills of exchange, promissory notes, endorsements, cheques and orders for money or goods purporting to be signed by or on behalf of the company and in all invoices, receipts and letters of credit of the company.

Fines are imposed on the company and its officers for non-compliance with s 114(1).

Officers' liability for use of name incorrectly

17.27 If an officer issues a business letter, cheque, order or invoice showing the name of the company incorrectly, that officer or any other person acting for the company, will be subject to a fine not exceeding £250, and be liable for the debts of the company in the transaction involved, if the company were to default.[3]

---

1 Of the 1963 Act.
2 See s 23 of the 1963 Act.
3 Ie the officer is only liable as surety for the company's debt under s 114(4). It is irrelevant to the question of liability whether or not the recipient of a company's cheque was actually misled by the incorrect use of the company name – see *Scottish and Newcastle Breweries Ltd v Blair* 1967 SLT 72.

REGISTERED OFFICE

17.28   A company must, at all times, maintain a registered office[1] in Ireland, to which all communications and notices may be addressed.[2] This requirement is necessary because the company, whilst being a legal person, is artificial and has no physical existence.

Particulars of the registered office must be delivered to the registrar prior to incorporation of the company. The registrar must also be notified of any change in its situation, within 14 days of the date of the change.

Registers and documents to be kept at the registered office

17.29   The following will usually be kept at the registered office:

(1) The Register of Members;
(2) Minute Books of General Meetings;
(3) Books of Account;
(4) Register of Directors and Secretary;
(5) Register of Directors' and Secretary's interests in shares;
(6) Register of Debenture Holders;
(7) Copies of instruments which create charges.

Service of proceedings on a company

17.30   Section 379(1) of the 1963 Act permits a document to be served on a company by leaving it at, or sending it by post to, the company's registered office.

---

1 Section 113 of the 1963 Act.
2 A company need not necessarily carry on its business from its registered office.

Chapter 18

COMPANY CONTRACTS AND THE POWERS OF ITS HUMAN AGENTS

FORM OF COMPANY CONTRACTS

18.1   A company is recognised by law as a legal person with almost the same powers as a human being to enter into contracts.

Notwithstanding its artificial existence, a company may enter into oral or written contracts. However, the company can only negotiate its contracts by means of human agents. As Denning LJ stated in *Bolton & Co Ltd v T. J. Graham & Sons Ltd*:[1]

> '... companies may in many ways be likened to human bodies. They have a brain and a nerve centre which control what they do. They also have hands that hold the tools and act in accordance with directions from the centre.
>
>   Some of the people in the company are mere servants and agents who are nothing more than hands to do the work and cannot be said to represent the directing mind or the will. Others are directors or managers who represent the directing mind and will of the company, and control what they do. The state of mind of these managers is the state of mind of the company and is treated by the law as such.'

These comments, made in the context of illustrating the criminal aspects of a company's activities, also show that, for all practical purposes, a company can only negotiate contracts by human persons acting under its authority, express or implied.[2]

A bill of exchange can be made, accepted or endorsed on behalf of the company by any person acting under its authority.[3]

A document or proceeding requiring authentication by a company, may be signed by a director, secretary or other authorised officer of the company, and need not be under its common seal.

The seal

18.2   The company's seal must be used only with the authority of the directors or of a committee of directors authorised by the directors on that behalf, and every instrument to which the seal is affixed must be signed by a director and countersigned by the secretary or by a second director or by some other person appointed by the directors for the purpose.[4]

---

1   [1957] 1 QB 159.
2   Section 38 of the 1963 Act.
3   Section 39.
4   Article 115 of Table A.

A company will generally not be bound if the seal is affixed without proper authority.

THE COMPANY'S HUMAN AGENTS

18.3   As mentioned in Chapter 1, the company has neither mind nor body, so cannot operate or enter into contracts without the assistance of human agents. These human agents will normally be the company's directors, officers, managers and other employees. Before considering the role of these intermediaries, it is useful to outline some relevant principles of the law underpinning these relationships. The area of law concerned is that of agency.

Agency law principles

18.4   Generally, only people who are parties to a contract can acquire rights and incur liabilities under it. This principle is known as privity of contract. The technical term 'privity' means, essentially, that a person will not be bound by any deal made by another, unless he personally took part in its negotiation.

Definition of agent

18.5   An agent, quite simply, is a person authorised to act on behalf of another. Accordingly, the law of agency contains the legal rules governing the relationships that arise when one person is authorised by another to perform certain legal tasks on his behalf, eg a manager on behalf of the company.

Fridman[1] suggests the following description of what agency involves:

> 'Agency is the relationship that exists between two persons where one, called the agent, is considered in law to represent the other, called the principal, in such a way as to be able to affect the principal's legal position in respect of strangers to the relationship by the making of contracts.'

The 'strangers' to the contract are usually termed 'third parties'. Thus, an agent is a person who is employed for the purpose of bringing his principal into contractual relations with third parties.

In the context of company contracts, the company is the principal; directors, officers and employees act as its agents in negotiating contracts on the company's behalf, with third parties (outsiders).

Authority of agent

18.6   There are three broad categories of agent, depending upon the amount or extent of authority vested in them by their principal.

These categories are:

---

1 G.H.L. Fridman *The Law of Agency* (Butterworths, 1971).

(1) *Universal Agents* – here the agent has an unlimited authority to act on behalf of his principal. In effect, he can bind his principal as if he were the principal himself. Such agents must be appointed by deed – a power of attorney. These appointments are relatively rare.

(2) *General Agents* – these agents have authority or power to bind their principals within certain limits. A company director has been held to be a general agent in *Hammond Properties Ltd v Gajdis*,[1] as has the manager of a public house in *Watteau v Fenwick*.[2]

(3) *Special Agents* – this type of agent has authority for only a specific purpose or occasion and is delegated limited powers.[3]

Most human agents negotiating contracts on behalf of companies would probably fall into the category of general agents, although the company may also employ special agents in connection with 'one-off' or specialist transactions. To discover the true nature of an agent's relationship with the principal, one must examine the extent of his authority.

Actual and ostensible authority

18.7   The actual extent of the agent's authority will depend upon:

(1) the express terms of his appointment by his principal; or

(2) the existence of authority implied by the law for particular legal relationships (usual authority).

Implied, or ostensible,[4] authority may exceed the agent's actual authority from his principal, thereby rendering the principal liable in contracts made by his agent outside the limits of his actual authority.

18.8   In *Watteau v Fenwick*, the manager of a public house was prohibited from ordering tobacco by his employer (principal). However, he ignored this prohibition and ordered tobacco on credit.

His employer was held liable to pay the seller because public house managers would usually have authority to place orders of this kind. The agent, therefore, had ostensible authority.

A principal is generally bound to third parties by the acts of his agents, whether within their actual, usual or ostensible authority.

Usual authority of company's agents

18.9   Actual authority is that which the company's agent actually possesses by virtue of the express terms of his appointment. Usual authority is that which is generally possessed by a particular class of agent.

---

1 [1968] 3 All ER 267.
2 [1893] 1 QB 346.
3 Eg an estate agent, solicitor, barrister, stockbroker, etc.
4 Sometimes also styled 'apparent' authority.

As the standard set of articles of association in Table A are widely used by companies,[1] it would be customary to refer to Table A to ascertain the usual authority of many of the company's agents, including its board of directors.

Board of directors

18.10 Article 80 of Table A provides that:

> 'the business of the company shall be managed by the directors ... subject to such directions ... as may be given by the company in general meeting: but no direction given by the company in general meeting shall invalidate any prior act of the directors which would have been valid if that direction had not been given.'

The directors may also 'exercise' all the powers of the company to borrow money,[2] and to mortgage or charge its undertaking, property and uncalled capital.

Internal limits on borrowing powers and lender protection

18.11 Article 79, in standard form, places a limit[3] on the directors' exercise of the company's borrowing powers. This upper limit is the nominal amount of the share capital of the company, unless the company, in general meeting, sanctions a loan exceeding this amount.

Suppose the directors of a company borrow money on the company's behalf in excess of the internal maximum limit, without obtaining prior authority from the shareholders by way of a resolution. What is the effect of this 'internal management' defect on the loan transaction?

18.12 These were the basis of the facts in the famous case of *Royal British Bank v Turquand*,[4] where Jervis CJ said:

> 'The (third) party here, on reading the deed of settlement would find, not a prohibition from borrowing, but a permission to do so on certain conditions. Finding that the authority might be made complete by a resolution, *he would have a right to infer the fact of a resolution* authorising that which, on the face of the document, appeared to be legitimately done. Consequently, persons dealing with a company are not concerned to inquire whether all matters of internal management have been complied with, if everything is apparently regular.' (author's emphasis)

This is known as the rule in *Turquand's* case or the Internal or Indoor Management rule.[5]

---

1 Either with or without alteration.

2 Article 79. Article 81 gives the directors the authority, by power of attorney, to delegate such powers as they think fit to any company, firm or person.

3 Apart from temporary loans obtained from the company's bankers in the ordinary course of business.

4 (1856) 6 E & B 327.

5 See G. McCormack 'The Indoor Management Rule in Ireland' *Law Society Gazette*, January/February 1985, pp 17–20.

The rule in *Turquand*'s case is an example of judicial creditor protection. It was applied in *Ulster Investment Bank Ltd v Euro Estates Ltd*[1] by Carroll J who stated:

> 'while persons dealing with a company are assumed to have read the public documents of the company, . . . They need not inquire into the regularity of the internal proceedings and may assume that all is being done regularly.'

Again, in *Allied Irish Banks Ltd v Ardmore Studios International (1972) Ltd,*[2] Finlay J upheld the plaintiff's contention that 'a person dealing with a limited liability company, and doing so bona fides, was not required to enquire into irregularities in the internal management of the company'.

Exceptions to the rule in Turquand's case

18.13   The rule does not apply when:

(1)   it is *known*[3] that the rules of internal management have not been complied with; or
(2)   the document upon which the person dealing with the company relies is a forgery;[4] or
(3)   an agent of the company has done something beyond any authority given him, or which he was held out as having;[5] or
(4)   the person dealing with the company has been put on enquiry;[6] or
(5)   the person dealing with the company is not an outsider. In *Hely-Hutchinson v Brayhead Ltd,*[7] however, the judgment suggests that where an insider like a director is dealing with the company qua outsider, he may still be able to claim the protection of the rule in *Turquand*'s case.

Protection of lenders[8] under art 79

18.14   Article 79 also provides for instances where directors exceed their borrowing powers. In fact, the relevant wording reflects and develops the principle underlying *Turquand*'s case by providing that:

> '. . . no debt incurred . . . in excess of [the internal] limit, shall be invalid or ineffectual, *except* in the case of express notice to the lender . . . at the time when the debt was incurred. . . . that the [internal] limit had been . . . exceeded.' (author's emphasis)

---

1   [1982] ILRM 57 (HC). See also *Cox v Dublin City Distillery (No 2)* [1915] 1 IR 345.
2   (Unreported) 30 May 1973 (HC).
3   *Howard v Patent Ivory Manufacturing Co* (1883) 38 ChD 156 and *AL Underwood Ltd v Bank of Liverpool and Martin* [1924] 1 KB 775.
4   *Ruben v Great Fingall Consolidated* [1906] AC 439, but see **29.20** and **29.21** below.
5   *Kreditbank Cassel v Schenkers* [1927] 1 KB 246.
6   *Houghton & Co v Nothard, Lowe and Wills Ltd* [1927] 1 KB 246.
7   [1967] 2 All ER 14.
8   The 'mechanics' of company borrowing and creditors' rights generally are dealt with in Part VIII.

Managing director

18.15   Articles 110 and 111 authorise the directors to appoint one (or more) of themselves to the office of managing director, and to confer upon him 'any of the powers exercisable by them'. Essentially therefore, the board can delegate all of its authority to a managing director, who in turn, will be able to negotiate contracts on behalf of the company.

Chairman

18.16   A company chairman usually has no executive authority, unless expressly appointed an executive chairman. The chairman's usual authority would be to chair company and directors' meetings and to sign the minutes of a previous meeting.

Individual directors

18.17   Individual directors' usual authority would be limited to witnessing the affixing of the company seal to a document.[1] However, they may also have contracts of employment with the company making them executive directors and thereby greatly increasing their actual authority.[2]

Company secretary

18.18   The development of the company secretary's role has already been detailed in Chapter 14. Since the *Panorama Developments* case, his ostensible authority to act on behalf of the company, has greatly increased.[3]

Shareholders

18.19   A shareholder has no usual authority to enter into contracts on behalf of the company.[4]

Third party protection and the doctrine of ostensible authority

18.20   In *Freeman & Lockyer v Buckhurst Park Properties (Mangal) Ltd,*[5] K and H formed the defendant company to purchase and resell a large estate. K, H and two nominees were appointed directors of the company. The articles provided for the appointment of a managing director, but none was appointed and K acted throughout as managing director with the knowledge of the board. K employed a firm of architects, the plaintiffs, to do certain work connected with developing the estate. The plaintiffs did this and then claimed from the company for payment of their fee. The court held that the company was bound

---

1 Article 115 of Table A.
2 The ostensible authority of non-executive directors would also be much wider than their actual authority.
3 See **14.34** and **18.25**.
4 See Chapters 4, 5 and 6.
5 [1964] 2 QB 480.

by acts done by a managing director within his ostensible or apparent authority and therefore liable to pay the fee.

Conditions necessary

18.21   In the *Freeman & Lockyer* case, Diplock LJ stated that the relevant law can be summarised by stating four conditions which must be fulfilled to entitle a contractor or third party to enforce against a company a contract entered into on behalf of the company by an agent who had no actual authority to do so. It must be shown:

(1) that a representation that the agent had authority to enter on behalf of the company into a contract of the kind sought to be enforced was made to the third party;

(2) that such representation was made by a person (or persons) who had 'actual' authority to manage the business of the company either generally or in respect of those matters to which the contract relates;

(3) that the third party was induced by such representation to enter into the contract, and in fact relied upon it; and

(4) that under its memorandum or articles of association the company was not deprived of the capacity either to enter into a contract of the kind sought to be enforced or to delegate authority to enter into a contract of that kind to the agent.

Managing directors and chairman

18.22   In the *Freeman & Lockyer* case, a person who had acted as managing director without being formally appointed, but with the knowledge of the board, was deemed to have the full (ostensible) authority of that office holder.

Again, in *Hely-Hutchinson v Brayhead Ltd* (see **18.13**), a person who was chairman of a company also acted as its de facto managing director; the board acquiescing afterwards by approving contracts negotiated by him. This person was deemed to have implied authority to do all such things as fall within the usual remit of a managing director's authority.

Thus, the authority of a managing director may be inferred from a course of dealings or from the conduct of the parties.

18.23   In *Kilgobbin Mink and Stud Farms Ltd v National Credit Co Ltd,*[1] Hamilton J seemed to extend the doctrine of ostensible authority to include a request made by a chairman and controlling shareholder to pay monies due to the company into the bank account of another company also controlled by himself.

This decision might have been easier to reconcile with established precedents had the request been made by a managing director (possessing wide usual authority) rather than a chairman (with limited usual authority – see **18.16** above). Again, it raises questions relating to the separate personality of the

---

1 (Unreported) 16 February 1978 (HC).

company. Accordingly, perhaps it should be interpreted narrowly as relating to its own peculiar facts.

Directors and managers

18.24   The doctrine of ostensible authority would seem to possess the potential to expand and encompass the activities of non-executive and executive directors, eg those styled finance and technical directors, senior (line) managers,[1] middle and junior management and, indeed, all employees. The ostensible authority of junior employees would, of course, be quite limited.

The company secretary

18.25   In the *Panorama Developments* case,[2] the company secretary hired cars for his own use by fraudulently representing that they were for the company. The court held that the company was liable as the secretary has ostensible (or apparent) authority to make a contract on the company's behalf for the hire of cars. However, in *UBAF Ltd v European American Banking Corp*,[3] it was held that the secretary had no apparent authority to make representations on the company's behalf in relation to a syndicated loan.

The secretary's ostensible authority is not as wide as that, for example, of a managing director. Perhaps it would be safe to assume he has only ostensible authority to bind the company in contracts relating to administration/internal management aspects of the company's affairs.[4]

The ultra vires doctrine and company agents

18.26   At common law, because of the doctrine of constructive notice, a contract which was ultra vires the company's objects was void. As a result, the other party possessed no rights under it against the company.

Because of the s 8 and reg 6 protection, detailed in Chapter 17, the other party can now enforce an ultra vires contract against the company. The doctrine of constructive notice has been virtually overturned by those statutory reforms whose aim was to protect company creditors.

This chapter has focused on company contracts entered into by human agents which were ultra vires the agents' authority, though not necessarily the company's objects. Where, for example, a company is empowered to borrow money, but the directors exceed an internal ceiling on borrowing, such a transaction is intra vires the company but ultra vires the directors. The judicial

---

1 Cf. the ostensible authority of a public house manager in *Watteau v Fenwick* [1893] 1 QB 346.

2 See **14.34** above.

3 [1984] QB 713.

4 The *Panorama Developments* case included elements of agency by estoppel and fraud. In his judgment, Lord Denning MR said: 'Mr Bayne was a fraud. But it was the company which put him in a position in which he was able to commit the fraud. So the defendants are liable'.

rule in *Turquand's* case protects the innocent third party lender in these circumstances; so, too, does art 79 of Table A (see **18.14** above).

Generally, if a company agent enters into any contract in excess of his actual authority, it is ultra vires the agent. The doctrine of ostensible authority, developed by judicial decisions, has the effect of rendering some such unauthorised transactions intra vires the agent's authority and enforceable against the company.

These distinctions between contracts ultra vires the company and those intra vires the company and merely ultra vires the company's agents, will be examined again in Part V, in the context of directors' liability.

PART V

DIRECTORS' PROCEEDINGS, DUTIES AND LIABILITIES

Chapter 19

DIRECTORS' PROCEEDINGS AND COMMON LAW DUTIES

DIRECTORS

19.1   In Chapter 14, the appointment, removal and roles of directors as office holders, quasi-trustees and agents was explained. Essentially, directors are the human 'managing agents' which make the concept of the 'non-human' company possible to operate in practice. The directors, acting collectively as the board, constitute the controlling 'mind' of the company.

A director can also have contract of service with the company, and then be an employee as well as an office holder, eg the managing director and the other executive directors.

The usual and ostensible authority of directors to enter into contracts on behalf of the company have already been outlined in Chapter 18. The focus in this chapter is on the proceedings of directors and their common law duties to the company and creditors.

PROCEEDINGS OF DIRECTORS

19.2   The proceedings of directors will usually be provided for in the articles of association. For example, art 101 provides that:

> 'the directors may meet together for the dispatch of business, adjourn and otherwise regulate their meetings, as they think fit. Questions arising at any meeting shall be decided by a majority of votes. Where there is an equality of votes, the chairman shall have a second or casting vote. A director may, and the secretary on the requisition of a director shall, at any time summon a meeting of the directors.'

The quorum necessary may be fixed by the directors, and unless so fixed, shall be two.[1] The directors themselves decide on their chairman[2] and they can change the chair as they wish.

Article 109 supplies a useful means of avoiding the need to hold formal meetings where the board is of one mind. Under this article, a resolution in writing, signed by all the directors, shall be as valid as it had been passed at a meeting of the directors duly convened and held.

Minutes of proceedings at directors' meetings must be kept in accordance with s 145 of the 1963 Act.

---

1 Article 102.
2 Article 104.

Committees

19.3   Articles 105 to 107 deal with the appointment of subcommittees of the board of management. Article 107 gives the chairman of a committee a second or casting vote. Apart from any such provision, motions are carried on majority decision.

Chairman's and managing directors' roles

19.4   The board of directors may, and often does, appoint a managing director of the company, delegating certain of their powers to him, principally the day-to-day management of the company. A managing director is answerable to the board and they may dismiss him or otherwise amend his delegated powers.[1] As mentioned in Chapter 18, there is a significant difference between the roles of a chairman of a board of directors and the managing director. The chairman is not, per se, a salaried employee of the company. He is an office holder. By contrast, the managing director has a contract of employment[2] with the company and, in the event of his dismissal, has recourse to the range of rights and remedies available to any fixed term contract employee in labour law.

DUTIES OF DIRECTORS

19.5   Directors,[3] as managing agents of a company, owe many duties to it as their principal. Early judicial decisions, such as *Percival v Wright*,[4] underlined the separate personality of the company by making it clear that directors' duties are owed to the company itself, and not the individual shareholders. As recently as 1989, the Supreme Court refused to grant shareholders the right to take a personal action against those alleged to have caused the value of their share holdings to decrease.[5]

Whilst it is possible that in the future a court may decide that directors owe a fiduciary duty to individual shareholders in very exceptional cases, the massive growth of directors' statutory duties generated by the Companies Act 1990 must make this judicial development less likely; particularly as some of the statutory duties benefit investors, as well as creditors. For example, the new rules regulating transactions involving directors and insider dealing rules will clearly benefit company shareholders (see **20.3** and **20.28** below).

---

1 Article 112.
2 See **14.30** above.
3 And, indeed, other company officers.
4 [1902] 2 Ch 421 – directors also owe their duties to the company qua directors, not qua shareholders – see *N.W. Transportation Co v Beatty* (1887) 12 App Cas 589.
5 *O'Neill v Ryan, Ryanair and Ors* – see **16.21** and the rule in *Foss v Harbottle*.

The company's best interests

19.6   Generally, directors are bound to act 'bona fide in what they consider – not what a court may consider – is the interests of the company'.[1] This effectively means that directors must act in the best interests of the company and not of its individual members. The definition of what constitutes the company's best interest is equated with the 'collective' interest of all its members, past, present and future. This judicial interpretation is illustrated in the cases of *Re Lee, Behrens and Co Ltd, Parke v Daily News Ltd* and *Hutton v West Cork Railway Co.* These cases were detailed in **17.8** and **17.9** above.

During 1996, a report on corporate governance in the UK by the 'Centre for Tomorrow's Company' noted that many chief executives and other directors considered it was their duty to concentrate on 'pleasing current shareholders'. The Centre then commented:

> 'In fact, directors' duties are owed to the company and not to any specific third party group. They must, as fiduciaries, have regard to the interest of shareholders, but that obligation is not related to the holders of shares at one particular time . . .
> For directors not to give due weight to all the company's key relationships may well be a breach of fiduciary duty since, without this, the company is exposing itself to undue risk, as well as missing opportunities to add long-term shareholder value through these relationships.'

Employees' interests

19.7   Section 52(1) of the 1990 Act indicates that directors owe a duty to consider 'the interests of the company's employees in general, as well as the interests of its members'. However, s 52(2) clarifies that:

> 'the duty [in s 52(1)] imposed on the directors shall be owed by them to the company (and the company alone) and shall be enforceable in the same way as any other fiduciary duty owed to a company by its directors.'

The section seems to have little practical effect on extending the directors' duties to persons, other than the company itself. However, the position of creditors is somewhat clearer.

The interests of creditors

19.8   In the *Frederick Inns* case,[2] the Supreme Court held that in cases of imminent[3] insolvency, the directors of a company also owe a duty to consider the interests of the company's creditors.[4]

---

1 Per Lord Greene MR in *Re Smith & Fawcett Ltd* [1942] Ch 304 (CA).
2 See **17.17**.
3 And actual.
4 See, generally, L. MacCann 'Directors' Duties: To Whom Are They Owed?' (1991) 9 ILT 3 30.

Directors' duties generally

19.9   It must now be clear that despite attempts to extend directors' duties to encompass the interests of employees and creditors, they are predominantly owed to the company itself.

The duties owed by directors to the company evolved through judicial decisions (or the common law) and have been extended and strengthened by statute.

Common law duties

19.10   Reflecting the dual roles of directors as (a) quasi-trustees[1] and (b) agents, their common law duties can be divided into the categories of (a) fiduciary duties, and (b) duties of care and skill.

Directors' fiduciary duties relate to their honesty; duties of care and skill refer to their competency.

Fiduciary duties

19.11   Directors' fiduciary duties have developed to deal with four specific aspects of their activities. These are:

(1) directors assuming responsibility for all company property and monies;
(2) directors not using their privileged positions to make a secret profit for themselves at the company's expense;
(3) directors at all times acting in the best interests of the company and avoiding conflicts of interest; and
(4) directors maintaining their independence by not fettering their discretion.

We shall now examine these specific fiduciary duties.

Responsibility for company property and monies

19.12   As quasi-trustees of the company's money and property, directors must account to the company for all its property, including its money, over which they exercise management and control.

Directors must return to the company any of its property which they have appropriated; any company money which they improperly paid out must be refunded.

19.13   In *Jackson v Munster Bank Ltd*,[2] it was held that a director's duty extends to taking action when he discovers misconduct by a fellow director. In that case, a director was held liable for remaining passive and omitting to take

---

1 See **14.7**.
2 (1885) 15 LR Ir 356.

appropriate remedial action when he became aware of breaches of their fiduciary duties to the company by fellow directors.

Not making a secret profit

19.14 Directors must not make a *secret profit* for themselves out of their position. If they do so, they must account for it to the company,[1] even though the profit concerned could not have been earned by the company. Where the company has not even had an opportunity of considering the business deal in question, and where there is no disclosure, the director will be bound to account for any profit he may have gained. For example, in *Industrial Development Consultants Ltd v Cooley*,[2] the company itself failed to obtain a business contract and hence could not be regarded as having been deprived of a business opportunity. Nevertheless, a (former) director was held liable to account for the profits he had made.

In the *Cooley* case, the defendant was the managing director, who, after being in negotiations with the Eastern Gas Board on behalf of his company, was later offered the opportunity to carry out the work in a personal capacity. Cooley then falsely informed the chairman that he wished to resign on grounds of ill health. He did so; then carried out the work himself and made a substantial profit.

19.15 The company was successful in making him account to them for these profits, on grounds of breach of a fiduciary duty he owed to the company. This decision was commented upon by Larkin J in *Canadian Aero Service v O'Malley*.[3] Larkin J said:

> 'What ... decisions [such as *IDC v Cooley*] indicate is an updating of the equitable principle whose roots lie in ... general standards ... namely, loyalty, good faith and avoidance of a conflict of duty and self-interest. Strict application against directors and senior management officials is simply recognition of the degree of control which their positions give them in corporate operations, a control which rises above day-to-day accountability to owning shareholders and which comes under some scrutiny only at annual general or at special meetings. It is a necessary supplement, in the public interest, of statutory regulation and accountability which themselves are, at one and the same time, an acknowledgement of the importance of the corporation in the life of the community and of the need to compel obedience by it and by its promoters, directors and managers to norms of exemplary behaviour.'

There is a tendency, in cases such as *Industrial Development Consultants Ltd v Cooley*, to blur the distinctions between the office of director and a director's role as an employee under a contract of employment with the company. For example, all employees are under an implied duty not to disclose confidential information, nor to solicit business from their employer's customers. Any

---

1 *Regal (Hastings) Ltd v Gulliver* [1942] 1 All ER 378.
2 [1972] 2 All ER 162.
3 (1974) 40 DLR (3d) 371.

employee who solicits orders from his employer's customers intending to meet the orders personally, rather than qua employee, would be in breach of an implied duty to serve his employer faithfully.[1] Accordingly, it could be argued that the managing director in the *Cooley* case was in breach of his duty to serve the company (his employer) faithfully as an executive director, rather than a specific fiduciary duty arising out of his holding of the office of director.

Avoiding conflicts of interest

19.16   Directors must exercise their powers honestly in the *interests of the company and not for themselves.* Accordingly:

(1) they must not place themselves in a position in which there is a *conflict* between their duties to the company and their personal interests; and
(2) they must not be interested, either directly or indirectly, in a contract with the company, unless the articles permit it. (Section 194 of the 1963 Act and Table A, arts 83 to 87 allow a director to contract with the company if certain conditions are fulfilled. The director must, however, disclose his interest[2] to the board.)

In order to prevent conflicts arising between directors' interests and those of the company, the Companies Act 1990 has imposed a new regulatory regime applicable to:

(1) transactions involving directors, including long-term service contracts,[3] substantial property deals, loans, credit arrangements and guarantees – Part III;
(2) disclosure of directors' interests in shares – Part IV; and
(3) insider dealing – Part V.

The provisions of Parts III to V of the 1990 Act, aimed at preventing possible conflict of interest situations, will be examined in Chapter 20.

Maintaining voting impartiality

19.17   Directors cannot validly make a contract as to how they will vote at future board meetings, ie they cannot fetter their discretion.[4]

The proper exercise of directors' fiduciary powers

19.18   When exercising their fiduciary powers on behalf of the company, directors must exercise them in *good faith* and for a *proper purpose.* In *Re Smith &*

---

1 *Arclex Optical Corporation v McMurry* [1958] Ir Jur Rep 65 (HC).
2 Any director may act in a professional capacity for the company as if he were not a director, except that he or his firm cannot act as auditors to the company.
3 See **14.31**.
4 *Clark v Workman* [1920] 1 IR 107 (ChD).

Fawcett Ltd,[1] the test of good faith was suggested as 'did the directors do what they honestly believed to be right [for the company]?'

In *Hogg v Cramphorn Ltd*,[2] directors, in an attempt to forestall a takeover bid, issued voting shares to a trust for the company's employees. The court held that the issue was ultra vires the directors' fiduciary powers. However, the directors' action was intra vires the company's powers and could be ratified by the company in general meeting, which it was.

19.19   Hoffmann LJ summarised the exercise of directors' powers recently in *Bishopsgate Investment Management Ltd v Maxwell*.[3] He said:

'If a director choses to participate in the management of the company and exercises powers on its behalf, he owes a duty to act *bona fides* in the interests of the company. He must exercise the power solely for the purpose for which it was conferred.'

Ross J, in *Clark v Workman*,[4] elaborated on the meaning of bona fides for directors. He said:

'In all cases bona fides is the test of the valid exercise of powers by trustees. An opportunity for deliberation in the full light of the facts and circumstances is impliedly required. I must say that I think it is hardly within the spirit of the articles that shareholders holding 55% of the shares should be allowed to declare their desire to sell at 12.30 o'clock, and that at 2.30 the chairman, who had previously refused to give any information, should disclose the names of the proposed transferees. We are not to forget the magnitude and importance of the proposed operation. It is a strong proposition to assert that a majority is to overbear and stifle a minority when the intention is to do such a serious thing as to give a controlling interest in one company to another company that is engaged in the same line of business, and that may be to some extent a rival company ...

When the test of bona fides comes to be applied, all these matters and the surrounding circumstances call for the most careful attention. Even the statutory powers of altering articles of association by a special resolution must be exercised subject to those general principles of law and equity which are applicable to all powers enabling majorities to bind minorities. They "must be exercised not only in the manner required by law, but also bona fide for the benefit of the company as a whole, and must not be exceeded. These conditions are always implied, and are seldom if ever expressed".[5] These observations (of Lord Lindley) refer to the exercise of powers by shareholders. They apply with augmented force when the powers are being exercised by directors ...'

---

1 [1942] Ch 304.

2 [1967] Ch 254. See also *Howard Smith Ltd v Ampol Petroleum Ltd* [1974] AC 821 (Privy Council).

3 [1993] BCC 120 (CA). In this case, it was held to be an improper use of a director's fiduciary powers when he used them to transfer the company's assets, without good reason, to a third party in which he had an interest.

4 See **19.17** above.

5 Ross J was quoting from Lord Lindley's judgment in *Allen v Gold Reefs Co of West Africa* [1900] 1 Ch 656.

Fiduciary powers obviously impinge on the honesty or otherwise of a director. His duties of care and skill, as an agent, rather than quasi-trustee, are concerned with competency levels (or perhaps the lack of them).

Duties of care and skill

19.20   The leading case on directors' duties of care and skill is *Re City Equitable Fire Insurance Co Ltd.*[1]

A managing director defrauded the company, and the liquidator sought to make the other directors, all of whom had acted honestly, liable in negligence. The liquidator's action failed. In his judgment, Romer J summarised the levels of care and skill required from directors at common law. He said:

> 'In order, therefore, to ascertain the duties that a person appointed to the board of an established company undertakes to perform, it is necessary to consider not only the nature of the company's business, but also the manner in which the work of the company is in fact distributed between the directors and the other officials of the company, provided always that this distribution is a reasonable one in the circumstances, and is not inconsistent with any express provisions of the articles of association. In discharging the duties of his position thus ascertained a director must, of course, act honestly; but he must also exercise some degree of both skill and diligence. To the question of what is the particular degree of skill and diligence required of him, the authorities do not, I think, give any very clear answer. It has been laid down that as long as a director acts honestly he cannot be made responsible in damages unless guilty of ... negligence in a business sense ...'

Romer J then went on to summarise the law on directors' competency under the headings of degree of skill, diligence and delegation.

Degree of skill

19.21   Romer J said:

> 'A director need not exhibit in the performance of his duties a greater *degree of skill than may reasonably be expected from a person of his knowledge and experience.* A director of a life insurance company, for instance, does not guarantee that he has the skill of an actuary or of a physician. In the words of Lindley MR: "If directors act within their powers, if they act with such care as is reasonably to be expected from them, having regard to their knowledge and experience, and if they act honestly for the benefit of the company they represent, they discharge both their equitable as well as their legal duty to the company". It is perhaps only another way of stating the same proposition to say that directors are not liable for mere errors of judgment.' (author's emphasis)

The subjectivity of this test was illustrated in *Dorchester Finance Co Ltd v Stebbing*,[2] where non-executive directors who had relevant experience and qualifications in accountancy and business were held liable in negligence for signing cheques

---

1   [1925] Ch 407.
2   [1989] BCLC 498.

in blank which gave the managing director the opportunity to misappropriate the company's money.

Diligence

19.22 A director *is not bound to give continuous attention to the affairs of his company.* His duties are of an intermittent nature to be performed at periodical board meetings, and at meetings of any committee of the board upon which he happens to be placed. He is not, however, bound to attend all such meetings, although he ought to attend whenever, in the circumstances, he is reasonably able to do so.

Notwithstanding his non-attendance at meetings, if a director receives notice of irregularities in company management, he is then under a duty to pursue the matter. Failure to take action, in these circumstances, will render him liable[1] to pay damages.

Delegation of responsibilities

19.23 To cite Romer J again, his comments on delegation of work were as follows:

> 'In respect of all duties that, having regard to the exigencies of business and the articles of association, may be properly left to some other official, *a director is*, in the *absence of grounds for suspicion, justified in trusting that official to perform such duties honestly.*' (author's emphasis)

CONCLUDING SUMMARY

19.24 The common law level of skill required from directors is therefore a subjective one, implying that there are no objective minimum qualifications necessary for persons to act as directors. Furthermore, a director is only expected to attend board meetings 'whenever, in the circumstances, he is reasonably able to do so'.

Again, a director may delegate many tasks to company officials, thereby relieving himself of responsibility for their implementation. However, a director may not avoid responsibility for delegated tasks, if there were grounds for suspicion about the official to whom he delegated the work.

19.25 The litigation which spawned directors' common law duties largely concerned the honesty of directors. This accounted for the growth of the specific fiduciary duties which have been identified above. Notwithstanding these judicial developments, we shall see in the next chapter how it has been necessary to strengthen directors' fiduciary duties by legislation.

---

1 *Jackson v Munster Bank Ltd, ex p Dease* (1885) 15 LR Ir 356.

The duties of care and skill are quite low; the litigation record evidencing more concern for directors behaving honestly than acting competently. Once again, the Companies Act 1990, with its onerous requirements on the keeping of accounts and its reckless trading provisions, will undoubtedly also increase directors' common law levels of skill and diligence.

Before focusing on directors' statutory duties in the next chapter, it has to be remembered that where directors are also company employees, eg managing and executive directors, they will owe separate and additional duties[1] to the company by virtue of their contracts of employment. The standards of *competency* enunciated in the *City Equitable* case, particularly those for diligence and, perhaps, *degree of skill*, should be interpreted as applying to the activities of office holders, ie non-executive director functions.

The aspects of the *City Equitable* judgment dealing with *delegation* would seem to be of wider application, as they reinforce Lord Halsbury's comments in *Dovey v Cory*[2] that:

> 'The business of life could not go on if people could not trust those who are put into a position of trust for the express purpose of attending to details of management.'

---

1 See M. Forde *Employment Law* (The Round Hall Press, 1992).
2 [1901] AC 477.

Chapter 20

STATUTORY STRENGTHENING OF DIRECTORS' DUTIES

THE COMPANIES ACT 1990

20.1 The Companies Act 1990 was of great significance to the law relating to directors. Reflecting the traditional focus of litigation involving directors, the Act introduced a new regulatory regime to strengthen directors' fiduciary duties (or honesty requirements). The new statutory provisions also increased directors' duties of care and skill. These aspects of the Act will be considered in this chapter. Its sections increasing the liability of directors will be examined in Chapter 21, and the new sanctions of restriction and disqualification orders in Chapter 22.

STRENGTHENING OF DIRECTORS' HONESTY REQUIREMENTS

20.2 The sections of the 1990 Act strengthening directors' common law fiduciary duties include ss 28 to 47 regulating transactions involving directors, and ss 53 to 66 requiring disclosure of share dealings by directors, secretaries and their families.

The insider dealing rules introduced by ss 107 to 121 are also most relevant to share dealings where a company director is involved.

TRANSACTIONS INVOLVING DIRECTORS (AND OTHERS)

20.3 Part III of the 1990 Act seeks to regulate a number of different transactions involving directors, connected persons and shadow directors. Sections 25 to 27 contain the relevant definitions, including those of 'connected persons' and 'shadow directors'.

Connected persons

20.4 Under s 26, a person (not already a director) is connected with a director of a company if, and only if, he is:

(1) the director's spouse, parent, brother, sister or child;
(2) a trustee acting for him, his family or company; or
(3) the director's partner.

Where another company is controlled by a director, that company is also a connected person. Such a company is generally one where the director can control more than 50 per cent of the voting shares.

Shadow directors

20.5 Section 27 introduces the term 'shadow director' to Irish law, defining it as 'a person in accordance with whose directions or instructions the directors of a company are accustomed to act'. The definition does not include a person giving professional advice to the directors.

Disclosure of interest in proposed contracts

20.6 Under s 194[1](1) of the 1963 Act, it:

> 'shall be the duty of a director ... who is in any way, whether directly or indirectly, interested in a contract or proposed contract with the company, to declare the nature of his interest at a meeting[2] of the directors of the company.'

Shadow directors must also disclose such interests, in writing, to the board.[3]

In *Hopkins v Shannon Transport Ltd*,[4] it was held that s 194 disclosure must be to an independent board of directors and not fellow directors who also had personal interests in the contract.

If a director (or shadow director) fails to disclose his interest in accordance with s 194, the contract is voidable and the director must account to the company for the personal profits he has made.[5]

Section 194 was extended by s 47 of the 1990 Act to require disclosure by directors of loans, quasi-loans, etc – see **20.20** below.

SPECIFIC TRANSACTIONS REGULATED

20.7 Part III of the 1990 Act makes provision for specific transactions which may give rise to potential conflict between a director's personal interest and that of the company.

These specific contracts include:

(1) contracts of employment or directors' service contracts;
(2) property transactions between the company and its directors;
(3) loans to directors;

---

1 As amended by ss 27 and 47 of the 1990 Act.
2 Section 194(2)–(7) deals with the procedural requirements for such a board meeting.
3 See s 27(3) of the 1990 Act.
4 (Unreported) 10 July 1972 (HC).
5 Compare *Guinness plc v Saunders* [1988] 2 All ER 940 (CA).

(4) contracts entered into by the company with a third party in which the director has an interest.

Directors' service contracts

20.8 The limitations on extending directors' service contracts, imposed by ss 28 and 50 of the 1990 Act, have already been detailed in **14.29** above.

The effect of these sections is to protect the company, and indirectly its investors, against a breach of his fiduciary duty by a director who might otherwise have placed his own personal interests above those of the company.

Substantial property transactions with directors

20.9 A property transaction is substantial if its value is the lower of £10,000 or 10 per cent of the company's net[1] assets shown in the most recent statutory accounts, but in no case less than £1,000.[2]

No transfer of any substantial non-cash asset, or any interest therein, can take place between a company and a director of the company, or of its holding company, or a person connected with such a director, unless it has first been approved by a resolution of the members in general meeting.

Effect of breach of s 29

20.10 Any arrangement[3] to transfer a non-cash asset made in contravention of s 29 is voidable at the option of the company, unless restitution to the company is no longer possible or avoidance would affect an innocent third party or the approval of the company in general meeting has been given within a reasonable period after the transaction.

Unless a director can show that he did not know the relevant circumstances[4] constituting a contravention, the director concerned and any director authorising such a transaction will be liable to repay to the company any gain he made and to indemnify the company for any loss it suffers.

Penalising the dealing in options to trade in certain shares and debentures

20.11 Section 31 of the 1990 Act makes it a criminal offence for directors, or any person acting on behalf of, or at the instigation of, a director, to deal in

---

1 The aggregate of the assets less the aggregate of all liabilities, including provisions for liabilities and charges.
2 See s 29(2).
3 And any transaction resulting from such an arrangement.
4 Or that he took all reasonable steps to secure the company's compliance with s 29 – see s 29(5).

options to buy or sell 'relevant'[1] shares in, or debentures of, the company or associated companies.

Prohibition of loans and credit to directors and connected persons

20.12   The 1963 Act did not prohibit the making of loans by companies to their directors, nor the granting of guarantees in respect of loans to directors by third parties. However, s 192[2] required particulars of such loans to be given in the company accounts, and then laid before the investors at the annual general meeting.

The 1963 Act did not provide for sanctions in the event of non-disclosure, s 192(3) simply placing a duty on the auditors, so far as they were reasonably able to do so, to include the required particulars in their report.

The 1990 Act introduces a much stricter regime. Sections 31 to 38 of that Act strictly regulate the provisions of loans, 'quasi-loans'[3] and other forms of credit granted by companies to their directors and persons connected with them. Unlike the 1963 Act, the 1990 legislation provides for criminal penalties and civil remedies in cases of non-compliance.

General prohibition on granting of credit to directors

20.13   Section 31(1) provides that, subject to the exceptional transactions specified in ss 32 to 37, all companies are prohibited from:

(1)   making a loan or quasi-loan to a director of the company or of its holding company or to a person connected with such a director; or

(2)   entering into a credit transaction as creditor for a director or a person so connected; or

(3)   entering into any guarantee or providing any security in connection with a loan, quasi-loan or credit transaction made by a third party to such a director or a person so connected.

'Permitted' credit transactions

20.14   The exceptional transactions permitted by ss 32 to 37 are set out below.

---

1   Defined in s 30(2).
2   Of the 1963 Act, as amended.
3   Defined in s 25(2)(a), (b) and (c). An example of a quasi-loan might be where a company allows a director to use its credit card for his personal purchases. The company pays the price of any purchases; in effect creating a loan to be repaid by the director.

Transactions below a certain value

20.15   Section 32 permits a company to 'lend' money to any of its directors or persons connected with them up to a maximum of 10 per cent of the net asset value[1] of the company.

Where the total amount outstanding to a company under such an arrangement exceeds 10 per cent of the net assets (in particular if the value of the relevant assets has fallen) and the directors become aware or ought reasonably to become aware that there exists such a situation, it is the duty of the company, its directors and any persons for whom the arrangements were made to amend the terms of the arrangements concerned within two months so that the total amount outstanding under the arrangements again falls within 10 per cent of the net asset value.[2]

Intra-group loans and transactions

20.16   Sections 34 and 35 permit loans and transactions between companies in the same group, notwithstanding that a director of one member company is connected with another.

Business transactions and advances on directors' expenses

20.17   By virtue of s 37, a company can trade on a normal basis with its directors and persons connected with them. Such transactions must be in the ordinary course of business and the credit terms must be no more favourable than would be reasonable for the company to offer to a third party of the same financial standing. Thus a director can be a trade debtor of his company in respect of purchases of the company's ordinary goods and services.

Section 36 permits a company to provide its directors with advances to meet expenses to be properly incurred by them on the company's behalf. If these advances are not used, they must be refunded within six months.

Civil[3] remedies for the making of prohibited loans, etc

20.18   Section 38(1) renders a transaction prohibited by s 31 voidable, unless this is not possible. In any event, the director concerned is liable to repay to the company any gain he has made and to indemnify it for any loss or damage resulting from the prohibited transaction.

Personal liability for company debts

20.19   If a company is being wound up and unable to pay its debts, and the court considers that loans to directors have contributed materially to the

---

1 Determined by reference to the last set of audited accounts – see s 29(2).

2 Section 33(1) and (2).

3 An officer of the company who authorises or permits the breach of s 31 will also be guilty of a criminal offence – see s 40.

company's insolvency, or substantially impeded its orderly winding up, the court, on the application of the liquidator, any creditor or contributory, may declare that director personally liable, without limitation of liability, for the debts and liabilities of the company.

In deciding whether to make such an order under s 39(1), the court will take into account amounts paid back prior to the winding up and will consider the extent to which the loans in question contributed to the insolvency or impeded the orderly winding up of the company.

DISCLOSURE OF TRANSACTIONS INVOLVING DIRECTORS, AND OTHERS, IN THE ACCOUNTS

20.20   Sections 41 to 47 of the 1990 Act contain the requirements for disclosure by companies of transactions involving directors and persons connected with them.

A company must disclose, in its accounts, particulars of transactions entered into or subsisting during the accounting period, by the company[1] to a director,[2] or to any person connected with the director.

Under s 41(8), the disclosure requirement applies whether or not:

(1) the transaction or arrangement was prohibited by s 31;
(2) the director (or connected person) was of this status at the time the transaction was made; and
(3) the company making the loan was a subsidiary company and the loan was to a director of its holding company.

When disclosure is not required

20.21   The general disclosure requirements are exempted in the cases of:

(1) licensed banks[3] or their holding companies in respect of loans to directors;
(2) certain inter-company transactions;[4]
(3) directors' service contracts.[5]

Specific 'low value' transactions are also exempted from disclosure by s 45, eg loans etc, if the outstanding balance did not exceed £2,500 for each category of transaction during the year.

---

1 Or its subsidiary.
2 Including a director of a holding company.
3 Section 41(6).
4 Section 41(7)(a).
5 Section 41(7)(b).

Particulars to be disclosed in companies' accounts

20.22   Section 42 sets out the particulars to be included in the accounts. In respect of each transaction,[1] the names of the persons involved, together with particulars of the principal terms, are to be disclosed in the annual accounts and, in the case of loans, the amounts outstanding at the start and end of the year, interest due, provisions made (if any) and the percentage of the company's net assets at the year end tied up in such loans. These general requirements relate to all companies, except licensed banks. Special rules for disclosure by licensed banks are contained in ss 44 and 45.

Where the particulars required by ss 41 to 43 are not supplied, under s 46 the auditors must include in their report such particulars so far as they are reasonably able to. This duty on auditors is similar to that in s 192(3) of the 1963 Act, which required disclosure in the auditors' report of loans to directors to the extent that these were not included in the accounts.

DISCLOSURE OF DIRECTORS' AND OTHERS' INTERESTS IN SHARES AND DEBENTURES

20.23   Sections 53 to 66 of the 1990 Act contain detailed provisions requiring disclosure by directors, shadow directors and company secretaries, of their interests in shares and debentures of the company.[2]

Share dealings by directors, secretaries and their families

20.24   Sections 54, 55 and 64 define the nature of interests to be disclosed. Generally, ss 53 to 66 require disclosure of beneficial interests of directors and secretaries for all companies.

Under s 53(1), directors, etc, must notify the company, *in writing*, of:

(1) interests held[3] on taking up the office;
(2) purchases and sales of shares[4] and debentures while holding that office.

Sanction for non-compliance

20.25   Section 53(7) provides a criminal sanction for non-compliance with s 53(1) and (2).

---

1 And also any agreement reached during the year for such a transaction.
2 Or other companies within the group.
3 Including those of his spouse or minor child.
4 Of the company, its holding company or subsidiary. The number of shares and the amount of the debentures must be given.

Register of directors' and other interests

20.26   Every company must keep a register[1] of interests notified under ss 53 to 58. Sections 60 to 62 contain the detailed provisions relating to this register, which must be open to inspection by members or the public.[2]

Disclosure of interests in directors' report or accounts

20.27   The notified information on directors' etc interests must be included in the directors' report or as a note to the accounts – see s 63.

A public company is also under a duty to notify the Stock Exchange of any information it receives on shares or debentures held by a director, shadow director or secretary.[3]

INSIDER DEALING BY CONNECTED PERSONS

20.28   In *Percival v Wright*, the directors bought investors' shares without disclosing to the vendors that the board were in negotiations on a take-over bid for the company which valued the shares at a price much higher than the directors paid the investors. The court refused to overturn these transactions, holding that the directors' fiduciary duty was owed to the company, and not the individual shareholders.

The insider dealing provisions in the 1990 Act now extend the directors' duty of disclosure to protect potential investors in the company. This protection is against the use by 'insiders' such as directors, of privileged information which:

(1)   they obtained by virtue of being connected with the company; and
(2)   is unpublished and could materially affect the trading price of the shares in question, if published, ie is 'price-sensitive'.

Persons who are closely connected with a company (insiders) and use 'price-sensitive' privileged information about that company to benefit them-selves in share dealings with 'outsiders', would engage in the practice known as 'insider dealing'.

The Stock Exchange Listing Agreement required directors of listed com-panies[4] to ensure that share dealings did not take place between parties, one of which did not have price-sensitive information, which was in the possession of the other. Sections 107 to 121 of the 1990 Act now make insider dealing unlawful.

---

1   Section 59.
2   Section 60(8).
3   Section 65.
4   See **10.15** above.

Unlawful dealing in securities by insiders

20.29 Section 108 makes it unlawful for a person who is, or has been during the preceding six months, connected with a company to deal in any securities of that company if, by reason of his connection with the company, he is in possession of unpublished price-sensitive information.

Section 107 defines both 'dealing' and 'securities'; the latter including, of course, shares and debentures.

Lawful dealings

20.30 The 1990 Act essentially makes it unlawful for *connected persons* to engage in dealings in securities, *unless* they give at least 21 days' notice to the Stock Exchange and the dealing takes place 7 to 14 days after the publication of the company's results.[1]

Connected persons

20.31 Section 108(11) makes it clear that a person is connected with a company and thus an insider if he is:

(1) an officer of the company, or other group company (subsidiary, holding company or fellow subsidiary); or
(2) a shareholder of the company or other group company; or
(3) a person who occupies a position which could reasonably be expected to give him access to inside information, ie persons having a professional, business or other relationship with the company or other group companies;
(4) an officer of a substantial shareholder (five per cent) in the company or other group company.

Section 107 contains a wide definition of 'officers'. It includes a director, secretary, or employee, liquidator, auditor, receiver, examiner or any person arranging a compromise between the company and its creditors.

Other companies and tippees

20.32 Persons connected with other companies[2] and individuals who receive 'tips'[3] or information from connected persons, can also be deemed to be 'insiders' for the purposes of insider dealing.

---

1 Interim or final – see s 108(10).
2 Section 108(2).
3 Section 108(3).

Liability for insider dealing

20.33 Under s 109, the insider will be liable to compensate any other party who sustained a loss[1] by virtue of his unlawful actions. The insider will also be liable to account to the company for any profit made by him out of dealing in the securities.

Time-limits

20.34 An action for recovery of profit or loss must be commenced within two years after the date of the completion of the unlawful transaction.[2]

Criminal sanctions

20.35 Exceptionally heavy criminal sanctions are imposed by ss 111 to 114; the maximum being imprisonment for 10 years and/or a fine of £200,000.

Exempt transactions

20.36 Section 110 provides that certain transactions are exempt from the insider dealing provisions of s 108. These include securities acquired:

(1) under a will or an intestacy;
(2) under an approved employee profit-sharing scheme;
(3) under the following transactions entered in good faith:
    (a) obtaining a share qualification by a director;
    (b) fulfilling obligations by a person under an underwriting agreement;
    (c) by personal representatives, trustees, liquidators, receivers or examiners in the performance of their duties;
    (d) by way of, or arising out of, mortgages or charges, pledges or liens on documents of title to securities.

Stock Exchange supervision of insider dealing regulations

20.37 The Stock Exchange is expected to 'police' the insider dealing rules and to report any apparent offences to the Director of Public Prosecutions (DPP).

The obligation to report to the DPP is imposed upon both the relevant authority of the exchange and its members. Relevant authority is defined in s 108 as the Stock Exchange's:

(1) board of directors, committee of management or other management body; or
(2) manager, however described.

---

1 Based on the share price differences arising out of the existence of the price-sensitive information.
2 Section 109(4).

The Minister and the court are also empowered, under s 115(3), (5) and (6), to direct a Stock Exchange authority to investigate a complaint of an alleged offence, and to make a report to the DPP.

Annual report

20.38   The Stock Exchange must present an annual report[1] to the Minister on its supervision of the insider dealing rules.

EU dimension

20.39   Section 116[2] contains provisions intended to encourage co-operation between member state national stock exchanges in combating insider dealing.

FRAUDULENT TRADING

20.40   The statutory[3] liability for fraudulent trading extends the duty of honesty owed by directors (and others) to creditors, as well as the company.

Any person guilty of fraudulent trading may be personally responsible, without limitation of liability, for all the debts and other liabilities of the company.

RAISING OF DIRECTORS' COMPETENCY LEVELS

20.41   At common law, the test of competency for directors is subjective. A director need not exhibit in the performance of his duties a greater degree of skill than may reasonably be expected from a person of his knowledge and experience. Here again, the 1990 Act has increased the duties of directors, particularly the 'proper books of account' and reckless trading provisions.

Keeping proper books of account

20.42   Section 202 of the 1990 Act requires proper books of account to be kept, whether in the form of documents, or otherwise.

Purpose of books of account

20.43   Every company must keep proper books of account that:

(1) correctly record and explain the transactions of the company;
(2) will at any time enable the financial position of the company to be determined with reasonable accuracy;

---

1 Section 120.
2 And s 119.
3 Section 138 of the 1990 Act – see **21.31** below.

(3) will enable the directors to ensure that any balance sheet, profit and loss account or income and expenditure account of the company complies with the requirements of the Companies Acts; and

(4) will enable the accounts of the company to be readily and properly audited.

Contents of books of account

20.44   Proper books of account are required to contain:

(1) entries from day to day of all sums of money received and expended by the company and the matters in respect of which the receipt and expenditure take place;

(2) a record of the assets and liabilities of the company;

(3) if the company's business involves dealing in goods:

    (a) a record of all goods purchased, and of all goods sold (except those sold for cash by way of ordinary retail trade), showing the goods and the sellers and buyers in sufficient detail to enable the goods and the sellers and buyers to be identified, and a record of all the invoices relating to such purchases and sales;

    (b) statements of stock held by the company at the end of each financial year and all records of stocktaking from which any such statement of stock has been, or is to be, prepared; and

(4) if the company's business involves the provision of services, a record of the services provided and of all the invoices relating thereto.

Criteria for proper books of account

20.45   If books of account are kept on a continuous and consistent basis, comply with the purpose and contents outlined above, give a true and fair view of the state of affairs of the company (see **24.20**), and explain its transactions, then they will be deemed to comply with s 202.

Personal liability of directors and officers

20.46   Directors and officers can incur both criminal and civil liabilities for failure to keep proper books of account, including unlimited personal liability for the debts of the company.[1]

Reckless trading

20.47   The concept of 'reckless trading' was introduced by s 138 of the 1990 Act.

Unlike fraudulent trading, reckless trading is confined to officers of the company, including directors, shadow directors, secretaries and auditors. All these officers can now be made personally liable to contribute to the assets of

---

1 See next chapter.

the company, thereby providing a further source of funds for creditors of insolvent companies.

The statutory definition[1] of 'reckless trading' in s 297A(1) and (2)[2] includes two tests. An officer of a company shall be deemed to have been knowingly a party to the carrying on of any business of the company in a reckless manner if:

'(a) he was a party to the carrying on of such business and, having regard to the *general knowledge, skill and experience that may reasonably be expected of a person in his position,* he ought to have known that his actions or those of the company would cause loss to the creditors of the company, or any of them; or

(b) he was a party to the contracting of a debt by the company and did not honestly believe on reasonable grounds that the company would be able to pay the debt when it fell due for payment as well as all its other debts (taking into account the contingent and prospective liabilities).'

The test in limb (a) breaks new legal ground by importing an *objective* test of 'general knowledge, skill and experience' that may reasonably be expected of a director. This test replaces a director's common law subjective test of skill. The effect of this reform must be to raise the competency levels expected from all directors.

20.48   The subjective test in (b) was referred to by Lynch J in *Re Hefferon Kearns Ltd (No 2)*[3] as:

'. . . a very wide ranging and indeed draconian measure and could apply in the case of virtually every company which becomes insolvent and has to cease trading for that reason. If, for example, a company became insolvent because of the domino effect of the insolvency of a large debtor, it would be reasonable for the directors to continue trading for a time thereafter to assess the situation and almost inevitably they would incur some debts which would fall within paragraph [b] before finally closing down. It would not be in the interests of the community that whenever there might appear to be any significant danger that a company was going to become insolvent, the directors should immediately cease trading and close down the business. Many businesses which might well have survived by continuing to trade coupled with remedial measures could be lost to the community.'

As a result of this subjective test, directors should be very careful as to the decisions they make when their company gets into financial difficulties. They are now, perhaps, under a duty to act prudently in such circumstances, recording and monitoring all relevant board decisions as evidence in case of future reckless trading proceedings being taken against them.

Again, the personal responsibility placed on directors to keep proper books of account increases their common law duties of care and skill.

---

1 Section 297A of the 1963 Act was inserted by s 138 of the 1990 Act.
2 Of the 1963 Act.
3 [1993] IR 3 191 (HC). See **21.26** below.

Chapter 21

LEGAL LIABILITIES OF DIRECTORS AND OTHERS

THE TWO PERSPECTIVES

21.1   There are two perspectives to the legal liabilities of company directors. The first dimension is directors' liability to the company itself as its managing agents for breach of their common law and/or statutory duties to it. The second is liability to third parties arising out of their dealings with them on behalf of the company.

DIRECTORS' LIABILITY TO THE COMPANY

21.2   The common law duties relating to directors' honesty and competency have been set out in Chapter 19. These were styled fiduciary duties and duties of care and skill respectively.

The Companies Act 1990 reinforced the common law honesty requirements by introducing a regulatory regime for a series of transactions between the directors and their principal, the company. The post-1990 regulatory and disclosure requirements for directors have been detailed in the previous chapter: which also notes the impact of ss 202[1] and 138[2] on levels of competency expected from directors.

Remedies against directors by the company

21.3 A breach of duty by the director is a wrong against the company. The company has the right to take legal action against the offending director(s). However, as the company is controlled by the directors who may have committed the wrong against it, there may be practical difficulties in the company[3] pursuing legal action against directors whilst they retain control of it. This situation is implicitly recognised in cases of statutory duties, where most remedies apply in the course of the winding up of the company.[4] Accordingly, breaches of statutory duties are probably of more benefit to the creditors of an insolvent company than to members of a solvent company with legal rights against its directors who actually control it. If, however, sufficient independent shareholders were aware of the directors' breach of duty, then they could replace the board by passing an ordinary resolution at a general meeting. The

---

1 Keeping proper books of account.
2 Liability for reckless trading.
3 Members are also unable to take action on behalf of the company, as the rule in *Foss v Harbottle* applies – see **16.19**.
4 See **21.16** below.

new directors could then pursue the company's rights of action against the (former) offending directors.

Relief of directors from liability for breach of duty

21.4   Since directors' duties are owed to the company, the members may, after full disclosure of the breach in question to a general meeting, *waive (or forgive) a director's breach of duty*. For example, in *Multinational Gas Petrochemical Co v Multinational Gas and Petrochemical Services Ltd*,[1] the court confirmed that members can, by resolution, waive a directors' breach of duty. Such a company resolution may also be a bar to a liquidator[2] pursuing that breach of duty against the director(s).

Section 391 relief

21.5   Section 391 of the 1963 Act empowers the court to relieve an officer, wholly or partially, from liability for negligence, default, breach of duty or breach of trust. This relief is only available where a court considers that the officer has acted honestly and reasonably and, that, having regard to all the circumstances of the case, he ought fairly to be excused.

Relief in the articles of association

21.6   Generally, a company cannot exempt any officer[3] from liability for negligence or breach of duty by provision in its articles of association, or in any other contract with him. It may, however, be possible to reduce directors' duties in the articles, thereby modifying their potential liability.[4] In addition, art 138 of Table A grants an indemnity by the company to any director or officer, for liabilities incurred in defending any proceedings in relation to his acts as a director where:

(1)   judgment is given in his favour; or
(2)   he is acquitted; or
(3)   relief is granted to him under s 391.

Insurance

21.7   Each director, or the company on their behalf, can effect insurance to cover at least some of their legal liability as directors[5] (and officers).

---

1 [1983] Ch 258.
2 Subsequently appointed to the company.
3 Or auditor – see s 200 of the 1963 Act.
4 See *Movitex Ltd v Bulfield* [1988] BCLC 104.
5 See next chapter.

DIRECTORS' LIABILITY TO OUTSIDERS AS AGENTS OF THE COMPANY

21.8 A company can only operate through using its human agents. Directors are a company's managing agents and, as such, will enter into many transactions with 'outsiders' on behalf of the company.

The powers and authority of directors have already been detailed in Chapters 17 and 18.[1] Accordingly, it is necessary now merely to outline the common law position.

Common law liabilities to outsiders

21.9 As companies are independent legal entities, generally, acts done for or contracts entered into by a director on the company's behalf are the responsibility of the company. In this situation, the company is the principal for whom the directors simply act as agents. Accordingly, where a director acts within the company's objects (or contractual power) and within the scope of his own authority, he will incur no personal liability for company contracts.

Ultra vires and unauthorised transactions

21.10 Where a contract is intra vires the company, but outside the scope of the director's authority,[2] prima facie, the company is not liable, but the director may be.[3] However, the company can ratify the director's unauthorised (ultra vires) action. Alternatively, the outsider may require rights against the company under s 8 of the 1963 Act, reg 6 of the 1973 Regulations and the rule in *Turquand*'s case.[4] If he does, then the company may sue the director.

If the director's action is ultra vires the company, as well as being outside his own authority, the company will not be able to ratify it. However, the validity of the contract between the company and the outsider may be upheld by s 8 or reg 6. Again, if so, the company will be entitled to claim damages from the director who exceeded his authority.

Personal contractual responsibility

21.11 Where a director accepts personal responsibility[5] under a contract, he can incur personal liability. This could arise, for example, where a director gives personal guarantees to a bank which makes a loan to his company.

---

1 Chapter 17 also explains the legal limits to a company's contractual capacity and the application of the 'ultra vires' doctrine to it.
2 Or even prohibited by the company.
3 For breach of warranty of authority.
4 And, perhaps, art 79 – see **18.11**.
5 Either expressly or by implication.

Tortious liability of a director

21.12   The general rule is that directors, as such, are not liable for the torts of the company. It is the company itself that is vicariously liable for the torts committed by its agents acting within the scope of their authority or employment.

The company may be liable in tort, even if the tortious act by its human agent is ultra vires,[1] or criminal. For example, the decision in *Lloyd v Grace Smith & Co*[2] confirms that a company may be vicariously liable in tort for a criminal act (fraud) committed by its employee.

If, however, a director (or officer) commits or gives instructions for the commission of a tort, he may be jointly liable with the company to the injured outsider. For example, a director who fraudulently or negligently misrepresented the future profits of his company to a bank when seeking a loan, might well be liable in tort to the lender in the event of the company failing to repay the loan.

Corporate crimes

21.13   A company, as a recognised legal entity, can commit crimes. Accordingly, the company will be liable for criminal acts of its agents; the 'mens rea' or necessary mental intention[3] of culpable directors or agents being ascribed or imputed to the company itself.[4]

The degree or extent to which the mental intention of directors and officers will be imputed to the company as its own 'intention' will depend on the nature of the charge, the relative position of the officer and other relevant facts and circumstances of the case.[5] None the less, companies have been convicted of crimes created both by statute[6] and at common law (see **4.5**).[7]

Individual directors and officers can also be convicted of corporate criminal offences.

Criminal sanctions in the Companies Acts against directors (and others)

21.14   There are many instances of sections of the Companies Acts prescribing offences for misconduct by directors and officers and maximum punishments in respect of them. For example, s 137 of the 1990 Act makes fraudulent trading a statutory criminal offence with a maximum punishment of seven years' imprisonment or a fine of £5,000 or both.

---

1   *Campbell v Paddington Corporation* [1911] 1 KB 869.
2   [1912] AC 716. On the tortious liability of companies generally, see B. MacMahon and W. Binchy *Irish Law of Torts* (Butterworths, second edition, 1989), Chapter 39.
3   *Tesco Supermarkets Ltd v Nattrass* [1972] AC 153.
4   Mens rea may not be necessary at all in offences of strict liability.
5   *R v ICR Haulage* [1944] KB 551.
6   *DPP v Kent & Sussex Contractors Ltd* [1944] KB 146 (Div Ct).
7   *R v ICR Haulage* (above).

Again, concealing information from the liquidator, falsification of company records and other forms of dishonesty may give rise to criminal liability under ss 293 and 295 of the 1963 Act. There is a duty on the liquidator to co-operate with the Attorney-General in prosecuting these offences – see **42.54** below.

Appendix B of this book illustrates a range of serious criminal offences committable by company directors.

Statutory liabilities of directors[1] to outsiders

21.15   The common law liabilities of company directors have been greatly increased by legislation. Furthermore, as many cases of statutory liability impact on directors in the event of the company's winding up, the line of demarcation between directors' duties to the company and responsibilities to outsiders becomes blurred. Since most cases of directors' liability in statute will become activated on the liquidation of the company, the main beneficiaries will be the creditors, rather than the company itself.[2] For example, the circumstances in which directors may become liable[3] personally for the debts of the company without limitation, include cases of:

(1)   fraudulent and reckless trading;[4]

(2)   failure to keep proper books of account;[5]

(3)   acting as a director whilst a restricted or disqualified[6] person, or taking instructions from such a person;

(4)   entering into a permitted credit transaction[7] with the company and where the company is subsequently wound up;[8]

(5)   the making of a declaration of solvency by a director under s 60(5) of the 1963 Act, in connection with the giving of financial assistance for the purchase of shares in the company;

(6)   the making of a declaration of solvency without having reasonable grounds prior to a voluntary winding up situation – s 256(6) of the 1963 Act, as amended;

(7)   the directors, by virtue of ss 197 and 198 of the 1963 Act and, as provided by the company's memorandum of association, having unlimited liability for the company's debts;

(8)   where 'misfeasance' is proved against directors or others they may be liable during the course of winding up the company under s 298 of the 1963 Act. Misfeasance includes the misapplication or retention of the money or property of the company, as well as a breach of duty or trust in relation to the company.

---

1   And others, eg shadow directors.

2   And, indirectly, its investors.

3   Also criminally, see ss 137, 203 and 40 of the 1990 Act.

4   Ibid, s 138.

5   Ibid, ss 202 to 204.

6   See Chapter 23.

7   Under s 32 of the 1990 Act. Directors can also incur liabilities under s 38 for breach of s 31 of the 1990 Act – see previous chapter.

8   Section 39 of the 1990 Act.

DIRECTORS' PERSONAL LIABILITY FOR THE DEBTS OF AN INSOLVENT COMPANY

21.16 Of the various instances where directors are made statutorily liable for the debts of the company, perhaps the most important, from a creditor's perspective, are:

(1) failure to keep proper books of account;
(2) reckless trading; and
(3) fraudulent trading.

Liability for failure to keep proper books of account

21.17 Under s 204(1) of the 1990 Act, if:

(1) a company that is being wound up and is unable to pay its debts has not kept proper books of account; and
(2) the court considers that this contravention has contributed to the company's financial decline,

the court may, on the application of the liquidator, or any creditor or contributory of the company, declare that any officers of the company who were at fault, shall be liable for all or part of the company's debts.

Defence

21.18 The court will not make such a declaration if it considers that an officer:

(1) took all reasonable steps to secure compliance by the company with s 202; or
(2) had reasonable grounds for believing, and did believe, that the responsibility for compliance had been delegated to a competent person, acting under the supervision or control of a director who had formally been allocated such responsibility.

Types of company losses

21.19 To give rise to personal liability under s 204, the failure to keep proper books must have either:[1]

(1) contributed to the company's inability to pay all of its debts; or
(2) resulted in substantial uncertainty as to the assets and liabilities of the company; or
(3) substantially impeded the orderly winding up of the company.

The first case brought against a director under s 204 resulted in him being declared liable to pay in excess of £90,000 under (3) above.

---

1 Section 204(1)(b).

Judicial interpretation

21.20 The first case under s 204 was *Mantruck Services Ltd (in liquidation); Mehigan v Duignan.*[1] In that case, Shanley J found that:

(1) the company was in breach of s 202 in failing to keep proper books of account;

(2) the company was unable to pay its debts at the date of its winding up;

(3) the breaches of s 202 resulted in:

    (a) substantial uncertainty as to the assets and liabilities of the company; and

    (b) substantially impeded the orderly winding up of the company;

(4) the respondent knowingly and wilfully authorised and permitted the breach of s 202, and could not avail of any defence.

When exercising its discretion under s 204, Shanley J felt the court must consider the extent to which the breach of s 202 resulted in financial loss and, if it did, whether or not such losses were reasonably foreseeable by the officer as a consequence of his action. He then held that, although it was not possible to separate out liabilities prior to winding up which resulted from the breach of s 202, the liquidator had spent 80 per cent of his time seeking to remedy the deficiencies in the books of the company. The cost of that proportion of the liquidator's time was £91,240 and was a loss reasonably foreseeable by the respondent as a consequence of his actions. Accordingly, Shanley J declared the respondent to be personally liable to the company for the £91,240.

21.21 In an article,[2] dealing with this case, it is suggested that, from an evidential viewpoint, an action under s 204 will in future be a far simpler and more attractive option to a liquidator than taking action in respect of alleged fraudulent and reckless trading.

However, it should be noted that the damages awarded in the *Mantruck Services* case were awarded solely on the basis of recompensing the liquidator for his time expended in preparing satisfactory books of account. No damages were awarded in respect of losses to the company creditors which might have resulted directly from the failure to keep proper books of account.

In view of the evidential difficulties in proving which company losses were directly traceable to the failure to keep proper books of account, perhaps liquidators will be considering the possibility of bringing actions for both failure to keep proper books of account *and* for reckless trading. Arguably, any directors who allow a company under their control to carry on business without proper books of account are trading recklessly in a literal and commercial sense. However, whether such actions would be deemed to be reckless within the objective test of 'recklessness' in s 297A(2)(a) is a moot point – see **21.29** below.

---

1 (Unreported) 8 October 1996 (HC).

2 M. Sanfey 'Personal Liability of Directors Under s 204 of the Companies Act, 1990' *The Bar Review*, November 1996, pp 50–54.

Liability for reckless trading

21.22 Officers' liability for reckless trading was introduced[1] into Irish law by s 33 of the Companies (Amendment) Act 1990, which was then repealed by s 138 of the Companies Act 1990. Section 138 inserted s 297A in the 1963 Act.

Who can initiate proceedings?

21.23 Section 297A(1) provides that if, either:

(1) in the course of winding up a company; or
(2) during examinership proceedings, it appears that an officer committed either reckless (or fraudulent) trading, the court, on the application of the *receiver, examiner, liquidator* or *any other creditor or contributory* of the company, may declare that such officer shall be personally liable.

What is reckless trading?

21.24 If it can be shown that a director or officer was *knowingly* a party to the carrying on of business in a reckless manner, then a court may hold them *personally* liable for the debts of the company.

The Act does not clearly define reckless trading but gives the following guidelines[2] as to what might constitute it:

(a) if a director or officer was party to the carrying on of the business in such a manner that, having regard to the general knowledge, skill and experience that may reasonably be expected of a person in his position, he ought to have known that his actions or those of the company would cause loss to the creditors – an objective test;
(b) if he was party to the contracting of a debt but did not honestly believe, on reasonable grounds, that the company would be able to pay the debt when it fell due for payment (including all contingent and prospective liabilities) – a subjective test.

In addition, an applicant to the court must prove that he has suffered loss or damage.[3]

Defence

21.25 Where an officer[4] has acted honestly and responsibly in relation to the affairs of the company, the court may relieve him of liability.[5]

The introduction of reckless trading makes it easier for liquidators and creditors to initiate successful actions and have directors made personally

---

1 Because of the inadequacies of the fraudulent trading measure – see L. Flynn 'Reckless Trading' *Irish Law Times*, August 1991, p 186.
2 In s 297A(2)(a) and (b).
3 As a result of the reckless (or fraudulent) trading – s 297A(3).
4 Or any person in the case of proceedings for fraudulent trading.
5 Section 297A(6).

responsible for the debts of the company. As reckless trading is not clearly defined, courts have discretion in applying both the subjective and objective tests in s 297A(2)(a) and (b) and deciding whether or not an officer has acted responsibly if pleading so as a defence under s 297A(6).

Judicial interpretation of reckless trading provisions

21.26 Lynch J used the defence in s 297A(6) to avoid what he labelled the 'draconian' effect of s 297A(2)(b) (the subjective test above), stating:

> 'It seems to me that the expression 'acted honestly and responsibly in relation to the conduct of the affairs of the company,' ... is wider (than the corresponding UK provision) and the court in this jurisdiction is given specific power to relieve such a director from any personal liability whatsoever.'

Lynch J's judgment was handed down in the case of *Re Hefferon Kearns Ltd (No 2): Dublin Heating Co Ltd v Hefferon and Others.*[1]

Hefferon Kearns Ltd[2] (the company) was a construction company in which the four defendants were the only members and directors. The company commenced trading in January 1989. Its initial trading losses were:

Year	Losses after	Amount in £000s
1989	6 months	73
	12 months	8
1990[3]	2 months	23
	4 months	39
	6 months	72

During May 1990, two directors personally borrowed £45,000 which they used to discharge company debts.

The directors expected to reduce the losses in summer 1990 (as they had done the previous year) but due to a dispute over contract payments, this did not happen. Instead, losses increased, and the August management accounts, when produced on 1 October, showed the company with a balance sheet deficit in excess of £400,000.

A meeting of creditors was called and it was resolved to have an examiner appointed. The examiner proposed a scheme of arrangement. It was a condition of the scheme that there should be no reckless trading proceedings taken against the directors. However, the plaintiff, who was owed £41,000, decided to sue, and this caused the scheme to collapse.

---

1 [1993] IR 3 191 (HC).

2 See article by L. McCann 'Reckless Trading Revisited', reviewing the case in *Irish Law Times*, February 1993, p 31.

3 Directors obtained bi-monthly management accounts from 1 January 1990.

Scope of s 297A

21.27 In an earlier application in the same proceedings,[1] Lynch J had held that this section was not retrospective and in the present case therefore only applied to acts committed between 29 August 1990 and 11 October 1990. Furthermore, s 297A applies individually and personally against officers of a company, rather than as a form of 'collective' responsibility on the board of directors.

Meaning of 'recklessness'

21.28 Lynch J held that in applying the *objective* test in s 297A(2)(a) to the facts, there was no evidence to show that the directors had been guilty of reckless trading.

Under s 297A(2)(a) – the objective test

21.29 Lynch J equated recklessness with gross carelessness. The test he applied was 'would a reasonable man have described the defendant's actions as reckless?' Again, the word 'knowingly'[2] has an effect on the definition of reckless. Because of it, recklessness required knowledge, or imputed knowledge, that the defendant's action would cause a loss to creditors; it would not be sufficient simply to show that there might have been some worry or uncertainty as to the ability to pay all the creditors. The judge continued:

> 'I think [knowingly] requires that the director is party to carrying on business in a manner which [he] knows very well involves an obvious and serious risk of loss or damage to others and yet ignores that risk because he does not really care ... because his selfish desire to keep his own company alive overrides any concern which he ought to have for others.'

Applying this objective test of recklessness to the facts of the case, the judge considered them mainly against the first director, T. Hefferon,[3] who was the de facto managing director.

Lynch J then found that, as Hefferon had reasonable grounds for believing that extra monies might be received to pay the company's creditors, he did not know that his actions would cause them loss. He had, therefore, not traded recklessly.

Under s 297A(2)(b) – the subjective test

21.30 The defendant's position was different using the subjective test. Under this test, where a person did not honestly believe, on reasonable grounds, that the company would be able to pay its debts as they fell due, he would be guilty of reckless trading.

---

1 *Re Hefferon Kearns Ltd (No 1)* [1992] ILRM 51, [1993] IR 3 177.
2 In s 297A(2)(a).
3 He also considered that his conclusions applied equally, if not more strongly, to the remaining directors.

Lynch J held that by continuing to trade after the board meeting on 27 September, the defendant:

> ' was ... a party to the contracting of debts, by the company ... when he knew that those debts ... could not be paid to the company as they fell due.'

Accordingly, Lynch J found that the defendant was deemed to have traded recklessly under s 297A(2)(b) but, as he had acted honestly and reasonably, absolved him from liability by invoking the defence in s 297A(6).

Liability for fraudulent trading

21.31 For a director to be made liable for the debts of his company on grounds of fraudulent trading, the court must be satisfied that he *was* knowingly a party to the carrying on of the business of the company either:

(1) with intent to defraud creditors;[1] or
(2) for any other fraudulent purpose.

The 'carrying out' of a business can include a single transaction. For example, in *Re Hunting Lodges Ltd*,[2] the directors arranged for the sale of the company's main asset (Dirty Nelly's Public House), at a time when the company was insolvent. In addition, £200,000 of the agreed price was paid 'under the table' to the directors personally. Carroll J held, inter alia, that this single act constituted the carrying on of the business in a fraudulent manner.

On the question of 'intent to defraud', Carroll J stated:

> '... it is not necessary that there should be a common agreed fraudulent intent. If each of the participants acts for a fraudulent purpose, then each may be liable.'

21.32 In *Re Kelly's Carpetdrome Ltd*,[3] financial records were destroyed, and company assets and stocks siphoned off. Costello J held that liability for fraudulent trading should extend to anybody who knew of or was involved in the act. Accordingly, he imposed liability, not only on the company officers (and members), but also on an outsider because:

> '... he ran the company and the directors did his bidding at every opportunity that he required them to do so.'

Other cases where officers were made personally liable for the debts of their companies after they had siphoned off its monies and assets were *Re Aluminium Fabricators Ltd*[4] and *Re Contract Packaging Ltd*.[5] In the latter case, a number of deposit accounts were excluded from the company's records, thereby resulting in the Revenue Commissioners being defrauded.

---

1 Of the company, or creditors of any other person.
2 [1985] ILRM 75.
3 (Unreported) 1 July 1983 (HC).
4 [1984] ILRM 399.
5 See the *Irish Times*, 16, 17 and 18 January 1992.

Section 297A(9) makes it clear that a person can be declared liable for fraudulent[1] trading even though:

(1) he is the subject of criminal proceedings;
(2) the activities complained of occurred outside of Ireland.

21.33 Section 297A(1) is an anti-avoidance measure. It seeks to prevent a person against whom a decree has been given, passing on property to a trustee or assignee. Section 297A(1) replaced s 297(1) in the 1963 Act, following the enactment of the 1990 Act.

Since s 297 was introduced in 1963, the high evidential requirements involved in proving fraud have limited the effectiveness of 'fraudulent trading' provisions to the more 'blatant' examples illustrated by the cases mentioned above.

When a court decided to impose personal liability on a defendant for fraudulent trading, it generally did so on the basis of individual culpability. However, the constitutionality of s 297(1) has come into contention.

21.34 In *O'Keeffe v Ferris, Ireland and the Attorney General*,[2] the plaintiff sought a declaration that s 297(1) of the 1963 Act was unconstitutional because it created a criminal offence which was not minor in nature and, accordingly, should only be tried before a jury. She also argued that the section was punitive in its effect and not merely compensatory.

Murphy J accepted that s 297(1) was withdrawing:

> '... in certain circumstances and to a certain extent the right of an executive to plead that he was acting as an agent of a corporate body and to make him personally liable in certain circumstances for the activities for which he was directly responsible.'

He further held that the legislature clearly intended to create a civil remedy to deal with the problems faced by liquidators, creditors and contributories arising out of fraudulent trading, which remedy should not be available within the realm of the criminal law.[3]

As Murphy J found that s 297(1) neither created a criminal offence nor infringed the constitution, Ms O'Keeffe appealed his decision to the Supreme Court. In February 1997,[4] the Supreme Court gave judgment on the constitutionality of s 297(1) of the 1963 Act; now s 297A(1)(b) following its amendment by the 1990 Act. It decided that the sanctions available under the legislation do not encroach on the constitution and dismissed the appeal.

---

1 Or reckless.
2 [1993] 3 IR 165.
3 See G. Duffy 'Fraudulent trading and the decision in *O'Keeffe v Ferris' Commercial Law Practitioner*, October 1994.
4 Noted in *The Bar Review*, March 1997, p 178.

Criminal sanctions for fraudulent trading

21.35 Section 297(1) of the Companies Act 1963, since its revision by the Companies Act 1990, is a new section which imposes criminal liability on persons for fraudulent trading. Under s 297(2), a person convicted, on indictment, will be liable to a maximum prison sentence of seven years and/or a fine not exceeding £50,000.

During May 1996, a former insurance and investment broker was sentenced to imprisonment for four years and three months for fraudulent trading. He had been charged with carrying on business with intent to defraud the creditors of the company by falsely pretending that he, as a director, was engaged in the business of investing monies entrusted to him when he knew the company was insolvent.

Another company director was sentenced to four years' imprisonment for fraudulent trading when convicted of fraud, false pretences and falsification of accounts.[1]

---

1 See *Irish Independent*, 24 October 1996, p 3.

Chapter 22

DIRECTORS' AND OFFICERS' PROFESSIONAL INDEMNITY INSURANCE

CLAIMS FOR COMPENSATION

22.1 Claims for compensation against directors and officers of companies in the USA are frequent. As directors and officers in that jurisdiction face a significant risk of being sued, it is not unusual for them to insist, as a condition of accepting appointment, that directors' and officers' professional indemnity (D&O) insurance be effected to protect them.

The position of directors and officers in Ireland is somewhat different. Traditionally, it is probably fair to assert that such persons did not consider themselves subject to any serious risk of being sued. However, since the coming into effect of the Companies Act 1990, their position has changed. The courts are, increasingly,[1] making orders compelling directors to accept personal responsibility for the debts of their companies. It is therefore a distinct possibility that a director or officer, quite innocently and with no dishonest or criminal intent, may breach his duties. He may give negligent advice or make an actionable mis-statement, or perhaps he may perform some act which exceeds his own powers[2] or those of the company.[3] Again, he may be accused of, for example, failure to supervise employees to whom responsibility has been delegated or simply plain errors of judgement. Moving on to breach of statutory duties, we have already seen[4] the increased responsibility thrust upon directors by the provisions of the Companies Act 1990. In particular, a director now faces unlimited personal liability for the debts of the company, if, for example, he has failed to ensure that it keeps proper books of account, or it has traded recklessly.

WHO IS ABLE TO SUE?

22.2 A preliminary matter which must be considered at this stage is who is likely or able to sue company directors.

It is easy to envisage a situation where the liquidator of an insolvent company initiates legal proceedings against the directors of the failed company. However, if a company is solvent, and the directors control the majority of

---

1 See previous chapter.
2 Or authority.
3 Eg authorising excessive company borrowings.
4 See previous chapter.

voting shares, it may be difficult to make them responsible for any wrongs committed by them against minority shareholders.

Legal proceedings against directors and officers by minority investors

22.3   Directors' duties are owed to the company. If they are in breach of their duties, the company may sue. This means, in practice, that the majority of shareholders must agree to bring the action. If the directors hold the majority of the shares or are in control of the company, they may feel secure or immune from risk. This is because of the rule in *Foss v Harbottle* which prevents minority shareholders suing for wrongs done to the company. However, as we saw in Chapter 16, minority investors now enjoy opportunities to take action against the directors through the apparent judicial exceptions to the rule.[1]

In *Daniels v Daniels*,[2] two directors, who were also majority shareholders, caused the company to sell land to one of their wives, for £4,250. The land was later resold for £120,000. The plaintiffs were minority shareholders, and alleged, not fraud, but that the directors had failed in their duty to the company by selling its land at less than its market value.

The court held that the rule in *Foss v Harbottle* should not permit directors to profit from their negligence, Templeman J stating:

> 'If minority shareholders can sue if there is fraud, I see no reason why they cannot sue where the action of the majority and the directors, though without fraud, confers some benefit on those directors and majority shareholders themselves. It would seem to me quite monstrous – particularly as fraud is so hard to plead and difficult to prove – if the confines of the exception to *Foss v Harbottle* were drawn so narrowly that directors could make a profit out of their negligence. The principle which may be gleaned from (authority) is that a minority shareholder who has no other remedy may sue where directors use their powers, intentionally or unintentionally, fraudulently or negligently, in a manner which benefits themselves at the expense of the company.'

22.4   In *Prudential Assurance Co Ltd v Newman Industries Ltd (No 2)*,[3] a case involving legal costs of about £750,000, the Court of Appeal suggested that a plaintiff bringing a derivative action be required, before proceeding with his action, to establish a prima facie case:

(1) that the company is entitled to the relief claimed; and
(2) that the action falls within the proper boundaries of the exception to the rule in *Foss v Harbottle*.

In order to determine (2), the judge may grant a sufficient adjournment to enable a general meeting to be convened so that the court can form a view in the light of the conduct of, and proceedings at, that meeting.

---

1 In *Foss v Harbottle*. Minority members also enjoy statutory protections of their rights.
2 [1978] Ch 406.
3 [1982] Ch 204.

The issue of legal costs will often affect minority shareholders. Because of them, shareholders will often be reluctant to pursue rights against directors. Here, too, the courts have been helpful.

22.5   In *Wallersteiner v Moir (No 2)*,[1] it was recognised that a minority shareholder who properly pursued a derivative action, could be indemnified by the company for the legal costs and expenses incurred because it is the company which would benefit if the action succeeded. As Denning MR stated:

'seeing that, if the action succeeds, the whole benefit will go to the company, it is only just that the minority shareholder should be indemnified against the costs he incurs on its behalf. If the action succeeds, the wrongdoing director will be ordered to pay the costs: but if they are not recovered from him, they should be paid by the company. .... But what if the action fails? Assuming that the minority shareholder had reasonable grounds for bringing the action – that it was a reasonable and prudent course to take in the interests of the company – he shall not himself be liable to pay the costs of the other side, but the company itself should be liable, because he was acting for it and not for himself. In addition, he should himself be indemnified by the company in respect of his own costs even if the action fails.'

Under s 205 of the 1963 Act, any member[2] of a company can complain to the court that the powers of the directors are being exercised in a manner oppressive to him. Any such person may also petition the court to wind up the company under s 213. In fact, the most serious risk to directors of being sued will usually arise when the company encounters financial difficulties, as happened in the *Hefferon Kearns* cases[3] which involved allegations of reckless trading.

Another example of directors' liability is s 23(11) of the 1983 Amendment Act. Under s 23(11), if shares are allotted without giving the existing shareholders a statutory right of pre-emption, the directors responsible will be liable to the shareholders directly for all loss, damage and expenses incurred by them.

Legal proceedings by non-members

22.6   Actions by creditors can arise when the company is in serious financial difficulty. Such actions can be taken by the creditors directly, or by a liquidator on behalf of all the company's creditors.

The many instances where a court can make company directors personally liable, for the debts of the company without limitation of liability, have already been dealt with in Chapter 21. Some of these actions may involve allegations of fraud against the directors or officers, eg an action for fraudulent trading under s 297A(1)(b) of the 1963 Act. However, if only one director is guilty of fraud, a D&O insurance policy may still cover an innocent director by treating

---

1 [1975] QB 373.
2 A minority of members can also apply to the court to appoint an inspector to investigate the affairs of the company under s 7 of the 1990 Act – see Chapter 27.
3 See previous chapter.

the wrongful act of his co-director as not being imputed to him (see **22.11** below).

22.7 Under s 298 of the 1963 Act, a court can award damages against a director where it appears during a winding up that he has been guilty of misfeasance or breach of trust in relation to the company. In an action taken under s 298, there is no need for the claimant to prove fraud in order to succeed in obtaining damages.

There are many other examples, particularly under the 1990 Act, of circumstances where breach of statutory duty by a company director or officer will render him liable to pay damages.

A further problem confronting directors is that statutory duties are imposed upon them nowadays, not only by the Companies Acts, but also by other business related legislation. Company directors could incur a legal liability for a breach of their statutory duties arising under such related statutes as:

The Safety, Health and Welfare at Work Act 1989
The Data Protection Act 1988
The Employment Equality Act 1977
The Anti-Discrimination Pay Act 1974
The Income Tax Act 1967
The Corporation Tax Act 1976
The Competition Act 1991
The Finance Act 1997

For example, competitors of the company may allege that they have suffered losses arising from anti-competitive practices by the company. If a director bears responsibility for any such practices, he could incur a personal liability. In reality though, as long as the company remains financially sound, the director is unlikely to be sued personally.

22.8 The Finance Act 1997 has created another risk for directors where company shares (or ownership) are transferred out of Ireland.

Prior to the 1997 Act, where an Irish resident company moved its central management and control from Ireland, ie became non-resident, it incurred no Irish tax liabilities as a result. Because of the 1997 Act, such a change will now result in the company being deemed to have disposed of its assets at market value for the purposes of capital gains tax.

If the company does not pay this tax, its former controlling director (and fellow group members of a subsidiary) may be obliged to pay on its behalf.

Because of related statutory and other legal responsibilities, in addition to claims for damages being taken against them by company members and creditors, directors may also be sued by company employees, government departments, new company owners and owners of property adjacent to that owned by the company.

Looking to the future, it seems likely that these extraneous legal liabilities of directors will increase, rather than diminish. For example, EU developments in the fields of employment and social security, environmental and competition law generally, may further extend the responsibilities of company directors. The fact that shareholders are currently tending to scrutinise company performance more closely may also lead to a rise in litigation against the directors of public companies.

Events giving rise to legal proceedings against directors

22.9 If one examines the circumstances in which directors have been sued, certain events can be identified as 'triggering' the legal action. The events which often give rise to the initiation of legal proceedings against directors and officers would usually be:

(1) the liquidation of the company;
(2) a change in ownership of the company's share capital;
(3) the sale of the company, or the acquisition of it by another company. In these cases, the purchasers will have had to base their assessment of company worth on facts and forecasts which, after the sale, may prove unrealistic. Again, in describing the company to be sold, the directors[1] may make representations, or give warranties, covenants or even indemnities which, should they prove to be inaccurate or breached, would result in their being sued;
(4) the death of the principal shareholder, leading to a change of control;
(5) the dishonesty of a director or officer;
(6) the resignation of a director;
(7) the consequence of poor trading results;
(8) the publication of an adverse official report on the company's affairs; and
(9) adverse publicity.

There can be little doubt that directors and officers of companies face real risks of being sued. Prudent directors and officers will seek to transfer much of this risk to an insurance company by effecting a Directors' and Officers' (D&O) Professional Indemnity insurance policy.

COVER PROVIDED BY D&O POLICIES

22.10 The terms of individual D&O insurance contracts will vary, but, generally, the following is an outline of the type of cover available to directors and officers.

---

1 Or shareholders.

The *indemnity* to directors and officers is against *loss* arising from any claim(s) made during the period of insurance by reason of any *wrongful act* in their respective capacities of directors and/or executive officers of the company.[1]

The policy is therefore on a 'claims made' basis. Claims resulting in a loss to the directors or officers because of a wrongful act will be indemnified by the insurer.

'Wrongful act' may be defined as any actual or alleged breach of duty, breach of trust, neglect, error, mis-statement, omission, breach of warranty or other act wrongfully done by any director or officer. It therefore covers breaches of fiduciary duty, negligence, and liability for directors and officers exceeding their authority as agents for the company. It would be usual for a deductible[2] of, say, £500 to apply to each claim.

Related, continuous or repeated wrongful acts may be deemed to constitute a single wrongful act.

'Loss' means such sums which the director or officer is legally liable to pay for any wrongful act. It would include damages, judgments, settlements and defined costs. It would not include fines, penalties or punitive damages, nor matters which may be deemed uninsurable under the law.

D&O policies usually have a limit of indemnity, eg £1 million. However, insurance cover may be purchased for limits of up to at least £15 million.

Policy exclusions

22.11   A number of exclusions are normal, which may vary from one insurer to another. Standard exclusions from D&O policy cover might include the following:

(1)   claims based upon or attributable to any director or officer gaining personal profit or advantage to which he was not legally entitled;
(2)   claims brought about or contributed to by the dishonesty of the directors or officers. Some insurers make it clear that it is the individual dishonest director or officer who is denied indemnity and that the exclusion does not apply to other directors and officers. For example, fraudulent actions by one director may not be imputed to his co-directors if they were not privy to them;
(3)   any personal guarantee or warranty (other than a warranty of authority) given by a director or officer;
(4)   claims which are insured by any other policy or policies;
(5)   bodily injury to any person or loss or damage to property;

---

1 Or of subsidiary companies.
2 A deductible, also known as an excess, is an amount which an insurance company is entitled to deduct from the payment of each claim under a policy.

(6) pollution, contamination, seepage, the emission of effluents of any kind into the atmosphere or any body of land, water, waterway or watercourse or any other form of pollution;

(7) libel or slander may also be excluded by some insurers.

Claims made against the directors by the majority of the shareholders for breach of duty may also be excluded from cover, in addition to any claims instigated by one director or officer against a fellow director or officer.

Basis of cover

22.12   The D&O policy may be in two parts. One part can cover the directors and officers in their personal capacity in circumstances where they cannot claim an indemnity from the company.

The second part of a D&O policy will reimburse the company in respect of costs and expenses it may have incurred in a successful defence of a director or officer under s 200 or s 391[1] of the 1963 Act. There may be an increased deductible for such claims, eg £5,000.

Section 200 and D&O policies

22.13   It has been suggested that as s 200 prohibits the company from exempting or indemnifying its directors and officers from liability, it should not be able to purchase professional indemnity insurance for them.

It is one matter to indemnify a director out of the company's assets. It is quite another to purchase insurance cover for non-criminal liabilities of directors, at a reasonable price or premium. Furthermore, in the event of a successful claim against the director, it would be the insurer, rather than the company, who indemnifies the director. It is therefore difficult to see how the purchase of D&O policy for their directors and officers can be a breach of s 200 by the company.

In the UK, the equivalent section of its companies legislation now provides, in s 310(3)(a) of the Companies Act 1985, that s 310 does not prevent a company from purchasing and maintaining D&O (or Auditors) Liability insurance. It would be sensible if s 200 was similarly amended to remove any doubts on this matter.

The future of D&O insurance

22.14   In a booklet[2] issued by a leading provider of this specialised form of insurance cover, AIG Europe confirm[3] that 'we are advised that the Directors

---

1 See previous chapter.
2 *Directors and Officers Liability Insurance. A Guide from AIG Europe* (AIG Europe (Ireland) Ltd, 1992).
3 Ibid, p 6. Pages 16–22 give examples of claims made against directors by shareholders, government departments, employees, new owners, creditors, and 'miscellaneous' persons.

and Officers Liability Insurance policy does not breach the prohibition of s 200'. They also point out that, based upon their claims experience, the world wide trend towards an increasing number of legal actions being initiated against company directors seems likely to be repeated in Ireland.

Under a heading, 'potential Irish D&O scenarios', the AIG booklet gives a sample of newspaper headlines taken from reported legal cases involving directors and officers. These headlines were printed in the *Irish Times* over a period of less than six months. They include:

'Directors accused of misapplying funds'[1]

'Insolvent firm kept on trading'[2]

'Non Executive directors fail to take stand against abuses'[3]

'Packaging firm directors accused of fraud and conspiracy'[4]

'Court orders directors to pay £647,543, house, car and boats forfeited'[5]

'Court orders directors not to leave country'[6]

'50 per cent shareholding, outvoted by casting vote, is minority shareholder entitled to sue under rule in *Foss v Harbottle*?'[7]

MODERN ATTITUDE TOWARDS DIRECTORS' RESPONSIBILITIES

22.15   The Companies Act 1990 has changed the modern attitude towards directors' responsibilities. This statute, quite rightly, recognises that directors constitute the controlling 'mind and hands' of a company, and it is they, rather than the owners/investors, who should be accountable for any wrong doings by the company.

The logical development arising from this new legal environment must be a recognition by directors of their roles as professional managers of companies, and an acceptance by them to be accountable for their actions. This scenario is likely to spawn litigation against directors, seeking to make them liable for the debts of companies which may have failed financially.

As a result, the prudent Irish company director of the third millennium should see D&O insurance as a necessity, rather than an optional extra.

---

1   11 December 1991.
2   6 December 1991.
3   17 December 1991.
4   16 January 1992.
5   18 January 1992.
6   4 February 1992.
7   13 April 1992.

CHAPTER 23

RESTRICTION AND DISQUALIFICATION OF DIRECTORS

THE COMPANIES ACT 1990

23.1 Under the 1963 Act, there was only one section which dealt with restricting persons from acting as directors. This was the little used s 184, whose provisions were limited to:

(1) circumstances where a person was found guilty of fraud or dishonesty; and
(2) in the case of companies in liquidation, where a person was found guilty of fraudulent trading.

Section 184 has now been replaced by Part VII of the Companies Act 1990.

Part VII of the 1990 Act introduced radical reforms in the treatment of directors and other officers who are found to have abused the privilege of trading with limited liability. These reforms are based on the recommendations of the Cork Committee[1] which stated, inter alia, that:

> 'to provide proper safeguards to the general public the law must also provide that those whose conduct has shown them to be unfit to manage the affairs of a company with limited liability shall, for a specific period, be prohibited from doing so.'

Part VII effectively implements the Cork Committee's recommendation by providing for the restriction and disqualification of directors.[2]

PART VII OF THE 1990 ACT

23.2 Part VII is divided into three chapters. These chapters deal with:

(1) *restrictions*[3] on directors of insolvent companies;
(2) *disqualification*[4] of directors; and
(3) *enforcement* provisions.[5]

---

1 Report of the Review Committee on Insolvency Law and Practice under the chairmanship of Sir Kenneth Cork (HMSO, 1982, Cmnd 8558).
2 See articles by H. Linnane 'Restrictions on and Disqualification of Directors' *ILT*, June 1994, p 132 and B.P. Farren 'Restrictions on Directors of Insolvent Companies' *The Bar Review*, Vol 2, Issue 8, June 1997, p 349.
3 Sections 149 to 158.
4 Sections 159 and 160.
5 Sections 161 to 169.

Restrictions on directors

23.3 Directors of insolvent companies which are wound up may only act as directors of other companies in restricted circumstances.

The provisions of Chapter 1 come into effect where, under s 149(1), *a company is being wound up and:*

(a) it is proved to the court at the commencement of the winding up that it is unable to satisfy its debts; or

(b) the liquidator certifies, or it is otherwise proved, to the court during the course of the winding up, that it is unable to pay its debts.

In *Re Verit Hotel and Leisure (Ireland) Ltd; Carway v Attorney General,*[1] the constitutionality of s 149(1)(b) was raised. This case made it clear that the fact that a s 150 (restriction) declaration might affect a person's ability to earn a livelihood was not a reason for declaring s 149(1)(b) unconstitutional. Carroll J held that nothing in s 149 warranted the interpretation that the liquidator's certificate was to be conclusive evidence of insolvency. Once this was established, the plaintiff's claim failed.

Any director or 'shadow director' of such a company (or anyone who was such within 12 months prior to the commencement of the winding up) is not to act as a director or secretary or be concerned in the promotion or management of any company for a period of 5 years, unless the company meets the specified[2] requirements as to its paid-up capital.

Effect of s 150 restriction declaration

23.4 Directors who are affected by these provisions[3] cannot act as directors of other companies during the five-year period unless, in the case of a public limited company, the nominal value of the allotted share capital is at least £100,000 or, in the case of a private company, £20,000 and in either case each allotted share and any premium is fully paid up in cash. The liquidator applied to the court to have two directors restricted in *Re E.P. Nolan Contractors (Longford) Ltd*[4] because the directors had failed to keep proper records, failed to hold annual meetings or to file annual returns. During the case, further irregularities came to light. As a result, the court restricted the two directors for five years.

Exemption and relief

25.5 Under s 150(2), a restriction declaration is not to be made where the court is satisfied that:

---

1 [1997] 1 ILRM 110.
2 Section 150(1).
3 Eleven persons were restricted during 1994, and 57 during 1995.
4 The *Irish Times*, 22 June 1996.

(1) the person concerned has acted honestly and reasonably in relation to the conduct of the affairs of the company and there is no other reason why it would be just and equitable to subject him to such restriction; or

(2) the person concerned was a director solely because he was nominated as such by a financial institution in connection with the giving of credit to, or the purchase of shares in, the company by that institution.

In *Re Cavan Crystal Group Ltd*,[1] the court held that the directors, other than the managing director who was responsible for falsifying VAT and PAYE returns, had acted honestly and responsibly, and as a result were not restricted.

Under s 152, a restricted person may apply to the court for relief. The court may grant such relief on whatever terms and conditions it sees fit.

Duties of liquidators and receivers

23.6 There is no obligation on the liquidator to notify the persons affected by these provisions of the fact that they are so affected. If, however, it appears to him that the interests of another company or its creditors may be placed in jeopardy, under s 151 a liquidator must inform the court that a restricted person is acting as a director or promoter of that other company. In fulfilling this duty, the liquidator will have access to a list of restricted persons, as a current register of such persons must be maintained by the registrar of companies.[2]

Section 154 makes it clear that the provisions of Chapter 1 applying to liquidators and winding up proceedings, also apply to receivers and receiverships.

Effect of restriction declarations on companies

23.7 A person who is declared a restricted person by the court must give 14 days' notice to a company appointing him as a director, notifying it that he is a restricted person.[3]

Restrictions on the company

23.8 Section 155 imposes a number of restrictions on any company where a restricted person is an officer. These restrictions preclude such a company from making use of the machinery provided under s 60 of the 1963 Act (whereby a company may provide financial assistance for the purchase of its own shares) and subjecting it to the same restrictions as are imposed by the 1983 Act on public limited companies in making allotments of shares other than for cash.

---

1 (Unreported) 26 April 1996 (HC).
2 Under s 153.
3 Section 155(5).

Where such a company allots a share which is not fully paid up, it is to be treated as if the whole of its nominal value and any premium had been received, but the allottee is liable to pay the company, in cash, the full amount which should have been received less the amount of any consideration paid.[1]

Relief for the company

23.9   Section 157 gives the court the power to grant relief to the company, or any person adversely affected by these restrictions. However, no such relief will be granted if the company was properly notified in advance by the restricted person.

Disqualification of directors

23.10   The second form of restraint imposed upon directors is a disqualification order.

Disqualification order

23.11   A disqualification order is an order made by the court, disqualifying a person from acting[2] as:

> '... an auditor, director or other officer, receiver, liquidator or examiner, or be in any way, whether directly or indirectly, concerned or take part in the promotion, formation or management of any company or any society registered under the Industrial and Provident Societies Acts, 1893 to 1978.'

Whilst a restriction declaration may impose conditions under which a person can act as a director or secretary, a disqualification order extends to prevent a person being employed by a company in a management position.

Disqualification may be either mandatory or discretionary.

Mandatory disqualification

23.12   Where a person is convicted on indictment of any indictable offence in relation to a company or one involving fraud or dishonesty, he shall be deemed to be disqualified for five years from the date of the conviction.[3]

The court, on the application of the prosecutor, has the discretion to vary the five-year disqualification period.

Discretionary disqualification

23.13   Discretionary disqualification may occur following an application to the court. The court may make an order where:

---

1 Section 156.
2 Or being appointed to act – see s 159.
3 Section 160(1)(b).

(1) a person has been guilty of *any* fraud in relation to a company, its members or creditors, while acting as promoter, auditor, officer, receiver, liquidator or examiner of the company;

(2) a person has been guilty, while acting in any of the roles mentioned in (1) of a breach of his duty as such;

(3) a person has been declared personally liable for a company's debts because of fraudulent or reckless trading;

(4) a person's conduct in any of the roles mentioned in (1) makes him unfit to be concerned in the management of a company;

(5) in consequence of an inspector's report under the Companies Acts a person is similarly unfit; or

(6) a person has been persistently in default in making returns, giving notices or filing documents with the registrar.

A person is presumed conclusively to have been persistently in default for the purpose of (6) if he has been found guilty of three or more such defaults.[1]

The managing director of a garage, Thomas O'Doherty, was found to have deliberately defrauded financial companies by purporting to sell cars that never existed. He was disqualified for a period of five years.[2]

At 31 December 1996, two notifications of disqualification orders had been lodged with the court. The names, addresses and periods of disqualification of these two former directors are recorded in the Companies Report 96.[3]

Who may apply for the making of a disqualification order?

23.14 An application for the making of a disqualification order may be made in any proceedings, civil or criminal, or independently under s 160. Such an application may be made by the Director of Public Prosecutions or any member, contributory, officer, employee, receiver, liquidator, examiner or creditor of the relevant company. However, only the DPP may apply on ground (5) and only the DPP and the registrar under ground (6) – see **23.13**.

Relief from disqualification order

23.15 Any disqualified person has the right to apply to the court for relief, which the court is empowered to grant on whatever terms and conditions it deems fit.

Enforcement and sanctions

23.16 When a person breaches the terms of either a restriction or disqualification order, he is liable to the following sanctions:

---

1 Section 160(2) and (3). See also s 160(9).
2 The *Irish Independent*, 24 October 1996.
3 Department of Enterprise, Trade and Employment (The Stationery Office, Dublin, August 1997, p 39). Pages 29–39 contain details of almost 100 persons who were subject to s 150 (restriction) declarations at the end of 1996.

(1) a person who is already subject to a restriction order becomes subject to a disqualification order for five years from the date of conviction;

(2) a person who is already subject to a disqualification order will have his period of disqualification extended by a period of 10 years from the date of his conviction or such other period as the court may decide;

(3) where a restricted person is or becomes a director of another company, which goes into insolvent liquidation during his restriction period, this can lead to the making of a disqualification order on that person;

(4) where a person is found to be guilty of breaching his restriction or disqualification, he will not be permitted to apply to the court for relief from his disqualification order.[1]

Civil consequences

23.17 Where a person breaches a restriction or a disqualification order there are two further civil consequences:

(1) the company will be entitled to recover from him 'as a simple contract debt' any consideration given to him by the company for an act done or services provided while he was acting in contravention of the order, eg remuneration paid to him;

(2) where the company is wound up while he is acting, or within a period of 12 months since his involvement, and if it is unable to pay its debts, that person may be made personally liable for all or part of the company's debts incurred while he was so acting.[2] An application may be made by a liquidator or a creditor to render that person liable.

Other directors

23.18 The other directors of a company which does not comply with the capital requirements of s 150(3) after it is notified by a person on whom a restriction order has been placed are also at risk financially. If the company is wound up and is unable to pay all its debts, its officers who knew, or ought to have known, of the restriction may be personally liable for all the debts of the company.[3]

Acting under direction of disqualified person

23.19 Any person who acts on an instruction from a person whom he knows is disqualified will be guilty of an offence which on conviction could lead to that person being, himself, disqualified. In addition, he may also be held personally liable for the debts of a company while he was acting on the instruction of the disqualified person.[4]

---

1 Sections 161 and 162.
2 Section 163.
3 Section 163(4).
4 Sections 164 and 165.

Register of orders

23.20   The registrar of companies is required to keep a register of disqualification orders, having been furnished with particulars by an officer of the court.[1]

Undischarged bankrupts

23.21   Section 183 of the 1963 Act dealing with an undischarged bankrupt acting as director has been replaced by a new section which prohibits an undischarged bankrupt acting as an officer, auditor, liquidator or examiner of a company or even acting in the management of a company. If an undischarged bankrupt is convicted of an offence, he, too, may become the subject of a disqualification order.[2]

---

1 Sections 167 and 168.
2 Section 169.

PART VI

MONITORING THE DIRECTORS' STEWARDSHIP OF THE COMPANY

Chapter 24

FINANCIAL RECORDS, ACCOUNTS AND REPORTS

BASIC FINANCIAL RECORDS

24.1 Prior to the 1963 Act, Irish companies were not legally required to keep proper books of account, although many would have done so as a matter of good commercial practice. However, s 147(1) of the 1963 Act provided that all companies had to keep basic financial records in the form of proper books of account showing:

(1) all income and expenditure;
(2) all sales and purchases; and
(3) the assets of the company.

BOOKS OF ACCOUNT

24.2 Section 147 has now been superseded by the more detailed and onerous requirements of s 202 of the 1990 Act. As a director could be held liable for the debts of the company if proper books of account are not kept, the requirements of s 202 have been dealt with in Chapter 20.

The books of account must be kept at the registered office of the company or at such other places as the directors think fit.[1] The books must be kept by the company for at least six years.

Section 202(4) stipulates that proper books of account shall only be deemed to be kept if they comply with subsections (1), (2) and (3),[2] and give a *true and fair view* of the state of affairs of the company and *explain its transactions.*

Books of account must be available for inspection at all reasonable times, without charge, by the officers (but not members) of the company and 'by any other persons entitled pursuant to the Companies Acts, to inspect the books of account of the company'.

24.3 In *Healy v Healy Homes Ltd*,[3] Kenny J held that a director of a company, when exercising his right to inspect the books of account, is entitled to be accompanied by an accountant, and, if necessary, make copies of these records. In his judgment, Kenny J stated:

---

1 See s 202(5) to (10).
2 See **20.42–20.44**.
3 [1973] IR 309 (HC).

'a director's right to inspect the books of account necessarily involves that an accountant nominated by him may do this ... when he is accompanied by the director or when the accountant has been given a written authority to do so ...'

The accountant may also be required to give a written undertaking that he will treat the knowledge gleaned from the books of account as confidential, using it only for the purpose of giving confidential advice to the director who employed him in relation to the matter with which he has been retained.

Sanctions for breach of s 202

24.4   The 1990 Act provides for both criminal and civil sanctions in respect of breaches of s 202.

Criminal sanctions

24.5   Section 202(10) makes it a criminal offence where a director 'fails to take all reasonable steps to secure compliance by the company ... or has, by his own wilful act been the cause of any default by the company'.

Defences

24.6   Section 202(10) sets out two defences to a director in these circumstances. First, if he can prove that he took all reasonable steps to secure compliance with s 202(1) to (4), he will have a good defence. Secondly, he may also escape responsibility if he can prove that he had reasonable grounds for believing, and did believe, that the task of keeping proper books of account had been delegated to an appropriate officer who was in a position to carry it out.

Officers

24.7   Section 203 includes similar provisions to impose criminal liability on 'officers' of the company. However, unlike s 202(10), s 203 will operate against officers only if:

(1)   the company being wound up and unable to pay its debts has contravened s 202; and
(2)   the contraventions have:
    (a)   contributed to the inability of the company to pay all its debts; or
    (b)   resulted in substantial uncertainty as to the assets and liabilities of the company; or
    (c)   substantially impeded the orderly winding up of the company.

An officer charged under s 203, may avail of the same two defences open to directors under s 202(10).

The maximum punishment for an officer is a £10,000 fine and/or five years' imprisonment.

Other criminal sanctions

24.8 Section 293(1) of the 1963 Act and s 243(1) of the 1990 Act create statutory offences relating to the hiding, concealment, destruction, mutilation and falsification of books of account by company officers.

Civil liability of officers for debts of the company

24.9 Under s 204 of the 1990 Act, officers of the company may incur civil liability for the debts of the company. This is a most important new remedy available to company creditors, against directors and other officers. Accordingly, s 204 has been dealt with in Chapter 21 in the context of directors' liabilities to company creditors. This chapter includes an analysis of the *Mantruck Services Ltd* case – the first arising under s 204 (see **21.20**).

THE ANNUAL ACCOUNTS

24.10 Investors do not generally have the right[1] to inspect their company's primary financial records. Accordingly, s 148 of the 1963 Act is an important plank in the context of investor protection.

Section 148 imposes a duty on directors to prepare annually a profit and loss account and a balance sheet. These accounts must be laid before the annual general meeting of the company and signed by at least two directors on behalf of the board.[2]

Reports by the directors and an independent auditor must be attached to the company accounts. Copies of the Balance Sheet with directors' and auditors' reports must be forwarded to members[3] at least 21 days before the AGM.

Group accounts

24.11 The preparation of group accounts for limited companies is governed by the European Communities (Companies) (Group Accounts) Regulations 1992[4] (the 1992 Regulations).

Under the 1992 Regulations, parent undertakings must prepare consolidated group accounts[5] detailing the state of affairs of the group as a whole. They must lay these group accounts before the AGM at the same time as their own accounts.

---

1 Unless granted by the articles of association, which would be rare.
2 Section 156 of the 1963 Act.
3 Special provision is made for single-member companies in reg 8 of the European Communities (Single-Member Private Limited Companies) Regulations 1994.
4 SI 1992/201. These regulations implemented the Seventh EU Company Law Directive.
5 In addition to their own accounts.

A parent undertaking is defined in the 1992 Regulations as one which has one or more subsidiary undertakings. 'Subsidiary undertaking' is also defined in reg 4: the definition using both ownership *and* control as criteria.

The 1992 Regulations also deal with the form, format and contents of group accounts. They also include accounting principles to be used in the cases of acquisitions and mergers.

Failure to prepare annual accounts

24.12   If the directors fail to prepare either individual company or group accounts, they are liable to criminal prosecution.[1]

Preparation of annual accounts

24.13   Section 149[2] of the 1963 Act deals with the content and form of company accounts. It has now, however, for most practical purposes, been replaced by provisions in the Companies (Amendment) Act 1986.

The 1986 Act applies generally to all limited[3] companies engaged in trading operations. When implementing the Fourth EC Company Law Directive,[4] it introduces a distinction between accounts prepared for company members, and 'filed' accounts. As illustrated (in **24.32** below), less information may have to be made available to the public than to shareholders.

Shareholders' accounts and filed accounts

24.14   Two sets of accounts may now be prepared under the 1986 Act. The first set are those which must be prepared for the AGM. These are *shareholders' accounts*, and must give a true and fair view of the profit[5] for the year and the state of affairs at the balance sheet date.

The second set of accounts must be filed in the Companies Registration Office by annexing them to the annual return.[6] These are *filed accounts*.

Under the 1986 Act, specified accounting principles are to be followed in the preparation of the accounts. Specified formats are also prescribed for the accounts. Certain information must be disclosed by way of notes to the accounts. 'Medium-sized' and small companies enjoy certain disclosure

---

1 See ss 148(3) and 158(7) of the 1963 Act. The fines were increased to £500 in the Companies (Amendment) Act 1982, Sch 1.
2 But not subsections (5) and (7).
3 See s 2 which specifies the types of companies which are outside the scope of this Act. These include unlimited companies. However, if the shareholders of any unlimited company are all limited liability companies, it must follow the accounts requirements for limited liability companies – see reg 7 of the European Communities (Accounts) Regulations 1993.
4 Directive 78/660/EEC.
5 Or loss.
6 See next chapter.

exemptions in respect of their accounts. Notwithstanding, each profit and loss account and balance sheet filed must give a true and fair view of the company's financial position. The requirement of accounts to give a true and fair view of the profit or loss and balance sheet of a company is described in the Act[1] as an 'overriding' or fundamental requirement.

Form and content of accounts

24.15 Prior to the 1986 Act, there had been few regulations on the format of accounts, although certain balance sheet groupings and disclosures were required by the 1963 Act, Sch 6.

The 1986 Act[2] changed this situation by prescribing statutory formats for the balance sheet and profit and loss accounts.

Formats

24.16 The formats to be followed are set out in Part I of the Schedule to the 1986 Act.

There are two types of format for the balance sheet, giving a choice between a vertical (list) and a horizontal layout.

Balance sheet layout

24.17 A balance sheet is drawn up in the vertical form when assets are shown at the top of the page, followed by liabilities, and capital at the bottom. In the horizontal form, liabilities and capital are shown on the left hand side of the page.

Format 1 in the Schedule is the vertical form and the more up to date and common format used. Information required by it includes details of:

A. Fixed Assets

    I.   Intangible assets

        1. Development costs
        2. Concessions, patents, licences, trade marks and similar rights and assets
        3. Goodwill
        4. Payments on account

    II. Tangible assets

        1. Land and buildings
        2. Plant and machinery
        3. Fixtures, fittings, tools and equipment
        4. Payments on account and assets in course of construction

---

1 In s 3(4).
2 Section 4.

III. Financial assets

    1. Shares in group companies
    2. Own shares
    3. Shares in related companies
    4. Loans to related companies
    5. Other investments other than loans
    6. Other loans

B. Current Assets

  I.   Stock

    1. Raw materials and consumables
    2. Work in progress
    3. Finished goods and goods for resale
    4. Payments on account

  II. Debtors

    1. Trade debtors
    2. Amounts owed by group companies
    3. Amounts owed by related companies
    4. Other debtors
    5. Called up share capital not paid
    6. Prepayments and accrued income

  III. Investments

    1. Shares in group companies
    2. Own shares
    3. Other investments

  IV. Cash at bank and in hand

C. Creditors: amounts falling due within one year
    1. Debenture loans
    2. Bank loans and overdrafts
    3. Payments received on account
    4. Trade creditors
    5. Bills of exchange payable
    6. Amounts owed to group companies
    7. Amounts owed to related companies
    8. Other creditors including tax and social welfare
    9. Accruals and deferred income

D. Net current assets (liabilities)

E. Total assets less current liabilities

F. Creditors: amounts falling due after more than one year under Headings 1 to 9 in C above.

G. Provisions for liabilities and charges

    I.   Pensions and similar obligations
    II. Taxation, including deferred taxation
    III. Other provisions

H. Capital and reserves

    I.   Called up share capital
    II. Share premium account
    III. Revaluation reserve
    IV. Other reserves

        1. The capital redemption reserve fund
        2. Reserve for own shares
        3. Reserves provided for by the articles of association
        4. Other reserves

    V. Profit and loss account.

All assets must be classified as either fixed or current. They must then be valued in accordance with statutory rules – see **24.22** below.

Profit and loss account layout

24.18 Choices of format also have to be made when preparing the profit and loss account. There are four formats which allow two methods of aggregating costs in the trading and profit and loss account, both of which can be in either vertical or horizontal form.

Every profit and loss account must show the amount of the profit or loss of the company on ordinary activities before taxation. This account must also show:

(1) separately, the aggregate amount of the dividends paid and the aggregate amount of the dividends proposed to be paid;
(2) any transfer between the profit and loss account and reserves;
(3) any increase or reduction in the balance on the profit and loss account since the immediately preceding financial year;
(4) the profit or loss brought forward at the beginning of the year; and
(5) the profit or loss carried forward at the end of the year.

Profit and loss account formats 1 and 3 use a functional approach whilst formats 2 and 4 show receipts and expenditure by their nature, rather than their function. For example, the following details are required under Format 1:

1. Turnover
2. Cost of sales
3. Gross profit or loss
4. Distribution costs
5. Administrative expenses
6. Other operating income
7. Income from shares in group companies
8. Income from shares in related companies
9. Income from other financial assets

10. Other interest receivable and similar income
11. Amounts written off, financial assets and investments held as current assets
12. Interest payable and similar charges
13. Tax or profit or loss on ordinary activities
14. Profit or loss on ordinary activities after taxation
15. Extraordinary income
16. Extraordinary charges
17. Extraordinary profit or loss
18. Tax on extraordinary profit or loss
19. Other taxes not shown under the above items
20. Profit or loss for the financial year.

Vertical and horizontal layouts

24.19   Both balance sheet and profit and loss accounts can be prepared in either vertical or horizontal layout. Whichever format is chosen, however, must be adopted in following years unless the directors are of the opinion that there are special reasons for a change.[1]

Accounting principles

24.20   The Statements of Standard Accounting Practice (SSAPs) are rules laid down on behalf of the accountancy bodies for the preparation of financial statements.

If an SSAP has been issued, accounts which do not comply with it may be presumed not to be true and fair. In *Lloyd Cheyham & Co Ltd v Littlejohn & Co*,[2] it was held that compliance with SSAP No 2[3] was strong (but not conclusive) evidence that accounts prepared presented a 'true and fair' view of the company. Furthermore, Wolfe J stated:

> 'third parties on reading the accounts are entitled to assume that they have been drawn up in accordance with approved practice, unless there is some indication in the accounts which clearly states that this is not the case.'

SSAP 2 had identified four fundamental accounting principles which must be followed if accounts are to show a true and fair view. These principles were:

(1)   going concern;
(2)   accruals;
(3)   consistency; and
(4)   prudence.

24.21   These principles are now included in s 5 of the 1986 Act, which provides that the amounts to be included in the accounts of a company shall be determined in accordance with the following principles:

---

1 See s 4(3) and (4).
2 [1987] BCLC 303 (QBD).
3 Issued in November 1971 and dealing with Disclosures of Accounting Policies.

(1) the company shall be presumed to be carrying on business as a going concern;

(2) accounting policies shall be applied consistently from one financial year to the next;

(3) the amount of any item in the accounts shall be determined on a prudent basis and in particular:

    (a) only profits realised at the balance sheet date shall be included in the profit and loss account; and

    (b) all liabilities and losses which have arisen or are likely to arise in respect of the financial year to which the accounts relate, or a previous financial year, shall be taken into account, including those liabilities and losses which only become apparent between the balance sheet date and the date on which the accounts are signed;

(4) all income and charges relating to the financial year to which the accounts relate shall be taken into account without regard to the date of receipt or payment; and

(5) in determining the aggregate amount of any item the amount of each individual asset or liability that falls to be taken into account shall be determined separately.

If it appears to the directors of a company that there are special reasons for departing from any of the principles specified in s 5, they may so depart, but particulars of the departure, the reasons for it and its effect on the balance sheet and profit and loss account of the company shall be stated in a note to the accounts, for the financial year concerned, of the company.[1]

Valuation rules

24.22 A company's accounts are often prepared on the historic cost principle. This involves valuing assets at their purchase price. Because of factors such as inflation, assets may be undervalued in accounts using the historic cost basis. An alternative method, known as current cost or replacement cost accounting, may give a more accurate view of a company's current worth.

A company may opt for either method under the 1986 Act. Part II of the Schedule sets out the rules to be followed where the historic cost method is used. If the company opts for the current cost method, Part III of the Schedule contains alternative accounting rules permitting certain assets to be revalued according to current cost, market value or any basis which appears to the directors to be appropriate in the circumstances of the company. However, if the current cost basis is used, the historical cost of assets must always be disclosed or ascertainable.[2] In *Carroll Industries plc v O'Cualacháin,*[3] Carroll J

---

1 Section 6.
2 See para 21(3) and (4) of the Schedule.
3 [1988] IR 705.

held that accounts prepared for taxation purposes must follow an historic[1] cost approach. In other cases, a company could choose either of the two methods.

Fixed and current assets

24.23   All assets are classified under the 1986 Act as either fixed or current – see AI to III and BI to IV of the prescribed balance sheet format illustrated at **24.17** above.

Part IV of the Schedule clarifies that fixed assets are those intended for use on a continuing basis in the company's activities. Assets not intended for such use are taken to be current assets.

Each individual asset, whether fixed or current, must be valued separately.

Parts II and III of the Schedule contain the detailed historical costs and current cost accounting rules for valuing fixed and current assets respectively.

Revaluation reserve

24.24   Any profit or loss arising on the revaluation of an asset under the current cost method must be credited or debited to a separate reserve. This reserve is styled the 'revaluation reserve'.[2]

Information required by way of notes to the accounts

24.25   Part IV of the Schedule to the 1986 Act prescribes additional information to be given as notes to the accounts or in a separate document annexed to them.

Balance sheet

24.26   Paragraphs 26 to 37 require information which either supplements information given with respect to any balance sheet item or is otherwise relevant to assessing the company's state of affairs in the light of the information so given. Paragraphs 26 to 37 deal with such matters as:

(1) share capital and debentures;
(2) fixed assets;
(3) financial assets and investments held as current assets;
(4) reserves and provisions;
(5) provisions for taxation;
(6) details of indebtedness;
(7) guarantees and other financial commitments.

---

1 A current cost accounting basis may, in some circumstances, produce a smaller amount of taxable profits.
2 See para 22 of the Schedule.

Profit and loss account

24.27 Paragraphs 39 to 43 require supplementary information in relation to the profit and loss account. This information deals with matters such as:

(1) separate statement of certain items of income and expenditure;
(2) particulars of tax and turnover;
(3) particulars of staff, including:
    (a) the average number of persons employed by the company in the financial year; and
    (b) the average number employed within each category of persons employed by the company.

Details of subsidiaries

24.28 Under s 16 of the 1986 Act, the company must also include a note to the accounts giving full information regarding subsidiary and associated companies.

Other information required in accounts

24.29 The 1963 Act requires particulars of directors' salaries and other payments to be given in the accounts or a statement annexed thereto. The 1990 Act provides for disclosure of transactions involving directors, and others, in the accounts.

Directors' salaries, etc

24.30 Section 191(1) of the 1963 Act prescribes the following information requirements for payments to directors:

(1) the aggregate amount of directors' emoluments;
(2) the aggregate amount of directors' and past directors' pensions;
(3) the aggregate amount of any compensation to directors or past directors for loss of office.

'Emoluments' is defined in s 191(2). It includes fees, commissions and sums paid to directors by way of expenses allowances insofar as those sums are charged to income tax.

Disclosures of transactions involving directors, and others

24.31 Sections 41 to 47 of the Companies Act 1990 provide for disclosures in respect of transactions involving directors. Directors' interests in shares, etc. must also be disclosed in their report or as a note to the accounts – see **20.20**.

Medium-sized and small private companies

24.32 Medium-sized and small private companies are defined in ss 8 and 9 of the 1986 Act.

Section 8, as amended by reg 4 of the European Communities (Accounts) Regulations 1993,[1] sets out the following criteria for defining medium and small private companies.

Tests to be satisfied

24.33   Companies have to satisfy *two* of the following three criteria:

	Medium-sized (not exceeding)	Small (not exceeding)
Balance sheet total	£6 million	£1.5 million
Turnover for the year	£12 million	£3 million
Average number of employees in the year	250	50

Some relief from disclosure is provided for medium-sized and small private[2] companies. These reliefs relate to the format of the accounts and the content of the notes to the accounts. They are detailed in ss 10, 11 and 12 of the Act.

Generally, both medium-sized and small companies are permitted to prepare 'shortened' profit and loss accounts for their members. In addition, a small company may also prepare an 'abridged' balance sheet. Both these types of company enjoy more concessions in relation to 'filed' accounts.

The information requirements for the annual return and the concessions available to small and medium-sized companies are detailed in **25.14**.

Directors' report

24.34   Section 158 of the 1963 Act requires that a directors' report be attached to the balance sheet of every company. This report must deal with:

(1) the state of affairs of the company, or, in the case of a holding company, of the company and its subsidiaries; and
(2) the proposed dividend; and
(3) the amount to be carried to reserves; and
(4) any change in the nature of the company's or its subsidiaries' business.

The report must also give a list of its subsidiaries and the nature of their businesses and a list of any bodies in which it holds more than 20 per cent in nominal value of shares carrying voting rights. It must also state where each subsidiary or body mentioned above is incorporated.

---

1 SI 1993/396.
2 Public companies do not qualify for size exemptions. These would therefore all be classified as large companies.

Under s 26 of the Electoral Act 1997, particulars of all donations made by the company exceeding £4,000 must be included in the directors' report (and the annual return).

The Safety, Health and Welfare at Work Act 1989 places a duty on directors to include in their report 'an evaluation of the extent to which the policy set out in the safety statement was fulfilled'.

Expanded directors' report

24.35　The directors' report was expanded by ss 13 and 14 of the 1986 Act, to require inclusion of the following matters:

(1) a fair review of the development of the business of the company and of its subsidiaries, if any, during the financial year ending with the relevant balance sheet date;
(2) particulars of any important events affecting the company or any of its subsidiaries, if any, which have occurred since the end of that year;
(3) an indication of likely future developments in the business of the company and of its subsidiaries, if any; and
(4) an indication of the activities, if any, of the company and its subsidiaries, if any, in the field of research and development.

Section 14 requires detailed information on any shares in the company which are acquired by:

(1) forfeiture or surrender in lieu of forfeiture;[1]
(2) the nominee of the company or a person given financial assistance by the company to buy its shares; or
(3) where any shares are made subject to a lien or other charge.[2]

Extra statement for directors of small or medium-sized companies

24.36　By virtue of s 18(2) of the 1986 Act, a copy of a balance sheet annexed to the annual return[3] must contain a statement by the directors that:

(1) they have relied on specified exemptions for small or medium-sized companies; and
(2) they have done so on the ground that the company is entitled to the benefit of those exemptions as a small company or (as the case may be) as a medium-sized company.

---

1 See Part VII of this book.
2 See s 14(d).
3 See Chapter 25.

Auditors' report

24.37 The auditors of a company must report to the members on the accounts examined by them, and on every balance sheet, profit and loss and group accounts laid before the company in general meeting.[1]

The auditors' report has to be read at the AGM and open to inspection by any member.

Contents of auditors' report

24.38 Section 193(4) of the 1990 Act provides that the auditors' report must state whether:

(1) the auditors have obtained all the information and explanations which, to the best of their knowledge and belief, are necessary for the purposes of the audit;
(2) in their opinion, proper books of account have been kept by the company;
(3) in their opinion, proper returns adequate for their audit have been received from branches of the company not visited by them;
(4) the company's balance sheet and profit and loss accounts are in agreement with the books of account and returns;
(5) if relevant, the company's group accounts have been prepared in accordance with the provisions of the Companies Acts and give a true and fair view of the company's[2] affairs and profit or loss for its financial year;
(6) in their opinion, a serious loss of capital as defined in s 40[3] has occurred.

Auditors must also notify the registrar if they find that proper books have not been kept.

Expanded auditors' report

24.39 Section 15 of the 1986 Act provides that the auditors have a duty, in preparing their report, to consider whether the information given in the report of the directors of the company relating to the financial year concerned is consistent with the accounts prepared by the company for that year, and the auditors must state in the report whether, in their opinion, such information is consistent with those accounts.

Special auditors' reports

24.40 Where the auditors of a medium-sized or small company are satisfied that the directors are entitled to rely on the filing concessions and that the accounts are properly prepared pursuant to the exemption provisions, the auditors must provide the directors with a written report stating:

(1) that the directors are entitled to file those accounts; and

---

1 Section 193(1) of the 1990 Act.
2 And its subsidiaries – see s 193(4)(e) and (f).
3 Of the Companies (Amendment) Act 1983 – see **13.35**.

(2) that the accounts are properly prepared as aforesaid.[1]

This written report must be accompanied by the auditors' report on the shareholders' accounts. These two reports together constitute the special report of the auditors required by s 18(3) of the 1986 Act. This special auditors' report must be filed with the company's balance sheet.

The auditors may also be requested to comment[2] on the profits available for distribution.

Recommendation in Partnership 2000

24.41 The agreement reached in 1997 between the social partners[3] has recommended that the requirement of a statutory audit be abolished for companies with a turnover of less than £100,000.

Profits available for distribution

24.42 At common law, a company could pay dividends out of the profits of any one year, without first making good the losses of previous years. This situation was altered by s 45 of the 1983 Act.

The rules on distribution of company profits are subject to the profit figure being based on properly prepared audited annual accounts – see s 49. In particular, s 49(3) provides that the following requirements apply where the last annual accounts constitute the only relevant accounts for a distribution of profits:

(1) the auditors must have stated in their report whether, in their opinion, the accounts were *properly prepared* ie unqualified;
(2) if the auditors' report is *not unqualified*, the auditors must have included a *statement* indicating that the distribution is in breach of the 1983 Act; and
(3) a copy of the accounts, auditors' report and statement, if any, indicating the illegality of the distribution, must have been delivered to the registrar.

Dividends

24.43 A dividend is the portion, received by a shareholder, of the company's distributable assets which have been divided among the members.

Most companies are formed with the objective of earning profits for their members. The company pays the shareholders dividends out of the distributable profits earned by it.

The payment of dividends is dealt with in Part VII of this book as a shareholders' right.

---

1 Section 18(4) of the 1986 Act.
2 Under s 49(3) of the 1983 Act.
3 Government, industry employers and trade unions.

When the directors propose payment of an attractive dividend to its share-holders at the AGM it is an indication of good management by them. As a result, the shareholders are more likely to approve the annual accounts.

Approval of annual accounts

24.44   When the accounts have been discussed at the AGM, it is usual that a resolution be proposed that they be 'adopted' or approved. When this resolution is passed, it can be regarded as a vote of confidence by the investors in the directors' management of their investment – the company.

If the investors were to reject the accounts, by not agreeing to approve them, this would be a most serious matter for the directors. It would, essentially, be an expression of the investors' lack of confidence in them.

Chapter 25

STATUTORY REGISTERS, BOOKS AND THE ANNUAL RETURN

MAINTAINING REGISTERS

25.1 As was shown in the previous chapter, each company must record transactions in proper books of account. In addition, they must also keep registers. The objective of keeping these registers is to record its members' investments and its creditors' loans and other debts. Maintaining registers also assists in the orderly conducting of each company's affairs.

STATUTORY REGISTERS

25.2 The Companies Acts make it compulsory for each company to maintain several registers. These include the register of members.

The register of members

25.3 Section 116(1)[1] of the 1963 Act makes it necessary for every company to record the following particulars in its register of members:

(1) the name and address of each member;
(2) in the case of a company having share capital, a statement of the shares held by each member distinguishing each share by its number (so long as it has a number) and the amount paid or agreed to be considered as paid on each share;
(3) the date at which each person was entered in the register as a member;
(4) the date at which any person ceased to be a member.

If there are more than 50 members, the register should be indexed.[2] Any member may inspect the register during business hours without charge; non-members must pay an appropriate charge. This facility must be available for at least two hours every day.[3] A copy may also be requested.

A company may close the register for 30 days in any year so long as it advertises the fact.[4] This will enable companies without computer facilities to make up a list of dividend recipients.

---

1 As amended by s 20 of the Companies (Amendment) Act 1982.
2 1963 Act, s 117.
3 Ibid, s 119.
4 Ibid, s 121.

The register of members may be located elsewhere than in the registered office. In fact, public companies quite often contract out the management of their register.

Other aspects of the register of members will be dealt with in Part VII.

Extra registers for plcs

25.4 A plc must also keep a *register of significant interests* under s 80 of the 1990 Act. This register is to record the acquisition and disposal of shareholdings in excess of five per cent of the company's shares by individuals acting alone or in concert.[1]

Again, s 81 empowers a plc to investigate the ownership of its shares. If it obtains relevant information, it must be recorded in a register of interests disclosed under s 81 – see Chapter 31.

Register of directors and secretaries

25.5 The register of directors and secretaries must contain the following[2] information:

(1) present and former Christian names and surnames; and date of both;
(2) residential address;
(3) nationality, if not Irish;
(4) business occupation;
(5) particulars of other directorships held currently or within the previous 10 years.

Similar disclosure obligations apply in relation to shadow directors as to ordinary directors.

The position is altered in the case of a company secretary because a body corporate may act as company secretary. The register must contain the following particulars relating to the secretary or, where there are two secretaries, in respect of each of them:

(1) in the case of an individual, his present Christian name and surname, any former Christian name and surname and his usual residential address; and
(2) in the case of a body corporate, the corporate name and registered office.

Any changes in this register must be notified to the registrar within 14 days.[3]

---

1 See ss 67 to 71 of the 1990 Act.
2 Section 195 of the 1963 Act, as amended by s 51 of the 1990 Act.
3 Section 8 of the Companies (Amendment) Act 1982.

Register of directors' interests in shares and debentures of the company

25.6   This register must be maintained by all companies[1] and show details of holdings which have to be notified[2] under s 53.

Whenever the company grants to a director or secretary a right to subscribe for shares in or debentures of the company, appropriate details must be included in this register.

The interests recorded in this register must be disclosed in the directors' report or in a note to the company's accounts.[3]

Register of debenture-holders

25.7   A debenture[4] is a contract of loan: an acknowledgement of a debt by a limited company.

Every company must keep a register[5] of holders of debentures of the company, and enter in it the:

(1) names and addresses of the debenture-holders; and
(2) the amount of debentures currently held by each.

Section 92 of the 1963 Act gives debenture-holders (and members) rights to inspect this register and to obtain copies of it and of any trust deed for securing an issue of debentures.

Debentures can be secured by a charge on the company's assets. If so, they may have to be registered under s 99. The registrar will give a certificate of registration which is conclusive evidence that s 99 has been complied with.

The *registrar* also maintains, *in relation to each company*, a register of charges[6] which is open to inspection by any person.

STATUTORY BOOKS AND MINUTES

25.8   Where a director discloses his interest in any contract made by or with the company, a copy of every declaration made and notice given under s 194[7] must be entered in a book which is kept for that purpose. This book must be open for inspection by company officers, investors and auditors, and must be produced at every general meeting of the company.

---

1 Section 59 of the 1990 Act.
2 By directors, secretaries and their families – see s 64.
3 Section 63 – see also previous chapter.
4 Debentures pay a fixed interest and are often long-dated – see Part VIII.
5 Section 91 of the 1963 Act.
6 See s 103 of the 1963 Act.
7 Of the 1963 Act.

Section 194 also applies to the interests of shadow directors.[1]

Minute books

25.9 Books must be maintained by companies, recording the minutes of all proceedings of general meetings and meetings of its directors or committees of directors.[2]

Investors are given a statutory right by s 146 to inspect the minute books recording the proceedings at general meetings.

ANNUAL RETURN

25.10 Section 125 of the 1963 Act makes it compulsory for every company having a share capital to make an annual return to the registrar of companies.

Information to be included in annual return

25.11 The information to be included in the annual return of a company having a share capital is prescribed in Part I of the Fifth Schedule to the 1963 Act. It includes:

(1) the address of the registered office of the company;
(2) (a) if the register of members is kept elsewhere than at the registered office of the company, the address of the place where it is kept;
    (b) if any register of holders of debentures of the company is kept elsewhere than at the registered office of the company, the address of the place where it is kept;
(3) a summary, distinguishing between shares issued for cash and shares issued as fully or partly paid up otherwise than in cash, specifying the following particulars:
    (a) the amount of the share capital of the company and the number of shares into which it is divided;
    (b) the number of shares taken from the incorporation of the company up to the date of the return;
    (c) the amount called up on each share;
    (d) the total amount of calls received;
    (e) the total amount of calls unpaid;
    (f) the total amount of the sum, if any, paid by way of commission in respect of any shares or debentures;
    (g) the discount allowed on the issue of any shares issued at a discount or so much of that discount as has not been written off at the date on which the return is made;

---

1 Companies Act 1990, s 27.
2 Section 145 of the 1963 Act.

(h) the total amount of the sums, if any, allowed by way of discount in respect of any debentures since the date of the last return;

(i) the total number of shares forfeited;

(4) particulars of the total amount of the indebtedness of the company in respect of all mortgages and charges which are required to be registered with the registrar of companies;

(5) a list:

(a) containing the names[1] and addresses of all persons who, on the 14th day after the company's annual general meeting for the year, are members of the company, and of persons who have ceased to be members since the date of the last return or, in the case of the first return, since the incorporation of the company;

(b) stating the number of shares held by each of the existing members at the date of the return, specifying shares transferred since the date of the last return (or, in the case of the first return, since the incorporation of the company) by persons who are still members and have ceased to be members respectively and the dates of registration of the transfers;

(6) particulars[2] relating to the persons who, at the date of the return, are the directors of the company and any person who is the secretary of the company.

Under the Electoral Act 1997, details of all donations made by the company which exceed £4,000 must also be included in the annual return.

Part II of the Fifth Schedule prescribes the format in which the information contained within the annual return is to be presented.

Companies not having a share capital

25.12 Under s 126, a company not having a share capital need only include the details required in (1), (2) and (6) (above) in its annual return.

Documents to be attached to the annual return

25.13 The following documents are required by s 7[3] to be submitted with the annual return:

(1) a certified copy of every *balance sheet, profit and loss account* and other documents and reports required by law to be attached to the balance sheet, ie filed accounts; and

(2) a certified copy of the *auditors' report.*

---

1 In alphabetical order or with an index attached.
2 Such as are required to be contained in the register of directors and secretaries.
3 Of the 1986 Amendment Act.

Private companies did not need to attach filed accounts to their annual returns under the 1963 Act. The 1986 Amendment Act removes this exemption. However, in doing so, it grants concessions to 'medium-sized' and 'small' private companies.

Medium-sized and small private companies

25.14   The criteria for defining medium-sized and small companies were set out in the previous chapter.

Concessions for medium-sized private companies

25.15   These companies are permitted[1] to annex an *abridged balance sheet*. An abridged balance sheet is less detailed than either Format 1 or 2 in the Schedule to the 1986 Amendment Act. The precise items to be omitted are specified in s 11(2).

Section 11(1) also permits[2] a company to attach a *shortened form of profit and loss account*. The items to be combined into one heading of 'gross profit or loss' are specified in s 11(1).

Section 12(2) also exempts medium-sized companies from the requirement to disclose particulars of turnover by way of note to the filed accounts, abridged or otherwise.

Concessions for small private companies

25.16   Section 10(1) of the 1986 Amendment Act permits small companies to prepare an *abridged balance sheet* for the purposes of both the shareholders and the filed accounts, subject to the requirement that it gives a 'true and fair' view of the company's state of affairs at the end of the year. The items to be deleted from the balance sheet are indicated in s 10(1). Using the horizontal layout in Format 2 of the Schedule, an abridged balance sheet under s 10(1) would require the following information:

Assets	**Liabilities**
A. *Fixed Assets*	A. *Capital and Reserves*
I. Intangible Assets	I. Called up share capital
II. Tangible Assets	II. Share Premium Account
III. Financial Assets	III. Revaluation reserve
	IV. Other Reserves
B. *Current Assets*	V. Profit and Loss Account
I. Stocks	
II. Debtors	B. *Provisions for Liabilities/Charges*
III. Investments	
IV. Cash at Bank and in Hand	C. *Creditors*

---

1 Section 11(2).
2 The directors may, if they wish, forego these concessions and annex full accounts.

Because of s 10(2), it is not necessary for a small company to annex either the profit and loss account, and/or the directors' report, to the filed accounts. All a small company, therefore, need attach to its annual return are the abridged balance sheet and the special auditors' report.[1]

Section 12 exemptions in relation to notes to the accounts

25.17 Section 12(1) exempts small companies from complying with paras 23 to 44 of the Schedule relating to notes to the accounts with the exception of:

Para	24	Details of accounting policies
	26	Information regarding share capital and debentures
	27	Allotments of shares
	33	Provision for taxation
	34	Details of indebtedness
	44	Details of foreign exchange; changes in accounting policy or errors in accounts.

Summary of 1986 Act concessions for medium-sized and small companies

25.18 The 1986 Act, whilst removing the exemption on filing accounts which private companies had enjoyed under s 128,[2] nevertheless has granted concessions to medium-sized and small companies in respect of both filed and shareholders' accounts. For example, medium-sized companies need file only a shortened profit and loss account and an abridged balance sheet.[3] They can also prepare a shortened profit and loss account for their shareholders.

Small companies are exempted from filing a profit and loss account and need only prepare a shortened balance sheet for filing[4] and for their members.[5]

Large companies

25.19 Private companies not qualifying as medium-sized or small companies can be classified as large companies. So, too, can all public limited companies.

Large[6] limited liability companies are not entitled to any concessions from the requirements of the 1986 Act. Accordingly, they must prepare full balance sheet and profit and loss accounts, and annex all other documents, notes and

---

1 See previous chapter.
2 Of the 1963 Act.
3 Under s 11(2).
4 Sections 10(2) and 12(1).
5 Section 10(1).
6 Except those excluded under s 2(1) and not enjoying the partial exemptions under s 2(2) and (3) of the 1986 Act.

reports, to both their shareholders and their filed accounts. These accounts will also have to be accompanied by expanded directors' and auditors' reports.[1]

Certificates to be attached by private companies

25.20   A private company must send a *certificate* with the annual return[2] confirming that the company has not invited the public to subscribe for its shares or debentures, and that its membership numbers do not exceed the 50 maximum in s 33.[3]

Time-limit for filing of annual return

25.21   The annual return must be completed within 60 days of the AGM and then immediately sent to the registrar.

There are serious sanctions available against both the company and its officers in the case of defaults in making returns. These sanctions may be brought and prosecuted by the registrar – see ss 125 and 127 of the 1963 Act and s 12[4] of the Companies (Amendment) Act 1982. Section 12 gives the registrar the power to strike off the register a company which fails to make annual returns for two consecutive years.

The maximum fine in s 125 was increased to £1,000 by s 244 of the 1990 Act.

During 1995, a total of 56 directors were convicted for failure to file annual returns under s 125.

---

1 See previous chapter and ss 18 and 15 of the 1986 Act.
2 Signed by both a director and the secretary.
3 Of the 1963 Act.
4 As amended by s 245 of the 1990 Act.

Chapter 26

THE AUDITOR'S ROLE AND RESPONSIBILITY

THE AUDITOR

26.1   An auditor is an independent professional who examines the books and financial records of a company.

Every company must appoint an auditor whose task it is to examine the books of account, annual accounts, group accounts (if any) and directors' report. He then makes a report on his findings to the members – the investors who own the company.

APPOINTMENT OF AUDITORS

26.2   The articles usually provide for the appointment of auditors and the auditing of the accounts of the company. For example, Table A, art 130 states:

> 'Auditors shall be appointed and their duties regulated in accordance with ss 160 to 163 of the Act.'

First auditors

26.3   The first auditors may be appointed by the directors[1] at any time before the first AGM. However, their appointment is subject to the power of the members in general meeting to remove them.

Subsequent auditors

26.4   As the function of the auditor is to check the books and accounts on behalf of the company owners, it is the investors in general meeting who have the powers to appoint and remove an auditor, and to fix his fee.

Section 160(1) provides that every company shall, at each general meeting, appoint an auditor(s) to hold office until the conclusion of the next AGM.

Retiring auditors

26.5   At any general meeting, a retiring auditor,[2] however appointed, will be re-appointed without any resolution being passed unless:

(1) he is not qualified for re-appointment; or

---

1 Section 160(6) of the 1963 Act.
2 See s 160(2) and (3) of the 1963 Act.

(2) a resolution has been passed at that meeting appointing somebody instead of him or providing expressly that he shall not be re-appointed; or

(3) he has given the company notice in writing of his unwillingness to be re-appointed.

Appointment by Minister

26.6 Where, at an AGM, no auditors are appointed, or re-appointed, the Minister may appoint a person to fill the vacancy.

Qualifications for appointment

26.7 Generally, under s 187(1) of the 1990 Act, a person will not be qualified to act as an auditor of a company[1] unless:

(1) he is a member of a body of accountants recognised by the Minister and holds a valid practising certificate from such a body; or

(2) he holds an accountancy qualification that is, in the opinion of the Minister, of no lesser standard and which would entitle him to be granted a practising certificate by that body if he were a member of it, and is for the time being authorised by the Minister to be appointed;[2] and

(3) the particulars required by ss 199 and 200[3] in respect of them have been forwarded to the registrar.

Recognition of accountancy bodies

26.8 The full set of rules governing qualification for auditing purposes and the information to be furnished to the registrar of companies is contained in Part X of the 1990 Act and the Companies Act 1990 (Auditors) Regulations.[4]

At the end of 1995, the following bodies of accountants were recognised by the Minister for Enterprise and Employment for auditing purposes under s 191 of the Companies Act 1990:

(1) The Institute of Chartered Accountants in Ireland;
(2) The Institute of Certified Public Accountants in Ireland;
(3) The Chartered Association of Certified Accountants;
(4) The Institute of Chartered Accountants in England and Wales;
(5) The Institute of Chartered Accountants of Scotland.

A further body, the Institute of Incorporated Public Accountants Limited, was recognised by the Minister in April 1996. In addition, an application for recognition was received by the Minister from the Association of International Accountants. This body had already been recognised by the UK authorities.

---

1 Or as a public auditor.
2 See additional categories in s 187(1)(a)(iii) to (vi).
3 Of the 1990 Act.
4 SI 1992/259.

Registration of auditors

26.9   Section 198 of the 1990 Act required the registrar to maintain a register of persons notified to him to be qualified for appointment as auditors. Accordingly, details of those members of the recognised bodies who are qualified to act as auditor of a limited company are retained in the Companies Registration Office and are available for public inspection on payment of the appropriate fee. Particulars of each member qualified for appointment as auditor of a company are submitted to the registrar on an annual basis. This is one of the conditions of recognition for accountancy bodies.

Each of the recognised bodies is also required to submit an annual report to the Minister giving details of the number of complaints received and the number and outcome of cases dealt with by its investigation, disciplinary, and appeals committees pertaining to members practising as auditors in the State. By the time the Companies Report for 1995 was issued by the Department of Enterprise and Employment, none of the five recognised bodies had supplied the required reports for the year 1995 and only one had supplied a report for 1994.

Individually recognised auditors

26.10   Fifty-nine individuals had obtained Ministerial authorisation[1] prior to 3 February 1983 and were authorised to continue as auditors on 31 December 1995.

Prosecution

26.11   During 1995, one person was fined £500 for acting as an auditor without being qualified to do so.

Persons disqualified from acting as auditors

26.12   Section 187(2) provides that the persons who are disqualified from being appointed as auditors include:

(1)   an officer or servant of the company;
(2)   a person who has been an officer or servant of the company within a period in respect of which accounts would fall to be audited by him if he were appointed auditor of the company;
(3)   a parent, spouse, brother, sister or child of an officer of the company;
(4)   a person who is a partner of or in the employment of an officer of the company;
(5)   a person who is disqualified from acting as an auditor of the company's holding company or any of its subsidiaries.

---

1   Granted under s 199 of the 1990 Act.

In addition, any former directors who are the subject of a disqualification[1] order, are also disqualified from being appointed to act as auditor of any company.

REMUNERATION OF AUDITORS

26.13   Generally, whoever appoints the auditor has the power to negotiate and agree his remuneration for the period of the appointment. Nevertheless, when the members appoint the auditors at the AGM, they usually authorise the directors to negotiate his remuneration and expenses.

TERMINATION OF AUDITOR'S APPOINTMENT

26.14   The auditor may voluntarily resign, or be removed and replaced against his wishes.

Resignation of an auditor

26.15   An auditor can resign before the expiry of his term of office if he serves written notice[2] on the company stating his intention to resign.

The notice must contain a statement of the circumstances giving rise to his resignation and a statement as to whether or not the auditor considers his reasons should be brought to the notice of the members or creditors of the company.

A similar procedure must be followed by an auditor who is unwilling to be re-appointed as auditor.

A resigning auditor is empowered[3] to requisition a general meeting of the company and to address it. He is also entitled to attend and be heard at:

(1) the annual general meeting at which, but for his resignation, his term of office would have expired; and
(2) any general meeting at which it is proposed to fill the vacancy caused by his resignation.

Removal and replacement of an auditor

26.16   Section 160(5) of the 1963 Act empowers the members of a company, by ordinary resolution at a general meeting, to remove an auditor[4] and appoint in his place any other person who has been nominated for appointment by any

---

1 See s 195 of the 1990 Act and Chapter 23.
2 Complying with the requirements of s 185(2), (3) and (4) of the 1990 Act.
3 By s 186 of the 1990 Act.
4 Other than the first auditor(s).

member of the company (and who is qualified to be an auditor and of whose nomination notice has been given).

Extended notice

26.17   Extended notice[1] is required for:

(1)   a resolution at an annual general meeting of a company appointing as auditor a person other than a retiring auditor or providing expressly that a retiring auditor shall not be re-appointed;

(2)   a resolution at a general meeting of a company removing an auditor before the expiration of his term of office; and

(3)   a resolution at a general meeting of a company filling a casual vacancy in the office of auditor.

An auditor is entitled to have his representations sent to members at the company's expense, prior to the meeting at which he is to be removed. He is also entitled to attend and address this meeting.

GENERAL POSITION OF AUDITORS

26.18   The relationship between an auditor and a company is not one of employer and employee. Instead, it is that of a professional independent accountant and his client.

Again, whilst an auditor is not ostensibly an officer of the company, where he has been guilty of fraud or breach of duty[2] in relation to the company's books and accounts, he may be treated as an 'officer' for both criminal and civil proceedings, eg the term 'officer' in s 138 of the 1990 Act includes 'any auditor, liquidator, receiver or shadow director'. Section 138 renders officers liable for reckless trading.

Auditors are not normally deemed to be the agents of the company.[3] They are, however, agents for the shareholders although members are not necessarily bound by notice of all matters given to or discovered by the auditors,[4] eg their knowledge of fraudulent acts of the directors.

AUDITORS' RIGHTS

26.19   Section 193(3) of the 1990 Act gives every auditor a statutory right of access at all reasonable times to the books, accounts and vouchers of the company. Auditors are also entitled to require from company officers and

---

1   Within the meaning of s 142 – see **15.26**.
2   *R v Shacter* [1960] 1 All ER 61 (CCA).
3   *Re Transplanters (Holding Co) Ltd* [1958] 2 All ER 711.
4   *Spackman v Evans* (1868) LR 3 HL 171.

employees such information and explanations[1] that are within their knowledge or can be procured by them if they think these are necessary for the proper discharging of their duties as auditors. The auditors are entitled to attend any[2] general meeting of the company and to receive all notices of, and other communications relating to, any general meeting which any investor in the company is entitled to receive and to be heard at any general meeting which they attend on any part of the business of the meeting which concerns them as auditors.[3]

AUDITORS' DUTIES

26.20   In *Nelson Guarantee Corporation Ltd v Hodgson*,[4] McCarthy J stated:

> 'The duties of an auditor must be determined by the contract and by no other test, for the relationship between an auditor and a company engaging him is solely a matter of contract ...'

The main task facing auditors is to make a report[5] to the investors on the accounts examined by them, and on every balance sheet and profit and loss account, and all group accounts, laid before the company in general meeting during their tenure of office.

In preparing his report, s 193(6) of the 1990 Act places the auditor under a general duty to carry out the audit with *professional integrity*. Whilst this statutory duty is not explained in detail, one would expect compliance with it to include the maintenance of auditing standards at least equal to the levels required by the professional accounting bodies.[6]

The auditors are also under a duty to make themselves acquainted with the company's articles of association.

In the *Nelson Guarantee* case, McCarthy J also suggested the following five principles as applying to the duties of an auditor:

(1) that the primary purpose in the engagement of an auditor is to obtain a report to the shareholders on the accounts of the company and the primary duty of the auditor is to make that report;

(2) that, in carrying out this primary duty, an auditor has to exercise reasonable care and skill in making inquiries and investigations which may include investigations and reports upon the conduct of employees of the company;

---

1 Section 196 also gives auditors powers to obtain information from subsidiary companies.
2 Section 193(6).
3 The auditors of a single-member company may request the holding of an AGM – see reg 8(3) of the European Communities (Single-Member Private Limited Companies) Regulations 1994.
4 [1958] NZLR 609 (Supreme Court of New Zealand).
5 Section 193(1).
6 Such as in the Statements of Standard Accounting Practice (SSAP) – see Chapter 24. They would also be expected to have an adequate knowledge of the Companies Acts 1963 to 1990.

(3) that an auditor is never bound to exercise more than reasonable care and skill;

(4) that what is reasonable care and skill in any particular case must depend upon the circumstances of that case;

(5) that, where there is cause for suspicion, more care is necessary but the test is still that of reasonable care and skill in the light of all the circumstances including those circumstances which arouse suspicion.

If proper books of account are not being kept

26.21 If the auditors form the opinion that proper books of account[1] are not being kept, and the breach is major or significant, they must:

(1) serve a notice on the company as soon as may be stating their opinion; and

(2) not later than seven days after the service of such notice on the company, notify the registrar of companies, in the prescribed form, of the notice.

During 1995, the registrar received 12 such notifications under s 194.

If the breach is minor or immaterial, or the situation has been rectified by the directors, the auditors need not serve the notices required above – see s 194(1) of the 1990 Act.

Directors' emoluments

26.22 If details of the directors' emoluments are not included in the accounts, as required by s 191 of the 1963 Act, it is the duty of the auditors to include in their report a statement giving the required particulars, insofar as they are reasonably able to do so.[2]

Auditors and the 1983 Act

26.23 Under the Companies (Amendment) Act 1983, the auditors are required to report on the *s 40 maintenance of capital provision*.[3] They may also be required to comment on several other matters, including profits available for distribution,[4] allotment of shares by a plc otherwise than for cash,[5] and the transfer of a non-cash asset to a plc by a shareholder.[6]

Again, on the re-registration of a private limited company as a plc, the registrar of companies must be furnished with a written statement[7] from the auditor expressing his opinion that the company's net assets are not less than the

---

1 As required by s 202 of the 1990 Act.
2 Section 191(8) of the 1963 Act.
3 See **13.35**.
4 See s 49(3) and (6), and **13.49** and **24.42**.
5 See s 30(5) to (8), and (12), and **10.31**.
6 Section 32, and **10.31**.
7 See section 9(3) of the 1983 Act.

aggregate of its called-up share capital and undistributable reserves (as defined by s 46(2)).

PENALTIES FOR FALSE STATEMENTS TO AUDITORS

26.24 Section 197 of the 1990 Act authorises the imposition of heavy criminal sanctions against officers who are convicted of giving false or misleading information to the company auditors.

CIVIL LIABILITY OF AUDITORS

26.25 When considering the civil liability of auditors in respect of mistakes made by them in carrying out their duties, one must consider the standard of care owed by them, and to whom it is owed.

Auditors' standard of care

26.26 An auditor must carry out his work with professional integrity[1] – this is now a statutory requirement. Earlier, in judicial parlance, Hanna J almost implied this general duty when stating[2] that:

> '... the duty upon an auditor is, under the circumstances of the particular case and of his employment, to exercise such skill and care as a diligent, skilled and cautious auditor would exercise according to the practice of the profession.'

An auditor who has been, or ought to have been, put on enquiry, is under a duty to make an exhaustive investigation of the matter in question.[3]

Auditors' liability under contract

26.27 Generally, where an auditor fails to perform his duties competently,[4] he will be liable to the company for any losses it may sustain as a result of his breach of contract.

Again, an auditor, if formally appointed by the articles or under s 160 of the 1963 Act, may be an 'officer' of the company[5] and liable to be proceeded against for misfeasance under s 298 of the 1963 Act.

Other examples where auditors may be liable to pay damages as company 'officers' include situations where there has been reckless trading (see **21.16** above) and failure by the company to keep proper books of account.

---

1 See **26.20** above.
2 In *Leech v Stokes* [1937] IR 787.
3 *Re Thomas Gerrard & Son Ltd* [1968] Ch 455.
4 Ie with reasonable care and skill.
5 *R v Shacter* [1960] 1 All ER 61.

In *Re Western Counties Steam Bakeries v Milling Co*,[1] the auditors were not formally appointed by the general meeting and the court held that 'informally' appointed auditors could not be made liable as 'officers' of the company.

Contracting out of liability

26.28 Any provision,[2] whether contained in the articles or in any contract with the company, exempting an auditor from, or indemnifying him against, any liability which would attach to him in respect of any negligence, default, breach of duty or breach of trust of which he may be guilty in relation to the company, is *void*.

An auditor may, however, be indemnified against the costs of defending such proceedings if the judgment is given in his favour.[3]

Auditors' liability in tort

26.29 A firm of auditors prepared accounts with the knowledge that they would be shown to a third person with the purpose of inducing him to invest in shares of that company. The third party invested in the company.

It turned out that the accounts had been incorrectly prepared by the auditors. The company was wound up within a year. The third party investor suffered a financial loss as a result.

In *Candler v Crane, Christmas & Co*,[4] it was held that, in these circumstances, the auditors did not owe a duty of care to third parties with whom they had no contractual obligation. As a result, the plaintiff investor was unable to recover his loss from the auditors in tort.

26.30 The law changed following the decision in *Hedley Byrne & Co v Heller & Partners*.[5] In this case, the court extended the auditors' duty beyond their contract with the company, to include a non-contractual duty of care in negligence to third parties such as potential investors relying upon the accounts to decide whether or not to buy that company's shares.

Irish cases such as *Kelly v Haughey Boland & Co*[6] and *John Sisk & Son v Flinn*[7] recognised this extended version of actionable auditor's negligence in Ireland. However, in the UK, the House of Lords decision in *Caparo Industries plc v Dickman*[8] seemed to restrict the auditors' duty of care to the company itself. The court felt that there was nothing in the statutory duties of an auditor to suggest that they were intended to protect the interests of the public at large

---

1 [1897] 1 Ch 617.
2 Section 200 of the 1963 Act as amended by 1983 Act, Sch 1, para 16.
3 See s 200(b).
4 [1951] 2 KB 164.
5 [1964] AC 465.
6 [1989] ILRM 373. See also *Securities Trust Ltd v Hugh Moore and Alexander Ltd* in **29.10**.
7 (Unreported) 18 July 1984 (HC).
8 [1990] 1 All ER 568.

or potential investors in the company. It also considered that the auditors' statutory duty was owed to the shareholders as a body, and not as individual shareholders.[1] However, in *ADT v BDO Binder Hamlyn*,[2] the auditors were held liable to an acquiring company *who clearly had relied upon* the accounts prepared by them and their professional advice. The damages awarded, including interest and costs, exceeded £100 million.

This decision seems to be a classic application of liability based on *Hedley Byrne v Heller & Partners*.

An appeal against the judgment was withdrawn in February 1997 following an agreed settlement at a lower figure, said to be within the auditors' professional indemnity insurance cover.

The extent to which Irish auditors owe a duty of care to third parties must now be uncertain, following the *Caparo* judgment.

Contracting out of liability for negligent acts

26.31 Generally, auditors cannot 'contract out' of their liability to third parties. This is because no contract exists between the auditors and such 'company outsiders'. As a result, a disclaimer in the auditors' contract with the company may not be a defence[3] against a third party action for damages based on their negligent acts – always assuming a duty of care is owed to them in the post-*Caparo* Irish scenario.

Auditors' concern over size of potential liability

26.32 Following the collapse of the PMPA Insurance Company in 1983, its outstanding claims liabilities were transferred to a new company, Primor plc. Two High Court decisions empowered Primor plc to pursue a claim for £175 million damages, plus interest, against the joint auditors of PMPA. During December 1995, the Supreme Court[4] overturned the two High Court decisions, dismissing what would have been Ireland's largest tortious claim because of unjustified delay by the plaintiffs.

Again, the failure of the Insurance Corporation of Ireland Insurance Co (ICI) led to the transfer of its outstanding liabilities to ICAROM plc.

ICAROM plc (and Allied Irish Banks), like Primor plc, sought damages against ICI's accountants. The case was settled out of court for an amount thought to

---

1 The interests of the individual shareholders could be protected indirectly by the company bringing an action against the auditors for professional negligence.
2 [1996] BCC 808.
3 See *John Sisk & Son v Flinn* where a qualification to the accounts succeeded as a defence against a third party.
4 In *Primor plc v Stokes Kennedy Crowley; Primor plc v Oliver Freaney & Co, The Irish Times*, 20 December 1995.

be £77 million during 1993. In the same year, the six largest accounting firms in the UK paid up to eight per cent of their audit fees in legal claims.[1]

26.33 From the size of these awards/settlements levels, it is understandable that the issue of legal liability is one of major concern to the auditing profession in Ireland (and the UK). In these two EU Member States, legal actions against auditors are particularly prevalent, with amounts of awards of damages running very high. By contrast, in Germany,[2] auditors are entitled to limit their liabilities arising out of an audit to DM500,000 (about £200,000), thereby reducing the incentive for litigation.

In December 1996, a conference was held in Brussels to consider a Green Paper on the role and liability of auditors within the EU. It will be interesting to see whether developments at an EU level can reduce legal liability and litigation levels for auditors in Ireland.

---

1 P. Boyle 'Accountants face rise in litigation' *Irish Press*, 22 February 1994.
2 Germany has a fundamentally different legal system to the UK and Ireland, being civil law, rather than common-law based.

Chapter 27

INVESTIGATIONS INTO A COMPANY'S AFFAIRS AND OWNERSHIP

APPOINTMENT OF INSPECTORS

27.1 Under ss 165 to 173 of the 1963 Act, the Minister had the power to appoint inspectors to investigate the affairs of a company.

Only four investigations were instigated by the Minister under the 1963 Act. Not surprisingly, therefore, ss 165 to 173 have been replaced by more effective provisions in the Companies Act 1990.

Generally, the directors, as a company's managing agents, enjoy almost complete control over the company's internal affairs. As a result, investors, and indeed, creditors, could encounter great difficulty in obtaining information concerning the company, if the directors chose not to be of help to them. Part II of the 1990 Act now allows members and creditors to apply to the courts seeking an investigation into the affairs of the company.

Section 7 empowers the courts to appoint inspectors who can investigate the company's affairs. Section 14 authorises the Minister to appoint inspectors to investigate a company's ownership without prior recourse to the courts.

INVESTIGATION OF A COMPANY'S AFFAIRS

27.2 Sections 7 and 8 transfer the power of ordering an investigation into the affairs of a company from the Minister to the court.

The court may appoint one or more *inspectors* to investigate the affairs of the company as directed by the court and to submit a report. The term 'affairs of the company' was judicially defined[1] as including the company's goodwill, its profits and losses, and its contracts and assets. This definition also embraces a company's shareholdings in, and ability to control the affairs of, a subsidiary or subsidiaries.

WHO CAN APPLY FOR APPOINTMENT OF INSPECTORS?

27.3 Section 7(1) permits the following persons to apply to the court for the appointment of inspectors to investigate a company:

---

1 In *R v Board of Trade, ex p St Martin's Preserving Co Ltd* [1965] 1 QB 603.

(1) in the case of a company having a share capital, either not less than 100 members or a member or members holding not less than one-tenth of the paid-up share capital of the company;

(2) in the case of a company not having a share capital, not less than one-fifth in number of the persons on the company's register of members;

(3) the company;

(4) a director of the company;

(5) a creditor of the company.

The court may require applicant(s) to give security of up to £10,000 for payment of the costs of the investigation.

Applications by the Minister

27.4   Section 8 empowers the court to appoint inspectors on the application of the Minister. Before it does so, however, the court must be satisfied that there are circumstances suggesting:

(1) that the company's affairs are being or have been conducted with intent to defraud its creditors or for other fraudulent or unlawful purposes or in a manner which is unfairly prejudicial to the interest of its members;

(2) that persons connected with the formation or the management of the company's affairs have been guilty of fraud, misfeasance or other misconduct towards it or its members; or

(3) that the company's members have not been given all the information relating to its affairs which they might reasonably expect.

On 16 September 1991, the High Court, on the application of the Minister, appointed Messrs Aidan Barry, accountant, and Ciaran Foley, barrister, as inspectors under s 8 to investigate the affairs of Siúcre Éireann cpt and certain related companies. The inspectors furnished their final report to the court on 25 February 1992.

DUTIES OF COMPANY OFFICERS AND AGENTS

27.5   All officers and agents are under a duty to assist appointed inspectors by:

(1) producing all relevant books and documents; and/or

(2) meeting the inspectors, when required; and

(3) giving the inspectors all the assistance which they are reasonably able to give.

Any answer given by a person to an inspector may be used against him.

Secret transactions

27.6 Section 10(3) gives inspectors power to obtain details of any 'secret' bank accounts and/or improper corporate transactions that may have taken place under the directors' stewardship.

Examination on oath

27.7 Under s 10(4), an inspector has the power to examine under oath any company officer or agent or both, and to administer the oath personally. The definition of 'officer' and 'agent' in s 10(7) includes past, as well as present, officers and agents. The term 'agents' includes the company's bankers, solicitors and auditors.

Related companies

27.8 With the approval of the court, the inspector may have his power extended under s 9 to include an investigation into related companies.

In *Lyons, Keleghan and Murphy v Curran*,[1] the inspector, Mr Curran, appointed under s 14 (see **27.14** below) extended his investigation to a company, Talmino, not named in his warrant of appointment, and without obtaining prior approval from the court under s 9.

The applicants sought to have the inspector's final report quashed on the grounds that there was no authority or power to investigate Talmino.

Blaney J held that the inspector had both the power and a duty to investigate Talmino under the terms of his appointment. He stated:

> 'In my opinion Section 9 applies to a situation different from that in which the respondent found himself in Talmino. The respondent had to investigate Talmino in order to fulfil the purpose for which he was appointed. That is very different from the position of an inspector availing of Section 9. Such an inspector simply 'thinks' it is necessary for the purposes of his investigation to investigate also the membership of another body corporate. He does not *know* that it is necessary, which was the respondent's position.' (author's emphasis)

INSPECTOR'S SANCTIONS

27.9 If any company officer or agent refuses to co-operate with an inspector, he may certify their refusal to the court. The court will then enquire into the matter, and, if necessary, punish the offender as if he had been guilty of contempt of court.

The court can also compel attendance before an inspector, the production of particular books or documents, or the answering of a particular question.

---

1 [1993] ILRM 375.

INSPECTOR'S REPORTS

27.10   Inspectors, if directed by the court, may have to submit interim reports to it. In any event, they must prepare a final report on the conclusion of their investigations, and for the court.

Copies

27.11   Section 11(3) makes provision for copies of the report to be made available to a number of interested parties, including the Minister, the company itself, auditors, shareholders, the applicants for the investigation and any person whose conduct has been referred to in the report.

The court may also decide that the inspector's report be printed and published. The inspector's report may be used in civil proceedings as evidence of the facts or of the inspector's opinion.

Section 18 provides for the admissability of evidence given to inspectors in subsequent legal proceedings. The Act does not, however, make it clear whether or not a witness is entitled to refuse to answer a question put to him by the inspector on the grounds that it might incriminate him.

In *Heaney v Ireland*,[1] Costello J suggests that the personal rights guaranteed by art 38 of the Constitution include privilege against self incrimination.

Acting upon the inspector's report

27.12   Having considered the inspector's report, the court can make any order it deems fit. Such orders might include:[2]

(1) an order for the winding up of the company; or
(2) an order for the purpose of remedying any disability suffered by any person whose interests were adversely affected by the conduct of the affairs of the company.

The Minister also has the power to present a petition for the winding up of the company, following an inspector's report.

EXPENSES OF INVESTIGATION INTO COMPANY'S AFFAIRS

27.13   The costs of the investigation will be paid initially by the Minister for Justice. However, the court may order the company, or the applicant, to

---

1   [1994] ILRM 420. See also *Rock v Ireland* (unreported) 10 November 1995 (HC), *AT & T Istel Ltd v Tully* [1993] AC 45 and P. Dillon-Malone 'The privilege against self-incrimination in the light of *Saunders v UK*' *The Bar Review*, February 1997, pp 133–134.
    ˙ɔn 12(1).

reimburse the Minister. If this were to happen, s 13(1) limits the amount payable by an applicant to £100,000.

In *Minister for Justice v Siúcre Éireann, Greencore plc*,[1] it was held that the Minister should, prima facie, be reimbursed the expenses by the company investigated. However, because Siúcre Éireann was controlled by the Minister for Finance prior to its 'privatisation', Lynch J decided that it would be unjust to penalise purchasers of shares by making that company reimburse the expenses.

If property is restored to any person as a result of the investigation, he may be ordered to contribute up to 10 per cent of its value towards the costs of the investigation.

Any person convicted or ordered to pay damages may also be ordered to repay all or part of the costs of the investigation.

INVESTIGATION BY AN INSPECTOR INTO THE OWNERSHIP OF A COMPANY

27.14 Section 14 *gives the Minister the power* to appoint one or more inspectors to investigate and report on the membership of any company. The purpose of this investigation is to determine the true persons who are financially interested in the success or failure of the company or who are able to control or influence company decisions. This power should enable the Minister to unveil some of the secrecy which surrounds nominee shareholdings.

The Minister also has the power to investigate a company's ownership without appointing an inspector (see **27.17** below).

When appointing an inspector under s 14, the Minister can specify the period of time or the specific matters to be investigated, in particular the enquiry may be limited to matters connected with particular shares or debentures.

An appointment may be made by the Minister where there are circumstances suggesting that it is necessary in the public interest – see s 14(2).

The initial appointments of inspectors under these powers were made during 1991.

27.15 The Minister for Industry and Commerce utilised these powers in September 1991. Then he decided to initiate an investigation into suspected irregularities which involved the purchase of shares in Sugar Distribution (Holdings) Ltd and their resale to Siúcre Éireann cpt at a substantial profit. This subsequently became known as the Greencore investigation.

The Minister appointed Maurice Curran, solicitor, under s 14, as an inspector to investigate the beneficial ownership of certain companies associated with Siúcre Éireann cpt and of certain of its debentures.

---

1 [1992] 2 IR 215.

During October 1991, the Minister appointed John Glacken, solicitor, as an inspector to investigate the true ownership and control of Hoddle Investments Ltd and Chestvale Properties Ltd arising out of the sale of a Ballsbridge site to Telecom Éireann, again at a substantial profit.

In *Desmond v Glackin (No 2)*,[1] the court held that the Minister must exercise his discretion to appoint an inspector in good faith.

Inspector's powers

27.16 An inspector appointed by the Minister has essentially the same powers[2] as those available to inspectors appointed by the court. The inspector's powers extend to examining the existence of arrangements which, though not legally binding, were observed in practice and relevant to the investigation.

The Minister has the power to direct the publication of part or all of the report.

MINISTER'S POWERS TO INVESTIGATE COMPANY OWNERSHIP

27.17 Section 15 gives the Minister the power, without appointing an inspector, to require any person whom he has reason to believe to have, or to be able to obtain for him, information as to the ownership of shares or debentures, to supply that information to him. This may be a less expensive and faster method of investigating company ownership than appointing an inspector.

'Ownership' is defined widely in s 15(2). Section 19 authorises the Minister to direct a body corporate to produce specified books and documents to him or to any authorised officer. The direction will be given by the Minister if he is of the opinion that there are circumstances suggesting that:

(1) the examination of the documents would assist in determining whether an inspector should be appointed;
(2) the affairs of the company have been conducted with intent to defraud creditors or investors, or for other fraudulent purposes;
(3) the affairs of the company are being conducted in a manner which is unfairly prejudicial to some part of its investors; or
(4) the company was formed for any fraudulent or unlawful purpose.

The power to obtain documents includes the power to take copies or extracts or require any person to give explanations. In addition, any person who does not have in his possession the documents must, if he knows, provide information as to their whereabouts.

[1993] 3 IR 67 (HC).
appropriate amendments – s 14(5).

In addition to requesting his own officers to carry out this work, the Minister may appoint outsiders to carry out this function, and such outsiders shall have the same rights, duties and obligations as officers.

On 14 December 1993, the Minister appointed Mr Peter Fisher, accountant, as an authorised officer under s 19 to examine the books and documents of County Glen plc. The authorised officer's report was submitted to the Minister on 23 December 1993, who immediately applied to the court for the appointment of an inspector under s 8. Arising out of this application, the High Court appointed Mr Frank Clarke, barrister, as an inspector to enquire further into certain of the affairs of County Glen plc.

Powers to enter and search premises

27.18 If the authorised officer, inspector or other person acting on behalf of the Minister can demonstrate reasonable grounds to suspect that there are, on any premises, books or documents which give information in relation to the ownership of shares and debentures, then, under s 20, he has the right to seek an order from the District Court for the Gardai, together with other named persons, to enter and search the premises for the purposes of obtaining the documents.

Any books or documents seized may be retained for a period of three months or, pending criminal proceedings commenced within that period, until their conclusion. Obstruction of the right of entry or search will constitute an offence.

Security of information obtained

27.19 Section 21 provides for the security of information obtained by the Minister as a result of using his powers under s 19 and/or s 20. There are also provisions in s 23 relating to *privileged* information.

Power to impose restrictions on shares

27.20 If it appears to the Minister that there is difficulty in finding out the relevant facts about the ownership of any share, the Minister may, by notice in writing, direct that the shares shall, until further notice, be subject to restrictions. Those restrictions are that:

(1) any transfer of the shares or rights to the shares shall be void;
(2) no voting rights shall be exercised in respect of the shares;
(3) the shareholder will not be entitled to participate in any rights issue;
(4) except in a liquidation, no dividend shall be paid in respect of the shares, whether in respect of capital or otherwise.

Any person aggrieved by the Minister's action can appeal to the court.[1]

The consequences of the Minister's action are dealt with in s 16(3) to (18). The court may, for example, on the application of the Minister, order the restricted shares to be sold.[2]

In such circumstances, the proceeds of the sale, less the related costs of the sale, will be paid into court for the benefit of the person who is beneficially interested in the shares. Such person may apply to the court for the proceeds to be paid to him.[3]

Criminal offence

27.21   Any person who exercises rights in relation to shares or debentures which are restricted, will be guilty of a criminal offence.[4]

Lifting of restrictions on shares

27.22   The restrictions can be lifted by order of the court or a direction by the Minister under s 16(6).

The restrictions will only be lifted if:

(1)   the relevant facts about the shares have been disclosed to the company, and no unfair advantage had accrued to any person as a result of the earlier non-disclosure; or

(2)   the shares are to be sold and the court or the Minister approves the sale.

LIMITS ON INVESTIGATING FOREIGN COMPANIES

27.23   Inspectors may be appointed by the court[5] to investigate foreign companies who carried on or are engaged in business within the State.

The court does not have the power to make a winding up order nor the Minister to seek such an order as a result of the inspector's report.

There are no powers available to investigate the ownership of foreign companies.

---

1 Section 16(5).
2 Section 16(8).
3 Section 16(9).
4 See s 16(14) to (17).
5 Section 17.

PART VII

INVESTORS' INDIVIDUAL RIGHTS AND RESPONSIBILITIES

Chapter 28

ACQUIRING AND RELINQUISHING COMPANY MEMBERSHIP

MEMBERSHIP

28.1 There are various ways by which a person can acquire shares in a company. Owning shares, of itself, does not confer membership status on the holder. To become a company member, the shareholder's name must be entered in the register of members.

WHO CAN BECOME MEMBERS?

28.2 Generally, any person of full contractual capacity can become a member. Some exceptional instances exist, though. These include membership by infants and companies, and the status of deceased and/or bankrupt members.

Infants and minors

28.3 Persons aged under 21 years used to be classified as infants for contracting purposes. The Age of Majority Act 1985 reduced this age to 18 and changed the classification to 'minors'.

A minor may enter into a contract to purchase shares. This contract will, however, be voidable at the minor's option.[1] Until such time as he rescinds the contract, the minor will be liable for any obligations arising out of the ownership of his shares, eg meeting a 'call' made upon shareholders by the directors.

A minor must exercise his option to withdraw from the company either before, or within a reasonable time after, attaining majority (18 years).

Notwithstanding the position of a minor at law, a company may provide expressly in the articles that a minor cannot be a member.

Companies

28.4 A company may be a member of *another* company if it is authorised to do so by its memorandum of association. There are, however, limitations on the extent to which a company can become:

(1) a member of itself; and

---

1 See R. Friel *The Law of Contract* (Round Hall Press, 1995), Chapter 5.

(2) a member of its holding company.

Buying its own shares

28.5 There are restrictions on a company either buying its own shares or giving loans for the purchase of its own shares. These restrictions have already been outlined in Chapter 13 in the context of protecting the capital base of the company (see **13.24** and **13.38**).

Purchasing the shares of its holding company

28.6 Section 224 of the 1990 Act empowers a subsidiary to acquire and hold shares in its holding company. This share holding is subject to the conditions set out in s 224(2). These include:

(1) the consideration for the purchase must be provided out of the profits of the subsidiary available for distribution; and
(2) following the share purchase:
    (a) the profits of the subsidiary available for distribution shall be restricted by a sum equal to the total cost of the shares acquired in its holding company; and
    (b) the subsidiary cannot exercise any voting rights in respect of the acquired shares.

The directors will be liable to repay the cost price of the shares to the subsidiary, if a winding up of that company commences within six months after the purchase and the company is unable to pay its debts.[1]

A return of the transaction must be made to the registrar[2] and, in the case of public companies, the Stock Exchange.[3] Section 228 empowers the Minister to make regulations governing the purchase of companies of their own shares or of shares in their holding company.

The European Communities (Public Limited Companies Subsidiaries) Regulations 1997 (the 1997 Regulations) implement Directive 92/101/EEC, which amends the Second Directive (Formation and Capital of Public Limited Companies) to apply conditions on the purchase of shares in a public limited company by subsidiaries of it.

Part XI of the 1990 Act had already substantially implemented Directive 92/101/EEC.

Regulation 4 of the 1997 Regulations extends the definition of subsidiary of a public limited company for the purposes of s 224 of the 1990 Act.

---

1 Section 225.
2 Section 226.
3 See ss 229 and 230.

Regulation 5 applies the conditions relating to acquiring shares by a public limited company itself, to the subscription, acquisition or holding of shares by any subsidiary in its parent plc.

Regulation 6 extends the provisions of s 14 of the Companies (Amendment) Act 1986, requiring information to be included in the directors' report regarding the acquisition by a company of its own shares, to include the acquisition by a subsidiary company of shares in its parent public limited company.

Deceased members

28.7 On the death of a shareholder, he ceases to be a member. Ownership of his shares, however, vests automatically in his legal personal representatives.

Bankrupt members

28.8 If a shareholder is made a bankrupt, the Official Assignee in Bankruptcy has the option of taking the shares. If the shares are 'onerous', ie a financial drain on the company, the Official Assignee can[1] disclaim the shares.

HOW PERSONS MAY BECOME MEMBERS

28.9 A person may become a member of a company either by subscribing to the memorandum of association or agreeing to become a member and having his name placed on the register of members.[2]

By subscribing to the memorandum

28.10 Those persons who sign the memorandum of association[3] are deemed to have agreed to become members. When the company's certificate of incorporation is issued by the registrar, the company must enter the subscribers' names in the register of members.[4]

By agreeing to become members

28.11 A person may agree to become a member either by:

(1) applying[5] for an allotment of shares and being allotted them; or

---

1 Within 12 months of their vesting in him – see Bankruptcy (Ireland) (Amendment) Act 1872, ss 97 and 98.
2 Section 31 of the 1963 Act.
3 Section 31(1) – see also Chapter 8.
4 Section 21(2).
5 See Chapter 10.

(2) taking a transfer of shares from an existing member. Such a transfer may
     be voluntary or involuntary; or

(3) by estoppel.

Transfer of shares

28.12 A voluntary transfer of shares takes place when the holder decides to
sell them and actually does so. An involuntary transfer occurs when the
shareholder dies and the property in his shares passes to his personal
representatives.

Directors' powers

28.13 Articles 22 to 28 of Table A[1] provide model internal company
guidelines affecting the transfer of shares. They give the directors of public
companies the right to decline to register a share transfer. As the purchaser of
shares will only become a member when his name is entered on the register of
members, the directors of a company may be given the power in its articles to
'block' a new member. For example, art 24 of Table A provides:

> 'The directors *may* decline to register the transfer of a share (not being a fully paid
> share) to a person of whom they do not approve, and they may also decline to
> register the transfer of a share on which the company has a lien. The directors may
> also decline to register any transfer of a share which, in their opinion, may imperil
> or prejudicially affect the status of the company in the State or which may imperil
> any tax concession or rebate to which the members of the company are entitled ...'
> (author's emphasis)

The directors of a private company may enjoy even greater powers to refuse
membership because of the limit on maximum number of members permitted
for private companies. For example, art 3 of Table A, Part II gives the directors
of a private company the power 'in their *absolute discretion, and without assigning
a reason therefore,* (to) decline to register any transfer of any shares ...' (author's
emphasis).

The procedures involved in share transfers will be dealt with in Chapter 31.
This will include judicial interpretation of the directors' 'blocking' powers.

Transmission of shares

28.14 The term 'transmission' is used to denote the involuntary transfer of
share ownership; in particular in the case of death or bankruptcy of a member.

Articles 29 to 31 of Table A, Part I contain the model guidelines. For example,
arts 30 and 31 stipulate that:

> '**30.** Any person becoming entitled to a share in consequence of the *death* or
> *bankruptcy* of a member may ... elect either to be registered himself as holder of the

---

1 Part I.

share or to have some person nominated by him registered as the transferee thereof, but the directors shall, in either case, have the same right to decline or suspend registration as they would have had in the case of a transfer of the share by that member before his death or bankruptcy, as the case may be. (author's emphasis)

31. If the person entitled elects to be registered himself, he shall deliver or send to the company a notice in writing signed by him stating that he so elects. If he elects to have another person registered, he shall testify his election by executing to that person a transfer of the share ...'

Estoppel

28.15 Any person who allows his name to remain on the register of members, or in other ways holds himself out as a member, may be legally estopped (or prevented) from denying that he is, in fact, a member.

Condition precedent to membership

28.16 In all cases of the acquisition of company membership, mere ownership of shares is not enough. It is the entering of the shareholder's name in the register of members which entitles him to membership. Thus, the entering of a person's name on the register is a condition precedent to becoming a member – see *Kinsella and Others v Alliance & Dublin Consumers Gas Company and Others.*[1]

REGISTER OF MEMBERS

28.17 Every company must maintain a register of members.[2] The register and index must be open to inspection by members and non-members. It is, therefore, possible to obtain details of the membership of a company, and to ascertain their liabilities.

The register is prima facie evidence that the persons named in it are members.[3]

Rectification of the register

28.18 Section 122 of the 1963 Act provides a remedy for any improper entry or omission of entry in the register. The remedy is 'rectification' or correction.

If the name of any person is, without sufficient cause, entered in or omitted from the register, or default is made, the person aggrieved, or any member of the company, may apply to the court for rectification of the register.

Rectification has been ordered by a court:

---

1 (Unreported) 5 October 1982 (HC).
2 See Chapter 25 for its contents.
3 Though not conclusive evidence – see s 124 of the 1963 Act.

(1) where a person was wrongfully removed from the register;
(2) where a person was put on the register, but had not agreed to take shares;
(3) where shares had been improperly surrendered;
(4) where a transfer had been forged.

Notice[1] of any rectification ordered by the court must be given to the registrar.

Trusts not to be entered in the register

28.18 Section 123 provides that no notice of any trust[2] shall be entered on the register or be receivable by the registrar.

Shares may, of course, be held in trust, but if there is a trust, then it is the trustee's name that is put on the register; he is nominally the shareholder and is liable to the company for calls even if the calls exceed the value of the trust property in his hands.

This means that a company is in no way concerned with the relation of its registered holders to anyone else. If they are, in fact, trustees, the company need not enquire whether they are acting within their powers in dealing with the shares. The company looks solely to the registered holders.

Article 7 of Table A, Part I elaborates upon s 123 by providing 'except as required by law, no person shall be recognised by the company as holding any shares upon any trust . . .'

Article 7 also makes it clear that s 123 will not preclude the company from requiring members to furnish the company with information as to the beneficial ownership of any share, when this is reasonably required by the company. This type of information may now be required under Part IV of the 1990 Act.

Even though the company may become aware that there are beneficial interests[3] in shares by reason of disclosure[4] under Part IV, it is prohibited by s 123 from noting any trusts in its register of members. In *Simpson v Molson's Bank*,[5] it was held that the company need not take any notice of a trust, even if it has constructive notice that it exists.

HOW PERSONS RELINQUISH MEMBERSHIP

28.19 A person may cease to be a member in the following ways and circumstances:

---

1 Section 122(5).
2 Express, implied or constructive.
3 Other than the members'.
4 See Chapter 31 and disclosure orders. Beneficial interests by directors, secretaries and their families must also be disclosed – see **20.24** above.
5 [1895] AC 270.

(1) by a *transfer of his shares*, duly registered – see Chapter 31. He will, however, be liable to contribute on the 'B' list if winding up commences within 12 months of the sale;[1]

(2) by *forfeiture*[2] of his shares through non-payment of *calls*, if permitted by the articles;

(3) by *sale* of the shares by the company under power given by its articles to enforce a *lien*.[3] The former member may remain a debtor of the company for any amount unpaid on his shares, if the articles so provide;

(4) by a valid *surrender*[4] of his shares by the member;

(5) on the *death, bankruptcy* or *mental incapacity*[5] of the member and appropriate notification of disclaimer by the official personal representatives;

(6) by *repudiation* (or cancellation) either:

    (a) by a *minor* under a voidable contract; or

    (b) by any member on grounds of fraud, misrepresentation mistake or irregular allotment.[6]

---

1 See Chapter 42.

2 See Chapter 30.

3 Ibid. A lien is a legal right to keep possession of someone's property and, if necessary, sell it, unless a debt owed by the property owner is paid.

4 Ibid.

5 See **31.36**.

6 See **10.33**.

Chapter 29

THE INVESTORS' STATUTORY CONTRACT

SIGNIFICANCE OF MEMBERSHIP

29.1   The means by which an investor acquires an interest in a company is by obtaining its shares. He subsequently becomes a member of that company when his name is entered in the register of members. The question now arises as to the significance of membership over mere share ownership.

In *Kinsella and Others v Alliance and Dublin Consumers Gas Company and Others*,[1] the court decided that only persons whose names are entered in the register of members are entitled to vote at a general meeting. In that case, Barron J stated:

> 'Persons entitled to stock (shares) must be registered in the register of share-holders. Until they are, they are not entitled to vote. This is a well established principle and I would be wrong not to follow it ...
>
>   The meeting was properly held on the basis of the register of shareholders as it then existed ... In the present case, all reasonable efforts were made to register transfers and the failure to register them is not a ground on which the plaintiffs are entitled to rely ...'

Clearly, membership is significant for investors who wish to exercise important rights attaching to their shares, such as attending company meetings and voting at them.

Corporate majority decisions and individual members' rights

29.2   The Companies Acts permit the majority of the members to control constitutional aspects of a company. We have already explained:

(1) company meetings and resolutions;[2]
(2) the democratic[3] nature of the voting underlying major company decisions.

A result of the democratic nature of corporate control may mean that individual shareholders, if outvoted on an issue, have no grounds for redress. A further extrapolation of this principle is that, if a member feels that the company has suffered a loss, it is the company who must pursue it. This is what the rule in *Foss v Harbottle*[4] entails.

Where, however, corporate majority decisions *wrongfully* affect members' individual rights, these individual or minority members are given some protection by:

---

1 (Unreported) 5 October 1982 (HC).
2 See Chapter 15.
3 See Chapter 16.
4 Ibid.

(1) the apparent judicial exceptions to the rule in *Foss v Harbottle*, and

(2) statutory provisions such as ss 205 and 213[1] of the 1963 Act.

As we focus on shareholders' and members' individual rights, it should not be forgotten that in some cases the exercise of these rights may be adversely affected by this democratic nature of company decision-making.

SHARES

29.3   In legal parlance, a share is a 'chose in action', ie a certain form of right or interest which cannot be possessed in a physical sense. The share certificate, issued to an investor, and showing his name, and type and amount of shares held, is evidence of an 'interest' possessed by him in the company.

What is a share?

29.4   A shareholder does not possess a 'share' in the property owned by the company. An incorporated association such as a registered company has a legal personality separate from its shareholders. It also owns its own property.[2]

Essential nature

29.5   A distinguishing feature of a share in a company is that the holder becomes a member of that company when his name is entered in the register of members. At this stage, therefore, we shall assume that all shareholders are registered as members and treat the terms 'shareholder' and 'member' as synonymous.

A person holding a share or shares in a company does not have any rights over the company's property. In *Att-Gen for Ireland v Jameson*,[3] the court held that no shareholder:

> 'has a right to any specific portion of the company's property, and save by, and to the extent of his *voting power* at a general meeting of the company, cannot curtail the free and proper disposition of it ...' (author's emphasis)

A shareholder does have rights: the right to a dividend in certain cases; the right to vote at meetings if he holds the appropriate type of shares, etc. But the company's property belongs to the company.

---

1 See Chapter 16.
2 See Chapters 3 and 4. A shareholder has, however, a share in the ownership of the company itself.
3 [1904] 2 IR 644 (ChD).

Essentially a contract

29.6   In *Borlands Trustee v Steel Bros*,[1] Farwell J defined a share as:

> 'the interest of a shareholder in the company, measured by a sum of money, for the purpose of liability, in the first place, and of interest in the second; but also consisting of a series of mutual covenants, entered into by all the shareholders inter se.'

Thus, a share consists of:

(1) *an interest*. In *IRC v Crossman*,[2] Russell LJ defined that interest in the company as being composed of rights and obligations which are defined by the Companies Act and by the memorandum and articles of association of the company; and

(2) a *series of mutual* provisions entered into by all *the shareholders* inter se.

29.7   In *Att-Gen for Ireland v Jameson*, the court further held that a shareholder:

> 'is entitled to a share of the company's capital and profits the former … being measured by a sum of money which is taken as the standard for the ascertainment of his share of the profits. If the company disposes of its assets, or if the latter be realised in a liquidation, he has a right to a proportion of the amount received after the discharge of the company's debts and liabilities. In acquiring these rights – that is, on becoming a member of the company – he is deemed to have simultaneously entered into a contract under seal to conform to the regulations contained in the articles of association … Whatever obligations are contained in the articles, he accepts the ownership of the share and the position of a member of the company, bound and controlled by them. He cannot divorce his money interest, whatever it may amount to, from these obligations. They are inseparable incidents attached to his rights, and the idea of a share cannot be complete without their inclusion.'

The 'mutual provisions' and 'rights and obligations' are clearly spelled out in s 25 of the 1963 Act. Section 25 provides that:

> 'the memorandum and articles shall, when registered, bind the company and the members thereof to the same extent as if they respectively had been signed and sealed respectively by each member and contained covenants by each member to observe all the provisions of the memorandum and of the articles.'

The s 25 contract

29.8   The definition of a share is clearly important in a commercial and economic sense. However, from its contractual perspective, the most significant factor is that a shareholder becomes a member of the company, with legal rights and obligations flowing from this relationship. These contractual relations mean that under s 25, the company's articles of association bind:

---

1   [1901] 1 Ch 279 (approved by Fitzgibbon LJ in *Casey v Bentley* [1902] 1 IR 376).
2   [1937] AC 26. In *Private Motorists Provident Society & Moore v Attorney-General* [1984] ILRM 988 (SC), it was held that a share itself also constitutes a property right which can be protected by the Constitution.

(1) the investors to the company;

(2) the company to investors (individually); and

(3) individual investors to other investors, who are deemed to have each covenanted under seal to observe the articles (and the memorandum).

The 's 25 contract' may be enforced[1] by and against both the company and the individual members.

29.9 The typical matters included in articles of association can be illustrated by Table A. Table A deals with the following important internal company matters:

Share Capital and Shares –	articles 2–46
Meetings –	articles 47–74
Directors –	articles 75–112
Secretary –	articles 113–114
Dividends & Reserves –	articles 116–124
Accounts –	articles 125–129
Capitalisation of Profit –	articles 130–131
Audit –	article 132
Notices –	articles 133–136
Winding Up –	article 137

The s 25 contract dealing with these internal company matters can *only be enforced* by a *member in his capacity as member*. For example, in *Eley v The Positive Government Security Life Assurance Co Ltd*,[2] a member acting as the company's solicitor was unable to rely on the articles as a contract of employment between the company and himself in that capacity. Eley had not been pursuing any claim as a member. He was an outsider in respect of his claim.

Astbury J, in *Hickman v Kent or Romney Marsh Sheep Breeders Association*,[3] said of outsiders:

> 'an outsider to whom rights purport to be given by the articles in his capacity as such outsider, whether he is or subsequently becomes a member, cannot sue on those articles treating them as contracts between himself and the company to enforce those rights.'

As a result, outsiders or third parties, generally, do not acquire rights under a s 25 contract, as they are not parties (or privy) to it.

29.10 In *Securities Trust Ltd v Hugh Moore & Alexander Ltd*,[4] the High Court held that where a third party had suffered loss because of an error in the articles of association supplied to him, the company did not owe him a duty of care in tort: the company's duty of care only extending to a shareholder who was supplied with the articles. As Davitt P stated:

---

1 *Clark v Workman* [1920] 1 IR 107 (ChD).

2 (1876) 1 ExD 88 (CA).

3 [1915] 1 Ch 881 (ChD).

4 [1964] IR 417.

'It can hardly be seriously contended that the defendant company owed a duty to the world at large to take care to avoid mistakes and printers' errors in the reprint of their articles.'

Alteration of the articles of association means, in effect, changing the terms of the s 25 statutory contract. Such a contract has been described judicially[1] as 'of the most sacred character' because it is on the faith of it that each investor advances his money.

Shareholders enjoy protection against changes in the articles. They can only be altered by a resolution passed by a 75 per cent majority of members. Even then, there are further protections for minority members – see Chapter 16.

As a result, each shareholder, as a member, is bound contractually to the company according to the terms set out in the articles of association. The shareholders are also contractually bound to each other to observe their respective rights and duties set out in the articles.

Shareholders' rights

29.11   The rights of a shareholder may include:

(1) *Dividends.* The right to receive a share of the company's distributable profits in the form of a dividend;[2]
(2) *Meetings.* The right to attend and vote at meetings of the company (if the type of share permits);
(3) *Directors.* The right to vote in the election or removal of directors, again if the type of share grants this right;
(4) *Information.* The right to receive a copy of the annual accounts and directors' and auditors' reports, at least 21 days before the AGM;
(5) *Changes in Memorandum and Articles of Association.* The right to vote on these alterations which might be necessary to:
   (a) increase the company's authorised share capital;
   (b) give the directors authority to allot shares; or
   (c) waive members' pre-emption rights;
(6) *Requisitions.* The right to requisition extraordinary general meetings if the statutory minimum number of minority members required can be mustered;
(7) *Rights and Bonus Issues.* The right to participate, in proportion to the number of shares held, in any rights or bonus issues of shares;
(8) *Transfer.* The right to transfer[3] the shares to a third party for consideration (ie by selling them) or by way of gift. This right will, however, be restricted for shareholders of private companies;

---

1 By Ross J in *Clark v Workman* [1920] 1 IR 107 (ChD).
2 See Chapter 30.
3 See Chapter 31.

(9) *Capital.* The right to receive, on the winding up of the company, their proportion of assets remaining (if any), after all the creditors have been paid.

Many of these rights may be amended or excluded by the articles, unless conferred by statute, eg (4) and (6). Other statutory rights include the shareholders' rights to inspect the register of members, to petition the court to appoint an inspector,[1] to vote to wind up the company voluntarily[2] and to petition the court for relief under s 205 of the 1963 Act, in cases of oppression (see **16.8**).

Shareholders' duties

29.12   The main duty of a shareholder recognises the fact that he is basically an investor. This is his duty to pay the amount which he has agreed to pay on his shares. This may involve payment of the full amount when the contract is agreed, ie when the shares are allotted to him.

Public subscriptions for shares

29.13   The methods of raising capital from the public, making payment for shares and the protection for investors in these transactions have been detailed in Chapter 10. This chapter also includes rules on the payment for shares by *non-cash consideration.*

Calls

29.14   Part only of a share may be payable on application or purchase. The remaining amount can be payable when a call is made by the directors on the shareholder of a partly-paid share – see next chapter.

Types of shares

29.15   Class rights and the differences between types of shares, such as ordinary and preference, were explained when dealing with the composition of the company's capital base, in Chapter 12.

Variation of class rights

29.16   The protections for shareholders in the event of the variation of the rights of their particular class of share were also detailed in Chapter 12.

---

1 See Chapter 25.
2 Section 251 of the 1963 Act – see Part X of this book.

Amount and numbering of shares

29.17   The memorandum of association must state the amount of the share capital of a limited liability company, divided into shares of a fixed amount, eg 250,000 shares of £1 each.[1]

Unless all the issued shares (or class of shares) are fully paid up and ranking pari passu (equally), each share must be numbered.[2]

Share certificates

29.18   A shareholder is furnished with a share certificate as evidence of his s 25 contract, and of his title to the shares. The share certificate contains few details; merely the shareholder's name, number and classes of shares held, etc.

Notwithstanding, as Lord Selborne LC declared in *Oakbank Oil Co v Crum:*[3]

> 'Each party must be taken to have made himself acquainted with the terms of the written contract contained in the articles of association ... He must also in law be taken ... to have understood the terms of the contract according to their proper meaning; and that being so, he must take the consequences, whatever they may be, of the contract which he has made.'

Object of certificate

29.19   A valid share certificate issued under seal, is prima facie evidence[4] of the investor's title to the shares. As a result, loss of a share certificate can cause difficulties for a shareholder in dealing with his shares. However, art 8 of Table A provides for the replacement of any share certificate which has been lost, defaced or destroyed.

Effect of certificate

29.20   The certificate has been defined as a statement that the company asserts that the person to whom it is granted is the registered shareholder entitled to the shares included in the certificate, and that the amount certified to be paid has been paid. As a result, the company may be estopped (prevented) from:

(1)   disputing the title of the registered holder, as happened in *Re Bahia and San Francisco Ry.*[5]

---

1   Section 6(4)(a) of the 1963 Act.
2   See s 80 of the 1963 Act.
3   (1882) 8 App Cas 65.
4   Section 87 of the 1963 Act.
5   (1868) LR3 QB 584. In this case, the registered holder left the share certificate with brokers who forged her signature to a transfer of the shares.

According to case-law, the company is *not* estopped from denying the title of the registered holder where an *officer* of the company issues a forged certificate. In *Ruben v Great Fingall Consolidated*,[1] Lord Macnaghten stated:

> 'Ruben and Ladenbury are the victims of a wicked fraud ... But their claim against the respondent company is, I think, simply absurd.
>
> The thing put forward as the foundation of their claim is a piece of paper which purports to be a certificate of shares in the company. This paper is false and fraudulent from beginning to end ... Every statement in the document is a lie. The only thing real about it is the signature of the secretary of the company who was the sole author and perpetrator of the fraud. No one would suggest that this fraudulent certificate could of itself ... bind or affect the company in any way. It is not the company's deed, and there is nothing to prevent the company from saying so ...
>
> The directors have never said or done anything to represent or lead to the belief that the thing was the company's deed. Without such a representation, there can be no estoppel.
>
> The secretary *who is a mere servant* ... has no authority to guarantee the genuineness or validity of a document which is not the deed of the company ...' (author's emphasis)

or

(2) alleging that the amount stated as being paid on the shares has not been paid. For example, if the certificate incorrectly states that the shares are fully paid up, the company cannot make a call upon the holder for the amount unpaid.[2]

Comment on case-law

29.21   The decision in *Ruben v Great Fingall Consolidated* in (1) above is based on a nineteenth-century judicial view of the company secretary's role. As pointed out in Chapter 14, the company secretary is no longer viewed as 'a mere servant or clerk', but as a company's chief administrative officer/ executive. Furthermore, there is no common law impediment to holding a company vicariously liable for the fraudulent acts of its employees.[3] Accordingly, it is questionable whether a modern judge would find that a company was not estopped from denying that it was liable for a share certificate issued fraudulently by its secretary – despite the precedent of the *Ruben* case.

Again, the case-law in (2) above – that the company is estopped from making a call on a shareholder where the share certificate wrongly stated that the shares were fully paid up – would result in the issuing of those shares at a discount. This situation is now prohibited by s 27(1) of the 1983 Act.

---

1 [1906] AC 439. The proper shareholder may, however, be able to sue the company for damages if the shares have been sold under the forged certificate to a person who purchases them in good faith.

2 *Burkinshaw v Nicholls* (1878) 3 App Cas 1004. Nor can the company place a transferee of them, without knowledge, on the list of contributories on the company going into liquidation – see *Bloomenthal v Ford* [1897] AC 156.

3 See *Lloyd v Grace Smith & Co* [1912] AC 716.

Where shares are allotted in contravention of s 27(1), the allottee will be liable to pay the company an amount equal to the amount of the discount, plus interest thereon at an appropriate rate.[1]

The term 'allottee' denotes the original purchaser of shares from the company. It is unlikely, therefore, that s 27 could be used by the company as a means of obtaining payment of the discount from a transferee, or at least a person who bought the shares from the allottee in good faith and for value without notice, in the event of the allottee failing to pay them. As a result, the common law position would appear to prevail in favour of transferees,[2] and the company would be estopped from alleging that the amount stated as being paid on the shares had not been paid.

Share warrants

29.22   A share certificate is not a negotiable instrument. If a company issues a share warrant instead of a certificate, the holder can transfer the ownership of his shares by handing over the warrant to a purchaser. Thus, a share warrant is a negotiable instrument like a cheque.

Private companies do not issue share warrants. Whilst s 88 empowers a company to issue share warrants, few, in fact, do so.

CONVERSION OF SHARES INTO STOCK

29.23   Sections 68 and 69 of the 1963 Act give a company the power to alter its share capital structure. In particular, the company may, by ordinary resolution, convert any paid up shares into stock, and reconvert any stock into paid up shares of any denomination.

Generally, the holders of the stock will have the same rights as if they held the shares from which the stock arose – see Table A, art 42.

---

1 Section 27(2).
2 Some doubts might exist in the case of involuntary transferees and, perhaps, instances where the allottee makes a gift of the shares to the transferee.

Chapter 30

DIVIDENDS AND CALLS ON SHARES

SHAREHOLDERS' RIGHTS AND LIABILITIES

30.1 Shareholders enjoy many rights and can incur several liabilities under their s 25 contracts. These have already been summarised in the previous chapter. We now focus on a shareholder's right to dividends and his liability to meet calls for payments on his shares.

SHAREHOLDERS' PRINCIPAL RIGHTS

30.2 The principal rights enjoyed by shareholders include:

(1) the right to attend and vote[1] at meetings;
(2) statutory rights to accounts and reports,[2] etc;
(3) the right to a dividend, if one is declared; and
(4) the right to receive a proportionate part of any surplus capital remaining after all the creditors have been paid in the event of the company being wound up.[3]

In Chapter 12, we explained which of these rights were enjoyed solely by preference and/or by ordinary shareholders. Generally, both these types of shareholders may be entitled to dividends.

Dividends

30.3 A dividend is the share, received by a shareholder, of the company's profits legally available for distribution[4] to its investors.

Every trading company has the implied power to pay dividends, subject to any restrictions imposed on it by its memorandum of association.

Right to a dividend

30.4 Generally, shareholders have no right to a dividend, even where the distributable profits are available, if the directors decide not to declare one. For example, art 116 of Table A provides:

> 'The company in general meeting may declare dividends, but no dividend shall exceed the amount recommended by the directors.'

---

1 See Chapter 15.
2 See Chapters 24 and 25. A wider range of shareholders' rights is also summarised in Chapter 29.
3 See Part X.
4 See Chapters 13 and 24.

The directors are also empowered by art 117 to pay to members such interim dividends as appear to them to be justified by the profits of the company.

In *Scott v Scott*,[1] a resolution, passed by the company in general meeting, that the directors should pay an interim dividend, was held to be inoperative.

An interim dividend is one passed on a date between two annual general meetings of the company. Clearly, from the judgment in *Scott v Scott*, reinforcing art 117, a majority of investors cannot compel the directors to declare an interim dividend.[2]

Again, art 118 of Table A stipulates that no dividend or interim dividend can legally be paid otherwise than in accordance with Part IV of the 1983 Act.

The provisions of Part IV which apply concern profits[3] available for distribution and restrictions on the distribution of assets.

The fundamental statutory rule is that a company cannot make a distribution except out of its accumulated realised profits, less its accumulated realised losses (see **13.49**).

Again, the directors may, before recommending any dividend, set aside out of the profits of the company such sums as they think proper as a reserve which shall, at the discretion of the directors, be applicable for any purpose to which the profits of the company may be properly applied, and pending such application may, either be employed in the business of the company, or be invested in such investments as the directors may lawfully determine. The directors may also, without placing the same to reserve, carry forward any profits which they may think it prudent not to divide.[4]

Amount of dividend payable

30.5   The dividends on preference shares are usually paid at a fixed rate, eg six per cent, whereas dividends paid to ordinary shareholders will vary according to the amount of the distributable profit. If there is only sufficient distributable profit to pay the fixed dividends to the preference shareholders, then the ordinary shareholders will not receive any dividend.

If the company has incurred a trading loss, it will not be able to pay dividends to either preference or ordinary shareholders.

The articles usually stipulate the amounts to be paid. For example, art 120 of Table A provides that, subject to the rights of special classes such as preference shareholders, 'all dividends shall be declared and paid according to the amounts paid (or credited as paid)' on the relevant shares.

---

1 [1943] 1 All ER 582.
2 Except, perhaps, in the case of fraud: *Thairlwall v Great Northern Railway Co* [1910] 2 KB 509.
3 Sections 45 and 45A – see Chapters 13 and 24.
4 Article 119 of Table A.

Mode of payment

30.6 The mode of payment for dividends is normally determined by the articles. For example, art 123 of Table A provides that any dividend payable in cash in respect of any shares may be paid by cheque or warrant sent through the post to the registered address of the member.

Shares in lieu of dividends

30.7 Investors can also be offered extra shares in lieu of dividend payments.

Effect of declaration of dividend

30.8 The declaration of a dividend creates a contract debt from the company to the shareholder. Because the articles of association bind the investors in a s 25 contract[1] as if they had covenanted under seal, the debt is in the nature of a specialty debt, and thus not barred for a period of 12 years.[2]

Dividends are no longer debts owed by the company if a winding up occurs. In this event, the shareholder's right to sue for his arrears of dividend is deferred until the debts of the company's trading creditors have been satisfied.[3]

FINANCIAL LIABILITIES OF SHAREHOLDERS

30.9 When a shareholder has paid the full nominal value for his shares, then, on the winding up of the company, he incurs no further liability – his liability being limited to the amount, if any, unpaid on his shares.[4]

Where any share is issued with less than the nominal value paid on allotment, it is partly paid. Generally, the company is entitled to require the unpaid amount of shares to be paid at any time. However, the articles usually make provision for such payments 'by instalments' to be made.

Whilst normally payment for shares is required in full, in the case of a newly formed company, the directors may consider that payment of the full value of each share is not required at once. Such issued 'partly paid' shares therefore are paid for by instalments. A request by the company to the shareholders for a part payment is known as a *call*. For example, the issuing company may require 50p per £1 share paid on allotment, followed by two further calls of 25p each.

---

1 See previous chapter.
2 *Re Belfast Empire Theatre of Varieties* [1963] IR 41.
3 *Wilson (Inspector of Taxes) v Dunnes Stores (Cork) Ltd* (unreported) 22 January 1976 (HC) – see also Part X.
4 See Chapter 4.

Making a call for payment

30.10   An example of a procedure for the making of calls is to be found in Table A, arts 15 to 21.

Article 15 empowers the directors from time to time to make calls upon the investors in respect of any money unpaid on their shares, (whether on account of the nominal value or by way of premium).

A call is made at the time the directors' resolution was passed.[1]

Calls should be made by directors equally on all shareholders. In *Alexander v Automatic Telephone Co*,[2] it was held to be an abuse of power, when directors made calls on shareholders other than themselves.

In *Galloway v Halle Concerts Society*,[3] Sargant J stated:

> 'Prima facie ... there is ... an implied condition of equality between shareholders in a company, and ... prima facie it is entirely improper for the directors to make a call on some members of a class of shareholders ... without making a similar call on all the other members of that class.'

Article 20 of Table A allows directors:

> 'on the issue of shares, [to] differentiate between the holders as to the amount of calls to be paid and the times of payment.'

Such powers must be used by the directors in good faith and for the benefit of the company.

Limits

30.11   There is a limit on the amount that can be called, ie no call shall exceed one-quarter of the nominal value of the share or be payable at less than one month from the date fixed for the payment of the last preceding call, and each member shall (subject to receiving at least 14 days' notice specifying the time or times and place of payment) pay to the company at the time or times and place so specified the amount called on his shares. A call may be revoked or postponed as the directors may determine.

Early payment of calls

30.12   Article 21 permits the early or advance payment of calls, and allows the directors to pay interest of up to five per cent on the money advanced.

---

1 See art 16 of Table A.
2 [1900] 2 Ch 56.
3 [1915] 2 Ch 233.

Late payment

30.13 Under art 18, a member may be liable to pay interest not exceeding five per cent for late payments, although the directors can waive payment of this interest.

Non-payment of calls

30.14 The company has sanctions against investors who do not meet calls made on them. These sanctions are:

(1) forfeiture;
(2) surrender; and
(3) lien.

Forfeiture of shares

30.15 A company can take the powers in its articles to forfeit shares as illustrated by arts 33 to 39 of Table A.

Notice of forfeiture

30.16 If an investor fails to pay any call[1] on the day appointed for payment thereof, the directors may, at any time whilst any part of the call remains unpaid, serve a notice on him requiring payment of so much of the call as is unpaid together with any interest which may have accrued.

The notice must name a further day (not earlier than 14 days from the date of service of the notice) on or before which the payment required by the notice is to be made, and shall warn that, in the event of non-payment at or before the time appointed, the shares in respect of which the call was made will be liable to be forfeited.

If the requirements of the notice are not complied with, the shares in question may be forfeited by resolution of the directors.[2]

Effect of forfeiture

30.17 A forfeited share may be sold or reissued on such terms as the directors think fit. An investor whose shares have been forfeited ceases to be a member of the company. Notwithstanding, art 37 imposes a liability on him to pay calls due at the date of forfeiture, unless these unpaid calls have been paid by a subsequent holder of them.

Section 43(1) of the 1983 Act imposes a time limit on a plc within which to sell shares which have been forfeited or surrendered. These shares must be sold

---

1 Or instalment of a call.
2 See art 35.

within three years. If not, they must be cancelled. This action would have the effect of reducing the amount of the plc's nominal share capital.[1]

Surrender of shares

30.18   An investor is only allowed[2] to voluntarily surrender his shares where they could have been forfeited and it is desired to avoid the formalities attached to forfeiture. Otherwise, a surrender would be classified as an unlawful reduction of the company's capital.

Lien on members' shares

30.19   A lien is a legal right to hold another person's goods/assets, and keep them until a debt owed by that person has been paid.

Normally, the articles[3] give the company a 'non-possessory' lien on the members' shares for non-payment of calls. For example, art 11 of Table A provides:

> 'The company shall have a first and paramount lien on every share (not being a fully paid share) for all monies (whether immediately payable or not) called or payable at a fixed time in respect of that share; but the directors may at any time declare any share to be wholly or in part exempt from the provisions of this regulation. The company's lien on a share shall extend to all dividends payable thereon.'

The company may enforce its security by selling the shares under powers given to it in arts 12 and 13.

If the proceeds of the sale exceed the amount owed on the shares, the balance must be paid to the member – see art 14.

Notice of other interests

30.20   Cases such as *Bradford Banking Co v Briggs*[4] and *Rearden v Provincial Bank of Ireland*[5] suggest that, although no notice of any trust or equitable interest in its shares is registerable[6] by the company, it must, nevertheless, take notice of such interests when a question of priorities to title arises between the company and a third party. This situation could arise in circumstances involving the exercise of a company's lien over an investor's shares.

Because of the possibilities of problems arising relating to third party interests, the remedy of forfeiture would seem to be a much more effective and practical remedy for non-payment of calls, than the exercising of a lien on the defaulting member's shares.

---

1 See Chapter 13.
2 If there is authority in the articles.
3 Section 44 of the 1983 Act also restricts a plc taking a lien or charge on its own shares.
4 (1986) 12 App Cas 29.
5 [1896] 1 IR 532 (ChD).
6 See Chapter 29.

Chapter 31

DISCLOSURE AND TRANSFERS OF SHAREHOLDERS' INTERESTS

THE REGISTER

31.1 We have already[1] seen that the interests of directors, secretaries and their families in the shares and debentures of the company must be noted in a register of directors' and secretaries' interests.

DISCLOSURE OF INTERESTS IN SHARES

31.2 The disclosure regime under the 1990 Act is contained in Part IV. It involves the *disclosure* of interests in shares in the following circumstances:

(1) share dealings by directors, secretaries and their families;
(2) in the case of individual and group acquisitions:
    (a) the disclosure of interests exceeding five per cent in the voting shares of a plc held by any person;
    (b) the notification of interests of concert parties in the shares of a plc;
    (c) the keeping of a register of notified interests of shares in a plc.

Share dealings by directors, secretaries and their families

31.3 The 1990 Act requires the disclosure of beneficial interests of directors, secretaries and their families – see Chapter 20. This requirement applies to both public and private companies.

Disclosure of significant interests in shares of a plc

31.4 Any person holding an interest in voting shares exceeding five per cent of the company's issued share capital, must notify a plc of their significant share holding[2] in it.

A person is deemed to be interested[3] in any shares:

(1) in which his spouse or minor child has an interest;
(2) held by a body corporate if:
    (a) the body corporate or its directors are accustomed to act in accordance with his directions or instructions; or

---

1 In Chapter 20.
2 Disposal of a significant share holding is also notifiable – see ss 72 and 73.
3 For notification purposes – see ss 72 and 73.

(b) he has the control of one-third or more of the voting power at that
      body corporate's general meetings;
(3) held under a concert party agreement of which he is a member (see **31.8**
    below).

Register of significant interests

31.5 Section 80 provides for the keeping of a register of notified significant
(five per cent) interests in shares by every plc. This register must be updated
within three days of a new notification being received.

There are detailed procedures contained in s 80 for the maintenance of this
register.

Investigations of interests in shares

31.6 If a plc knows, or has reasonable cause to believe, that a person was
interested in its voting shares during the preceding three years, it may, by
written notice, ask him to confirm or deny the holding. If he confirms the
holding, the company may require him to provide further details.[1]

If the recipient of a notice fails to give the information within such a time
period as the company may specify, the company may apply to the court for an
order directing that the rights attaching to the shares in question be restricted.[2]

A plc must include in its s 80 register of significant interests, information which
it receives in response to notification enquiries made by it. The information
must be entered in a separate part of the register.[3]

Members of a public limited company holding at least 10 per cent of the voting
paid-up share capital can also require the company to investigate any interests
in its voting shares.[4]

After the investigation has been completed, the company must make available a
report to its investors at its registered office. Interim reports must be made
available at three-monthly intervals until a final report is made.[5]

The register of significant interests, and any company investigation report
required by s 84, must be made available for inspection to members and other
persons. Copies of such documents must also be made available by the
company on payment of a fee.[6]

---

1 Section 81.
2 Section 85.
3 Section 82.
4 Section 83.
5 Section 84.
6 Section 88.

Notification of thresholds to Stock Exchange

31.7 The 1990 Act also implemented the EU Major Holdings Directive[1] whose objective is to harmonise the rules relating to information publishable when a major holding in a listed company is acquired or sold.

If a person acquires or disposes of an interest in an Irish public limited company which results in an ownership threshold of 10 per cent, 25 per cent, 50 per cent or 75 per cent being exceeded or reduced below, that person must, in addition, to notifying the company of the change in interest, also notify the Stock Exchange.

The Stock Exchange is required to publish the information within three days of the receipt of the declaration.[2]

Notification of interests of concert parties

31.8 A concert party is an arrangement whereby several people or companies work together to acquire another (target) company through a takeover bid.[3]

Parties acting in concert must keep each other informed[4] of all relevant facts in relation to interests held in a plc.

They must also notify the company of the names and addresses of the parties to their takeover agreement.[5] Thus, disclosure is now required by parties acting in concert both to each other and to the company.

Disclosure orders for interests in private companies

31.9 A disclosure order is defined in s 98 of the 1990 Act as an order of the court which obliges:

(1) any person whom the court believes to have or to be able to obtain any information as to:
   (a) persons interested at present, or at any time during a period specified in the order, in the shares or debentures of a company;
   (b) the names and addresses of any of those persons;
   (c) the name and address of any person who acts or has acted on behalf of any of those persons in relation to the shares or debentures,
   to give such information to the court; or

---

1 Directive 88/627/EEC of 12 December 1988.
2 Section 91. See also ss 92 to 96 which deal with, inter alia, obligation of professional secrecy, immunity from suit and the application and amendment of the 1984 Regulations mentioned in Chapter 10.
3 See s 73 for detailed statutory definition.
4 See ss 74 and 75.
5 See s 74(4) and (5).

(2) any person whom the court believes to be, or at any time during a period specified in the order to have been, interested in shares or debentures of a company to confirm that fact or (as the case may be) to indicate whether or not it is the case and, where he holds any interest[1] in such shares or debentures, to give such further information as the court may require; or

(3) any person interested specified in the order, to disclose the information required in (1) above.

Exempted companies

31.10 Section 97 provides that a disclosure order will *not* be available against the following companies:

(1) plcs;
(2) building, industrial and provident societies; and
(3) any body corporate which is prohibited by statute or otherwise from making any distribution of its income or property among its members while it is a going concern or when it is in liquidation.

Who can apply for a disclosure order?

31.11 Any person who has a financial interest in a company may apply to the court for a disclosure order.

A person with a financial interest is defined as a member, contributory, creditor, employee, co-adventurer, examiner, lessor, lessee, licensor, licensee, liquidator or receiver in relation to the company or a related company.

The court will only make the disclosure order if:

(1) it deems it just and equitable to do so; and
(2) it is of the opinion that the financial interest of the applicant is or will be prejudiced by the non-disclosure of any interest in the shares or debentures of the company.

Notice of the order must be sent to the parties specified in s 102. These include the registrar of companies.

Scope of disclosure order

31.12 Section 100 sets out details of what information must be disclosed by the addressee of a disclosure order. The interests to be disclosed under s 100 include those of beneficiary under a trust and of a person, who, though not a shareholder, can influence and control the exercise of the rights of the named shareholder.

---

1 Or has, during that period, held any interest.

Where information on interests held in shares, etc is furnished to the applicant for a disclosure order, or to a company, the court may impose such restrictions[1] on the publication of this information as it thinks fit.

Contravention of disclosure order

31.13 Where the addressee fails to comply with the terms of a disclosure order, his rights under the non-disclosed shares become unenforceable, unless the court is satisfied that his failure to comply was accidental or due to some other sufficient cause.[2]

TRANSFER OF SHARES

31.14 A transfer of shares may take place voluntarily or involuntarily, ie compulsorily. An example of a voluntary transfer is where the shareholder sells the shares or makes a gift of them. An involuntary transfer is one that takes place automatically on the death, bankruptcy or insanity of the member.

Sections 81 to 84 of the 1963 Act make it clear that there are two distinct stages in the process of completing both voluntary and involuntary transfers of shares. These stages are:

(1) assignment of his interest by the holder to the transferee; and
(2) registration of the transferee as a member of the company, ie the entering of his name in the register of members.

Assignment of interest

31.15 Sections 81 and 82 provide that it shall not be lawful for any company to register a transfer of shares (or debentures) unless a proper instrument of transfer has been delivered to the company. In other words, if, and when, the seller completes the proper instrument of transfer, ie a Stock Transfer Form, this first stage of the transaction is in order and complete.

The Stock Transfer Form

31.16 Section 79 of the 1963 Act classifies shares as personal (rather than real) estate and 'transferable in the manner provided in the articles of the company.'

Articles 22 and 23 of Table A provide:

'**22.** The instrument of transfer of any share shall be executed by or on behalf of the transferor and transferee, and the transferor shall be deemed to remain the

---

1 Section 103(4).
2 Section 104.

holder of the share until the name of the transferee is entered in the register in respect thereof.

23. Subject to such of the restrictions of these regulations as may be applicable, any member may transfer all or any of his shares by instrument in writing in any usual or common form or any other form which the directors may approve.'

Whilst article 23 permits the use of 'any other form which the directors may approve', under the Stock Transfer Act 1963, there is a standard 'Stock Transfer Form' used for the transfer of shares. However, it is the contents of the form that are essential, and any form embodying these contents would probably suffice.

Contents[1]

31.17   The main details required by the Stock Transfer Form include:

(1)   amount of the consideration money;
(2)   full name of undertaking, ie the company whose shares are being transferred;
(3)   full description of security, eg ordinary shares;
(4)   number or amount of shares;
(5)   the name(s) of registered holder(s). The address should be given if there is only one holder. If the transfer is not being made by the registered holders, the capacity of the person(s) making the transfer must be indicated, eg on the death of the member, his shares would be transferred by the executors[2] named in his will;
(6)   the name(s) and address(es) of the person(s) to whom the security is transferred;
(7)   signature(s) of transferor(s) to the following declaration: 'I/We hereby transfer the above security out of the name(s) aforesaid to the person(s) named ...'.

The transfer also requests that such entries be made in the register of members as is necessary to give effect to the transfer.

There are also parts[3] of the form which must be stamped by the selling and buying brokers and the certifying Stock Exchange.

The effect of the computerised CREST system on the Stock Transfer Form is mentioned in **31.33**.

---

1   See P. Egan, A. Gilvarry and M. Graham *Irish Company Secretarial Precedents* (Jordans, 1993), pp 98 and 99, for example of Stock Transfer Form.
2   See **31.36** below.
3   There is also a section dealing with a certificate required where the transfer is not liable to ad valorem stamp duty.

Procedure

31.18 The transferor signs the completed Stock Transfer Form and delivers it to the transferee (or his brokers), together with the original share certificates.[1]

The share transfer is then completed by insertion of the name of the transferee, who may be the person who now owns the shares beneficially, or his nominee. Following this, the transfer form is lodged with the company secretary or the registrar who performs the function of registration. In a company with articles in the form of Table A (see art 24), the directors may refuse to register the transfer of shares.

Consequences

31.19 As between the parties, the transaction will be completed on the exchange of the share certificates and transfer form for the consideration, unless the contract for the purchase of the shares expressly provides otherwise. Assuming that it does not, the transaction is at the end of phase 1. The legal position of both parties is now clearly stated in art 22 of Table A which stipulates that 'the transferor shall be deemed to remain the holder of the share until the name of the transferee is entered in the register of members'. In other words, despite the transfer of ownership of the shares, the transferor still remains the member.

Registration of the transferee

31.20 The transfer is complete as between the transferor and transferee at the end of phase 1. However, the transfer is not complete as between the company and the parties at that stage: registration of the transferee's name is required for this.

Section 83 of the 1963 Act places the onus on the company to enter the name of the transferee in its register of members 'on the application of the transferor'. As illustrated in the outline contents of the Stock Transfer Form above (see **31.17**), this form includes a request by the transferor to the company to make the necessary entries in the register to give effect to the transfer. However, the directors are not bound to approve the proposed transfer.

Directors' powers to refuse registration in private companies

31.21 As we saw in Chapter 28, the directors of private companies are given the power by art 3 of Table A, Part II, 'in their absolute discretion, and without assigning any reasons therefor, [to] decline to register the transfer of any share'.

---

1 Or instead, a Stock Transfer Form certificated as provided for in s 85 of the 1963 Act. This may be necessary if the seller is retaining some shares or where there are several transferees.

In *Re Smith and Fawcett Ltd,*[1] the articles gave directors absolute discretion to refuse to register any transfer of shares. Fawcett died. His executor applied to have the deceased's shares registered in his name. Smith refused to register a transfer of the full holding, but offered to register part and to buy the balance.

The court held that the power to refuse registration need not be limited to matters personal to the transferee, and that the only limitation on that power was that, being fiduciary, it must be exercised bona fide in the interests of the company. The court then concluded that it could see no reason for saying that the director's action was *not* bona fide in this case.

31.22 In *Re Hafner, Olhausen v Powderly,*[2] the articles gave the directors absolute and uncontrolled discretion and without assigning any reason, to refuse to register shares. The plaintiff claimed that the effect of the directors' refusal to register him was to prevent him, should he become a member, from questioning the level of fees the directors were being paid. Sullivan CJ held:

> 'There can be little doubt that, if the transfer to the plaintiff had been registered, he would at the next meeting of shareholders have challenged the action of the directors in fixing such salaries, and there can be little doubt that this was in the minds of the directors when they decided to refuse the plaintiff's application. It may be, that the plaintiff, while not a member of the company, would be entitled to apply to the court for a declaration that the resolutions authorising these salaries were void, and offer an injunction to restrain the directors from paying them, but even if that be so, the directors would realise that the plaintiff would be more likely to make such an application if he was a member.
>
> We are satisfied that the learned judge was entitled to come to the conclusion, as an inference of fact, that a desire that the payment of these salaries should not be questioned by the plaintiff was a motive actuating the directors' refusal to register the transfer to the plaintiff, and, in the absence of any evidence that would indicate a different motive – and there was no such evidence beyond a general statement by each director that it was in the interest of the company that registration of the transfer should be refused – we think that conclusion is unassailable. That a refusal actuated by such a motive could not be supported as a decision arrived at by the directors bona fide in exercise of the power conferred upon them ... is not denied.'

The court had little difficulty deciding that the directors' exercise of their discretion was not bona fide.[3]

Summary – private company share transfers

31.23 If a shareholder wishes to dispose of his shares in a private limited company, he must make application to the company by means of a duly executed transfer form. But the directors are not bound to approve the proposed transfer. It will be recalled that one of the three distinguishing

---

1 [1942] 1 All ER 524, [1942] Ch 304. Smith and Fawcett each held 50 per cent of the issued share capital of the company.
2 [1943] IR 426 (SC).
3 And that, by their conduct, they had waived a pre-emption clause.

features of a private limited company is that it restricts the right to transfer its shares. In other words, the company's shares are not freely marketable on the stock market in the same way as the shares of a public company. Thus, if the directors do not approve of the transferee, they will refuse the holder's application to transfer his shares to him, and their decision is final. No reasons need be given for their refusal, provided that the directors are acting in good faith and for the benefit of the company.

Directors' powers to refuse registration in plcs

31.24 Unlike the shares in a private company, those in a plc are generally freely transferable. However, here, too, the directors possess the power to refuse registration of a transfer, but their power of refusal is less than that enjoyed by the directors of private companies. For example, under art 24[1] of Table A, the directors of a plc have a discretion to decline to register the transferee. In *Re Dublin North City Milling Co Ltd*,[2] the articles provided that the directors, on behalf of the company, may decline to register any transfer. A shareholder purchased additional shares in the company and the directors refused to register the transfer. In his judgment, Meredith J said:

'I dislike mystery, but I think the law is wise in refusing to compel directors to disclose their reasons for accepting or declining a transfer. The directors have kept themselves within the rule, and the reasons operating on their minds are not disclosed, and I cannot speculate or guess as to what they were. There could not have been anything dishonourable, or anything approaching personal unfitness on the part of [the shareholder] But I am of opinion that the law allows the directors to hold their tongues. It allows them to say that everything was done honestly and bona fide in the interests of their company; and they have unanimously decided that it is not for the interest or advantage of the company that these shares should be transferred to [the shareholder] and according to my view I have no power to make them say more.

If [the shareholder] had made a clear, definite charge against the directors of corruption, or conspiracy, or dishonesty, I should have had them examined before me; and if I came to the conclusion that they had not acted fairly and honestly, I should compel them to register the transfer. There is no proof that these directors did not act in the way that they were entitled to act under the articles.'

Meredith J concluded that, even though the transferee was already a member,[3] the board had acted bona fide.

From this judgment, it would appear that the courts are reluctant to interfere in instances where directors are exercising the powers to refuse registration under either art 24 or art 3 of Table A.

---

1 See Chapter 28.
2 [1909] 1 IR 179.
3 In *Tangney v Clarence Hotel Co Ltd* [1933] IR 51 (HC), it was held that a restriction on transfer to an undesirable person could not be applied to a person who was already a member of the company.

Notice of refusal to register

31.25   Section 84 of the 1963 Act stipulates that, if the company refuses to register a transfer, it must, within two months after the date on which the transfer is lodged with it, send the transferee notice of the refusal.

If the company does not issue this notice of refusal under s 84, its right to refuse registration will probably be considered unenforceable.

Delays

31.26   In *Re Sussex Brick Co*,[1] it was held that where default or unnecessary delay takes place in entering the transferee's name in the register, the court can order both rectification of the register and payment of damages, even if the company is being wound up.

Consequences of non-registration

31.27   There is no implied condition in a contract for the sale of shares that the company will register the purchaser as a member.[2]

Until a share transfer is registered, the transferor holds them as nominee for the transferee. This is a trust relationship which is recognised in equity but not in law. Section 123 of the 1963 Act specifies that no notice of a trust shall be entered on the register of members.

The transferor will be obliged to account to the transferee for any benefit he may receive.

Non-registration and subsequent transfers

31.28   When only phase 1 of the transfer process is completed, the company having refused to register the transferee, the rights of the parties are:

(1) the transferor, as the registered holder of the shares, is the legal owner; and
(2) the transferee, whilst beneficially entitled to the shares, has merely an equitable interest.

Competing claims

31.29   Disputes can arise between the registered holder of the shares and a claimant asserting a prior equity, or between two competing equitable interests in the shares.

---

1 [1904] 1 Ch 598.
2 *Casey v Bentley* [1902] 1 IR 376 (CA).

Generally, all rights of a registered holder, as legal owner of the shares, will prevail over a prior equitable claimant, if the registered holder gave valuable consideration for the shares and had no notice of the prior equitable interest.[1]

Where there is a conflict between two equitable interests in the same shares, the rules of equity apply as follows:

(1) where the equities are equal, the first to register has priority;
(2) where the equities are equal and neither is registered, the first in time prevails.

It is therefore important that shares are registered as soon as possible. Such registration will only prevail, however, if the transferee is a purchaser for value without prior notice of the equities, ie the third party interests. Thus, the interest of a recipient of the shares as a gift would not be protected by registration.

To be without prior notice of equities means that there must have been no reason in the manner of the conduct of the transaction which would have put a reasonable transferee on enquiry. For example, if the transferee is handed the original share certificates or good forgeries of them, there would be no apparent reason to put him on enquiry. As a result, the company may be estopped from denying the validity of a forged certificate – see **29.20**.

Whilst the handing over of share certificates is not absolutely necessary, if they are missing, the transferee is put on enquiry. In fact, companies would normally refuse to register share transfers where the original share certificates do not accompany the completed Stock Transfer Form – see art 25 of Table A.

Forged transfers

31.30 If a transfer is forged, and the company registers the transferee, the true owner remains entitled to be put back on the register.[2] Where the company issues a certificate on foot of the forged transfer, and any person acts on the faith of it and suffers damage, the company may be liable.

Certification of transfer

31.31 If a shareholder wishes to transfer only part of his holding, a new share certificate will be required. Section 85 of the 1963 Act provides for this situation by making available to the company a procedure by which it can certificate the transfer of shares. For example, if A has 10,000 shares and sells 5,000 to B, he can deliver the certificate and transfer form to the company. The company will then stamp on the transfer form (before it is handed to B) 'certificate for 10,000 shares has been lodged at the company's office'.

---

1 See also **32.15**.
2 *Sheffield Corporation v Barclay* [1905] AC 392. However, the company can claim an indemnity from the person responsible for perpetrating the fraudulent transfer.

On registration of the transfer, the company prepares two new certificates for 5,000 shares each for A and B.

A 'certified transfer' under s 85 is, of course, accepted by the Stock Exchange as a good delivery of the shares.

Rights issues[1] and voluntary share transfers

31.32 Where a company makes a rights issue of new shares, they generally include a renounceable letter by means of which the recipients can sell and transfer them.

The letter usually states that the allottee is entitled to a certain number of shares upon acceptance but it will have printed on it a letter of renunciation and an application for registration. If the allottee wishes to sell his rights or gift them to somebody else, he signs the renunciation form and delivers it to the transferee. The latter can also sign and pass it on to someone else.

Eventually, the application for registration will be completed and sent to the company.

Computerised transfers of shares

31.33 In July 1996, a new computerised system for settling sales and purchases of shares was introduced into both the UK and Irish Stock Exchanges. This system is known as CREST.

In Ireland, CREST has replaced the former Talisman system which involved the use of a nominee stock exchange company called Sepon Ltd.

CREST is intended to bring the systems in the UK and Ireland up to the best international standards. It will achieve this aim by making settlement cheaper, faster and more secure.

Under CREST, each investor, if he elects, will be able to hold his share certificates in electronic form as a computer record, rather than on paper.

The introduction of CREST meant that ss 79 and 81 of the 1963 Act and s 2(1) of the Stock Transfer Act 1963 needed to be amended. This was done by reg 4(1) of the Companies Act 1990 (Uncertified Securities) Regulations 1996[2] (the 1996 Regulations). Regulation 4(1) now permits the evidencing and transferring of title to securities without a written instrument, provided the procedures set out in the 1996 Regulations are followed.

A new vocabulary

31.34 In the 1996 Regulations, the computer based system and procedures are known as the *relevant system*. The legal framework underlying the operation

---

1 See Chapter 10.
2 SI 1996/68.

of the relevant system, together with the criteria which the operator and the relevant system must meet, are contained in these lengthy regulations.

A unit of a security which may be transferred is referred to as an *uncertificated unit*.

A security, the units of which may become uncertificated, is known as a *participating security*.

An issuer which issues a participating security may be referred to as a *participating issuer*. Instructions sent by means of the relevant system will be known as *dematerialised instructions*.

The 1996 Regulations outlined

31.35 Chapter II of the 1996 Regulations deals with a range of matters relating to transfers of title to securities (including transfers of uncertified holdings, transfers from uncertificated to certificated holdings and vice-versa) through a dematerialised system; the recording and registration of these transfers and the obligations imposed on participating issuers.

Chapter III provides for the approval of an operator by the Minister or recognition by him of an operator already approved by a competent authority of a Member State of the EU. The Minister may delegate these approval and supervisory functions to a designated body, if he so wishes.

Provision is made in Chapter IV to prevent persons sending dematerialised instructions from denying particular matters relating to them. This chapter also compels persons receiving such instructions to accept, with certain exceptions, that the information contained in them, and matters relating to them, are correct.

Chapter V details certain notices to be issued in respect of minority shareholdings resulting from a take-over situation, whilst supplementary provisions designed to overcome evidential problems which may arise in relation to system entries, are included in Chapter VI.

The *Schedule* to the Regulations sets out the requirements for approval and continuing operation of a person as an operator within the CREST system.

The practical consequence of the new stock exchange system is that much of the administrative work associated with share transfers is devolved to the exchange's member firms (identified in Appendix A of this book).

Involuntary share transfers

31.36 Sections 81 and 82 of the 1963 Act make provision for the involuntary transfer of shares and the registration of persons as members, who become entitled to this status by operation of the law. For example, on the death of a member, his shares vest in his personal representatives: on a member's bankruptcy, they vest in the Official Assignee in Bankruptcy.

Articles 29 to 32 of Table A set out the requirements for the personal representatives and Official Assignee. They must either:

(1) elect to be entered on the register themselves; or
(2) have some other person nominated by them registered as the transferee of the shares in question.

The two stages of assignment and registration are also involved in these cases, and the directors have the same rights to decline or suspend registration as they enjoyed against the original members.

Compulsory purchase of shares

31.37 When a company is in financial difficulties, the remedy may mean reconstruction, takeover or merger. These corporate remedies can affect the individual rights of shareholders. For example, if at least 80 per cent of the investors accept a takeover bid, then the acquiring company may compel the minority to transfer their shares on the same terms – see Chapter 40.

SHARE WARRANTS

31.38 There is another way that the membership of a company can be transferred. This is through the use of share warrants. Under s 88,[1] a company may, where the articles so permit, issue a warrant stating that the bearer is entitled to the shares specified therein. Transfer is effected by mere delivery.[2] As a result, share warrants, unlike share certificates, are negotiable instruments. However, few companies issue share warrants.

---

1 Of the 1963 Act.
2 Section 88(3) – see Chapter 29.

PART VIII

CREDITORS' RIGHTS AGAINST THE COMPANY AND ITS OFFICERS

Chapter 32

COMPANY CREDITORS AND THEIR SECURITIES (CHARGES)

CREDITORS

32.1 In Chapter 2, the twin objectives of company law were identified. These objectives are the protection of two classes of persons, ie investors and creditors.

Investors provide the investment capital of the company by purchasing shares and becoming members. It is the members who actually own the company. Shareholders have an interest in the company which they own.

Creditors are persons to whom the company is indebted. This indebtedness may have arisen out of a trading transaction. More frequently, however, when the term creditor is used in company law, it refers to a person who has loaned money to the company, often taking security for the loan in the form of a charge on the company's assets. Creditors may, therefore, be unsecured or secured.

Secured creditors are usually known as debenture-holders (see **32.10** below).

Creditors, unlike shareholders, do not have an interest in the company; instead they have a claim against the company for repayment of the monies owed to them.

Creditors' rights generally

32.2 The rights of shareholders have already been examined in Parts II, III, IV, VI, and VII. The statutory rules (see Part IV, Chapter 13) relating to maintenance of company capital, whilst offering some protection to investors, are designed primarily to protect the interests of company creditors: creditors being given a right to object to a permitted reduction of capital under s 72 of the 1963 Act.

Not only are creditors given the right to object to changes in the company's capital structure which affect their interest; they are also given the right to object to certain major corporate decisions. By virtue of s 8(2) of the 1963 Act, any debenture-holder may apply to the court to restrain the company from acting ultra vires. Again, s 10(3) and (7) entitle certain debenture-holders to apply to the court to block a proposed alteration of the company's objects clause.

Apart from bestowing separate rights on creditors to take action when their financial interest in the company is threatened, the Companies Acts also provide for much of the information which has to be made available to members, to be also provided for creditors.

Company information for creditors

32.3   The general requirements for companies to deliver information to the registrar of companies and/or publish it in *Iris Oifigiúil*, renders certain company information public and therefore accessible to both members and creditors. For example, any person can obtain details of all company charges, by inspecting the register of charges. This register is maintained by the registrar of companies.

Copies of a company's memorandum and articles of association – its constitutional documents – must also be forwarded to the registrar. Consequently, these are 'public documents'. Creditors can inspect these documents and extract such information as they consider necessary.

Again, in addition to sending them to members, s 159 provides that a company must send a copy of its balance sheet and directors' and auditors' reports to every debenture holder.

The companies legislation, therefore, provides for minimum levels of information to be made available to creditors, both indirectly and directly, to assist them negotiate and manage their transactions with the company.

32.4   In Chapter 2, we identified the range of creditors' or third party interests arising out of company transactions. We shall now focus on the distinctions between the different types of creditor.

For all practical purposes, company creditors can be classified into the following categories:

(1) unsecured; or
(2) preferential; or
(3) secured.

Unsecured creditors

32.5   A wide range of third party interests fall under this heading. For example, where a company buys raw material from suppliers it is likely that the latter will be an unsecured creditor of the company until paid. Where builders and painters are employed to repair and paint the company premises, these parties will also be unsecured creditors until the prices agreed for their services have been remitted to them.

Even employees can be classified as unsecured creditors for arrears of wages and salaries, although their rights have been elevated to that of preferential creditors for at least part of their outstanding salaries and holiday pay in s 285 of the 1963 Act.

Preferential creditors

32.6 Section 285[1] lists a series of unsecured debts which are elevated to preferential status, ie they rank above the unsecured creditors and creditors whose debts are secured by a floating (but not a fixed) charge.

Section 285 grants priority on certain amounts due in respect of:[2]

(1) various claims by employees and unpaid taxes due to the Revenue Commissioners; and,

(2) damages for personal injuries to employees.

Secured creditors

32.7 Creditors who possess some mortgage, charge or lien on the company's property are termed 'secured'. The most common situation giving rise to a secured transaction with a company is when the latter wishes to raise funds by loan capital, ie by borrowing money, often from a bank.

A COMPANY'S BORROWING POWERS

32.8 All trading companies have, by implication, the power to borrow money to finance the company's business. In many cases, the power to borrow will be specifically granted by the memorandum of association. It might be thought that a sole trader or a partnership would find it easier to borrow money since the trader or the partners in a firm are personally liable. This is not so. By the device of a 'floating charge' (see **32.18** below) a company may borrow money, and give as security a general charge over the whole of the company's assets. This general security does not interfere with the company's trading transactions, and only 'crystallises' into a fixed charge in certain circumstances.

As stated above, a power to borrow money is an implied prerogative of every trading company, but the memorandum or the articles may restrict this power by setting out the purposes for which money may be borrowed. They may direct how the directors can exercise this power. Any borrowing which is not covered by the power given is, prima facie, ultra vires.

A non-trading company cannot borrow money unless the power to do so is conferred by the memorandum of association. If borrowing is beyond the powers of the company, the lender is the one who finds himself in difficulty, not the company. The lending and the borrowing constitute a contract between the company and the lender, but if the borrowing is beyond the powers granted to the company, the contract is void.

32.9 At common law, the lender was not entitled to sue the company for non-payment under an ultra vires lending contract. In Chapter 17, it was

---

1 As amended by s 10 of the 1982 Act.
2 See **42.49** for fuller details.

shown how creditors are now protected against lending which is ultra vires the company's memorandum of association by s 8 of the 1963 Act and reg 6 of the European Communities (Companies) Regulations 1973. These statutory reforms will allow most lenders to pursue repayment of their loans to a company, even if the transaction was ultra vires.

A lender's contract may be intra vires the company's objects but outside the authority of the directors or managers who negotiated the loan. Where, for example, the directors borrow money in excess of a limit in the company's articles, this transaction would be intra vires the company but ultra vires the directors' powers. The judicial rule in *Turquand*'s case may also protect a lender in these circumstances (see **18.11**).

Directors' common law and statutory liabilities to third party creditors have been detailed in Chapter 21. For the purposes of redress by creditors, the defence of ultra vires is now hardly likely to be an effective one for any company, whether the contract is for borrowing money, or for the provision of any goods or services.

When a company borrows money, the written terms of the transaction are contained in a document called a debenture. The creditor who lends the company the money is known as a debenture-holder.

DEBENTURES

32.10   Whilst, strictly speaking, a debenture is the document by which the company acknowledges its indebtedness under a loan, the term is also used generally to describe the loan transaction.

Chitty J, in *Levy v Abercorris Slate and Slab Company*,[1] described a debenture as:

> 'a document which either creates a debt or acknowledges it, and any document which fulfils either of these conditions is a debenture. I cannot find any precise legal definition of the term . . .'

Debentures and shares

32.11   Because debentures are not capital, the rules of capital maintenance do not apply to them. Accordingly:

(1) a company's capacity to purchase its own debentures is not restricted, unlike the purchase of its own shares; and

(2) interest due on debentures may be paid out of capital, whereas dividends on shares can only be paid out of distributable profits; and

(3) unlike shares, debentures may be issued at a discount – see s 99(9) of the 1963 Act. However, such debentures cannot subsequently be exchanged for fully paid shares of an equal nominal value.

---

1 (1887) 37 ChD 260.

Despite these fundamental differences between shares and debentures, there are also similarities. For example, a typical debenture will be one of a series similar to a class of shares. Debentures are transferable in the same manner as shares. Debentures may be issued to the public. If so, a prospectus may be required. Debentures may also be quoted on the Stock Exchange.

Because shares and debentures are both essentially vehicles of investment in a company, potential investors will be concerned with balancing the potential for capital appreciation in shares and the degree of risk associated with them, with the yield and security offered by debentures (and, indeed, preference shares).

The types and forms of debentures are dealt with in Chapter 33.

Security for company borrowing

32.12 When a company has the power to borrow, it also has the power to charge its property as security for repayment of the loan.

In *General Auction, Estate & Monetary Co v Smith*,[1] the memorandum of a trading company did not contain a power to borrow. The court held that the company, being a trading company, had implied power to borrow and charge its property.

Debentures can be issued with or without security. For example, s 2(1) of the 1963 Act defines a debenture as 'including stocks, bonds and any other securities of a company, whether constituting a charge on the assets or not'.

Debentures, once issued by the company, are often classified under the generic name of 'charges'.

CHARGES

32.13 A charge may be broadly defined as a guarantee of security for a loan, for which assets of the company are pledged as collateral. It includes a mortgage.

Unless registered[2] with the registrar of companies within 21 days of its creation, the security conferred on the company's asset will be void against the liquidator and any creditor of the company.

Thus, if a charge securing any issue of debentures is not registered within 21 days, the lender loses out. The company has the money loaned, but a failure to register by the company will render the charge or security for the loan invalid.

---

1 [1891] 3 Ch 432.
2 Sections 99 to 102 of the 1963 Act, as amended. Section 106 sets out circumstances where the time for registration of a charge may be extended – see next chapter.

MORTGAGES AND FIXED CHARGES

32.14 Money borrowed by a company may be secured by a range of charges, including:

(1) charges by way of legal (or equitable) mortgage;
(2) fixed charges; and
(3) floating charges.

Charges by way of mortgage

32.15 A legal mortgage is where the company, as mortgagor, executes a deed transferring the ownership of the property to the lender (mortgagee). The company retains an equitable right in the property. On repayment of the loan and interest, the company will be able to recover ownership of the property.

Where, instead of transferring the ownership of the property, the company merely deposits the title deeds with the lender, this would constitute an equitable rather than a legal mortgage. Here, the lender possesses an equitable, instead of a legal, interest in the charged property.

Legal and equitable interests

32.16 Where a person holds a legal interest, eg the registered owner of land, his title is good against all other persons. However, when a person has an equitable title to land and goods, his interest might be defeated by a subsequent bona fide purchaser for value without notice of his interest.

All charges are equitable. What the chargee obtains is not ownership (or legal title), but the equitable right to claim the charged property in satisfaction of his secured debt, if unpaid. In legal theory, therefore, a legal mortgage would not be technically classified as a charge. However, in practice it often is.

Fixed charges

32.17 A fixed charge is one which attaches to a specific asset belonging to the company, eg a factory, plant and machinery. Although the company can deal with the asset in the usual course of its business, it is subject to the charge at all times. In short, the charge is attached to a specific and named asset.

The asset must be sufficiently identified and any necessary formalities observed for the creation of the charge. Essentially, a fixed charge prevents the company from selling or otherwise disposing of the specified property without the consent of the holders of the charge.

FLOATING CHARGES

32.18 A floating charge is a charge on a class[1] of assets present and future, which, in the ordinary course of business, changes from time to time, eg the stock, or a fleet of motor vehicles. The company is free to deal with that class of assets until the holders of the charge take steps to enforce their security. A floating charge 'floats like a cloud over the assets' but does not settle on them unless and until certain circumstances intervene to threaten those assets, when it 'crystallises' and becomes fixed as a charge on the assets. Thus, in the case of *Re Yorkshire Woolcombers Association*,[2] the characteristics of a floating charge were said to be:

(1) a charge on both present and future assets;
(2) the assets are constantly changing from time to time in the ordinary course of the business; and
(3) until the holder of the charge takes some steps to enforce the security, it floats.

A floating charge is, therefore, an equitable interest on some or all of the present and future property of the company: it is, however, subject to the company's power to deal with the assets in the course of its business. As Henchy J stated succinctly in *Re Keenan Bros Ltd*:[3]

'A floating charge, so long as it remains floating, avoids the restricting (and in some cases, paralysing) effect on the use of the assets of the company resulting from a fixed charge. While a charge remains a floating one, the company may, unless there is agreement to the contrary, deal with its assets in the ordinary course of business just as if there were no floating charge ...'

Until the charge crystallises, the company can utilise its assets in the ordinary course of business. Any assets disposed of in this way cease to be subject to the floating charge, whilst any new assets of the same type acquired by the company become subject to it.

Crystallisation of a floating charge

32.19 A floating charge remains suspended until such time as it 'crystallises'. To quote Henchy J[4] again:

'Crystallisation occurs on the happening of some event, such as the appointment of a liquidator which shows that the company is no longer in business, or until the chargee intervenes. At that point, the floating charge is said to crystallise and the rights of the chargee become the same as if he had got a fixed charge; thereafter the company cannot deal with the assets in question except subject to the charge.'

Thus, crystallisation of a floating charge will occur:

---

1 Rather than a specific.
2 [1903] 2 Ch 284.
3 [1985] IR 401 (SC).
4 Ibid.

(1) if winding up of the company commences; or

(2) if the company defaults *and* the debenture-holders take steps to enforce their security either by appointing a receiver or applying to the court to do so.

In the absence of express provision in the debenture to the contrary, crystallisation will not occur automatically, simply because the company ceases to carry on business.[1] In fact, the parties to a debenture are free[2] to stipulate whatever events they agree should cause a floating charge to crystallise.

Effect of crystallisation

32.20 On crystallisation, the floating charge automatically becomes a fixed charge, thereby attaching to the assets which it had previously floated (or hovered) over. This transformation has the effect of transferring equitable title to the debenture-holder of all the property comprised in the floating charge.[3]

De-crystallisation

32.21 In the case of *Re Holidair Ltd*,[4] the Supreme Court, rather surprisingly, held that a floating charge, which crystallised on the appointment of a receiver, de-crystallised on the subsequent appointment of an examiner[5] to the same company.

Advantages to companies of floating charges

32.22 There are two major advantages to companies from using floating charges as security for company borrowing. First, assets can be charged which would not be suitable or acceptable for a fixed charge, eg a large stock-in-trade.

Secondly, whilst the assets are subject to the floating charge, they can be dealt with, and even disposed of,[6] by the company, in the ordinary course of its business.

Disadvantages to lenders

32.23 A floating charge may be deemed invalid under ss 288[7] and 289 of the 1963 Act or lose its priority under s 98.

---

1 *Halpin v Cremin* [1954] IR 19 (HC).
2 *Re Brightlife Ltd* [1987] Ch 200, [1987] 2 WLR 197.
3 *Tempany v Hynes* [1976] IR 101 (SC).
4 [1994] 1 ILRM 481.
5 See **37.34**.
6 See *Re Old Bushmills Distillery Co Ltd* [1897] 1 IR 488 (CA).
7 As amended by s 136 of the 1990 Act.

Avoidance under ss 288 and 289

32.24   Where a company is being wound up, a floating charge created within the 12 months before the commencement of the liquidation will be invalid,[1] unless it is proved (by the lender) that the borrowing company was solvent, immediately after the charge was created.

Where the floating charge is created in favour of a connected person,[2] the 12-month period in s 288 is extended to 2 years.

Section 289 provides for the situation where a company is being wound up and during the preceding 12-month period discharged any debts to an officer by creating a floating charge in his favour. Here again, the floating charge will be invalid unless it can be proved that the company was solvent immediately after creation of the charge.

Solvency

32.25   The term 'solvency' normally means a company's assets must exceed its liabilities. In *Re Creation Printing Co Ltd, Crowley v Northern Bank Finance Corporation Ltd & Anor,*[3] the meaning of this term in the context of ss 288 and 289 was addressed by Kenny J. He stated:

> ' "solvent" and "insolvency" are ambiguous words. It has now been established by decided cases that, for the purposes of s 288 . . ., the test to be applied . . . is whether the company was able to pay its debts as they became due. The question is not whether its assets exceed in estimated value its liabilities, or whether a business man would have regarded it as solvent.'

Loss of priority under s 98

32.26   Section 98 of the 1963 Act provides that a receiver must use any assets he obtains on foot of a floating charge, to pay preferential creditors, before using the balance (if any) to make payments to the holder of the floating charge.

Generally, in the distribution of assets in a winding up, whilst fixed charges take priority over preferential creditors, floating charges do not.[4]

Commercial risks

32.27   In addition to the risks to his security posed by ss 288, 289, and 98, the floating chargee may also be affected by unprofitable company trading.

Unprofitable trading may gradually reduce the amount of the assets which are securing the loan. A debenture holder may not be aware that his security is

---

1 There is a saving, however, in relation to money actually paid or the value of goods or services supplied as consideration to the company for its creation – see s 288(1) and (2) and Chapter 42.
2 As defined in s 288(4), eg a director, shadow director or a related company.
3 [1981] IR 353 (SC).
4 Section 285(7)(b) of the 1963 Act. See also Chapter 42.

deteriorating unless he is closely in touch with the workings of the company. He must then go through certain formalities in order to enforce his security; all causing loss of time. Thus, some of his security may have been eaten away by the time he has brought his action, or petitioned the court for a winding up order or the appointment of a receiver or manager. Only when this has been done will the floating charge crystallise and become fixed.

Reservation of title clauses[1]

32.28 Where a seller of goods to the company 'reserves title' to these goods until payment, a floating charge may not, on crystallisation, attach to those specified goods, because the supplier has a better claim than the borrowing company to those goods. For example, where a floating chargee has a charge over raw materials to be used by the company, he may find that on crystallisation of his charge, it does not attach to the raw materials in question because the supplier of the goods has retained title to them until he has been paid, by a reservation of title clause. Such a clause may even allow the supplier, if unpaid, to remove the goods from the company's premises, in priority to the floating chargee's rights.

The unpaid seller may lose his rights if the goods become mixed, eg where wool supplied became woven into carpets. Again, if the unpaid seller had reserved merely 'equitable' (rather than legal) ownership of the goods, his interest may require registration[2] as a charge under s 99 of the 1963 Act.

Subsequent fixed charges

32.29 Because debenture-holders with a floating charge have implicitly authorised the company to deal with the assets charged, their interests may be postponed to a subsequent fixed charge on the property if the fixed chargee had no notice of their prior floating charge. Registration of the charge will constitute constructive notice.

Negative pledge[3] clauses

32.30 To protect themselves from the borrowing company creating sub-sequent fixed (or other) charges over the assets ranking in priority to them, lenders usually include 'negative pledge clauses' in the debentures creating their floating charge. Such a clause will be effective against subsequent secured

---

1 Known as 'Romalpa' Clauses since the case of *Aluminium Industrie Vaassen BV v Romalpa Aluminium Ltd* [1978] 1 WLR 676.

2 *Re Bond Worth* [1979] 3 All ER 919. Problems may also arise for the unpaid seller if the goods are re-sold and he seeks to claim the proceeds of the sale – see *Re W.J. Hickey Ltd (in Receivership); Uniacke v Cassidy Electrical Supply Co Ltd* [1988] IR 126 (HC).

3 Such a clause might be drafted thus: 'The company shall not create any mortgage, charge or lien ranking pari passu with or in priority to the floating charge hereby created.'

creditors, providing they have actual notice of the clause. As a negative pledge does not have to be registered under s 99, it is unlikely that constructive notice extends to include it.[1]

In *Re Holidair Ltd* (see **37.34**), the Supreme Court held that an examiner is not bound by a negative pledge clause.

FIXED OR FLOATING CHARGE?

32.31   There can be circumstances when a floating charge has advantages for a lender over a fixed charge. For example, suppose that money is lent to a company on the security of the stock and book debts. If the charge is a fixed charge, the security will diminish as the stock and the book debts are sold and called in respectively, until the time when they have disappeared from the books in their original form and amount. The fact that new stock and new book debts have taken their place in the ordinary course of business is immaterial. If the charge is a floating charge, the stock and the book debts remain subject to the charge from day to day, however much they fluctuate, and the security will remain reasonably stable unless there is a pre-determined (and generally fraudulent) attempt to run down both.

Although a floating charge has some advantage to a lender, in view of the range of risks mentioned above which can imperil the security of assets subject to the charge, it is clear that the fixed charge offers a superior form of security. Because of this, disputes have arisen as to whether a particular charge in a debenture is fixed or floating, particularly in the case of book debts.[2]

Disputes over whether charges are fixed or floating can be of especial concern to the preferential creditors; in particular the Revenue Commissioners. Section 115 of the Finance Act 1986 stipulated that even if book debts were deemed to be fixed charges, they would no longer be entitled to priority over debts to the Revenue Commissioners. Section 115 was amended by s 174 of the Finance Act 1995. Under s 174, where a person holds a fixed charge on book debts, he may be liable to pay tax if the company fails to pay any amount for which it is liable.

---

1 See *Coveney v Persse* [1910] 1 IR 194.
2 See next chapter.

Chapter 33

DEBENTURES, REGISTRATION AND PRIORITY OF CHARGES

THE DEBENTURE

33.1   There are two principal ways by which a company can raise capital. These are by the issue of shares to investors and by the issue of debentures to lenders of money. The rights of investors[1] are very different to the rights of lenders, who are (usually) secured creditors of the company. The contract evidencing the loan between the lender and the borrowing company is known as a debenture.

TYPES OF DEBENTURES

33.2   If the company decides to raise money by the issue of debentures, it may be either:

(1) a *single* debenture between the company and a particular lender; or
(2) a whole *series* of debentures issued by the company to members of the public. Such debentures will usually have the same terms and rank pari passu (equally), although they need not necessarily each be issued for the same amount.

Where a series of debentures is issued to the public, the statutory provisions relating to prospectuses will apply. If the debentures are listed on the Stock Exchange, the Exchange's regulations will apply – see Chapter 10.

Registered and bearer debentures

33.3   A debenture is usually registered in the books of the company in the name of the person who has lent the money to the company. But a company may issue 'bearer debentures' which are transferable by delivery under the rules relating to negotiable instruments.

Redeemable and perpetual debentures

33.4   Some debentures are issued for a fixed period of time. When this elapses, the lender may call for redemption of the loan, ie repayment of it. These types of debenture are styled *redeemable*. By contrast, a *perpetual* debenture is one in which the principal sum only becomes repayable at the winding up of the company – see s 94. It is also possible to issue debentures payable on demand.

---

1 See Part VII of this book.

FORMS OF DEBENTURE

33.5   A debenture is an instrument issued by the company, by which it agrees to repay a loan at a specified time. Before repayment, the company will agree to pay interest in the agreed manner and amount, charging the company's property as security for those payments and promising to comply with the various conditions contained in, or endorsed on, the instrument.

The charge

33.6   An example of the wording of an instrument creating the charge might be:

> 'The company has agreed with the lender to charge all its undertaking property and assets whatsoever and wheresoever both present and future including its uncalled capital for the time being and goodwill with payment to the lender of all moneys due or to become due by the company to the lender either as principal or surety to the lender.'[1]

The conditions

33.7   The conditions might also include additional details of fixed and/or floating charges including a negative pledge[2] clause.

If the debenture is one of a series, a condition will be included that all debentures are to rank pari passu.

'Pari passu' means that all the debentures of the series are to be paid rateably, so that if there are insufficient company funds to repay them all, each receives a similar proportion. If the debentures were not expressly 'pari passu', each would be payable according to the date of issue or, if all issued at the same time, in numerical order.

Again, the conditions will generally stipulate the circumstances in which the principal loan becomes immediately payable, eg:

(1)   if the company makes default for a period of, say, 14 days, in the payment of interest; or

(2)   if a receiver is appointed.

The conditions will usually also give the debenture holder the power to appoint a receiver[3] and manager. Without this express power, they could not appoint a receiver without first applying to the court.

---

1   See Specimen Bank 'All Monies' debentures giving a fixed and floating charge in *Jordans Irish Company Secretarial Precedents* (Jordans, 1993), pp 162–166.
2   See **32.30**.
3   See next chapter.

Interpretation of wording

33.8   A debenture may describe the property and the type of charge. The fact that a particular charge is described as a fixed charge is not conclusive evidence that it is so. The court, on the construction of the document as a whole, may hold it to be a floating charge. This happened in *Re Lakeglen Construction Ltd*,[1] where future book debts were held to be a floating charge. However, in *Re Keenan Bros Ltd (in Liquidation)*,[2] the Supreme Court classified book debts as a fixed charge when the debenture expressed them to be so and restricted the borrower's freedom to deal with them by requiring it to pay all monies it received in respect of those debts into separate designated accounts. Again, in *Re A.H. Masser Ltd*,[3] the High Court, following the same reasoning as the Supreme Court, held that the debenture placed such restrictions on the use of book debts that they were in the nature of a fixed charge.

33.9   In *Re Holidair Ltd*,[4] the Supreme Court approved *Re Keenan* and confirmed that, when determining whether a charge is fixed or floating, the instrument as a whole must be considered.

When book debts are being considered, the significant question is whether the company can deal with its book debts in the ordinary way. Whilst the debenture provided for payment of book debts to be made into selected banks, it did not provide for any restriction on the withdrawal of monies from these bank accounts. In this case, therefore, the charge on the book debts was a floating one.

Trustees for the debenture-holders

33.10   When a series of debentures is issued to the public, the company will enter into an agreement with trustees to act on behalf of the debenture-holders and watch over their interest.

There is great value in appointing such trustees, since by this method, the trustee can act immediately instead of having to await separate instructions from the individual debenture-holders. If property of the company has been used as security to cover the loans of the debenture-holders, the trustee will usually call for the title deeds to such property.

The trust deed will provide, inter alia, for payment of remuneration to the trustees and the calling by them of meetings of debenture-holders.

The principal function of the trustees is to ensure that the terms of the debenture are honoured by the company, and to safeguard generally the interests of the debenture-holders. Whilst so acting, the trustees must carry out their functions prudently and competently. Any clauses in the trust deed

---

1 [1980] IR 347 (HC).
2 [1985] ILRM 641.
3 (Unreported) 6 October 1986 (HC).
4 [1994] 1 ILRM 481.

seeking to exempt the trustees from, or to indemnify them against, liability for breach of trust or failure to exercise proper care and diligence, may be void – see s 93 of the 1963 Act.

REGISTRATION OF CHARGES SECURING DEBENTURES

33.11   By s 99(1) of the 1963 Act, every charge for the purpose of securing an issue of debentures is void as against the liquidator and any creditor of the company, unless particulars of the charge, verified in the prescribed manner, are delivered to the registrar of companies within 21 days after the date of its creation.

Section 99(2) identifies several specific types of charges which must be notified. These include:

(1) a charge on book debts of the company;
(2) a floating charge on the undertaking or property of the company;
(3) a charge on uncalled share capital of the company;
(4) a charge on calls made but not paid;
(5) a charge on land;
(6) a charge on good will.

33.12   Charges which are not included in the headings set out in s 99(2) are not registerable under s 99(1). Thus, charges not created by the company, but arising by operation of the general law, need not be registered. However, a deposit of title deeds to land, creating an equitable interest, must be registered because the charge is a contractual one.[1]

As mentioned in Chapter 32, whether or not reservation of title clauses need to be registered, depends on their terms.

Register of charges

33.13   The registrar of companies must keep,[2] in relation to each company, a register of charges notified to him. This register is open to inspection by any person, and contains the following particulars of a company's debentures:

(1) the total amount secured by the whole series; and
(2) the dates of the resolutions authorising the issue of the series, and the date of the covering deed, if any, by which the security is created or defined; and
(3) a general description of the property charged; and
(4) the names of the trustees, if any, for the debenture-holders.

---

1 See *Re Farm Fresh Frozen Foods Ltd* [1980] ILRM 131 and *Re Wallis & Simmonds (Builders) Ltd* [1974] 1 All ER 561.
2 Sections 103 to 105 of the 1963 Act.

The registrar will issue a certificate confirming that he has received the required particulars of the charge. This certificate is conclusive evidence that the statutory registration requirements have been complied with.[1]

If and when the debt in relation to the charge has been repaid, the registrar, on evidence being supplied to him, may enter on the register a memorandum of satisfaction that the undertaking or property has been released[2] from the charge.

Extension of registration time and correction of errors in the register

33.14 Section 106 of the 1963 Act allows the company, or any person interested in the charge, to apply to the court to:

(1) extend the time for registration of the charge; or
(2) rectify any omission or mis-statement of any particulars which were delivered.

Any order granted by the court under s 106 may be made subject to a condition that it is not to affect the rights of secured creditors or a liquidator acquired against the property prior to registration.[3]

Register of debenture-holders

33.15 Every company which issues a series of debentures must keep a register of holders, entering in it the names and addresses of each debenture-holder and the amount of debentures currently held by each. This register may be kept on computer records.[4]

Debenture-holders are given rights by s 92 to inspect the register and to obtain copies from it and the trust deed.

TRANSFER OF DEBENTURES

33.16 Generally, debentures may be transferred in a similar manner to shares: ss 79 to 90[5] provide for the transfer and evidence of title to *both* shares and debentures. Section 81 makes it clear that it shall not be lawful to register a transfer of shares or debentures unless a proper instrument of transfer has

---

1 Section 104. See also *Lombard & Ulster Banking (Ireland) Ltd v Amarec Ltd (in Liquidation)* (1978) 112 ILTR 1 (HC).
2 See s 105.
3 See *Re International Retail Ltd* (unreported) 19 September 1979 (HC).
4 See s 91 of the 1963 Act and s 4 of the 1977 Act.
5 Of the 1963 Act.

been delivered to the company. Section 83 provides for registration of the transfer by the company at the request of the transferor.[1]

Transfer generally 'subject to equities'

33.17 When a debenture is transferred, unless the contrary is expressly provided for in the debenture,[2] the transferee takes the debenture 'subject to equities', ie subject to any rights enjoyed by others. Thus, the transferee will not be in a better position than the transferor.[3]

If there are rights enjoyed by others in the property or assets charged, then the law must provide for the resolution of disputes relating to their claims. This is done through the rules relating to priority.

Priority of charges

33.18 A legal mortgage will rank before a previous equitable interest where it was acquired by a bona fide purchaser for value without notice of the earlier interest.

Priority is governed between equitable charges by the date or order of their creation, the charge created first ranking in priority. This rule has been modified in relation to floating charges and subsequent fixed charges.

A floating charge will be postponed to any subsequently created fixed charge regardless of notice, because the nature of a floating charge permits the company to deal with the assets which are subject to the charge.[4]

Effect of registration on priorities

33.19 Any charge which is not registered within 21 days, in accordance with s 99 of the 1963 Act, is void. As a result, it will lose all entitlement to priority which it might otherwise possess.

Registration gives constructive notice to subsequent chargees. In *Wilson v Kelland*,[5] however, it was held that registration of a charge, whilst it gave constructive notice of the charge, did not give the same notice of the terms contained in the deed creating it. An example of constructive notice is given at **13.42**.

Generally, a registered charge will have priority over an earlier unregistered charge (which is void), even if the later charge had notice of the earlier unregistered charge. However, if the subsequent chargee expressly agrees to

---

1 See Chapter 31.
2 See *Hilger Analytical Ltd v Rank Precision Industries and Others* [1984] BCLC 301.
3 *Re China Steamship Co, ex p Mackenzie* (1869) LR 7 Eq 240.
4 See negative pledge clauses (discussed at **32.30**).
5 [1910] 2 Ch 306.

subordinating his rights to those of the earlier unregistered chargee, the latter can regain priority by obtaining late registration of his charge under s 106.[1]

RE-ISSUE OF DEBENTURES

33.20 Debentures which have been redeemed by the company may be re-issued under s 95 of the 1963 Act. The re-issued debentures will rank pari passu with the original issue unless:

(1) the articles or any contract provide to the contrary; or
(2) the company has carried out some act showing its intention that the debentures be cancelled.

Subject to the saving of rights of certain mortgagees, on the re-issue of redeemed debentures, the transferee shall be entitled to the same priorities as if the debentures had never been redeemed.[2]

DEBENTURE STOCK

33.21 Debenture stock is also a debt, generally secured by a trust deed. It is sub-divisible, and is often issued frequently in a series of transferable debenture stocks that are registered and transferred in a similar manner to shares. In fact, the distinction between a debt secured by debenture and debenture stock[1] is rather like that between shares and stock (see **29.23**).

DEBENTURE-HOLDERS' REMEDIES

33.22 Whilst, in theory, debentures can be issued without security, in commercial practice few are.

In the next chapter, we shall focus on the rights of both unsecured and secured creditors against the company.

DEBTS DUE FROM DEBENTURE-HOLDERS

33.23 If the holder of debentures owes money to the company, and the company, in turn, cannot pay him monies due under the debenture in full, the

---

1 See **33.14**. *Re Clarets Ltd; Spain v McCann and Stonehurst Bank (Ireland) Ltd* [1978] ILRM 215.
2 See ss 95 and 96.
3 The liability of the company is regarded as a liability to pay an annuity rather than as a liability to repay a loan forever under a perpetual debenture.

holder cannot normally set off his debt against the debenture. Such trans-actions should generally be kept separate and distinct.

However, where a floating chargee is owed money by the company, Kenny J held in *Re Russell Murphy*[1] that a right of set off[2] may operate over the assets subject to the charge, before the charge crystallises.

---

1 [1976] IR 15.
2 Set off is defined at **42.29**.

Chapter 34

CREDITORS' REMEDIES AGAINST THE COMPANY – CONSEQUENCES OF RECEIVERSHIP

RIGHTS OF ACTION

34.1   If a creditor, at any stage of his transaction with the company, considers some event has occurred which makes it less likely that the company will be able to (re)pay him the monies owed, he has certain legal rights of action. These rights of action will depend on whether the creditor is unsecured or secured.

UNSECURED CREDITORS' REMEDIES

34.2   The most obvious remedy is for the creditor to immediately demand payment of the monies owed to him by the company.

When a creditor, who is owed at least £1,000, leaves a written demand for payment of it at the registered office of the company, and the company does not pay it within three weeks, that creditor may be able to petition the court to wind up the company under s 213 of the 1963 Act. The grounds for the petition would be that the company is unable to pay its debts.

This is a drastic remedy for the unsecured creditor. It is further complicated by the fact that unsecured creditors are discriminated against on the liquidation of a company. Creditors whose debts are secured by fixed charges, preferential creditors and floating chargees, are entitled to be paid out of the assets of a liquidated company, in priority to the unsecured creditors.

Because of their low priority in the distribution of company assets, unsecured creditors are unlikely to be paid out of the liquidated assets of an insolvent company. Their most realistic source of redress would, therefore, be to sue the company's officers.[1]

Secured creditors (or debenture-holders) are in a much stronger legal position to obtain repayment of their debts from the company, without having to seek its winding up.

DEBENTURE-HOLDERS' REMEDIES

34.3   As an alternative to petitioning for the winding up of the company, a debenture-holder will have several other remedies available to him. These are often set out in the debenture deed, and include the rights:

---

1 See Chapter 36.

(1) to take possession of the charged property and, subsequently, sell it without the assistance of the court;
(2) to apply for a court order to sell the charged property in their possession;
(3) to receive and apply the income from the possessed property to discharge the loan; or
(4) to appoint a *receiver* under the terms of the debenture, or apply to the court to appoint one.

The appointment of a receiver is the most frequently used remedy.

Appointment of receiver

34.4 A receiver may be appointed either by a mortgagee, by debenture-holders (or trustees on their behalf), or by the court.

The most common form of appointment is that made directly by the debenture-holder(s); most instruments containing a condition empowering the debenture-holders to appoint a receiver without recourse to a court order.

Power is usually also given to the trustees to appoint a receiver, or, alternatively, to approve the appointment of a receiver nominated by the holders of the majority in value of the outstanding debentures in the series.

Appointment under a fixed charge

34.5 A debenture with a fixed charge will normally set out the circumstances when a power of sale[1] will arise, eg if payment of interest on the loan is in arrears or if winding up commences. The receiver appointed by the trustees will collect the income from the charged property until it can be sold.

Appointment under a floating charge

34.6 Generally, default by the company on repayment of either principal or interest will crystallise a floating charge and convert it into a fixed charge.

If expressly provided for in the trust deed, the receiver may be appointed without an application to the court.

Jeopardy

34.7 In *Angelis v Algemene Bank Nederland (Ireland) Ltd*,[2] Kenny J seems to suggest that the debenture-holders can also appoint a receiver directly whenever their security is in jeopardy. Kenny J stated:

> 'It is not necessary to cite authority for the proposition that when the assets charged by a debenture are in danger of seizure, a debenture holder may immediately appoint a receiver.'

---

1 A power of sale and the power to appoint a receiver is conferred on mortgagees and registered chargees whose mortgages are created by deed – see ss 17 to 23 of the Conveyancing Act 1881.
2 (Unreported) 4 July 1974 (HC).

Appointment by the court

34.8 If the debenture does not contain a provision for the direct appointment of a receiver, the holders may petition the court[1] to do so on one of the following grounds:

(1) that the principal sum or interest payable is in arrears;
(2) that an event has occurred on which, under the terms of issue of the debentures, the security becomes enforceable against the company; or
(3) whilst there has been no actual breach of a condition in the debenture of the company, nevertheless, that the chargee's security is in jeopardy or imperilled, eg when liquidation is likely because creditors are pressing for payment.

Qualifications of receiver

34.9 Any fit person may be appointed a receiver. In practice, the appointee will usually be an experienced accountant. The following persons are, however, prohibited from being appointed as receiver by ss 314 and 315 of the 1963 Act, as amended by s 170 of the 1990 Act:

(1) any body corporate;
(2) an undischarged bankrupt;
(3) a person who is, or who has within 12 months of the commencement of the receivership been, an officer (including auditors) or servant of the company;
(4) a parent, spouse, brother, sister or child of an officer of the company;
(5) a person who is a partner of or in the employment of an officer or servant of the company;
(6) a person who is not qualified for appointment as receiver of the property of a related company.

Notice of appointment

34.10 The person who appoints the receiver under a debenture, or who obtains a court order for his appointment, must, within seven days of appointment, publish notice of it in *Iris Oifigiúil* and in at least one local daily newspaper. Section 107(1)[2] also makes provision for the registrar of companies to be notified at the same time.

Invoices and letterheads

34.11 Where a receiver of the property of a company has been appointed, every invoice, order for goods or business letter issued by or on behalf of the company or the receiver or the liquidator of the company, being a document in

---

1 See *Alexander Hull & Co Ltd v O'Carroll, Kent & Co* (1955) 89 ILTR 70.
2 Of the 1963 Act.

which the name of the company appears, must contain a statement that a receiver has been appointed.[1]

Notifications and information

34.12   Section 319 of the 1963 Act also stipulates that where a receiver of substantially the whole of the property of a company is appointed on behalf of debenture-holders secured by a floating charge:

(1)   the receiver must immediately send notice to the company of his appointment;
(2)   the company must then, within 14 days[2] after receipt of the notice, make out and submit to the receiver a statement in the prescribed form as to the affairs of the company; and
(3)   within two months after receipt of the statement, the receiver must forward to the registrar of companies, to the court, to the company, to any trustees for the debenture-holders on whose behalf he was appointed and, so far as he is aware of their addresses, to all such debenture-holders, a copy of the statement and of any comments he sees fit to make on it.

The receiver's specific statutory tasks are detailed in **35.10** below.

Powers of receivers and managers

34.13   If it is necessary to carry on the company's business in addition to realising the chargees' security, the appointee must be expressly appointed receiver and manager. This would be the case where the creditors' security embraced the entire undertaking and business of the company, rather than being confined to a single asset. Section 323 of the 1963 Act stipulates that unless the contrary intention appears, any reference in the Act to a receiver of the property (or part of it) of a company, includes a reference to the receiver and manager of that property.

The typical powers of a receiver and manager appointed by the debenture-holders might be:

(1)   to take possession of, collect and get in the property charged by the debentures, and, for that purpose, to take all the proceedings in the name of the company or otherwise as may seem expedient;
(2)   to carry on or concur in carrying on the business of the company, and, for that purpose, to raise money on the premises charged in priority to the debentures or otherwise;
(3)   to sell or concur in selling any of the property charged by the debentures after giving to the company at least seven days' notice of his intention to sell, and to carry any such sale into effect by conveying in the name or on behalf of the company or otherwise;

---

1   Section 317(1) of the 1963 Act.
2   Or such longer period as may be allowed by the receiver or the court.

(4) to make any arrangement or compromise which he or they shall think expedient in the interest of the debenture-holders.

A receiver/manager may also be granted express powers [1] to:

(1) borrow money for the company's business; and/or
(2) dismiss and employ staff; and/or
(3) insure and repair company property.

Application to court for directions or objections

34.14 Section 316(1)[2] of the 1963 Act gives the following persons the right to apply to the court for directions in relation to any matter connected with the exercise of the receiver's powers:

(1) the receiver himself;
(2) an officer of the company;
(3) a member of the company;
(4) employees of the company comprising at least half in number of the persons employed in a full-time capacity by the company;
(5) a creditor or creditors of the company owed at least £10,000 in aggregate;
(6) a liquidator;
(7) a contributory,

and, on any application, the court may give such directions, or make such order declaring the rights of persons before the court or otherwise, as the court thinks just.

An application by any of these persons, other than by the receiver himself, would have to be supported by such evidence that the applicant is being unfairly prejudiced by any actual or proposed action or omission of the receiver, as the court may require.

Application of monies realised

34.15 All monies received or realised by a receiver must[3] be applied in or towards satisfaction pari passu of the debts due to the debenture-holders.

EFFECT OF APPOINTMENT OF A RECEIVER

34.16 When a receiver is appointed by the debenture-holders, the following effects flow immediately from the appointment:

(1) any floating charge crystallises and becomes a fixed charge on the assets over which it was created;

---

1 Receivers/managers will also possess such ancillary powers as are incidental to the exercise of their express powers.
2 As amended by s 171 of the 1990 Act.
3 Subject to the order of application of receipts in s 24(8) of the Conveyancing Act 1881.

(2) the powers of the directors to control the management of the company are suspended. This suspension, however, only relates to powers over assets over which the receiver is appointed. Directors retain their powers where these are exercisable over assets not controlled by the receiver;[1]

(3) the receiver may, if the interests of the debenture-holders so require, sell the property charged, or make any compromise which he considers expedient in the interests of the debenture-holders;

(4) contracts of employment between the company and its employees may not be automatically terminated.[2] A receiver has, however, the power to terminate such contracts of employment, if he considers this action necessary (see **34.24** below);

(5) other existing contracts of the company remain valid and binding on it (see **34.21** below).

THE STATUS OF A RECEIVER

34.17   When a receiver has been appointed, a fundamental matter which must be clarified is whether he is an agent of the company or an officer of the court. The answer to this question depends on the manner of his appointment.

Receivers appointed by the debenture-holders

34.18   A receiver appointed by a debenture-holder or holders would, in the absence of express provision to the contrary, be the agent of the debenture-holder(s). However, to protect the debenture-holders against being held liable for the actions of a receiver appointed by them, most debenture instruments would contain a clause making any receiver appointed on the basis of it, the agent of the company. As a result, the company, not the debenture-holders, will be responsible for the receiver's wrongful acts (if any). It will also be liable to pay him his remuneration.

Receivers appointed by the court

34.19   Whilst most receivers will be appointed by the debenture-holders, occasionally, one will be appointed by the court.

A receiver appointed by the court is an officer and agent of the court. As the court cannot be liable, at common law the receiver is personally liable on his

---

1 *Wymes v Crowley* (unreported) 27 February 1987 (HC). The directors' powers are automatically reinstated if, and when, the receivership ends – see next chapter.

2 At common law, contracts of employment were automatically terminated by the appointment of a receiver. The European Communities (Safeguarding of Employees' Rights on Transfer of Undertakings) Regulations 1980, SI 1980/306, changes the common law position; at least in the context of transfers of undertakings. The decision in *Griffiths v Secretary of State for Social Services* also seems to revise the common law position – see **34.24** below.

contracts, and entitled to be indemnified out of the assets of the company in priority[1] to the rights of the debenture-holders.

The receiver and company contracts

34.20 The appointment of a receiver can have implications for both existing and new company contracts.

Existing contracts

34.21 Generally, existing contracts remain binding on the company, although a receiver cannot be held liable under them. In fact, the receiver can repudiate or cancel such contracts unless to do so would:

(1) adversely affect the subsequent realisation of the company's assets; or
(2) injure the company's good will[2] if it were to trade again.

When the receiver decides that existing contracts are to be continued and performed by the company, he does not thereby incur a personal liability[3] in respect of them. This position differs for new contracts.

New contracts

34.22 Section 316(2) of the 1963 Act renders the receiver personally liable on any new contract entered into by him in the performance of his functions, unless the contract expressly provides that the receiver is not to be liable.

Section 316 further provides that if the receiver is held liable for a new company contract, he will be entitled to an indemnity out of the company assets.

Substituting new for existing contracts

34.23 A supplier of goods or services to the company may insist on payment of his arrears as a condition for the continuation of his obligation to supply under a new contract. For example, in *W & L Crowe Ltd & Anor v E.S.B.*,[4] it was held that the E.S.B. were entitled to refuse to enter into a new contract with the receiver to supply power to the company, unless the monies owed to them under their existing contract were paid. The E.S.B. were also not prepared to accept the receiver's undertaking to accept personal responsibility for electricity bills under the new contract proposed.

---

1 *Burt, Boulton & Hayward v Bull* [1895] 1 QB 276.
2 *Re Newdigate Clothing Co Ltd* [1912] 1 Ch 468.
3 Unless the receiver expressly accepts personal responsibility for the continuation of the existing company contract.
4 (Unreported) 9 May 1984 (HC).

Contracts of employment

34.24   Where a receiver is appointed by the court, the contracts of employees are automatically terminated. If this happens, the dismissed employees may be able to sue for damages for wrongful dismissal.[1]

Where the receiver is appointed directly by the debenture-holders, it was held in *Griffiths v Secretary of State for Social Services*,[2] that an employee's contract of employment was not automatically terminated, unless his continued employment (as managing director) was inconsistent with the role and functions of the appointee.

---

1 *Reed v Explosives Co Ltd* (1887) 19 QBD 264.
2 [1974] QB 468.

Chapter 35

THE RECEIVER'S RIGHTS AND DUTIES – PREMATURE ENDING OF HIS POWERS

RIGHTS OF RECEIVER

35.1 The rights of a receiver may be considered under the headings of remuneration, indemnity and relief from liability for defects in his appointment.

Remuneration

35.2 Section 318[1] deals with the remuneration of the receiver. The remuneration of the receiver is normally a matter for the receiver and the person appointing him. However, the court may, on application by a liquidator, creditor or member of the company, fix the receiver's remuneration. This provision applies even where the remuneration has already been agreed between the receiver and the person appointing him.

Indemnification

35.3 A prudent receiver will seek to have included, in his contract with debenture-holders, a clause indemnifying him against any claims or proceedings which might be brought against him as a result of the receivership.

In addition, receivers are entitled[2] to an indemnity out of company assets if they incur a personal liability for company contracts.

Defective appointment

35.4 Where it is discovered subsequently that there was a defect in the charge purporting to appoint a receiver, s 316(3) gives the court the power, if it thinks fit, to order that the receiver is wholly or partially relieved from liability for his actions under the defective appointment.

RECEIVER'S DUTIES

35.5 Receivers, irrespective of the method of their appointment, are regarded as being in a fiduciary relationship with those who appointed them. Consequently, the receiver's relationship with the debenture-holders is a

---

1 Of the 1963 Act.
2 Ibid, s 316 – see previous chapter.

fiduciary one, and he must exercise his powers of receivership[1] in *good faith and for their proper purposes.*

Duty when selling property

35.6   Whilst the receiver's primary duty is owed to the debenture-holders as agent of the company, he owes a secondary duty to the company (and to a guarantor of its indebtedness).[2] This common law duty has been strengthened by s 316A(1)[3] of the 1963 Act which provides that a receiver, on selling company property, must exercise 'all reasonable care to obtain the best price reasonably obtainable for the property as at the time of the sale.'

Section 316A(2) further provides that if a receiver is in breach of s 316A(1), he will lose any rights he might have had to be compensated or indemnified by the company for his breach of statutory duty.

Sale of non-cash assets

35.7   Section 316A(3) prohibits a receiver from selling a non-cash asset of the requisite value to an officer of the company unless he has given at least 14 days' notice of his intention to do so to all creditors of the company who are known to him or who have been intimated to him.

Duties in applying the proceeds of sale of assets

35.8   Section 98 of the 1963 Act makes provision for the payment by a receiver of the debts of preferential creditors, when he has been appointed under a floating charge.

Under s 98, when a receiver is appointed on behalf of debenture-holders under a floating charge or possession is taken by or on behalf of the debenture-holders of any property under a charge, then, even if the company is not at that time being liquidated, the preferential debts under s 285 must be paid out of the assets coming into the hands of the receiver in priority to any principal or interest payable under the debentures. Any preferential payments made by the receiver under this section can, of course, be recouped, so far as may be, out of the assets of the company available for the general creditors.

Where the receiver sells assets which are the subject of a fixed charge or a legal mortgage, his duty is to apply the proceeds in the discharge of the monies due to the debenture-holders. Any surplus is payable to the company, as s 98 only applies to assets subject to a floating charge.

---

1 He must also exercise a general duty of care by, for example, obtaining the best possible price which the circumstances of a sale permit – see *McGowan v Gannon* [1983] ILRM 516.
2 *Standard Chartered Bank Ltd v Walker* [1982] 3 All ER 938.
3 As amended by s 172 of the 1990 Act.

Duty to report misconduct

35.9 Section 299(2) of the 1963 Act imposes a duty on liquidators to report criminal behaviour by company officers and members to the Director of Public Prosecutions, and to assist him prosecute the offenders. This duty was extended to receivers by s 179 of the 1990 Act.

Receiver's specific statutory tasks

35.10 Sections 319 and 320 specify the procedures to be adopted when a receiver, appointed on behalf of holders of debentures secured by a floating charge, *takes over the whole, or substantially the whole, of the property of a company.* Such a receiver is required by the Act to take the following steps.

Notification

35.11 The receiver must notify the company immediately of his appointment.

Statement of particulars

35.12 Within 14 days after receipt of the notice or such longer period as he, or the court, may allow, the receiver must obtain from the company a statement showing particulars of:

(1) the assets;
(2) the debts and liabilities;
(3) the names and residences of the creditors;
(4) the securities held by the respective creditors;
(5) the dates on which the various securities were given;
(6) such other information as may be prescribed.

Verification of particulars

35.13 The statement of particulars must be submitted and verified by the affidavit (or statutory declaration where the appointment is under a deed) of one or more of the directors of the company and by the secretary at the date of the appointment. In addition, the receiver may require any of the following persons to submit and verify the statements:

(1) present or past officers of the company;
(2) anyone who has taken part in the formation of the company within a year of the receiver's appointment;
(3) persons employed by the company within the past year and who are, in the opinion of the receiver, capable of giving the information required;
(4) anyone employed within the preceding year as an officer in another company which itself took part in the management of the main company.

Any person making the statement and affidavit (or statutory declaration) is entitled to be paid by the receiver, out of his receipts, any costs and expenses which the receiver considers reasonable. He may appeal to the court if dissatisfied.

Persons not complying with these verification requirements are liable to criminal sanctions of up to three years' imprisonment and/or a fine not exceeding £5,000.

Copies to registrar and debenture-holders

35.14 Within two months of receipt of this statement of particulars, the receiver must send copies of it, together with any comments he sees fit to make, to the registrar of companies, the court,[1] the company, to any trustees for the debenture-holders on whose behalf he was appointed and, so far as he is aware of their addresses, to all debenture-holders.

Delivering of half-yearly returns to the registrar

35.15 Section 321 of the 1963 Act provides that every receiver, within one month after the expiration of six months from the date of his appointment and every subsequent six months (and again within one month of ceasing to act as receiver), must send to the registrar of companies an abstract in the prescribed form showing:

(1) the assets of the company of which he has taken possession, since his appointment;
(2) their estimated value;
(3) the proceeds of sale of any such assets since his appointment;
(4) his receipts and payments during the period of six months, or for the broken period when he ceases to act;
(5) the aggregate amounts of his receipts and payments during all preceding periods since his appointment.

In addition to making these returns, the receiver must, of course, render proper accounts of his receipts and payments to the persons to whom he is responsible, in accordance with the terms of his appointment.

Sections 319 and 320 (at **35.10** above) apply where the receiver takes over the whole of the company's property. Where a receiver is appointed *other than over substantially all of the company's assets* so that ss 319 and 320 do not apply, he still must file half-yearly accounts with the registrar of companies containing the same particulars as those required under s 319. On ceasing to act, a receiver must file a final return.

---

1 If appointed by the court.

Enforcement of receiver's duty to make returns

35.16   The court is empowered under s 322, on an application being made, to direct a receiver to make good any default in making returns. In particular, s 322 specifies the receiver's default:

(1) in failing to file, deliver or make any return,[1] account or other documents within 14 days after the service on him of a notice requiring him to do so; or

(2) in failing to provide proper accounts, to vouch his receipts and payments and to pay over the balance due to the liquidator of the company.

Applications for the purpose of (1) above may be made to the court by any member or creditor of the company or by the registrar of companies, and on the grounds in (2) by the liquidator. The court may provide for the costs of the application to be borne by the receiver.

Liabilities of receivers

35.17   The main legal liabilities of receivers are likely to arise out of contracts entered into by them on behalf of the company. Their liability for existing and new company contracts has been explained in **34.21**.

Application to the court for directions

35.18   If a receiver is unsure as to the legality of a course of action, he has the right, under s 316 of the 1963 Act, to apply to the court for directions (see **34.14**).

PREMATURE TERMINATION OF RECEIVER'S POWERS

35.19   A receiver's powers may be brought to an end before he has accomplished his task of utilising or realising the company's assets under his control to pay the debenture-holders. This premature termination of a receiver's powers may be brought about either voluntarily or involuntarily. A receiver may resign voluntarily. He may also be involuntarily removed by the court.

Resignation

35.20   Section 322C[2] of the 1963 Act makes provision for the resignation of a receiver. A receiver of the property of a company appointed under the powers contained in any instrument may resign, provided he has given one month's notice to:

---

1   Or to give any notice which he is required to deliver.
2   As inserted by s 177 of the 1990 Act.

(1) the holders of floating charges over all or any part of the property of the company;

(2) the company or its liquidator; and

(3) the holders of any fixed charge over all or any part of the property of the company.

If any receiver resigns without giving the notice prescribed by s 322C, he will be liable to a maximum fine of £1,000.

Removal

35.21   In addition to voluntary resignation, the Act also provides for the involuntary removal of a receiver. Section 322A(1)[1] empowers the court, on cause shown, to remove[2] a receiver and appoint another in his place.

The court may also remove a receiver on the application of the liquidator – see **35.24** below.

RECEIVERS, EXAMINERS AND LIQUIDATORS

35.22   A *receiver* is an appointee of the secured creditors[3] (debenture-holders). His primary function is to take over (and, if necessary, sell) the assets of the company which have been mortgaged or charged by it as security for repayment of the debenture-holders' loan.

The exercising of his rights over the charged assets by the receiver may, but not necessarily must, result in the winding up of the company.

An *examiner*[4] is appointed by the court, usually at the request of the company's officers, who are seeking his appointment to protect the company against its secured creditors. The examiner's function is to examine the financial affairs and prospects of the company, and to report back to the court on its prospects for survival, ie how it can avoid liquidation.

A *liquidator*[5] may be appointed by either investors or creditors. His task is to terminate the 'life' of the company by winding it up, liquidating its assets and distributing them in accordance with the law.

Effect on receiver of appointment of examiner

35.23   Section 6(1) of the Companies (Amendment) Act 1990 provides that where an examiner is appointed to a company and a receiver is already in

---

1 Inserted by s 175 of the 1990 Act.
2 Section 322A(2) sets out the procedure to be followed. This includes giving the receiver at least seven days' notice before the hearing of such proceedings.
3 Or by the court on their behalf.
4 See Part IX.
5 See Part X.

control of the whole or any part of the property or undertaking of that company, the court may make such order as it thinks fit, including an order as to any or all of the following matters:

(1) that the receiver shall cease to act as such from a date specified by the court;

(2) that the receiver shall, from a date specified by the court, act as such only in respect of certain assets specified by the court;

(3) directing the receiver to deliver all books, papers and other records, which relate to the property or undertaking of the company and are in his possession or control, to the examiner within a period to be specified by the court;

(4) directing the receiver to give the examiner full particulars of all his dealings with the property or undertaking of the company.

The Supreme Court has held that the appointment of an examiner will de-crystallise a floating charge over a company's book debts.[1]

Effect on receiver of appointment of liquidator

35.24   The subsequent appointment of a liquidator over a company whose property is under the control of a receiver, does not automatically affect the receivership. However, s 322B[2] of the 1963 Act gives a court the power to terminate or limit the receivership on the application of the liquidator.

On the application of a liquidator, in these circumstances, the court may:

(1) order that the receiver shall cease to act as such from a date specified by the court, and prohibit the appointment of a new receiver; or

(2) order that the receiver shall act as such only in respect of certain assets specified by the court.

The court may, on receipt of an application made either by the liquidator or by the receiver, cancel or amend an order made under s 322B(1).

---

1 See **37.34**.

2 Inserted by s 176 of the 1990 Act.

Chapter 36

UNSATISFIED CREDITORS' REMEDIES AGAINST THE COMPANY'S MEMBERS AND OFFICERS

CREDITORS' REMEDIES

36.1 Because of the separate legal personality[1] of the company, the general rule is that creditors of the company only have redress against company assets to obtain (re)payment of any monies owing to them by the company.

Any unsecured or secured creditor owed at least £1,000 has the right to petition for the winding up of the company. When a company is liquidated, the law provides for priority of payment to secured over unsecured creditors. For example, after the holders of any fixed charges have realised their security, the liquidator will use the remaining company assets realised to repay the company's creditors in the following order:

(1) preferential creditors;
(2) creditors secured by floating charges;
(3) unsecured creditors.

As mentioned in Chapter 2, in many company liquidations, the Revenue Commissioners, though preferential creditors, are often left unpaid because of the lack of company assets. In this context, the likelihood of floating chargees and unsecured creditors being paid is very slim. In many liquidations, the unsecured creditors will not be paid.

UNSATISFIED CREDITORS' REMEDIES AGAINST THE MEMBERS

36.2 The reason why the unsatisfied creditors remain unpaid during (and after) a liquidation is clearly the insufficiency of company assets to pay them. Can these unsatisfied creditors now seek to reclaim their monies from the company's members?

In Chapter 4, we explained how the principle of limited liability protected the members of a company from being held liable for the debts of the company which they own. Once every member has fully paid up the nominal value of each share he holds, then his liability to company creditors is generally extinguished. Thus, the principle of limited liability, allied to the separate personality of the company, confers an immunity on members against claims by unsatisfied creditors of the company.

---

1 See Chapter 3.

As was illustrated in Chapter 6, corporate personality is likened to a veil. This veil of incorporation prevents unsatisfied creditors from pursuing legal action against company members, even though the identities of the members and the number of shares which they hold can be ascertained.

It is only in exceptional cases that unsatisfied company creditors can successfully pursue a claim against the members. These exceptional cases have arisen as a result of the courts and the legislature[1] 'lifting' the veil of incorporation.

The rare instances where unsatisfied creditors are able to pursue company members might be where the company was originally formed or used for a fraudulent purpose. Members of companies which traded with less than the minimum number of members required by s 36 of the 1963 Act, may also be held personally responsible for the company's unpaid debts.

Immunity of members

36.3   The Joint Stock Companies Act 1844 and the Limited Liability Act 1855 permitted the registration of companies as separate legal persons with limited liability for their investors. The purpose of these Acts was to encourage enterprise by offering the protection of limited liability to investors or company members. The few exceptional cases where investors' immunity against unsatisfied company creditors' claims have been breached by the 'lifting of the veil' during the past 150 years, would seem to suggest that the nineteenth century legislation has been most successful in protecting investors against claims by unsatisfied creditors of the company.

UNSATISFIED CREDITORS' CLAIMS AGAINST DIRECTORS AND OFFICERS

36.4   Although investors, as company members, are protected, essentially, against claims made by unsatisfied creditors of the company, the legislature has opened up new avenues of redress for creditors against the managing agents of the company, ie its directors and officers.

In Ireland, of the 147,058 companies registered at 31 December 1995, 134,769 (92 per cent) were private limited companies. Many directors of private companies will also be major[2] shareholders in them. Accordingly, it is worth noting that even though a private company member may be protected, qua member, against the claims of unsatisfied company creditors, that same individual, as a director, or officer, might be held liable[3] for the debts of the company.

---

1 See Chapter 6 for details.
2 Possibly controlling shareholders.
3 Qua director or officer.

Directors' and officers' liabilities towards creditors

36.5 The right of an unsatisfied company creditor to pursue directors and officers depends on whether or not these managing agents are legally liable for the debts of the company.

We have already detailed the duties and liabilities of company directors and officers in Chapters 19 to 23. From the perspective of an unsatisfied creditor of the company, perhaps the most important likely sources[1] of redress will arise out of either a director's failure to keep proper books of account; reckless or fraudulent trading; or breach of a restriction or disqualification order.

Failure to keep proper books of account

36.6 Section 204(1) of the 1990 Act provides that when a company is being wound up, is unable to pay all of its debts and has failed to keep proper books of account, and the court considers that such contravention has contributed to the company's inability to pay all of its debts or has resulted in substantial uncertainty as to the assets and liabilities of the company or has substantially impeded the orderly winding up thereof, the court, on the application of the liquidator or any creditor or contributory of the company, may declare that any one or more of the officers and former officers of the company who are in default shall be personally liable, without any limitation of liability, for all, or part of the debts of the company.

Directors' and officers' liability under s 204 has already been analysed in **21.17**, including the implications of the *Mantruck Services* case.

The advantage of s 204 to an unsatisfied creditor is that he, or the liquidator, can seek to supplement the paucity of company assets by making the directors and officers personally liable for the company's debts.

Reckless and fraudulent trading

36.7 Section 138 of the 1990 Act also provides that:

'If in the course of winding up of a company or in the course of proceedings under the Companies (Amendment) Act 1990, it appears that—

(a) any person was, while an officer of the company, knowingly a party to the carrying on of any business of the company in a reckless manner; or
(b) any person was knowingly a party to the carrying on of any business of the company with intent to defraud creditors of the company, or creditors of any other person or for any fraudulent purpose;

the court, on the application of the receiver, examiner, liquidator or any creditor or contributory of the company, may, if it thinks it proper to do so, declare that such person shall be personally responsible, without any limitation of liability, for all or any part of the debts or other liabilities of the company as the court may direct.'

---

1 See **21.15** for other examples of statutory redress.

Thus, the company assets available to meet the claims of unsatisfied creditors can be supplemented by obtaining contributions:

(1) from officers of the company who were knowingly privy to the carrying on of any business of the company in a reckless manner; or

(2) any person who was knowingly a party to fraudulent trading.

The case-law on these statutory reckless and fraudulent trading provisions was examined in Chapter 21.

Restriction and disqualification

36.8   Any director who has been acting in breach of a restriction declaration or disqualification order, may be made personally liable for all or part of the company's debts[1] – thereby providing a further source of funding for unsatisfied company creditors.

The post-1990 legal environment

36.9   The Companies Act 1990 has greatly increased the potential liability of a company's human managing agents towards the unsatisfied creditors of the company. As a result, such creditors now enjoy a much greater chance of recovering some, if not all, of their unsatisfied claims against the company from its directors and officers. The fact that directors and officers can effect insurance[2] to indemnify themselves against many of these potential claims, further improves the creditors' position. In fact, the likely reaction of unpaid company creditors will be to pursue the directors and officers, rather than the members, for recovery of their unsatisfied claims against the company. This reaction is a practical acknowledgement of the strength of the veil of incorporation and the effectiveness of the investors' immunity from liability for the debts of their companies.

---

1 See **23.17**.

2 See Chapter 22.

PART IX

PROTECTION AVAILABLE TO A COMPANY AGAINST ITS CREDITORS

Chapter 37

EXAMINERSHIP AND ITS EFFECTS ON CREDITORS' RIGHTS

THE EFFECT OF EXAMINERSHIP

37.1   The prospect of losing a valuable beef trade outlet as a result of a United Nations embargo on trade with Iraq led to financial difficulties for companies within the Goodman International Group.[1] To protect these companies from their creditors, special sittings of the Oireachtas took place in August 1990, to process the parliamentary stages of the Companies (Amendment) Act 1990.[2] The 1990 Amendment Act provided for the placing of a company facing temporary financial difficulties under the protection of the court, whilst an examiner is appointed to look into its affairs.

The effect of the process of examinership is to allow a company in difficulty the opportunity of obtaining court protection from its creditors for at least three months whilst the examiner attempts to put in place a financial rescue package to save the company.

If the examiner considers that the company is viable, he may propose a scheme of arrangement involving the creditors accepting less than the amounts owed to them by the company. The court will have to approve such a scheme before it becomes binding.

Where the examiner forms the opinion that the company has no chance of survival, he is likely to propose its winding up.

We now focus on the detailed provisions in the legislation.

POWER OF THE COURT

37.2   Where it appears to the court that:

(1) a company is or is likely to be unable to pay its debts; and
(2) no resolution subsists for the winding up of the company; and

---

1 In August 1990, this group's debts were estimated to be about £450 million. Many of the creditors were foreign banks whose loans were unsecured.
2 This Act was, in effect, an early enactment of Part IX of the Companies Bill which was being processed at the time. This Bill subsequently became the Companies Act 1990. Sections 180 and 181 of the 1990 Act amended the 1990 Amendment Act, revising the practical working of examinership in the light of several months' experience.

(3) no order has been made for the winding up of the company,

it may appoint an examiner to the company for the purpose of examining the state of the company's affairs.[1]

In particular, the court may make an order if it considers that such action would be likely to facilitate the survival of the company, either whole or part, as a going concern.

The Act does not include criteria to guide the court in assessing whether a company is likely to survive. In *Re Atlantic Magnetics Ltd*,[2] Finlay CJ suggested:

> 'does the evidence lead to the conclusion that in all the circumstances, it appears worthwhile to order an investigation by the examiner into the company's affairs and see can it survive, there being some reasonable prospect of survival.'

Keane J, in *Re Butler Engineering Ltd*,[3] refined the term 'some reasonable prospect of survival' to 'an identifiable possibility' that the company will survive as a going concern if an examiner is appointed; a refinement approved by Budd J in *Re Westport Property Construction Co Ltd*.[4]

In deciding whether to make an order under s 2, the court may also have regard to whether the company has sought from its creditors significant extensions of time for the payment of its debts, from which it could reasonably be inferred that the company was likely to be unable to pay its debts.

37.3 A company will be deemed to be unable to pay its debts if:

(1) it is unable to pay its debts as they fall due;
(2) the value of its assets is less than the amount of its liabilities, taking into account its contingent and prospective liabilities; or
(3) s 214(a) or (b) of the 1963 Act applies to the company – see Chapter 41.

For example, during February 1997, an interim examiner (see **37.6** below) was appointed over Bell Lines. In the petition to appoint him, the court was informed that the company had a surplus of assets over liabilities of £8 million. However, without access to further working capital which it required, the company was in a position where it was likely that it would be unable to pay its debts as they fell due. Nevertheless, it was felt that Bell Lines was capable of surviving as a going concern.

The court appointed the interim examiner to facilitate the orderly re-structuring of the company.

---

1 And performing the appropriate duties in relation to the company – see s 2 of the 1990 Amendment Act, as amended by s 181 of the 1990 Act.
2 [1993] 2 IR 561 (SC).
3 (Unreported) 1 March 1996 (HC).
4 (Unreported) 13 September 1996 (HC).

Related companies

37.4   Where the court appoints an examiner to a company, it may, at the same or any time thereafter, make an order:

(1)   appointing the examiner to be examiner to a related company; or
(2)   conferring on the examiner, in relation to such company, all or any of the powers or duties conferred on him in relation to the original company.

Section 4(5) of the 1990 Amendment Act stipulates that a company will be related to another company if:

(1)   that other company is its holding company or subsidiary; or
(2)   more than half in nominal value of its equity share capital is held by the other company and companies related to that other company; or
(3)   more than half in nominal value of the equity share capital of each of them is held by members of the other; or
(4)   that other company or companies related to that other company are entitled to control the exercise of more than one half of the voting power at any general meeting of the company; or
(5)   the businesses of the companies have been so carried on that the separate business of each company, or a substantial part thereof, is not readily identifiable; or
(6)   if there is another corporate body to which both companies are related.

37.5   Before deciding to appoint the examiner to a related company, the court will have regard to whether the making of the order would be likely to facilitate the survival of the company, or of the related company, or both, as a going concern.

A related company to which an examiner is appointed will also be deemed to be under the protection of the court for the period beginning on the date of the making of an order and continuing for the period during which the company to which it is related is under protection.

Where an examiner is appointed to two or more related companies, he will have the same powers and duties in relation to each company, taken separately, unless the court directs otherwise.

Interim examiner

37.6   The court has the power, if it considers it necessary, to appoint an interim examiner pending an adjourned hearing of a petition.

Security for costs

37.7   The court may refuse to hear a petition to appoint an examiner presented by a contingent or prospective creditor until such security for costs has been given as the court thinks reasonable, and until a prima facie case for the protection of the court has been established.

Examiner's liability for company contracts

37.8 The legal position of an examiner resembles that of a receiver. For example, under s 13(6), he is personally liable on any contract entered into by him in the performance of his duties (whether the contract is entered into by him in the name of the company or in his own name as examiner or otherwise) unless the contract provides that he is not to be personally liable on such contract.

Right to indemnity

37.9 Section 13(6) also provides that if the examiner does incur a personal liability for company contracts, he will be entitled to an indemnity in respect of that liability, out of the assets of the company.

Qualifications of an examiner

37.10 A person will only be qualified to act as an examiner of a company, if he is qualified to act as its liquidator – see **42.5**.

WHO CAN PETITION THE COURT?

37.11 Generally, the following[1] may petition the court to appoint an examiner:

(1) the company; or
(2) the directors of the company; or
(3) a creditor, or contingent or prospective creditor (including an employee), of the company; or
(4) members of the company holding, at the date of the presentation of a petition, not less than one-tenth of such of the paid-up capital of the company as carries at that date the right of voting at general meetings of the company; or
(5) by all or any of those parties, together, or separately.

The petition presented to the court must:

(1) nominate a person to be appointed as examiner; and
(2) be supported by such evidence as the court may require for the purpose of showing that the petitioner has good reason for requiring the appointment of an examiner.[2]

---

1 See s 3 of the 1990 Amendment Act, as amended by s 180 of the 1990 Act.
2 Where the petition is presented by the company or its directors, it must include a statement of the assets and liabilities of the company (in so far as they are known to them) as they stand on a date not earlier than seven days before the presentation of the petition. The directors and their professional advisers must also observe the utmost good faith when applying for a protection order – see *Re Wogans (Drogheda) Ltd (No 2)* (unreported) 7 May 1992 (HC).

The petition must also be accompanied:

(1) by a consent signed by the person nominated to be examiner; and
(2) if proposals for a compromise[1] or scheme of arrangement in relation to the company's affairs have been prepared for submission to interested parties for their approval, by a copy of the proposals.

Notification of examiner's appointment

37.12   Section 12(1) prescribes that notice of the petition to appoint an examiner must be delivered in the appropriate form, *by the petitioner*, to the registrar of companies.

By the examiner

37.13   Section 12(2) imposes a duty on the examiner to immediately notify the public of:

(1) his appointment and the date thereof; and
(2) the date, if any, set for the hearing of the matters arising out of his report (see **38.2** below).

The examiner must notify the public by publishing the notices in *Iris Oifigiúil* and in at least two local daily newspapers. The time-limits for publishing these notices are:

(1) 21 days after his appointment, in the case of *Iris Oifigiúil*; and
(2) three days after this appointment, for the local daily newspapers. He must also send the registrar of companies a copy of the order appointing him within three days.

In letterheadings etc

37.14   Every invoice, order for goods or business letter issued by or on behalf of the company, being a document on or in which the name of the company appears, must contain the statement 'under the protection of the court'.

CONSEQUENCES OF EXAMINERSHIP

37.15   Section 5(1) of the 1990 Amendment Act provides that for three months[2] after the presentation of the petition, the company is deemed to be under the protection of the court.

---

1 See Part X.
2 Or such extension as is permitted by s 18(3) and (4) of the 1990 Amendment Act.

Company immunities

37.16 When a company is deemed to be under the protection of the court, the immunities enjoyed by it include:

(1) no proceedings for the winding up of the company may be commenced or resolution for winding up passed in relation to that company. Any resolution so passed shall be of no effect;

(2) no receiver over any part of the property or undertaking of the company may be appointed, or, if so appointed before the presentation of a petition shall, subject to s 6 (see **37.17** below), be able to act;

(3) no attachment, sequestration, distress or execution can be put into force against the property or effects of the company, except with the consent of the examiner;

(4) where any claim against the company is secured by a charge on the whole or any part of the property, effects or income of the company, no action may be taken to realise the whole or any part of such security, except with the consent of the examiner;

(5) no steps may be taken to repossess goods in the company's possession under any hire-purchase agreement except with the consent of the examiner;

(6) where any person other than the company, such as a guarantor, is liable to pay all or any part of the debts of the company:
    (a) no attachment, sequestration, distress or execution can be put into force against the property or effects of such person in respect of the debts of the company; and
    (b) no proceedings of any sort may be commenced against such person in respect of the debts of the company;

(7) no order for relief against oppression will be made under s 205 of the 1963 Act against the company in respect of complaints as to the conduct of the affairs of the company or the exercise of the powers of the directors prior to the presentation of the petition;

(8) no set off between separate bank accounts of the company can be effected, except with the consent of the examiner.

Receivers

37.17 Section 6(1) of the Act clarifies the effect of the appointment of an examiner on an existing receivership.[1]

Provisional liquidators

37.18 Where an examiner is appointed to a company and a provisional liquidator stands appointed to that company, the court may make such order as it thinks fit, including an order as to any or all of the following matters:

---

1 See **35.23**.

(1) that the provisional liquidator be appointed as examiner of the company;
(2) appointing some other person as examiner of the company;
(3) that the provisional liquidator shall cease to act as such from the date specified by the court;
(4) directing the provisional liquidator to deliver all books, papers and other records, which relate to the property or undertaking of the company or any part thereof and are in his possession or control, to the examiner within a period to be specified by the court;
(5) directing the provisional liquidator to give the examiner full particulars of all his dealings with the property or undertaking of the company.

POWERS OF EXAMINER

37.19   Sections 7 and 8 of the 1990 Amendment Act deal specifically with the powers of an examiner.

Essentially, s 7 confers on an examiner the powers and rights of an auditor of the company. An examiner may seek the production of documents and evidence, without reference to the court. He may also attend meetings, convene and chair board meetings, and take appropriate remedial action if he discovers detrimental conduct (see **37.25** below) by the company or its agents. He may certify expenses and apply to the court for specific directions.

With the consent of the court, an examiner may also be empowered to:

(1) deal with company property that is subject to a charge;
(2) seek a transfer of the directors' powers. These would include their power to borrow on the company's behalf.

Murphy J clarified the powers of the examiner over directors in *Re Edenpark Construction Ltd.*[1] He stated:

'in the absence of some particular order of the High Court, the examiner may not usurp the functions of the board of directors ... and it is the board or its officials who will continue to manage the business of the company during the period of protection and the continuance of the examinership.'

Further powers of the court over company management

37.20   If the examiner finds:

(1) that the affairs of the company are being conducted, or are likely to be conducted, in a manner which is calculated or likely to prejudice the interests of the company or of its employees or of its creditors as a whole; or
(2) that it is expedient, for the purpose of preserving the assets or of safeguarding the interests of the company or its employees or its creditors as a whole, that the carrying on of the business of the company by its

---

1 (Unreported) 17 December 1993 (HC).

directors or management should be curtailed or regulated in any particular respect; or

(3) that the company, or its directors, have resolved that such an order should be sought; or

(4) any other matter in relation to the company the court thinks relevant,

he may apply to the court. The court may then, if it considers it is just and equitable to do so, make an order under s 9 that all or any of the functions or powers which are vested in or exercisable by the directors shall be performable or exercisable only by the examiner. Such an order may provide that the examiner shall have all or any of the powers that he would have if he were a liquidator appointed by the court in respect of the company.

Seeking the production of documents and evidence

37.21   Officers and agents of the company are under a duty by s 8 to produce for the examiner all books and documents which are in their custody or power, to attend before him when required and otherwise to give to him all assistance in connection with his functions which they are reasonably able to give.

If the examiner considers that a person, other than an officer or agent, may be in possession of any information, he may require that person to produce any books or documents in his custody or power relating to the company, to attend before him and otherwise to give to him all assistance which he is reasonably able to give.

Examination on oath

37.22   An examiner may examine, on oath, officers, agents or any other persons, in relation to the company's affairs. He may also:

(1) administer an oath; and

(2) reduce the answer of such persons to writing, and require their signatures of them.

Any person who refuses to produce books, etc. when requested to do so by the examiner, will be liable to punishment as if he had been guilty of contempt of court.

'Agents' include bankers, solicitors and auditors of the company.

Directors' statement of affairs

37.23   Within seven days of the appointment of an examiner, the directors must submit[1] to him a statement of affairs of the company.

---

1 Section 14(1).

The statement must, insofar as is reasonably possible to do so, show particulars of the company's assets, debts and liabilities, the names and addresses of its creditors, the securities held by them, the dates when the securities were respectively given and such further information as may be prescribed or as the court may direct.

Meetings

37.24 An examiner is entitled to reasonable notice of, to attend and be heard at, all meetings of the board of directors of a company and all general meetings of the company to which he is appointed.

An examiner also has the power to convene, set the agenda for, and preside at meetings of the board of directors and general meetings of the company and to propose motions or resolutions and to give reports to such meetings.

Discovery of detrimental conduct

37.25 Section 8(3) gives an examiner power to require a director to produce for him all documents in the director's possession or control, relating to an unauthorised bank account. An unauthorised bank account is one into or out of which there has been paid:

(1) any money which has resulted from or been used in the financing of any transaction, arrangement or agreement, particulars of which have not been disclosed in the accounts of any company as required by law; or
(2) any money which has been in any way connected with any act or omission which, on the part of that director, constituted misconduct (whether fraudulent or not) towards that company or its investors.

Remedies

37.26 Section 7(5) gives the examiner full power to take whatever steps are necessary to halt, prevent or rectify any detrimental conduct by the company's officers, employees, investors or creditors.

Certification of expenses

37.27 Section 29(2) provides that, unless the court otherwise orders, the remuneration, costs and expenses of an examiner shall be paid and the examiner shall be entitled to be indemnified in respect of them out of the revenue of the business of the company or the proceeds of realisation of its assets (including investments).

Whilst an examiner, insofar as is reasonably possible, should make use of the staff and services of the company, he may, if necessary, appoint or employ persons to assist him.

Section 10(1) makes it clear that any liabilities incurred during the 'protection period' [1] will be treated as expenses properly incurred for the purpose of s 29. Such liabilities are those certified by the examiner, to have been incurred in circumstances where, in the opinion of the examiner, the survival of the company as a going concern during the protection period would otherwise have been seriously prejudiced.

37.28   In *Re Edenpark Construction Ltd,* (see **37.19** above) Murphy J only took into account liabilities incurred by the company after the appointment of the examiner. He excluded any costs arising out of the presentation of the petition to appoint the examiner. The result of this judgment was a reduction of 20 per cent in the fees presented by the examiner.

Sections 10 and 29 were also considered by the Supreme Court in *Re Don Bluth Entertainment Ltd and Related Companies.*[2] Here, it was held that certified expenses, properly incurred by an examiner under ss 29 or 10, rank in priority to both unsecured and secured creditors.

Applications to the court for direction

37.29   Sections 7(6) and (7) and 13(7) make provision for questions arising in the course of the examinership to be determined by application to the court.

Power to deal with charged property

37.30   Section 11(1) empowers the examiner, with the approval of the court, to dispose of property already secured by a floating charge. However, the court will have to be satisfied that the exercise of his power by the examiner is likely to facilitate the survival of the company, or any part of it, as a going concern, before it authorises him to take priority over the floating charge.[3]

Fixed charge and mortgage holders, and the owners of goods held under a hire-purchase agreement, are dealt with in s 11(2) and (4). In these cases, if property or goods are sold by the examiner, the court can determine the open market value of the company asset sold, and order the company to make good any deficiency in price to the holder of the security.

The right to seek a transfer of the directors' powers

37.31   As mentioned above, s 9 gives the court further powers to transfer 'all or any' of the directors' powers to the examiner. These powers include the right to borrow money on the company's behalf. The court may, when sanctioning the transfer of directors' borrowing powers, also order that such borrowings

---

1 Ie the time the company is under the protection of the court.
2 *Irish Times Law Reports* 4 July 1994.
3 See s 11(1) and (3).

may be certified as 'expenses' of the examinership under s 10. If this is done, it will give a 'certified lender' priority over earlier secured creditors.

EFFECT OF EXAMINERSHIP ON CREDITORS' RIGHTS

37.32 The whole purpose of the examinership process is to give the company temporary protection against creditors exercising their legal rights and remedies against the company's assets.

The effects of the appointment of an examiner on a receiver have already been outlined (see **35.23**). Let us now consider the individual positions of the various types of creditors.

Costs of examinership paramount

37.33 Section 29(3) gives first priority to the remuneration, costs and expenses of an examiner which have been sanctioned by order of the court. Such costs must be paid in full before any other claim, secured or unsecured, under any compromise or scheme of arrangement or in any receivership or winding up of the company.

In *Re Atlantic Magnetics Ltd,*[1] the Supreme Court held that the costs[2] of examinership take priority over fixed, as well as floating charges.

Secured creditors

37.34 Section 5(2)(d) provides that a secured creditor can take no action to realise the whole or any part of the charged assets, except with the consent of the examiner.

In *Re Holidair Ltd,*[3] a bank's instruction to the borrowing company to lodge the proceeds of its book debts into a designated bank account after an examiner was appointed, was held to be a breach of s 5(2)(d).

This Supreme Court judgment also suggests that floating charges which have crystallised, will de-crystallise on the appointment of an examiner, and that an examiner can ignore a negative pledge clause.[4]

Where an examiner is given the power to borrow money and to certify such borrowings as 'expenses' under s 10, these expenses will rank before earlier secured creditors, whether fixed or floating. Because of this threat to their underlying security, secured lenders in the United Meat Packers examinership[5]

---

1 [1993] 2 IR 561.
2 Incurred under ss 29 and 10 – see the *Don Bluth* case (at **37.28** above). They also take priority over the rights of fixed charge holders, etc, in s 11(2) and (4).
3 [1994] 1 ILRM 481.
4 See **32.30**.
5 (Unreported) 2 March 1992 (HC), 13 March 1992 (SC).

refused to lend further monies to the company to enable it to survive during the protection period. As a result, the examiner was unable to facilitate the continued survival of the company. This, in turn, led to a withdrawal of the court's protection for the company.

Unsecured creditors

37.35   Unsecured creditors' remedies of petitioning for the winding up of the company or initiating legal proceedings against it to obtain judgment for its debt, cannot[1] be utilised while the company is under the protection of the court.

---

1 See s 5(2) and (3) of the 1990 Amendment Act.

Chapter 38

THE EXAMINER'S OPINION AND THE FUTURE OF THE COMPANY

DUTY OF EXAMINER

38.1   The primary duty of an examiner is to conduct an examination of the affairs of the company and report back to the court.

The examiner must report[1] to the court within 21 days, or such longer period as the court may allow.

INFORMATION IN EXAMINER'S REPORT

38.2   Section 16[2] provides that the examiner's report must contain the following information:

(1)   the names and permanent addresses of the officers of the company and, insofar as the examiner can establish, any person in accordance with whose directions or instructions the directors of the company are accustomed to act;

(2)   the names of any other bodies corporate of which the directors of the company are also directors;

(3)   a statement as to the affairs of the company, showing, insofar as is reasonably possible to do so, particulars of the company's assets, debts and liabilities (including contingent and prospective liabilities) as at the latest practicable date, the names and addresses of its creditors, the securities held by them and the dates when the securities were respectively given;

(4)   such other matters as the examiner thinks relevant or the court directs.

Examiner's opinions

38.3   The examiner must also *express opinions* on whether:

(1)   any deficiency between the assets and the liabilities of the company has been satisfactorily accounted for or, if not, whether there is evidence of a substantial disappearance of property that is not accounted for;

---

1 The examiner must deliver a copy of his report to the company. Copies may also have to be supplied to interested parties, ie creditors or members of the company – see s 15(3), (4) and (5) of the 1990 Amendment Act.
2 Ibid, s 16, as amended by s 180 of the 1990 Act.

(2) the company, and the whole or any part of its undertaking, would be capable of survival as a going concern and a statement of the conditions which he feels are essential to ensure such survival, whether as regards the internal management and controls of the company or otherwise;

(3) the formulation, acceptance and confirmation of proposals for a compromise or scheme of arrangement would facilitate such survival;

(4) an attempt to continue the whole or any part of the undertaking of the company would be likely to be more advantageous to the members as a whole and the creditors as a whole, than a winding up of the company;

(5) the facts disclosed would warrant further inquiries with a view to proceedings[1] for fraudulent or reckless trading, or both;

(6) his work would be assisted by a direction of the court extending the role or membership of any creditors' committee.[2]

Examiner's recommendation

38.4   The examiner's report must conclude with recommendations as to the course he thinks should be taken in relation to the company including, if warranted, draft proposals for a compromise or scheme of arrangement.

The future course of examinership proceedings will differ according to whether the examiner's opinion expressed in his report is positive or negative.

When the examiner's report expresses a positive opinion, the examiner has concluded that the company, or at least a part of it, is capable of surviving as a going concern. In this event, the examiner prepares a report under s 18; puts forward a rescue package to the creditors and investors, and seeks the approval of the court under s 24. If, and when, the court approves this package, the examinership effectively comes to an end.

When the examiner's report expresses a negative opinion, the examiner has concluded that the company, or at least a part of it, is incapable of surviving as a going concern. In these circumstances, the court will immediately hold a hearing under s 17 to consider the future of the company (see **38.17** below).

WHEN EXAMINER'S RECOMMENDATION IS POSITIVE

38.5   Where the examiner is of the opinion that the company is capable, at least in part, of survival as a going concern, and an attempt to continue the company would be likely to be more advantageous to the members as a whole, and to the creditors as a whole, than a winding up of the company, the examiner must formulate proposals under s 18 for a *compromise or scheme of arrangement*[3] with the company's creditors. In doing so, he must convene and

---

1 Both criminal and civil for fraudulent trading.
2 See **38.10** below.
3 See Chapter 39.

preside at meetings of investors and creditors to consider his proposals. He then reports to the court within 42 days of his appointment, or such longer period as the court may allow.

Examiner's report under s 18

38.6 An examiner's report under s 18 must include the following details:

(1) the proposals placed before the required meetings;
(2) any modification of those proposals adopted at any of those meetings;
(3) the outcome of each of the required meetings;
(4) the recommendation of the committee of creditors, if any;
(5) a statement of the assets and liabilities of the company as at the date of his report;
(6) a list of the creditors of the company, the amount owing to each creditor, the nature and value of any security held by any such creditor, and the priority status of preferential creditors;
(7) a list of the officers of the company;
(8) his recommendations;
(9) such other matters as the examiner deems appropriate or the court directs.

Copies of the report must be delivered to the company, and other interested parties, on receipt of their written request.

Avoidance of certain company contracts

38.7 Where a compromise or scheme of arrangement is being devised by the examiner as a 'rescue package', the company may, subject to the approval of the court under s 20, affirm or repudiate any contract under which some element of performance, other than the payment of money, remains outstanding either by the company or the other contracting party.

Any contracting party who suffers loss or damage as a result of such avoidance under s 20(1) will be deemed to be an unsecured creditor for the value of his loss or damage.

The proposed rescue package

38.8 Section 22 sets out the requirements in relation to an examiner's proposals to 'rescue' the company. Proposals for a compromise or scheme of arrangement must:

(1) specify each class of members and creditors of the company;
(2) specify any class of members and creditors whose interests or claims will not be impaired by the proposals;
(3) specify any class of members and creditors whose interests or claims will be impaired by the proposals;

(4) provide equal treatment for each claim or interest of a particular class unless the holder of a particular claim or interest agrees to less favourable treatment;

(5) provide for the implementation of the proposals;

(6) if the examiner considers it necessary or desirable to do so to facilitate the survival of the company as a going concern, specify whatever changes should be made in relation to the management or direction of the company, or in the memorandum or articles of the company;

(7) include such other matters as he thinks appropriate.

A statement of the assets and liabilities of the company at the date of the proposals must be attached. There must also be attached a description of the financial outcome of a winding up of the company for each class of members and creditors.

Impairment

38.9   A creditor's claim against the company will be impaired if he receives less in payment than the full amount due to him on the appointment of the examiner.

In *Jetmara Teo*,[1] it was held that where the creditors claim is to be paid in full, but only by means of instalments, that claim will be deemed to be impaired for the purposes of s 24(2)(c) of the 1990 Amendment Act. Section 24(2) gives an impaired creditor the right to be heard by the court when the examiner presents his proposals to it for confirmation (see **38.12** below).

A member's interest in the company is impaired if:

(1) the nominal value of his shareholding in the company is reduced;

(2) he is entitled to a fixed dividend in respect of his shareholding in the company, and the amount of that dividend is reduced;

(3) he is deprived of all or any part of the rights accruing to him by virtue of his shareholding in the company;

(4) his percentage interest in the total issued share capital of the company is reduced; or

(5) he is deprived of his shareholding in the company.

Committee of creditors

38.10   Under s 21, an examiner may, and if so directed by the court, must, appoint a committee of creditors to assist him in the performance of his functions.

The committee of creditors must consist of not more than five members, including the holders of the three largest unsecured claims who are willing to serve.

---

1 (Unreported) 10 May 1991 (HC).

The examiner will have to provide the committee with a copy of any rescue proposals. The committee may express an opinion on the proposals on its own behalf or on behalf of the creditors or classes of creditors whom it represents.

When the examiner has put together his proposed rescue package, he must call a meeting of all members and creditors to consider it.

Plenary meetings

38.11 At plenary meetings of members and creditors summoned under s 23, the examiner's proposals can be modified, but only with his consent.

Proposals will be deemed to have been accepted by a meeting of members, or of a class of members, if a majority of the votes validly cast at that meeting, whether in person or by proxy, are cast in favour of the resolution for the proposals.

The examiner's proposals shall be deemed to have been accepted by a meeting of creditors or of a class of creditors when a majority in number representing a majority in value of the claims represented at that meeting have voted, either in person or by proxy, in favour of the resolution for the proposals.

Confirmation by the court

38.12 Section 24 makes it necessary for the examiner to present his proposals for a compromise or scheme of arrangement to the court for its confirmation. The court can confirm these proposals, or approve them subject to modification. It may also refuse to approve them.

The court will not confirm any proposals unless:

(1) it can be shown that at least one class of members and one class of creditors whose interests or claims would be impaired by implementation of the proposals have accepted the proposals; or
(2) the proposals are fair and equitable in relation to any class of members or creditors that has not accepted the proposals and whose interests or claims would be impaired by implementation; and
(3) the proposals are not unfairly prejudicial to the interests of any interested party.

The court will also refuse to confirm the proposals if their primary purpose is the avoidance of payment of tax due.

Objections

38.13 At the court hearing to consider the examiner's proposals, any member or creditor who claims that his rights would be impaired, may object to confirmation of the rescue package by the court on the grounds set out in s 25. These grounds are:

(1) irregularities in or at the plenary meetings of members or creditors;

(2) that acceptance of the proposals by the meeting was obtained by improper means;

(3) that the proposals were put forward for an improper purpose;

(4) that the proposals unfairly prejudice the interests of the objector(s).

If the court upholds such an objection, it may order that the decision in question be set aside. The court may then order that another plenary meeting be convened.

Court's decision

38.14 Once the court confirms the examiner's proposals, they become binding on all creditors and members, and on the company.

If the court refuses to confirm the proposed rescue package, it may order the winding up of the company or make any other order it deems fit.

Revocation on grounds of fraud

38.15 Section 27 entitles the company, or any interested party, within 180 days after the confirmation of the proposals by the court, to apply to the court for revocation of confirmation on the grounds that it was procured by fraud. The court, if satisfied that such was the case, may revoke the confirmation on such terms and conditions as it thinks fit.

CESSATION OF PROTECTION ORDER

38.16 When a compromise or scheme of arrangement confirmed by the court comes into effect, the protection of the court for the company will cease. So, too, will the examiner's appointment – see s 26.

WHEN EXAMINER'S REPORT IS NEGATIVE

38.17 If the examiner's report expresses the opinion that:

(1) the company is not capable of survival as a going concern, or

(2) a compromise or scheme of arrangement would not facilitate its survival; or

(3) an attempt to continue the whole or part of the undertaking of the company would not be likely to be more advantageous to the members or the creditors as a whole, than a winding up of the company; or

(4) there is evidence of a substantial disappearance of property that is not adequately accounted for, or of other serious irregularities in relation to the company's affairs,

the court will hold a hearing, under s 17, to consider the implications of the report. At this hearing, the following parties will be entitled to appear and be heard:

(1) the examiner;
(2) the company;
(3) creditors or members;
(4) any person against whom the report suggests misconduct.

Power of the court

38.18 Following a hearing under s 17(1), the court may make such orders as it thinks fit. For example, it may make an order for:

(1) the discharge of all or some of the company assets from the protection of the court;
(2) the sale of the whole or part of the company's assets, and, if necessary for that purpose, the appointment of a receiver;
(3) the formulation by the examiner of proposals for a compromise or scheme of arrangement and the convening of meetings to consider them;
(4) the holding of a board meeting or general meeting to consider such matters as the court direct;
(5) the winding up of the company.

Once the court makes an order under s 17, the examiner must deliver a copy of it to the registrar of companies, for registration.

PART X

FINANCIAL ARRANGEMENTS AND RESTRUCTURING; CHANGE(S) IN OWNERSHIP AND WINDING UP OF COMPANIES

Chapter 39

FINANCIAL ARRANGEMENTS BETWEEN THE COMPANY, ITS CREDITORS AND MEMBERS

PAYMENT OF OUTSTANDING COMPANY DEBTS

39.1   In Part IX, we looked at a recent legal development which permits a company to protect itself against its creditors by petitioning the court to appoint an examiner; an official who, if he considers the company could be saved as a going concern, is entitled to place a financial rescue package for the company before the court, for its approval. In this way, a company could be maintained as a going concern by coming to a compromise or arrangement with its creditors, in respect of their debts.

Apart from examinership, s 201 of the 1963 Act also facilitates a company coming to an arrangement with its creditors over payment of outstanding company debts.

SECTION 201 SCHEMES OF ARRANGEMENT AND COMPROMISES

39.2   An arrangement can be defined as a scheme drawn up by a company to offer ways of paying its debts so as to avoid winding up proceedings.

Section 201 makes provision for the court to sanction a proposed compromise or arrangement between a company and its members and/or creditors.

In *Re Savoy Hotel Ltd*,[1] the court made it clear that it would not approve a proposed arrangement unless it was supported by the company itself.

In *Re National Farmers Union (NFU) Development Trust*,[2] over 85 per cent of the members voted in favour of a scheme in which their rights were surrendered without compensation. The court held that the scheme was neither a compromise nor an arrangement, because both these processes required a measure of 'give and take' from both sides.

A compromise is, essentially, an agreement between two sides, where each gives way a little to settle a dispute. A compromise can only be reached when the parties had previously been in dispute. An arrangement does not require the existence of a prior dispute. In fact, s 201(7) defines an 'arrangement' as including a reorganisation of the share capital of the company by the consolidation of shares of different classes or by the division of shares into shares of different classes or by both those methods.

---

1   [1981] 3 All ER 646.
2   [1973] 1 All ER 135.

Who may apply to the court?

39.3   The company itself, or any creditor[1] or member of the company may apply to the court to sanction a proposed arrangement under s 201. However, creditors or members may need, at least, the approval of the company if they wish to apply to the court on their own – see *NFU Development Trust* case (in **39.2**).

The applicant(s) will submit a document to the court detailing the terms of the scheme, and enclosing a copy of the explanatory statement to be issued to members and creditors before the appropriate meeting(s) (see **39.4** below). On receipt of this application, the court may, on such terms as seems just, stay all proceedings against the company for as long as it thinks fit.

When the application is successful, the court will order the holding of meetings between the interested parties to discuss the proposed scheme of arrangement.

The statutory meetings

39.4   Section 201(1) stipulates that the court may:

> 'order a meeting of the creditors or class of creditors, or of the members of the company or class of members, as the case may be, to be summoned in such manner as the court directs.'

In fact, the court will not approve[2] a scheme, unless proper class meetings have been held.

Class meetings

39.5   All unsecured creditors will generally form a single class unless some of them are to be treated differently from the rest. In such circumstances, separate class meetings will have to be held.

In *Pye (Ireland) Ltd*,[3] a substantial unsecured creditor was also a substantial shareholder. Because there was not a separate class meeting held for unsecured creditors who were also shareholders, the court refused to sanction the scheme.

Information for members and creditors

39.6   Every notice summoning the relevant meeting(s) which is sent to a creditor or member, must also include a statement[4] explaining the effect of the arrangement; in particular, stating any material interests of the directors of the company, whether as directors or as members or as creditors of the company or otherwise, and the effect on them of the compromise.

---

1 Or liquidator when the company is being wound up.
2 *Re Hellenic & General Trust Ltd* [1975] 3 All ER 382.
3 (Unreported) 11 March 1985 (HC).
4 Section 202(1)(b) and (3) also provide for the disclosure and notification of certain information in advertisements.

This statement must also disclose whether the directors are being treated differently to other persons holding similar interests.

Where the proposed compromise affects the rights of debenture-holders of a company, the statement must give the same explanation in relation to the trustees of any deed for securing the issue of the debentures as it is required to give in relation to the company's directors.[1]

Approval of members and creditors

39.7 After the holding of the required meetings and class meetings, the scheme will need to obtain the support of interested parties before being sent to the court for its approval.

The scheme must be approved by:

(1) a majority in number of those voting at each meeting of:
   (a) creditors; or
   (b) class of creditors; or
   (c) members; or
   (d) class of members; and
(2) who represent 75 per cent in value of the relevant shares or amounts owed.

When these approvals have been obtained, a further application is made to the court for its approval of the scheme.

COURT SANCTION OF SCHEME

39.8 The detailed scheme and the responses of the interested parties will be considered by the court. Even if a class of members does not vote in favour, the court may still sanction the scheme if it is satisfied that one class, eg ordinary shareholders, has no interest whatever in the remaining company assets.[2]

Once the court sanctions the arrangement, it then becomes binding on all interested parties. However, as Murnaghan J stated in *Re John Power & Son Ltd*:[3]

> 'the sanction to be given by the court must be a real sanction ... no majority ... can carry an arrangement which a fair and impartial mind would not sanction.'

Objections by minorities

39.9 While the scheme is being considered, s 203(1)(e) empowers the court to make provision for dissenting minorities.

---

1 Section 202(2).
2 As happened in *Tea Corporation Ltd; Sorsbie v Tea Corporation Ltd* [1904] 1 Ch 12 (CA).
3 [1934] IR 412.

AMALGAMATIONS

39.10   An amalgamation is where two or more companies join together to form a single new company.

Section 203 also makes it clear that the court can, if necessary, also approve a scheme for the reconstruction or amalgamation of any two or more companies whilst considering a proposal under s 201. In this event, the court order may provide for any of the following:

(1) the transfer to a new 'transferee' company of the whole or any part of the undertaking and of the property or liabilities of any 'transferor' company;
(2) the allotting or appropriation by the transferee company of any shares, debentures, or other like interests in that company[1];
(3) the continuation by or against the transferee company of any legal proceedings pending, by or against any transferor company;
(4) the dissolution, without winding up, of any transferor company;
(5) such incidental, consequential and supplemental matters as are necessary to secure that the reconstruction or amalgamation will be fully and effectively carried out.

Registration of the court order

39.11   The approval of the court for either a scheme of arrangement or amalgamation will not take effect until an office copy of its order has been delivered to the registrar of companies.

A copy of the court order must also be attached to every copy of the memorandum of association issued after the order was made.

USES FOR SCHEMES OF ARRANGEMENT

39.12   A scheme of arrangement is a useful instrument for making changes to the rights of members and creditors in the light of a company's financial difficulties. For example, it has been used to vary the rights attached to debentures and preference shares, and to reconstruct the capital of a company. However, the court will not permit the s 201 procedure to be used to circumvent the safeguards for minority interests available generally,[2] where there is a reduction of capital or a variation of class rights.

The usefulness of s 201 schemes of arrangement has diminished as a result of the examinership procedures detailed in Chapters 37 and 38.

---

1 Which under the arrangement are to be allotted or appropriated by the transferee company 'to or for any person' – see s 203(1)(b).
2 See Chapter 13.

Reconstructions

39.13   A reconstruction of a company takes place when it restructures its finances by transferring its assets to a new company. The s 201 procedure can also be used[1] to facilitate reconstruction and amalgamation of companies.

Where the scheme provides for the transfer of company assets to a new company, with little other change, this process is often referred to as 'reconstruction'. For example, in addition to effecting compromises or arrangements with creditors and members,[2] ss 201 and 203 will permit the transferring of their rights to another transferee company which then issues shares or takes over liabilities in return for the cancellation of existing rights against the first company. Section 260 provides for reconstruction, where the first company is already in voluntary liquidation (see **39.15** below).

Amalgamations

39.14   Sections 201 and 203 can also be used to amalgamate two companies as an alternative to a takeover under s 204.[3] In *Re Hellenic & General Trust Ltd,*[4] the court would not permit a scheme of arrangement to circumvent provisions similar to those in s 204, which were designed to protect dissenting members from having their shares compulsorily acquired.

RECONSTRUCTIONS UNDER SECTION 260

39.15   Section 260 of the 1963 Act gives the liquidator, in a members' voluntary winding up situation, the power to sell the 'whole or part of' the business or property of a company, and to accept shares in the transferee company, as consideration for that sale. In fact, s 260(1) stipulates that the liquidator may enter into:

> 'any other arrangement whereby the members of the transferor company may, in lieu of receiving cash, shares, policies or other like interests, or in addition thereto, participate in the profits of or receive any other benefit from the transferee company.'

Procedure

39.16   Under s 260, if a company is being, or is proposed to be, wound up voluntarily, and its property intended to be transferred or sold to another company, the liquidator of the first company (the transferor company) may, with the sanction of a *special resolution* of that company, receive in compensation

---

1   Under s 203.
2   By changing their rights in or against the company.
3   In this event, the Mergers, Takeovers and Monopolies (Control) Act 1978 may also apply – see s 14 and Chapter 40.
4   [1975] 3 All ER 382.

for the transfer or sale, 'shares, policies or other like interests in the transferee company, for distribution among the members of the transferor company'.

Any sale or arrangement under s 260(1) will be binding on the members of the transferor company.[1]

Effect of winding-up order

39.17   If an order is made within a year for the winding up of the company by the court, the special resolution becomes invalid unless sanctioned by the court.[2] This allows for the protection of creditors who might otherwise be prejudiced by the reconstruction.

Dissenting members' rights

39.18   If any member who did not vote for the special resolution expresses his dissent in writing, addressed to the liquidator, and leaves it at the registered office of the company within seven days after the passing of the special resolution, he may require the liquidator either:

(1) to abstain from carrying the resolution into effect; or
(2) to purchase his interest, 'at a price to be determined by agreement or by arbitration'.[3]

The arbitration procedure is that laid down in the Companies Clauses Consolidation Act 1845.[4]

If the liquidator elects to purchase the dissenting member's interest, the purchase money must be paid before the company is dissolved.[5]

A company cannot, by provisions in either its memorandum or articles of association, deprive dissenting shareholders of these rights.

SECTION 260 AND A CREDITORS' VOLUNTARY WINDING UP

39.19   In a members' voluntary winding up, the company is in a position to pay all its creditors in full. This is not the position, however, in a creditors' voluntary winding up. Because of this, s 271 stipulates that the liquidator cannot proceed with a s 260 reconstruction unless he also obtains the sanction of either the court or the creditors.[6]

---

1 Section 260(2).
2 Section 260(5).
3 Section 260(3).
4 Section 260(6).
5 Section 260(4).
6 Through their representatives on the committee of inspection – see s 268.

AMALGAMATIONS GENERALLY

39.20   An amalgamation results in the joining together of two (or more) companies to form a single new company. As illustrated above, an amalgamation may be carried out under ss 201 to 203, as a scheme of arrangement with creditors, or under s 260 in the course of a voluntary liquidation.

A takeover or merger may also result in an amalgamation. However, in these cases, the reason for the takeover may have nothing to do with the creditors of the company. Takeovers often take place because the bidding company sees a company of profit-making potential and wishes to acquire a controlling interest in it. As takeovers and mergers are, essentially, changes of company ownership and control, rather than arrangements with company creditors, we shall deal with them separately in Chapter 40.

Chapter 40

COMPANY TAKEOVERS AND MERGERS

INTRODUCTION

40.1 The term 'takeover' is usually used to describe a bid to purchase the majority or all of the shares in a 'target' company by another company.

If the bid is not contested, the transaction will be described as a merger. This would happen, for example, where a private company with few controlling shareholders 'agrees' to the proposed takeover. However, a takeover bid may be contested where one public company seeks to take over a second public company with a multiplicity of shareholders.

TAKEOVER PROCEDURE

40.2 Generally, the bidding company will offer to purchase all the shares in the target company either for cash or in exchange for its own shares. This offer will be conditional on acceptance by a stated percentage of the shareholders. When that percentage acceptance level has been reached, the offer becomes unconditional and binding on the acquiring company.

POWER TO COMPULSORILY ACQUIRE SHARES OF MINORITY

40.3 In some instances, a minority of shareholders in the target company may not wish to sell their shares. This could be problematic for a bidding company which wants to acquire a wholly owned subsidiary. In these circumstances, s 204 of the 1963 Act, gives the bidding company the power to acquire shares of dissenting members, when the bid has been accepted by a majority of 80 per cent.

If, within four months, the offer of the bidding company is accepted by holders of not less than 80 per cent in value of the shares affected,[1] the bidding company may buy the shares of any dissenting member by giving him two months' notice after the end of the four-month period.

If the bidding company wishes to compulsorily acquire shares, under s 204(1), it must offer the dissenting minority the same terms as the majority have already accepted.[2]

---

1 Excluding those already held by the bidding company at the date of the offer – see s 204(2).
2 See *Re Carlton Holdings* [1971] 2 All ER 1082, [1971] 1 WLR 918.

Rights of dissentient members

40.4 Once a member has received notice from the bidding company that it wishes to compulsorily purchase his shares, he has the right to apply to the court, within one month, seeking an order disallowing the purchase.

Section 204(1) gives the court power to disallow the compulsory purchase if it thinks fit to do so. Generally, once the takeover bid is fair and the procedural requirements of s 204 have been followed, the court will be reluctant to grant relief[1] to the dissenting shareholder. In *Securities Trust Ltd v Associated Properties Ltd*,[2] it was suggested that the dissenting members should also have been given particulars of the takeover, including the method of carrying it out and its consequences.

Onus of proof

40.5 The burden of showing that the compulsory purchase of the dissentients' shares is unfair, lies on the applicant.[3] In *Re Sussex Brick Co*,[4] Vaisey J stated that it was difficult to 'predicate unfairness' where the good faith of the transferee company is not challenged, and there is no case of intentional misleading of the offeree shareholders. The fact that an applicant may be able to demonstrate that the takeover scheme is open to criticism or is capable of improvement, is not enough to discharge the onus of proof which lies on the applicant.[5]

In *Re Grierson, Oldham and Adams Ltd*,[6] the court held that the test of the fairness of an offer is not whether it is fair to the individual shareholder, but whether it is fair to the body of shareholders as a whole. In that case, where holders of 99 per cent of the shares had approved the scheme and the price was slightly above market value, it was held that there was no unfairness.

The market price of the shares on the Stock Exchange is cogent, but not conclusive, proof of the true value of shares.[7]

Proving unfairness

40.6 Generally, the dissenting shareholders must establish affirmatively that, notwithstanding the view of the majority, the scheme is unfair. Thus, the onus is on an applicant to adduce evidence showing the takeover scheme to be patently and obviously unfair. This was done in the case of *Re Bugle Press Ltd*.[8]

---

1 *McCormick v Cameo Investments Ltd* [1978] 1 ILRM 191 (HC).
2 (Unreported) 19 November 1980 (HC).
3 *Re Hoare & Co Ltd* (1933) 150 LT 374.
4 [1961] 1 All ER 772.
5 Ibid.
6 [1967] 1 All ER 192.
7 Ibid.
8 [1960] 3 All ER 791 (CA).

In this case, a company had three shareholders. Two of these shareholders (A and B) each held 45 per cent of the shares: the third (C) 10 per cent. A and B formed a new company. This company then made an offer for the shares of the old company. A and B accepted the takeover bid. The new company then served notice[1] on C, who had dissented.

C opposed the compulsory purchase of his shares on the ground that it was an expropriation of his interest because the two shareholders of the new company were the persons who held 90 per cent of the shares in the old company. The Court of Appeal accepted C's evidence and held that the bidding company could not compulsorily acquire his shares, Harman J stating:

> 'In my judgment this is a barefaced attempt to evade that fundamental rule of company law which forbids the majority of shareholders, unless the articles so provide, to expropriate a minority. It would be all too simple if all one had to do was to form a £2 company and sell to it one's shares and then force the outsider to comply. If the point had been taken earlier, I, for one, should have been prepared to hold that this case never came within s 209 at all. Indeed, no serious attempt to comply with the section has ever been made here. ...
>
> [The applicant proves his case] ... quite simply by showing that the transferee company is nothing but a little hut built round his two co-shareholders and that the so-called scheme was made by themselves as directors of the company with themselves as shareholders and the whole thing, therefore, is seen to be a hollow sham. It is then for the company to show that nevertheless there is some good reason why the scheme should be allowed to go on. The company, whether because they do not wish to go into the witness-box and be cross examined or for some other reason, do not file any evidence at all ... There is in my judgment no case to answer. The applicant has only to shout and the walls of this Jericho fall flat. I am surprised that it was thought that so elementary a device would receive the court's approval ...'

Dissentients' opportunity to sell

40.7   Section 204(4) gives the dissentients an opportunity to sell their shares to the bidding company, even where that company does not wish to exercise its powers of compulsory purchase under s 204(1).

This offer to buy under s 204(4) must be on the same terms as the remaining 80 per cent were acquired.

LEGAL CONTROLS OVER PROFITEERING

40.8   Takeovers and mergers present an opportunity for directors and shareholders to make sizeable profits. Accordingly, there are a number of controls in place to prevent conflict of interest situations arising and secret

---

1   Under s 209 of the Companies Act 1948, the UK equivalent of s 204.

profits being earned. These controls[1] include ss 187 and 188 of the 1963 Act which deal with compensation for loss of office by directors following a transfer of the company's shares, undertaking or property.

Compensation for loss of office on mergers etc

40.9   Section 187 of the 1963 Act makes it necessary for directors to obtain the approval of the company in general meeting, for any payments of compensation to them for loss of office on the merger, takeover or amalgamation of the company.

Where a director receives such compensation without approval of the general meeting, he holds the amount received in trust for the company.

Section 188 contains provisions imposing a duty on directors to disclose payments to be made to them in connection with the transfer of shares, where the transfer involves an offer being made to the general body of shareholders. Where a director is in breach of s 188, he will be subject to a fine of £125. Any amounts received by him will be deemed as being held in trust for persons who sold their shares as a result of the offer.

The City Code on Takeovers and Mergers

40.10   As mentioned in **40.1** above, it is the prior agreement of the parties to an amalgamation of companies that distinguishes the process of merger from that of takeover. Mergers are usually the result of an agreed takeover bid, perhaps with the directors being involved in negotiations on behalf of the members.

In a takeover, there are likely to be unrepresented dissenting shareholders who may need protection.

In the case of a take over bid for shares of public companies listed on the Stock Exchange, the City Code on Takeovers and Mergers applied. This non-statutory code of practice operated amongst investment banks and intermediaries.

The main purpose of the Code[2] was to ensure that, in a takeover bid, all shareholders were treated in the same way. Information given to them had to be adequate, accurate and made available to all shareholders concerned.

---

1 The fiduciary duties of directors are also relevant – see Chapter 19. So, too, are the statutory rules on insider dealing detailed in Chapter 21. The statutory restrictions which prohibit a company from giving financial assistance for the purchase of its own shares could also prevent a company assisting a 'friendly' third party to out-bid the bidding companies. These restrictions are dealt with in Chapter 13.

2 Which consists of General Principles, Detailed Rules and Practice Notes in the form of specific rulings.

The operation of the Code was supervised by a panel, who could give rulings on disputed issues which arose in the course of takeover bids.

The City Code and s 204

40.11   The Code generally supplemented the statutory takeover rules in s 204 until the Irish Takeover Panel began exercising its functions on 1 July 1997.

THE IRISH TAKEOVER PANEL

40.12   The Irish Takeover Panel Act 1997 provides for the appointment of a Takeover Panel to monitor and supervise takeovers and certain other transactions in relation to securities, mainly in public companies quoted on the Irish Stock Exchange.

The designation of a Takeover Panel has two main objectives:

(1) to protect shareholders in situations where takeovers or other relevant transactions (eg substantial acquisitioning of shares) are contemplated and/or put into effect; and
(2) to provide support and credibility for the Irish financial market following the separation of the Irish Stock Exchange from London.

The Irish Panel published its takeover rules just prior to assuming its regulatory functions.

Whilst the 'voluntary' self-regulatory regime administered by the London Panel only applied to Irish listed companies, the statutory based rules of the Irish Panel will also apply to Irish companies quoted on the Exploration Securities or the Developing Companies Markets.[1]

'Takeover' is defined as an agreement or transaction whereby control of a company is, or may be, acquired. 'Control' means the holding, directly or indirectly, of securities of a company, which confers not less than 30 per cent of the voting rights in that company.

40.13   Under the 1997 Act,[2] the Panel has a general power to make appropriate rules. In particular, the Act obliges the Panel to make rules on the following three issues:

(1) the requirement that a person or persons acting in concert who acquire control of a company make a 'mandatory offer' for the remaining securities of the company. The rule made by the Panel for this purpose is similar to the City Code's mandatory offer rule;
(2) the interaction between the rules and the requirements of the mergers legislation (see **40.23** below); and

---

1 See **10.17**.
2 See N. Hyland, 'The Irish Takeover Panel Act 1997', *Bar Review*, Vol 2, Issue 9, July 1997, p 408.

(3) the speed with which a person or persons acting in concert may make a 'substantial acquisition of securities' below the control threshold. The rules made by the Panel for this purpose follow the form of the London rules.

Generally, as expected, the Irish Panel's General Principles and Rules on Takeovers are broadly similar to the London City Code which they replaced.

Rulings and directions

40.14   The Irish Panel has the power, of its own accord or at the request of an interested person, to make a ruling as to whether any activity or proposed activity complies with the general principles and the rules. To ensure that the general principles and the rules are complied with, the Panel also has an extensive power to give a direction to any party to a takeover to do or refrain from doing any act.

If the Panel believes that a ruling or direction made by it has not been complied with, it may apply to the High Court for an order enforcing the ruling or direction.

Appeals

40.15   An appeal against a rule, ruling or direction of the Irish Panel is normally only by way of an application to the High Court for a judicial review.

In addition to the investor protection granted by the General Principles and Rules of the Irish Takeover Panel, shareholders in certain companies may be further protected by the European Communities (Mergers and Divisions of Companies) Regulations 1987.

THE EUROPEAN COMMUNITIES (MERGERS AND DIVISIONS OF COMPANIES) REGULATIONS 1987

40.16   These Regulations, SI 1987/137, implement the Third[1] and Sixth[2] EU Company Law Directives. They apply only to plcs and to some unregistered companies.

The Regulations define mergers and divisions. Both involve the transfer of the assets and liabilities of plcs (transferor companies) to other public companies (acquiring companies), or, in some cases, to companies formed specifically for the purpose of the merger or division.

---

1 Directive 78/855/EEC.
2 Directive 82/891/EEC.

The transfer of the assets and liabilities of the transferor company must be in exchange for shares in the acquiring company, with or without additional cash payment.

Procedure

40.17 Generally, the directors of the companies involved must draw up draft terms of the merger or division. These must be approved by a special resolution passed at a general meeting or class meetings of each company.

The court has the power to make an order for the protection of the interests of dissenting shareholders.

The Regulations also provide for the directors to draw up written explanatory reports, and for companies to appoint an independent person to examine the draft terms indicating, inter alia, whether or not the proposed merger or division is fair and reasonable.

Liability of directors and independent persons

40.18 The directors and independent persons may incur personal liability[1] for any losses suffered by shareholders as a result of untrue statements in the draft terms, or any reports prepared by them. They may also be liable for losses caused by misconduct in the preparation for, or implementation of, the transactions involved.

Confirmation by the court

40.19 When all the shareholders involved have given their approval, application must be made to the court by all companies involved, for an order confirming the draft terms.

Creditors have a right to object to the making of a court order confirming the draft terms. On hearing them, the court may dispose of the consent of creditors on condition that the company pays their debts. The court may also order the acquiring company to purchase the shares of dissenting shareholders at a price fixed by the court.

If the transaction is caught by the Mergers, Takeovers and Monopolies (Control) Act 1978, the court may delay the making of its order 'until the Minister's intention is clear' (see **40.24** below).

Copy to registrar

40.20 A copy of the confirmation order must be delivered to the registrar and notice of such delivery published in *Iris Oifigiúil* within 14 days.

---

1 They may also be subjected to criminal sanctions.

The European Communities (Safeguarding of Employees' Rights on Transfer of Undertakings) Regulations 1980

40.21 These 1980 Regulations[1] implement the EU's Acquired Rights Directive[2] and transfer automatically to the transferee company any obligations to employees arising under collective agreements entered into by the transferor company.

Controlling the economic impact of mergers and takeovers

40.22 In the Irish Independent Business Supplement of 10 July 1997, a strategic merger was mentioned between United Drug and Dublin Drug. On page 12 it was reported:

> 'The board have agreed a share swap which values Dublin Drug at £15·1 million, but the acquisition is conditional on acceptance by at least 80% of Dublin Drug shareholders *and* regulatory clearance under the Merger Act and Competition Act.' (author's emphasis)

This newspaper report illustrates clearly that mergers are not simply a matter for the respective shareholders and company law; aspects of competition law have to be considered as well.

The State has an interest in ensuring that takeovers or mergers do not result in monopoly conditions prevailing within a market, thereby harming the consumer by reducing competition. The Mergers, Takeovers and Monopolies (Control) Act 1978[3] gives the government powers to act to prevent such a situation arising.

The Mergers, Takeovers and Monopolies (Control) Act 1978 (the 1978 Act)

40.23 The 1978 Act enables the Minister to prohibit, or to permit subject to conditions, certain takeovers and mergers which would impede competition.

A merger is defined in s 1(3)(a) as arising where 'two or more enterprises, at least one of which carries on business in the State, come under common control'. Common control means one enterprise obtaining the right to appoint or remove a majority of the board of the other; or acquiring a substantial part of the assets of the other so as to result in the buyer being in a position to substantially replace the vendor in the business in which the latter was engaged immediately before the acquisition. Common control can also exist after the acquisition of a substantial bloc (about 25 per cent) of voting shares.

---

1 SI 1980/306.
2 77/187/EEC of 14 February 1977.
3 As amended by the Restrictive Practices (Amendment) Act 1987.

The 1978 Act, generally, only applies to mergers and takeovers where the turnover of the two enterprises exceeds £20 million.[1] However, if the Minister considers the public interest warrants it, he may declare that the Act is to apply to a particular merger or takeover which does not reach the statutory minimum turnover[2] threshold.

Procedure

40.24 Every takeover or merger is deferred until the Minister has had the time to consider whether or not he should make an order prohibiting it on grounds of being anti-competitive.

A circular is available from the Department setting out the relevant information which has to be submitted to the Minister.

The initial notification to the Minister must be made within one month of there having been a viable offer, which if accepted, would bring the enterprises under common control.[3] As a result, the ownership of the assets involved in a takeover or merger will not be transferred until:

(1) the Minister has confirmed that he will not be making a prohibition order; or
(2) the Minister has made a conditional order; or
(3) three months have elapsed from the date of notification of all the information required by the Minister. If, however, within the first month, the Minister requires further information, the three months will not start to run until the Minister receives that information.

Section 14 of the Competition Act 1991 empowers the Minister, where he is of the opinion that there is an abuse of a dominant position,[4] to request the Competition Authority to carry out an investigation on his behalf. The Minister will then consider the findings of the Authority's report, before making his decision.

The Competition Act 1991

40.25 Section 4(1) of the Competition Act 1991 is modelled on art 85 of the Treaty of Rome. It defines a number of prohibited anti-competitive agreements which have as their object the prevention or distortion of competition or trade within the State.

---

1 This threshold does not apply to newspapers because of the Mergers, Takeovers and Monopolies (Control) Act (Newspapers) Order 1979, SI 1979/17.
2 Or assets. The gross assets threshold for the two (or more) enterprises involved is £10 million. These thresholds are regularly revised upwards.
3 See T. O'Connor 'Notifying the Irish Regulatory Authorities of a Merger or Takeover' *Commercial Law Practitioner,* June 1994, pp 156–158.
4 As defined in s 5 of the Competition Act 1991.

Section 4(1) prohibits and declares void any of the anti-competitive agreements indicated in it. As mentioned in **40.29** below, s 4 has been deemed to embrace agreements for a merger or takeover, with or without restrictive covenants or 'non-compete' clauses.

Section 4(2) established the Competition Authority (CA) with a view to monitoring such agreements. With effect from 23 June 1997, the CA is located at Parnell House, 14 Parnell Street, Dublin 1, telephone 01–804–5400.

The CA has the power to grant a licence in the case of any agreement or category of agreement. Before granting a licence, the CA may invite any Minister concerned with the matter to offer such observations as he may wish to make.

Powers of the Competition Authority

40.26 The CA may confirm that an agreement is not, in its opinion, a prohibited one. This statement would be classified as a *certificate*. The CA may also state that even though the agreement submitted offends s 4(1), it approves of it on grounds of the resulting benefits. This type of statement is styled a *licence*.

A licence may have conditions attached and be for a limited period of time. Effectively, a licence legalises a prohibited agreement under s 4(1).

Sanctions available to aggrieved persons

40.27 Section 6 of the 1991 Act gives any person who is 'aggrieved' as a result of an agreement prohibited by s 4(1), the right to institute legal proceedings for damages (including exemplary damages) and other judicial remedies against any undertaking which is a party to such an agreement.

Defences

40.28 If a CA certificate is in place, an aggrieved person, whilst entitled to initiate legal proceedings, will not be awarded damages.

When a CA licence has been issued, an aggrieved person is debarred from mounting a legal challenge to the terms of the agreement.

The 1978 and 1991 Acts

40.29 In the *Woodchester* case,[1] the CA stated that, in its view, a merger was not automatically outside the scope of the Competition Act[2] by virtue of its having

---

1 Competition Authority Decision No 6 of 4 August 1992.
2 For further information, see T. O'Connor *Competition Law Source Book* (Round Hall Sweet & Maxwell, 1996), vols 1 and 2.

been approved by the Minister under the Mergers, Takeovers and Monopolies (Control) Act 1978.

The CA, however, indicated that unless the market following the merger was likely to be fairly concentrated, it would not regard the merger as offending s 4(1) of the Competition Act. Even where the market was to be concentrated, the CA considered that it would not deem a merger offensive in the absence of barriers to entry by new firms, or if there was a significant level of competition from imports. Some of these indicators from the CA appeared in draft quasi legislative form during 1997 (see **40.30** below).

The first merger to be found offensive by the CA[1] under s 4 of the Competition Act, was the proposed acquisition of the entire share capital of Cooley Distillery by Irish Distillers Group plc. This case further highlighted the question as to whether proposed mergers needed to be notified to both the Minister under the 1978 Act and the CA under the 1991 Act. There appears to be an overlap between these Acts which may involve parallel notifications[2] of mergers. This overlapping situation may be eased somewhat by the CA granting notification exemptions for categories of acquisitions which do not contravene the 1991 Act. Guidelines in connection with such exemptions are being issued under the Competition (Amendment) Act 1996.

The Competition (Amendment) Act 1996[3]

40.30 Under the Competition (Amendment) Act 1996, the CA is empowered to issue notification exemption certificates for *categories of agreements* which, in its opinion, do not contravene the law. These will be known as 'category certificates' and will constitute a form of 'negative block clearances'.

During May 1997, the CA published a draft list of conditions which companies must meet if they require an automatic approval for a merger[4] agreement. Generally, under these proposed conditions, following a merger the combined market share of the four largest companies in the market should be less than 40 per cent, unless there are no significant barriers on entry to that market, or there is a reasonable prospect of future competition from imports.

The CA also proposes accepting the practice of including a 'non-compete' provision in merger and buy out agreements. For example, in the case of a standard business, the seller can be restrained from competing for a maximum of two years. This period of restraint can be extended up to five years in the event of the business involving significant and secret technical knowledge.

---

1 See Decision No 285 of 25 February 1994.

2 See P. Massey and P. O'Hare *Competition Law and Policy in Ireland* (Oak Tree Press, 1996), Chapter 10.

3 This Act extended the Competition Act 1991 and the Mergers, Takeovers and Monopolies (Control) Act 1978 (as amended).

4 Or buy out. A 'buy out' is the expression used to indicate the purchase of a controlling interest in a company.

In order to qualify for a 'category certificate', a non-compete agreement must also be confined to the geographical area within which the business operates.

Abuse of a dominant position

40.31   Section 5 of the Competition Act 1991 (by analogy with art 86 of the Treaty of Rome) prohibits any abuse by an undertaking of a dominant position. The acquisition of one competitor by another may lead to an abuse of a dominant position.

INTRA-EU AND INTERNATIONAL TRADING

40.32   If a takeover or merger in any Member State could result in an anti-competitive situation arising within the EU, as a trading area, rather than in Ireland alone, the EU Commission (or any interested party) could take action under art 86 of the Treaty of Rome to prevent this 'abuse of a dominant position'.

In the *Continental Can* case,[1] the European Court of Justice held that mergers came within the provisions of art 86 of the Rome Treaty. However, at an EU level, arts 85 and 86 have been superseded by special legislation dealing with multi-State mergers. This legislation is the EU Merger Control Regulation[2] which came into force on 21 September 1990. It applied only to mergers where the aggregate world wide turnover of all the parties involved exceeded 5,000 million ECUs, and the aggregate Community-wide turnover of each of at least two of the undertakings involved exceeded 250 million ECUs. These thresholds were reduced to 2,500 million and 100 million ECUs respectively by EC Regulation No 1310/97,[3] thus reinforcing merger control at EU level.

The EU Merger Control Regulation excludes the jurisdiction of (national) Irish law for any merger coming within its scope. Thus, the specially created Merger Task Force in DG IV of the Commission has exclusive jurisdiction for large intra-EU mergers.

On 15 December 1996, Boeing and McDonnell Douglas Airlines announced their intention to merge into the world's largest aircraft manufacturer in a transaction valued at over $14 billion (£9.5 billion). This transaction placed Boeing, already with 60 per cent of the market, well ahead of its main rival in commercial aircraft manufacture, Europe's Airbus Industrie consortium, which had, at the time, a 20 per cent share of this strategically important aerospace industry.

---

1 *Europemballage and Continental Can Co v EC Commission* [1973] ECR 215.

2 4064/89. It is based on arts 87 and 235 of the Treaty of Rome. Article 235 allows the Council 'to take action ... where ... necessary to attain the objectives of the Treaty, including the maintenance of effective competition in the Common Market.'

3 Amending Regulation No 4064/89 on Control of Concentrations between Undertakings published in OJ No L 180 of 9 July 1997, p 1.

In May 1997, after a five-month investigation of the proposed transaction, the European Commission's Competition Commissioner, Karel Van Miert, objected forcefully to the merger. In a strongly worded, 40-page 'statement of objections', the Commissioner highlighted his concern at Boeing's inevitable stranglehold on the global market for new passenger planes which would seriously undermine the position and viability of Europe's manufacturer, Airbus Industrie. The Commissioner reminded Boeing that if the EU found the deal anti-competitive it could, under EU competition law, fine Boeing 10 per cent of its turnover and fine any European companies doing business with the US group.

At the end of July, after a summer of intense negotiations involving the US Federal Trade Commission and US Vice-President, Al Gore, EU Commissioner Van Miert announced that a deal had been struck with Boeing permitting the EU Commission to agree in principle to the merger thus averting a potentially disastrous EU–US trade war. Under this deal, Boeing agreed to abandon its 20-year single supplier contracts with three big US Airlines – American, Continental and Delta – signed in the wake of the December merger and pledged not to sign any new exclusive accords for 10 years. On Wall Street, Boeing and McDonnell Douglas stock rose strongly on the news from Brussels and was continuing to do so at the time of writing.[1]

During June 1997, the Commission began an investigation into the proposed merger between Guinness plc and Grand Metropolitan plc. The US authorities also decided to launch an investigation into this planned 'mega' merger.

Both European and US competition authorities were particularly interested in ascertaining whether the merged company,[2] GMG Brands, would enjoy a dominant position on their whiskey markets.

A proposal by the USA relating to the extra-territorial application of their anti-trust legislation in the EU was being considered by the EU Commission during 1997.

---

1 See *The Irish Times*, 16 December 1996, 23 May and 24 July 1997.

2 Under the proposed merger, Guinness shareholders retain their shares in Guinness (to be renamed GMG Brands), and Grand Metropolitan shareholders receive one new GMG Brands ordinary share for each Grand Metropolitan share. A capital repayment to shareholders was also proposed.

Chapter 41

INITIATION OF WINDING-UP PROCEDURE BY CREDITORS, MEMBERS AND OTHERS

LIMITED LIABILITY COMPANIES

41.1   Limited liability companies are legal entities created under the law by following a registration procedure. The 'lives' of such companies can also be brought to an end by the occurrence of certain events or procedures leading to their dissolution.

METHODS OF DISSOLUTION

41.2   A company which is defunct may be struck off the Companies Register for:

(1) failure to carry on business;[1] or
(2) failure to submit accounts.[2]

The registrar initiates these actions and will publish details in *Iris Oifigiúil.*

A company which is transferring assets to another company under a scheme for reconstruction or amalgamation may, under s 203(1)(a), be dissolved without winding up, if the court so orders.

The most common procedure for dissolving a company is to wind it up or liquidate it. Three months after registration of the liquidators' final return,[3] the liquidated company will be dissolved.

Until a company is dissolved, it continues its existence as a corporate entity.

METHODS OF WINDING UP

41.3   There are two methods of winding up. These are compulsory winding up by the court and voluntary winding up. A voluntary winding up may be initiated either by investors or by creditors of the company.

---

1 Section 311 of the 1963 Act. This process may be reversible, though. See K. Mooney 'Restoring Companies to the Register' *Bar Review*, Vol 2, Issue 6, April 1997, pp 266–268.
2 Section 12 of the 1982 Act.
3 See ss 263 and 273 of the 1963 Act.

Winding up by the court

41.4 The Companies Acts give the court certain powers to intervene in the running of a company, and to order that it should be wound up in certain circumstances.

Grounds for compulsory winding up

41.5 The court may order the winding up of a company in the following circumstances, set out in s 213:[1]

(1) if the company has, by special resolution, resolved that it be wound up by the court. In *Re Galway and Salthill Tramway Co,*[2] it was held that the directors of a company cannot present a winding up petition in the name of the company without the authority of a general meeting. It is the company, and not the directors, who must resolve that it be wound up by the court.

The members can, in general meeting, however, ratify the directors' actions:

(2) where a newly formed company does not commence its business within a year from incorporation, or a company suspends its business activities for a whole year;

(3) where the number of investors is reduced below the statutory minimum of two for private[3] and seven for public companies.

The circumstances set out in (1) to (3) above can be classified as *procedural* grounds for winding up a company. Section 213(e) to (g) contains the following *substantive* grounds for winding up:

(4) if the company is *unable to pay its debts*;

(5) if the court is of the opinion that it is *just and equitable* that the company should be wound up; and

(6) if the court is satisfied that the *company's affairs are being conducted in a manner oppressive* to any member or his interests.

Inability to pay its debts

41.6 Section 214[4] explains the circumstances in which a company will be deemed to be unable to pays its debts. There are three situations envisaged:

(1) if a creditor is owed a sum exceeding £1,000 by the company, and has served on the company, by leaving it at the registered office of the company, a demand in writing requiring the company to pay the sum due, and the company has for three weeks thereafter neglected to pay the sum or to secure or compound for it to the reasonable satisfaction of the creditor.

---

1 Of the 1963 Act.
2 [1918] 1 IR 62 (HC).
3 Other than single-member companies.
4 As amended by s 123 of the 1990 Act.

In *Re Shannon Transport Systems Ltd*,[1] the High Court held that a petition to wind up a company on grounds of inability to pay its debts may be dismissed if the court decides that a genuine dispute is in existence between the parties as to the amount owed. Again, in *Re Pageboy Couriers Ltd*,[2] the court dismissed a petitioner's claim to wind up the company, because his claim (for £5,000 director's fees) had at all times been disputed by the company on substantial grounds.

Keane J considered the factors which a court should consider in deciding whether or not to refuse a petition to wind up the company in *Truck and Machinery Sales Ltd v Marubeni Kumatsu Ltd*.[3] His view was that even if the debt was disputed on substantial grounds by the company, if the latter is insolvent, the court may refuse to restrain the petition to wind it up, thereby protecting the interests of the legitimate creditors.

If the company is insolvent and no genuine dispute over the debt exists, the court is likely to grant the petition. As Costello J stated in *Re Dubned Exports Ltd*:[4]

'I have come to the conclusion that the dispute ... is not a bona fide one and that Dubned Exports Ltd is now insolvent. It would be wrong, in these circumstances, not to grant the petitioner the relief ... to which he is entitled.'

Opposition by the company's creditors to the winding up will be considered by the court but will not be the deciding factor. In *Re Irish Tourist Promotions Ltd*,[5] the company was wound up despite the creditors' objections. However, Costello J granted a petition to wind up the company in *Re Bula Ltd*,[6] saying:

'the petitioner's prima facie right to an order has not been displaced in any of the evidence. I take into account the fact that the majority of creditors in value and in number, favour this course to be adopted ...'

(2) where a creditor obtains a judgment or court order against the company in satisfaction of a debt, but is unable to obtain payment from the company because of its lack of assets; or

(3) if the creditor proves to the satisfaction of the court that the company is unable to pay its debts. The creditor may be able to do this by proving that:

    (a) the company is not able to pay its debts as they fall due. This is known as the 'commercial insolvency' test; or

    (b) the company's assets are less than its liabilities – the 'balance sheet' test.

---

1 (Unreported) 3 February 1975 (HC).

2 [1983] ILRM 510.

3 (Unreported) 23 February 1996 (HC). See article by MacCann 'Restraining a petition to wind up a company' *Bar Review*, Vol 1, Issue 2, August 1996, pp 6 and 9.

4 (Unreported) 9 May 1986 (HC).

5 (Unreported) 22 April 1974 (HC). As regards the position of creditors in subsidiary companies, see *Re Southard & Co* [1979] 1 WLR 1198.

6 (Unreported) 18 July 1986 (HC).

In utilising both these tests, the company's contingent and prospective liabilities must be taken into account.

Just and equitable grounds

41.7   Winding up for just and equitable reasons is treated as a separate ground for granting a petition under s 213(f). The court will not make the order winding up the company, unless there is a special reason for so doing.

Examples of instances where the court has granted petitions on just and equitable grounds include:

(1) where the substratum (or main objects) of the company are gone, eg inability to obtain a patent which it was the main object of the company to work.[1] However, if there are two or more main objects, inability to achieve one of them does not necessarily justify winding up the company;[2]

(2) where there is deadlock, ie perpetual disagreement, between two members, each of whom controls 50 per cent of the company's voting power.[3] The court's reasoning here transposes the mutual trust and confidence necessary for the working of a partnership to the working of a small private company. Under the Partnership Act 1890, the court has the power to dissolve a partnership if the partners are deadlocked.

In *Re Irish Tourist Promotions Ltd*,[4] there was deadlock in the management of the company. Notwithstanding, the creditors believed that they had a better chance of being paid if the company was not wound up. Despite the creditors' wishes, Kenny J ordered the winding up of the company because its management was deadlocked.

(3) where the circumstances disclose some underlying obligation in good faith and confidence that the petitioner should participate in the management of the company as long as it continues in business.[5]

In *Re Murph's Restaurant Ltd*,[6] one director was effectively excluded from participation in management of the company by two other directors who were brothers. The court held this was grounds for winding up under s 213. It would not make an order under s 205 because of the fundamental breakdown in the relationship;

(4) misapplication of company funds, eg where the directors withhold information from the shareholders in circumstances giving rise to suspicion.

---

1   *Re German Date Coffee Co* (1882) 20 Ch D 169.
2   *Re Kitson & Co Ltd* [1946] 1 All ER 435.
3   *Re Yenidje Tobacco Co Ltd* [1916] 2 Ch 426.
4   (Unreported) 22 April 1974 (HC).
5   See *Ebrahimi v Westbourne Galleries Ltd* [1973] AC 360.
6   [1979] ILRM 141.

In *Re Newbridge Sanitary Laundry Ltd*,[1] the managing director, who was a large shareholder, refused to account for monies received by him for the company. Two shareholders presented a petition to wind up the company.

Sir Ignatius O'Brien LC stated that the 'just and equitable' ground was to be viewed as a completely separate heading in the context of the substantive grounds set out in (the equivalent of) s 213. He then ordered that the company be wound up, despite the ratification of the managing director's actions by the members in general meeting;

(5) where the objects of the company are essentially illegal[2] or fraudulent.[3] However, the whole object of the company must be fraudulent: mere fraud in carrying on aspects of the company's business will not, of itself, justify a winding up;[4]

(6) where the business is being carried on for the benefit of the debenture-holders only.[5]

Oppression of a member

41.8 Section 213(g) provides that a company may be wound up by the court if it is satisfied that the company's affairs are being conducted, or the powers of the directors are being exercised, in a manner oppressive to any member or in disregard of his interests as a member and that, despite the existence of an alternative remedy, winding up would be justified in the general circumstances of the case.

The court may, however, dismiss a petition to wind up under s 213(g) if it is of the opinion that proceedings under s 205 would be more appropriate. Section 205 gives the court a wide range of remedies.[6]

Who may petition the court to wind up the company?

41.9 Section 215 provides that an application to the court for the compulsory winding up of the company may be initiated either by:

(1) any creditor;
(2) any contributory;[7]
(3) in the case of oppression, any person entitled to apply for an order under s 205. This will generally be members; and
(4) the company itself.

---

1 [1917] 1 IR 237.
2 *R v Registrar of Joint Stock Companies ex p More* [1931] 2 KB 197 – a case involving the sale of tickets for the Irish Hospital Sweepstake.
3 *Re T.E. Brinsmead & Sons* [1897] 1 Ch 45.
4 *Re Medical Battery Co* [1894] 1 Ch 444.
5 *Re Chic Ltd* [1905] 2 Ch 345.
6 See **16.9**.
7 Ie any person liable to contribute to the assets of the company in the event of it being wound up – see **42.21**.

A company will rarely present a petition itself. The majority of petitions to wind up a company compulsorily will be presented by the creditors.

Any creditor seeking to wind up the company must provide security for the costs of the petition and also satisfy the court that there is a prima facie case for winding up.

Petitions by contributories, by the Minister and by members

41.10 Section 215(a), (d) and (e) sets out the restricted circumstances in which contributories, the Minister and members may petition the court to wind up the company.

Effect of winding-up order

41.11 Irrespective of who initiates a winding-up petition, once an order is made to wind up a company, s 223 makes it clear that it will operate in favour of all creditors and all contributories, as if made on their joint petition.

Effects of application to wind up

41.12 Any creditor or contributory (or the company itself) may apply to the court under s 217 to stop or restrain legal proceedings against the company whilst the petition is being considered by the court. The court may admit such a stay in legal proceedings on such terms and for such time as it thinks fit.

Any transfer of shares or disposition of company property after the commencement of the winding up, will be void under s 218, unless validated by the court. As the purpose of s 218 is to ensure, as far as possible, that the insolvent company's assets are all available for distribution amongst its creditors, the court will exercise the power of making a validation order sparingly. Generally, it will only do so in favour of persons dealing with the company in good faith and without notice, and when the transaction benefits the general body of creditors.[1]

Commencement of winding up by the court

41.13 A winding up by the court will be deemed to have commenced at the time of the presentation of the petition for winding up, unless a resolution has previously been passed for a voluntary winding up. In this event, the winding up will have commenced at the time of the passing of the resolution.[2]

There were 29 compulsory liquidations by order of the court in 1995, and eight in 1996.

---

1 See *In re John Daly & Co Ltd* (1887–88) 19 LR Ir 83 and *Re Ashmark Ltd (No 2)* (unreported) 8 December 1989 (HC). In the latter case, the court clarified that the disposition of a cheque only takes place when it is honoured: the writing of the cheque is not a disposition.
2 Section 220.

Members' voluntary winding up

41.14 Section 251 sets out the circumstances in which the members can initiate the voluntary winding up of the company.

Circumstances in which company may be wound up voluntarily

41.15 A company may be wound up voluntarily:

(1) when the period, if any, fixed for the duration of the company, has expired or an event which the articles prescribes for the dissolution of the company has happened and the resolution[1] has been passed at a general meeting that the company be wound up voluntarily; or

(2) if the company has passed a special resolution that it be wound up voluntarily; or

(3) if the company resolves in general meeting that it cannot, by reason of its liabilities, continue in business and that it be wound up voluntarily.

Publication of resolution

41.16 When a company resolves to be wound up, it must give notice, within 14 days, in *Iris Oifigiúil.*[2]

Commencement of winding up

41.17 A voluntary winding up is deemed to commence at the time of the passing of the resolution.[3]

Consequences of voluntary winding up

41.18 From the commencement of a voluntary liquidation, the company ceases to carry on business but the corporate state and corporate powers of the company continue until it is dissolved. In certain circumstances where it would be beneficial to the winding up, the company may continue in business. Any alteration in the status of members or transfer of shares must, from the commencement of the winding up, be authorised by the liquidator.[4]

Statutory declaration of solvency

41.19 Where it is proposed to wind up a company voluntarily, the directors of the company, or a majority of them, must make a statutory declaration to the effect that they have enquired in full into the affairs of the company and have formed the opinion that the company will be able to pay its debts in full within a period not exceeding 12 months from the commencement of the winding up. This declaration must be made within 28 days immediately preceding the date of the resolution for winding up and be delivered to the registrar of companies

---

1 This may be an ordinary resolution unless the articles prescribe otherwise.
2 Section 252.
3 Section 253.
4 Sections 254 and 255.

by the date of the passing of the resolution. It must embody a statement of the company's assets and liabilities at the last practical date[1] before the making of the declaration.

Independent verification

41.20   Section 256 was amended by s 128 of the 1990 Act to make provision for independent verification of the directors' declaration. Section 256(3) and (4) stipulates that verification must be by a person 'qualified at the time of the report to be appointed, or to continue to be, auditor of the company.' The independent auditor's report will have to confirm that the directors' opinion on solvency is a reasonable one.

Objections by creditors

41.21   If, within 28 days of the passing of the resolution for winding up being advertised in *Iris Oifigiúil*, a creditor applies to the court and the court is satisfied that the creditor, together with any creditors supporting him, represents one-fifth at least in number or value of the creditors of the company, and the court is of the opinion that the company is unlikely to be able to pay its debts within the specified period, then it may order that the provisions of the Act relating to a creditors' voluntary winding up[2] shall apply instead of the provisions relating to a members' voluntary winding up. If such an order is given by the court, then the company must, within 28 days, deliver a copy of the order to the registrar of companies. If no objections are made by creditors, then the liquidation will be known as 'a members' voluntary winding up' and the provisions of the Act in relation to a members' voluntary winding up shall apply.[3]

Liability of directors for declaration of solvency

41.22   Where, despite the directors' statutory declaration of solvency, the company is subsequently unable to pay its debts, the directors will be liable. Section 256(8) and (9) gives the liquidator, or any creditor or contributory of the company, the right to apply to the court. The court may then declare that a director who was a party to the declaration, without having reasonable grounds for his opinion, shall be personally liable without limitation for the debts of the company.

Appointment of liquidator

41.23   The members control the appointment of the liquidator in a members' voluntary winding up. The role of a liquidator appointed by the members is detailed in Chapter 43.

---

1 Which must, in any event, be not more than three months.
2 See Chapter 44.
3 Sections 257 to 264 – see Chapter 43.

There were 254 members' liquidations in 1995, and 258 during 1996.

Creditors' voluntary winding up

41.24 If no declaration of solvency is made, or if the creditors object successfully to a declaration of solvency, a voluntary liquidation will proceed as a creditors', rather than a members' winding up. Again, if during a members' voluntary winding up, the liquidator is of the opinion that the company will be unable to pay its debts, the winding up will convert to a creditors' liquidation.[1]

Initiation of a creditors' voluntary winding up

41.25 To initiate a creditors' voluntary winding up, the directors must convene a general meeting of members and pass a resolution to wind up the company.

Under s 266 of the 1963 Act, the company must call a meeting of creditors on the day that the resolution to wind up is passed, or on the following day. The notice of the meeting must be advertised in at least two daily newspapers circulating in the district where the registered office or principal place of business of the company is situated. Notice of the meeting must have been sent to creditors at least 10 days before the date of the meeting. A statement of affairs and a list of creditors' with the estimated amounts due to them, must be laid before the meeting of creditors by the directors. One director must preside over the meeting.

Appointment of liquidator

41.26 At both the company members' meetings and creditors' meeting mentioned above (see **41.25**), a person may be nominated as liquidator. If both meetings nominate a different person, then the person nominated at the creditors' meeting will be the liquidator. If no one is nominated at the creditors' meeting, the person nominated at the company meeting will be the liquidator. Where different people are nominated at both meetings and any director, member or creditor wishes, he may apply to the court for an order that the person nominated as liquidator by the company be made liquidator, instead of, or jointly with, the person nominated by the creditors.[2]

The role of the liquidator in a creditors' voluntary winding up is outlined in Chapter 44.

There were 494 creditors' voluntary liquidations carried out in 1995, and 552 during 1996.

---

1 Section 261 – see Chapter 43.
2 Or, indeed, that some person, other than the creditors' nominee, be appointed liquidator – s 267(2).

Chapter 42

THE OFFICIAL LIQUIDATOR'S ROLE

WINDING-UP ORDERS

42.1 The overwhelming majority of compulsory winding-up orders are initiated by creditors.

Once the winding-up order has been made by the court, a copy must be sent[1] immediately to the registrar of companies for registration.

CONDUCTING THE WINDING-UP PROCEEDINGS

42.2 The court appoints a liquidator[2] to conduct the proceedings of the winding-up. In fact, the court may appoint a provisional[3] liquidator at any time after the presentation of a winding-up petition and before the appointment of the official liquidator.

Actions stayed

42.3 Once the winding-up order has been made, or a provisional liquidator appointed, all actions or legal proceedings against the company can only proceed with the leave of the court.[4]

The statement of affairs

42.4 Within 21 days of the making of the winding-up order or appointment of a provisional liquidator,[5] a statement of affairs must[6] be submitted by the company to the liquidator giving particulars of:

(1) the assets;
(2) the debts and liabilities;
(3) the names, residences and occupations of the creditors;
(4) the securities held by the respective creditors;
(5) the dates on which the various securities were given;

---

1 By the company – see s 221.
2 Or liquidators.
3 Whose powers may be restricted or limited by the court – see s 226(2).
4 Section 222.
5 Or within such extended period as the court may permit – s 224(3).
6 Unless the court thinks fit to order otherwise – s 224(1).

(6) such other information as may be prescribed by the court.

The statement of affairs must be filed and verified[1] by one or more directors and by the secretary or by any of the following persons whom the court may require:

(1) any officer or past officer of the company;
(2) anyone who has taken part in the formation of the company within a year before the date of the winding-up order;
(3) anyone employed by the company within the past year who is, in the opinion of the court, capable of giving the information required;
(4) anyone employed within the past year as an officer in another company which itself was an officer[2] of the main company.

Any person who is a creditor or contributory of the company may, at all reasonable times, inspect the statement of affairs and take a copy or extract therefrom.

Appointment of official liquidator

42.5 Section 300 of the 1963 Act disqualifies any body corporate from appointment as liquidator to a company. Nor can a disqualified director under s 160 of the 1990 Act be appointed a liquidator. Statutory reforms were also enacted during 1990 to ensure the impartiality of individuals appointed to be liquidators.

Impartiality

42.6 Section 146 of the 1990 Act inserted a new s 300A in the 1963 Act. Section 300A disqualifies the following 'connected' persons from being eligible for appointment as liquidator. Connected persons include:

(1) a person who is, or who has been within 12 months of the commencement of the winding up, an officer or servant (including auditor) of the company;
(2) except with the leave of the court, a parent, spouse, brother, sister or child of an officer of the company;
(3) a person who is a partner or in the employment of an officer or servant of the company;
(4) a person who is similarly connected with any other body corporate which is that company's subsidiary or holding company or a subsidiary of that company's holding company.

Again, s 301 makes it a criminal offence to bribe any member or creditor of the company to secure an appointment as its liquidator. Furthermore, under s 301A, any creditor (or other person) who has a connection with the proposed

---

1 By affidavit.
2 Acting through its own directors and officers and influencing the management of the main company.

liquidator, must disclose it to the meeting before voting on a resolution to appoint a liquidator.

Subject to the statutory disqualification and disclosure requirements relating to liquidators, the court may make any order it thinks fit to give effect to the wishes of the creditors and contributories on the appointment of a liquidator.

Publicity

42.7   Within 21 days after his appointment, the liquidator must publish notice of it in *Iris Oifigiúil.* He must also deliver a copy of the court order appointing him, to the registrar of companies.[1]

Section 303 of the 1963 Act also provides that every invoice, order for goods or business letter issued by or on behalf of the company, must contain a statement that it is being wound up. Section 303 applies to voluntary as well as compulsory liquidations.

Title

42.8   The liquidator should be described by the title of, for example, 'Official Liquidator of Delta Ltd', rather than by his personal name.

Terms of appointment

42.9   The court may determine whether the liquidator should give any security on his appointment. His remuneration will be fixed by the court.

Any acts done by the liquidator will be valid even if it is discovered afterwards that there was some defect in his appointment.

Position

42.10   The liquidator is appointed to act as an agent of the company. However, as Kenny J stated in *Re Belfast Empire Theatre of Varieties Ltd:*[2]

> 'While a liquidator may be a trustee for the company ... he is not ... a trustee in any sense of the word for its members and creditors. The true position is that he is an agent with fiduciary obligations arising from his office and with statutory duties imposed on him [by the Companies Acts 1963–90]. If the company has not been dissolved he may be ordered to pay damages or compensation [under s 298] and if the company has been dissolved he may be sued for breach of these statutory duties.'

Resignation and removal of liquidator

42.11   Section 228(c) provides that a liquidator appointed by the court may resign or, on cause shown, be removed by the court.

---

1 Section 227.
2 [1963] IR 41 (HC).

When the court makes an order to pool the assets of related companies which are being wound up compulsorily (see **42.35** below) it may, under s 141(3) of the 1990 Act, remove any liquidator of any of the companies and appoint any person to act as liquidator of any one or more of the companies.

Any vacancy which occurs in the office of liquidator will be filled by the court.

Procedures to be followed by liquidators

42.12   Section 312 of the 1963 Act extends the rule making authority of the courts to apply to the winding up of companies, whether compulsorily or voluntarily. Accordingly, a number of Rules of the Supreme Court apply to the liquidation procedure, the most important of which are the 1986 Rules, SI 1986/115.

Under these Rules, the liquidator must lodge all monies received by him into a special account within seven days from their receipt. Failure to do this will render him liable to pay compensation.

The Rules also provide for the signing of cheques, and the selling of company property by the liquidator. They also set out procedures for summoning meetings of creditors and contributories.

Procedure for calling meetings

42.13   Where the court so directs, the liquidator must summon a meeting of creditors or separate meetings of creditors and contributories, for the purpose of deciding whether a committee of inspection should be appointed to act with the liquidator and, if so, who is to be appointed to that committee. Where the creditors and contributories cannot agree on this question, the court may decide the matter as it thinks fit.

Committees of inspection

42.14   If the decision is taken to appoint a committee of inspection under the Act, it will be composed of creditors in such proportions as directed by all of the creditors and contributories and, in the event of disagreement, as determined by the court. This committee will meet at the times set out by it, and any member of the committee or the liquidator may call a meeting at any time.

The committee will act on a decision of the majority of the members present provided there is a majority of the full committee at the meeting. Any member of the committee may resign by giving signed notice in writing to the liquidator. If a member becomes bankrupt or absents himself from five consecutive meetings, his place becomes vacant. Also, a member may be removed by an ordinary resolution at a meeting of creditors if he represents creditors, or contributories if he represents contributories, of which seven days' notice has been given.

On a vacancy occurring, the liquidator will call a meeting of the creditors or contributories to appoint, by resolution, a person to fill the vacancy.[1]

Powers of the liquidator

42.15   The statutory powers of a liquidator are contained in s 231[2] of the 1963 Act. Basically, the liquidator's powers are divided into the categories of those exercisable without the approval of the court or the committee of inspection, and those exercisable with prior court or committee approval.

Without prior approval

42.16   Without the prior sanction of the court or the committee of inspection, the liquidator has power:

(1)   to sell real and personal property by public auction or by private contract. However, the liquidator cannot sell by private contract a non-cash asset worth at least £1,000[3] to an officer of the company, unless he has given at least 14 days' notice of his intention to all creditors of the company;[4]

(2)   to do all acts and execute deeds, receipts, etc, and use the seal of the company where necessary;

(3)   to prove for calls when a contributory has been adjudged bankrupt;

(4)   to draw, endorse and accept bills of exchange;

(5)   to raise money on the security of the assets of the company;

(6)   to give security for costs in any proceedings commenced by the company;

(7)   to appoint an agent to do any business which the liquidator is unable to do himself; and

(8)   to do all such things as are necessary for the winding up of the company and distributing the assets.

With prior approval

42.17   With the sanction of the court or the committee of inspection, the liquidator has the power:

(1)   to bring or defend any action or proceeding on behalf of the company;

(2)   to carry on the business so far as may be necessary for the beneficial winding-up of the company;

(3)   to appoint a solicitor to assist him;

(4)   to pay any classes of creditors in full;

(5)   to make any compromise or arrangement with creditors;

(6)   to compromise all calls and liabilities to calls and debts and liabilities between the company and contributories (see **42.20** below).

---

1   Section 233.
2   As amended by s 124 of the 1990 Act.
3   See s 29(2) of the 1990 Act.
4   See s 124 of the 1990 Act and s 231(2)(a) of the 1963 Act.

Duties of the liquidator

42.18 The principal duty of the liquidator is to collect or get in the company property and pay its debts. His specific tasks include the following:

(1) to take the property of the company into his custody;
(2) to settle the list of contributories;
(3) to admit or reject proof of debts;
(4) to realise the company assets;
(5) to pay the debts of the company in the order prescribed by ss 284 and 285;
(6) to distribute the surplus (if any) amongst the contributories;
(7) to co-operate with the court in ensuring that irregularities he uncovers in the conduct of the company's affairs are brought to the attention of the appropriate authorities.

We shall now consider these specific tasks in more detail.

Duty to take company's property into his custody

42.19 Section 229 makes it incumbent upon the liquidator, when appointed, to take into his custody or control all the 'property and things in action to which the company is, or appears to be, entitled'.

If, at any stage, there is no liquidator, the property will be deemed to be in the custody of the court.

In order that the liquidator may bring or defend, in his official name, any action or proceedings relating to the company's property, the court may, on the application of the liquidator, direct that all or any of the property be vested in his name.[1]

Thus, although the company property does not automatically vest in the liquidator on his appointment, the court may make an order vesting all or any of the company's property in him.

Duty to settle list of contributories

42.20 One of the first duties of a liquidator is to settle the list of contributories. However, where it appears to the court that it will not be necessary to make calls on or adjust the rights of contributories, the court may dispense with the settlement of a list of contributories. Subject to this, the court shall, 'as soon as may be after a winding-up order', settle a list of contributories.

In settling the list of contributories, the court will distinguish between persons who are contributories in their own right and persons who are contributories as being representatives of or liable for the debts of others.

---

1 Section 230.

Meaning of contributory

42.21   The term 'contributory' means every person[1] who is liable to contribute to the assets of the company in the event of it being wound up. The main categories of contributory are likely to be present and past members.

Present members' liability

42.22   A present member is liable as a contributory up to:

(1) the amount (if any) *unpaid on his shares* in the case of a limited liability company;
(2) the amount undertaken to be contributed by him to the assets of the company in the case of a company *limited by guarantee*, plus any sums unpaid on shares held by him;
(3) the full amount needed to pay off the debts and liabilities of the company in the case of an unlimited company.

Past members' liability

42.23   A past member is liable on a similar basis to a present member where:

(1) it appears to the court that existing members are unable to make the payments required of them; and
(2) they ceased to be members within 12 months before the commencement of winding up; and
(3) the debts and liabilities were contracted while the past members were members.

Lists of contributories[2]

42.24   There are, generally, two lists of contributories. Present members are put on the 'A' list, whilst past members are placed on the 'B' list.

Rectification

42.25   Any person who has been wrongly placed on the list of contributories may apply to the court to rectify the list.

Liability of contributories

42.26   A contributory's liability does not cease on his death; it passes to his personal representatives.

---

1 See ss 208 to 211 of the 1963 Act.
2 The rules on contributories outlined in this chapter apply, generally, to both compulsory and voluntary winding-up procedures.

Directors as contributories

42.27 Where the liability of a company's directors has been made unlimited under the provisions of ss 197 and 198 of the 1963 Act, then, in addition to his liability to contribute as an ordinary member, a director may be liable to make a further contribution if:

(1) he has been a director within one year of the commencement of the winding up;

(2) the debts and liabilities were incurred before he ceased to be a director; and

(3) the court deems it necessary that he contribute in order to satisfy the debts and liabilities of the company.[1]

Duty to admit or reject proof of debts

42.28 Debts which must be proved by creditors include 'all debts payable on a contingency, and all claims against the company, present or future, certain or contingent, ascertained or sounding in damages'.[2]

The Act requires a just estimate to be made, so far as possible, of the value of debts which do not bear a certain value.

Bankruptcy rules and set off

42.29 Section 284 applies the same rules as bankruptcy to a winding-up situation with regard to:

(1) the respective rights of secured and unsecured creditors;

(2) debts provable; and

(3) the valuation of annuities and future and contingent liabilities.

The application of the bankruptcy rules also means that set off provisions also apply in a winding up. 'Set off' means the use of a debt owed by a creditor to the company to reduce a debt owed to him by the company.

Where there have been mutual dealings between a creditor and the company, the debt due from one can be set off against the debt due from the other, and the creditor need only prove for the balance.

Time-limits

42.30 Debts which are 'stale' and statute barred[3] under the Statute of Limitations 1957 will be rejected by the liquidator.

---

1 Section 207(2).

2 Section 283(1).

3 See also s 283(2) regarding dividends declared more than six years previously.

Procedure for ascertaining creditors

42.31   The court will direct the publishing of an advertisement fixing a time within which the creditors are to furnish the liquidator with particulars of their claims.[1]

The liquidator then decides which debts are allowable without further evidence, and which require to be proved.

The Rules of the Supreme Court provide a procedure for adjudicating on disputes concerning these 'provable' debts. Under this procedure, the decision of the court examiner (usually a court registrar or the Master of the High Court) will put the liquidator in a position of being able to assess the total amount owing by the company to all creditors.

Duty to realise the company assets

42.32   The primary task of the liquidator is to 'liquidate' the assets of the company and use them to pay the proved debts of its creditors.

In realising the company assets, the liquidator will be assisted by the court. For example, the court has the power to order contributories (and others) to pay their debts to the company[2] by lodging money into a bank to the account of the liquidator.

When the liquidator suspects that a director is likely to remove company assets from the State, or to dissipate those assets, he can apply to the court for a *Mareva* injunction to prevent him from doing so. The court may also order the director to disclose the location of assets which are the subject of a *Mareva* injunction.

Maximising company assets

42.33   It could be argued that the liquidator also has a duty to maximise the company's assets. He is given statutory assistance in doing this by provisions relating to him obtaining contributions from:

(1)   directors and others under their personal liability for:
    (a)   failure to keep proper books of account;[3]
    (b)   fraudulent and reckless trading;[4]
    (c)   misfeasance or other breach of duty or trust in relation to the company;[5] and
(2)   related companies.

---

1   Section 241 gives the court the power to exclude creditors not proving in time.
2   See ss 237 to 243. Other court powers include those of summoning persons for examination, compelling attendance of officers at meetings, and ordering the costs of winding up to be paid out of assets – ss 244 to 249.
3   See Chapters 20 to 23.
4   Ibid.
5   See s 298, as amended by s 142 of the 1990 Act. Directors of subsidiary companies may also be liable under s 148 of the 1990 Act.

Related companies

42.34   Section 140 of the 1990 Act empowers the liquidator or any creditor or contributory of any company that is being wound up, to apply to the court for an order that:

> 'any company that is or has been related to the company being wound up shall pay to the liquidator ... an amount equivalent to the whole or ... any of the debts provable in that winding-up.'

This is, potentially, one of the most significant provisions in the 1990 Act. On receipt of an application under it, the court may, if satisfied that it is just and equitable to do so, order the related company to pay the liquidator an amount equivalent to the whole or part of the liabilities of the company being wound up.

Section 140(2) sets out the criteria to be used by the court in deciding whether it is just and equitable to make an order. These tests are:

(1)   the extent to which the related company took part in the management of the company being wound up;
(2)   the conduct of the related company towards the creditors of the company being wound up;
(3)   the effects such an order would be likely to have on the creditors of the related company concerned.

It is not sufficient for the person seeking the order simply to prove that the companies are related or that the creditors of the company being wound up have relied on the fact that the other company is or has been related to the first-mentioned company. There must be clear evidence that the circumstances that gave rise to the winding-up are attributable to the actions or omissions of the related company.

For the purpose of the Act, a company is related on a number of tests including the normal subsidiary/holding company tests and tests which could apply to a consortium joint venture or common ownership relationship. In addition, a test in relation to the manner in which the separate businesses of the company are or are not identifiable can also be applied.[1] A company can be related if there is another company to which it and the company being wound up are related.

Pooling of assets of related companies

42.35   Section 141 of the 1990 Act provides for the pooling of the assets of related companies where both are being wound up. On the application of the liquidator of any of the companies, the court may make an order, on just and equitable grounds, that the companies be wound up together as if they were one company.

---

1 See s 140(5)(a) to (f).

The criteria used by the court in deciding whether or not to make such an order include:

(1) the extent to which the circumstances that gave rise to the winding-up of any of the companies are attributable to the actions or omissions of any of the other companies; and

(2) the extent to which the businesses of the companies have been intermingled.[1]

In deciding the terms and conditions of an order under s 141, the court will have particular regard to the interests of those persons who are members of some, but not all, of the related companies.

Minimising the company's liabilities

42.36 In addition to increasing the number of sources from which a liquidator can seek contributories to boost the company's assets, he is also given statutory assistance in minimising the company's liabilities in respect of 'antecedent and other transactions'.[2] For example, certain floating charges may be automatically rendered void, transactions which fraudulently prefer one creditor to another may be avoided, and onerous property or unprofitable contracts may be 'disclaimed'. Any transfer of company assets after the commencement of the winding-up may also be rendered void by the court (see **41.12**).

Avoidance of floating charges

42.37 Under s 288 of the 1963 Act, as amended by s 136 of the 1990 Act, certain floating charges created within the 12 months prior to the commencement of the winding-up shall be invalid unless it is proved that the company was solvent immediately after the charge was created.

The onus is on the holder of the charge to prove that the company was solvent at the time. As Kenny J stated in *Re Creation Printing Co Ltd; Crowley v Northern Bank Finance Corporation Ltd*:[3]

> 'When a floating charge . . . is created and the company is ordered, or resolves, to be wound up within 12 months afterwards, the burden of establishing that the company was solvent at the date of the debenture rests on the debenture holder. The charge is invalid unless something is proved. Therefore, the proving of the conditions which exempt the charge from invalidity rests on the holder of the charge.'

If the company was not solvent, the floating charge may still be valid to the extent of any money advanced or paid or the actual price or value of goods (or services) sold to the company in consideration for the charge (interest may also

1 See s 141(3) to (6).
2 See ss 286 to 292 of the 1963 Act.
3 [1981] IR 353 (SC).

be payable at the annual rate of five per cent). However, to be valid, such a transaction must take place at the time of, or subsequently to the creation of the charge. In *Re Daniel Murphy Ltd*,[1] Kenny J cited, with approval, the principle that any cash paid to a company 'at the time of the creation of the charge' cannot mean on the stroke of the clock or even within the same 24 hours. It is not a question of the clock; it is a question of what are the circumstances of each particular case and what is the real substance of the transaction. Judges are not prepared to 'strain' the words of a provision like this to invalidate bona fide transactions carried out honestly in accordance with the usual course of business.

Floating charges and connected persons

42.38   Where a floating charge has been granted in favour of a connected person, the period for invalidity is extended to two years. Generally, the term 'connected person' includes directors, shadow directors, directors' spouses and family members, related companies, etc.[2]

Floating charges and officers

42.39   Section 289 renders certain floating charges in favour of an officer invalid unless the company was solvent immediately after the charge was created, if the company is wound up within 12 months of the transaction.

Fraudulent preferences

42.40   Under s 286 of the 1963 Act, as amended by s 135 of the 1990 Act, any act disposing of company property or assets within six months of its winding-up will be deemed a 'fraudulent preference' and, thus, invalid. The six months period is extended to two years where the transaction is in favour of a 'connected' person. The onus of proof is on a connected person to prove that the preference was not fraudulent. In other cases, the onus of proof is on the liquidator. To discharge this burden of proof, the liquidator will have to prove that the transaction had, as its dominant intention, the giving of a preference to one creditor over other creditors. The liquidator failed to discharge this burden of proof in *Corran Construction Co Ltd v Bank of Ireland Finance Ltd*,[3] but succeeded in *Kelleher v Continental Irish Meat Ltd*,[4] where there were irregularities surrounding the formalities of the transaction.

In two cases, the liquidator was able to have transactions held as invalid by the court where the directors intended to prefer themselves over other creditors of the company.[5]

---

1 [1964] IR 1 (HC).
2 See s 288(4).
3 (Unreported) 8 September 1976 (HC).
4 (Unreported) 9 May 1978 (HC).
5 *Re Welding Plant Ltd* (unreported) 27 June and 25 July 1984 (HC) and *Re Station Motors Ltd* (unreported) 22 November 1984 (HC).

Disclaimer of onerous property and contracts

42.41   Section 290 of the 1963 Act empowers the liquidator to disclaim, with leave of the court, any property burdened with onerous covenants, unprofitable contracts or shares in companies. This power enables a liquidator to take effective action in stopping the financial haemorrhaging of the company's assets as a result of its existing contractual obligations. In these circumstances, the liquidator would be under a duty to act to minimise the company's liabilities.

Getting in the company's assets

42.42   Clearly, in getting in the company's assets, the liquidator must not only collect outstanding monies owed to the company by its creditors and contributories, he must also maximise the pool of assets by seeking other sources of funds from directors, related companies, etc. He must also minimise the company's liabilities by disclaiming onerous or unprofitable company contracts and avoiding any fraudulent preferences and certain floating charges.

Once the company's assets have been collected, the next task of the liquidator is to pay the company's creditors.

Duty to pay the company's debts

42.43   Whether the debts of the company can be paid in full or not, obviously depends on whether the company was solvent on winding up.

Where the company is solvent

42.44   The liquidator's duty in this situation is to pay all creditors' debts in full, and then distribute the surplus assets amongst the contributories/members in accordance with their rights.

Where the company is insolvent

42.45   Where there are insufficient assets available to the liquidator to pay all creditors, his duty is to pay secured creditors with fixed charges first, then apply the remaining assets to pay other creditors in the order laid down by s 285.

Secured creditors with fixed charges

42.46   In Chapter 32, the various types of charges or security were explained.

A secured creditor with a fixed charge has several courses of action available to him. He may realise his security and prove for the balance (if any) of his debt. He may also surrender his security and prove for the whole amount or value and retain his security and prove for the balance.

Costs of the liquidation

42.47   The liquidator must retain a sum to meet the costs of the liquidation,[1] before paying any of the remaining debts. Section 244 gives the court the power to order the costs of winding up to be paid out of company assets, where the company is insolvent.

Section 281 provides that in a voluntary liquidation, all costs, charges and expenses properly incurred in the winding up, including the remuneration of the liquidator, shall be payable out of the assets of the company in priority to all other claims.

However, if the liquidator initiates legal proceedings against the former directors or controllers of the company, and fails in them, the costs of the successful defendant(s) may take priority even over the liquidator's own legal costs and remuneration in the liquidation: the Supreme Court deciding[2] that where an action is brought by a company after liquidation, the costs of the successful defendant (whether they fall within s 281 or s 285 of the 1963 Act) rank in priority to all other claims.

Section 285 ranking of debts

42.48   After the costs of the liquidation have been paid or provided for, the liquidator must pay the debts of the company in the following order:

(1) preferred creditors;
(2) floating chargees;
(3) unsecured creditors;
(4) members and contributories of the company.

Preferential creditors

42.49   The creditors whose claims are preferred under s 285(2)[3] include claims for:

(1) 12 months' rates levied by local authorities;
(2) 12 months' income and corporation tax levied by the Revenue Commissioners;
(3) four months' wages and salaries of employees, subject to a maximum of £2,500;[4]
(4) accrued holiday pay owed to employees;
(5) 12 months' social welfare contributions;
(6) compensation and damages for uninsured accidents to employees;[5]
(7) sickness or pensions payments due to employees;

---

1 Which would include his own remuneration.
2 In *Comhlucht Páipéar Riomhaireachta Teo v Udarás Na Gaeltachta* [1990] 1 IR 320.
3 As amended.
4 See s 285(3), (4) and (5).
5 A director was held to be an employee in *Re Dairy Lee Ltd* [1976] IR 314.

(8) redundancy payments, claims for minimum notice and for unfair dismissal.[1]

42.50 Section 285(14) provides that the priority accorded to these preferential debts will only apply if they have been notified to the liquidator or become known to him within six months after the advertisements inviting claims have been published in at least two local daily newspapers. In *In the Matter of H. Williams (Tallaght) Ltd (in Receivership and Liquidation)*,[2] Geoghegan J stated that s 285(14) could not be extended to include constructive knowledge. What was required was actual notification or actual knowledge by the liquidator. The court had no implied power to extend the time limit imposed by statute.

If these preferred debts have been notified to him in time and cannot be paid in full, the liquidator will pay them pari passu. All preferential creditors rank equally amongst themselves – s 285(7)(a).

Floating chargees

42.51 Although floating chargees are secured creditors, their rights have been ranked below those of preferential creditors by s 285(7)(b). Accordingly, it is only if the liquidator still has funds after paying all the preferential creditors in full, that he will be able to make payments to the floating chargees.

Where there are insufficient assets to pay all the floating chargees, their priority will be based on the date of creation of their charges – the earliest created floating chargees being paid first.

Unsecured creditors

42.52 It is only if there are funds remaining after paying the floating chargees in full that the claims of unsecured creditors will be met.

Unsecured creditors' claims rank pari passu amongst themselves.

In an insolvent liquidation, the unsecured creditors are very vulnerable and unlikely to be paid their debts.

Members and contributories of the company

42.53 In a solvent liquidation, any surplus remaining after paying all the company's creditors must be distributed amongst the members according to their rights and interests.[3]

---

1 Under the Redundancy Payments Acts 1967–1979, the Minimum Notice and Terms of Employment Act 1973 and the Unfair Dismissals Act 1977, respectively.
2 [1997] *Irish Times Law Reports*, 27 January.
3 Section 275 of the 1963 Act.

In a compulsory winding up, it is the court which would adjust the rights of members amongst themselves and order the distribution of the surplus amongst them.[1] However, this task would be undertaken by the liquidator himself in a members'[2] or creditors'[3] voluntary winding up.

Duty to co-operate with the court and the relevant authorities

42.54 Section 299 of the 1963 Act provides for the prosecution of criminal offences committed by officers and members of a company.

In a winding up by the court, the court may direct the liquidator to refer possible offences to the Director of Public Prosecutions (DPP). In doing so, the liquidator is under a duty to give the DPP all the information and assistance he deems necessary.

In a voluntary winding up, the onus is on the liquidator himself to report any possible criminal offences to the Attorney-General (A-G). Again, he must co-operate fully with the Attorney-General in prosecuting these offences. If the liquidator fails to report an irregularity to the Attorney-General, the court may direct him to do so on the application of any person interested in the winding up.[4]

TERMINATION OF LIQUIDATION AND DISSOLUTION OF THE COMPANY

42.55 When the liquidator has completely wound up the affairs of the company, he applies to the court, who will make an order that the company be dissolved.[5]

An office copy of the court order must be sent to the registrar within 21 days.

---

1 Section 242.
2 See Chapter 43.
3 See Chapter 44.
4 See s 299(3) to (5).
5 Section 249(1).

Chapter 43

MEMBERS' VOLUNTARY LIQUIDATION PROCEDURES

MEMBERS' VOLUNTARY WINDING UP

43.1 A members' voluntary winding up is not hostile to the company because the liquidation procedure is controlled by the members.

Section 258 of the 1963 Act empowers the company in general meeting to appoint one or more liquidators.[1] It may also fix their remuneration.

Effect of liquidator's appointment

43.2 On the appointment of the liquidator(s), all the powers of the directors cease, unless the general meeting or the liquidator sanctions their continuance.

Duties and powers of liquidator

43.3 The function of the liquidator appointed by the members is to realise all the company's assets, pay all its creditors, and, as the company was solvent, to distribute the surplus assets amongst its members and contributories (if any) according to their class rights. As a result, many of the official liquidator's specific duties, detailed in Chapter 42, will also be applicable to the members' liquidator. For example, ss 283 to 313 of the 1963 Act apply to every mode of winding up and deal with such matters as:

(1) proof and ranking of claims;
(2) effect of winding up on antecedent and other transactions; and
(3) methods of dissolution.

43.4 Sections 275 to 282 apply to all voluntary liquidations, whether controlled by members or creditors. Under s 276, the liquidator may:

(1) in the case of a members' voluntary winding up, with the sanction of a special resolution of the company, and, in the case of a creditors' voluntary winding up,[2] with the sanction of the court or the committee of inspection or (if there is no such committee) a meeting of the creditors, exercise any of the powers given to a liquidator in a winding up by the court to:
   (a) pay any classes of creditors in full;
   (b) make any compromise or arrangement with creditors or persons claiming to be creditors; or

---

1 It may fill any vacancies which arise in the office of liquidator in a similar manner – s 259.
2 See next chapter.

(c) compromise[1] all calls and liabilities to calls, debts and liabilities capable of resulting in debts, and all claims, present or future, certain or contingent, ascertained or sounding only in damages, and all questions in any way relating to or affecting the assets or winding up of the company, on such terms as may be agreed, and take any security for the discharge of any such call, debt, liability or claim, and give a complete discharge in respect thereof;

(2) without sanction, exercise any of the other powers given to the liquidator in a winding up by the court;

(3) exercise the power of the court of settling a list of contributories, and the list of contributories shall be prima facie evidence of the liability of the persons named therein to be contributories;

(4) exercise the power of the court of making calls;

(5) summon general meetings of the company for the purpose of obtaining the sanction of the company by resolution or for any other purpose he may think fit;

(6) pay the debts of the company and adjust the rights of the contributories amongst themselves.[2]

The liquidator or any contributory or creditor may apply to the court to determine any question arising in the winding up of a company, or to exercise all or any of the powers which the court might exercise if the company were being wound up by the court.[3]

Duty to call meetings

43.5 Sections 262 and 263 make provision for annual meetings and a final meeting.

Annual meetings

43.6 The liquidator is under a duty to summon a general meeting of the company each year. He must lay before that meeting an account of his acts and dealings and of the conduct of the winding up during the preceding year. A copy of this report must be sent to the registrar within seven days of the holding of the annual meeting.

Final meeting

43.7 When the affairs of the company are fully wound up and all the creditors paid as forecast in the declaration of solvency, the liquidator must make up a final account, call a general meeting of the company and lay the final accounts before that meeting.

---

1 See s 279 regarding the binding of creditors by arrangements.
2 See s 275 on rules for distribution of company assets.
3 Section 280.

Within one week after the final meeting, the liquidator must send a copy of his final account to the registrar of companies, together with a formal return of the holding of that meeting.

Dissolution of the company

43.8   Three months after the registrar receives the liquidator's final account and return of the holding of the final meeting, the company is deemed to be dissolved.[1]

Powers of the liquidator in a reconstruction

43.9   Section 260 gives the liquidator specific powers to facilitate a reconstruction of the company. Where the whole or part of the business (or property) of the company being wound up is proposed to be transferred to another company (the transferee company), the liquidator may accept shares or other like interests in the transferee company as consideration for the sale of any property of the company being liquidated, provided sanction has been given by that company in the form of a special resolution. Dissenting shareholders, if any, may request the liquidator to purchase that part of their interest which their shares represent, providing they express their dissent in writing addressed to the liquidator within seven days after the passing of the resolution. In such circumstances, the price payable for their shares is to be determined by agreement or by arbitration.

If the liquidator elects to purchase the members' interests, the purchase money must be paid before the company is dissolved. Unless specifically provided to the contrary, the purchase money will be deemed to be part of the costs and expenses of winding up.

If company is insolvent

43.10   The whole basis underlying allowing members to control the winding up of their company is the fact that the directors have certified that the company is solvent and in a position to pay all its creditors.

If, therefore, the liquidator is at any time of the opinion that the company will not be able to pay its debts in full within the period stated in the declaration of solvency, he must:

(1) summon a meeting of creditors for a day not later than 14 days after the day on which he formed that opinion;
(2) send notices of the creditors' meeting to the creditors by post not less than seven days before the day on which that meeting is to be held;

---

1 Section 263(4).

(3) cause notice of the creditors' meeting to be advertised, at least ten days before the date of the meeting, once in *Iris Oifigiúil* and once at least in two daily newspapers circulating in the locality in which the company's principal place of business was situated during the relevant period; and

(4) during the period before the day on which the creditors' meeting is to be held, furnish creditors free of charge with such information concerning the affairs of the company as they may reasonably require.

Section 261(2) makes it necessary for the liquidator also:

(1) to make out a statement as to the affairs of the company, including a statement of the company's assets and liabilities, a list of the outstanding creditors and the estimated amount of their claims;

(2) to lay that statement before the creditors' meeting; and

(3) to attend and preside at that meeting.

Consequence for the winding-up procedure

43.11   As from the day on which the creditors' meeting is held under s 261, the winding up becomes a creditors' winding up.[1]

Appointment of new liquidator by creditors

43.12   The creditors may appoint a liquidator at their meeting to replace the members' appointee. However, such a replacement will not affect the validity of any action previously taken by the members' appointee as liquidator.

Annual and final meetings

43.13   Section 264 makes provision for alternative arrangements relating to the calling of annual and final meetings, when the liquidator is of the opinion that the company is unable to pay its debts.

---

1 See next chapter.

Chapter 44

CREDITORS' VOLUNTARY WINDING-UP PROCEDURES

INTRODUCTION

44.1 A creditors' voluntary winding up may appear to be a 'hostile' liquidation, but this may not really be the case.

The main difference between a 'member's' and a 'creditor's' voluntary liquidation is that, in the former, the members are allowed to control the winding up process because the directors have made a 'statutory declaration of solvency'. In effect, the directors are certifying that the company is solvent and will be able to pay the debts of all its creditors.

If, however, the directors cannot make this declaration, then any voluntary liquidation will be a creditors' winding up.

Sections 266 to 273 of the 1963 Act are special provisions applicable to a creditors' voluntary winding up.

MEETING OF CREDITORS

44.2 On the day the company members pass the resolution to wind up the company, a meeting of creditors must also take place, under s 266.[1]

Appointment of liquidator

44.3 If there is a difference of opinion between the creditors and the members as to who is to be appointed liquidator, it is the creditors' wishes that will prevail.[2] Thus, whilst it is the members who control the appointment of a liquidator in a members' voluntary winding up, it is the creditors who do so when the company is not solvent.

In both a members' and creditors' winding up, the chairman of any meeting at which a liquidator is appointed must, within seven days of the meeting, notify the liquidator in writing of his appointment, unless the liquidator or his duly authorised representative is present at the meeting where the appointment is made.[3]

The appointment of a liquidator in a voluntary winding up will be of no effect unless the person nominated has, prior to his appointment, given his written

---

1 See **41.25**.
2 Ibid, and s 267.
3 Section 276A.

consent to the appointment.[1] He must also, within 14 days of his appointment, give the registrar of companies notice of his appointment.

44.4 The remuneration[2] of the liquidator is fixed by the committee of inspection or, if there is no committee, by the creditors. If any creditor or contributory feels that the remuneration is excessive, he may apply to the court to amend the remuneration. Such an application must be made within 28 days of the fixing of the remuneration by the creditors or the committee of inspection (see **44.6** below).

Any vacancy[3] in the office of liquidator may be filled by the creditors.

The court may, on cause shown, remove a liquidator and appoint another in his place.[4]

Effect of appointment of liquidator

44.5 When the liquidator is appointed, all powers of the directors cease, except so far as the committee of inspection or creditors sanction their continuance.

Committee of inspection

44.6 No committee of inspection is necessary in a members' voluntary winding up. However, in a creditors' voluntary winding up,[5] a committee of inspection may be appointed to assist the liquidator.

Composition

44.7 The creditors, at their s 266 meeting, may appoint a committee of inspection comprising not more than five persons nominated by the creditors' meeting and three persons nominated by the company.[6]

The creditors can object to any of the persons appointed by the company and, if so, those persons cannot act unless the court so directs.[7]

Procedures

44.8 Generally, a committee of inspection in a creditors' voluntary winding up will operate under the same s 233 procedures as a committee of inspection appointed to assist an official liquidator.[8]

---

1 Section 276A.
2 Section 269. All costs of voluntary winding up, including the liquidator's remuneration, have priority over all other claims – see s 281.
3 Section 270.
4 Section 277.
5 As in a winding up by the court.
6 Section 268(1).
7 Section 268(2).
8 See **42.14**.

DUTIES OF THE LIQUIDATOR

44.9   The basic duties of a liquidator appointed by the creditors will be similar to those imposed on other voluntary liquidators.[1] However, s 271 provides that the powers of the liquidator to accept shares as consideration for the sale of company property in a reconstruction will only apply in a creditors' winding up provided sanction is obtained from either the court or the committee of inspection.[2]

Annual meetings

44.10   After the first year of the liquidation and each subsequent year, the liquidator must hold a general meeting of the company and a meeting of the creditors[3]. He must present an account of his acts and dealings during the preceding year to both meetings. He must also send a copy of the account to the registrar within seven days of the later of the two meetings.[4]

Final meetings

44.11   When the affairs of the company are fully wound up, the liquidator must present an account[5] of the winding up, showing how the winding up has been conducted and how the assets of the company have been disposed of, to a general meeting of the company and a meeting of the creditors. Each meeting must be called by advertising in two daily newspapers circulating in the district where the registered office of the company is situated, setting out the time, place and objects of the meeting. Such advertisements must be published at least 28 days before each meeting. The liquidator must send the account to the registrar within one week of the later of the two meetings. If a quorum is not present at either meeting, the liquidator must notify the registrar that a meeting was summoned and that a quorum was not present.

Dissolution of the company

44.12   Three months after the registrar has received the liquidator's final account and notification of the holding of the final meetings, the company is deemed to be dissolved,[6] unless the court, on the application of the liquidator or any interested party, makes an order deferring the date at which the dissolution of the company is to take effect.

---

1 See Chapter 42.
2 Under s 260 – see Chapter 43.
3 Within three months of the end of each year.
4 Section 272.
5 He must also send this account to the registrar – see s 273.
6 Section 273(4) and (5).

APPENDICES

Appendix A

THE IRISH STOCK EXCHANGE AND ITS MEMBER FIRMS

The primary functions of a stock exchange are to give companies a means of raising capital from institutional[1] investors to fund their enterprises (usually to finance further business expansion), and to provide these investors with a means of sharing in the profits of successful companies.

The Irish Stock Exchange used to be the Irish Unit of the International Stock Exchange of the UK and Ireland. However, the Stock Exchange Act 1995 separated the Irish Unit from the consolidated exchange and resulted in the creation of the Irish Stock Exchange Ltd.

The Irish Stock Exchange is a company limited by guarantee. Its member firms are its guarantors.

Only member firms are permitted to buy and sell quoted shares directly on the Stock Exchange. A member wishing to sell his shares in a plc will do so by using the services of a member firm.

Under the Stock Exchange Act 1995, the Central Bank is empowered to act as supervisor of the Irish Stock Exchange.

The Irish Stock Exchange is more limited than its US or UK counterpart, with fewer than 80 companies quoted. Of these, about 60 are on the Official List: mainly, large financial and industrial companies. The shares of the remaining companies are traded on the Exploration Securities Market (ESM) and the recently created Developing Companies Market.

The official equity index produced by the Exchange 'ISEQ' is calculated once a minute during the trading day (8.30 am to 5.30 pm). The ISEQ indices include all Official List equity shares, but excludes those of foreign registered companies.

During February 1997, the Irish stock market rose through the 3,000 ISEQ Overall Index, reflecting a strong demand from investors for all leading financial and industrial stocks. On 16 June 1997,[2] the ISEQ Overall Index had reached 3,359, reflecting a market capitalisation of £27.9 billion.

Relevant details of the Stock Exchange and its member firms[3] are:

> Irish Stock Exchange
> 28 Anglesea Street
> Dublin 2
>
> Telephone +353 1 6778808
> Fax   +353 1 6776045

---

1 The reduction in capital gains tax to 20 per cent from December 1997 is likely to extend share ownership of public companies amongst private investors.

2 By 8 December 1997 the Index had reached an all-time high of 4009.

3 As at 16 June 1997.

FIRM & ADDRESS	TELEPHONE	FAX
AIB CAPITAL MARKETS PLC AIB International Centre PO Box 2750, IFSC, Dublin 1	353–1–8740222	353–1–6054067
B.C.P. STOCKBROKERS 72 Upper Leeson Street, Dublin 4	353–1–6684688	353–1–6684246
BLOXHAM STOCKBROKERS 2/3 Exchange Place International Financial Services Centre Dublin 1	353–1–8291888	353–1–8291877
BLOXHAM STOCKBROKERS 12 Marlboro Street, Cork	353–1–21–270697	353–1–21–276036
BLOXHAM STOCKBROKERS 46 Cecil Street, Limerick	353–61–414065	353–61–419750
BUTLER & BRISCOE 3 College Green, Dublin 2	353–1–6777348	353–1–6777044
BUTLER & BRISCOE 7 Lower Rowe Street, Wexford	353–53–22187	
CREDIT SUISSE FIRST BOSTON (EUROPE) LTD Cabot Square, London E14 4QJ	44–171–5164049	44–171–5163879
CAMPBELL O'CONNOR & CO 8 Cope Street, Dublin 2	353–1–6771773	353–1–6791969
J & E DAVY 49 Dawson Street, Dublin 2	353–1–6797788	353–1–6712704
FEXCO STOCKBROKING LTD 12 Ely Place, Dublin 2	353–1–6611800	353–1–6610800
GARBAN BUTLER 3 College Green, Dublin 2	353–1–6707367	353–1–6707377
GOODBODY STOCKBROKERS 122 Pembroke Road, Dublin 4	353–1–6670400	353–1–6670280
MONEY MARKETS INTERNATIONAL 26 Lower Baggot Street, Dublin 2	353–1–6766277	353–1–6765250
W & R MORROGH 74 South Mall, Cork	353–21–270647	353–21–277581
N.C.B. STOCKBROKERS LTD 3 George's Dock International Financial Services Centre Dublin 1	353–1–6115611	353–1–6115766
RIADA STOCKBROKERS LTD ABN Amro House, IFSC, Dublin 1	353–1–6093700	353–1–6093711
UBS LIMITED 100 Liverpool Street, London EC2M 2RH	44–171–9013240	44–171–9013983

Appendix B

POTENTIAL CRIMINAL LIABILITIES OF COMPANY DIRECTORS

The more serious criminal offences committable by company directors include the following:

Nature of Offence	Source	
Fraudulent trading	s 297	1963 Act
Insider dealing	s 114	1990 Act
Failing to notify the company in writing of interests[1] in its shares or debentures	s 53	1990 Act
Failure to ensure notification *by agent* of acquisition or disposal of company shares or debentures	s 58	1990 Act
Misleading statements to company auditors	s 197	1990 Act
Failure to keep proper register of directors and secretaries, and to allow inspection of it	s 51	1990 Act
Failure to ensure that proper books of account[2] are maintained	s 202	1990 Act
Failure to keep proper books of account in a company which is subsequently wound up	s 203	1990 Act
Failure to co-operate with an inspector looking into the affairs of the company	s 10	1990 Act

---

1 Including those of his spouse and children – see s 64 of the 1990 Act. A director also commits an offence if he fails to disclose payments made to him in connection with company shares or fails to disclose his interest in company contracts – see ss 188 and 194 of the 1963 Act.

2 There are other offences in relation to the preparation of accounts. See ss 148, 149 and 158 of the 1963 Act and s 22 of the 1986 Amendment Act.

Nature of Offence	Source	
Incorrect statements in a prospectus	ss 44, 46 and 50	1963 Act
Offences prior to and during winding up (16 offences listed in s 293), eg non-co-operation with liquidator	s 293	1963 Act
Frauds committed by officers of companies which have gone into liquidation	s 295	1963 Act
Destruction, mutilation or falsification of company documents	s 243	1990 Act
Breach of restriction declaration	s 161	1990 Act
Breach[1] of disqualification order	s 161	1990 Act

---

1 Any person who acts under the direction of a disqualified director also commits a criminal offence – see s 164 of the 1990 Act.

Appendix C

ADDITIONAL READING

Company Law Review Group, First Report, Government of Ireland (Stationery Office, Dublin, 1995).

Companies Report 96 (Department of Enterprise and Employment, Stationery Office, Dublin 1997).

T.B. Courtney *The Law of Private Companies* (Butterworth (Ireland) Ltd, 1994).

B. Doolin *A Casebook on Irish Company Law* (Gill & MacMillan, 1987).

P. Egan *Irish Corporate Procedures* (Jordans, 1992).

M. Forde *Company Law* (Mercier Press, 1992).

M. Forde *The Law of Corporate Insolvency* (Round Hall Press, 1993).

D. Hogan, B. O'Neill, and J. Bowen-Walsh *Combined Companies Acts, 1963–1990* (Bastow Charleton Publications, 1991).

R. Keane *Company Law in the Republic of Ireland* (Butterworth (Ireland) Ltd, 1991).

I. Lynch, J. Marshall, and R. O'Ferrall *Corporate Insolvency and Rescue* (Butterworth (Ireland) Ltd, 1996).

L. MacCann *A Casebook on Company Law* (Butterworth (Ireland) Ltd, 1991).

L. MacCann *Companies Acts 1963–1990* (Butterworth (Ireland) Ltd, 1993).

P. Ussher *Company Law in Ireland* (Sweet & Maxwell, 1986).

INDEX

References are to paragraph numbers.

Accounts
annual, *see* Annual accounts
books of account
  availability of   24.2
  civil liability of officers for debts of
    company   24.9
  competency levels of directors
    20.42–20.46
  contents of   20.44
  criminal sanctions   24.5–24.8
  criteria for   20.45
  failure to keep, liability for
    21.17–21.21, 36.6
  generally   24.2–24.3
  personal liability of directors and
    officers   20.46
  purpose of   20.43
  sanctions for breach of s 202
    24.4
disclosure of transactions in
  generally   20.20
  particulars to be disclosed   20.22
  when not required   20.21
Agents
contractual capacity of   1.23
directors as   14.9–14.10
human, *see* Human agents
investigation into company's affairs
  duties relating to   27.5–27.8
  examination on oath   27.7
  related companies   27.8
  secret transactions   27.6
managing   1.16
Allotment of shares, *see* Public
subscription
Amalgamation
generally   39.20
meaning   1.36, 39.10
registration of court order   39.11
schemes of arrangement, use for
  39.14
Annual accounts
accounting principles   24.20–24.21
approval of   24.44

auditors' report   24.37–24.41
directors' report   24.34–24.36
dividends   24.43
failure to prepare   24.12
form and content of   24.15–24.19
generally   24.10
group accounts   24.11
medium-sized companies   24.32–
  24.33
notes to accounts, information
  required by way of   24.25–
  24.28
other information required in
  24.29–24.31
preparation of   24.13–24.14
profits available for distribution
  24.42
small private companies   24.32–
  24.33
valuation rules   24.22–24.24
Annual general meeting (AGM)
adjourned   15.6
generally   15.2, 15.3
notice   15.4
waiver of notice   15.5
Annual report
insider dealing regulations, Stock
  Exchange supervision of
  20.38
Annual return
companies not having share
  capital   25.12
documents to be attached to
  25.13–25.17
information to be included in
  25.11
large companies   25.19
medium-sized companies, summary of
  1986 Act concessions for
  25.18
private companies, certificates to be
  attached by   25.20
requirement to make   25.10
small companies, summary of 1986 Act
  concessions for   25.18

Annual return – *cont.*
  time-limit for filing   25.21
Appeal
  Irish Takeover Panel, ruling or
    direction of   40.15
  salomon case   3.4
Articles of association
  alteration of   16.2
  formation of company, procedures
    for   8.11
  public nature of   2.12
  relief of directors from liability for
    breach of duty   21.6
  remuneration of promoters   9.13
Artificial nature of company
  company capital and initial
    finance   1.10
  generally   1.7
  human agents of company   1.8–1.9
Assets
  insolvent company, of, creditors'
    rights against   1.28–1.29
  property of company, as   4.9
Auditors
  1983 Act and   26.23
  appointment of
    first auditors   26.3
    generally   26.2
    minister, by   26.6
    persons disqualified from acting
      26.12
    qualifications for   26.7–26.11
    subsequent auditors   26.4–26.6
  civil liability of
    contract, liability under   26.27–
      26.28
    contracting out of liability for
      negligent acts   26.31
    generally   26.25
    size of potential liability, concern
      over   26.32–26.33
    standard of care   26.26
    tort, liability in   26.29–26.30
  contract, liability under   26.27–
    26.28
  contracting out of liability for
    negligent acts   26.31
  directors' emoluments, duties relating
    to   26.22
  duties of   26.20–26.23
  extended notice   26.17

false statements to, penalties for
  26.24
first   26.3
general position of   26.18
individually recognised   26.10
meaning   26.1
penalties for false statements to
  26.24
persons disqualified from acting as
  26.12
proper books of account not being
  kept, duties relating to   26.21
prosecution   26.11
qualifications for appointment
  26.7–26.10
recognition of accountancy bodies
  26.8
registration of   26.9
removal of   26.16–26.17
remuneration of   26.13
replacement of   26.16–26.17
report of
  contents of   24.38
  expanded   24.39
  generally   24.37
  recommendation in Partnership
    2000   24.41
  special   24.40
resignation of   26.15
retiring   26.5
rights of   26.19
standard of care   26.26
subsequent   26.4–26.6
termination of appointment of
  extended notice   26.17
  generally   26.14
  removal of auditor   26.16–26.17
  replacement of auditor   26.16–
    26.17
  resignation of auditor   26.15
tort, liability in   26.29–26.30

Bankruptcy
  bankrupt members   28.8
Board of directors
  usual authority of   18.10
Books
  account, of, *see* Accounts
  minute books   25.9

Books – *cont.*
  statutory books and minutes   25.8–
    25.9
Borrowing
  internal limits on powers   18.11–
    18.12
  lender protection   18.11–18.12,
    18.14
  potential opportunities, formation of
    company may increase   4.11
  powers of company   32.8–32.9
  security for   32.12
Business
  commencement of, *see*
    Commencement of business
  name, *see* Name of company

CREST
  introduction of   31.33–31.34
Capital
  artificial nature of company   1.10
  authorised   12.11
  circulating capital, meaning   12.7
  extraordinary meeting following
    serious loss of   13.35–13.36
  fixed capital, meaning   12.7
  gearing   12.6
  investment capital
    balance sheet position   12.3
    meaning   12.2
  issued   12.12
  loan capital
    capital employed   12.5
    meaning   12.4
  maintenance of   2.13–2.14
  meaning   12.1–12.9
  nominal   12.11
  paid-up   12.13
  public company
    methods of raising   10.7–10.11
    minimum share capital for   8.6,
      8.17
    offer for sale   10.8
    placing   10.9
    public offer   10.10
    rights issue   10.11
  reserve   12.14
  share, *see* Share capital
  uncalled   12.13
  working capital, meaning   12.8

Capital base
  protection of, *see* Share capital
Care and skill
  directors, duties of   19.20–19.21
Chairman
  ostensible authority, doctrine of
    18.22–18.23
  proceedings of directors, role relating
    to   19.4
  usual authority of   18.16
Change of status
  generally   8.20
  limited company, conversion of
    8.27
  private company
    change from public company
      into   8.23–8.24
    re-registration as public
      company   8.25–8.26
  public company
    change into private company
      8.23–8.24
    re-registration of private company
      as   8.25–8.26
  single-member company
    change from   8.22
    change to   8.21
  unlimited company, conversion of
    8.27
Charges
  fixed
    floating charges distinguished
      from   32.31
    meaning   32.17
    receiver, appointment of   34.5
  floating
    advantages to companies of
      32.22
    crystallisation of   32.19
    de-crystallisation   32.21
    disadvantages to lenders   32.23–
      32.30
    effect of crystallisation   32.20
    fixed charges distinguished
      from   32.31
    meaning   32.18
    receiver, appointment of   34.6
  meaning   32.13
  mortgage, by way of
    generally   32.15
    legal and equitable interests
      32.16

Charges – *cont.*
  range of   32.14
Chief administrative officer
  functions of company secretary as
    14.35
Circulating capital
  meaning   12.7
City Code on Take-overs and Mergers
  main purpose of   40.10
  s 204, and   40.11
Class rights, *see* Shares
Classes of shares, *see* Shares
Close companies
  meaning   6.10
  penetrating veil   6.10
Commencement of business
  European Economic Interest
      Groupings   11.10
  generally   11.1
  non-Irish company
    accounts   11.5
    cessation of business in Ireland
      11.6
    details of external companies
      11.8
    generally   11.4
    Irish branches   11.7
    publicity   11.5
  other business associations   11.9–
    11.10
  pre-trading contract, liability of
      director for   11.3
  trading certificate   11.2
Committees
  proceedings of   19.3
Common law
  directors, duties of
    avoiding conflicts of interest
      19.16
    company property, responsibility
      for   19.12–19.13
    fiduciary duties   19.11
    generally   19.10
    maintaining voting impartiality
      19.17
    monies, responsibility for   19.12–
      19.13
    secret profit, not making   19.14–
      19.15
  liabilities to outsiders
    generally   21.9

personal contractual
    responsibility   21.11
  tortious liability of director
      21.12
  ultra vires and unauthorised
      transactions   21.10
misrepresentations, investors'
    remedies for
  concealment   10.45
  directors, remedies against
      10.44
  fraud, damages for   10.42
  generally   10.39
  limits on rescission   10.41
  negligence, damages for   10.43
  promoters, remedies against
      10.44
  rescission   10.40
promoter, remedies of company
    against   9.6, 9.10, 10.44
Companies
  contracts, *see* Contracts
  human agents, *see* Human agents
  insolvent, *see* Insolvent company
  management, *see* Management
  meetings, *see* Meetings
  name, *see* Name of company
  partnerships compared with
    advantages   5.6
    disadvantages   5.7
    unincorporated business
        association, partnership as
        5.5, 5.8
  private, *see* Private companies
  public, *see* Public companies
  sole traders compared with
    advantages   5.3
    carrying on business   5.2–5.4
    disadvantages   5.4
Companies Registration Office
  register of business names maintained
      by   7.2
Company officer
  meaning   14.34
  See also Officers
Company secretary
  appointment of   1.20, 14.38
  authority of   14.36
  chief administrative officer, functions
      as   14.35
  disclosure, general duty of   14.24

Company secretary – *cont.*
  ostensible authority, doctrine of
    18.25
  qualifications required   14.37
  register of   25.5
  role of   14.34–14.38
  share dealings by   20.24–20.25
  traditional judicial attitude to
    14.34
  usual authority of   18.18
Compensation
  professional indemnity insurance
    22.1
Competition
  Act of 1991   40.25
  abuse of dominant position   40.31
Competition Authority
  category certificates   40.30
  powers of   40.26
  sanctions available to aggrieved
    persons   40.27–40.28
Compulsory purchase
  investors, rights and responsibilities
    of   1.15
Concealment
  common law remedy, as   10.45
Concert parties
  notification of interests of   31.8
Conflicts of interest
  common law duties of directors
    19.16
Connected persons
  insider dealing by   20.28–20.39
  meaning   20.4
Constitutional documents
  public nature of   2.12
Contracts
  auditors' liability under   26.27–
    26.28
  company can sue and be sued in its
    own name   4.5
  constructive notice   17.2
  contractual capacity of company
    1.23
  contractual powers
    company powers   17.7–17.12
    constitutional documents   17.1–
      17.2
    creditors and ultra vires
      doctrine   17.15–17.22
    investors and ultra vires
      doctrine   17.13–17.14

  modern objects clauses, evolution
    of   17.5–17.6
  ultra vires transactions, effect of
    17.3–17.4
  examiner's liability for   37.8–37.9
  form of   18.1–18.2
  objects clauses
    alteration of   17.14
    drafting   17.4
    modern, evolution of   17.5–17.6
  pre-trading, *see* Pre-trading contracts
  receiver, status of   34.20–34.24
  seal   18.2
  service, *see* Service contracts
Control of company
  democratic   15.31
  interests, other than investors'
    interests, to be considered
    16.25
  minority investors
    judicial protection for   16.4–16.8
    other examples of statutory
      protection   16.19
    rule in *Foss v Harbottle*   16.20–
      16.24
    s 205 remedy for oppression by
      majority   16.9–16.16
  nature of   1.24
  taking of decisions
    articles of association, alteration
      of   16.2
    corporate rights versus individual
      rights   16.3
    generally   16.1
Corporate crimes
  legal liabilities of directors   21.13–
    21.14
Corporate personality
  concept of
    effect of incorporation   3.1–3.10
    veil of incorporation, *see* Veil of
      incorporation
  incorporation, *see* Incorporation
  Salomon's case, separate legal
    personality and
    case on appeal   3.4
    essence of judgment   3.5
    generally   3.2
    importance of *Salomon* decision
      3.10
    liquidator's contention   3.3

Corporate personality – *cont.*
  Salomon's case, separate legal
    personality and – *cont.*
    one-man companies   3.6
    subsequent case-law   3.7–3.9
    separate   1.4–1.5
  veil of incorporation, *see* Veil of
    incorporation
Corporation tax
  single rate of   4.13
Court
  examiner, powers relating to, *see*
    Examiner
  receiver, appointment of   34.8,
    34.19
  share capital, permitted reduction
    in   13.6, 13.11–13.12
  veil lifted by   6.6–6.7
  winding up by, *see* Winding up
Credit
  advances on directors' expenses
    20.17
  business transactions   20.17
  connected persons, to, prohibition
    of   20.12
  directors, to, prohibition of   20.13
  intra-group loans and transactions
    20.16
  permitted transactions   20.14
  transactions below certain value
    20.15
Creditors
  borrowing powers of company
    32.8–32.9
  capital base, protection of, *see* Share
    capital
  charges, *see* Charges
  company information for   32.3–
    32.4
  debentures, *see* Debentures
  directors and others, rights against
    1.30
  examinership, effect of
    costs of examinership
      paramount   37.33
    generally   37.32
    secured creditors   37.34
    unsecured creditors   37.35
  insolvent company's assets, rights
    against   1.28–1.29
  interests of, duties of directors relating
    to   19.8

intervention powers   2.15
  nature of   32.1
  preferential   32.6
  protecting company against   1.32–
    1.34
  protection available to company
    against, *see* Examiner
  protection of
    creditors' powers to intervene
      2.15
    maintenance of company's
      capital   2.13–2.14
    nature of   2.11
    priorities in distribution   2.20
    public nature of constitutional
      documents   2.12
    ranking of creditors' claims   2.19
    recovery against company, creditors'
      rights of   2.16–2.19, 2.21–
      2.23
    secured creditors   2.17
    unsecured creditors   2.18
  ranking of claims of   2.19
  recovery against company
    debenture, meaning   2.16
    generally   2.16
    other rights   2.21–2.23
    ranking of creditors' claims   2.19
    secured creditors   2.17
    significance of two 1990 Acts
      2.22–2.23
    unsecured creditors   2.18
  reduction of share capital, objections
    relating to   13.9–13.10
  remedies of
    directors, claims against   36.4–
      36.9
    generally   36.1
    members, against   36.2–36.3
    officers, claims against   36.4–36.9
  rights against company   1.26–1.29
  rights of   32.2
  rights of action   34.1
  secured   2.17, 32.7
  ultra vires doctrine, and
    generally   17.15
    position of company   17.22
    s 8 protection   17.16–17.22
  unsatisfied
    directors, claims against   36.4–
      36.9

Creditors – *cont.*
  unsatisfied – *cont.*
    members, remedies against
      36.2–36.3
    officers, claims against   36.4–36.9
    unsecured
      examinership, effect of   37.35
      meaning   32.5
      recovery, rights of   2.18
      remedies of   34.2
    voluntary winding up   41.24–41.26,
      44.1–44.12
    winding up, rights relating to   1.31
Crimes
  corporate, legal liabilities of
    directors   21.13–21.14
Criminal liability
  misrepresentations, for
    defence   10.51
    generally   10.50
Criminal sanctions
  books of account, relating to   24.5–
    24.8
  fraudulent trading, liability for
    21.35
  insider dealing, liability for   20.35

D&O policies, *see* Professional indemnity
  insurance
Damages
  fraud, for   10.42
  misfeasance, for, fiduciary position of
    promoter   9.9
  negligence, for   10.43
Death
  deceased members   28.7
Debenture-holders
  debts due from   33.23
  receiver, appointment of, *see* Receiver
  register of   25.7, 33.15
  remedies of   33.22, 34.3–34.15
  trustees for   33.10
Debentures
  bearer   33.3
  charge   33.6
  conditions   33.7
  debenture stock   33.21
  disclosure of directors' interest in
    directors' report or accounts, in
    20.27

  generally   20.23
  register of directors' and other
    interests   20.26
  sanction for non-compliance
    20.25
  share dealings   20.24–20.25
  forms of   33.5–33.10
  interpretation of wording   33.8–
    33.9
  meaning   2.16, 32.10, 33.1
  penalising dealing in options to trade
    in   20.11
  perpetual   33.4
  re-issue of   33.20
  redeemable   33.4
  register of directors' interests in
    25.6, 31.1
  registered   33.3
  registration of charges securing
    correction of errors in register
      33.14
    extension of registration time
      33.14
    generally   33.11
    register of charges   33.13
  security for company borrowing
    32.12
  shares, and   32.11
  transfer of
    generally   33.16
    priority of charges   33.18–33.19
    subject to equities   33.17
  types of   33.2–33.4
Debts
  compromising company debts
    1.35–1.36
  debenture holders, due from
    33.23
  directors' liability for   1.18, 20.19
  insolvent company, of, directors'
    personal liability for
    failure to keep proper books of
      account   21.17–21.21
    fraudulent trading   21.31–21.35
    generally   21.16
    reckless trading   21.22–21.30
  liquidator, duties of   42.28–42.31
  loans for purchase of company's own
    shares   13.45
  outstanding, payment of   39.1

Defence
 failure to keep proper books of
   account   21.18
 misrepresentations, criminal liability
   for   10.51
 reckless trading, relating to   21.25
Deferred shares
 meaning   12.20
Developing Companies Market (DCM)
 entry requirements for access to
   10.17
 price-sensitive information, disclosure
   of   10.17
Diligence
 directors, duties of   19.22
Directors
 agents, as   14.9–14.10
 appointment by members
   assignment of office by directors
     14.26
   defects in appointment   14.19
   disclosure   14.23–14.24
   disqualification of directors
     14.20
   emoluments, disclosure of   14.23
   first directors   14.14
   generally   1.16, 14.13
   increase in numbers of directors
     14.17
   letter headings, particulars to be
     shown in   14.25
   loans to directors   14.22
   reduction in numbers of
     directors   14.17
   removal of directors   14.18
   remuneration of directors   14.21
   rotation of directors   14.16
   salaries, disclosure of   14.23
   subsequent directors   14.15
 assignment of office by   14.26
 authority of   14.33
 board of, usual authority of   18.10
 books of account, personal liability
   for   20.46
 care and skill, duties of   19.20–
   19.21
 common law remedies against
   10.44
 connected persons
   meaning   20.4
 credit to
   advances on expenses   20.17

 business transactions   20.17
 general prohibition on granting
   of   20.13
 permitted credit transactions
   20.14
 transactions below certain value
   20.15
 creditors' rights against   1.30
 debentures
   disclosure of interest in   20.23–
     20.27
   penalising dealing in options to
     trade in   20.11
 debts of company, personal liability
   for   20.19
 defects in appointment   14.19
 delegation of responsibilities   19.23
 diligence   19.22
 disclosure
   accounts, particulars to be disclosed
     in   20.22
   debentures, interest in   20.23–
     20.27
   emoluments, of   14.23
   general duty of   14.24
   generally   20.20
   interest in proposed contracts
     20.6
   salaries, of   14.23
   shares, interest in   20.23–20.27
   when not required   20.21
 disqualification of
   application for making order
     23.14
   civil consequences   23.17–23.19
   Companies Act 1990   23.1
   discretionary disqualification
     23.13
   enforcement   23.16
   generally   1.19, 14.20
   mandatory disqualification
     23.12
   order   23.10–23.11
   Part VII of 1990 Act   23.2–23.21
   register of orders   23.20
   relief from order   23.15
   sanctions   23.16
   undischarged bankrupts   23.21
 duties of
   avoiding conflicts of interest
     19.16

Directors – *cont.*
  duties of – *cont.*
    common law duties   19.10–19.17
    company property, responsibility
      for   19.12–19.13
    company's best interests   19.6
    creditors' interests   19.8
    employees' interests   19.7
    fiduciary duties   19.11
    generally   1.17, 19.5, 19.9
    maintaining voting impartiality
      19.17
    monies, responsibility for   19.12–
      19.13
    secret profit, not making   19.14–
      19.15
  election by investors   1.16
  emoluments
    auditors' duties relating to   26.22
    disclosure of   14.23
  examiner, powers of, *see* Examiner
  fiduciary powers, proper exercise
    of   19.18–19.19
  first   14.14
  fraudulent trading, liability for
    20.40, 21.31–21.35, 36.7
  generally   19.1, 19.24–19.25
  honesty requirements, strengthening
    of   20.2
  income tax   4.13
  increase in numbers of   14.17
  intra-group loans and transactions
    20.16
  letter headings, particulars on   7.6,
    14.25
  liability of
    breach of duty, relief from liability
      for   21.4–21.6
    common law liabilities to
      outsiders   21.9–21.12
    company debts, for   1.18
    corporate crimes   21.13–21.14
    failure to keep proper books of
      account   21.17–21.21, 36.6
    fraudulent trading   21.31–21.35
    generally   21.2
    insolvent company, debts of
      21.16–21.35
    insurance   21.7
    outsiders as agents of company,
      to   21.8–21.15

  potential criminal liabilities
    App B
  reckless trading   21.22–21.30
  remedies by company   21.3
  statutory liabilities to outsiders
    21.15
  two perspectives   21.1
  lifting veil of incorporation
    legal liability of directors   6.18
    peeping behind veil   6.8
    statutory   6.17
  loans to   14.22, 20.12
  managing, *see* Managing director
  meaning   14.5–14.6
  monitoring management of
    company   1.21
  ostensible authority, doctrine of
    18.24
  particulars on letter headings   7.6,
    14.25
  personal contractual responsibility
    21.11
  potential criminal liabilities of
    App B
  pre-trading contracts, liability for
    11.3
  proceedings of
    chairman, role of   19.4
    committees   19.3
    generally   19.2
    managing director, role of   19.4
  professional indemnity insurance
    claims for compensation   22.1
    cover provided by D&O policies
      22.10–22.14
    events giving rise to legal
      proceedings against
      directors   22.9
    minority investors, legal
      proceedings by   22.3–22.5
    modern attitude towards directors'
      responsibilities   22.15
    non-members, legal proceedings
      by   22.6–22.8
    who is able to sue   22.2–22.9
  prohibition of loans and credit to
    20.12
  quasi-trustees, as   14.7–14.8
  raising of competency levels
    generally   20.41
    keeping proper books of
      account   20.42–20.46

Directors – *cont.*
  raising of competency levels – *cont.*
    reckless trading   20.47–20.48
  reckless trading, liability for   20.47–
    20.48, 21.22–21.30, 36.7
  reduction in numbers of   14.17
  register of   25.5
  remedies against   21.3
  removal of
    generally   14.18, 14.27
    natural justice   14.28
  remuneration of   14.21
  report of
    expanded   24.35
    generally   24.34
    small or medium-sized companies,
      extra statement for   24.36
  restriction of
    civil consequences   23.17–23.19
    Companies Act 1990   23.1
    effect of restriction declaration
      23.4, 23.7–23.9
    enforcement   23.16
    exemption and relief   23.5
    generally   23.3
    liquidators, duties of   23.6
    Part VII of 1990 Act   23.2–23.21
    receivers, duties of   23.6
    sanctions   23.16
  role of   14.4–14.10
  rotation of   14.16
  salaries, disclosure of   14.23
  service contracts
    1990 Act limitations on   14.31
    authority of directors   14.33
    entry into   1.16
    generally   14.29
    inspection of   14.32
    managing director's contract
      14.30
    regulation of   20.8
  shadow, transactions involving
    20.5
  shares
    disclosure of interest in   20.23–
      20.27
    penalising dealing in options to
      trade in   20.11
  statutory strengthening of duties of
    accounts, disclosure of transactions
      in   20.20–20.22

Companies Act 1990   20.1
fraudulent trading   20.40
honesty requirements   20.2
insider dealing by connected
  persons   20.28–20.39
raising of competency levels of
  20.41–20.48
shares and debentures, disclosure of
  interest in   20.23–20.27
specific transactions regulated
  20.7–20.19
transactions involving directors (and
  others)   20.3–20.6
subsequent   14.15
substantial property transactions
  with   20.9–20.10
tortious liability of director   21.12
transactions involving
  connected persons   20.4
  disclosure of interest in proposed
    contracts   20.6
  generally   20.3
  shadow directors   20.5
unsatisfied creditors' claims
  against   36.4–36.9
usual authority of   18.17
Disclosure
  accounts, in
    generally   20.20
    particulars to be disclosed   20.22
    when not required   20.21
  company secretary, general duty
    on   14.24
  directors
    accounts, particulars to be disclosed
      in   20.22
    debentures, interest in   20.23–
      20.27
    emoluments   14.23
    general duty on   14.24
    generally   20.20
    interest in proposed contracts
      20.6
    salaries   14.23
    shares, interest in   20.23–20.27
    when not required   20.21
  order
    contravention of   31.13
    scope of   31.12
    who can apply for   31.11
  promoter, fiduciary relationship of
    9.5

Disclosure – *cont.*
  share purchases, of   13.34
  shares, interests in
    application for order   31.11
    concert parties, notification of
      interests of   31.8
    contravention of order   31.13
    exempted companies   31.10
    generally   31.2
    private companies, disclosure orders
      for interests in   31.9
    register of significant interests
      31.5–31.6
    scope of order   31.12
    share dealings by directors,
      secretaries and their
      families   31.3
    significant interests in shares of
      plc   31.4
    Stock Exchange, notification of
      thresholds to   31.7
Disclosure of interests
  investors, rights and responsibilities
    of   1.13
Discount
  prohibition against issuing shares at
    generally   13.46
    issuing shares at premium   13.48
    payment by instalments   13.47
Disqualification of directors, *see*
  Directors
Dissolution of company
  nature of   1.39
Distribution
  meaning   13.50
  priorities in   2.20
Dividends
  amount payable   30.5
  annual accounts   24.43
  effect of declaration of   30.8
  generally   30.3
  loans for purchase of company's own
    shares   13.45
  mode of payment   30.6
  payment only out of profits
    distribution, meaning   13.50
    generally   13.49
    public companies, profits of
      13.51
    relevant accounts   13.53
    specialist companies   13.52

  right to   30.4
  shares in lieu of   30.7
Documents
  constitutional   17.1–17.2
  examiner seeking production of
    37.21
  lodgement of   8.13
  registered office, kept at   17.29

Emoluments of directors
  auditors' duties relating to   26.22
  disclosure of   14.23
Employees
  directors, duties of   1.22, 19.7
Estoppel
  membership, acquisition of   28.15
European Communities
  Admissions Directive   10.4
  EC (Stock Exchange) Regulations
    1984   10.3–10.6
  Interim Reports Directive   10.6
  Listing Particulars Directive   10.5
  mergers and divisions of
    companies   40.16–40.31
European Economic Interest Groupings
  (EEIGS)
  nature of   11.10
European Union
  insider dealing regulations, Stock
    Exchange supervision of
    20.39
  intra-EU and international trading
    40.32
  See also European Communities
Evidence
  examiner, powers of   37.21
Examiner
  appointment of
    notification of   37.12–37.14
    receiver, effect on   35.23, 37.17
  certification of expenses   37.27–
    37.28
  cessation of protection order
    38.16
  charged property, power to deal
    with   37.30
  consequences of examinership
    37.15–37.18
  costs of examinership paramount
    37.33

Examiner – *cont.*
  court, power of
    contracts, examiner's liability
        for   37.8–37.9
    generally   37.2–37.3
    interim examiner   37.6
    negative report, relating to
        38.18
    qualifications of examiner   37.10
    related companies   37.4–37.5
    security for costs   37.7
  creditors' rights, effect of
      examinership on
    costs of examinership
        paramount   37.33
    generally   37.32
    secured creditors   37.34
    unsecured creditors   37.35
  direction, application to court for
      37.29
  directors
    right to seek transfer of powers
        of   37.31
    statement of affairs of   37.23
  discovery of detrimental conduct
      37.25–37.26
  effect of examinership   37.1
  examination on oath   37.22
  expenses, certification of   37.27–
      37.28
  interim   37.6
  management of company, further
      powers of court over   37.20
  meaning   35.22
  meetings   37.24
  petitioning court
    notification of examiner's
        appointment   37.12–37.14
    who can petition   37.11–37.14
  powers of   37.19–37.31
  provisional liquidator, effect of
      appointment on   37.18
  remedies   37.26
  report of
    cessation of protection order
        38.16
    information in report   38.2–38.4
    negative   38.17–38.18
    opinions   38.3
    positive recommendation   38.5–
        38.15

    primary duty   38.1
    recommendation   38.4
    seeking production of documents and
        evidence   37.21
Expenses
  examiner, of   37.27–37.28
  investigation into company's affairs,
      of   27.13
Expert
  misrepresentation, liability for
      10.47
External interests
  examples of   2.4
  nature of   2.4–2.5
External relationships
  compromising company debts
      1.35–1.36
  corporate restructuring   1.35–1.36
  creditors, *see* Creditors
  dissolving company   1.39
  mergers   1.37
  nature of   1.25
  take-overs   1.37
  winding up   1.38–1.39
Extraordinary general meeting (EGM)
  business at   15.12
  following serious loss of capital
      13.35–13.36
  generally   15.2, 15.10
  notice   15.11
  s 40 requirements to call   13.36

Families
  share dealings by   20.24–20.25,
      31.3
Fiduciary relationship of promoter, *see*
    Promoters
Finance
  initial   1.10
Financial arrangements
  amalgamations, *see* Amalgamations
  court sanction of scheme
    generally   39.8
    objections by minorities   39.9
  debts, *see* Debts
  mergers, *see* Mergers
  reconstructions   39.13, 39.15–39.18
  s 201 schemes of arrangement and
      compromises
    approval of members and
        creditors   39.7

Financial arrangements – *cont.*
  s 201 schemes of arrangement and
    compromises – *cont.*
    generally   39.2
    information for members and
      creditors   39.6
    statutory meetings   39.4–39.5
    uses for   39.12–39.14
    who may apply to court   39.3
  takeovers, *see* Takeovers
Financial records
  basic   24.1
  books of account, *see* Accounts
Fixed capital
  meaning   12.7
Fixed charge
  meaning   2.19
Fixed charges
  floating charges distinguished
    from   32.31
  meaning   32.17
  receiver, appointment of   34.5
Floating charge
  meaning   2.19
Floating charges
  advantages to companies of   32.22
  crystallisation of
    effect of   32.20
    meaning   32.19
  de-crystallisation   32.21
  disadvantages to lenders
    avoidance under ss 288 and 289
      32.24
    commercial risks   32.27
    generally   32.23
    loss of priority under s 98   32.26
    negative pledge clauses   32.30
    reservation of title clauses   32.28
    solvency   32.25
    subsequent fixed charges   32.29
  fixed charges distinguished from
    32.31
  meaning   32.18
  receiver, appointment of   34.6
Foreign companies
  limits on investigating   27.23
Forfeiture
  shares held by or on behalf of public
    company   13.15
Formation of company
  approval of proposed company
    name   8.12

articles of association   8.11
change of status
  generally   8.20
  limited company, conversion of
    8.27
  public company changed into
    private company   8.23–8.24
  re-registration of private company as
    public company   8.25–8.26
  single-member company, change to
    or from   8.21–8.22
  unlimited company, conversion
    of   8.27
factors affecting choice of corporate
  form   8.8–8.19
increasing potential borrowing
  opportunities   4.11
lodgement of documents   8.13
make up of register of companies
  8.19
memorandum of association   8.10
new public limited company,
  minimum share capital for
  8.6, 8.17
off the shelf companies   8.14
private company   8.5, 8.7
procedures for
  approval or proposed company
    name   8.12
  articles of association   8.11
  generally   8.9
  memorandum of association
    8.10
promoters, *see* Promoters
public company   8.5, 8.6
publication in *Iris Oifigiúil*
  8.15
single-member private company
  8.16
unlimited company   8.18
Fraud
  damages for   10.42
  minority investors, judicial protection
    for   16.5–16.6
Fraudulent trading
  criminal sanctions for   21.35
  directors' liability for   20.40, 21.31–
    21.35, 36.7
  officers' liability for   36.7
  statutory liability for   20.40

Gearing
  meaning   12.6
Gratuitous payments
  company's power to make   17.8–17.10
Groups of companies
  lifting veil of incorporation   6.16
Guarantee
  company limited by
    conversion of unlimited
      company   8.27
    nature of   8.3
    registration   8.3
    single-member private company
      8.16
  company purchasing own shares
    13.39

Hardship
  minority investors, judicial protection
    for   16.7
Holding companies
  peeping behind veil   6.2
  purchase by subsidiary of shares in
    13.33, 28.6
Human agents
  actual authority of   18.7–18.8
  agency law principles   18.4–18.7
  agent, meaning   18.5
  authority of   18.6
  company organisation by means of
    company secretary   1.20
    directors   1.16–1.19
    employees   1.22
    generally   1.11
    investors' rights and
      responsibilities   1.12–1.15
    managing agents   1.16–1.19
    monitoring directors' management
      of company   1.21
    officers   1.16–1.19
  company secretary, *see* Company
    secretary
  contracts, legal power to enter
    into   1.9
  directors, *see* Directors
  general agent, authority of   18.6
  generally   18.3
  ostensible authority of
    extent of   18.7–18.8

third party protection and doctrine
    of   18.20–18.25
  promoter   1.8
  special agent, authority of   18.6
  ultra vires doctrine and   18.26
  universal agent, authority of   18.6
  usual authority of
    board of directors   18.10
    chairman   18.16
    company secretary   18.18
    exceptions to rule in *Turquand's*
      case   18.13
    generally   18.9
    individual directors   18.17
    internal limits on borrowing
      powers   18.11–18.12
    lender protection   18.11–18.12,
      18.14
    managing director   18.15
    shareholders   18.19

Income tax
  directors   4.13
  shareholders   4.13
Incorporation
  company can sue and be sued in its
    own name   4.5
  effect of   3.1–3.10
  facilitating transfer of investors'
    interests   4.12
  perpetual succession, company has
    4.10
  potential borrowing opportunities,
    formation of company may
    increase   4.11
  property, company can own
    company assets   4.9
    generally   4.6–4.8
  Salomon's case, separate legal
    personality of company and
    case on appeal   3.4
    essence of judgment   3.5
    generally   3.2
    importance of *Salomon* decision
      3.10
    liquidator's contention   3.3
    one-man companies   3.6
    subsequent case-law   3.7–3.9

Incorporation – *cont.*
    taxation implications   4.13
    veil of, *see* Veil of incorporation
Indemnity
    examiner, of   37.9
    insurance, *see* Professional indemnity
        insurance
    receiver, of   35.3–35.4
Independent expert
    property, valuation by   9.10
Infants
    members, as   28.3
Initial finance
    artificial nature of company   1.10
Insider dealing
    connected persons, by   20.28–20.39
    exempt transactions   20.36
    liability for
        criminal sanctions   20.35
        generally   20.33
        time-limits   20.34
    Stock Exchange supervision of
        regulations
        annual report   20.38
        EU dimension   20.39
        generally   20.37
    unlawful dealing in securities
        connected persons   20.31
        generally   20.29
        lawful dealings   20.30
        other companies and tippees
        20.32
Insolvent company
    assets of, creditors' rights against
        1.28–1.29
    debts of, directors' personal liability
        for
        failure to keep proper books of
            account   21.17–21.21
        fraudulent trading   21.31–21.35
        generally   21.16
        reckless trading   21.22–21.30
Inspection
    minute books, of   15.28
    service contract of director   14.32
Insurance
    directors' liability to company   21.7
    professional indemnity, *see*
        Professional indemnity insurance
Interests
    company's best interests   19.6

    creditors, of   19.8
    employees, of   19.7
    external   2.4–2.5
    internal   2.2–2.3
Internal interests
    examples of   2.3
    nature of   2.2–2.3
Investigation
    company officers and agents, duties of
        examination on oath   27.7
        generally   27.5
        related companies   27.8
        secret transactions   27.6
    company's affairs, of   27.2
    expenses of   27.13
    foreign companies, limits on
        investigating   27.23
    inspectors
        applications by Minister   27.4
        appointment of   27.1
        reports of   27.10–27.12
        sanctions of   27.9
        who can apply for appointment
            of   27.3
    ownership
        entry and search of premises
        27.18
        inspector's powers   27.14–27.16
        lifting restrictions on shares
        27.22
        Minister's powers   27.17–27.22
        security of information obtained
        27.19
        shares, power to impose restrictions
            on   27.20–27.21
    reports of inspectors
        acting upon   27.12
        copies   27.11
        generally   27.10
Investment capital
    balance sheet position   12.3
    meaning   12.2
Investors
    capital base, protection of, *see* Share
        capital
    directors, appointment of   1.16,
        14.13–14.26
    disclosure of interests   1.13
    limitation of liability
        nature of   2.7
        price paid for   2.8

Investors – *cont.*
  limited liability of   1.6
  minority
    investigation into affairs of
        company   16.17
    judicial protection for   16.4–16.8
    legal proceedings against directors
        and officers by   22.3–22.5
    other examples of statutory
        protection   16.19
    petitioning for winding up   16.18
    rule in *Foss v Harbottle*   16.20–
        16.24
    s 205 remedy for oppression by
        majority   16.9–16.16
  misrepresentations
    criminal liability for   10.50–10.51
    investors' remedies for   10.37–
        10.49
  protection of
    generally   2.6
    limitation of liability   2.7–2.8
    need for   10.1
    other protections   2.9
    price paid for limitation of
        liability   2.8
  public companies, in
    contractual aspects of public
        subscriptions   10.25–10.36
    criminal liability for
        misrepresentations
        10.50–10.51
    national investment markets
        10.12–10.17
    need for protection   10.1
    prospectuses   10.18–10.24
    public company formation
        procedures   10.2–10.11
    public subscriptions, contractual
        aspects of   10.25–10.36
    remedies for
        misrepresentations
        10.37–10.49
    statement in lieu of
        prospectus   10.52
  remedies for misrepresentations
    common law remedies   10.39–
        10.45
    generally   10.37
    investors' remedies   10.38
    statutory remedies under s 49
        10.46–10.49
  rights and responsibilities of
    compulsory purchase   1.15
    disclosure of interests   1.13
    generally   1.12
    transfer of interests   1.14
  shareholders, *see* Shareholders
  statutory contract of
    conversion of shares into stock
        29.23
    membership, significance of
        29.1–29.2
  shares, *see* Shares
  transfer of interests
    incorporation facilitates   4.12
    rights and responsibilities   1.14
  ultra vires doctrine and
    alteration of objects clause   17.14
    generally   17.13
Invitation to treat
  prospectus issued to public deemed to
      be   10.25
Iris Oifigiúil
  publication in   8.15

Legal personality of company, *see*
    Corporate personality
Letter headings
  directors' particulars on   7.6, 14.25
  notification of examiner's
      appointment   37.14
Liability
  directors, of
    breach of duty, relief from liability
        for   21.4–21.6
    common law liabilities to
        outsiders   21.9–21.12
    company debts, for   1.18
    corporate crimes   21.13–21.14
    failure to keep proper books of
        account   21.17–21.21, 36.6
    fraudulent trading   21.31–21.35
    generally   21.2
    insolvent company, debts of
        21.16–21.35
    insurance   21.7
    outsiders as agents of company,
        to   21.8–21.15
    potential criminal liabilities
        App B
    reckless trading   21.22–21.30

Liability – *cont.*
  directors, of – *cont.*
    remedies by company   21.3
    statutory liabilities to outsiders
      21.15
    two perspectives   21.1
  insider dealing, for
    criminal sanctions   20.35
    generally   20.33
    time-limits   20.34
  limited, *see* Limited liability
  pre-trading contracts, for   11.3
Lifting veil, *see* Veil of incorporation
Limited company
  conversion of unlimited company
    into   8.27
  guarantee, *see* Guarantee, company
    limited by
  shares, *see* Shares, company limited by
Limited liability
  investors, of   1.6
  memorandum of association
    generally   4.2
    registration of company, effect
      of   4.3
  nature of   2.7, 4.1
  price paid for   2.8
  principle of   1.2
Limited liability company
  methods of dissolution   41.2
  nature of   41.1
Liquidator, *see* Official liquidator
Listed Market
  listing rules   10.15
  nature of   10.14
Loan capital
  capital employed   12.5
  meaning   12.4
Loans
  connected persons, to, prohibition
    of   20.12
  directors, to   14.22, 20.12
  intra-group   20.17
  prohibited, civil remedies for making
    of   20.18
  prohibition of   20.12
  purchase of company's own shares, for
    breach of s 60 procedures, effect
      of   13.41
    conditions for valid loans or
      guarantees   13.39

    debts   13.45
    dividends   13.45
    generally   13.38
    objections   13.40
    permitted loans under s 60
      13.43
    public companies, restriction on
      13.44
    third party notice of breach
      13.42

Management
  company secretary, *see* Company
    secretary
  court's powers over   37.20
  day-to-day   14.3
  directors, *see* Directors
  investors, *see* Investors
  members, *see* Members
  monitoring directors' management of
    company   1.21
  ownership distinguished from   3.12
  second tier of   14.3
  underlying relationships   14.1–14.3
Managers
  ostensible authority, doctrine of
    18.24
  powers of   34.13–34.15
Managing agents
  directors, *see* Directors
  role of   1.16
Managing director
  ostensible authority, doctrine of
    18.22–18.23
  proceedings of directors, role relating
    to   19.4
  service contract of   14.30
  usual authority of   18.15
Market purchase
  meaning   13.27
  off-market purchase, meaning
    13.28
Meetings
  adjourned   15.24
  annual general
    adjourned   15.6
    business at   15.8
    generally   15.2, 15.3
    location of   15.9
    notice   15.4

Meetings – *cont.*
  annual general – *cont.*
    waiver of notice   15.5
  democratic control of company
    15.31
  examiner, powers of   37.24
  extraordinary general
    business at   15.12
    following serious loss of capital
      13.35–13.36
    generally   15.2, 15.10
    notice   15.11
  inspection of minute books   15.28
  minutes of   15.27–15.28
  power to order holding of   15.13
  proceedings at general meetings
    adjournment   15.17
    chairman   15.16
    generally   15.14
    proxies   15.19
    quorum of members   15.15
    voting   15.18
  resolutions
    adjourned meetings   15.24
    amendments   15.25
    copies of   15.29
    extended notice   15.26
    ordinary   15.21
    registration of   15.29
    special   15.22–15.23, 15.30
    types of   15.20
    unanimous agreement   15.23
  single-member companies   15.7
  types of   15.1
Members
  agreeing to become   28.11
  bankrupt   28.8
  companies
    buying own shares   28.5
    holding company, purchasing
      shares of   28.6
    limitations   28.4
  corporate majority decisions   29.2
  deceased   28.7
  directors, appointment of   14.13–
    14.26
  individual members' rights   29.2
  infants   28.3
  legal relationship with company
    14.12

  membership
    condition precedent to   28.16
    how persons relinquish   28.19
    nature of   28.1
    significance of   29.1–29.2
  methods of becoming
    agreeing to become members
      28.11
    condition precedent to
      membership   28.16
    estoppel   28.15
    generally   28.9
    subscribing to memorandum
      28.10
    transfer of shares   28.12–28.13
    transmission of shares   28.14
  minors   28.3
  register of
    generally   25.3, 28.17
    rectification of   28.18
    trusts not to be entered in   28.18
  role of   14.11
  unsatisfied creditors' remedies
    against   36.2–36.3
  voluntary winding up   41.14–41.23,
    43.1–43.13
  who can become   28.2–28.8
  See also Investors
Memorandum of association
  company powers   17.7–17.12
  formation of company, procedures
    for   8.10
  limited liability and
    generally   4.2
    registration of company, effect
      of   4.3
  objects clause   17.1
  public nature of   2.12
  subscribing to   28.10
Mergers
  changes in company ownership by
    1.37
  City Code on Takeovers and
    Mergers   40.10–40.11
  compensation for loss of office
    40.9
  controlling economic impact of
    40.22
  European Communities   40.16–
    40.31
  intra-EU and international trading
    40.32

Mergers – *cont.*
  meaning   1.37
Minimum subscription
  prospectus, contents of   10.21
Minority investors
  investigations into affairs of
      company   16.17
  judicial protection for
    bona fide for benefit of company as
        whole   16.5–16.6
    generally   16.4
    hardship, cases of   16.7
    other minority remedies   16.8
  legal proceedings against directors
      and officers by   22.3–22.5
  other examples of statutory
      protection   16.19
  rule in *Foss v Harbottle*
    apparent judicial exceptions to
        16.23
    application of rule   16.22
    derivative action   16.24
    generally   16.20–16.21
    policy reasons underlying   16.20
  s 205 remedy for oppression by
      majority
    examinership   16.16
    generally   16.9
    offending conduct   16.11–16.12
    only available to investors   16.10
    proceedings in camera   16.15
    remedies available to court
        16.14–16.15
    second limb   16.13
Minority protection
  change from public company into
      private company   8.24
Minors
  members, as   28.3
Minute books
  maintenance of   25.9
Misconduct
  receiver's duty to report   35.9
Misfeasance
  damages for, fiduciary position of
      promoter   9.9
Misrepresentations
  criminal liability for
    defence   10.51
    generally   10.50

investors' remedies for
  common law remedies   10.39–
      10.45
  generally   10.37
  investors' remedies   10.38
  statutory remedies under s 49
      10.46–10.49
Money
  common law duties of directors
      19.12–19.13
  company's power to lend   17.11
Monitoring
  accounts, *see* Accounts
  annual accounts, *see* Annual accounts
  auditors, *see* Auditors
  directors' management of
      company   1.21
  investigation, *see* Investigation
  registers, *see* Registers
Mortgage
  charges by way of   32.15–32.16

Name of company
  change of   17.25
  directors' particulars on
      letterheadings   7.6
  generally   17.23
  memorandum of association   17.23
  mistaken registration   7.7
  officers' liability for use of name
      incorrectly   17.27
  passing off   7.8–7.10
  power to dispense with word
      'limited'   17.24
  proposed, approval of   8.12
  publication of   17.26
  registration of business names
    information to be registered   7.2
    mistaken registration   7.7
    partnerships   7.2
    penalties   7.4
    publication of registered business
        name   7.5
    refusal to register name   7.3
    sole traders   7.2
  restrictions on choice of
    passing off   7.8–7.10
    significance of name   7.1–7.7
    tort of passing off   7.8–7.10
  significance of   7.1
  tort of passing off   7.8–7.10

National investment markets
  investors in public companies,
    protection for   10.12–10.17
Natural justice
  directors, removal of   14.28
Negligence
  damages for   10.43
Non-Irish company
  accounts   11.5
  cessation of business in Ireland
    11.6
  commencement of business   11.4–
    11.8
  details of external companies   11.8
  Irish branches   11.7
  publicity   11.5

Objects clauses
  alteration of   17.14
  Bell Houses clause   17.6
  catch-all clause   17.6
  drafting of, effect of ultra vires
    doctrine on   17.4
  memorandum of association,
    statement in   17.1
  modern, evolution of   17.5–17.6
Off the shelf company
  formation of   8.14
Off-market purchase
  meaning   13.28
Offer for sale
  method of raising capital, as   10.8
Officers
  books of account, personal liability
    for   20.46
  fraudulent trading, liability for
    36.7
  insurance, *see* Professional indemnity
    insurance
  investigation into company's affairs,
    duties relating to
      examination on oath   27.7
      generally   27.5
      related companies   27.8
      secret transactions   27.6
  liability for use of name
    incorrectly   17.27
  peeping behind veil   6.8
  professional indemnity insurance
    claims for compensation   22.1

cover provided by D&O policies
    22.10–22.14
  events giving rise to legal
    proceedings against
    directors   22.9
  minority investors, legal
    proceedings by   22.3–22.5
  modern attitude towards directors'
    responsibilities   22.15
  non-members, legal proceedings
    by   22.6–22.8
  who is able to sue   22.2–22.9
  reckless trading, liability for   21.22–
    21.30, 36.7
  See also Directors
Official liquidator
  appointment of   42.5–42.11
  co-operation with court and relevant
    authorities   42.54
  company assets
    duty to realise   42.32
    maximising   42.33–42.35
  contributories, duty to settle list of
    42.20–42.27
  debts, duty to admit or reject proof
    of   42.28–42.31
  dissolution of company   42.55
  duties of   42.18
  meaning   35.22
  minimising company's liabilities
    42.36–42.42
  payment of company's debts
    42.43–42.53
  powers of   42.15–42.17
  procedures to be followed by
    42.12–42.14
  property, duties relating to   42.19
  provisional, effect of examiner's
    appointment on   37.18
  receiver, effect of appointment on
    35.24
  removal of   42.11
  resignation of   42.11
  Salomon case   3.3
  termination of liquidation   42.55
  winding up
    conducting proceedings   42.2–
      42.54
    orders   42.1
One-man company, *see* Single-member
  company

Ordinary resolution
  meaning   15.21
Ordinary shares
  meaning   12.18
  non-voting   12.19
  preference shares distinguished
    from   12.21
Origins of company law
  statutory framework   1.1–1.3
Ostensible authority
  company secretary   18.25
  directors   18.24
  managers   18.24
  managing director   18.22–18.23
  third party protection and doctrine
    of   18.20–18.25
Outsiders
  liability of directors to, *see* Directors
Ownership
  investigation into
    entry and search of premises
      27.18
    inspector, by   27.14–27.16
    lifting restrictions on shares
      27.22
    Minister's powers   27.17–27.22
    security of information obtained
      27.19
    shares, power to impose restrictions
      on   27.20–27.21
  management distinguished from
    3.12
  nature of   1.24
  property of company   4.6–4.9

Partnership
  advantages for   5.6
  disadvantages for   5.7
  fundamental advantages enjoyed by
    companies   5.12
  meaning   5.5
  trading in   5.5–5.8
  unincorporated business association,
    as   5.5, 5.8
Passing off
  liability for tort of   7.8–7.10
Penalties
  registration of business names,
    relating to   7.4
Pensions
  company powers   17.12

Placing
  method of raising capital, as   10.9
Pre-emption rights
  concept of   10.24
Pre-incorporation contracts
  pre-trading contracts distinguished
    from   9.16
  promoters and   9.15
Pre-trading contracts
  liability of directors for   11.3
  pre-incorporation contracts
    distinguished from   9.16
Preference shares
  meaning   12.17
  ordinary shares distinguished from
    12.21
Price
  limitation of liability, payment for
    2.8
Private companies
  change from public company into
    minority protection   8.24
    special resolution   8.23
  directors' powers to refuse registration
    in   31.21
  disclosure orders for interests in
    31.9
  formation of   8.7
  nature of   8.7
  re-registration as public company
    balance sheet   8.25
    special resolution   8.25
    third party rights   8.26
  share transfers   31.23
  single-member, formation of   8.16
Professional indemnity insurance
  claims for compensation   22.1
  cover provided by D&O policies
    basis of cover   22.12–22.13
    future of D&O insurance   22.14
    generally   22.10
    policy exclusions   22.11
  modern attitude towards directors'
    responsibilities   22.15
  who is able to sue
    events giving rise to legal
      proceedings against
      directors   22.9
    generally   22.2
    minority investors, legal
      proceedings by   22.3–22.5

Professional indemnity insurance – *cont.*
  who is able to sue – *cont.*
    non-members, legal proceedings
      by   22.6–22.8
Profits
  available for distribution   24.42
  payment of dividends only out of
    distribution, meaning   13.50
    generally   13.49
    public companies, profits of
      13.51
    relevant accounts   13.53
    specialist companies   13.52
  public companies, of   13.51
  recovery of, fiduciary position of
    promoter   9.8
  secret profit, common law duty of
    directors not to make   19.14–
    19.15
Promoters
  common law remedies of company
    against   9.6, 9.10, 10.44
  fiduciary relationship
    common law remedies of
      company   9.6
    damages for misfeasance   9.9
    disclosure, duties of   9.5
    effect of breaching 1983 Act
      9.11
    meaning   9.4
    misfeasance, damages for   9.9
    recovery of profits   9.8
    rescission   9.7
    statutory rights of company   9.10
  meaning   1.8, 9.1, 9.2–9.3
  pre-incorporation contracts, position
    relating to   9.15
  remuneration of
    articles of association, provision
      in   9.13
    information in prospectus   9.14
    legal right to recover expenses, lack
      of   9.12
    prospectus, information in   9.14
Property
  assets of company   4.9
  charged, examiner's power to deal
    with   37.30
  common law duties of directors
    19.12–19.13
  company ownership of   4.6–4.9

directors
  common law duties of   19.12–
    19.13
  substantial property transactions
    with   20.9–20.10
independent expert, valuation by
  9.10
liquidator, powers of   42.19
receiver's duty when selling   35.6–
  35.7
Prospectus
  contents of
    generally   10.20
    minimum subscription   10.21
    registration   10.23
    reports to be attached   10.22
  meaning   10.18
  nature of   10.18
  persons named without authority
    10.48
  pre-emption rights   10.24
  public offers   10.19
  remuneration of promoters,
    information on   9.14
  statement in lieu of   10.52
Protection
  capital base, of, *see* Share capital
  creditors, of, *see* Creditors
  investors, of, *see* Investors
Public companies
  advantages of   8.6
  capital
    methods of raising   10.7–10.11
    minimum share capital   8.6, 8.17
  change into private companies
    minority protection   8.24
    special resolution   8.23
  formation of   8.6, 10.2–10.11
  minimum share capital   8.6, 8.17
  nature of   8.6
  offer for sale   10.8
  placing   10.9
  profits of   13.51
  protection for investors in
    contractual aspects of public
      subscriptions   10.25–10.36
    national investment markets
      10.12–10.17
    need for protection   10.1
    prospectuses   10.18–10.24
  public company formation
    procedures   10.2–10.11

Public companies – *cont.*
  protection for investors in – *cont.*
    public subscriptions, contractual
      aspects of   10.25–10.36
    public offer   10.10
    re-registration of private companies as
      balance sheet   8.25
      special resolution   8.25
      third party rights   8.26
    rights issue   10.11
Public offer
  meaning   10.19
  method of raising capital, as   10.10
Public subscription
  allotment stage, protecting public
    investors at
      allotment procedures   10.28
      directors' authority   10.27
      generally   10.26
      minimum subscription   10.29
    contractual aspects of   10.25–10.36
    other remedies and protections
      10.36
    payment for allotted shares
      directors' liabilities   10.32
      generally   10.30
      non-cash consideration   10.31
    returns of allotments   10.34
    shareholders' liability   10.35
    void allotment   10.33
    voidable allotment   10.33
Purchasing own shares, *see* Shares

Quasi-trustees
  directors as   14.7–14.8

Receiver
  appointment of
    court, by   34.8, 34.19
    effect of   34.16
    fixed charge, under   34.5
    floating charge, under   34.6
    generally   34.4
    jeopardy   34.7
    notice of   34.10–34.12
  company contracts   34.20–34.24
  court, appointment by   34.8, 34.19
  defective appointment   35.4

  directions, application to court for
    35.18
  duties of   35.5–35.18
  effect of appointment of   34.16
  enforcement of duty to make
    returns   35.16
  examiner
    appointment of, effect on receiver
      of   35.23, 37.17
    meaning   35.22
  indemnification   35.3–35.4
  liabilities of   35.17
  liquidator
    appointment of, effect on receiver
      of   35.24
    meaning   35.22
  meaning   35.22
  misconduct, duty to report   35.9
  non-cash assets, sale of   35.7
  powers of   34.13–34.15
  premature termination of powers of
    generally   35.19
    removal   35.21
    resignation   35.20
  property, duty when selling   35.6–
    35.7
  registrar
    copies of statement of particulars
      to   35.14
    delivery of half-yearly returns to
      35.15
  removal of   35.21
  remuneration   35.2
  resignation   35.20
  returns, enforcement of duty to
    make   35.16
  rights of   35.1–35.4
  sale
    non-cash assets, of   35.7
    proceeds of sale of assets, duties in
      applying   35.8
  specific statutory tasks
    copies to registrar and debenture
      holders   35.14
    delivery of half-yearly returns to
      registrar   35.15
    generally   35.10
    notification   35.11
    statement of particulars   35.12
    verification of particulars   35.13
  status of
    company contracts   34.20–34.24

Receiver – *cont.*
status of – *cont.*
  court, receiver appointed by
    34.19
  debenture holders, receiver
    appointed by   34.18
  generally   34.17
Reckless trading
  concept of   20.47–20.48
  defence   21.25
  directors' liability for   20.47–20.48,
    21.22–21.30, 36.7
  judicial interpretation of
    provisions   21.26
  meaning   21.24
  objective test   21.29
  officers' liability for   21.22–21.30,
    36.7
  recklessness, meaning   21.28
  scope of s 297A   21.27
  subjective test   21.30
  who can initiate proceedings   21.23
Reconstruction
  meaning   1.36, 39.13
  schemes of arrangement, use for
    39.13
  under s 260
    creditors' voluntary winding up
      39.19
    dissenting members' rights
      39.18
    generally   39.15
    procedure   39.16
    winding-up order, effect of
      39.17
Recovery against company
  creditors' rights of
    debenture, meaning   2.16
    fixed charge, meaning   2.19
    floating charge, meaning   2.19
    generally   2.16
    ranking of creditors' claims   2.19
    secured creditors   2.17
    unsecured creditors   2.18
Redeemable shares
  meaning   13.17
  redemption of
    cancellation of shares on   13.19
    capital redemption reserve fund
      13.20
    conditions for   13.18

    payment of premium on
      redemption   13.21
    re-issuing of treasury shares
      13.23
    treasury shares   13.22
Reduction of share capital, *see* Share
  capital
Registered companies
  advantages for   5.10
  disadvantages for   5.11
  nature of   5.9
Registered office
  documents to be kept at   17.29
  generally   17.28
  registers to be kept at   17.29
  service of proceedings on
    company   17.30
Registers
  debenture-holders, of   25.7, 33.15
  debentures, directors' interests in
    25.6, 31.1
  directors and secretaries, of   25.5
  extra registers for plcs   25.4
  maintaining   25.1
  members, of
    generally   25.3, 28.17
    rectification of   28.18
    trusts not to be entered in   28.18
  shares, directors' interests in   25.6,
    31.1
  significant interests, of   31.5–31.6
  statutory   25.2–25.7
Registration
  auditors, of   26.9
  business names, of
    partners   7.2
    penalties   7.4
    publication of registered business
      name   7.5
    refusal to register name   7.3
    sole traders   7.2
  choice of company type
    generally   8.1
    guarantee, companies limited by
      8.3
    shares, companies limited by   8.2
    unlimited companies   8.4
  debentures, of, *see* Debentures
  guarantee, companies limited by
    8.3
  lodgement of documents   8.13

Registration – *cont.*
make up of register of companies
8.19
memorandum of association, of
4.3
prospectus, contents of 10.23
re-registration of private company as
public company
balance sheet 8.25
special resolution 8.25
third party rights 8.26
registered companies
advantages 5.10
disadvantages 5.11
generally 5.9
registered office
documents to be kept at 17.29
generally 17.28
registers to be kept at 17.29
service of proceedings on
company 17.30
resolutions, of 15.29
shares, companies limited by 8.2
transfer of shares, *see* Shares
Related companies
court, power of 37.4
peeping behind veil 6.5
Remedies
creditors, of
directors, claims against 36.4–
36.9
generally 36.1
members, remedies against
36.2–36.3
officers, claims against 36.4–36.9
creditors, protection of, *see* Creditors
debenture holders, of 33.22, 34.3–
34.15
directors, against 21.3
examiner, of 37.26
investors, protection of, *see* Investors
misrepresentations, for
common law remedies 10.39–
10.45
generally 10.37
investors' remedies 10.38
statutory remedies under s 49
10.46–10.49
promoter, against 9.6, 10.44
public subscription, relating to
10.36

unsecured creditors, of 34.2
Remuneration
auditors, of 26.13
promoters, of
articles of association, provision
in 9.13
legal right to recover expenses, lack
of 9.12
prospectus, information in 9.14
receiver, of 35.2
Reports
auditors, of, *see* Auditors
directors, of, *see* Directors
examiner, of, *see* Examiner
inspector, of
acting upon 27.12
copies 27.11
generally 27.10
prospectus, contents of 10.22
Rescission
misrepresentations, investors'
remedies for
generally 10.40
limits on rescission 10.41
promoter, fiduciary relationship of
9.7
Resolutions
adjourned meetings 15.24
amendments 15.25
copies of 15.29
extended notice 15.26
ordinary 15.21
registration 15.29
special
meaning 15.22
unanimous agreement 15.23
when required 15.30
types of 15.20
Restriction of directors, *see* Directors
Return, *see* Annual return
Rights issue
method of raising capital, as 10.11

Salaries
directors, of, disclosure of 14.23
Sanctions, *see* Criminal sanctions
Schemes of arrangement, *see* Financial
arrangements
Scope of company law
statutory framework 1.1–1.3

Seal
  use of   18.2
Secretary, *see* Company secretary
Section 201 schemes of arrangement, *see*
    Financial arrangements
Security for costs
  examiner, court's power relating
      to   37.7
Separate legal personality, *see*
    Incorporation
Service contracts
  directors, of
      1990 Act limitations on   14.31
      authority of directors   14.33
      entry into   1.16
      generally   14.29
      inspection of   14.32
      regulation of   20.8
  managing director, of   14.30
Shadow director
  meaning   20.5
Share capital
  alteration of   13.54–13.55
  authorised capital   12.11
  diminution of   13.55
  direct reduction of, restrictions on
      generally   13.2
      permitted use of share premium
          fund   13.4
      share premium fund treated as
          capital   13.3
  forfeiture, etc under s 43   13.15
  giving loans for purchase of own
      shares
      breach of s 60 procedures, effect
          of   13.41
      conditions for valid loans or
          guarantees   13.39
      debts   13.45
      dividends   13.45
      generally   13.38
      objections   13.40
      permitted loans under s 60
          13.43
      public companies, restriction on
          13.44
      third party notice of breach
          13.42
  increase in   13.55
  issued capital   12.12
  meaning   12.9, 12.10

  minimum, formation of public
      company   8.6, 8.17
  nominal capital   12.11
  other capital maintenance rules
      13.37–13.53
  paid-up capital   12.13
  permitted reduction in, under s 72
      application to court   13.6
      court order for reduction
          13.11–13.12
      fairness between competing class
          rights   13.7
      generally   13.5
      objections by creditors   13.9–
          13.10
      shareholders' liability for reduced
          shares   13.12
      variation of class rights   13.8
  profits, payment of dividends only out
      of
      distribution, meaning   13.50
      generally   13.49
      public companies, profits of
          13.51
      relevant accounts   13.53
      specialist companies   13.52
  protection of capital base
      extraordinary meeting following
          serious loss of capital
          13.35–13.36
      other capital maintenance rules
          13.37–13.53
      statutory rules   13.1
  re-registration under s 15   13.14
  reserve capital   12.14
  share premium fund
      permitted use of   13.4
      treated as capital   13.3
  statutory capital maintenance rules
      company purchasing own shares,
          restrictions on   13.24–13.34
      indirect reduction of share capital,
          prevention of   13.16
      redemption of redeemable
          shares   13.17–13.23
  statutory rules protecting   13.1
  uncalled capital   12.13
Share premium fund
  permitted use of   13.4
  treated as capital   13.3

Shareholders
  dividends
    amount payable   30.5
    effect of declaration of   30.8
    generally   30.3
    mode of payment   30.6
    right to   30.4
    shares in lieu of   30.7
  duties of   29.12
  financial liabilities of
    forfeiture of shares   30.15–30.19
    generally   30.9
    making call for payment   30.10–30.13
    non-payment of calls   30.14
    notice of other interests   30.20
  liabilities of   30.1
  principal rights of   30.2–30.8
  reduced shares, liability for   13.12
  rights of   12.26, 29.11, 30.1
  usual authority of   18.19
Shares
  allotment of, *see* Public subscription
  amount of   29.17
  CREST   31.33–31.34
  calls
    early payment of   30.12
    generally   29.14
    late payment   30.13
    limits   30.11
    making call for payment   30.10–30.13
    non-payment of   30.14
  certificates
    effect of   29.20
    generally   29.18
    object of   29.19
  chose in action, as   29.3
  class rights
    competing, fairness between   13.7
    issuing of additional shares of
      similar class   12.24
    meaning   12.16
    objections to alteration of   12.23
    s 38 procedure   12.25
    variation of   12.22–12.25, 13.8, 29.16
  classes of
    articles of association   12.15
    class rights   12.16

    ordinary shares
      meaning   12.18
      non-voting   12.19
      preference shares distinguished
        from   12.21
    preference shares
      meaning   12.17
      ordinary shares distinguished
        from   12.21
  comment on case-law   29.21
  company limited by
    conversion of unlimited company
      into   8.27
    nature of   8.2
    registration   8.2
    single-member private company   8.16
  company purchasing own shares
    acquisition of membership   28.5
    contingent purchase contracts   13.29
    disclosure of share purchases   13.34
    failure to redeem or purchase own
      shares, effect of   13.32
    holding company, purchase by
      subsidiary of shares in   13.33, 28.6
    loans for   13.38–13.45
    market purchase   13.27
    off-market purchases   13.28
    payments by company for own
      shares   13.31
    purchasing shares under 1990
      Act   13.26
    release of company's right to buy
      own shares   13.30
    restrictions on   13.24–13.34
    s 41 of 1983 Amendment Act   13.25
    transfer of company's right to buy
      own shares   13.30
  compulsory purchase of   31.37
  contract, as   29.6–29.7
  conversion into stock   29.23
  debentures and   32.11
  deferred shares   12.20
  directors' interest in, disclosure of
    directors' report or accounts,
      disclosure of interests in   20.27
    generally   20.23

Shares – *cont.*
  directors' interest in, disclosure of –
    cont.
    register of directors' and other
      interests   20.26
    sanction for non-compliance
      20.25
    share dealings   20.24–20.25
  disclosure of interests in
    application for order   31.11
    concert parties, notification of
      interests of   31.8
    contravention of order   31.13
    exempted companies   31.10
    generally   31.2
    private companies, disclosure orders
      for interests in   31.9
    register of significant interests
      31.5–31.6
    scope of order   31.12
    share dealings by directors,
      secretaries and their
      families   31.3
    significant interests in shares of
      plc   31.4
    Stock Exchange, notification of
      thresholds to   31.7
  dividends, *see* Dividends
  essential nature   29.5
  forfeiture of
    effect of   30.17
    generally   30.15
    notice of   30.16
  in lieu of dividends   30.7
  involuntary share transfers   31.36
  lien on members' shares   30.19
  meaning   29.4–29.7
  non-voting ordinary shares   12.19
  notice of other interests   30.20
  numbering of   29.17
  ordinary shares
    meaning   12.18
    non-voting   12.19
    preference shares distinguished
      from   12.21
  penalising dealing in options to trade
    in   20.11
  preference shares
    meaning   12.17
    ordinary shares distinguished
      from   12.21

  public subscriptions for   29.13
  purchasing own shares, *see* company
    purchasing own shares, above
  redeemable, *see* Redeemable shares
  register of directors' interests in
    25.6, 31.1
  restrictions on
    lifting of   27.22
    power to impose   27.20–27.21
  rights issues   31.32
  s 25 contract   29.8–29.10
  share warrants   29.22, 31.38
  stock, conversion into   29.23
  surrender of   30.18
  transfer of
    1996 Regulations outlined   31.35
    assignment of interest   31.15–
      31.18
    certification of transfer   31.31
    compulsory purchase of shares
      31.37
    computerised   31.33–31.34
    consequences   31.19
    directors' powers to refuse
      registration   31.21–31.22
    forged transfers   31.30
    generally   28.12–28.13, 31.14
    involuntary   31.36
    non-registration   31.27–31.29
    notice of refusal to register
      31.25–31.26
    private company share transfers
      31.23
    refusal of registration in plcs
      31.24
    registration of transferee   31.20
    rights issues   31.32
    voluntary share transfers   31.32
  transmission of   28.14
  types of   29.15
  voluntary share transfers
    31.32
  warrants   29.22, 31.38
Single-member company
  annual general meeting   15.7
  change from   8.22
  change to   8.21
  formation of   8.1, 8.16
  meetings   15.7
  Salomon case   3.6

Skill
    care and, directors' duties of
        19.20–19.21
    degree of   19.21
Sole traders
    advantages of operating in business
        as   5.3
    capital, restricted scope for raising
        5.4
    carrying on business as   5.2–5.4
    disadvantages for   5.4
    fundamental advantages enjoyed by
        companies   5.12
    unlimited liability for debts of
        business   5.4
Solvency
    meaning   32.25
Special resolution
    meaning   15.22
    unanimous agreement   15.23
    when required   15.30
Status, change of, *see* Change of status
Statutory framework
    summary   1.1–1.3
Statutory registers, *see* Registers
Stock Exchange
    Admissions Directive   10.4
    EC (Stock Exchange) Regulations
        1984   10.3–10.6
    insider dealing regulations,
        supervision of
        annual report   20.38
        EU dimension   20.39
        generally   20.37
    Interim Reports Directive   10.6
    Listing Particulars Directive   10.5
    member firms   App A
    notification of thresholds to   31.7
Strangers, *see* Third parties
Subsidiaries
    peeping behind veil   6.3
    purchase of shares in holding
        company   13.33
Succession
    perpetual, company has   4.10

Takeovers
    changes in company ownership by
        1.37
    City Code on Takeovers and
        Mergers   40.10–40.11

compensation for loss of office
    40.9
compulsory acquisition of shares of
    minority
    dissentient members, rights of
        40.4
    dissentients' opportunity to sell
        40.7
    generally   40.3
    onus of proof   40.5–40.6
controlling economic impact of
    40.22
European Communities   40.16–
    40.31
generally   40.1
intra-EU and international trading
    40.32
Irish Takeover Panel
    appeals   40.15
    powers of   40.12–40.13
    rulings and directions   40.14
legal controls over profiteering
    40.8–40.11
meaning   1.37, 40.1
procedure   40.2
takeover bid, compulsory purchase
    following   1.15
See also Mergers
Taxation
    corporation tax   4.13
    income tax   4.13
    shareholders, of   4.13
Third parties
    company purchasing own shares,
        notice of breach relating to
        13.42
    interests   2.4–2.5
    ostensible authority and
        chairman   18.22–18.23
        company secretary   18.25
        conditions necessary   18.21
        directors   18.24
        generally   18.20
        managers   18.24
        managing director   18.22–18.23
    re-registration, effect of   8.26
    relationships, *see* Third party
        relationships
    strangers to contract termed as
        18.5

Third party relationships
  compromising company debts
    1.35–1.36
  corporate restructuring   1.35–1.36
  creditors, *see* Creditors
  dissolving company   1.39
  mergers   1.37
  nature of   1.25
  takeovers   1.37
  winding up   1.38–1.39
Time-limits
  filing annual return   25.21
  insider dealing, liability for   20.34
Torts
  auditors' liability in   26.29–26.30
  company can sue and be sued in its
    own name   4.5
  passing off   7.8–7.10
Trading
  fraudulent, *see* Fraudulent trading
  reckless, *see* Reckless trading
Trading certificate
  commencement of business   11.2
Transfer of interests
  investors
    incorporation facilitates transfer
      4.12
    rights and responsibilities of
      1.14
Transfer of shares, *see* Shares
Trust
  register of members, not entered
    in   28.18
Trustees
  debenture holders, for   33.10

Ultra vires doctrine
  company agents, application to
    18.26
  creditors and
    generally   17.15
    position of company   17.22
    s 8 protection   17.16–17.22
  investors and
    alteration of objects clause   17.14
    generally   17.13
  objects clauses, effect on drafting
    of   17.4
  outsiders as agents of company,
    directors' liability to   21.10

transactions, effect of   17.3–17.4
Unincorporated association
  electing to trade as   8.1
  partnership, *see* Partnership
Unlimited company
  conversion into limited company and
    vice versa   8.27
  formation of   8.18
  nature of   8.4
Unlisted Securities Market (USM)
  formation of   10.16
  nature of   10.16
Unsecured creditors, *see* Creditors
Untrue statement
  meaning   10.49

Veil of incorporation
  creditors, protection of   2.21
  directors
    legal liability of   6.18
    peeping behind veil   6.8
    statutory lifting of veil   6.17
  extending   6.11
  ignoring   6.12–6.14
  lifting
    conclusions on   6.15–6.18
    extending veil   6.11
    groups of companies at common
      law   6.16
    ignoring veil   6.12–6.14
    legal liability of directors   6.18
    nature of metaphor   6.1–6.18
    peeping behind veil   6.2–6.9
    penetrating veil   6.10
    statutory, and directors   6.17
  nature of   1.5
  peeping behind
    court, veil lifted by   6.6–6.7
    directors   6.8
    nature of   6.2–6.4
    officers   6.8
    purpose of   6.9
    related companies   6.5
  penetrating   6.10
  protection given to members by
    3.11
Voting
  common law duties of directors
    19.17